Lieutenant-General Sir Rowland Hill. K.C.B.

from the portrait by G. Dawe. R.A.

A HISTORY OF THE
PENINSULAR WAR

BY

CHARLES OMAN, K.B.E.

M.A. Oxon., Hon. LL.D. Edin.

FELLOW OF THE BRITISH ACADEMY
MEMBER OF PARLIAMENT FOR THE UNIVERSITY OF OXFORD
CHICHELE PROFESSOR OF MODERN HISTORY
AND FELLOW OF ALL SOULS COLLEGE, OXFORD

VOL. VI

SEPTEMBER 1, 1812—AUGUST 5, 1813

THE SIEGE OF BURGOS
THE RETREAT FROM BURGOS
THE CAMPAIGN OF VITTORIA
THE BATTLES OF THE PYRENEES

WITH MAPS AND ILLUSTRATIONS

The Naval & Military Press Ltd

Published by

The Naval & Military Press Ltd
Unit 5 Riverside, Brambleside
Bellbrook Industrial Estate
Uckfield, East Sussex
TN22 1QQ England

Tel: +44 (0)1825 749494

www.naval–military–press.com
www.nmarchive.com

PREFACE

IT is seldom that the last chapter of a volume is written seven years after the first has been finished ; and when this does happen, the author is generally to blame. I must ask, however, for complete acquittal on the charge of dilatoriness or want of energy. I was writing the story of the Burgos Campaign in July 1914 : in August the Great War broke out : and like every one else I applied for service in any capacity in which a man of fifty-four could be useful. By September 4th I was hard at work in Whitehall, and by a queer chance was the person who on September 12th drafted from very inadequate material the long *communiqué* concerning the battle of the Marne. For four years and six months I was busy in one office and another, and ended up my service by writing the narrative of the Outbreak of the War, which was published by the Foreign Office in February 1919. My toils at the desk had just finished when it happened that I was sent to the House of Commons, as Burgess representing the University of Oxford, after a by-election caused by the elevation of my predecessor, Rowland Prothero, to the Upper Chamber. Two long official tours in the Rhineland and in France combined with parliamentary work to prevent me writing a word in 1919. But in the recess of 1920 I was able to find time to recommence Peninsular War studies, and this volume was finished in the autumn and winter of 1921 and sent to the press in January 1922.

It was fortunate that in the years immediately preceding the Great War I had been taking repeated turns

round the Iberian Peninsula, so that the topography of
very nearly all the campaigns with which this volume
deals was familiar to me. I had marvelled at the
smallness of the citadel of Burgos, and the monotony of
the plains across which Wellington's retreat of 1812 was
conducted. I had watched the rapid flow of the Zadorra
beside Vittoria, marked the narrowness of the front of
attack at St. Sebastian, and admired the bold scenery of
the lower Bidassoa. Moreover, on the East Coast I had
stood on the ramparts of Tarragona, and wondered
at the preposterous operations against them which
Sir John Murray directed. But there are two sections
of this volume in which I cannot speak as one who has
seen the land. My travels had never taken me to the
Alicante country, or the scene of the isolated and
obscure battle of Castalla. And—what is more important—I have never tramped over Soult's route from
Roncesvalles to the gates of Pampeluna, or from
Sorauren to Echalar. Such an excursion I had planned
in company with my good friend Foster Cunliffe, our
All Souls Reader in Military History, who fell on the
Somme in 1916, and I had no great desire to think of
making it without him. Moreover, the leisure of the
times before 1914 is now denied me. So for the greater
part of the ten-days' Campaign of the Pyrenees I have
been dependent for topography on the observations
of others—which I regret. But it would have been
absurd to delay the publication of this volume for
another year or more, on the chance of being able to
go over the ground in some uncovenanted scrap of
holiday.

I have, as in previous cases, to make due acknowledgement of much kind help from friends in the completion
of this piece of work. First and foremost my thanks

are due to my Oxford colleague in the History School, Mr. C. T. Atkinson of Exeter College, who found time during some particularly busy weeks to go over my proofs with his accustomed accuracy. His criticism was always valuable, and I made numerous changes in the text in deference to his suggestions. As usual, his wonderful knowledge of British regimental history enabled me to correct many slips and solecisms, and to make many statements clearer by an alteration of words and phrases. I am filled with gratitude when I think how he exerted himself to help me in the midst his own absorbing duties.

In the preceding volumes of this work I had not the advantage of being able to read the parts of the Hon. John Fortescue's *History of the British Army* which referred to the campaigns with which I was dealing. For down to 1914 I was some way ahead of him in the tale of years. But his volumes of 1921 took him past me, even as far as Waterloo, so that I had the opportunity of reading his accounts of Vittoria and the Pyrenees while I was writing my own version. This was always profitable—I am glad to think that we agree on all that is essential, though we may sometimes differ on matters of detail. But this is not the most important part of the aid that I owe to Mr. Fortescue. He was good enough to lend me the whole of his transcripts from the French Archives dealing with the Campaign of 1813, whereby I was saved a visit to Paris and much tedious copying of statistics and excerpting from dispatches. My own work at the *Archives Nationales* and the Ministry of War had only taken me down to the end of 1812. This was a most friendly act, and saved me many hours of transcription. There are few authors who are so liberal and thoughtful for the benefit of their colleagues in study. It will be noted in the Appendix that quite a large proportion of my statistics come from papers lent me by Mr. Fortescue.

As to other sources now first utilized in print, I have to thank Mr. W. S. D'Urban of Newport House for the loan of the diary of his ancestor Sir Benjamin D'Urban—most valuable for the Burgos retreat, especially for the operations of Hill's column. Another diary and correspondence, which was all-important for my last volume, runs dry as a source after the first months of 1813. These were the papers of Sir George Scovell, Wellington's cypher-secretary, from which so many quotations may be found in volume V. But after he left Headquarters and took charge of the newly formed Military Police ['Staff Corps Cavalry'] in the spring before Vittoria, he lost touch with the lines of information on which he had hitherto been so valuable. I owe the very useful reports of the Spanish Fourth Army, and the Marching Orders of General Giron, to the kindness of Colonel Juan Arzadun, who caused them to be typed and sent to me from Madrid. By their aid I was able to fill up all the daily *étapes* of the Galician corps, and to throw some new light on its operations in Biscay.

To Mr. Leonard Atkinson, M.C., of the Record Office, I must give a special word of acknowledgement, which I repeat on page 753, for discovering the long-lost 'morning states' of Wellington's army in 1813, which his thorough acquaintance with the shelves of his department enabled him to find for me, after they had been divorced for at least three generations from the dispatches to which they had originally belonged. Tied up unbound between two pieces of cardboard, they had eluded all previous seekers. We can at last give accurately the strength of every British and Portuguese brigade at Vittoria and in the Pyrenees.

I could have wished that the times permitted authors to be as liberal with maps as they were before the advent of post-war prices. I would gladly have added detailed plans of the combats of Venta del Pozo and Tolosa to my illustrations. And I am sorry that for maps of Tarragona, and Catalonia generally, I must refer readers back to my fourth volume. But books of research have now to be equipped with the lowest possible minimum of plates, or their price becomes prohibitive. I do not think that anything really essential for the understanding of localities has been left out. I ought perhaps to mention that my reconstructions of the topography of Maya and Roncesvalles owe much to the sketch-maps in General Beatson's *Wellington in the Pyrenees,* the only modern plans which have any value.

To conclude, I must express, now for the sixth time, to the compiler of the Index my heartfelt gratitude for a laborious task executed with her usual untiring patience and thoroughness.

CHARLES OMAN.

OXFORD,
   June 1922.

CONTENTS

SECTION XXXIV

THE BURGOS CAMPAIGN

CHAPTER   PAGE

I. Wellington in the North : Burgos Invested. September 1812 1

II. The Siege of Burgos. September 19–October 30, 1812 . 21

III. Wellington's Retreat from Burgos. (1) From the Arlanzon to the Douro. October 22–30 52

IV. Hill's Retreat from Madrid. October 25–November 6 . 87

V. Operations round Salamanca. November 1–15 . . 111

VI. Wellington's Retreat from the Tormes to the Agueda. November 16–20 143

VII. Critical Summary of the Campaigns of 1812 . . 167

SECTION XXXV

I. Winter Quarters. November–December 1812—January 1813 181

II. The Troubles of a Generalissimo. Wellington at Cadiz and Freneda 194

III. Wellington and Whitehall 214

IV. The Perplexities of King Joseph. February–April 1813 . 239

V. The Northern Insurrection. February–May 1813 . . 252

VI. An Episode on the East Coast, April 1813. The Campaign of Castalla 275

SECTION XXXVI

THE MARCH TO VITTORIA

I. Wellington's Plan of Campaign 299

II. Operations of Hill's Column. May 22–June 3, 1813 . 313

III. Operations of Graham's Column. May 26–June 3, 1813 . 322

IV. Movements of the French. May 22–June 4, 1813 . 334

V. The Operations around Burgos. June 4–14, 1813 . . 346

VI. Wellington crosses the Ebro. June 15–20, 1813 . . 364

VII. The Battle of Vittoria, June 21, 1813 : The First Stage 384

VIII. The Battle of Vittoria : Rout of the French . . 413

SECTION XXXVII

THE EXPULSION OF THE FRENCH FROM SPAIN

CHAPTER   PAGE

I. Wellington's Pursuit of Clausel. June 22–30, 1813 . 451

II. Graham's Pursuit of Foy. June 22–31, 1813 . . 470

III. The East Coast. Murray at Tarragona. June 2–18, 1813 488

IV. Wellington on the Bidassoa. July 1–12, 1813 . . 522

V. Exit King Joseph. July 12, 1813 546

SECTION XXXVIII

THE BATTLES OF THE PYRENEES

I. The Siege of St. Sebastian : the First Period, July 12–25 557

II. Soult takes the Offensive in Navarre. July 1813 . . 587

III. Roncesvalles and Maya. July 25, 1813 . . . 608

IV. Sorauren. July 28, 1813 642

V. Soult's Retreat. Second Battle of Sorauren. July 30 . 681

VI. Soult Retires into France. July 31–August 3, 1813 . 707

APPENDICES

I. British Losses at the Siege of Burgos. September 20–
October 21, 1812 741

II. The French Armies in Spain. Morning State of
October 15, 1812 741

III. Strength of Wellington's Army during and after the
Burgos Retreat. October–November 1813 . . 745

IV. British Losses in the Burgos Retreat . . . 747

V. Murray's Army at Castalla. April 1813 . . . 748

VI. Suchet's Army at Castalla 749

VII. British Losses at Biar and Castalla 750

VIII. Wellington's Army in the Vittoria Campaign . . 750

IX. Spanish Troops under Wellington's Command. June–
July 1813 753

X. The French Army at Vittoria 754

XI. British and Portuguese Losses at Vittoria . . . 757

XII. French Losses at Vittoria 761

XIII. Sir John Murray's Army in the Tarragona Expedition 762

XIV. Suchet's Army in Valencia and Catalonia. June 1813 763

XV. Spanish Armies on the East Coast. June 1813 . . 764

XVI. The Army of Spain as reorganized by Soult. July 1813 765

CHAPTER   PAGE
XVII. British Losses at Maya and Roncesvalles.   July 25,
        1813   768

XVIII. British Losses at Sorauren.   July 28, 1813   .   .   769

XIX. British Losses at the Second Battle of Sorauren and
        the Combat of Beunza.   July 30, 1813 .   .   .   770

XX. British Losses in Minor Engagements.   July 31–
        August 2, 1813   772

XXI. Portuguese Losses in the Campaign of the Pyrenees .   773

XXII. French Losses in the Campaign of the Pyrenees .   .   774

INDEX   775

MAPS AND PLANS

I. Plan of Siege Operations at Burgos.   Septem-
        ber–October 1812   .   .   .   .   *To face* 48

II. Operations round Salamanca.   November 1812   ,,   130

III. Battle of Castalla   .   .   .   .   .   ,,   274

IV. General Map of Northern Spain for the
        Burgos and Vittoria Campaigns .   .   *End of volume*

V. Plan of the Battle of Vittoria   .   .   *To face* 434

VI. Plan of the Siege of St. Sebastian   .   .   ,,   584

VII. General Map of the Country between Bayonne
        and Pampeluna .   .   .   .   .   .   ,,   606

VIII. Combat of Roncesvalles   .   .   .   .   ,,   622

IX. Combat of Maya   .   .   .   .   .   .   ,,   636

X. First Battle of Sorauren.   July 28   .   .   ,,   640

XI. Second Battle of Sorauren and Combat of
        Beunza.   July 30   .   .   .   .   .   ,,   670

ILLUSTRATIONS

Portrait of Sir Rowland Hill   .   .   *Frontispiece*

King Joseph at Mortefontaine   .   .   *To face page* 544

SECTION XXXIV

THE BURGOS CAMPAIGN

CHAPTER I'

WELLINGTON IN THE NORTH : BURGOS INVESTED
AUGUST 31st—SEPTEMBER 20th, 1812

THE year 1812 was packed with great events, and marked in
Spain no less than in Russia the final turn of the tide in the
history of Napoleon's domination. But the end was not yet :
when Wellington entered Madrid in triumph on August 12th,
the deliverance of the Peninsula was no more certain than was
the deliverance of Europe when the French Emperor evacuated
Moscow on October 22nd. Vittoria and Leipzig were still
a year away, and it was not till they had been fought and won
that the victory of the Allies was secure. The resources of the
great enemy were so immense that it required more than one
disaster to exhaust them. No one was more conscious of this
than Wellington. Reflecting on the relative numbers of his
own Anglo-Portuguese army and of the united strength of all
the French corps in Spain, he felt that the occupation of Madrid
was rather a *tour de force*, an admirable piece of political propaganda, than a decisive event. It would compel all the scattered
armies of the enemy to unite against him, and he was more than
doubtful whether he could make head against them. ' I still
hope,' he wrote to his brother Henry, the Ambassador at Cadiz,
' to maintain our position in Castille, and even to improve our
advantages. But I shudder when I reflect upon the enormity
of the task which I have undertaken, with inadequate powers
myself to do anything, and without assistance of any kind from
the Spaniards [1] . . . . I am apprehensive that all this may turn
out but ill for the Spanish cause. If, for any cause, I should be
overpowered, or should be obliged to retreat, what will the

[1] August 23, from Madrid, *Dispatches*, ix. p. 374.

world say ? What will the people of England say ? . . . That we made a great effort, attended by some glorious circumstances ; that from January 1st, 1812, we had gained more advantages for the cause, and had acquired more extent of territory by our operations than any army ever gained in such a period of time against so powerful an enemy ; but that unaided by the Spanish army and government, we were finally overpowered, and compelled to withdraw within our old frontier.'

It was with no light heart that Wellington faced the strategical problem. In outline it stood as follows. Soult was now known to be evacuating Andalusia, and it was practically certain that he would retire on Valencia, where he would join King Joseph and Suchet. Their three armies would produce a mass of veteran troops so great that even if every division of the Anglo-Portuguese army were concentrated, if Hill came up from Estremadura and Skerrett's small force from Cadiz, it would be eminently doubtful whether Madrid could be held and the enemy thrust back. The French might advance 85,000 strong, and Wellington could only rely on 60,000 men of his own to face them—though he might scrape together three or four divisions of Spanish troops in addition [1]. It was true that Suchet might probably refuse to evacuate his Valencian viceroyalty, and that occupation for him might be found by utilizing Maitland's expeditionary force at Alicante, and Elio's Murcian army. But even if he did not join Soult and King Joseph in a march on Madrid, the armies of the South and Centre might put 65,000 men into the field.

But this was only half the problem. There was Clausel's Army of Portugal, not to speak of Caffarelli's Army of the North, to be taken into consideration. Clausel had some 40,000 men behind the Douro—troops recently beaten it is true, and known to be in bad order. But they had not been pursued since the Allied army turned aside for the march on Madrid, and had now been granted a month in which to pull themselves together. Nothing had been left in front of them save Clinton's 6th Division at Cuellar, and a division of the Galicians at Valladolid.

---

[1] Certainly Carlos de España and Morillo, probably some of the Galicians, and even some of Elio's or Ballasteros' troops from the South, if they proved able to feed themselves and march.

And now the vexatious news had come that Clausel was on the move, had chased the Galicians out of Valladolid, and was sending flying columns into the plains of Leon. It was clear that he must be dealt with at once, and there was no way to stop his annoying activity, save by detaching a considerable force from Madrid. If unopposed, he might overrun all the reconquered lands along the Douro, and even imperil the British line of communication with Salamanca and Portugal. If, as was possible, Caffarelli should lend him a couple of divisions from the Army of the North, he might become a real danger instead of a mere nuisance.

This was the reason why Wellington departed from Madrid on August 31st, and marched with the 1st, 5th and 7th Divisions, Pack's and Bradford's Portuguese, and Bock's and Ponsonby's dragoons—21,000 sabres and bayonets—to join Clinton, and thrust back Clausel to the North, before he should have leisure to do further mischief. There was, as he conceived, just time enough to inflict a sharp check on the Army of Portugal before the danger from the side of Valencia would become pressing. It must be pushed out of the way, disabled again if possible, and then he would return to Madrid for the greater game, leaving as small a containing force as possible in front of the Northern army. He summed up his plan in a confidential letter in the following terms : ' All the world [the French world] seems to be intending to mass itself in Valencia ; while I am waiting for their plans to develop, for General Hill to march up from Estremadura, and for the Spanish armies to get together, I shall hunt away the elements of Marmont's [i. e. Clausel's] army from the Douro. I shall push them as far off as I can, I shall try to establish proper co-operation between the Anglo-Portuguese detachment which I must leave on this side and the Galician Army, and so I shall assure my left flank, when I shall be engaged on the Valencian side [1].'

Here then, we have a time-problem set. Will it be possible to deal handsomely with the Army of Portugal, to put it completely out of power to do harm, before Soult shall have reached Valencia, reorganized his army, and joined King Joseph in

---

[1] *Dispatches,* ix. p. 424, to General Dumouriez, to whom Wellington often sent an illuminating note on the situation.

what Wellington considered the inevitable scheme of a march
on Madrid ? The British general judged that there would be
sufficient time—and probably there might have been, if everything had worked out in the best possible way. But he was
quite conscious that events might prove perverse—and he
shuddered at the thought—as he wrote to his brother in Cadiz.

The last precautions taken before departing for the Douro
were to draw up three sets of instructions. One was for Charles
Alten, left in command of the four divisions which remained
in and about Madrid [1], foreseeing the chance of Soult's marching
on the capital without turning aside to Valencia—' not at all
probable, but it is necessary to provide for all events.' The
second was for Hill, who was due to arrive at Toledo in about
three weeks. The third was for General Maitland at Alicante,
whose position would obviously be very unpleasant, now that
Soult was known to be evacuating Andalusia and marching on
Valencia to join Suchet and King Joseph. Soult's march altered
the whole situation on the East Coast: if 50,000 more
French were concentrated in that direction, the Alicante force
must be in some danger, and would have to observe great
caution, and if necessary to shut itself up in the maritime
fortresses. ' As the allied forces in Valencia and Murcia '—
wrote Wellington to Maitland—' will necessarily be thrown
upon the defensive for a moment, while the enemy will be
in great strength in those parts, I conclude that the greater
part of those forces will be collected in Alicante, and it would
be desirable to strengthen our posts at Carthagena during this
crisis, which I hope will be only momentary [2].' Another
dispatch, dated four days later, adverts to the possibility that
Soult may fall upon Alicante on his arrival in the kingdom of
Valencia. Maitland is to defend the place, but to take care that
all precautions as to the embarking his troops in the event of
ill-success are made. He is expected to maintain it as long as
possible ; and with the sea open to him, and a safe harbour, the
defence should be long and stubborn, however great the numbers
of the besiegers [3].

With these instructions drawn out for Maitland, Wellington

[1] *Dispatches*, ix. pp. 390–1. Alten had the 3rd, 4th, Light, and España's
divisions.   [2] *Dispatches*, ix. p. 377.   [3] Ibid., ix. pp. 383–4 and 386–7.

finally marched for the North. His conception of the situation
in Valencia seems to have been that Soult, on his arrival, would
not meddle with Alicante : it was more probable that he and
King Joseph would rather take up the much more important
task of endeavouring to reconquer Madrid and New Castile.
They would leave Suchet behind them to contain Maitland,
Elio and Ballasteros. It would be impossible for him to lend
them any troops for a march on Madrid, while such a large
expeditionary force was watching his flank. The net result
would be that ' by keeping this detachment at Alicante, with
Whittingham's and Roche's Spaniards, I shall prevent too
many of the gentlemen now assembled in Valencia from
troubling me in the Upper Country [New Castile] [1].'

Travelling with his usual celerity, Wellington left Madrid
on August 31st, was at Villa Castin on the northern side of the
Guadarrama pass on September 2nd, and had reached Arevalo,
where he joined Clinton and the 6th Division on September 3rd.
The divisions which he was bringing up from Madrid had been
started off some days before he himself left the capital. He
passed them between the Escurial and Villa Castin, but they
caught him up again at Arevalo early on the 4th, so that he
had his fighting force concentrated on that day, and was
prepared to deal with Clausel.

The situation of affairs on the Douro requires a word of
explanation. Clausel, it will be remembered, had retired from
Valladolid on July 30, unpursued. He was prepared to retreat
for any length—even as far as Burgos—if he were pressed. But
no one followed him save Julian Sanchez's lancers and some
patrols of Anson's Light Cavalry brigade. Wherefore he halted
his main body on the line of the Arlanza, with two divisions at
Torquemada and two at Lerma ; some way to his left Foy, with
two divisions more, was at Aranda, on the Upper Douro, where
he had maintained his forward position, because not even
a cavalry patrol from the side of the Allies had come forward
to disquiet him. In front of Clausel himself there was soon
nothing left but the lightest of cavalry screens, for Julian
Sanchez was called off by Wellington to New Castile: when he
was gone, there remained Marquinez's guerrilleros at Palencia,

---

[1] Ibid., ix. p. 398.

and outposts of the 16th Light Dragoons at Valtanas : the
main body of G. Anson's squadrons lay at Villavanez, twenty
miles behind[1]. The only infantry force which the Allies had
north of the Douro was one of the divisions of the Army of
Galicia, which (with Santocildes himself in command) came
up to Valladolid on August 6th, not much over 3,000 bayonets
strong. The second of the Galician divisions which had
descended into the plain of Leon was now blockading Toro.
The third and most numerous was still engaged in the interminable siege of Astorga, which showed at last some signs of drawing
to its close—not because the battering of the place had been
effective, but simply because the garrison was growing famished.
They had been provisioned only as far as August 1, and after
that date had been forced upon half and then quarter rations.
But the news of the disaster of Salamanca had not, as many
had hoped among the Allies, scared their commander into
capitulation.

Clausel on August 1 had not supposed it possible that he
would be tempted to take the offensive again within a fortnight.
His army was in a most dilapidated condition, and he was
prepared to give way whenever pressed. It was not that his
numbers were so very low, for on August 1st the Army of
Portugal only counted 10,000 less effectives than on July 15th.
Though it had lost some 14,000 men in the Salamanca campaign,
it had picked up some 4,000 others from the dépôt at Valladolid,
from the many small garrisons which it had drawn in during
its retreat, and from drafts found at Burgos.[2] Its loss in cavalry
had been fully repaired by the arrival of Chauvel's two regiments
from the Army of the North, and most of the fugitives and
marauders who had been scattered over the country-side after
the battle of July 22nd gradually drifted back to their colours.
It was not so much numbers as spirit that was wanting in the

---

[1] The best account of all this is in the diary for August of Tomkinson
of the 16th Light Dragoons, who was in charge of the outlying party that
went to Valtanas.

[2] The actual numbers (as shown in the tables given in vol. v, Appendix xi
—which I owe to Mr. Fortescue's kindness) were July 15, 49,636 ; August 1,
39,301. The deficiency of about 600 cavalry lost had been more than
replaced by Chauvel's 750 sabres. There was a shortage of twenty guns of
the original artillery, but Chauvel had brought up six.

Army of Portugal. On August 6 Clausel wrote to the Minister
of War at Paris that he had halted in a position where he could
feed the troops, give them some days of repose, and above all
re-establish their morale[1]. 'I must punish some of the men,
who are breaking out in the most frightful outrages, and so
frighten the others by an example of severity ; above all I must
put an end to a desire, which they display too manifestly, to
recross the Ebro, and get back nearer to the French frontier.
It is usual to see an army disheartened after a check : but it
would be hard to find one whose discouragement is greater than
that of these troops : and I cannot, and ought not, to conceal
from you that there has been prevailing among them for some
time a very bad spirit. Disorders and revolting excesses have
marked every step of our retreat. I shall employ all the means
in my power to transform the dispositions of the soldiers, and
to put an end to the deplorable actions which daily take place
under the very eyes of officers of all grades—actions which the
latter fail to repress.'

Clausel was as good as his word, and made many and severe
examples, shooting (so he says) as many as fifty soldiers found
guilty of murders, assaults on officers, and other excesses[2]. It
is probable, however, that it was not so much his strong punitive
measures which brought about an improved discipline in the
regiments, as the fortnight of absolutely undisturbed repose
which they enjoyed from the 1st to the 14th of August. The
feeling of demoralization caused by the headlong and disorderly
retreat from Salamanca died down, as it became more and more
certain that the pursuit was over, and that there was no serious
hostile force left within many miles of the line of the Arlanza.
The obsession of being hunted by superior forces had been the
ruinous thing : when this terror was withdrawn, and when the
more shattered regiments had been re-formed into a smaller
number of battalions, and provided in this fashion with their
proper proportion of officers[3], the troops began to realize that

---

[1] Dispatch printed in *King Joseph's Correspondence*, ix. p. 64.

[2] Clausel to Clarke, August 18th, 1812.

[3] The 2nd, 4th, 6th, and 25th Léger, the 1st, 15th, 36th, 50th, 62nd, 65th,
118th, 119th, 120th Line had to cut themselves down by a battalion each :
the 22nd and 101st, which had been the heaviest sufferers of all, and had
each lost their eagle, were reduced from three to one battalion each. There

they still formed a considerable army, and that they had been
routed, but not absolutely put out of action, by the Salamanca
disaster.

Yet their morale had been seriously shaken; there was still
a want of officers; a number of the rejoining fugitives had come
in without arms or equipment; while others had been heard
of, but had not yet reported themselves at their regimental
head-quarters. It therefore required considerable hardihood on
Clausel's part to try an offensive move, even against a skeleton
enemy. His object was primarily to bring pressure upon the
allied rear, in order to relieve King Joseph from Wellington's
attentions. He had heard that the whole of the Anglo-Portu-
·guese army, save a negligible remnant, had marched on
Madrid; but he was not sure that the Army of the Centre
might not make some endeavour to save the capital, especially
if it had been reinforced from Estremadura by Drouet. Clausel
knew that the King had repeatedly called for succours from the
South; it was possible that they might have been sent at the
last moment. If they had come up, and if Wellington could
be induced to send back two or three divisions to the Douro,
Madrid might yet be saved. The experiment was worth risking,
but it must take the form of a demonstration rather than
a genuine attack upon Wellington's rear. The Army of Portugal
was still too fragile an instrument to be applied to heavy work.
Indeed, when he moved, Clausel left many shattered regiments
behind, and only brought 25,000 men to the front.

There was a second object in Clausel's advance: he hoped
to save the garrisons of Astorga, Toro, and Zamora, which
amounted in all to over 3,000 men. Each of the first two was
being besieged by a Spanish division, the third by Silveira's Portuguese militia. The French general judged that none of the investing forces was equal to a fight in the open with a strong flying
column of his best troops. Even if all three could get together,
he doubted if they dared face two French divisions. His scheme
was to march on Valladolid with his main body, and drive out
of it the small Spanish force in possession, while Foy—his senior
division-commander—should move rapidly across country with

had been seventy-four battalions in the Army of Portugal on July 1st : on
August 1st there were only fifty-seven.

some 8,000 men, and relieve by a circular sweep first Toro, then Astorga, then Zamora. The garrisons were to be brought off, the places blown up : it was useless to dream of holding them, for Wellington would probably come to the Douro again in force, the sieges would recommence, and no second relief would be possible in face of the main British army.

On August 13th a strong French cavalry reconnaissance crossed the Arlanza and drove in the guerrilleros from Zevico : on the following day infantry was coming up from the rear, pushing forward on the high-road from Torquemada to Valladolid. Thereupon Anson, on that evening, sent back the main body of his light dragoons beyond the Douro, leaving only two squadrons as a rearguard at Villavanez. The Galician division in Valladolid also retired by the road of Torrelobaton and Castronuevo on Benavente. Santocildes—to Wellington's disgust when it reached his ears—abandoned in Valladolid not only 400 French convalescents in hospital, but many hundred stand of small arms, which had been collected there from the prisoners taken during the retreat of Clausel in the preceding month. This was inexcusable carelessness, as there was ample time to destroy them, if not to carry them off. French infantry entered Valladolid on the 14th and 15th, apparently about 12,000 strong : their cavalry, a day's march ahead, had explored the line of the Douro from Simancas to Tudela, and found it watched by G. Anson's pickets all along that front.

The orders left behind by Wellington on August 5th, had been that if Clausel came forward—which he had not thought likely—G. Anson was to fall back to the Douro, and if pressed again to join Clinton's division at Cuellar. The retreat of both of them was to be on Segovia in the event of absolute necessity. On the other hand, if the French should try to raise the sieges of Astorga or Zamora, Santocildes and Silveira were to go behind the Esla[1]. Clausel tried both these moves at once, for on the same day that he entered Valladolid he had turned off Foy with two divisions—his own and Taupin's (late Ferey's)—and a brigade of Curto's *chasseurs*, to march on Toro by the road through Torrelobaton. The troops in Valladolid served to

---

[1] See ' Memorandum for General Santocildes ' of August 5. *Dispatches*, ix. pp. 344-5.

cover this movement : they showed a division of infantry and 800 horse in front of Tudela on the 16th, and pushed back Anson's light dragoons to Montemayor, a few miles beyond the Douro. But this was only a demonstration : their cavalry retired in the evening, and Anson reoccupied Tudela on the 20th. It soon became clear that Clausel was not about to cross the Douro in force, and was only showing troops in front of Valladolid in order to keep Anson and Clinton anxious. He remained there with some 12,000 or 15,000 men from August 14th till September 7th, keeping very quiet, and making no second attempt to reconnoitre beyond the Douro. Anson, therefore, watched the line of the river, with his head-quarters at Valdestillas, for all that time, while the guerrilleros of Saornil and Principe went over to the northern bank and hung around Clausel's flank. Clinton, on his own initiative, moved his division from Cuellar to Arevalo, which placed him on the line of the road to Madrid via the Guadarrama, instead of that by Segovia. This Wellington afterwards declared to be a mistake : he had intended to keep the 6th Division more to the right, apparently in order that it might cross the Douro above Valladolid if required[1]. It should not have moved farther southward than Olmedo.

Foy meanwhile, thus covered by Clausel, made a march of surprising celerity. On the 17th he arrived at Toro, and learned that the Galicians blockading that place had cleared off as early as the 15th, and had taken the road for Benavente. He blew up the fort, and took on with him the garrison of 800 men. At Toro he was much nearer to Zamora than to Astorga, but he resolved to march first on the remoter place—it was known to be hard pressed, and the French force there blockaded was double that in Zamora. He therefore moved on Benavente with all possible speed, and crossed the Esla there, driving away a detachment of the Galician division (Cabrera's) which had come from Valladolid, when it made an ineffectual attempt to hold the fords. On the 20th August he reached La Baneza, some sixteen miles from Astorga, and there received the tiresome news that the garrison had surrendered only thirty-six hours before to Castaños. The three battalions there, worn down by

[1] *Dispatches*, ix. pp. 389-90.

famine to 1,200 men, had capitulated, because they had no suspicion that any help was near. The Spanish general had succeeded in concealing from them all knowledge of Foy's march. They laid down their arms on the 18th, and were at once marched off to Galicia : Castaños himself accompanied them with all his force, being fully determined not to fight Foy, even though his numbers were superior.

The French cavalry pushed on to Astorga on the 21st, and found the gates open and the place empty, save for seventy sick of the late garrison, who had been left behind under the charge of a surgeon. It was useless to think of pursuing Castaños, who had now two days' start, wherefore Foy turned his attention to Zamora. Here Silveira, though warned to make off when the enemy reached Toro, had held on to the last moment, thinking that he was safe when Foy swerved away toward Astorga. He only drew off when he got news on the 22nd, from Sir Howard Douglas, the British Commissioner with the Galician army, to the effect that Foy, having failed to save Astorga, was marching against him. He retired to Carvajales behind the Esla, but was not safe there, for the French general, turning west from Benavente, had executed a forced march for Tabara, and was hastening westward to cut in between Carvajales and the road to Miranda de Douro on the Portuguese frontier. Warned only just in time of this move, Silveira hurried off towards his own country, and was within one mile of its border when Foy's advanced cavalry came up with his rear-guard near Constantin, the last village in Spain. They captured his baggage and some stragglers, but made no serious endeavour to charge his infantry, which escaped unharmed to Miranda. Foy attributed this failure to Curto, the commander of the light horse : ' le défaut de décision et l'inertie coupable du général commandant la cavalerie font perdre les fruits d'une opération bien combinée ' (August 23rd)[1]. This pursuit had drawn Foy very far westward ; his column turning

---

[1] The best account of all this is not (as might have been expected) in Foy's dispatches to Clausel, but in a memorandum drawn up by him in 1817 at the request of Sir Howard Douglas, and printed in an appendix at the end of the life of that officer (pp. 429–30). Sir Howard had asked Foy what he intended to do on the 23rd–27th August, and got a most interesting reply.

back, only reached Zamora on August 26th : here he drew off the garrison and destroyed the works. He states that his next move would have been a raid on Salamanca, where lay not only the British base hospital, but a vast accumulation of stores, unprotected by any troops whatever. But he received at Zamora, on the 27th, urgent orders from Clausel to return to Valladolid, as Wellington was coming up against him from Madrid with his whole army. Accordingly Foy abandoned his plan, and reached Tordesillas, with his troops in a very exhausted condition from hard marching, on August 28th. Clausel had miscalculated dates—warned of the first start of the 1st and 7th Divisions from Madrid, he had supposed that they would be at Arevalo some days before they actually reached it on September 4th. Foy was never in any real danger, and there had been time to spare. His excursion undoubtedly raised the spirit of the Army of Portugal : it was comforting to find that the whole of the Galicians would not face 8,000 French troops, and that the plains of Leon could be overrun without opposition by such a small force. On his return to join the main body Foy noted in his diary that Clausel had been very inert in face of Anson and Clinton, and wrote that he himself would have tried a more dashing policy—and might possibly have failed in it, owing to the discouragement and apathy still prevailing among many of the senior officers of the Army of Portugal [1].

Wellington had received the news of Clausel's advance on Valladolid as early as August 18th, and was little moved by it. Indeed he expressed some pleasure at the fact. ' I think,' he wrote to Lord Bathurst, ' that the French mean to carry off the garrisons from Zamora and Toro, which I hope they will effect, as otherwise I must go and take them. If I do not, nobody else will, as is evident from what has been passing for the last two months at Astorga [2].' He expressed his pleasure on hearing that Santocildes had retired behind the Esla without fighting, for he had feared that he might try to stop Foy and get beaten. It was only, as we have already seen, after he obtained practical certainty that Soult had evacuated Andalusia, so that no expedition to the South would be necessary, that he

[1] Diary of Foy, in Girod de l'Ain's *Vie militaire du Général Foy*, p. 182.
[2] Wellington to Bathurst, August 18th.

turned his mind to Clausel's doings. And his march to Arevalo and Valladolid was intended to be a mere excursion for a few weeks, preparatory to a return to New Castile to face Soult and King Joseph, when they should become dangerous. From Arevalo he wrote to Castaños to say that ' it was necessary to drive off Marmont's (i.e. Clausel's) army without loss of time, so as to make it possible to turn the whole of his forces eventually against Soult.' He should press the movement so far forward as he could ; perhaps he might even lay siege to Burgos. But the Army of Galicia must come eastward again without delay, and link up its operations with the Anglo-Portuguese. He hoped to have retaken Valladolid by September 6th, and wished to see Castaños there, with the largest possible force that he could gather, on that date [1]. The Galician army had returned to Astorga on August 27th, and so far as distances went, there was nothing to prevent it from being at Valladolid eleven days after, if it took the obvious route by Benavente and Villalpando.

The troops from Madrid having joined Clinton and the 6th Division at Arevalo, Wellington had there some 28,000 men collected for the discomfiture of Clausel, a force not much more numerous than that which the French general had concentrated behind the Douro, for Foy was now back at Tordesillas, and the whole Army of Portugal was in hand, save certain depleted and disorganized regiments which had been left behind in the province of Burgos. But having the advantage of confidence, and knowing that his enemy must still be suffering from the moral effects of Salamanca, the British general pushed on at once, not waiting for the arrival on the scene of the Galicians. On the 4th the army marched to Olmedo, on the 5th to Valdestillas, on the 6th to Boecillo, from whence it advanced to the Douro and crossed it by various fords between Tudela and Puente de Duero—the main body taking that of Herrera. The French made no attempt to defend the line of the river, but—rather to Wellington's surprise—were found drawn up as if for battle a few miles beyond it, their right wing holding the city of Valladolid, whose outskirts had been put in a state of defence, their left extending to the ground about the village

[1] Wellington to Castaños, September 2. *Dispatches*, ix. p. 394.

of La Cisterniga. No attempt was made to dislodge them with the first divisions that came up : Wellington preferred to wait for his artillery and his reserves ; the process of filing across the fords had been tedious, and occupied the whole afternoon.

On this Clausel had calculated : he was only showing a front in order to give his train time to move to the rear, and to allow his right wing (Foy) at Simancas and Tordesillas to get away. A prompt evacuation of Valladolid would have exposed it to be cut off. On the following morning the French had disappeared from La Cisterniga, but Valladolid was discovered to be still held by an infantry rearguard. This, when pushed, retired and blew up the bridge over the Pisuerga on the opposite side of the city, before the British cavalry could seize it. The critics thought that Clausel might have been hustled with advantage, both on the 6th and on the morning of the 7th, and that Foy might have been cut off from the main body by rapid action on the first day [1]. Wellington's cautious movements may probably be explained by the fact that an attack on Clausel on the 6th would have involved fighting among the suburbs and houses of Valladolid, which would have been costly, and he had no wish to lose men at a moment when the battalion-strengths were very low all through the army. Moreover, the capture of Valladolid would not have intercepted the retreat of the French at Simancas, but only have forced them to retire by parallel roads northward. At the same time it must be owned that any loss of life involved in giving Clausel a thorough beating on this day would have been justified later on. He had only some 15,000 men in line, not having his right-wing troops with him that day. If the Army of Portugal had been once more attacked and scattered, it would not have been able to interfere in the siege of Burgos, where Wellington was, during the next few weeks, to lose as many men as a general action would have cost. But this no prophet could have foreseen on September 6th.

It cannot be said that Wellington's pursuit of Clausel was pressed with any earnestness. On the 8th his advanced cavalry

[1] See especially Sir Howard Douglas's *Memoirs*, pp. 206–7, and Tomkinson's diary, p. 201. Napier is short and unsatisfactory at this point, and says wrongly that Clausel abandoned Valladolid on the night of the 6th. His rearguard was certainly there on the 7th.

were no farther forward than Cabezon, seven miles in front of
Valladolid, and it was not till the 9th that the 6th Division,
leading the infantry, passed that same point. Wellington
himself, with the main body of his infantry, remained at Valladolid till the 10th. His dispatches give no further explanation
for this delay than that the troops which had come from Madrid
were fatigued, and sickly, from long travel in the hot weather,
and that he wished to have assurance of the near approach of
the Army of Galicia, which was unaccountably slow in moving
forward from Astorga[1]. Meanwhile he took the opportunity
of his stay in Valladolid to command, and be present at,
a solemn proclamation of the March Constitution. This was
a prudent act; for though the ceremony provoked no enthusiasm whatever in the city[2], where there were few Liberals
in existence, it was a useful demonstration against calumnies
current in Cadiz, to the effect that he so much disliked the
Constitution that he was conspiring with the *serviles*, and
especially with Castaños, to ignore or even to overthrow it.

While Wellington halted at Valladolid, Clausel had established
himself at Dueñas, fifteen miles up the Pisuerga. He retired
from thence, however, on the 10th, when the 6th Division and
Anson's cavalry pressed in his advanced posts, and Wellington's
head-quarters were at Dueñas next day. From thence recon
naissances were sent out both on the Burgos and the Palencia
roads. The latter city was found unoccupied and—what was
more surprising—not in the least damaged by the retreating
enemy. The whole of Clausel's army had marched on the
Burgos road, and its rearguard was discovered in front of
Torquemada that evening. The British army followed, leaving
Palencia on its left, and head-quarters were at Magaz on the
12th. Anson's light dragoons had the interesting spectacle
that afternoon of watching the whole French army defile across
the bridge of the Pisuerga at Torquemada, under cover of
a brigade of *chasseurs* drawn up on the near side. Critics

---

[1] Castaños's explanation was that Wellington's letter of August 30, telling
him to march on Valladolid, did not reach him till the 7th September, along
with another supplementary letter to the same effect from Arevalo of
September 3.

[2] 'The proclamation was made from the town-hall in the square : few
people of any respectability attended.' Tomkinson, p. 202.

thought that the covering force might have been driven in, and jammed against the narrow roadway over the bridge[1]. But the British brigadier waited for artillery to come up, and before it arrived the enemy had hastily decamped. He was pursued as far as Quintana, where there was a trifling cavalry skirmish at nightfall.

At Magaz, on the night of the 12th, Wellington got the tiresome news that Santocildes and Castaños, with the main body of the Army of Galicia, had passed his flank that day, going southward, and had continued their way towards Valladolid, instead of falling in on the British line of march. Their junction was thus deferred for several days. Wellington wrote in anger, 'Santocildes has been six days marching: he was yesterday within three leagues of us, and knew it that night; but he has this morning moved on to Valladolid, eight leagues from us, and unless I halt two days for him he will not join us for four or five days more[2].' As a matter of fact the Galicians did not come up till the 16th, while if Santocildes had used a little common sense they would have been in line on the 12th September.

The pursuit of Clausel continued to be a very slow and uninteresting business: from the 11th to the 15th the army did not advance more than two leagues a day. On the 13th the British vanguard was at Villajera, while the French main body was at Pampliega: on the 14th Anson's cavalry was at Villadrigo, on the 15th at Villapequeña, on the 16th near Celada, where Clausel was seen in position. On this day the Galicians at last came up—three weak divisions under Cabrera, Losada, and Barcena, with something over 11,000 infantry, but only one field-battery and 350 horse. The men looked fatigued with much marching and very ragged: Wellington had hoped for 16,000 men, and considering that the total force of the Galician army was supposed to be over 30,000 men, it seems that more might have been up, even allowing for sick, recruits, and the large garrisons of Ferrol and Corunna.

The 16th September was the only day on which Clausel

---

[1] Tomkinson, p. 203.

[2] Wellington to Henry Wellesley, Magaz, September 12. *Dispatches*, ix. p. 422.

showed any signs of making a stand : in the afternoon he was found in position, a league beyond Celada on favourable ground. Wellington arranged to turn his left flank next morning, with the 6th Division and Pack's brigade ; but at dawn he went off in haste, and did not stop till he reached Villa Buniel, near Burgos. Here, late in the afternoon, Wellington again out-flanked him with the 6th Division, and he retreated quite close to the city. On the 18th he evacuated it, after throwing a garrison into the Castle,. and went back several leagues on the high-road toward the Ebro. The Allies entered Burgos, and pushed their cavalry beyond it without meeting opposition. On the 19th the Castle was invested by the 1st Division and Pack's brigade, while the rest of Wellington's army took position across the road by which the French had retreated. A cavalry reconnaissance showed that Clausel had gone back many miles : the last outposts of his rear were at Quintanavides, beyond the watershed which separates the basin of the Douro from that of the Ebro. His head-quarters were now at Briviesca, and it appeared that, if once more pushed, he was prepared to retreat *ad infinitum*. Wellington, however, pressed him no farther : throwing forward three of his own divisions and the Galicians to Monasterio and other villages to the east of Burgos, where a good covering position was found, he proceeded to turn his attention to the Castle.

This short series of operations between the 10th and the 19th of September 1812 has in it much that perplexes the critical historian. It is not Clausel's policy that is interesting—he simply retired day after day, whenever the enemy's pursuing infantry came within ten miles of him. Sometimes he gave way before the mere cavalry of Wellington's advanced guard. There was nothing in his conduct to remind the observer of Ney's skilful retreat from Pombal to Ponte Murcella in 1811, when a rearguard action was fought nearly every afternoon. Clausel was determined not to allow himself to be caught, and would not hold on, even in tempting positions of considerable strength. As he wrote to Clarke before the retreat had begun, ' Si l'ennemi revient avec toute son armée vers moi, je me tiendrai en position, quoique toujours à peu de distance de lui, afin de n'avoir aucun échec à éprouver.' He suffered no check because he always made off before he was in the slightest danger of being brought to action. It is difficult to understand Napier's enthusiasm for what he calls 'beautiful movements'[1]; to abscond on the first approach of the enemy's infantry may be a safe and sound policy, but it can hardly be called brilliant or artistic. It is true that there would have been worse alternatives to take—Clausel might have retreated to the Ebro without stopping, or he might have offered battle at the first chance ; but the avoidance of such errors does not in itself constitute a very high claim to praise. An examination of the details of the march of the British army during this ten days plainly fails to corroborate Napier's statement that the French general ' offered battle every day ' and ' baffled his great adversary.' His halt for a few hours at Celada on September 16th was the only one during which he allowed the allied main body to get into touch with him late in the day ; and he absconded before Wellington's first manœuvre to outflank him [2].

The thing that is truly astonishing in this ten days is the extraordinary torpidity of Wellington's pursuit. He started by waiting three days at Valladolid after expelling the French ; and he continued, when once he had put his head-quarters in motion, by making a series of easy marches of six to ten miles a day, never showing the least wish to hustle his adversary or to bring him to action [3]. Now to manœuvre the French army to beyond Burgos, or even to the Ebro, was not the desired end—it was necessary to put Clausel out of action, if (as Wellington kept repeating in all his letters) the main allied army was to return to Madrid within a few weeks, to watch for Soult's

[1] Napier, iv. p. 335.

[2] Napier was not with the main army during this march, the Light Division being left at Madrid. On the other hand Clausel had been very polite to him, and lent him some of his orders and dispatches (Napier, iv. p. 327). I fancy he was repaid in print for his courtesy. The diaries of Tomkinson, Burgoyne, D'Urban, and Sir Howard Douglas do not give the impression that the French ever stayed to manœuvre seriously, save on the 16th.

[3] Head-quarters were at Valladolid, September 9; Cigales, September 10; Dueñas, September 11; Magaz, September 12; Torquemada, September 13; Cordovilla, September 14; Villajera, September 15; Pampliega, September 16; Tardajos, September 17; Villa Toro, September 18. Ten stages in about 80 miles !

offensive. To escort the Army of Portugal with ceremonious politeness to Briviesca, without the loss to pursuers or pursued of fifty men, was clearly not sufficient. Clausel's troops, being not harassed in the least, but allowed a comfortable retreat, remained an ' army in being ' : though moved back eighty miles on the map, they were not disposed of, and could obviously come forward again the moment that Wellington left the north with the main body of his troops. Nothing, therefore, was gained by the whole manœuvre, save that Clausel was six marches farther from the Douro than he had been on September 1st. To keep him in his new position Wellington must have left an adequate containing army : it does not seem that he could have provided one from the 28,000 Anglo-Portuguese and 11,000 Galicians who were at his disposition, and yet have had any appreciable force to take back to Madrid. Clausel had conducted his raid on Valladolid with something under 25,000 men ; but this did not represent the whole strength of the Army of Portugal : after deducting the sick and the garrisons there were some 39,000 men left—of these some were disarmed stragglers who had only just come back to their colours, others belonged to shattered corps which were only just reorganizing themselves in their new *cadres*. But in a few weeks Clausel would have at least 35,000 men under arms of his own troops, without counting anything that the Army of the North might possibly lend him. To contain him Wellington would have to leave, in addition to the 11,000 Galicians, at least three British divisions and the corresponding cavalry—say 16,000 or 18,000 men. He could only bring back some 10,000 bayonets to join Hill near Madrid. This would not enable him to face Soult.

But if Clausel had been dealt with in a more drastic style, if he had been hunted and harassed, it is clear that he might have been disabled for a long time from taking the offensive. His army was still in a doubtful condition as regards morale, and there can be little reason to doubt, that if hard pressed, it would have sunk again into the despondency and disorder which had prevailed at the beginning of the month of August. The process of driving him back with a firm hand might, no doubt, have been more costly than the slow tactics actually adopted ; but undoubtedly such a policy would have paid in the end.

There is no explanation to be got out of Wellington's rather numerous letters written between the 10th and the 21st. In one of them he actually observes that ' we have been pushing them, but not very vigorously, till the 16th [1],' without saying why the pressure was not applied more vigorously. From others it might perhaps be deduced that Wellington was awaiting the arrival of the Galician army, because when it came up he would have a very large instead of a small superiority of force over the French. But this does not fully explain his slowness in pursuing an enemy who was evidently on the run, and determined not to fight. We may, as has been already mentioned, speak of his wish to avoid loss of life (not much practised during the Burgos operations a few days later on !) and of the difficulty of providing for supplies in a country-side unvisited before by the British army, and very distant from its base-magazines. But when all has been said, no adequate explanation for his policy has been provided. It remains inexplicable, and its results were unhappy.

[1] Wellington to Sir E. Paget, September 20. *Dispatches*, ix. p. 436.

SECTION XXXIV: CHAPTER II

THE SIEGE OF BURGOS. SEPTEMBER 19TH—OCTOBER 20TH, 1812

THE Castle of Burgos lies on an isolated hill which rises straight out of the streets of the north-western corner of that ancient city, and overtops them by 200 feet or rather more. Ere ever there were kings in Castile, it had been the residence of Fernan Gonzalez, and the early counts who recovered the land from the Moors. Rebuilt a dozen times in the Middle Ages, and long a favourite palace of the Castilian kings, it had been ruined by a great fire in 1736, and since then had not been inhabited. There only remained an empty shell, of which the most important part was the great Donjon which had defied the flames. The summit of the hill is only 250 yards long : the eastern section of it was occupied by the Donjon, the western by a large church, Santa Maria la Blanca : between them were more or less ruined buildings, which had suffered from the conflagration. Passing by Burgos in 1808, after the battle of Gamonal, Napoleon had noted the commanding situation of the hill, and had determined to make it one of the fortified bases upon which the French domination in northern Spain was to be founded. He had caused a plan to be drawn up for the conversion of the ruined mediaeval stronghold into a modern citadel, which should overawe the city below, and serve as a half-way house, an arsenal, and a dépôt for French troops moving between Bayonne and Madrid. Considered as a fortress it had one prominent defect : while its eastern, southern, and western sides look down into the low ground around the Arlanzon river, there lies on its northern side, only 300 yards away, a flat-topped plateau, called the hill of San Miguel, which rises to within a few feet of the same height as the Donjon, and overlooks all the lower slopes of the Castle mount. As this rising ground— now occupied by the city reservoir of Burgos—commanded so much of the defences, Napoleon held that it must be occupied, and a fort upon it formed part of his original plan. But the Emperor passed on ; the tide of war swept far south of Madrid ; and the full scheme for the fortification of Burgos was never carried out ; money—the essential thing when building is in hand—was never forthcoming in sufficient quantities, and the actual state of the place in 1812 was very different from what it would have been if Napoleon's orders had been carried out in detail. Enough was done to make the Castle impregnable against guerrillero bands—the only enemies who ever came near it between 1809 and 1812—but it could not be described as a complete or satisfactory piece of military engineering. Against a besieger unprovided with sufficient artillery it was formidable enough : round two-thirds of its circuit it had a complete double *enceinte*, enclosing the Donjon and the church on the summit which formed its nucleus. On the western side, for about one-third of its circumference, it had an outer or third line of defence, to take in the lowest slopes of the hill on which it lies. For here the ground descended gradually, while to the east it shelved very steeply down to the town, and an external defence was unnecessary and indeed impossible.

The outer line all round (i.e. the third line on the west, the second line on the rest of the circumference) had as its base the old walls of the external enclosure of the mediaeval Castle, modernized by shot-proof parapets and with tambours and palisades added at the angles to give flank fire. It had a ditch 30 feet wide, and a counterscarp in masonry, while the inner *enceintes* were only strong earthworks, like good field entrenchments ; they were, however, both furnished with palisades in front and were also 'fraised' above. The Donjon, which had been strengthened and built up, contained the powder magazine in its lower story. On its platform, which was most solid, was established a battery for eight heavy guns (*Batterie Napoléon*), which from its lofty position commanded all the surrounding ground, including the top of the hill of San Miguel. The magazine of provisions, which was copiously supplied, was in the church of Santa Maria la Blanca. Food never failed— but water was a more serious problem ; there was only one well, and the garrison had to be put on an allowance for drinking from the commencement of the siege. The hornwork of San Miguel, which covered the important plateau to the north, had never been properly finished. It was very large; its front was composed of earthwork 25 feet high, covered by a counter-scarp of 10 feet deep. Here the work was formidable, the scarp being steep and slippery; but the flanks were not so strong, and the rear or gorge was only closed by a row of palisades, erected within the last two days. The only outer defences consisted of three light *flèches*, or redans, lying some 60 yards out in front of the hornwork, at projecting points of the plateau, which commanded the lower slopes. The artillery in San Miguel consisted of seven field-pieces, 4- and 6-pounders: there were no heavy guns in it.

The garrison of Burgos belonged to the Army of the North, not to that of Portugal. Caffarelli himself paid a hasty visit to the place just before the siege began, and threw in some picked troops—two battalions of the 34th[1], one of the 130th; making 1,600 infantry. There were also a company of artillery, another of pioneers, and detachments which brought up the whole to exactly 2,000 men—a very sufficient number for a place of such small size. There were nine heavy guns (16- and 12-pounders), of which eight were placed in the Napoleon battery, eleven field-pieces (seven of them in San Miguel), and six mortars or howitzers. This was none too great a provision, and would have been inadequate against a besieger provided with a proper battering-train: Wellington—as we shall see—was not so provided. The governor was a General of Brigade named Dubreton, one of the most resourceful and enterprising officers whom the British army ever encountered. He earned at Burgos a reputation even more brilliant than that which Phillipon acquired at Badajoz.

The weak points of the fortress were firstly the unfinished condition of the San Miguel hornwork, which Dubreton had to maintain as long as he could, in order that the British might not use the hill on which it stood as vantage ground for battering the Castle; secondly, the lack of cover within the works. The Donjon and the church of Santa Maria could not house a tithe

---

[1] One of the regiments withdrawn to the north after suffering at Arroyo dos Molinos, see vol. iv. p. 603.

of the garrison ; the rest had to bivouac in the open, a trying experience in the rain, which fell copiously on many days of the siege. If the besiegers had possessed a provision of mortars, to keep up a regular bombardment of the interior of the Castle, it would not long have been tenable, owing to the losses that must have been suffered. Thirdly must be mentioned the bad construction of many of the works—part of them were mediaeval structures, not originally intended to resist cannon, and hastily adapted to modern necessities : some of them were not furnished with parapets or embrasures—which had to be extemporized with sandbags. Lastly, it must be remembered that the conical shape of the hill exposed the inner no less than the outer works to battering : the lower *enceintes* only partly covered the inner ones, whose higher sections stood up visible above them. The Donjon and Santa Maria were exposed from the first to such fire as the enemy could turn against them, no less than the walls of the outer circumference. If Wellington had owned the siege-train that he brought against Badajoz, the place must have succumbed in ten days. But the commander was able and determined, the troops willing, the supply of food and of artillery munitions ample—Burgos had always been an important dépôt. Dubreton's orders were to keep his enemy detained as long as possible—and he succeeded, even beyond all reasonable expectations.

Wellington had always been aware that Burgos was fortified, but during his advance he had spoken freely of his intention to capture it. On September 3rd he had written, ' I have some heavy guns with me, and have an idea of forcing the siege of Burgos—but that still depends on circumstances[1].' Four days later he wrote at Valladolid, ' I am preparing to drive away the detachments of the Army of Portugal from the Douro, and I propose, if I have time, to take Burgos[2].' Yet at the same moment he kept impressing on his correspondents that his march to the North was a temporary expedient, a mere *parergon* ; his real business would be with Soult, and he must soon be back at Madrid with his main body. It is this that makes so inexplicable his lingering for a month before Dubre-

[1] Wellington to Castaños. *Dispatches*, ix. p. 394.
[2] Wellington to George Murray. *Dispatches*, ix. p. 398.

ton's castle, when he had once discovered that it would not fall, as he had hoped, in a few days. After his first failure before the place, he acknowledged it might possibly foil him altogether. Almost at the start he ventured the opinion that ' As far as I can judge, I am apprehensive that the means I have are not sufficient to enable me to take the Castle.' Yet he thought it worth while to try irregular methods : 'the enemy are ill-provided with water ; their magazines of provisions are in a place exposed to be set on fire. I think it possible, therefore, that I have it in my power to force them to surrender, although I may not be able to lay the place open to assault[1].'

The cardinal weakness of Wellington's position was exactly the same as at the Salamanca forts, three months back. He had no sufficient battering-train for a regular siege : after the Salamanca experience it is surprising that he allowed himself to be found for a second time in this deficiency. There were dozens of heavy guns in the arsenal at Madrid, dozens more (Marmont's old siege-train) at Ciudad Rodrigo and Almeida. But Madrid was 130 miles away, Rodrigo 180. With the army there was only Alexander Dickson's composite Anglo-Portuguese artillery reserve, commanded by Major Ariaga, and consisting of three iron 18-pounders, and five 24-pounder howitzers, served by 150 gunners—90 British, 60 Portuguese. The former were good battering-guns ; the howitzers, however, were not—they were merely short guns of position, very useless for a siege, and very inaccurate in their fire. They threw a heavy ball, but with weak power—the charge was only two pounds of powder : the shot when fired at a stout wall, from any distance, had such weak impact that it regularly bounded off without making any impression on the masonry. The only real use of these guns was for throwing case at short distances. ' In estimating the efficient ordnance used at the Spanish sieges,' says the official historian of the Burgos failure, ' these howitzers ought in fairness to be excluded from calculation, as they did little more than waste invaluable ammunition[2].' This was as well known to Wellington as to his subordinates, and it is inexplicable that he did not in place of them bring up

---

[1] Wellington to Lord Bathurst. *Dispatches*, ix. p. 442.
[2] Jones, *History of the Peninsular Sieges*, i. p. 473.

from Madrid real battering-guns : with ten more 18-pounders he would undoubtedly have taken the Castle of Burgos. But heavy guns require many draught cattle, and are hard to drag over bad roads : the absolute minimum had been taken with the army, as in June. And it was impossible to bring up more siege-guns in a hurry, as was done at the siege of the Salamanca forts, for the nearest available pieces were not a mere sixty miles away, as on the former occasion, but double and triple that distance. Yet if, on the first day of doubt before Burgos, Wellington had sent urgent orders for the dispatch of more 18-pounders from Madrid, they would have been up in time ; though no doubt there would have been terrible difficulties in providing for their transport. It was only when it had grown too late that more artillery was at last requisitioned—and had to be turned back not long after it had started.

Other defects there were in the besieging army, especially the same want of trained sappers and miners that had been seen at Badajoz, and of engineer officers[1]. Of this more hereafter :—the first and foremost difficulty, without which the rest would have been comparatively unimportant, was the lack of heavy artillery.

But to proceed to the chronicle of the siege. On the evening on which the army arrived before Burgos the 6th Division took post on the south bank of the Arlanzon : the 1st Division and Pack's Portuguese brigade swept round the city and formed an investing line about the Castle. It was drawn as close as possible, especially on the side of the hornwork of San Miguel, where the light companies of the first Division pushed up the hill, taking shelter in dead ground where they could, and dislodged the French outposts from the three *flèches* which lay upon its sky-line. Wellington, after consulting his chief engineer and artillery officers, determined that his first move must be to capture the hornwork, in order to use its vantage-ground for battering the Castle. The same night (September 19–20) an assault, without any preparation of artillery fire, was made upon it. The main body of the assailing force was composed of Pack's Portuguese, who were assisted

[1] There were eight rank and file of the Royal Military Artificers only, of whom seven were hit during the siege, and five R.E. officers in all.

by the whole of the 1/42nd and by the flank-companies [1] of
Stirling's brigade of the 1st Division, to which the Black Watch
belonged. The arrangement was that while a strong firing party
(300 men) of the 1/42nd were to advance to the neighbourhood
of the hornwork, ' as near to the salient angle as possible,' and
to endeavour to keep down the fire of the garrison, two columns
each composed of Portuguese, but with ladder parties and
forlorn hopes from the Highland battalion, should charge at the
two demi-bastions to right and left of the salient, and escalade
them. Meanwhile the flank-companies of Stirling's brigade
(1/42nd, 1/24th, 1/79th) were to make a false attack upon the
rear, or gorge, of the hornwork, which might be turned into
a real one if it should be found weakly held.

   The storm succeeded, but with vast and unnecessary loss of
life, and not in the way which Wellington had intended. It
was bright moonlight, and the firing party, when coming up
over the crest, were at once detected by the French, who opened
a very heavy fire upon them. The Highlanders commenced
to reply while still 150 yards away, and then advanced firing
till they came close up to the work, where they remained for
a quarter of an hour, entirely exposed and suffering terribly.
Having lost half their numbers they finally dispersed, but not
till after the main attack had failed.   On both their flanks the
assaulting columns were repulsed, though the advanced parties
duly laid their ladders : they were found somewhat short, and
after wavering for some minutes Pack's men retired, suffering
heavily. The whole affair would have been a failure, but for
the assault on the gorge. Here the three light companies—140
men—were led by Somers Cocks, formerly one of Wellington's
most distinguished intelligence officers, the hero of many a
risky ride, but recently promoted to a majority in the 1/79th.
He made no demonstration, but a fierce attack from the first.
He ran up the back slope of the hill of St. Miguel, under
a destructive fire from the Castle, which detected his little
column at once, and shelled it from the rear all the time that
it was at work. The frontal assault, however, was engrossing

   [1] By an odd misprint in Wellington's *Supplementary Dispatches*, xiv.
p. 120, the order is made to allot the flank-*battalions* instead of the flank-
companies to the task.

the attention of the garrison of the hornwork, and only a weak guard had been left at the gorge. The light companies broke through the 7-foot palisades, partly by using axes, partly by main force and climbing. Somers Cocks then divided his men into two bodies, leaving the smaller to block the postern in the gorge, while with the larger, he got upon the parapet and advanced firing towards the right demi-bastion. Suddenly attacked in the rear, just as they found themselves victorious in front, the French garrison—a battalion of the 34th, 500 strong —made no attempt to drive out the light companies, but ran in a mass towards the postern, trampled down the guard left there, and escaped to the Castle across the intervening ravine. They lost 198 men, including 60 prisoners, and left behind their seven field-pieces [1]. The assailants suffered far more—they had 421 killed and wounded, of whom no less than 204 were in the 1/42nd, which had suffered terribly in the main assault. The Portuguese lost 113 only, never having pushed their attack home. This murderous business was the first serious fighting in which the Black Watch were involved since their return to Spain in April 1812 ; at Salamanca they had been little engaged, and were the strongest British battalion in the field—over 1,000 bayonets. Wellington attributed their heavy casualties to their inexperience—they exposed themselves over-much. ' If I had had some of the troops who have stormed so often before [3rd and Light Divisions], I should not have lost a fourth of the number [2].'

The moment that the hornwork had fallen into the power of the British, the heavy guns of the Napoleon battery opened such an appalling fire upon it, that the troops had to be withdrawn, save 300 men, who with some difficulty formed a lodgement in its interior, and a communication from its left front to the ' dead ground ' on the north-west side of the hill, by which reliefs could enter under cover.

The whole of the next day (September 20) the garrison kept

[1] This narrative of the assault, not very clearly worked out in Napier— is drawn from the accounts of Burgoyne, Jones, the anonymous ' Private Soldier of the 42nd ' [London, 1821], and Tomkinson, the latter the special friend and confidant of Somers Cocks.

[2] Wellington to Lord Bathurst. *Dispatches*, ix. pp. 443–4.

up such a searching fire upon the work that little could be
done there, but on the following night the first battery of the
besiegers [battery 1 on the map] was begun on a spot on the
south-western side of the hill, a little way from the rear face of
the hornwork, which was sheltered by an inequality of the
ground from the guns of the Napoleon battery. It was armed
on the night of the 23rd with two of the 18-pounders and three
of the howitzers of the siege-train, with which it was intended to
batter the Castle in due time. They were not used however at
present, as Wellington, encouraged by his success at San
Miguel, had determined to try as a preliminary move a second
escalade, without help of artillery, on the outer *enceinte* of
the Castle. This was to prove the first, and not the least disheartening, of the checks that he was to meet before Burgos.

The point of attack selected was on the north-western side
of the lower wall, at a place where it was some 23 feet high.
The choice was determined by the existence of a hollow road
coming out of the suburb of San Pedro, from which access in
perfectly dead ground, unsearched by any of the French guns,
could be got, to a point within 60 yards of the ditch. The
assault was to be made by 400 volunteers from the three
brigades of the 1st Division, and was to be supported and
flanked by a separate attack on another point on the south
side of the outer *enceinte*, to be delivered by a detachment of
the caçadores of the 6th Division. The force used was certainly
too small for the purpose required, and it did not even get
a chance of success. The Portuguese, when issuing from the
ruined houses of the town, were detected at once, and being
heavily fired on, retired without even approaching their goal.
At the main attack the ladder party and forlorn hope reached
the ditch in their first rush, sprang in and planted four ladders
against the wall. The enemy had been taken somewhat by
surprise, but recovered himself before the supports got to the
front, which they did in a straggling fashion. A heavy musketry
fire was opened on the men in the ditch, and live shells were
rolled by hand upon them. Several attempts were made to
mount the ladders, but all who neared their top rungs were
shot or bayoneted, and after the officer in charge of the assault
(Major Laurie, 1/79th) had been killed, the stormers ran back

to their cover in the hollow road. They had lost 158 officers and men in all—76 from the Guards' brigade, 44 from the German brigade, 9 from the Line brigade of the 1st Division, while the ineffective Portuguese diversion had cost only 29 casualties. The French had 9 killed and 13 wounded.

This was a deplorable business from every point of view. An escalade directed against an intact line of defence, held by a strong garrison, whose morale had not been shaken by any previous artillery preparation, was unjustifiable. There was not, as at Almaraz, any element of surprise involved; nor, as at the taking of the Castle of Badajoz, were a great number of stormers employed. Four hundred men with five ladders could not hope to force a well-built wall and ditch, defended by an enemy as numerous as themselves. The men murmured that they had been sent on an impossible task; and the heavy loss, added to that on San Miguel three days before, was discouraging. Many angry comments were made on the behaviour of the Portuguese on both occasions [1].

Irregular methods having failed, it remained to see what could be done by more formal procedure, by battering and sapping up towards the enemy's defences on the west side of the Castle, the only one accessible for approach by parallels and trenches. The plan adopted was to work up from the hollow road (from which the stormers had started on the last escalade) in front of the suburb of San Pedro. The hollow road was utilized as a first parallel; from it a flying sap (b on the map) was pushed out up-hill towards the outer *enceinte* in a diagonal line. The object was to arrive at it and to mine it (at the place marked I on the map). When the working party had got well forward, a point was chosen in the sap at a distance of 60 feet from the wall, and the mine was started from thence. All this was done under very heavy fire from the Castle, but it was partly kept down by placing marksmen all along the parallel, who picked off many of the French gunners, and of the infantry who lined the parapet of the outer *enceinte*. Sometimes the return fire of the place was nearly silenced, but many of the

---

[1] For a dispute between the chief engineer, Burgoyne, who blamed the Portuguese, and some officers in the Portuguese service who resented his words, see Wellington, *Supplementary Dispatches*, xiv. p. 123.

British marksmen fell. The work in the flying sap was made very costly by the fact that the trench, being on very steep ground, had to be made abnormally deep [September 23–6].

Meanwhile, on the hill of San Miguel, a second battery (No. 2 on the map) was dug out behind the gorge of the dismantled hornwork, and trenches for musketry (*a.a* on the map) were constructed on the slope of the hill, so as to bring fire to bear on the flank and rear of the lower defences of the Castle. The French heavy guns of the Napoleon battery devoted themselves to incommoding this work; their fire was accurate, many casualties took place, and occasionally all advance had to cease. A deep trench of communication between the batteries on San Miguel and the attack in front of San Pedro was also started, in order to link up the two approaches by a short line: the ground was all commanded by the Castle, and the digging went slowly because of the intense fire directed on it.

Meanwhile battery No. 1 on San Miguel at last came into operation, firing with five howitzers (the 18-pounders originally placed there had been withdrawn) against the palisades and flank of the north-western angle of the outer *enceinte* of the Castle. These inefficient guns had no good effect; it was found that they shot so inaccurately and so weakly that little harm was done. After firing 141 rounds they stopped, it being evident that the damage done was wholly incommensurate with the powder and shot expended [September 25]. This first interference of the British artillery in the contest was not very cheering either to the troops, or to the engineers engaged in planning the attack on the Castle. The guns in battery 1 kept silence for the next five days, while battery 2, where the 18-pounders had now been placed, had never yet fired a single shot. Wellington was now staking his luck on the mine, which was being run forward from the head of the flying sap.

This work, having to be cut very deep, as it was to go right under the ditch, and being in the hands of untrained volunteers from the infantry, who had no proper cutting tools, advanced very slowly. The soil, fortunately, was favourable, being a stiff argillaceous clay which showed no disposition to crumble up: the gallery was cut as if in stone, with even and perpendicular

sides and floor, and no props or timbering were found necessary. The main hindrance to rapid work, over and above
the unskilfulness of the miners, was the foul air which accumulated at the farther end of the excavation : many times it was
necessary to withdraw the men for some hours to allow it to
clear away. At noon on September 29 the miners declared that
they had reached the foundations of the wall, and this seemed
correct enough, for they had come to a course of large rough
blocks of stone, extending laterally for as far as could be probed.
It is probable, however, that the masonry was really the
remains of some old advanced turret or outwork, projecting
in front of the modern *enceinte*. For when the end of the mine
was packed with twelve barrels, containing 90 lb. of powder
each, well tamped, and fired at midnight, the explosion brought
down many stones from the front of the wall, but did not
affect the earth of the rampart, which remained standing
perpendicular behind it. There seemed, however, to be places,
at the points where the broken facing joined the intact part
of the wall, where men might scramble up. Accordingly the
storming-column of 300 volunteers who had been waiting for
the explosion, was let loose, under cover of a strong musketry
fire from the trenches. A sergeant and four men went straight
for one of the accessible points, mounted, and were cast down
again, three of them wounded. But the main body of the
forlorn hope and its officer went a little farther along the wall,
reached a section that was wholly impracticable for climbing,
and ran back to the trenches to report that the defences were
uninjured. The supports followed their example. The loss,
therefore, was small—only 29 killed and wounded—but the
moral effect of the repulse was very bad. The men, for the
most part, made up their minds that they had been sent to
a hopeless and impossible task by the errors of an incompetent staff. The engineers declared that the stormers had
not done their best, or made any serious attempt to approach
the wall.

Wellington must by now have been growing much disquieted about the event of the siege. He had spent ten days
before Burgos, but since the capture of the hornwork on the
first night had accomplished absolutely nothing. There were

rumours that the Army of Portugal was being heavily reinforced, and these were perfectly true. By the coming up from
the rear of drafts, convalescents, and stragglers, it had received
some 7,000 men of reinforcements, and by October 1 had
38,000 men with the colours—more than Wellington counted,
even including the Galicians. Souham was now in command :
he had been on leave in France at the time of the battle of
Salamanca, but returned in the last days of September and
superseded Clausel. There had been in August some intention
of sending Masséna back to the Peninsula, to replace the
disabled Marmont. Clarke, the Minister of War, dispatched
him to Bayonne on his own responsibility, there being no time
to consult Napoleon, who was now nearing Moscow [1]. When
the Emperor had the question put to him he nominated Reille [2],
but by the time that his order got to Spain Souham was in full
charge of the army, and was not displaced till the campaign
was over. Masséna never crossed the frontier to relieve him,
reporting himself indisposed, and unable to face the toils of
a campaign : his nomination by Clarke was never confirmed,
and he presently returned to Paris. Hearing of the gathering
strength of the Army of Portugal, Wellington remarked that
he was lucky—the French were giving him more time than he
had any right to expect [3] to deal with Burgos. Meanwhile
he showed no intention, as yet, either of abandoning the siege
or of taking back to Madrid the main part of his army, as he
had repeatedly promised to do in his letters of early September.
Soult and the King were not yet showing in any dangerous
combination on the Valencian side, and till they moved
Wellington made up his mind to persevere in his unlucky siege.
It is clear that he hated to admit a failure, so long as any
chance remained, and that he was set on showing that he could
' make bricks without straw.'

   The mine explosion of the 29th–30th had been a disheartening
affair ; but Wellington had now resolved to repeat this form of
attack, aiding it however this time by the fire of his insignificant siege-train. A second mine had already been begun,

[1] Clarke to Marmont of August 18, and to Masséna of August 19.
[2] Napoleon to Clarke, Moscow, September 12.
[3] See Wellington to Hill of October 2. *Dispatches*, ix. p. 463.

against a point of the outer *enceinte* (II in the map) somewhat
to the south of that originally attacked by the first. This
was pushed with energy between September 30 and October 4;
but at the same time an endeavour was made to utilize, for
what it was worth, the direct fire of artillery, at the shortest
possible distance from the walls. On the night of September 30–
October 1 a battery for three guns (No. 3 in the map) was
commenced, slightly in advance of the 1st Parallel in the Hollow
Road, no more than some sixty-five yards from the French
defences. The garrison, not having been troubled with any
battery-building on this front before, suspected nothing, and
at dawn on October 1 the earthwork was completed, and the
carpenters were beginning to lay the wooden platforms on
which the 18-pounders were to stand. With the coming of the
light the enemy discovered the new and threatening work, and
began to concentrate upon it every gun that he could bring to
bear. The platforms however were completed, and at 9 o'clock
the artillery hauled the three heavy guns, which were Wellington's sole effective battering-tools, into their places. The
sight of them provoked the French to redoubled activity : shot
shell and musketry fire were directed upon the front of the
battery from many quarters, its parapet began to fly to pieces,
and the loss among the artillerymen was heavy. Before the
embrasures had been opened, or a single shot had been fired
from the three guns, the enemy's fire had become so rapid and
accurate that the work had become ruined and untenable.
Two of the 18-pounders had been cast down from their carriages
and put out of action—one had a trunnion knocked off, the
other (which had been hit eleven times) was split in the muzzle.
Only one of the three remained in working order. Without
having fired even once, two of the three big guns were disabled !
It was a bad look out for the future [October 1].

Wellington, however, ordered a second battery to be constructed, somewhat to the left rear of the first (No. 4 in the map),
and behind instead of before the parallel. The position chosen
was one on to which many of the French guns could not be
trained, while it was equally good with battery No. 3 for playing
on the outer *enceinte*. After midnight [October 1–2] the two
disabled and one intact 18-pounders were dragged out of the

abandoned battery and taken to the rear. Next morning,
however, a new disappointment was in store for Wellington :
the French detected battery No. 4, and opened upon it, with
all guns that could reach it, such an accurate and effective fire
that the parapet, though revetted with wool-packs, soon began
to crumble, and the workmen had to withdraw. ' It became
evident that under such a plunging fire no guns could ever be
served there [1].' All hopes of breaching the lower *enceinte* from
any point on its immediate front had to be abandoned—and
meanwhile the heavy artillery had been ruined.

The next order issued was that the solitary intact 18-pounder
and the other gun with the split lip—which had been mounted
on a new carriage—should be hauled back to the hill of San
Miguel and put into their original place, battery No. 1. The
night during which they were to be removed was one of
torrential rain, and the working parties charged with the duty
gradually dropped aside and sought shelter, with the exception
of those detailed from the Guards' brigade and the artillery.
At dawn on October 3 the guns had not reached their destination, and had to be shunted beside the salient of the hornwork,
to hide them from the enemy during the day. Wellington,
justly vexed with the shirking, ordered the defaulters to be
put on for extra duty, and the names of their officers to be
formally noted. This day was lost for all work except that of
the mine, which advanced steadily but slowly, long intervals
of rest having to be given in order to allow for the evaporation
of foul air in its inner depths (October 3). On the following
night, however, the 18-pounders were got into battery No. 1, and
about the same time the engineer officers reported that the
mine (now eighty-three feet long) had got well under the wall
of the outer *enceinte*. The 4th of October was therefore destined
to be an eventful day.

At dawn, battery No. 1 opened on the wall, where it had
been damaged by the first mine on September 29th, using the
two 18-pounders and three howitzers. The effect was much
better than could have been expected : the 18 lb. round-shot
(of which about 350 were used) had good penetrating power,
and the already shaken wall crumbled rapidly, so that by

---

[1] Jones, i. p. 329.

four in the afternoon there was a practicable breach sixty feet long.

Wellington at once arranged for a third assault on the outer *enceinte*, telling off for it not details from many regiments, as on the previous occasion, but—what was much better— a single compact battalion, the 2/24th. Only the supports were mixed parties. At 5 p.m. the mine was fired, with excellent effect, throwing down nearly 100 feet of the rampart, and killing many of the French. Before the dust had cleared away, the men of the 2/24th dashed forward toward both breaches, with great spirit, and carried them with ease, and with no excessive loss, driving the French within the second or middle *enceinte*. The total loss that day was 224, of which the assault cost about 190, the other casualties being in the batteries on San Miguel and in the trenches. But the curious point of the figures is that the 2/24th, forming the actual storming-column, lost only 68 killed and wounded ; the supports, and the work- men who were employed to form a lodgement within the conquered space, suffered far more heavily. Dubreton reports the casualties of the garrison at 27 killed and 42 wounded [October 4].

In the night after the storm the British, after entrenching the two breaches, began to make preparations to sap forward to the second *enceinte*, which being ditchless and not faced with masonry, looked less formidable than that which had already been carried, though it was protected by a solid row of palisades. Meanwhile the artillery officers proposed that battery No. 2 on San Miguel should be turned against a new objective, the point where the walls of the second and the inner lines met, immediately in front of the hornwork, in the re-entering angle marked III in the map. Battery No. 1 was meanwhile to play on the palisades of the second *enceinte*. This it did with some success. At 5 o'clock in the evening, however, there was an unexpected tumult in the newly-gained ground. Dubreton, misliking the look of the approaches which the assailants were beginning to run out from the breaches, ordered a sortie of 300 men, who dashed out most unexpectedly against the lodgements in front of the northern breach (No. I), and drove away the workmen with heavy loss, seizing most of their tools, overthrowing the gabions, and shovelling earth into the trench. They gave way when the covering party came up, and retired, having done immense mischief and disabled 142 of the besiegers, while their own loss was only 17 killed and 21 wounded. This was an unpleasant surprise, as showing the high spirit and resolution of the garrison ; but the damage was not so great but that one good night's work sufficed to repair it : the loss of tools was the most serious matter—the French had carried off 200 picks and shovels which could not be replaced, the stock (as usual in Peninsular sieges) being very low[1].

On the 6th and 7th the besiegers again began to sap forward towards the second *enceinte*, with the object of establishing a second parallel on its glacis, but with no great success. There was little or no effective fire from the batteries on San Miguel ·to keep down the artillery of the besieged, and the work at the sap-head was so deadly that the engineers could hardly expect the men to do much : however, the trench was driven forward to within thirty yards of the palisades. So useless were the howitzers in No. 2 battery that two of them were removed, and replaced by two French field-pieces from those captured in the hornwork on September 20 ; these, despite of their small calibre, worked decidedly better. The heavy guns in the Napoleon Battery devoted themselves to keeping down the fire of the two surviving 18-pounders in battery No. 2, and on the 7th knocked one from its carriage and broke off one of its trunnions. This left only one heavy piece in working order ! But the artisans of the artillery park, doing their best, rigged up both the gun injured on this day and that disabled on October 1 upon block carriages, with a sort of cradle arrangement to hold them up on the side where a trunnion was gone ; and it was found that they could be fired, if a very reduced charge was used. When anything like the full amount of powder was employed, they jumped off their carriages, as was natural, considering that they were only properly attached to them on one side. Of course, their battering power was hopelessly reduced by the small charge. The artillery diarists of the siege call them

---

[1] Indeed the besiegers had largely depended on a dépôt of French picks and shovels found by chance in the town of Burgos, after the siege had begun.

'the two *lame* guns' during the last fortnight of their employment.

On October 8 Dubreton, growing once more anxious at the sight of the advance of the trenches toward the second *enceinte*, ordered another sally, which was executed by 400 men three hours after midnight. It was almost as successful as that of October 5. The working party of Pack's Portuguese and the covering party from the K.G.L. brigade of the 1st Division were taken quite unawares, and driven out of the advanced works with very heavy loss. The trench was completely levelled, and many tools carried away, before the supports in reserve, under Somers Cocks of the 1/79th—the hero of the assault on the Hornwork—came up and drove the French back to their palisades. Cocks himself was killed—he was an officer of the highest promise who would have gone far if fate had spared him, and was the centre of a large circle of friends who have left enthusiastic appreciations of his greatness of spirit and ready wit[1]. The besiegers lost 184 men in this unhappy business, of whom 133 belonged to the German Legion : 18 of them were prisoners carried off into the Castle[2]. The French casualties were no more than 11 killed and 22 wounded—only a sixth part of those of the Allies.

We have now (October 8) arrived at the most depressing part of the chronicle of a siege which had been from the first a series of disappointments. After the storm of the lower *enceinte* on October 4, the British made no further progress. The main cause of failure was undoubtedly the weakness of their artillery, which repeatedly opened again from one or other of the two San Miguel batteries, only to be silenced after an hour or two of conflict with the heavy guns on the Donjon. But it was not only the small number of the 18-pounders which was fatal to success—they had run out of powder and shot ; a great deal of the firing was done with second-hand missiles—French 16 lb. shot picked out of the works into which they had fallen.

---

[1] See especially Tomkinson, an old comrade of Cocks in the 16th Light Dragoons, pp. 211–17.

[2] Wellington says 18 prisoners in his return. Dubreton claimed to have taken 2 officers and 36 men in his report. Possibly the difference was mortally wounded men, who were captured but died.

The infantry were offered a bonus for each one brought to the artillery park, and 426 were paid for. More than 2,000 French 8 lb. and 4 lb. shot were also bought from the men, though these were less useful, being only available for field-guns, which were of little use for battering. But in order not to discourage the hunting propensities of the soldiers, everything brought in was duly purchased. Shot of sorts never wholly failed, but lack of powder was a far more serious problem—it cannot be picked up second-hand. There would have been an absolute deficiency but for a stock got from a most unexpected quarter. Sir Home Popham and his ships were still on the Cantabrian coast, assisting the operations of Longa and Mendizabal against the Army of the North. The squadron had made its headquarters at Santander, the chief port recovered from the French, and communications with it had been opened up through the mountains by the way of Reynosa. On September 26 Wellington had written to Popham[1] to inquire whether powder could not be brought from Santander to Burgos, by means of mule trains to be hired at the port. The Commodore, always helpful, fell in with the idea at once, and succeeded in procuring the mules. On October 5th 40 barrels of 90 lb. weight each were brought into camp : considering the distance, the badness of the roads, and the disturbed state of the country, it cannot be denied that Popham did very well in delivering it only ten days after Wellington had written his request, and eight days after he had received it. Other convoys from Santander came later. It is a pity that Wellington did not think of asking for heavy ship guns at the same time. But he had written to the Commodore on October 2 that ' the means of transport required to move a train either from the coast or from Madrid (where we have plenty) are so extensive that the attempt would be impracticable[2].'

The idea of requisitioning ship guns had been started on the very first day of the siege (September 20) by Sir Howard Douglas, who had lately come from Popham's side, and maintained that by the use of draught oxen, supplemented by man-handling in difficult places, the thing could be done. But Wellington would hear nothing of it, maintaining that matters

[1] *Dispatches*, ix. p. 450.   [2] Ibid., ix. p. 465.

would be settled one way or another before the guns could possibly arrive. After the disaster to batteries 3 and 4 on October 2nd he—too late—altered his opinion, and consented that an appeal should be made to Popham. The Commodore rose to the occasion, and started off two 24-pounders on October 9th, which by immense exertions were dragged as far as Reynosa, only 50 miles from Burgos, by October 18th, and had passed the worst part of the road. But at Reynosa they were turned back, for Wellington was just raising the siege and preparing to retire on Valladolid. It is clear that if they had been asked for on September 20 instead of October 3rd—as Howard Douglas had suggested—they and no doubt another heavy gun or so, could have been brought forward in time for the last bombardment, and might have turned it into a success. But guns might also have come from Madrid : Wellington did not think it wholly impossible to move artillery from the Retiro arsenal. For, ere he left it on August 31, he had instructed Carlos de España that the best guns there should be evacuated on to Ciudad Rodrigo, if ever Soult and King Joseph should draw too close in [1]. It is true that he observed that the transport would be a difficult matter, and that much would have to be destroyed, and not carried off. But it is clear that he thought that *some* cannon could be moved. The strangest part of the story is that his own brother-in-law, Pakenham, wrote to him from Madrid offering to send him twelve heavy guns over the Somosierra, pledging himself to manage the transport by means of oxen got in the Madrid district. His offer was rejected [2]. It seems that the conviction that the Castle of Burgos would be a hard nut to crack came too late to Wellington. And when he did realize its strength, he did not reconsider the matter of siege artillery at once, but proceeded to try the methods of Badajoz and Almaraz, mere *force majeure* applied by escalade, instead of thinking of bringing up more guns. He judged— wrongly as it chanced—that he would either take the place by sheer assault, or else that the French field army would interfere before October was far advanced. Neither hypothesis turned

---

[1] See Wellington to Castaños of 7 October. *Dispatches*, ix. p. 477.

[2] See Napier, iv. p. 412, who had the fact from Sir Edward Pakenham's own mouth.

out correct, and so he had the opportunity of a full month's siege, and failed in it for want of means that might have been procured, if only he had made another resolve on August 31st, or even on September 20. But even the greatest generals cannot be infallible prophets concerning what they will require a month ahead. The mistake is explicable, and the critic who censures it over-much would be presumptuous and unreasonable [1].

But to return to the chronicle of the unlucky days between October 8th and October 21st. The working forward by sap from the third *enceinte* towards the second practically stood still, after the second destructive sally of the French against the new approaches. This is largely accounted for by the steepness of the ground, which made it necessary to dig trenches of extraordinary depth, and by the setting in after October 7 of very rainy weather, which made the trenches muddy rivers, and the steep banks of earth and breaches so slippery that it was with great difficulty that parties could find their way about and move to their posts [2]. But the unchecked power of the French artillery fire counted for even more, and not least of the hindrances was the growing sulkiness of the troops. ' Siege business was new to them, and they wanted confidence ; sometimes they would tell you that you were taking them to be butchered. The loss, to be sure, was sometimes heavy, but it was chiefly occasioned by the confused and spiritless way in which the men set about their work, added to the great depth we were obliged to excavate in the trenches, to obtain cover from the commanding fire of the enemy [3].'

Meanwhile the batteries on San Miguel, when they had ammunition, and when they could put in a few hours' work before being silenced by the fire from the Donjon, continued to pound away at the re-entering angle in the second *enceinte*

---

[1] Howard Douglas's proposal to get up big guns at once on September 20 is detailed at length in his biography, pp. 210–11. Napier has a good deal to say on it. Jones and Burgoyne tell nothing about it, but they were evidently nettled at the idea that Douglas, who had no official position in the army, should have raised a proposal and got Wellington to listen to it. I fancy that Douglas is one of the officers alluded to by Burgoyne (*Correspondence*, i. p. 234) as unauthorized persons, who volunteered useless advice. Gomm, p. 287, says, ' we have set to work idly without having the means we might have commanded.'

[2] Burgoyne, i. p. 220.   [3] Ibid., i. p. 233.

(III in the map), and with more effect than might have been
expected, for this section of the defences turned out to have
been built with bad material, and crumbled even under such
feeble shooting as that of Wellington's ' lame ' 18-pounders.
The French on several days had first to silence the English
battery, and then to rebuild the wall with sandbags and earth
under a musketry fire from the trenches (*a–a* in the map) upon
San Miguel, from which they could not drive the sharp-shooters
of the besiegers. It was thought later—an *ex post facto* judgement—that the best chance of the Allies would have been to
attempt a storm on this breach when first it became more or
less practicable. The delay enabled the besieged to execute
repairs, to scarp down the broken front, and to cut off the
damaged corner by interior retrenchments.

Meanwhile, since doubts were felt as to the main operation
of storming the new breach, No. III, subsidiary efforts were
made to incommode the enemy in other ways. At intervals
on the 9th, 10th, and 11th red-hot shot were fired at the church
of Santa Maria la Blanca, where it was known that the French
magazine of food lay. The experience of the Salamanca forts
had led the artillery officers to think that a general conflagration
might be caused. But the plan had no success ; the building
proved to be very incombustible, and one or two small fires
which burst out were easily extinguished. Another device
was to mine out from the end houses of the city towards the
church of San Roman, an isolated structure lying close under
the south-east side of the Castle, which the French held as an
outwork. Nothing very decisive could be hoped from its
capture, as if taken it could only serve as a base for operations
against the two *enceintes* above it [1]. But, as an eye-witness
remarked, at this period of the siege any sort of irregular scheme
was tried, on the off chance of success. By October 17 the
mine had got well under the little church. A more feasible plan,
which might have done some good if it had succeeded, was to
run out a small mine or fougasse from the sap-head of the trench

---

[1] Alexander Dickson remarks in his diary, p. 772, ' This was done to
please General Clinton, and had nothing to do with the attack.' Clinton's
troops were opposite this side of the Castle, and had as yet not been
entrusted with any important duty.

in front of breach I to the palisades of the second *enceinte*.   It was a petty business, no more than two barrels of powder being used, and only slightly damaged an angle of the work in front when fired on October 17.   An attempt to push on the sap after the explosion was frustrated by the musketry fire of the besieged.

On the 18th the engineers reported that the church of San Roman was completely undermined, and could be blown up at any moment.   On the same morning the one good and two lame 18–pounders in battery 2 on San Miguel swept away, not for the first time, the sandbag parapets and *chevaux de frise* with which the French had strengthened the breach III.   They were then turned against the third *enceinte*, immediately behind that breach, partly demolished its ' fraises,' and even did some damage to its rampart.   This was as much as could have been expected, as the whole of the enemy's guns were, as usual, turned upon the battering-guns, and presently obtained the mastery over them, blowing up an expense-magazine in No. 2, and injuring a gun in No. 1.   But in the afternoon the defences were in a more battered condition than usual, and Wellington resolved to make his last attempt.   Already the French army outside was showing signs of activity; and, as a precaution, some of the investing troops—two brigades of the 6th Division— had been sent forward to join the covering army.   If this assault failed, the siege would have to be given up, or at the best turned into a blockade.

The plan of the assault was drawn up by Wellington himself, who dictated the details to his military secretary, Fitzroy Somerset, in three successive sections, after inspecting from the nearest possible point each of the three fronts which he intended to attack [1].

Stated shortly the plan was as follows :

(1) At 4.30 the mine at San Roman was to be fired, and the ruins of the church seized by Brown's caçadores (9th battalion), supported by a Spanish regiment (1st of Asturias) lent by Castaños.   A brigade of the 6th Division was to be ready in the streets behind, to support the assault, if its effect looked promising, i.e. if the results of the explosion should

[1] Jones, i. p. 357.

injure the *enceinte* behind, or should so drive the enemy from
it that an escalade became possible.

(2) The detachments of the Guards' brigade of the 1st Division,
who were that day in charge of the trenches within the captured
outer *enceinte*, and facing the west front of the second *enceinte*,
were to make an attempt to escalade that line of defence, at the
point where most of its palisades had been destroyed, opposite
and above the original breach No. I in the lower *enceinte*.

(3) The detachments of the German brigade of the 1st Division,
who were to take charge of the trenches for the evening in
succession to the Guards, were to attempt to storm the breach III
in the re-entering angle, the only point where there was an
actual opening prepared into the inner defences.

From all the works, both those on St. Miguel and those to
the west of the Castle, marksmen left in the trenches were to
keep up as hot a musketry fire as possible on any of the enemy
who should show themselves, so as to distract their attention
from the stormers.

The most notable point in these instructions was the small
number of men devoted to the two serious attacks. Provision
was made for the use of 300 men only in the attack to be made
by the Guards : they were to move forward in successive
rushes—the first or forlorn hope consisting of an officer and
twenty men, the supports or main assaulting force, of small
parties of 40 or 50 men, each of which was to come forward only
when the one in front of it had reached a given point in its
advance. Similarly the German Legion's assault was to be led
by a forlorn hope of 20, supported by 50 more, who were only
to move when their predecessors had reached the lip of the
breach, and by a reserve of 200 who were to charge out of
the trench only when the support was well established on the
rampart.

Burgoyne, the senior engineer present, tells us that he protested all through the siege, at each successive assault, against
the paucity of the numbers employed, saying that the forlorn
hope had, in fact, to take the work by itself, since they had
no close and strong column in immediate support ; and if the
forlorn hope failed, ' the next party, who from behind their
cover have seen them bayoneted, are expected to valiantly

jump up and proceed to be served in the same way.' He reminded Wellington, as he says, that the garrison at Burgos was as large as that at Ciudad Rodrigo, where two whole divisions instead of 500 or 600 men had been thrown into the assault. The Commander-in-Chief, condescending to argument for once, replied, ' why expose more men than can ascend the ladders [as at the Guards' attack] or enter the work [as at the breach in the K.G.L. attack] at one time, when by this mode the support is ordered to be up in time to follow the tail of the preceding party[1] ? ' And his objection to the engineer's plea was clinched by the dictum, ' if we fail we can't lose many men.' This controversy originally arose on the details of the abortive storm of September 22, but Burgoyne's criticism was even more convincing for the details of the final assault on October 18. The number of men risked was far too small for the task that was set them.

The melancholy story of the storm runs as follows. On the explosion of the mine at San Roman, punctually at 4.30, all three of the sections of the assault were duly delivered. At the breach the forlorn hope of the King's German Legion charged at the rough slope with great speed, reached the crest, and were immediately joined by the support, led most gallantly by Major Wurmb of the 5th Line Battalion. The first rush cleared a considerable length of the rampart of its defenders, till it was checked against a stockade, part of the works which the French had built to cut off the breach from the main body of the place. Foiled here, on the flank, some of the Germans turned, and made a dash at the injured rampart of the third line, in their immediate front : three or four actually reached the parapet of this inmost defence of the enemy. But they fell, and the main body, penned in the narrow space between the two *enceintes,* became exposed to such an overpowering fire of musketry that, after losing nearly one man in three, they finally had to give way, and retired most reluctantly down the breach to the trenches they had left. The casualties out of 300 men engaged were no less than 82 killed and wounded[2],

---

[1] For this dialogue, told at length, see Burgoyne's *Correspondence*, ed. Wrottesley, i. p. 235.

[2] So I make out from the returns, but Beamish's and Schwertfeger's

among the former, Wurmb, who had led the assault, and among the latter, Hesse, who commanded the forlorn hope, and was one of the few who scaled the inner wall as well as the outer.

The Guards in their attack, 100 yards to the right of the breach, had an even harder task than the Germans, for their storm was a mere escalade. It was executed with great decision: issuing from the front trench they ran up to the line of broken palisades, passed through gaps in it, and applied their ladders to the face of the rampart of the second *enceinte*. Many of them succeeded in mounting, and they established themselves successfully on the parapet, and seized a long stretch of it, so long that some of their left-hand men got into touch with the Germans who had entered at the breach. But they could not clear the enemy out of the *terre-pleine* of the second *enceinte*, where a solid body of the French kept up a rolling fire upon them, while the garrison of the upper line maintained a still fiercer fusillade from their high-lying point of vantage. The Guards were for about ten minutes within the wall, and made several attempts to get forward without success. At the end of that time a French reserve advanced from their left, and charging in flank the disordered mass within the *enceinte* drove them out again. The Guards retired as best they could to the advanced trenches, having lost 85 officers and men out of the 300 engaged. The French returned their casualties at 11 killed and 30 wounded.

Wellington's dispatch, narrating the disaster, gives the most handsome testimonial to the resolution of both the bodies of stormers. 'It is impossible to represent in adequate terms the conduct of the Guards and the German Legion upon this occasion. And I am quite satisfied that if it had been possible to maintain the posts which they gained with so much gallantry, these troops would have maintained them[1].' But why were 600 men only sent forward, and no support given them during the precious ten minutes when their first rush had carried them within the walls? Where were the brigades to which the stormers belonged? It is impossible not to subscribe to

Histories of the K.G.L. both give the lesser figure of 75—still sufficiently high !

[1] Wellington to Lord Bathurst, October 26.

Burgoyne's angry comment that 'the miserable, doubting, unmilitary policy of small storming-parties' caused the mischief[1]. He adds, 'large bodies encourage one another, and carry with them confidence of success: if the Castle of Badajoz was stormed with ten or twelve ladders, and not more than 40 or 50 men could mount at once, I am convinced that it was only carried because the whole 3rd Division was there, and the emulation between the officers of the different regiments got their men to mount; although we lost 600 or 700 men, it caused success—which eventually saves men.'

The third section of the assault of October 18, the unimportant attack on the church of San Roman, had a certain measure of success. The mine, though it did not level the whole building, as had been hoped, blew up the terrace in front of, and part of its west end. Thereupon the French evacuated it, after exploding a mine of their own which brought down the bell-tower and much more, and crushed a few of the caçadores and Spaniards[2] who were ahead of their comrades. The besiegers were able to lodge themselves in the ruins, but could make no attempt to approach the actual walls of the second enceinte. So the 6th Division remained behind, within the streets of Burgos, and never came forward or showed themselves.

Such was the unhappy end of this most unlucky siege. All through the day of the assault there had been heavy skirmishing going on at the outposts of the covering army; Souham was at last on the move. On the 19th the Guards' brigade and the K.G.L. brigade of the 1st Division marched to join the 5th and 7th Divisions at the front, leaving only the line brigade (Stirling's) to hold the trenches on the north and west sides of the Castle. Two-thirds of the 6th Division had already gone off in the same direction before the storm: now the rest followed, handing over the charge of Burgos city and the chain of picquets on the east side of the Castle to Pack's Portuguese. There was

[1] Burgoyne's *Correspondence*, i. p. 236.
[2] Dubreton and Belmas speak of a 'grand nombre d'Anglais écrasés,' the latter says 300! (Belmas, iv. pp. 501 and 548). Putting aside the fact that there were no *English* here at all, we may remark that Burgoyne (i. p. 226) says that *three* Spaniards were buried in the ruins, and that the loss of the Portuguese in the whole affair is put at 8 killed, 44 wounded, and 2 missing in Wellington's report.

little doing in the lines this day—the French built up the oft-destroyed parapet of breach III with sandbags, and made an incursion into the church of San Roman, driving out the Portuguese guard for a short time, and injuring the lodgement which had been made in the ruins. But they withdrew when the supports came up.

On the 20th, news being serious at the front—for Souham showed signs of intending to attack in force, and it was ascertained that he had been reinforced by great part of the Army of the North, under Caffarelli in person—Wellington gave orders to withdraw the guns from the batteries, leaving only two of the captured French pieces to fire an occasional shot. All transportable stores and ammunition were ordered to be loaded up. There was some bickering in San Roman this day, but at night the Portuguese were again in possession of the much-battered church.

On the 21st came the final orders for retreat. The artillery were directed to burn all that could not be carried off—platforms, fascines, &c.—to blow up the works on San Miguel, and to retire down the high-road to Valladolid. The three 18-pounders were taken a few miles only. The roads being bad from heavy rain, and the bullocks weak, it was held that there was no profit in dragging about the two guns which had lost trunnions and were practically useless. The surviving intact gun shared the fate of its two 'lame' fellows : all three were wrecked[1], their carriages were destroyed, and they were thrown out on the side of the road. The artillery reserve, now reduced to the five ineffective 24-lb. howitzers, then continued its retreat.

On the night of the 21st–22nd, Pack's brigade and the other troops left to hold the works retired, the covering army being now in full retreat by various roads passing through or around the city. The main column crossed at the town bridge—the artillery with wheels muffled with straw to deaden their rumbling—risking the danger of being shelled in the darkness by the Castle, which had several guns that bore upon it. The

---

[1] By knocking off their remaining trunnions, which made them permanently useless. Some of the captured French field-guns from the hornwork were also destroyed.

long series of mishaps which constituted the history of the
siege of Burgos ended by the failure of the plan for the
explosions on San Miguel : the French found there next day
more than twenty barrels of powder intact. The arsenal in
the town was fired when the last troops had passed, but was
only partly consumed. Next morning (October 22) the advanced
guard of the Army of Portugal entered Burgos, and relieved
the garrison after thirty-five days of siege. Dubreton had still
nearly 1,200 effective men under arms : he had lost in his
admirable and obstinate defence 16 officers and 607 men, of
whom 304 were killed or died of their wounds. The corresponding total British casualty list was no less than 24 officers and
485 men killed, 68 officers and 1,487 men wounded and missing
[the last item accounting for 2 officers and 42 men]. Almost
the whole of the loss came from the ranks of the 1st Division
and Pack's Portuguese, the 6th Division troops having had
little to do with the trenches or assaults [1].

The external causes of the raising of the siege will be dealt
with in their proper place—the strategical narrative of the
general condition of affairs in both the Castiles which opens the
next chapter. Here it remains only to recapitulate the various
reasons which made the siege itself a failure. They have been
summed up by several writers of weight and experience—John
Jones, the official historian of the sieges of Spain, John Burgoyne the commanding engineer, William Napier, and Belmas
the French author, who (using Jones as a primary authority)
told its story from the side of the besieged. Comparing all
their views with the detailed chronicle of the operations of
those thirty-five eventful days, the following results seem to
emerge.

(1) Burgos would not have been a strong fortress against an
army provided with a proper battering-train, such as that
which dealt with Ciudad Rodrigo or Badajoz. But Wellington
—by his own fault as it turned out in the end—had practically
no such train at all : three 18-pound heavy guns were an absurd
provision for the siege of a place of even third-rate strength. If
Wellington had realized on September 20 that the siege was
to last till October 21, he might have had almost as many guns

[1] For detailed losses see table in Appendix I.

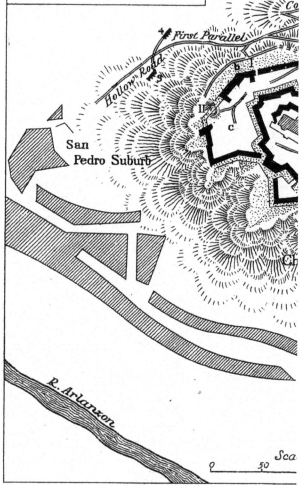

BURGOS

*Arabic figures indicate
Batteries; Roman, Breaches*
a-a *Musketry trenches on·S.t
Miguel*
b *Approaches to Breaches* I & II
c *Advanced trenches of the
British*
N *Napoleon Battery*
D *Donjon*
S.M.B. *S.Maria la Blanca*

First Parallel

Hollow Road

San
Pedro Suburb

San
Pedro Suburb

R. Arlanzon

0   50   Sca

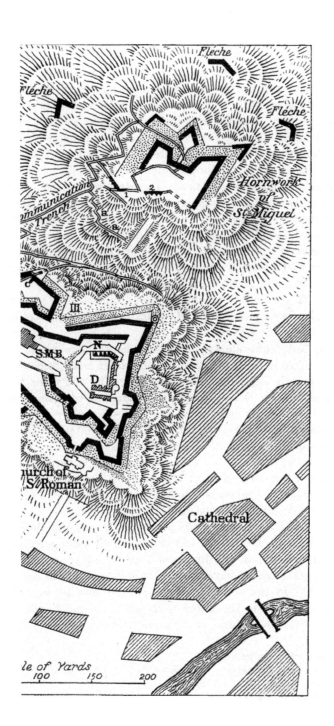

Flèche

Flèche

Flèche

Flèche

Hornwork
of
St Miguel

Communication Trench

1   2

a
a
c

c

III

S.M.B.

N

D

urch of
St Roman

Cathedral

Scale of Yards
100   150   200

as he pleased. But the strength of Burgos was underrated at the first; and by the time that it was realized, Wellington considered (wrongly, as it turned out) that it was too late to get the necessary ordnance from the distant places where it lay.

(2) Encouraged by the experience of Badajoz and Almaraz, Wellington and his staff considered that an imperfect fortification like the Castle of Burgos might be dealt with by escalade without artillery preparation. The Hornwork of San Miguel was taken on this irregular system; but the attempts against the *enceintes* of the Castle failed. Burgoyne is probably right in maintaining that the repeated failures were largely due to the general's reluctance to put in large masses of men at once, owing to his wish to spare the lives in units already worked down to a low strength by long campaigning. The principle ' if we fail we can't lose many men ' was ruinous. On October 18 the place *must* have fallen if 3,000 instead of 600 men had been told off for the assault.

(3) Notwithstanding the lack of artillery, Burgos might have been taken if Wellington had owned a large and efficient body of engineers. But (as at Badajoz, where he had made bitter complaints on this subject [1]) the provision of trained men was ludicrously small—there were just five officers of Royal Engineers [2] with the army, and eight ' Royal Military Artificers '. The volunteers from the Line, both officers and men, used as auxiliaries, were not up to the work required of them. It was a misfortune that none of the divisions before Burgos had experience of siege-work, like that which the Light, 3rd, and 4th Divisions (all left at Madrid) had been through.

(4) After the heavy losses in the early assaults the rank and file, both the British and still more the Portuguese, were much discouraged. As Burgoyne says, ' the place might have been, and ought to have been, taken if every one had done his duty [3].' In the actual assaults splendid courage was often displayed, but in the trench-work there was much sulkiness, apathy, and even shirking. ' Our undertaking, every night that

---

[1] See vol. v. pp. 255–6.

[2] Burgoyne commanding, John Jones the historian, Captain Williams, and Lieutenants Pitts and Reid.

[3] Burgoyne, i. p. 230.

we broke ground, appeared most pitiful : there was scarcely
a single instance where at least double the work was not projected, with sufficient men and tools collected, that was afterwards executed, owing to the neglect and misconduct of the
working parties. It was seldom that the men could be induced
to take out their gabions and set to work, and I myself placed
at different times hundreds of gabions with my own hands,
and then *entreated* the men to go and fill them, to no purpose.'
The engineers blamed the men—the men blamed the engineers,
who, as they grumbled, were by unskilful direction ' sending
them out to be butchered [1].' All this, in the end, was due to
the want of artillery for proper preparation, and of trained
sappers.

(5) Burgoyne, D'Urban, and other observers are probably right
in saying that the failure of the assaults was partly due to the
bad principle of composing the storming-parties of drafts from
many different corps, collected, under officers whom they did
not personally know, from the units that chanced to be on
duty that day. The one case where a brilliant success was
scored with small loss, was seen when a whole battalion, the
2/24th, carried the outer *enceinte* on October 4.

(6) Wellington's doubts, expressed almost from the first, as
to the practicability of the affair that he had taken in hand,
were known to many officers, and affected the general morale.

(7) Dubreton deserves unstinted praise. A general of more
ordinary type, such as Barrois at Ciudad Rodrigo, would have
lost Burgos for want of the extraordinary resourcefulness,
determination, and quick decision shown by this admirable
governor. His garrison must share his glory : the French 34th
certainly got in this siege a good *revanche* for their last military
experience, the surprise of Arroyo dos Molinos.

---

[1] Ibid., i. p. 233. There is much more in this interesting page of
Burgoyne's explanation of the failure, which I have not space to quote.

SECTION XXXIV: CHAPTER III

WELLINGTON'S RETREAT FROM BURGOS: OCTOBER— NOVEMBER 1812. (1) FROM THE ARLANZON TO THE DOURO: OCTOBER 22—OCTOBER 30

HAVING completed the depressing chronicle of the leaguer of the Castle of Burgos, it is necessary that we should turn back for a week or two, to examine the changing aspect of external affairs, which had affected the general strategical position in Spain while the siege lingered on. It will be remembered that the original scheme for the campaign had been that, after the Army of Portugal had been pushed back to the Ebro, a great part of Wellington's field force should return to Madrid, to pick up the divisions left there, and the corps of Hill, before Soult and King Joseph should begin to give trouble on the side of Valencia. Only a containing force was to have been left behind, to aid Castaños and his Galicians in keeping Clausel (or his successor Souham) out of mischief, while more important movements were on foot in New Castile[1]. As to the command of this containing force there was a difficulty: Wellington was not at all satisfied with the way in which Clinton had handled the troops left on the Douro in August, and it seems doubtful whether he wished to give him a far more important commission in the first half of October, when he was the natural person to be chosen for it. For at this time none of the other senior officers who had served in the recent campaigns were available: Beresford, Stapleton Cotton, and Picton were all three invalided at the moment. Graham, the best of them all, had returned to England. Hill could not be removed from the charge of his old army in the South. Of the five divisions before Burgos four were commanded by brigadiers acting in the position of *locum tenens*[2]: most of the brigades

[1] See above, pp. 3–4.

[2] Pringle was commanding the 5th Division (Leith being wounded); Bernewitz the 7th (Hope having gone home sick on September 23): Campbell, in charge of the 1st since Graham was invalided, was off duty himself

were, in a similar fashion, being worked by colonels for want of
a sufficient number of major-generals to go round. But after
October 11th the formal difficulty was solved : there was now
available an officer whom it was fitting to leave in charge against
Souham, viz. Sir Edward Paget, who came up to the front on
that day, after having been three years absent from the Peninsula ; he had last served under Wellington at the Passage of the
Douro in 1809, where he lost an arm. He had now come out
nominally to succeed Graham at the head of the 1st Division,
but also with the commission to act as second-in-command in
the event of the illness or disabling of the general-in-chief.
Paget was known as a good soldier, and had served with dis-
tinction during the Corunna retreat; but he had never been
trusted with the management of a large force, and had little
knowledge either of the army which Wellington had trained,
or of the parts of Spain in which the campaign was now going
on.   Moreover, Wellington disliked on principle the idea of
having a second-in-command, occupying to a certain extent
a position independent of his own.

The separate containing force never came into existence,
because Wellington never left the North or returned to Madrid,
though rumours were afloat after Paget's arrival that he was
about to do so without delay. Why, contrary to his own expressed intentions did he never go South ? The answer must
certainly be that down to a very late period of the siege he
continued to keep in his mind the idea of returning to Madrid [1],
but that he was distracted from his purpose by several considerations. The first was the abominable weather in October,
which made the prospect of a long forced march distasteful—the
army was sickly and would suffer. The second was his insufficient realization of the nearness of the danger in the South :
he thought that Hill was in a less perilous position than was
actually the case. The third was that he was beginning to mark
the growing strength of the Army of Portugal, which lay in his
own front, and to see that he could not hope to ' contain ' it by
any mere detachment, if he departed for the South with his

for illness when relieved by Paget. Bock commanded the Cavalry Division
vice Stapleton Cotton, wounded at Salamanca.
  [1] Clearly expressed in letters as late as that to Hill of October 12.

main body. Souham's host was no longer a spent force, which
eould be ignored as a source of danger; if Wellington took
away two or three divisions, the officer left in charge in the
North would be at once assailed by very superior numbers.
He did not like the idea of trusting either Clinton or Paget with
the conduct of a retreat before an enemy who would certainly
press him fiercely. In addition, there was the lingering hope that
Burgos might fall : if it were captured the situation would be
much improved, since the allies could use it as a sort of *point
d'appui*—to use the terminology of the day—on which the containing army could rest; and the enemy would be forced to
detach heavily for the investment of the place.

By the day of the last assault (October 18) Wellington had
clearly lingered too long, for very large reinforcements had just
come up to join Souham, who on that morning was in a position
to evict from before Burgos not only any mere ' covering force '
that might be left opposite him, but the whole 35,000 men
which formed the total of the allied host. For by now the Army
of Portugal was recruited up to a strength of 38,000 men present
with the colours : it had also just received the disposable battalions of the Bayonne Reserve, a strong brigade of 3,500 men
under General Aussenac, and what was more important still—
Caffarelli had appeared at Briviesca with the main field-force
of the Army of the North. The operations of Home Popham,
Mendizabal, Mina and Longa, which had detained and confused the French troops in Biscay and Navarre for the whole
summer, had at last reached their limits of success, and having
patched up affairs on the coast, and left some 20,000 men to
hold the garrison places, and to curb the further raids of the
British commodore and the Spanish bands, Caffarelli had come
southwards with the whole of his cavalry—1,600 sabres,—three
batteries, and nearly 10,000 infantry, forming the greater part
of the divisions of Vandermaesen and Dumoustier. There were
something like 50,000 French concentrated between Pancorbo
and Briviesca on October 18th [1], while Wellington—allowing

[1] Viz. (figures of the Imperial Muster Rolls for October 15) Army of
Portugal 32,000 infantry, 3,400 cavalry ; Army of the North : Chauvel's
cavalry brigade (lent to the Army of Portugal since July) 700 sabres,
Laferrière's cavalry brigade 1,600 sabres, parts of Abbé's and Dumoustier's

for his losses in the siege—had not more than 24,000 Anglo-Portuguese and 11,000 Spaniards in hand. The arrival of the Army of the North not only made the further continuance of the siege of Burgos impossible, but placed Wellington in a condition of great danger. It is clear that his campaign in the North had only been able to continue for so long as it did because Popham, Mina, and the Cantabrian bands had kept Caffarelli employed for a time that exceeded all reasonable expectation. It was really surprising that a small squadron and 10,000 half-organized troops, of whom a large part were undisciplined guerrillero bands, and the rest not much better, should have held the 37,000 men of the Army of the North in play for three months. But the combination of a mobile naval force, and of local levies who knew every goat-path of their native mountains, had proved efficacious in the extreme. It had taken Caffarelli the whole summer and much of the autumn to vindicate his position, and recover the more important strategical points in his wide domain. Even when he was marching on Burgos there was fierce fighting going on round Pampeluna, on which Mina had pressed in more closely when he heard of the departure of the general-in-chief. The Cantabrians and Navarrese did marvels for Wellington, and their work has never been properly acknowledged by British writers.

It is clear that the whole situation would have been different if Wellington had brought up to the North in September the 16,000 veteran British troops left at Madrid. For want of them he was in a state of hopeless inferiority to his immediate opponents. And yet at the same time they were useless at Madrid, because Hill—even with their aid—was not nearly strong enough to keep Soult and King Joseph in check. Wellington had in all at this time some 55,000 Anglo-Portuguese troops under arms and at the front; but they were so dispersed that on both

divisions 9,500 infantry. Allowing another 2,000 for artillery, sappers, &c., the total must have reached 53,000. Belmas says that Caffarelli and Souham had only 41,000 men. Napier gives them 44,000. Both these figures are far too low. No one denies that Caffarelli brought up about 10,000 men; and the Army of Portugal, by the return of October 15, had 45,000 effectives, from whom there are only to be deducted the men of the artillery park and the 'équipages militaires.' It must have taken forward 40,000 of all arms. See tables of October 15 in Appendix II.

theatres of war he was inferior to his enemies. He had 24,000 himself in Old Castile—Hill some 31,000 in New Castile ; each of the two halves of the army could count on the help of some 10,000 or 12,000 Spaniards [1]. But of what avail were the 35,000 men of all nations at Burgos against the 50,000 French under Souham and Caffarelli, or the 48,000 men of all nations near Madrid against the 60,000 of Soult and the King ? The whole situation would have been different if a superiority or even an equality of numbers had been established against one of the two French armies ; and it is clear that such a combination could have been contrived, if Wellington had adopted other plans.

There can be no doubt that the excessive tardiness of Soult's evacuation of Andalusia was the fact which caused the unlucky distribution of Wellington's forces in October. The Marshal, it will be remembered, only left Granada on September 16th, and did not come into touch with the outlying cavalry of the Valencian Army till September 29–30, or reach Almanza, where he was in full connexion with Suchet and King Joseph, till October 2. There was, therefore, no threatening combination of enemies on the Valencia side till thirteen days after the siege of Burgos had begun ; and Wellington did not know that it had come into existence till October 9th, when he received a dispatch from Hill informing him that the long foreseen, but long deferred, junction had taken place. If it had occurred—as it well might have—three weeks earlier, there would have been no siege of Burgos, and Wellington would have been at Madrid, after having contented himself with driving the army of Portugal beyond the Douro. It is probable that he would have done well, even at so late a date as October 9th, if he had recognized that the danger in front of Madrid was now pressing, and had abandoned the siege of Burgos, in order to make new arrangements. Souham was not yet in a condition to press him, and Caffarelli's 10,000 men had not arrived on the scene. But the last twelve days spent before Burgos ruined his chances.

---

[1] Wellington on the 11,000 Galicians, Hill on Carlos de España (4,000 men), Penne Villemur and Murillo (3,500 men), and the Murcian remnants under Freire and Elio, which got separated from the Alicante section of their Army and came under Hill's charge, about 5,000.

On getting Hill's dispatch Wellington pondered much—but came to an unhappy decision. In his reply he wrote, ' I cannot believe that Soult and the King can venture to move forward to attack you in the position on the Tagus, without having possession of the fortresses in the province of Murcia [Cartagena and Chinchilla] and of Alicante ;—unless indeed they propose to give up Valencia entirely. They would in that case [1] bring with them a most overwhelming force, and you would probably have to retire in the direction given to General Alten [i.e. by the Guadarrama Pass, Villa Castin, and Arevalo] and I should then join you on the Adaja. If you retire in that direction, destroy the new bridge at Almaraz. . . . I write this, as I always do, to provide for every event, not believing that these instructions are at all necessary [2].'

In a supplementary letter, dated two days later, Wellington tells Hill that he imagines that the autumn rains, which have made the siege of Burgos so difficult, will probably have rendered the rivers of the South impassable. ' I should think that you will have the Tagus in such a state as to feel in no apprehension in regard to the enemy's operations, be his numbers what they may [3].' Yet though he does not consider the danger in the South immediate or pressing, he acknowledges that he ought to bring the siege of Burgos to an end, even though it be necessary to raise it, and to give up the hope of its capture. But the continual storms and rains induced him to delay his departure toward the South : ' I shall do so as soon as the weather holds up a little.' On the same day (October 12) he wrote to Popham to say that if he had to march towards Madrid, he expected that Souham would follow him, but that Caffarelli must on no account be allowed to accompany Souham. At all costs more trouble must be made in Cantabria and Biscay, to prevent the Army of the North from moving. Popham must not withdraw his squadron, or cease from stimulating the Northern insurgents [4]. Wellington was not aware that Caffa-

---

[1] i. e. if they brought up Suchet's troops from Valencia, beside their own armies.

[2] Wellington to Hill, October 10. *Dispatches*, ix. p. 82.

[3] Wellington to Hill, October 12. Ibid., p. 485.

[4] Wellington to Popham, October 12. Ibid., p. 486.

relli was already on the move, and that the diversion in the North —through no fault of the officers in charge of it—had reached its limit of success.

The moment had now arrived at which it was necessary at all costs to come to some decision as to the movements of the Army at Burgos, for Caffarelli (though Wellington knew it not) had started for Briviesca, while Soult and King Joseph were also getting ready for an immediate advance on Madrid, which must bring matters in the South to a head. But relying on letters from Hill, dated October 10th, which stated that there was still no signs of movement opposite him, Wellington resolved on October 14 to stay yet another week in the North, and try his final assault on Burgos : it came off with no success (as will be remembered) on the 18th of that month. He was not blind to the possible consequences to Hill of a prompt advance of the French armies from Valencia, but he persuaded himself that the weather would make it difficult, and that he had means of detaining Soult and Joseph, if they should, after all, begin the move which he doubted that they proposed to make.

The scheme for stopping any forward march on the part of the French had two sections. The first was to be executed by the Anglo-Spanish Army at Alicante. Maitland had fallen sick, and this force of some 16,000 men was now under the charge of General John Mackenzie. To this officer Wellington wrote on October 13th : ' In case the enemy should advance from Valencia into La Mancha, with a view to attack our troops on the Tagus, you must endeavour to obtain possession of the town and kingdom of Valencia.' He was given the option of marching by land from Alicante, or of putting his men on shipboard and making a descent from the sea on Valencia [1]. The second diversion was to be executed by Ballasteros and the Army of Andalusia. Wellington wrote to him that he should advance from Granada, cross the Sierra Morena with all his available strength, and place himself at Alcaraz in La Mancha [2]. He ought to have at least 12,000 men, as some of the Cadiz troops were coming up

---

[1] Wellington to Mackenzie, October 13. *Dispatches*, ix. p. 487.

[2] See Wellington to Hill of October 14, and Wellington to Popham of October 17. Ibid., pp. 490 and 495.

to join him. Such a force, if placed on the flank of Soult and the King, when they should move forward for Almanza and Albacete, could not be ignored. And Wellington hoped to reinforce Ballasteros with that part of the Murcian Army, under Elio and Freire, which had got separated from the Alicante force, and had fallen back into the inland. There were also irregular bodies, such as the division of the Empecinado, which could be called in to join, and if 20,000 men lay at Alcaraz, Soult could not go in full force to assail Hill in front of Madrid. He must make such a large detachment to watch the Spaniards that he would not have more than 30,000 or 35,000 men to make the frontal attack on the Anglo-Portuguese force, which would defend the line of the Tagus. Against such numbers Hill could easily hold his ground.

It may be objected to these schemes that they did not allow sufficient consideration to the power of Suchet in Valencia. Mackenzie's force, of a very heterogeneous kind, was not capable of driving in the detachments of the Army of Aragon, which still lay cantoned along the Xucar, facing the Allies at Alicante. Suchet was able to hold his own, without detaining any of the troops of Soult or of King Joseph from their advance upon Madrid. Mackenzie's projected expedition against the city of Valencia had no chance of putting a check upon the main manœuvre that the French had in hand.

But the use of Ballasteros, whose movement must certainly have exercised an immense restraining power upon Soult and King Joseph, if only it had been carried out, was an experiment of a kind which Wellington had tried before, nearly always with disappointing results. To entrust to a Spanish general an essential part of a wide strategical plan had proved ere now a doubtful expedient. And Ballasteros had always shown himself self-willed if energetic; it was dangerous to reckon upon him as a loyal and intelligent assistant in the great game. And at this moment the captain-general of Andalusia was in the most perverse of moods. His ill temper was caused by the recent appointment of Wellington as commander-in-chief of all the Spanish armies, a measure to which the Cortes had at last consented, after the consequences of the battle of Salamanca and the occupation of Madrid had prepared public opinion for this momentous step. It had been bitterly opposed at the secret session when it was brought forward, but there could no longer be any valid excuse for putting off the obviously necessary policy of combining all military effort in the Peninsula, by placing the control of the whole of the Spanish armies in the hands of one who had shown himself such a master of the art of war.

Wellington's nomination as Generalissimo of the Spanish armies had been voted by the Cortes on September 22nd, and conveyed to him before Burgos on October 2nd. He had every intention of accepting the offer, though (as he wrote to his brother Henry [1]) the change in his position would not be so great in reality as in form, since Castaños and most of the other Spanish generals had of late been wont to consult him on their movements, and generally to fall in with his views. There had been exceptions, even of late, such as Joseph O'Donnell's gratuitous forcing on of battle at Castalla, when he had been specially asked to hold back till the Anglo-Sicilian expedition began to work upon the East Coast. But it would certainly be advantageous that, for the future, he should be able to issue orders instead of advice. Meanwhile he could not formally accept the post of general-in-chief without the official leave of the Prince Regent, and prompt information of the offer and a request for permission to accept it, were sent to London. The Cortes, foreseeing the necessary delay, had refrained from publishing the decree till it should be certain that Wellington was prepared to assume the position that was offered him. But the fact soon became known in Cadiz, and was openly spoken of in the public press. Wellington continued to write only letters of advice to the Spanish generals, and did not assume the tone of a commander-in-chief as yet, but his advice had already a more binding force. There was no opposition made to him, save in one quarter— but that was the most important one. Ballasteros, as Commander of the 4th Army and Captain-General of Andalusia, burst out into open revolt against the Cortes, the Regency, and the commander-in-chief elect.

This busy and ambitious man had taken up his abode in

---

[1] *Dispatches,* ix. p. 467.

Granada, after Soult's departure on September 23rd, and since then had not stirred, though Wellington had repeatedly asked him to advance into La Mancha with his available force, and to put himself in touch with Elio, Penne Villemur, and Hill. But Ballasteros was suffering from an acute attack of megalomania : after years of skulking in the mountains and forced marches, he was now in the position of a viceroy commanding the resources of a great province.   Though Andalusia had been cleared of the French by no merit of his, but as a side-effect of the battle of Salamanca, he gave himself the airs of a conqueror and deliverer, and fully believed himself to be the most important person in Spain.   As an acute observer remarked, ' Ballasteros wanted to begin where Bonaparte ended, by seizing supreme authority, though he had performed no such services for his fatherland as the French general.   He spared no effort to attach his army to his person, and to win its favour sacrificed without hesitation the whole civil population.   The land was drained of all resources, but he found new means of extorting money.   His officers went from town to town exacting a so-called " voluntary contribution " for the army.   Those who gave much were put in his white book as patriots—those who did not were enrolled in his black book as supporters of King Joseph.   He wanted to collect all the troops in Andalusia into a great army, with himself as commander.   But the Regency directed him, in accordance with Wellington's advice, to march at once with the troops immediately available and take post in La Mancha [1].'

Then came the news of Wellington's nomination as commander-in-chief.   Ballasteros thought the moment favourable for an open bid for the dictatorship.   Instead of obeying the orders sent, he issued on October 23rd a manifesto directed to the Regency, in which he declared that Wellington's appointment to supreme power was an insult to the Spanish nation, and especially to the Spanish Army.   He openly contemned the decree, as dishonourable and debasing—Spaniards should never become like Portuguese the servants of the foreigner.   If— what he could not believe—the national army and the nation itself should ratify such an appointment, he himself would

[1] Schepeler, pp. 672-3.

throw up his post and retire to his home. At the same time there was an outburst of pamphlets and newspaper articles inspired by him, stating that England was to be feared as an oppressor no less than France ; and all sorts of absurd rumours were put about as to the intentions of the British Government and the servility of the Cortes.

Ballasteros, however, had altogether mistaken his own importance and popularity : budding Bonapartes must be able to rely on their own troops, and he—as the event showed—could not. The Cortes took prompt measures for his suppression: one Colonel Rivera, a well-known Liberal, was sent secretly to Granada to bear to Virues, the second in command of the 4th Army, orders to arrest his chief, and place him in confinement. And this was done without any difficulty, so unfounded was the confidence which Ballasteros had placed in his omnipotence with the army. Virues and the Prince of Anglona, his two divisional generals, carried out the arrest in the simplest fashion. On the morning of October 30th they ordered out their troops for a field day on the Alcala road, save a battalion of the Spanish Guards, who had not belonged to Ballasteros's old army, and had no affection for him. This regiment surrounded his residence, and when he issued out the picquet refused him passage, and Colonel Rivera presented him with the warrant for his arrest. There was some little stir in Granada among the civil population, but the army made no movement when Virues read the decree of the Cortes to them. Before he well understood what had happened, Ballasteros was on his way under a guard to the African fortress of Ceuta. He was afterwards given Fregenal in Estremadura as the place of his detention.

But all this happened on October 30th, and meanwhile the Army of Andalusia had remained motionless, though Wellington had believed that it had marched for La Mancha as early as October 5th[1]. Nearly a month had been lost by Ballasteros's

---

[1] Wellington to Hill, October 5. *Dispatches*, ix. p. 469 : ' I do not write to General Ballasteros, because I do not know exactly where he is : but I believe he is at Alcaraz. At least I understand he was ordered there [by the Regency]. Tell him to hang upon the left flank and rear of the enemy, if they move by Albacete toward the Tagus.'

perversity, and when he was finally arrested and his troops became available, it was too late ; for Hill had been forced to retreat, and Madrid was about to fall into the hands of the French, who had advanced through La Mancha unmolested. The Fourth Army was put under the command of the Duke del Parque, the victor of Tamames, but the vanquished of Alba de Tormes in the campaign of 1809. It marched early in November to its appointed position at Alcaraz; but it was of no use to have it there when the enemy had changed all his positions, and had driven Hill beyond the Guadarrama into the valley of the Douro.

Wellington's arrangements for the defence of Madrid were therefore insufficient as the event proved, for three reasons. The diversion from Alicante was too weak—Suchet alone was able to keep Maitland in check. The main Spanish force which was to have co-operated with Hill never put in an appearance, thanks to the disloyal perversity of its general. And, thirdly, the autumn rains, which had so incommoded Wellington before Burgos, turned out to be late and scanty in New Castile. The Tagus and its affluents remained low and fordable almost everywhere.

As late as the 17th October Wellington had no fears about Hill's position. The probability that the enemy from Valencia would advance upon Madrid, as he wrote on that morning, seemed diminishing day by day—reinforcements were coming up from the South to Hill, and Ballasteros was believed to be already posted in La Mancha, 'which renders the enemy's movement upon the Tagus very improbable [1].' On the 19th, when his last assault on the Castle of Burgos had just been beaten off, and he was thinking of retreat, came much less satisfactory news from Hill. The enemy seemed to be drawing together : they had laid siege to the Castle of Chinchilla, and it was not impossible that they were aiming at Madrid, perhaps only with a view of forcing the abandonment of the siege of Burgos, perhaps with serious offensive intention. If so, Wellington might be caught with not one but both of the halves of his army exposed to immediate attack by a superior enemy, who was just assuming the offensive. And the total force of the French was appalling—50,000 men on the Northern field of

---

[1] Wellington to Popham. *Dispatches*, ix. p. 494.

operations, 60,000 on the other—while the united strength of all the available troops under Wellington's orders was about 80,000, of whom 25,000 were Spaniards, whose previous record was not in many cases reassuring. He had often warned the ministers at home that if the French evacuated outlying provinces, and collected in great masses, they were too many for him [1]. But that ever-possible event had been so long delayed, that Wellington had gone on, with a healthy and cheerful opportunism, facing the actual situation of affairs without taking too much thought for the morrow. Now the conjunction least to be desired appeared to be at length coming into practical existence and it remained to be seen what could be done.

As for his own army, there was no doubt that prompt retreat, first beyond the Pisuerga, then beyond the Douro, was necessary. Souham had already made his first preliminary forward movement. On the evening of October 18th a strong advance guard, consisting of a brigade of Maucune's division, pushed in upon the front of the allied army at the village of Santa Olalla, and surprised there the outlying picket of an officer and thirty men of the Brunswick-Oels, who were nearly all taken prisoners. The heights above this place commanded the town of Monasterio, wherefore Wellington directed it to be evacuated, and drew in its line to a position slightly nearer Burgos, for it was clear that there were heavy forces behind the brigade which had formed the French attacking force [2].

On the 19th he was in order of battle with all his army except the troops left before Burgos—Pack's Portuguese, a brigade of the 6th Division, and three weak battalions from the 1st Division. The position extended from Ibeas on the Arlanzon, through Riobena to Soto Palacios, and was manned by the 1st, 5th, and 7th Divisions, two brigades of the 6th, Bradford's Portuguese, Castaños's Galicians, and all the cavalry —about 30,000 men. Wellington expected to be attacked on the 20th, and was not prepared to give back till he had ascertained what force was in his front. He knew that the Army of

[1] See above, pp. 1–2.

[2] Wellington says in his Dispatch to Lord Bathurst of October 26 that the Brunswick officer disobeyed orders, and was taken because he did not retire at once, as directed.

Portugal had been reinforced, but was not sure whether the report that Caffarelli had come up with a large portion of the Army of the North was correct or no.

Souham's movement on the 18th had been intended as the commencement of a general advance : he brought up his whole force to Monasterio, and he would have attacked on the 20th if he had not received, before daybreak, and long ere his troops were under way, a much-delayed dispatch from King Joseph. It informed him that the whole mass of troops from Valencia was on the march for Madrid, that this movement would force Wellington to abandon the siege of Burgos and to fall back, and that he was therefore not to risk a general action, but to advance with caution, and pursue the allied force in front of him so soon as it should begin to retreat, when it might be pressed with advantage.[1] He was to be prepared to link his advance with that of the armies from the South, which would have columns in the direction of Cuenca. Souham was discontented with the gist of this dispatch, since he had his whole army assembled, while Caffarelli was close behind, within supporting distance, at Briviesca. He thought that he could have fought with advantage, and was probably right, since he and Caffarelli had a marked superiority of numbers, though Wellington's positions were strong.

Balked of the battle that he desired, he resolved to make a very strong reconnaissance against the allied centre, to see whether the enemy might already be contemplating retreat, and might consent to be pushed back, and to abandon Burgos. This reconnaissance was conducted by Maucune's and Chauvel's (late Bonnet's) divisions and a brigade of light cavalry : it was directed against Wellington's centre, in front of the villages of Quintana Palla and Olmos, where the 7th division was posted. Maucune's troops, forming the front line of the French, were hotly engaged in this direction, when Wellington, seeing that the main body of the enemy was very remote, and that the two vanguard divisions had ventured far forward into his ground, directed Sir Edward Paget with the 1st and 5th divisions— forming his own left wing—to swing forward by a diagonal movement and take Maucune in flank. The French general

---

[1] Souham to Clarke, October 22.

discovered the approaching force only just in time, and retreated in great haste across the fields, without calling in his
tirailleurs or forming any regular order of march. Each regiment made off by its own way, just early enough to escape
Paget's turning movement. The British horse artillery arrived
only in time to shell the last battalions; the infantry was too
far off to reach them. Dusk fell at this moment, and Paget
halted : if there had been one hour more of daylight Maucune
and Chauvel would have been in an evil case, for they were still
some distance from their own main body on the Monasterio
position, and the British cavalry was coming up in haste. The
reconnaissance had been pushed recklessly and too far—in
accordance with the usual conduct of Maucune, who was (as
his conduct at Salamanca had proved) a gallant but a very
rash leader. The losses on both sides were trifling—apparently
about 80 in the French ranks[1], and 47 in the British 7th division.
Paget's troops did not come under fire.

. On the morning of the 21st Wellington received a letter of
Hill's, written on the 17th, which made it clear to him that he
must delay no longer. It reported that the enemy were very
clearly on the move—the whole of Drouet's corps was coming
forward from Albacete, the castle of Chinchilla had fallen into
the hands of the French on Oct. 9th, and—what was the most
discomposing to learn—Ballasteros had failed to advance into
La Mancha : by the last accounts he was still at Granada.
He would certainly come too late, if he came at all. The only
compensating piece of good news was that Skerrett's brigade
from Cadiz was at last near at hand, and would reach Talavera
on the 20th. Elio, from his forward position at Villares,
reported that Suchet's troops opposite Alicante were drawing
back towards Valencia ; possibly they were about to join Soult
and King Joseph, who were evidently coming forward. Hill
was inclined to sum up the news as follows: ' The King, Soult,
and Suchet having united their armies are on the frontiers of
Murcia and Valencia, and appear to be moving this way. It is

---

[1] This is the figure given by Colonel Béchaud in his interesting narrative
of the doings of Maucune's division (*Études Napoléoniennes*, ii. p. 396).
Martinien's lists show 3 casualties of officers only, all in the 86th of
Maucune's division.

certain that a considerable force is advancing toward Madrid, but I think it doubtful whether they will attempt to force their way to the capital.' Meanwhile he had, as a precautionary measure, brought up the troops in cantonments round Madrid to Aranjuez and its neighbourhood, and had thrown forward a cavalry screen beyond the Tagus, to watch alike the roads from Albacete and those from Cuenca.

The mere possibility that Soult and the King were advancing on Madrid was enough to move Wellington to instant retreat : if he waited for certainty, he might be too late. And his own position in front of Souham and Caffarelli was dangerous enough, even if no more bad news from the South should come to hand. Accordingly on the afternoon of the 21st orders were sent to Pack to prepare to raise the siege of Burgos, when the main army in its backward movement should have passed him. The baggage was to be sent off, the stores removed or burned in the following night. The divisions in line opposite Souham were to move away, after lighting camp fires to delude the enemy, in two main columns, one on each side of the Arlanzon. The northern column, composed of the 5th Division, two-thirds of the Galician infantry, the heavy dragoons of Ponsonby (late Le Marchant's brigade) and the handful of Spanish regular cavalry, was to skirt the northern side of the city of Burgos, using the cross-roads by Bivar and Quintana Dueñas, and to retire to Tardajos, beside the Urbel river. The southern and larger column, consisting of the 1st, 7th, and 6th Divisions (marching in that order), of Bradford's Portuguese and the remainder of the Galicians, was to move by the high road through Villa Fria, to cross the town-bridge of Burgos (with special caution that silence must be observed, so as not to alarm the garrison of the Castle) to Frandovinez and Villa de Buniel. Here they would be in touch with the other column, which was to be only two miles away at Tardajos. Anson's cavalry brigade was to cover the rear of this column, only abandoning the outposts when the infantry should have got far forward. They were to keep the old picquet-line till three in the morning. Bock's German dragoons and the cavalry of Julian Sanchez formed a flank guard for the southern column : they were to cross the Arlanzon at Ibeas, five miles east of Burgos, and to retire parallel to the infantry line of march, by a circuit on cross-roads south of Burgos, finally joining the main body at Villa de Buniel [1].

All this complicated set of movements was carried out with complete success : the army got away without arousing the attention of the French of Souham, and the column which crossed the bridge of Burgos, under the cannon of the Castle [2], was never detected, till a Spanish guerrilla party galloped noisily across the stones and drew some harmless shots. Since the enemy was alarmed, the rear of the column had to take a side-path. Pack filed off the troops in the trenches, and got away quietly from the investment line. In the morning the two infantry columns were safely concentrated within two miles of each other at Tardajos and Villa de Buniel. There being no sign of pursuit, they were allowed some hours' rest in these positions, and then resumed their retreat, the northern column leading, with the 5th Division at its head, the southern column following, and falling into the main road by crossing the bridge of Buniel. The 7th Division formed the rearguard of the infantry ; it was followed by Bock's dragoons, Anson and Julian Sanchez bringing up the rear. On the night of the 22nd the army bivou-acked along the road about Celada, Villapequeña, and Hornillos ; the light cavalry, far behind, were still observing the passages of the Arlanzon at Buniel and of the Urbel at Tardajos.

The French pursuit was not urged with any vigour on this day. The departure of Wellington had only been discovered in the early morning hours by the dying down of the camp fires along his old position [3]. At dawn Souham advanced with caution ; finding nothing in front of it, his vanguard under Maucune entered Burgos about 10 o'clock in the morning, and exchanged congratulations with Dubreton and his gallant garrison. The light cavalry of the Army of Portugal pushed out along the roads north and south of the Arlanzon : those on the right bank found the three broken 18-pounders of Wellington's battering train a few miles outside of Burgos, and went as far

---

[1] For details see Wellington's Order of March in *Supplementary Dispatches*, xiv. pp. 144–5.

[2] The wheels of the artillery were all muffled with straw. The cavalry went at a walk.

[3] So Colonel Béchaud's narrative, quoted above, and most valuable for all this retreat.

as the Urbel, where they came on the rear vedettes of the Allies. Those on the left bank obtained touch with Anson's outlying picquet at San Mames, and drove it back to the Buniel bridge.

The 23rd October, however, was to be a day of a much more lively sort. Souham and Caffarelli, having debouched from Burgos, brought all their numerous cavalry to the front, and at dawn it was coming up for the pursuit, in immense strength. There were present of the Army of Portugal Curto's light horse, Boyer's dragoons, and the brigade formerly commanded by Chauvel now under Colonel Merlin of the 1st Hussars. These, by the morning state of October 15th, made up 4,300 sabres. The Army of the North contributed the bulk of its one—but very powerful—cavalry brigade, that of Laferrière, 1,650 strong.[1] Thus there were nearly 6,000 veteran horsemen hurrying on to molest Wellington's rear, where the covering force only consisted of Anson's and Bock's two brigades and of the lancers of Julian Sanchez—1,300 dragoons British and German[2], and 1,000 Spaniards admirable for raids and ambushes but not fit to be placed in battle line. Ponsonby's dragoons and the regular squadrons of the Galician army were far away with the head of the column. To support the cavalry screen were the two horse-artillery batteries of Downman and Bull, and the two Light Battalions of the German Legion from the 7th Division, under Colonel Halkett, which were left behind as the extreme rear-guard of the infantry.

All day the main marching column of the allied army laboured forward unmolested along the muddy high road from Celada del Camino to Torquemada, a very long stage of some 26 miles : Wellington seldom asked his infantry to make such an effort. What would have happened to Clausel's army if the

---

[1] These figures look very large—and exceed Napier's estimate of 5,000 sabres. But I can only give the strength of the French official returns, viz. Curto's division 2,163, Boyer's division 1,373, Merlin's brigade 746, Laferrière's brigade 1,662 ; total 5,944. All these units were engaged that day, as the French narrative shows, except that 4 only of the 6 squadrons of gendarmerie in Laferrière's brigade were at the front.

[2] Owing to losses at Garcia Hernandez and Majadahonda the Germans were only 4 squadrons, under 450 effective sabres. The Light Dragoons of Anson, all three regiments down to 2-squadron strength, made up about 800.

British had marched at this rate in the week that followed the
battle of Salamanca ?   Behind the infantry column, however,
the squadrons of the rearguard were fighting hard all day long, to
secure an unmolested retreat for their comrades.   This was the
most harassing and one of the most costly efforts that the
British cavalry was called upon to make during the Peninsular
War.   The nearest parallel to it in earlier years was the rearguard action of El Bodon in September 1811 [1].   But there the
forces engaged on both sides had been much smaller.

The French advanced guard consisted of Curto's light cavalry
division of the Army of Portugal, supported by Maucune's
infantry division.   It had started at dawn, and found the
British cavalry vedettes where they had been marked down on
the preceding night, at the bridge of Villa Buniel.   They retired
without giving trouble, being in no strength, and the morning
was wearing on when the French came upon Wellington's
rearguard, the horsemen of Anson and Julian Sanchez, and
Halkett's two German battalions, a mile or two east of Celada,
holding the line of the Hormaza stream.   Anson was in position
behind its ravine, with a battalion of the light infantry dispersed along the bushes above the water, and the cavalry in
support.   Julian Sanchez was visible on the other side of the
Arlanzon, which is not here fordable, beyond Anson's right :
on his left, hovering on hills above the road, was a small
irregular force, the guerrilla band of Marquinez [2].   The ground
along the Hormaza was strong, and the infantry fire surprised
the enemy, who were stopped for some time.   They came on
presently in force, and engaged in a bickering fight : several
attempts to cross the ravine were foiled by partial charges of
some of Anson's squadrons.   Wellington says in his dispatch
that the skirmishing lasted nearly three hours, and that Stapleton Cotton, who had recently come up from the Salamanca
hospital cured of his wound, made excellent dispositions.   But
the odds—more than two to one—were far too great to permit
the contest to be maintained for an indefinite period ; and when,

[1] See vol. iv. pp. 565–9.

[2] Who was not himself any longer at their head, having been killed in
a private quarrel some weeks before. His men were this day under his
lieutenant Puente (Schepeler, p. 680).

after much bickering, the French (O'Shee's brigade of Curto's division) at last succeeded in gaining a footing beyond the Hormaza, Anson's squadrons went off in good order. The ground for the next five or six miles was very unfavourable for a small detaining force, as the valley of the Arlanzon widened out for a time, and allowed the enemy space to deploy his superior numbers. Nevertheless the light dragoons turned again and again, and charged with more or less success the pursuing Chasseurs. While Curto's .division was pressing back ˙ the British brigade in front, Merlin's brigade, pushing out on the French right, ascended the hills beyond Anson's left flank, and there found and drove off the partida of Marquinez. The fugitive guerrilleros, falling back for support towards the British, came in upon the flank of the 16th Light Dragoons with French hussars in close pursuit, and mixed with them. The left squadron of the 16th was thrown into confusion, and suffered heavily, having some thirty casualties ; and the commander of the regiment, Colonel Pelly, and seven of his men were taken prisoners. As Curto was pushing on at the same time, Anson's brigade was much troubled, and was greatly relieved when it at last came in sight of its support, Bock's German Heavy Dragoons and Bull's battery, posted behind a bridge spanning a watercourse near the lonely house called the Venta del Pozo. The two battalions of Halkett, who had been retiring under cover of Anson's stubborn resistance, were now some little way behind Bock, near the village of Villadrigo. On seeing the obstacle of the watercourse in front of them, and the British reserves behind it, the cavalry of the Army of Portugal halted, and began to re-form. Anson's harassed brigade was permitted to cross the bridge and to join Bock.

At this moment there came on the scene the French cavalry reserves, Boyer's dragoons and the three regiments of the Army of the North, which were commanded that day not by their brigadier Laferrière (who had been injured by a fall from his horse) but by Colonel Faverot of the 15th Chasseurs. Souham, who had arrived in their company as had Caffarelli also, gave orders that the pursuit was not to slacken for a minute. While the cavalry of Curto and Merlin were re-forming and resting, the newly arrived squadrons were directed to drive in the

British rearguard from its new position. The brigade of Faverot was to attack in front, the dragoons of Boyer were to turn the hostile line, by crossing the watercourse some way to their right, and to fall on its flank and rear. So great was the superiority in numbers of the attacking party that they came on with supreme confidence, ignoring all disadvantages of ground. Faverot's brigade undertook to pass the bridge in column, in face of Bock's two regiments drawn up at the head of the slope, and of Bull's battery placed on the high road so as to command the crossing. Boyer's dragoons trotted off to the right, to look for the first available place where the water should allow them a practicable ford.

What followed was not in accordance with the designs of either party. Souham had intended Boyer and Faverot to act simultaneously ; but the former found the obstacle less and less inviting the farther that he went on : he rode for more than a mile without discovering a passage, and finally got out of sight of Souham and the high road [1]. Meanwhile Faverot had advanced straight for the bridge, and had begun to cross it. Of his three regiments the Berg lancers led, the 15th Chasseurs came next, the Legion of Gendarmerie brought up the rear. They were ten squadrons in all, or some 1,200 sabres. As each squadron got quit of the bridge it formed up in line, the first to pass to the right of the road, while those which followed successively took ground to the left, between the chaussée and the bank of the Arlanzon. Eight squadrons had got into position before the British line gave any signs of movement on the hillside above.

It is clear that to cross a bridge in this fashion was a reckless manœuvre. If Bock had charged when two or three squadrons only had passed[2], he must have crushed them in the act of deployment, and have jammed the rest of the French column at the bridgehead in a position of helpless immobility. That no such charge was made resulted from a curious chance. Stapleton Cotton, who was still conducting the retreat, had placed Bull's battery at a point on the slope where he judged that it

---

[1] To Caffarelli's high disgust : see his dispatch to Clarke of October 30, where he calls Boyer's action a ' fatalité que l'on ne peut conçevoir.'

[2] As Lumley did at Usagre against L'Allemand, see vol. iv. p. 412.

fully commanded the bridge, with Bock's four squadrons on its
right.   Then Anson's brigade, not in the best of order after its
long pursuit by the enemy, trotted over the bridge and came up
the slope.   Cotton intended that it should deploy on the left
of the guns, but the retreating regiments, before the directions
reached them, turned to the right and began to form up behind
Bock's line.   The general at once sent them orders to cross to
the left and prolong the line on the other side of Bull's battery.
By some extraordinary blunder the leading regiment (perhaps
to shorten its route) passed to the left in front of the guns,
instead of moving behind them.   It was thus masking the
battery just at the moment that the French, to the surprise of
every one, began to cross the bridge.   There was considerable
confusion in changing the march of the light dragoons, and before they were cleared off and the front of the battery was free,
several French squadrons were across the ravine and forming
up.   The artillerymen then opened, but in their hurry they
misjudged the elevation, and not one shot of the first discharge
told.   The second did hardly better; more French were passing
every moment, and Cotton then directed the cavalry to charge,
since the enemy was becoming stronger and stronger on the
near side of the bridge.

The charge was delivered in échelon of brigades; Bock's
two regiments, who had been awaiting orders for some time,
got away at once, and fell upon the left of the French—the
gendarmes and the left squadrons of the Chasseurs.   Anson's six
squadrons started somewhat later, and having tired horses—
after their long morning's fight—came on at a much slower
pace.   They found themselves opposed to the Lancers and the
right squadrons of the Chasseurs.   There was such a perceptible space between the two attacks, that some of the French
narratives speak of the British charge as being made by a front
line and a reserve.   The numbers engaged were not very unequal [1]

[1] Anson's brigade fought, it is said, with only 600 sabres out of its
original 800, owing to heavy losses in the morning, and to the dropping
behind of many men on exhausted horses, who did not get up in time to
form for the charge.   Bock's brigade was intact, but only 400 strong.   Of
the French brigade 1,600 strong on October 15 by its ' morning state '
two squadrons out of the six of gendarmes were not present, so that the
total was probably 1,250 or so engaged.

—probably 1,200 French to 1,000 British—but the former were all fresh, while the larger half of the latter (Anson's brigade) were wearied out—man and horse—by long previous fighting.

All accounts—English and French—agree that this was one of the most furious cavalry mêlées ever seen : the two sides broke each other's lines at various points—the 1st K.G.L. Dragoons rode down their immediate opponents, the 2nd got to a standing fight with theirs : Anson's regiments, coming on more slowly on their jaded mounts, made no impression on the Lancers and Chasseurs opposite them. The whole mass fell into a heaving crowd ' so completely mixed that friend could hardly be distinguished from foe—the contest man to man lasted probably a long minute, during which the ground was strewn with French, and our own loss was heavy in the extreme.' General Bock was at one time seen defending himself against six Frenchmen, and was barely saved by his men. Beteille, the Colonel of the French Gendarme Legion, received, it is said, twelve separate wounds, and was left for dead. The combat was ended by the intervention of the two rear squadrons of the Gendarmes, who had not crossed the bridge when the charge began ; they came up late, and fell upon the flank and rear of the 2nd Dragoons of the K.G.L. This last push settled the matter, and the British brigades broke and fell back[1].

They were not so disheartened, however, but that they rallied half a mile to the rear, and were showing fight when Boyer's dragoons came tardily upon the scene—they had at last found a passage over the ravine, and appeared in full strength on the flank. It was hopeless to oppose them, and the wrecks of the two British brigades fell back hastily towards their infantry support, Halkett's two Light Battalions of the German Legion, which had been retreating meanwhile towards Villadrigo, marching in column at quarter distance and prepared to form square when necessary. The need now came—the leading regiment of Boyer's Dragoons turned upon the rear battalion—the 1st—and charged it : the square was formed in good time, and the attack was beaten off. The battalion then

---

[1] Most of this detail is from the admirable account of von Hodenberg, aide-de-camp to Bock, whose letter I printed in *Blackwood* for 1913. There is a good narrative also in Martin's *Gendarmerie d'Espagne*, pp. 317–19.

retired, falling back upon the 2nd, which had nearly reached
Villadrigo. Both then retreated together, covering the broken
cavalry, and had gone a short distance farther when the French
renewed the attack. Both battalions formed square, both were
charged, and both repulsed the attack of the dragoons with
loss. The enemy, who had still plenty of intact squadrons,
seemed to be contemplating a third charge, but hesitated, and
finally Bock's and Anson's men having got back into some
sort of order, and showing a front once more, the squares
retired unmolested, and marched off in company with the
cavalry. The French followed cautiously and gave no further
trouble. It was now dark, and when the pursuit ceased the rearguard halted for two hours, and resuming its march about
ten o'clock, finally reached the bridge of Quintana del Puente,
outside Torquemada, at two o'clock next morning.

Thus ended a costly affair, which might have proved much
more perilous had the French been better managed. But
though their troopers fought well enough, their generals failed
to get such advantage as they should out of their superior
numbers. It is to be noted that both Curto and Boyer have
very poor records in the memoirs of Marmont, Foy, and other contemporary writers, who speak on other occasions of the ' inertie
coupable ' and ' faute de décision ' of the one, and call the other
' bon manœuvrier, mais n'ayant pas la réputation qui attire la
confiance aveugle du soldat ': Napoleon once summed them
up as ' mauvais ou médiocres [2],' along with several other
generals. It seems clear, at any rate, that they should have
accomplished more, with the means at their disposal. The
damage inflicted on the British rearguard was much smaller
than might have been expected—only 230 in all, including
5 officers and 60 men taken prisoners [2]. It is probable indeed

---

[1] Details are worth giving. The 2nd Dragoons K.G.L. had 52 casualties,
the 1st 44. In Anson's brigade the 11th Light Dragoons lost 49, the 12th
only 20, the 16th 47. The officers taken prisoners were Colonel Pelly and
Lieutenant Baker of the 16th, Major Fischer (mortally wounded) of the
1st Dragoons K.G.L., and Captain Lenthe and Lieutenant Schaeffer of
the 2nd Dragoons K.G.L. The two infantry battalions had 18 casualties,
of whom 13 were men missing, apparently skirmishers cut off in the fight
earlier in the day on the Hormaza, or footsore men who had fallen behind.

[2] In a conversation with Foy (see life of the latter, by Girod de l'Ain,

that the pursuers suffered no less ; for, though their official report spoke of no more than about a hundred and fifty casualties, Faverot's Brigade alone had almost as many by itself, showing a list of 7 killed and 18 officers and 116 men wounded. But the regimental lists give 35 French cavalry officers in all disabled that day, 5 in Curto's division, 5 in Merlin's Brigade, 5 in Boyer's Dragoons, and 2 on the staff, beside the 18 in Faverot's Brigade. This must indicate a total loss of nearly 800, applying the very moderate percentage of casualties of men to officers that prevailed in Faverot's regiments to the other corps. The engagement had been most honourable to the two cavalry brigades of Wellington's rearguard, and not less so to the German Legion light infantry. An intelligent observer— not a soldier—who saw the whole of the fighting that day remarked, ' I twice thought Anson's Brigade (which was weak in numbers and much exhausted by constant service) would have been annihilated ; and I believe we owe the preservation of that and of the heavy German brigade to the admirable steadiness of Halkett's two Light Battalions. . . . We literally had to fight our way for four miles, retiring, halting, charging, and again retiring. I say *we* because I was in the thick of it, and never witnessed such a scene of anxiety, uproar, and confusion. Throughout the whole of this trying occasion Stapleton Cotton behaved with great coolness, judgement, and gallantry. I was close to him the whole time, and did not observe him for an instant disturbed or confused [1].' At the end of the fight one officer in a jaded regiment observed to another that it had been a bad day. His friend replied that it had been a most honourable day for the troops, for at nightfall every unwounded man on an efficient horse was still in line and ready to charge again. There had been no rout, no straggling, and no loss of morale.

p. 141) when he said that *all* the cavalry generals of the Army of Portugal except Montbrun, Fournier, and Lamotte were ' mauvais ou médiocres '— these others being Curto, Boyer, Cavrois, Lorcet, and Carrié.

[1] H. Sydenham to Henry Wellesley, printed in *Wellington Supplementary Dispatches*, vii. pp. 464–5. Sydenham understates, however, the available force when he says that Anson had only 460 sabres and Bock only two squadrons. Hodenberg diminishes less, but still too much, when he gives Bock 300 sabres and Anson 600. The real numbers are given above.

While the combat of Venta del Pozo was in progress the main body of the army had been resting in and about Torquemada, undisturbed by any pursuit, so well had the rearguard played its part. Next morning (October 24th) it marched off and crossed the Carrion river by the bridges of Palencia, Villamuriel, and Dueñas. Behind this stream Wellington was proposing to check the enemy for at least some days. He chose it, rather than the Pisuerga, as his defensive line for tactical reasons. If he had stayed behind the Pisuerga, he would have had the Carrion and its bridges in his immediate rear, and he was determined not to fight with bridge-defiles behind him. In the rear of the Carrion there were no such dangerous passages, and the way was clear to Valladolid. It was fortunate that, after the lively day on the 23rd, the French made no serious attempt at pursuit upon the 24th, for there were many stragglers that morning from the infantry. Torquemada was the centre of a wine-district and full of barrels, vats, and even cisterns of the heady new vintage of 1812 ; many of the men had repaid themselves for a twenty-six mile march by over-deep potations, and it was very hard to get the battalions started next morning.[1] Napier says that ' twelve thousand men at one time were in a state of helpless inebriety : ' this is no doubt an exaggeration, but the diaries of eye-witnesses make it clear that there was much drunkenness that day.

Wellington's new position extended from Palencia on the Carrion to Dueñas on the Pisuerga, below its junction with the first-named river. He intended to have all the bridges destroyed, viz. those of Palencia, Villa Muriel, and San Isidro on the Carrion, and those of Dueñas and Tariego on the Pisuerga. He placed one of the Galician divisions (Cabrera's) in Palencia and south of it, supported by the 3/1st from the 5th Division. Another Galician division (Losada's) continued the line southward to Villa Muriel, where it was taken up by the 5th Division—now under General Oswald who had recently joined. The 1st, 6th, and 7th Divisions prolonged the line

---

[1] Napier, iv. p. 361. Corroboration may be had on p. 120 of the *Journal* of Green of the 68th, who says that his colonel was much puzzled to know how so many men had succeeded in getting liquor, and that one soldier was drowned in a vat, overcome by the fumes of new wine.

down the Pisuerga. Behind the rivers, all the way, there was a second line of defence, formed by the dry bed of the Canal of Castile, which runs for many miles through the valley : it was out of order and waterless, but the depression of its course made a deep trench running parallel with the Carrion and Pisuerga, and very tenable. It must be noted that Palencia lay to the wrong side of the Carrion for Wellington's purpose, being on its left or eastern bank. It had, therefore, either to be held as a sort of *tête de pont*, or evacuated before the enemy should attack. The Spanish officer in command resolved to take the former course, though the town was indefensible, with a ruinous mediaeval wall : he occupied it, and made arrangements for the blowing up of the bridge only when his advanced guard should have been driven out of Palencia and should have recrossed the river.

Souham, who had pushed his head-quarters forward to Magaz this day, resolved to try to force the line of the Carrion. Two divisions under Foy—his own and that of Bonté (late Thomières)—were to endeavour to carry Palencia and its bridge. Maucune, with the old advanced guard, his own division and that of Gauthier [1], was to see if anything could be done at the bridges of Villa Muriel and San Isidro. Foy had Laferrière's cavalry brigade given him, Maucune retained Curto's light horse. The main body of the army remained in a mass near Magaz, ready to support either of the advanced columns, if it should succeed in forcing a passage.

Unfortunately for Wellington, everything went wrong at Palencia. Foy, marching rapidly on the city, drove away the few squadrons of Galician cavalry which were observing his front, and then burst open one of its rickety gates with artillery fire, and stormed the entry with Chemineau's brigade. The Galician battalions in the town, beaten in a short street fight, were evicted with such a furious rush that the British engineer officer with the party of the 3/1st, who were working at the

---

[1] This was Bonnet's old division : Chauvel had been commanding it since Bonnet was disabled at Salamanca. But he had been wounded by a chanee shot at Venta del Pozo on the 23rd, and Gauthier, his senior brigadier, had taken it over.

bridge, failed [1] to fire the mine, whose fuse went wrong. Most
of them were taken prisoners. Colonel Campbell of the 3/1st,
who had been sent to support the Spaniards, fell back towards
Villa Muriel, judging the enemy too strong to be resisted, and
the routed Galicians had to be covered by Ponsonby's heavy
dragoons from the pursuit of the French cavalry, who spread
over the environs of Palencia and captured some baggage
trains, British and Spanish, with their escorts.

Thus Souham had secured a safe passage over the Carrion
and it mattered little to him that his other attack farther
south had less decisive success. Here Maucune, always a very
enterprising—not to say reckless—commander had marched
against the two bridges of Villa Muriel and San Isidro. He
led his own division towards the former, and sent that of
Gauthier against the latter. The 5th Division had an infantry
screen of light troops beyond the river—this was pushed in,
with some loss, especially to the 8th Caçadores. Both bridges
were then attacked, but each was blown up when the heads
of the French columns approached, and a heavy fire, both of
artillery and of musketry, from the other bank checked their
further advance. Gauthier then turned east in search of a
passage, and went coasting along the bank of the Pisuerga for
some miles, as far as the bridge of Tariego (or Baños, as the
British accounts call it). This had been prepared for destruction like the other bridges, but the mine when exploded only
broke the parapets and part of the flooring. The French
charged across, on the uninjured crown of the arch, and
captured some 40 of the working party [2] : they established
themselves on the opposite bank, but advanced no farther ;
here the British had still the lower course of the Pisuerga to
protect them, while Gauthier had no supports near, and halted,
content to have captured the bridge, which he began to repair.

Meanwhile, the bridge of Villa Muriel having been more
efficiently blown up, Maucune dispersed his voltigeur companies
along the river-bank, brought his artillery up to a favourable

---

[1] Some 27 men of the 3/1st, taken prisoners here, represent this party
in the casualty list of October 25. The battalion was not otherwise
seriously engaged.

[2] Who were drawn from the 4th, 30th, and 44th.

position, and entered on a long desultory skirmish with Oswald, which lasted for some hours. During this time he was searching for fords—several were found [1], but all were deep and dangerous. About three o'clock in the afternoon a squadron of cavalry forded one of them, apparently unobserved, reached the western bank, and rolled up a company of the 1/9th which it caught strung out along the river bickering with the skirmishers on the other side. An officer and 33 men were taken prisoners [2]. This passage was followed by that of eight voltigeur companies, who established themselves on the other side, but clung to the bank of the river, the British light troops having only retired a few score of yards from it. Having thus got a lodgement beyond the Carrion, Maucune resolved to cross in force, in support of his voltigeurs. Arnauld's brigade passed at the ford which had first been used, Montfort's at another, to the left of the broken bridge, farther down the stream. The French seized the village of Villa Muriel, and established themselves in force along the dry bed of the canal, a little to its front. Wellington had expected that Maucune would come on farther, and intended to charge him with the whole 5th Division when he should begin to ascend the slope above the canal. But when, after an hour or more, the enemy made no advance, it became necessary to assume the offensive against him, since Foy was now across the Carrion at Palencia, and, if he commenced to push forward, he might drive the Spanish troops between him and Villa Muriel into Maucune's arms. The latter must be expelled before this danger should arise: wherefore at about 4 o'clock a brigade of Losada's Spaniards was sent against the right of the French division, while Pringle's brigade attacked its front along the bed of the canal. The Spaniards made no progress—they were indeed driven back, and rallied with difficulty by Wellington's friend General Alava, who was severely wounded. To replace them the British brigade of Barnes was brought up, and told to

[1] For a romantic story of how one was discovered see Napier, iv. p. 363, a tale which I have not found corroborated in any other authority.

[2] I had not been able to make out how the 1/9th came to lose these prisoners till I came on the whole story in the Autobiography of Hale of the 1/9th, printed at Cirencester 1826, a rare little book, with a good account of this combat. He is my best source for it on the British side.

storm Villa Muriel—Spry's Portuguese supporting. After a stiff fight Pringle and Barnes swept all before them : the enemy yielded first on the right, but held out for some time in the village, where he lost a certain number of prisoners. He finally repassed the fords, and sought safety in the plain on the eastern bank, where the French reserves were now beginning to appear in immense force. 'Their numbers were so great that the fields appeared to our view almost black [1].' Wellington wrote home that he had hitherto under-estimated Souham's force, and only now realized that the Army of the North had brought up its infantry as well as its cavalry. He, naturally, made no attempt to pursue the enemy beyond the Carrion, and the fight died down into a distant cannonade across the water [2].

The combat of Villa Muriel cost the 5th Division some 500 casualties—not including 43 men of the 3/1st, hurt or taken in the separate fight at Palencia, or a few casualties in Ponsonby's dragoons in that same quarter. Maucune's losses were probably not far different—they must certainly have exceeded the ' 250 killed or wounded, 30 prisoners and 6 drowned ' of the official report : for one of Maucune's regiments—the 15th Line—had 200 casualties by itself [3]. Foy at Palencia lost very few men—though his statement of ' three or four ' as their total can hardly be correct. He had taken 100 prisoners (27 of them British), and killed or wounded 60 more, mostly Galicians [4]. The balance of the day's losses was certainly against the Allies.

Moreover, despite of Maucune's repulse, the result of the day's fighting was much to Wellington's detriment, since (though the loss of the bridge of Tariego mattered little) the capture of Palencia ruined his scheme for defending the line of the Carrion. Souham's whole army could follow Foy, and turn the left flank of the Allies behind that river. Wherefore Wellington first threw back the left flank of the 5th Division

---

[1] Hale, p. 95, quoted above.

[2] I have been using for the French side mainly the elaborate and interesting narrative of Colonel Béchaud of the 66th, recently published in *Études Napoléoniennes*, ii. pp. 405–11.

[3] See Béchaud, p. 410.

[4] These modest figures of Foy's report to Souham are much exaggerated in most French narratives of the affair.

en potence, to make a containing line against Foy, while its right
flank still held the line of the river about Villa Muriel. Under
cover of this rearguard; he remainder of the army evacuated
its positions on each side of Dueñas at dawn on the 26th, and
marched down the Pisuerga to Cabezon, where it passed the
river at the bridge of that place and retired to the opposite
side. The 5th Division followed (unmolested by the enemy)
in the early morning : at night the entire allied army had
retired across the broad stream, and was lining its left bank
from Valladolid upward, with that city (held by the 7th Division)
as the supporting point of its southern flank, and its northern
resting on the Cubillas river. This was one of the most surprising and ingenious movements that Wellington ever carried
out. On the 23rd he was defending the right bank of the Pisuerga
—on the 24th he was on the other side and defending its left
bank in a much stronger position. He was in no way sacrificing
his communications with Portugal or Madrid, since he had
behind him two good bridges over the Douro, those of Tudela
and Puente Duero, with excellent roads southward and westward to Medina del Campo, Arevalo, and Olmedo. The enemy
might refuse to attack him, and march down the west bank of
the Pisuerga towards the Douro, but Wellington had already
provided for the destruction of the three bridges of Simancas,
Tordesillas, and Toro, and the Douro was now a very fierce
and broad barrier to further progress, twice as difficult to cross
as the Pisuerga. On the other hand, if Souham should make
up his mind to come down the Pisuerga on its eastern bank, by
the restored bridge of Tariego, there was an excellent fighting
position along the Cubillas river. But the roads on this side
of the Pisuerga were bad, and the country rough, while on the
western bank the ground was flat and fertile, and the line of
march easy.

Souham, therefore, advanced as was natural from Palencia
southward, on the right bank of the Pisuerga ; on the 26th he
withdrew Maucune and Gauthier to that side, and on the 27th
felt the position of Cabezon, which he decided to be impregnable,
and left alone. He placed the infantry of the Army of the
North opposite it, and moved southward with the rest of his
forces. On the 28th he tried the passage of Valladolid, after

driving out a battalion of Portuguese caçadores from the suburb beyond the Pisuerga, and cannonading the 51st across the bridge. Here too the obstacles looked most formidable, and the French, pursuing their march, came to the bridge of Simancas, which was blown up in their faces by Colonel Halkett, whose brigade of the 7th Division had been placed in this part of the British line. Halkett then sent on one of his three battalions (the Brunswick-Oels) to Tordesillas.

This was all quite satisfactory to Wellington, who had been able to give his troops two days' rest, and who saw that the enemy, despite of his superior numbers, seemed to be brought to a nonplus by the position behind the Pisuerga. But the next evening (October 29) brought very untoward news. Foy's division now formed the advance-guard of the Army of Portugal: it reached and occupied Tordesillas, where the bridge (like that of Simancas) had its main arch destroyed. A mediaeval tower on the south bank of the ruined structure was held by a half-company of the Brunswick-Oels infantry as an outlying picquet: the rest of the battalion was encamped in a wood some hundreds of yards behind. Considering that the river was broad and swift, and that all boats had been carefully destroyed, it was considered that the passage was impossible. Foy thought, however, that it was worth making the hazardous attempt to cross: he called for volunteers, and collected 11 officers and 44 men, who undertook to attempt to ford the Douro by swimming and wading. Their leader was Captain Guingret of the 6th Léger, one of the minor historians of the war. They placed their muskets and ammunition on a sort of raft formed of planks hastily joined, which certain good swimmers undertook to tow and guide. At 4 o'clock in the afternoon the 55 adventurers pushed off the raft, and plunged into the water, striking out in a diagonal direction. Meanwhile Foy brought down his divisional battery to the shore, and began shelling the tower at the bridge-end. The starting-point had been well chosen, and the raft and swimmers were borne across the stream with surprising speed, and came ashore a few yards from the tower, which, all naked and with arms many of which had been soaked in the water and would not fire, they proceeded to attack. The lieutenant in charge of the Brunswick picquet and his men lost their heads in the most disgraceful fashion ; perhaps they were demoralized by the artillery playing on them—at any rate, after firing some ill-directed shots, they ran off—two were captured in the tower, nine others outside it. The swimmers, now shivering with cold, for the afternoon was bleak, took possession of the bridgehead, and Foy's sappers at the other end of the broken arch began to hurry forward ropes to establish a communication with the captured tower [1].

The major in command of the Brunswick battalion, half a mile off, behaved as badly as the subaltern at the tower. He should have come down in force and thrown the handful of naked men into the river. Instead of doing so he put his corps under arms in the edge of the wood, and sent information to his brigadier asking for orders. By the time that Halkett heard of the matter, a rough communication had been made across the shattered bridge, and the French were streaming over. Nothing was done, save to move reinforcements from the 7th Division to block the two roads that diverge from the bridgehead south and west.

This extraordinary feat of Guingret's party, one of the most dashing exploits of the Peninsular War, altered Wellington's position, much for the worse. The enemy had now secured a crossing on the Douro opposite his extreme left wing. He had already begun to move troops in this direction, when he saw Foy pushing forward past Simancas, and on the morning of the 29th had resolved to leave Valladolid and make a general shift westward, parallel to the enemy. Soon after dawn the bridge of Cabezon was blown up, and the British right wing retired, under cover of the troops still holding Valladolid. When the right wing (the 5th Division and the Galicians) had passed to the rear of that city, and were nearing the Douro bridges (Tudela and Puente de Duero) behind it, the centre of the British line (1st, 6th, and Pack's Portuguese) followed, and finally the left (two brigades of the 7th Division) evacuated Valladolid after destroying the Pisuerga bridge, and passed the Douro in the wake of the centre. All this was done with no

---

[1] There is a full account of this business in Foy's dispatch to Souham of the next morning, in which occur all the facts given by Guingret in his own little book. That officer's narrative must be taken as fully correct.

molestation from the enemy, and at nightfall on the 29th every man was on the south of the Douro, and its bridges had been blown up after the rearguards had passed.

Wellington had been intending to hold the line of that great river till he should have certain news of how Hill—of whose operations the next chapter treats—was faring in the south. Since he knew that the troops from Madrid were coming to join him, he had purposed to maintain himself behind the Douro till Hill came up to the Adaja. The news of the passage of Foy at Tordesillas was therefore very vexatious ; but his counter-move was bold and effective. Before the enemy had fully repaired the bridge, or got any large force across it, he marched to Rueda with the 1st, 6th, and 7th Divisions, and advanced from thence to the heights opposite Tordesillas, where he formed line of battle only 1,200 yards from the Douro, and threw up a line of redoubts, so strong that the enemy dared not push on. The first brigade to move out from the bridge would obviously be destroyed, and there was no room for large forces to deploy and attack. The enemy saw this, and instead of debouching constructed a defensive bridgehead at Tordesillas [1].

Souham indeed, having occupied Valladolid and drawn up to the line of the Douro, remained quiescent for six days. It looked as if his offensive movement had come to an end. The main cause of his halt was that Caffarelli, having assisted him in driving Wellington back to the Douro, refused to follow him further, declaring that he must go back at once to the North, from whence the most unsatisfactory news was reaching him day by day. Both about Pampeluna, and round Bilbao, which the Spaniards had once more seized, things were in a most dangerous condition. After barely visiting Valladolid he turned on his heel, and marching fast was back at Burgos again on November 6th [2]. Deprived of the strong cavalry brigade and the two infantry divisions of the Army of the North, Souham was no longer in a condition to press Wellington

---

[1] All this from Burgoyne, i. p. 244. Napier does not mention the earthworks, which were batteries for six guns each.

[2] There he wrote his dispatch, concerning the late combats, to Clarke. Napier never mentions Caffarelli's departure—a curious omission.

recklessly. He had now well under 40,000 men, instead of nearly 50,000, with which to assail the Allies in their new and strong position. Wherefore, he resolved to wait till he had news that Soult and King Joseph were drawing near from the South. The King's dispatches had told him to avoid a general action, and to wait for the effect of the great diversion that would soon be developing against Wellington's rear. Hence, mainly, came the halt, which caused his adversary to think for some days that he might be able to draw at the line of the Douro the limit of the French advance.

The first half of the retreat from Burgos was now at an end. To understand the manœuvres of the second half, we must first explain the doings of Soult, King Joseph, and General Hill in New Castile during the last week of October.

SECTION XXXIV : CHAPTER IV

HILL'S RETREAT FROM MADRID

THE crisis in front of Madrid, where Hill stood exposed to attack from the mass of French forces in the kingdom of Valencia, developed late. We have already seen that the first dispatch from the South which disquieted Wellington only reached him on the 19th October, and that it was not till the 21st that he realized that all his plans for hindering a French advance on Madrid were ineffective, and that Hill was in serious danger.

The long delay in Soult's evacuation of Andalusia was—as has been already remarked—the ultimate cause of the late appearance of the advancing columns of the enemy in front of Madrid. It was not till September 30 that the advanced cavalry of the Army of the South got into touch with the outlying vedettes of Treillard's dragoons, at Tobarra near Hellin. Four days later Soult was in conference with King Joseph, and the Marshals Jourdan and Suchet who had come out to meet him, at Fuente la Higuera, some fifty miles farther on the road toward Valencia. They met with various designs, though all were agreed that the Allies must be driven out of the capital as soon as possible. Suchet was mainly anxious to get the Army of the South, and the King also, out of his own viceroyalty. Joseph's troops were wasting his stores, and harrying the peasantry, whose shearing he wished to reserve for himself. Soult's men were notoriously unruly, and at the present moment half famished, after their long march through a barren land. The Duke of Albufera was anxious to see them all started off for Madrid at the earliest possible moment. His only personal demand was that he should be allowed to borrow a division from one or the other army ; for, when they should be gone, he thought that he would have barely enough men to hold off Mackenzie and the Spaniards of the Murcian army. He promised, and produced, large convoys of food for the service of the Armies of the South and Centre,

but pleaded that in order to make his only base and arsenal—
the city of Valencia—quite safe, it was necessary that they
should leave him 5,000 extra troops : in especial he pleaded for
Palombini's division, which had originally been borrowed from
his own army of Aragon. Jourdan—as he tells us in his memoirs[1]
—maintained that it was necessary to turn every possible man
upon Madrid, and that Suchet could defend himself against
his old enemies with his own army alone. He might, if hard
pressed, call down some troops from Catalonia.

But the real quarrel was between Soult and King Joseph. The
first was in a sullen and captious mood, because the King had
caused him to evacuate his much-prized viceroyalty in Andalusia, by refusing to join him there in September. But Joseph
was at a much higher pitch of passion ; not only did he still
remember all Soult's disobedience in July and August, which
(as he thought) had led to the unnecessary loss of Madrid, but
he had a new and a much more bitter grievance. Some time
before the Army of the South reached Valencia, he had become
possessed of the dispatch to the minister of war which Soult had
written on August 12th, in which he hinted that the King was
meditating treachery to his brother the Emperor, and had
opened up negotiations with the Cortes in order to betray the
French cause[2]. This document—as has been explained above—
had been given by Soult to a privateer captain bound from
Malaga to Toulon, who had been forced to run into the harbour
of Valencia by the British blockading squadron. Not knowing
the contents of the document, the captain had handed it over
to the King, when he found him at Valencia. Thus Joseph was
aware that the Marshal had accused him, on the most flimsy
evidence, of betraying his brother. He was justly indignant,
and had contemplated, in his first outburst of rage, the arrest
and supersession of Soult. His next impulse had been to send off
his confidential aide-de-camp Colonel Deprez, to seek first the
minister of war at Paris, and then the Emperor himself in
Russia[3], with his petition for vengeance. ' Je demande justice.

---

[1] p. 437.　　　　　　　　[2] See vol. v. pp. 538-9.

[3] Deprez, travelling with great speed, reached Paris and interviewed
Clarke on September 21. The Minister, who was no friend of Soult's,
told him that neither he himself nor the King could dare to depose the

Que le Maréchal Soult soit rappelé, entendu, et puni[1].' If his
enemy had appeared at Valencia early in September, he would
probably have taken the most extreme measures against him.
But three weeks had gone by, his anger had had time to cool,
and he could realize the danger of attempting to seize and deport
a marshal whose army was double the size of his own and
Suchet's combined, and who had a powerful faction to support
him among his own generals. Joseph hoped that a mandate
for Soult's recall and disgrace would soon be on its way from
Russia, and meanwhile curbed his temper, ignored the Marshal's
recent charges of treachery, and contented himself with treating
him with coldness, and overruling many of his proposals, on
the mere formal ground of discipline. He was the commander-
in-chief, and could accept or reject the suggestions of a subordinate as he pleased. Soult was no longer three hundred miles
away, as he had been in June, and orders given by a superior
on the spot could be enforced, unless the Marshal were prepared
to break out into open insubordination.

There was no difference of opinion as to the necessity for
marching on Madrid. But wrangling arose as to the amount
of troops that would be needed for the operation. Soult said
that every possible man would be required, and wished to march
with the entire Army of the South on San Clemente and Ocaña,
while he suggested that the King, with the Army of the Centre
and a large detachment taken from Suchet, should move by
Requeña and Cuenca. Suchet protested in the most vigorous
fashion against being stripped of any of his divisions, and
maintained that it was rather necessary that he should be lent
5,000 men from the Armies of the Centre or the South. The
King and Jourdan refused to consider the latter proposition,
but agreed that Suchet would require all his own troops, and
that none should be taken from him. Yet approving of the
double movement on Madrid, they declared that the Army of

Marshal without the Emperor's permission. Deprez then posted on to
Moscow, and overtook the Emperor there on October 18. Napoleon in
his reply practically ignored the quarrel, contented himself with administering a general scolding to all parties, and directed them to ' unite, and
diminish as far as possible the evils that a bad system had caused.' But
who had inaugurated the system ? He himself !

[1] Joseph to Clarke, September 7.

the Centre was too small to operate by itself, and that Soult should make over to it Barrois's division and a brigade of light cavalry, to bring it up to the necessary strength. Soult protested loudly : the Emperor had entrusted the army of the South to him ; he was responsible for it ; it was one and indivisible, and so forth [1].

Joseph then put the matter to him in the form of a simple order to set these troops on a certain route on a certain day. The Marshal did not dare to disobey, but stated that he regarded them as still belonging to his army, and should continue to expect reports from their commanders. This left him with a force of five infantry and three cavalry divisions, disencumbered of his sick, and of 2,000 old, weakly, or time-expired men, who marched to Valencia to join the next convoy that Suchet should send to France. Their total (omitting Barrois and the cavalry taken off by Joseph) made up 30,000 infantry, 6,000 horse, and with engineers, artillery, train, &c., just 40,000 men. The Army of the Centre on October 15th showed (including Palombini, the King's Guard and the Spaniards) about 15,000 present under arms, to which must be added Barrois and the two cavalry regiments that accompanied him [2], making 6,000 men between them. Thus the total force with which Joseph and Soult marched on Madrid was over 60,000 men [3].

The object of dividing the advancing army into two columns was not merely to make it more easy for the troops to find food in a desolate country, but much more to carry out a strategical plan. If the whole army had moved by the high road through La Mancha, it would have had no power to communicate with the Army of Portugal. The King's idea was that the northern column, which marched by Cuenca, and which he himself accompanied, would ultimately get into touch with Souham, who had been directed—by dispatches which reached him too late or not at all—to follow Wellington in such a way that he would be able to outflank him on the Upper Douro, and open up communications by the route of Aranda, the Somosierra Pass,

[1] See Soult to Joseph of October 11, and other days.
[2] Which were the 27th Chasseurs and 7th Polish Lancers.
[3] For details see Table of the Army of Spain of the date October 15th, in Appendix II to this volume.

and Guadalajara, with the main French Army. But Souham, when he commenced his advance against Wellington on October 18th, had no order from the King later than a letter of October 1st, written before Soult had arrived in the kingdom of Valencia. He received no more dispatches while engaged in his pursuit of Wellington, and was unaware of Joseph's later plans, so that when he reached Valladolid he made no endeavour to feel to his left, towards Aranda, but rather extended himself to his right, in the direction of Tordesillas and Toro, a movement which took him entirely away from the direction in which the King hoped to find him. They did not get into touch, or combine their operations in any way, till November had arrived. At the same time the advance of a large body of troops by the route of Cuenca turned out most profitable in the end to the French strategy, for it was precisely this flanking column, of great but unknown strength, which compelled Hill to abandon his intention of defending the lines of the Tagus or the Tajuna. However he might place himself opposite Soult's army coming from the South, he had this threatening force beyond his eastern flank, turning his positions by roads too remote for him to guard.

King Joseph had proposed to commence his march upon Madrid at the earliest possible moment—at the interview with the three marshals at Fuente la Higuera he had named the 9th October as the date for starting. But Soult declared, after a few days, that this was impossible, owing to the necessity for collecting the convoys that Suchet was sending him, replenishing his ammunition, and bringing up his rearmost troops. The division of Conroux had picked up the yellow fever, by plundering out of its route, during the march through Murcia. It had been left in quarantine, some days behind the rest of the army, and would take time to come up. It is probable that Soult was not really wasting time of set purpose ; but the King was certainly under the impression that he was doing so, and their correspondence was most acrimonious[1]. Special offence was given by Joseph's withdrawing Drouet from the Army of the South, and entrusting him with the command of that of the Centre. But when Soult murmured at this and other things,

[1] Joseph to Soult, Valencia, October 12.

the King sent him a laconic letter of ten lines, telling him that if he refused to obey orders he had better resign his command and go to Paris, where he would have to give account for all his doings. The Marshal, as on previous occasions when the question of his resignation had been pressed home [1], avoided this simple solution of the problem, and yielded a grudging obedience in the end.

Soult's army was at this time cantoned with its right wing about·Almanza, Yecla, and Fuente la Higuera, and its left wing —now about to become its advanced guard—in and around the large town of Albacete. A detachment from this wing had been for the last ten days attacking the isolated rock-fortress of Chinchilla, the only inland stronghold which was held by the Spaniards in the kingdom of Murcia. It was a Gothic donjon on an inaccessible cliff, only formidable because of its position, and manned by a trifling garrison. It might have held out indefinitely, having a resolute governor, a certain Colonel Cearra. But on October 9th, in a frightful thunderstorm, lightning struck the donjon, killed 15 soldiers, wounded many more, set the place on fire, and disabled the governor [2]. The garrison capitulated in sheer dismay, and the use by the French of the high road between Albacete and Almanza was no longer incommoded by the existence of this petty fortress.

King Joseph with the Army of the Centre marched out from Valencia on October 17th, and had his head-quarters at Requeña on the road to Cuenca on the 19th. On the 23rd he reached that ancient and much dilapidated city, and found it already in the hands of Drouet, who had arrived there on the 20th with Barrois's division and the cavalry brigade of Avy from the Army of the South : he had expelled from it Bassecourt's 3,000 Murcian troops. Soult had started on the 15th from Albacete, and had sent off Drouet's detachment from San Clemente to Cuenca, while he himself marched by Belmonte on Tarancon and Santa Cruz de la Zarza, which he reached on October 25th. He

---

[1] See above, vol. v. p. 332.

[2] Napier and Jourdan say that Cearra was killed ; but he only suffered concussion of the brain, and survived to tell Schepeler (p. 688) how his sword and its sheath were melted into one rod of metal by the lightning which ran down the side of the couch on which he was lying at the moment.

had not got into real touch with the enemy till, on the last-named day, the cavalry on the right of his advance came into contact with Freire's Murcian horse in front of Tarancon, and those on his left ran into the vedettes of Long's British dragoons in front of Ocaña. During the time of his advance these troops had been retiring in front of him, from Consuegra, Toboso, Almonacid, Belmonte, and other places in La Mancha, where they had been providing a long screen of posts to observe his movements. They had, by Hill's orders, retired from the 18th onward before the French cavalry, without allowing themselves to be caught up. It was only immediately in front of the Tagus that they slackened down their pace, and allowed the French to discover them. There was a smart skirmish in front of Ocaña on October 25th, between Bonnemain's brigade and the 9th and 13th Light Dragoons and 10th Portuguese cavalry. The allied squadrons were pushed back towards Aranjuez with the loss of some 30 men, Erskine, who was in command of the cavalry division, refusing to make a stand or to bring up his reserves. His management of the troops was (not for the first time) much criticized by eye-witnesses[1], but it must be remembered that Hill had directed him not to commit himself to a serious action. On the same day Freire's horse were turned out of Tarancon by Perreymond's chasseurs.

The position of the commander of Wellington's detached corps in front of Madrid had become a very responsible one between the 15th, when Soult's advance began, and the 24th, when the enemy came up to the line of the Tagus and developed his attack. Fortunately Hill was in close touch with his chief : so well was the line of communication between them kept up, that it only took two days for a letter from Burgos to reach Madrid—and vice versa. When the army had come back from the Arlanzon to the Douro, the time became even shorter. Wellington received at Cabezon on the evening of October 27th dispatches that Hill had written on the morning of the 26th[2]. This contrasts wonderfully with the slow travelling of French correspondence—Souham got at Briviesca on October 17 a letter written by King Joseph at Valencia on October 1st. It had been

---

[1] See, e. g., Schepeler (p. 689), who was present.
[2] See *Dispatches*, ix. p. 518.

obliged to travel by the absurdly circuitous route of Tortosa, Saragossa and Tudela. Truly the guerrilleros made concerted movements of French armies singularly difficult.

On the 17th October Hill had already got off his first letter of alarm to Wellington, saying that Soult was certainly on the move; by the 19th he knew that there was a column moving upon Cuenca, as well as the larger force which was advancing by San Clemente and Belmonte. He asked for orders, but meanwhile had to issue his own, in consonance with earlier directions received from Wellington. These presupposed two conditions which had not been realized—that the fords of the Tagus would be impassable, and that Ballasteros's Andalusian army would already have crossed the Sierra Morena to Alcaraz and be lying on Soult's flank. But their general directions were still practicable : the line of the Tagus was to be defended unless the enemy were in overwhelming strength : if (contrary to Wellington's expectation) the whole French force in Valencia should advance, and its numbers prove greater than Hill could hope to check, he had been directed to evacuate Madrid, and to fall back beyond the Guadarrama, in order to join his chief on the Adaja, south of Valladolid, in Old Castile [1]. The first thing necessary was to discover the strength of the enemy—all accounts sent in by the Spaniards agreed that it was very great, and in particular, that the column going by Cuenca was no mere detachment, but a solid and considerable force. Meanwhile Wellington, even as late as October 12 [2], had been informing Hill that his design of marching down on Madrid with three divisions, when the siege of Burgos should be either successfully concluded or else abandoned, was still retained. Any morning a dispatch might come to say that the commander-in-chief, with 15,000 men, was on his way to Valladolid ; and therefore the army in front of Madrid must be ready for him, concentrated and in marching order. For if he came in person with such a reinforcement, Soult and King Joseph could be fought and beaten, whenever they made their appearance.

On October 15th, when the French advance had actually begun, the allied troops in New Castile were disposed with an

---

[1] This is clearly stated in Wellington's note to Hill of October 10. *Dispatches*, ix. p. 481.   [2] Ibid., p. 485.

outer screen, mainly consisting of Spanish troops, and a central nucleus of Hill's own Anglo-Portuguese placed in cantonments between Madrid and the Tagus. Bassecourt was at Cuenca with 3,000 men; Elio, with Freire's Murcian horse and a weak division of infantry—5,000 men in all—was watching the high roads from Albacete and Requeña to Madrid, in front of Tarancon. Penne Villemur's cavalry with Morillo's infantry—3,500 men at the most—lay across the great chaussée from Andalusia, about Herencia and Madridejos[1]. These troops formed the outer screen—not taking account of the Empecinado, who was (as usual) on the borders of New Castile and Aragon, worrying Suchet's garrisons in the latter kingdom. Behind Penne Villemur, and south of the Tagus, were Long's British and H. Campbell's Portuguese cavalry brigades, in La Mancha, at Toboso, Villacanas, and other places. All the rest of the British troops were north of the Tagus, in the triangle Madrid–Toledo–Fuentedueñas, as were also D'Urban's Portuguese horse and Carlos de España's Spanish infantry division. When the advance of Soult and King Joseph developed itself, Hill drew everything back behind the Tagus, save Bassecourt's division at Cuenca, which being evicted from that place by Drouet on the 20th did not retire towards Madrid, but went up into the mountains, and ultimately by circuitous routes rejoined the Alicante army.

On the 25th October, when Soult's advanced cavalry had driven Long and Freire from Ocaña and Tarancon, Hill had his whole force, British, Portuguese and Spanish, arrayed in what he intended to be his preliminary fighting position along the Tagus. The extreme right was formed by Skerrett's 4,000 men from Cadiz, who had got up to the front just in time to take their share in the fighting. They lay at Toledo and Añover. Then came the four brigades of the British 2nd Division, two of them at Aranjuez—which was held as a sort of *tête de pont* south of the river—and two at Colmenar de Orija. The line beyond them was prolonged by Penne Villemur and Morillo about Belmonte de Tajo and the fords of Villamanrique. Elio and Freire, who

---

[1] When Penne Villemur moved in, and went behind the Tagus, I cannot make out exactly. But it was before October 25th, as at that time Erskine's British cavalry had no longer any screen in front of them.

had retired across the bridge of Fuentedueñas after being driven out of Tarancon, was in charge of the upper Tagus from that point to Sacedon. Behind this front line lay the reserves— the 3rd and 4th Divisions close together at Valdemoro and Cienpozuelos, behind Aranjuez; the Light Division at Arganda; Carlos de España at Camporeal; Hamilton's Portuguese division at Chinchon. Of the cavalry, Long and Campbell's Portuguese, after being turned out of Ocaña, had fallen back on Aranjuez: D'Urban's Portuguese were at Arganda, Slade's brigade at Morata, Victor Alten's at Getafé[1]. One march would concentrate the whole of the Allies, horse and foot—save Elio and Skerrett's detachment alone—to defend the passage of the Tagus at either Aranjuez or Fuentedueñas, the two crossing-places which Hill judged that Soult would take into consideration, when he attempted to force the line of the river. About 36,000 men would be available, of whom 28,000 were Anglo-Portuguese and 8,000 Spaniards.

Soult, however, kept perfectly quiescent in front of Aranjuez and Fuentedueñas on the 26th–27th. He had still his cavalry to the front, but his infantry divisions were only coming up in succession: Conroux's in especial, being still in quarantine owing to the yellow fever, was very far behind. But it was not merely the late arrival of his rear that kept Soult motionless: he was waiting for the Cuenca column to bring pressure to bear upon Hill's flank, and did not intend to commit himself to any important engagements until the whole French army was in line. He expressed to King Joseph his opinion that the Allies were drawn out upon too long a front, and that a bold thrust at Aranjuez would probably succeed, when the attention of Hill should be drawn away to the East by the appearance of the Cuenca column in the direction of Fuentedueñas. Meanwhile he proceeded to make his preparations for attacking Aranjuez on the 28th.

Such an attack was never delivered, because Hill, on the evening of the 27th, made up his mind that he must not fight upon the Tagus[2]. For this determination there were three

---

[1] All these dispositions come from a table of routes sent to D'Urban by Jackson, Hill's chief of the staff (Quartermaster-general), on the 24th.

[2] Jackson, Q.M.G., to D'Urban, 27th night: ' Sir Rowland has deter-

causes. The first was that the river still remained so low, the
autumn rains having been very scanty hitherto, that it was
fordable in many places. The mere breaking of the bridges at
Aranjuez and Fuente Dueñas did not make it impassable, as
Wellington and Hill himself had expected would be the case
by the end of October. Secondly, if the line of the Tagus were
forced at any point, the troops strung out along it had a very
dangerous retreat before them, owing to the fact that the Tajuna,
a stream not much smaller than the Tagus itself in this part of
its course, runs behind it and parallel to it at a distance of only
eight or ten miles. The number of spots where the Tajuna
could be crossed, by fords, bridges, or ferries, were very few,
and it was to be feared that bodies of troops abandoning
positions on the Tagus, and retreating to the next line, might
find themselves pressed against the Tajuna at impassable
sections of its course, and so might be destroyed or captured
if the enemy pursued with vigour. Thirdly—as Soult expected
—the movement of the King and the column from Cuenca had
now begun to exercise pressure on Hill's mind. He had already
moved two British brigades of the 2nd Division to Fuente
Dueñas, replacing them at Aranjuez by Skerrett's force, which
left Toledo. But what if the King should cross the Tagus not at
Fuente Dueñas but above it, where the river was only observed
by Elio's Murcians ? They certainly could not stop him, and
the whole Tagus line would be turned.

Hill's resolve was now to defend not the Tagus but the line,
running North and South, of the Henares and the Jarama (the
river formed by the union of the Tajuna and Manzanares), from
Guadalajara to the point near the Puente Larga where the
Jarama falls into the Tagus. On the 28th Skerrett evacuated
Aranjuez, and all the other troops fell back in similar fashion.
This position left the allied army still covering Madrid, and with
a safe retreat to the passes above it, should things go ill. The
new disposition of forces was as follows : Toledo had been
handed over to the *partida* of El Medico, since no French
reconnaissances had come in this direction, and it was clear
that the enemy had no serious intentions on this flank. The

mined to concentrate behind the Jarama, on account of the state of the
fords upon the Tagus, and their number,' &c.

extreme right wing of the army was formed by the 4th Division, now once more under General Cole, who had come up, cured of his wound, from the Salamanca hospital. It lay at Añover, behind the point where the Jarama flows into the Tagus, with its flank covered by the Gunten river and some of Long's dragoons. Next in line, six miles to the North, was Skerrett's force, holding the Puente Larga, the main passage over the Jarama river, two miles north of Aranjuez. Beyond him were the 3rd Division and Hamilton's Portuguese about Valdemoro and St. Martin de la Vega. Then came the Light Division at Alcalá de Henares [1]: Carlos de España's and Morillo's Spaniards were in their company. Elio's Murcians were directed to fall back on Guadalajara. So much for the infantry : the cavalry was kept out in front, with orders to keep a line of vedettes on the Tagus till they should be driven in, and then to hold the course of the Tajuna in a similar fashion, before breaking its bridges and falling back on to the Henares and Jarama, the real fighting line. But nothing was to be risked, and the main body of each brigade was to keep itself in front of a practicable cross-ing, by which it could retreat when the enemy should have shown himself in force. ' Sir Rowland,' wrote his Quarter-master-General, ' wishes you to keep the posts on the Tajuna, and those in front of it (on the Tagus), as long as you can with safety. Cover the line of the Henares *as long as you can.*' [2] Slade's, Long's, and Campbell's Portuguese squadrons had the right, covering the river bank from Aranjuez to Villamanrique with their vedettes, D'Urban, Victor Alten, and Penne Villemur held the left, from Villamanrique up stream.

On Oct. 28th the French cavalry, having detected the dis-appearance of Hill's infantry, crossed the Tagus both at Aran-juez and Fuente Dueñas in force, whereupon the allied horse retired behind the Tajuna and broke all of its bridges. Soult at once commenced to repair the bridges of Aranjuez, and brought

[1] They had been at Arganda behind the Tajuna on the previous day, when Hill was still thinking of defending the line of the Tagus. See *Diary of Leach*, p. 287.

[2] Jackson to D'Urban, October 27 : ' Keep your patrols on the Tagus as long as they can with prudence stay there, with orders to follow the march of your main body.' On the next day the order is varied to that quoted above.

an infantry division forward into the town on the 29th, but made
no serious effort to feel Hill's position behind the Jarama and
Tajuna, being determined not to involve himself in heavy
fighting till King Joseph and the column from Cuenca were up
in line. The head of the Army of the Centre, however, reached
Fuente Dueñas this same day, and began to pass [1], meeting (of
course) with no opposition. But the reconstruction of the bridge
took some time, and D'Erlon's infantry was not across the Tagus
in any force till the next day. The King himself rode to Ocaña,
conferred there with Soult, and made arrangements for a general
forward movement upon the 30th. There would have been
heavy fighting upon the 30th–31st, if Hill had been permitted
to make a stand on his chosen position with the 40,000 men
whom he had placed in line between Alcala and Añover. He
had now all his troops concentrated except Elio's Murcians, who
lay out in the direction of Guadalajara with no enemy in front
of them. But on the morning of the 29th Hill received a dispatch from Wellington, dated from Cabezon on the night of the
27th, which upset all the arrangements made hitherto. The
important paragraph of it ran as follows: ' The enemy are
infinitely superior to us in cavalry, and from what I saw to-day
very superior in infantry also. We must retire, and the Douro
is no barrier for us. If we go, and cannot hold our ground beyond
the Douro, your situation will become delicate. We certainly
cannot stand against the numbers opposed to us in any situation,
and it appears to me to be necessary that you, as well as we,
should retire. The only doubt which I entertain is about the
road which you should take, and that doubt originates in the
insufficiency of this army to stop the army opposed to it for
a sufficient time to allow you to reach the Adaja. I propose to
remain on the Pisuerga to-morrow (October 28) and as long as
I can upon the Douro, and then to retire by Arevalo. God
knows whether I shall be able to remain on either river ! ; and if
I cannot, your retreat should be by the valley of the Tagus.

---

[1] Owing to disgraceful carelessness on the part of a brigadier of the
British 2nd Division much of the boat-bridge of Fuente Dueñas (which had
been brought over to the north bank) had not been burnt when the troops
retired. Many boats were intact ; some of the French swam over, and
brought back several of them. (D'Urban MSS.)

If I can remain, we should join as arranged by previous letters. If I can remain on the Pisuerga to-morrow, I shall pass the Douro on the 29th, and shall probably be able to prevent the enemy from crossing in force till the 1st November, in which case I shall reach Arevalo on the 3rd. You will not receive this letter till the 29th. You will arrive at the Escurial, probably on the 31st, at Villacastin on the 2nd, at Arevalo on the 4th. . . . If I should not be able to hold my ground either on the Pisuerga or the Douro, I shall apprise you of it at the first moment, and shall suggest your line of retreat. . . . Your march, as proposed (i.e. via the Guadarrama) at least as far as Villacastin, would be secure, whereas that by Talavera, &c., would not, till you shall cross the Tagus. Do not order the bridge at Almaraz to be taken up or destroyed, till you are certain you do not want it.' [1] The dispatch ended by directing Hill to bring on with him Carlos de España's, Morillo's, and Penne Villemur's Spaniards, but to order Freire, Elio, and Bassecourt to join Ballasteros by the route of Toledo, while the Empecinado had better go to his old haunts in the mountains beyond Guadalajara.

This was a most alarming dispatch for Hill. Just as he had assumed his fighting position, and was expecting to be attacked by Soult on the following day, he received orders to retire without a moment's delay. And what was worst of all, he was told that the line of retreat indicated to him would not improbably prove dangerous or impossible, and that he might, within the next day or so, get a counter-order, directing him to retire by the line of the Tagus and Almaraz, since a junction with Wellington behind the Adaja might prove impossible. But a retreat across the front of the enemy, on the route Navalcarnero–Talavera–Almaraz, would clearly be most dangerous, since the left wing of the Army (the Light Division, D'Urban, Alten and the Spaniards) would have forty miles to march before they were clear of the advancing columns of the French, debouching from Aranjuez. And to make matters worse, the enemy was terribly strong in cavalry, and the countryside south of Madrid was very favourable to the mounted arm. If the army should march at once for the road by the Guadarrama, and when it had reached the neighbourhood of Madrid or the Escurial should get

[1] Wellington to Hill, Cabezon, October 27. *Dispatches*, ix. pp. 518-19.

the news that the route to Villacastin and Arevalo had been blocked, it would be almost impossible to turn off on to the Tagus line or to make for Almaraz. The only chance left would be to take the bad mountain-road to Avila, and thence to the upper Tormes, a choice that no officer could contemplate without dismay in October.

There was one plea that might have been urged in favour of an instant move toward Talavera and the Tagus route (the right wing to march by Illescas and Fuensalida, the left by Madrid and Navalcarnero), but it was a plea of which neither Wellington nor Hill seems to have thought. Supposing that Hill's 40,000 men after uncovering and evacuating Madrid should place themselves behind the Alberche, in and about Talavera, it was difficult to believe that Soult and King Joseph would dare to march north to join Souham and to trouble Wellington. They could hardly leave 40,000 men behind them uncontained, and would probably have to halt and to face toward Hill, so as to cover the capital. This threat to their flank and their rear might force the enemy to come to a stop, and might secure Wellington's rear as effectually as a junction with him at Arevalo behind the Adaja. But on the other hand there were two considerations which tended to make any use of the Tagus route undesirable, save on compulsion and as a *pis aller*. The first was that the whole valley from Toledo to Almaraz was in a state of dreadful exhaustion, with half its land untilled and its population living on the edge of starvation. To subsist there would be difficult. The second and more important was that the enemy might conceivably leave Soult and the Army of the South to hold Madrid and contain Hill's force, and then would still possess 20,000 men—of the Cuenca column—who might be sent by the Guadarrama and Villacastin to take Wellington in the rear. It would be of little use to bring the enemy to a standstill in the direction of Madrid, if he could still spare a detachment which would make Wellington's position in Old Castile hopelessly untenable, and might even put him in grave danger of being overwhelmed.

But ' sufficient for the day is the evil thereof ' was no doubt the reflection of Rowland Hill, a pious man well acquainted with his Bible. He had for the present a clear order to march for the

Escurial, the Guadarrama, and Arevalo. That it might be cancelled if certain circumstances, over which he had no control, should occur on the Douro, was an unpleasant possibility, which did not come into consideration on the 29th of October. Accordingly he gave orders for instant retreat. There was little immediate danger to his left wing, since the French column in front of it, at Fuente Dueñas, had to pass first the defiles of the Tajuna and then those of the Jarama, and all the bridges on both were destroyed or ready for destruction. The right wing was in a much more delicate situation, since it was separated from Soult at Aranjuez only by the Jarama. The outposts of the two armies were in close touch with each other at the Puente Larga, with nothing but the river between; and the 4th Division at Añover had to pass behind the force holding the Puente Larga in order to get into the Madrid road. Supposing that bridge were forced too soon, Cole would be driven off in an eccentric line of retreat toward Toledo and Talavera.

While, therefore, all the rest of the army was set in motion for the Escurial at dawn on the 30th, Skerrett was ordered to stand still at the Puente Larga, and to hold it at all costs till the rest of the allied right wing should have got clear. Meanwhile the troops about Alcalá (the Light Division, España and Morillo) marched round the north side of Madrid without entering the city, and continuing their course all day and part of the night, were on the upper Manzanares, about the palace of El Pardo by 12 p.m. At the same time the troops about Valdemoro (3rd Division, Hamilton's Portuguese, and the bulk of the cavalry) retired past the south side of Madrid, and reached Aravaca, on its west side two miles out, by night. Here Hill established his head-quarters. The 4th Division, from Añover, which had the longest march of all, had been started off before the bulk of the army, on the night of the 29th, not at dawn on the 30th like the rest. It fell into the main road at Valdemoro before daybreak, much fatigued; while halting there the weary men discovered more wine than was good for them—the population had fled and left their cellars exposed for the first comer. There was a terrible amount of drunkenness, and so much straggling, when the division marched off at noon, that many hundreds of men, hidden in houses in a state of absolute

incapacity to move, were left behind [1]. The division, minus
its drunkards, joined the rest of the right wing at Aravaca that
night. Cole remained behind himself—while his troops marched
on—to supervise the defence of the Puente Larga. He had been
told to take on Skerrett's brigade as a part of his division till
further orders, and naturally stopped with the rearguard.

By the night of the 30th all the army was concentrated beyond
Madrid, without having seen an enemy or suffered any molestation, save Skerrett's detachment, which was. fighting all day at
the Puente Larga for the protection of the rest. Soult, as Hill
had expected, had resolved to force the line of the Jarama and
Tajuna that day. But while on the right his cavalry felt forward only to the Tajuna and its broken bridges, on the left he
was already in touch with his enemy, for the Puente Larga is
only two miles outside Aranjuez, from which the approach to it
lies along one of the great avenues of planes that form part of
the royal Park between the Tagus and Jarama.

The Puente Larga is an immensely long bridge of 16 arches,
for the Jarama in winter is a very broad river. Its southern
end is commanded by a slight rising ground, its northern lies in
the flat and ends in a causeway, by which the road finally
mounts up on to the plateau of Valdemoro. Thus it would have
been easier to defend from the south than from the north, as
Skerrett had to do. An attempt had been made to blow up one
of the centre arches of the bridge, but though two mines had
been laid, their explosion on the morning of the 30th did not
make a complete breach, one parapet and a broad section of the
footway beside it remaining intact. The engineer officer in
charge, holding that there was no time to make another mine,
had a breastwork covered by an abattis thrown up across the
northern end of the bridge. Here then was a sort of terrace
with balustrades and stone seats, where the bridge and causeway met. Behind the breastwork and the terrace Skerrett
placed his two companies of the 95th Rifles and part of the

---

[1] See for this Wachholz (of the Fusilier brigade), Schepeler, Purdon's
history of the 47th, &c. Wachholz's Brunswick Company straggled so
that of 60 men he found only 7 with him at night. Several were lost for
good. Wellington put the colonel of the 82nd under arrest, because he
had lost 80 men this day.

2/47th, while behind the nearer part of the causeway there was room for the supports, the rest of the 47th and the 2/87th in close column. The ridge of the causeway almost completely sheltered them from fire from the French side of the river, even from the most elevated ground. Three guns of Braun's Portuguese battery were prepared for action on the right end of the terrace, behind the hastily extemporized breastwork. Half a mile to the rear, at the north end of the causeway, was Skerrett's reserve, composed of the 3rd batt. of the First Guards, the 20th Portuguese, and the remaining three pieces of Braun's battery. The whole defending force of five battalions and six guns was somewhat under 4,000 strong.

Soult was not certain whether Hill was intending to fight on the line of the Jarama, or whether he had merely to drive in a rearguard. The day was very misty from dawn onward, and at 9 o'clock in the morning rain began, and fell continuously till night. Thus the Marshal could not see in the least what sort of a force was opposed to him, and his cavalry, exploring up and down the river bank, were unable to find any practicable fords, or to give him any information as to whether there were allied troops holding the entire course of the Jarama. After some hours, therefore, Soult sent forward Reymond's division [1] with orders to force the Puente Larga, as he had been informed that it was still passable owing to the failure of the mines. A battery took post on the rising ground at the south end of the bridge, and shelled the breastwork and the Portuguese guns, while the voltigeur companies of the 12th Léger strung themselves out along the river bank, and commenced a long bickering fusillade with Skerrett's men across the water. The artillery and musketry fight went on for some hours, till Braun's three pieces ceased firing for want of ammunition. Thinking this a favourable moment, Soult sent part of the 12th Léger against the bridge—the head of the column never reached the narrow pass at the half-broken eighth arch, suffering so much from the musketry that it fell back in disorder before getting half-way across. Another regiment, or the same reformed, attempted a similar rush a few minutes later, and was repulsed in the same fashion. Thereupon Soult ordered the attack to cease, 'seeing,'

[1] D'Erlon's old division now commanded by this brigadier.

as he says in his dispatch, ' that we were wasting ammunition to no effect.' He drew off both his guns and his voltigeurs, and the combat came to an end. A French officer appeared on to the bridge with a white flag a little later, and got permission to remove the many wounded lying at its south end. After dark Skerrett withdrew very quietly, leaving dummy sentries on the bridge head and the causeway, who were only detected as straw-stuffed greatcoats at dawn next morning. The brigade, there-fore, had an undisturbed march all night, and halted next morning on the Prado of Madrid, where it was allowed a few hours of rest. Its loss had been about 3 officers and 60 men killed and wounded, of whom 40 were in the 2/47th and 11 in the rifle companies. The French had five officers and about 100 men killed and wounded [1]. The whole fight was much what the combat of the Coa would have been in 1810, if Craufurd had fought behind and not before the bridge of Almeida.

Soult had deduced, from the stubborn way in which the Puente Larga was defended, that Hill was standing to fight a general action behind the Jarama. He made during the night preparations for bringing up much artillery and constructing bridges, but discovered at dawn that his exertions had been unnecessary. Cavalry under Pierre Soult were pushed out as far as Valdemoro, and captured there some 300 drunken stragglers belonging to the 4th Division, who had not thought fit to follow Skerrett when he passed through. The day was one of dense fog, and the younger Soult never got in touch with Hill's rearguard, but picked up a rumour that Wellington was expected at Madrid that day, with two divisions from Burgos, and that the whole allied army was prepared to deliver battle in a position outside the capital. In consequence, his brother the Marshal held back, and contented himself with bringing up

[1] Always a reckless falsifier of his own losses (he said that he had only lost 2,800 men at Albuera !), Soult wrote in his dispatch that he had only about 25 wounded at the Puente Larga. The figure I give above is that of the staff-officer d'Espinchel, whose memoirs are useful for this campaign. By far the best English account is that of H. Bunbury of the 20th Portuguese (*Reminiscences of a Veteran*, i. pp. 158–63). I can only trace three of the five French officers in Martinien's lists—Pillioud, Caulet, Fitz-James, but do not doubt d'Espinchel's figures though his account of the combat is hard to fit in with any English version. He speaks with admiration of the steadiness of the defence.

the entire Army of the South to the Jarama, while he sent his false news to King Joseph and Jourdan. He proposed that the Cuenca column should make no attempt to force the higher course of the Tajuna, where all the bridges were broken, and behind which lay the equally tiresome obstacle of the Henares, but should come round to Aranjuez and cross by the Puente Larga. Jourdan advised compliance, remarking that the forcing of the lines of the Tajuna and Henares and the making of bridges upon them might take many days. To save time the right wing came round to join the left [1].

This was a godsend to Hill, as it resulted in no pursuit being made on the 81st ; the French advanced cavalry only entered Madrid on the 1st November, and the second of that month had arrived before any infantry reached the capital. By that day the allied army was over the Guadarrama, and well on its way to Villacastin and Arevalo. The evacuation of Madrid was accompanied with many distressing incidents : the people were in despair at seeing themselves about to fall back once more into the power of the 'Intrusive King'. Many of the notables had committed themselves so openly to the patriotic cause that they thought it wise to depart in company with Hill's army. An order to burn the considerable stores of provisions which could not be brought off led to a riot—the lower classes were on the edge of starvation, and the sight of good food being wasted led them to make a disorderly rush on the magazines, to drive away the commissaries, and to carry off the flour and salt meat which was being destroyed. Probably it would have been wise to permit them to do so without making difficulties ; as the stores, once dispersed, could hardly have been gathered in again by the enemy. The explosion of the Arsenal in the Retiro fort was a more absolute necessity, but the Madrileños murmured greatly that the large building of La China, the porcelain manufactory, was blown up along with the surrounding earthworks. The mines, it may be incidentally remarked, were so carelessly laid that two commissariat officers were killed by the first of them that went off, and the last nearly made an end of Captain Cleeves, K.G.L., the artillery officer in charge

---

[1] All this from Soult's dispatch to the King of October 31, from Valdemoro, and Jourdan's to Clarke from Madrid of November 3rd.

of the business. He was severely scorched, and barely escaped with his life [1].

The rearguard of the British Army quitted the mourning city by noon on the 31st October : the head of the column was already on that day at the Escurial. On November 1st the passage of the Guadarrama began, and on the 3rd the last cavalry brigade, bringing up the rear, was over the mountains. Not a sign had been seen of the enemy, whose advanced light cavalry only reached Galapagar, five miles south of the Escurial upon the 2nd. The weather, however, was very bad, rain falling day after day, and this must serve as an inadequate excuse for the fact that straggling had already begun, and that a certain number of men dropped so far behind that they fell into the hands of the tardily-appearing enemy. But the loss of these laggards, for the most part the selected bad characters of each battalion, was a small price to pay for an unmolested retreat. Hill's spirits rose, hour by hour, as he received no letter from Wellington to say that the retreat to Arevalo had become impossible, or that the line of the Douro had been lost. These terrible possibilities might—so far as he knew—have come into existence at any moment on the 1st, 2nd, or 3rd of November. On the 4th the whole army from Madrid was concentrated at Villacastin, so close to Wellington's position behind the Douro at Rueda that dispatches could now get through from him to Hill in less than twelve hours. The cavalry of the extreme rear-guard—the 2nd Hussars K.G.L., who had left the Escurial only on the 3rd, had barely seen the enemy's advanced vedettes on that day, and were not overtaken by them till late on the 4th. The pursuit was slow, cautious, and not executed by any very large body of horse. Hill, therefore, granted his troops a very necessary rest of twelve hours at Villacastin.

At last, however, on the evening of November 4th, when the worst possibilities seemed to have passed by, and nothing could any longer prevent Hill from joining Wellington, discouraging news, so long expected, at last came to hand. A dispatch from Rueda informed Hill that his chief had determined to retreat from the line of the Douro, for reasons which will be explained

[1] See *Diary of Swabey, R.A.*, p. 428, in *Journal of the Artillery Institution*, vol. xxii.

in the next chapter, and that the position in which he intended
to fight was that in front of Salamanca, where he had faced and
beaten Marmont in July. This being so, there was no reason to
bring up Hill's corps to Arevalo. Since a junction between the
two halves of the army was now secure, the troops from Madrid
should save themselves an unnecessary détour to the north, by
turning off the *chaussée* to Valladolid and taking the cross-road
by Belayos, Villanueva de Gomes, and Peñaranda. This would
bring them to Alba de Tormes, where they would find themselves
in touch with Wellington's own troops, which would move, by
La Nava and Cantalpino, to the San Cristobal position outside
Salamanca.

This march therefore Hill executed. On the 4th he had at
last heard of the appearance of Soult's cavalry, and that same
evening his extreme rearguard, the 2nd Hussars of the K.G.L.
had a slight engagement with French squadrons near Villacastin.
But nothing was known of the main body of the enemy's
infantry, nor was it even certain whether the Army of the South
and the Army of the Centre were both pursuing by the route
of the Guadarrama. Soult, as a matter of fact, had only made
up his mind to cross the mountains by that route on the 3rd, and
nothing but the light cavalry of his brother was near Hill's
rear. On the 4th, 5th, and 6th November his main body was
coming up, and he was in force at Arevalo on the last-named
day. Only the horse of his advanced guard had followed Hill
on the Peñaranda road. The object of the move on Arevalo
was to seek for the Army of Portugal, of which no certain news
had yet been obtained. The Duke of Dalmatia supposed however that it had to be looked for on the side of Tordesillas, and
wished to communicate with it before he pressed Hill too closely.
For if the latter had united with Wellington—as was very
possible—he might have found himself in face of more than
60,000 men, and he had but 40,000 of his own, since the Army of
the Centre was not yet up in line. The King himself with his
Guards followed Soult after a short interval, but the three
infantry divisions (Barrois, Palombini, Darmagnac) which had
formed the column that marched from Cuenca, were far behind.
Palombini's division, which had been told off to act as the rearguard, was observing the accumulation of Spanish troops near

Guadalajara, where Elio and Freire had now been joined by the Empecinado, who had come in from the direction of Aragon. They had united at the Puente de Aunion and Sacèdon, a few miles south-east of Guadalajara, on the upper Tagus. There were now 8,000 or 9,000 enemies in this quarter, still quite close to Madrid, and Joseph and Jourdan had to come to a difficult decision. If a garrison were left in Madrid, and a strong column sent to evict Elio from his position, the Army of the Centre would have few troops left who could follow Soult in the pursuit of Wellington. But if the whole Army of the Centre marched by the Guadarrama, there was nothing to prevent Elio from coming down to reoccupy Madrid, and the political effect of the evacuation of the capital would be detestable, for it would look as if the whole French army was but a flying column incapable of holding what it had won [1]. After some hesitation the King and Jourdan resolved that the military necessity of taking forward every available man to crush Wellington was all-important. If Soult alone joined the Army of Portugal in Old Castile the French in this direction would not outnumber the combined forces of Wellington and Hill, and might be brought to a stand—perhaps even beaten. The 20,000 men of the Cuenca column must be brought forward at all costs to secure a numerical superiority for the French arms in the North. Madrid therefore must be abandoned, and the infantry of the King's army marched out of it on the 6th and 8th November, Palombini bringing up the rear once more. Even the sick and Joseph's Spanish courtiers had to be taken on, with a comfortless assurance that they might in the end be dropped at Valladolid [2]. On the 8th the leading division of the Army of the

[1] The importance of the second evacuation of Madrid is brought out by no historian of the war except Vacani, vi. pp. 188–90. Napier barely mentions it. A curious story of the fate of certain English prisoners of Hill's army, who were forgotten in prison, and came out again to liberty when the French army moved on, may be found in the autobiography of Harley of the 47th Regiment.

[2] Napier (iv. p. 373) says that Joseph left a garrison and his impedimenta in Madrid—I can find no trace of it in the contemporary accounts, e. g. of Romanos (*Memorias de un Setenton*) or of Harley who was about the town during the second week of November. Vacani distinctly says that Joseph had to take on even his sick (vi. p. 190). Cf. also Arteche, xi. pp. 309–12.

Centre reached Villacastin by forced marches, the rear did not get up till the 10th[1]. Thus it is clear that on November 5th, when Hill executed his flank movement on Fontiveros and Penaranda, there was nothing near him save Soult's advanced cavalry, supported at an interval by the infantry of the Army of the South, while the Army of the Centre had not even left Madrid. If Wellington had but known this, it might have brought about a change in his orders; but—as cannot too often be repeated—the 'fog of war' sometimes lies very thick around a general at the moment when he has to make his crucial decision, and on these two days the enemy *might* have been closed up, instead of being strung out in detachments over a hundred miles of mountain roads. A few days after the French left Madrid the Empecinado came down to the capital and occupied it—Elio had gone off, according to Wellington's original orders, to place himself in communication with the Army of Andalusia (now no longer under Ballasteros) and took post in La Mancha. Bassecourt reoccupied Cuenca. There was not a French soldier left in New Castile, and all communication between Soult and King Joseph on one side and Suchet in Valencia on the other, were completely broken off.

[1] Napier, iv. p. 373, says that Joseph went by the route of Segovia to Castile. I cannot think where he picked up this extraordinary idea. Jourdan's dispatch of November 10 from Peñaranda gives all the facts. It was on the 5th, near Villacastin, that Soult told Joseph that Hill was about to be joined by Wellington and that the two might crush him. The King at once sent orders to Drouet to come up by forced marches from Madrid. The Army of the Centre started next day. Palombini did not get off till the 8th (Vacani, vi. p. 190), but the head of the column reached Villacastin that same day.

SECTION XXXIV: CHAPTER V

THE BURGOS RETREAT. THE OPERATIONS ROUND SALAMANCA. NOVEMBER 1—NOVEMBER 15, 1812

WHEN we turned aside to narrate the operations round Madrid, and Hill's retreat across the Guadarrama Pass, we left Wellington and his army on November 1st drawn up on the south side of the Douro, with head-quarters at Rueda. Their right flank was covered by the Adaja, the cavalry of their left flank was opposite Toro, where the French were visible in some force, and were known to be repairing the bridge which had been destroyed on October 30th. It was evident that the main body of the enemy still lay about Tordesillas, Simancas, and Valladolid, but its exact strength was not ascertainable. A rumour had crossed the river that Caffarelli and the Army of the North were already returning to their own regions beyond Burgos; it was a true rumour, but Wellington could get no confirmation for it[1]. Till the facts were ascertained, he was bound to consider it probable that the whole body of the enemy—nearly 50,000 strong—which had pursued him since October 22nd was still in his front[2]. With such a force he considered himself unable to cope, if once it crossed the river whose line he was defending. 'They are infinitely superior to us in cavalry, and from what I saw to-day (October 27) were superior in infantry also. We must retire therefore, and the Douro is no barrier for us.' He held on however in the position that he had taken up on October 30 till November 5, partly because he was wishing to cover as long as possible Hill's march to join him from Madrid, partly because Souham made no attempt for some days to debouch in force across the bridges of Tordesillas or Toro.

Wellington to Hill, November 3. *Dispatches*, ix. p. 532.

[2] His first definite information as to this was from a Spaniard who on November 4 saw 3,000 French infantry marching through Torquemada towards Burgos (*Dispatches*, ix. p. 544). Even so late as November 8th he did not rely on this important news as correct.

Meanwhile the near approach of Hill and the force from Madrid, with Soult's army in pursuit, was modifying the position from day to day. By November 4th Hill, as we have already seen, was at Villacastin with all his five infantry divisions, and the 7,000 or 8,000 Spaniards of Morillo and Carlos de España. He was being followed by the French, but reported that day that he had so far seen no more than four regiments of cavalry and two battalions of infantry. Was this the advanced guard of the whole 60,000 men whom Soult and King Joseph had brought against Madrid, or was it a mere corps of observation? 'I do not think it clear,' wrote Wellington to Hill, at 9 o'clock on the morning of November 5th, 'that the enemy is following you in force. I conceive these four regiments and two battalions to have been sent only to see what you are doing.'[1] This day Wellington could have united himself to Hill without any fear of being hindered by either of the French armies, and could have had the whole of his 65,000 men concentrated between Medina del Campo and Arevalo within thirty-six hours. The enemy, though their two armies taken together outnumbered him by more than 25,000 men, could not possibly unite within a similar time. He had, therefore, the position which enterprising generals most desire, that of lying between the two fractions of a hostile force, which cannot combine easily, and of being able to bring superior numbers against either one of them. One can speculate without much difficulty as to what Napoleon would have done in a similar posture of affairs.

But Wellington, after mature consideration, resolved that it would not be prudent to unite the two halves of his army and to march against one or other of his enemies. It is fortunate that he has left a record of the reasons which prevented him from doing so. They are contained in a dispatch to Lord Bathurst dated November 8th, when he had already committed himself to a wholly different policy. If he were to march with his own army, he wrote, to join Hill about Arevalo, with the object of falling upon the heads of Soult's columns as they debouched on Villacastin, Souham could cross the Douro unopposed behind him at Toro, whose bridge was now repaired,

---

[1] From Rueda, November 5, morning. *Dispatches*, ix. p. 537.

and get behind his left flank. While he was engaged with Soult and the King, who might conceivably have 50,000 men at the front[1], and be able to offer a good resistance, Souham could close in on his rear, and after cutting him off from Salamanca and his magazines, could attack him, while he was committed to the contest with the army from Madrid.

On the other hand, if he took the second alternative, and brought Hill's column up to Medina del Campo and Tordesillas, Souham would keep north of the Douro, and could not be assailed : ' the enemy would not attempt to pass so long as we remained in our position.'   But meanwhile Soult and the King, being unopposed by Hill, might cut him off from his base and magazines, because the line Villacastin–Fontiveros–Salamanca is shorter than that from Tordesillas to Salamanca. ' The enemy would have had the shortest line to the Tormes by Fontiveros, if they had preferred to march in that direction rather than to follow the march of Sir Rowland Hill's troops.'

This last argument, it must be confessed, seems disputable, for not only are the roads Rueda–Fuente Sauco–Salamanca and Rueda–Pitiegua–Salamanca as a matter of fact no longer than the road Villacastin–Fontiveros–Peñaranda–Salamanca[2], but they were in all respects better roads, through a level country, while the route which Wellington assigns to the enemy (and which Hill actually pursued) passes through much more difficult and hilly regions, and was but a cross-country line of communications. It would seem doubtful also whether there was any probability that the enemy, granting that he had his whole force concentrated at the front, would dare to take this route, since it was the one which made a junction

----

[1] They had really not the 50,000 on which Wellington speculated (' 45,000 men I should consider rather below the number ' (*Dispatches*, ix. p. 544)) but 60,000 or very nearly that number. But, on the day when Wellington was writing, their rear had not even started from Madrid, and Soult's 40,000 men were strung out all along the road.

[2] As a matter of fact, using the best map of 1812 available to me (Nantiat's), it would seem that the line Rueda–Fuente Sauco–Salamanca is about 50 miles, that by Rueda–Nava del Rey–Pitiegua–Salamanca about 55 miles, while the route suggested for the French, circuitous and running in more than one place by country cross-paths, is over 65 miles long, not to speak of its being a worse route for topographical reasons.

with Souham and the Army of Portugal most difficult to him. Soult and Joseph were very badly informed as to the exact situation of their friends from the North, but it was clear that they would have to be looked for rather in the direction of Tordesillas and Valladolid than in that of Salamanca. As a matter of fact, even after Wellington's retreat, Soult took the trouble to move on Arevalo, instead of marching on Fontiveros and Penaranda, for the sole purpose of getting into communication with Souham, whose co-operation was all-important to him.

But putting this particular objection aside, it seems certain that if Wellington had concentrated opposite Souham, behind the Douro, Soult and the King could not have been prevented from getting into touch with the Army of Portugal by taking the route Villacastin, Segovia, Olmedo, keeping the Adaja between them and the Allies, and making for the upper passages of the Douro (Tudela, &c.), which Wellington had surrendered to Souham on October 30th. This fact is conclusive against the policy of drawing up Hill to Rueda and making a move against the northern enemy. Though a march by Soult and Joseph against Salamanca was improbable, there were perfectly sound reasons for rejecting this particular combination.

As much cannot be said on purely strategical grounds for Wellington's resolution to retreat on Salamanca instead of making a blow at Soult—his old original plan of September and October. Supposing that he had left nothing more than a screen along the Douro to 'contain' Souham — say the Galicians and a little cavalry—he could have joined Hill at or near Arevalo on the 5th or 6th, and have calculated on a couple of days' start before the Army of Portugal could have followed him—it had to concentrate from scattered cantonments and to cross on one or other of two ill-repaired bridges. Meanwhile Soult would have been caught on the 6th with his 40,000 men strung out on many miles of mountain road, and with his supports (the Army of the Centre) still at Madrid—they did not even start for the Guadarrama till that same day. It is clear that the Duke of Dalmatia would have had to retreat in haste, under pain of suffering a disaster: his advance guard might very possibly have been cut up and maltreated,

and he would have had to fall back on the passes, where food
was unobtainable, and long sojourn impossible.

This would have been the Napoleonic method of dealing with
the situation.   But it would be absurd to blame Wellington
for not adopting such a plan.   Now, as always, he had to play
the safer game, simply because he could not afford to take
risks.   Napoleon could face with indifference the loss of 5,000
or 10,000 men from a forced march in bad weather, ending in
an operation that miscarried—such had been his march
against Sir John Moore in December 1808.   Wellington could
not.   The season at the moment was singularly unfavourable
for a sudden offensive stroke, involving rapid movement.   The
troops were almost worn out: Hill's column had only just
terminated a fatiguing retreat, the troops from Burgos had
only been granted five days' rest since the end of a similar
march.   The number of sick (about 17,000) was alarming, and
many battalions were already reduced to 250 or 300 bayonets.
What was worse, straggling had shown itself in the most
vexatious form, not only among the troops of Wellington's
own column, but among Hill's divisions, which ought to have
done better after their long sojourn in quiet cantonments
round Madrid.   A sudden dash to surprise Soult by forced
marches upon Villacastin would have been very costly, even
before the fighting began.   And if the Marshal refused to
stand, and simply retired in haste toward the Army of the
Centre, it would be impossible to push him far.   Meanwhile
Souham would be across the Douro, and threatening Salamanca,
or approaching Wellington's own rear.   After all there remained
the cardinal fact that the enemy had a great numerical
superiority: it was even over-estimated in Wellington's own
mind, since he thought that Caffarelli and the Army of the
North were still at Valladolid.

Hence came his final decision to retreat by easy marches
toward the strong positions about Salamanca, leaving the
offensive to the enemy, and granting them the opportunity
of uniting their two long-separated armies.   Wellington's own
plea in favour of this resolve must be quoted—' The two corps
of this army, particularly that which has been in the North,
are in want of rest.   They have been continually in the field,

and almost continually marching, since the month of January last; their clothes and equipments are much worn, and a period in cantonments would be very useful to them. The cavalry likewise are weak in numbers, and the horses rather low in condition. I should wish to be able to canton the troops for a short time, and I should prefer the cantonments on the Tormes to those farther in the rear. I do not know exactly what the force of the enemy is. The Army of Portugal have about 36,000 men, of which 4,000 is cavalry [1]. The Army of the North have 10,000 men, of which 1,200 is cavalry. It is hard to judge of the exact extent of Soult's force. It is reported that the enemy brought from Valencia to the Tagus from 40,000 to 45,000 men, but I should consider this to be rather below the number that the Armies of Andalusia and the Centre could bring up, without any troops from the Armies of Aragon and Valencia [2]. Soult is particularly strong in good cavalry, and there are several more regiments in the Army of the Centre. It will remain to be seen what number of troops can be brought to operate against our position (on the Tormes): as unless Madrid should be again abandoned to its fate by the King, he must make arrangements to resist the attacks which Elio and the guerrilleros (the Empecinado, El Medico, &c.) will make on that city, even if General Ballasteros should not move forward in La Mancha. I propose therefore to wait at present on the Tormes, till I shall ascertain more exactly the extent of the enemy's force. If they should move forward, I can either bring the contest to a crisis on the positions of San Christoval, or fall back to the Agueda, according to what I shall at the time consider to be best for the cause [3].'

Wellington's estimate of a total force for the enemy of rather more than 90,000 men was not far out, for if he wrongly supposed that Caffarelli might still be at the front with his 10,000 men,

[1] An under-estimate by several thousands. Wellington did not know of Aussenac's brigade from Bayonne, over 3,000 men, which had now been attached provisionally to the Army of Portugal.

[2] The total which marched was 60,000, so Wellington was even more correct than he supposed in his notion that 45,000 was too small a figure.

[3] Wellington to Lord Bathurst, Pitiegua, November 8. *Dispatches*, ix. pp. 544–5.

he underrated the total of the Armies of the South and Centre
very considerably. They had not merely the something over
45,000 men of which he wrote, but nearly 60,000. But he was
under the impression that King Joseph would probably leave
a large detachment to defend Madrid ; and if the enemy came
forward against the line of the Tormes with anything less than
70,000 men, he was prepared to defend it. His own force,
counting Hill, but allowing for the losses on the retreats from
Burgos and Madrid, which would amount to about 2,000 at the
most, would be not far below that same figure, including 18,000
Spaniards. But the strength of the position would compensate
for the inferior value of these auxiliaries in line of battle. Just
at this moment Wellington was not at all contented with the
Galicians, whose conduct at Palencia and Villa Muriel had
irritated him. ' I was sorry to observe,' he wrote to Lord
Bathurst, ' that in the affair of the 25th October, although the
Spanish soldiers showed no want of spirit or of disposition to
engage the enemy, they were totally unable to move with the
regularity and order of a disciplined body—by which alone
success can be hoped for in any contest with the French[1].'

There were three possibilities before Wellington when he
had made up his mind to retire to the Tormes. The French
might be contented with having driven him out of New Castile
and away from the Douro, and press him no farther. This
would be quite probable, if they had made up their minds to
detach a large force to hold Madrid. Or, secondly, they might
come up against him to Salamanca, with a force no greater
than his own. In this case he was prepared to fight, and hoped
to come well out of the business. Thirdly, there was the chance
that they might bring forward every available man, and try
to evict him from his chosen position : if they were in very
great strength he must yield, and go back to the Agueda and
the shelter of Ciudad Rodrigo, much contrary to his desire.
But he was not intending to give way, and to involve himself
in the difficulties of a retreat during the cold and rainy month
of November, until he should be convinced that the French
were too strong for him and that a rearward move was inevitable.
In the Salamanca positions he could force them to show their

[1] *Dispatches*, ix. p. 520.

strength, and yet have the power to draw off if that strength proved to be overpowering.

The retreat towards Salamanca commenced on November 5th, when Wellington both directed Hill to move on Fontiveros and Flores de Avila instead of on Arevalo, and also began to shift his own troops south-westward from the position about Rueda. On this day the 5th Division and Ponsonby's cavalry brigade marched for Alaejos. The rest of the Army were warned that their movement would begin next day [1]. It was well to keep Souham beyond the Douro, by continuing to show great strength in his front, till Hill should have got some way westward. There was no sign of activity in the enemy's cantonments, save that troops seemed to be moving towards Toro along the road on the north bank parallel with the river [2]. The retreat was therefore carried out in a leisurely fashion on the 6th–7th–8th: on the 6th Wellington's head-quarters were at Torrecilla de la Orden, on the 7th and 8th at Pitiegua. The divisions, covered by a cavalry rearguard, and with other cavalry on their flank, thrown out to observe the French at Toro, marched by several converging roads, some going through Alaejos, others through Castrejon and Vallesa, others by Fresno and Cantalpino [3]. There was no hurry, as there was no pursuit, and by the evening of the 8th all were safely placed in their old positions of June, north of the Tormes, in a semicircle from Aldea Lengua to San Cristobal. The weather being still very cold and rainy, as many of the troops were quartered in the villages as possible, and some as far back as Salamanca town; but many had to bivouac in the open. After several nights spent in position, dysentery and rheumatism, which had already been thinning the ranks, became more common than ever.

Hill's column, meanwhile, having left the main road at Villacastin on the 4th and having followed the bad cross-paths between Belayos and Fontiveros, got into a better route at

[1] Wellington to Hill, Rueda, November 5. *Dispatches*, ix. p. 537.
[2] Ibid., p. 539.
[3] I cannot find the details of the marching orders of the divisions; but from personal diaries I seem to deduce that the 5th and 7th Divisions marched by Alaejos, the 1st and 6th by Castrejon and Vallesa, while the cavalry not only provided a rearguard but kept out flank detachments as far as Cantalapiedra on one side and the lower Guarena on the other.

the latter place, which it reached after a very fatiguing march on the night of the 5th. D'Urban's Portuguese horse, covering the north flank of the retreat, had a narrow escape of being cut off from the main column, near Villanueva de Gomez, by Soult's advanced cavalry, which was pushing up northward to Arevalo, but D'Urban got across their front in time. Hill's Spanish divisions did not follow the same road as the British, but had moved from Villacastin to Arevalo on the 4th, covered by their own cavalry (Penne Villemur): on the 5th they marched from Arevalo to Fontiveros and rejoined Hill's head-quarters [1]. They had moved along two sides of a triangle, the British only along the base—but the advantage of a good road as opposed to a very bad one compensated for the difference of miles covered. Presumably the order to Hill to take the wretched by-paths that he followed was dictated by the idea that, if these routes were neglected, Soult might send a column along them, and anticipate Hill on the upper Tormes. Nothing of the kind was attempted; the Marshal's only preoccupation at this time was that he must at all costs look for the Army of Portugal, and his explorations were directed north, toward Arevalo. Hill's rear was only followed by a vanguard of light cavalry, which behaved with great caution, and contented itself with gathering up stragglers, who fell behind the column by their own fault or from exhaustion. Soult claims to have taken some 600 of them [2], a figure which English authorities reduce by about half: some scores of drunkards were undoubtedly captured in the wine vaults of Villacastin [3].

On the 6th Hill's column marched from Fontiveros to Peña-randa, the Light Division and Morillo forming the infantry rear-guard, covered at a distance by Long's and Victor Alten's squadrons. On the 7th the stage covered was from Peñaranda to Coca (not far from Garcia Hernandez) within easy reach of the Tormes, whose passage it was evident would be made without any interference by the enemy. On the 8th, the day

---

[1] All this from the detailed routes of march in the dispatches of Jackson (Hill's Q.M.G.) to D'Urban on November 4–5–6.

[2] See his dispatch of November 8 from Flores de Avila.

[3] For an adventure with these rascals, who threatened to shoot one of Hill's aides-de-camp, see Schepeler, p. 691.

on which Wellington entered the San Cristobal position, Hill crossed the Tormes at Alba, leaving Howard's brigade of the 2nd Division and Hamilton's Portuguese to hold that town, which lies on the east bank of the river. It was intended to maintain Alba as a sort of *tête de pont* to cover the bridge. Though dominated by heights a few hundred yards away [1], it was extremely suitable for defence against an enemy unprovided with heavy artillery. It was surrounded by an old Moorish wall, with gaps that could easily be blocked, and its castle, a solid donjon, completely commanded and protected the bridge. Slade's cavalry brigade remained out as a screen in front of Alba, to watch for the approach of the enemy. When the rest of the troops had crossed the Tormes, Wellington directed Hill to send him the 3rd, 4th, and Light Divisions, España's Spaniards, and Victor Alten's and D'Urban's cavalry. The force left under his lieutenant was now to consist, as in the early summer, of nothing more than the old Estremaduran corps—the 2nd Division, Hamilton's Portuguese, the British cavalry of Slade and Long, the Portuguese cavalry of Campbell and the Spanish squadrons of Penne Villemur—about 20,000 men of the three nations. These remained behind Alba, in the woods above the Tormes. The troops requisitioned from Hill moved up to Calvarisa de Arriba, Machacon, and other villages in the angle of the Tormes facing Huerta, from whence they could be drawn into the San Cristobal position, by the fords of Aldea Lengua and Santa Marta, if necessary. The whole army, not much under 70,000 strong, was now formed in line from San Cristobal to Alba, waiting to see whether the advance of the enemy would be by the eastern or the northern bend of the river.

The French were slow in making their appearance, and still slower in developing their intentions. For some days there was little more than cavalry seen in front of Wellington's position. The reason of their tardy appearance was that Soult had carried out his design of uniting with the Army of Portugal before attempting to press the Allies. On the 8th he was still at Arevalo in person, with the main body of his

---

[1] The ground on which Del Parque had fought his unlucky battle in 1809.

infantry : light cavalry alone had followed Hill. Only on the preceding night had his scouts, pushing out in the direction of Medina del Campo, succeeded in discovering Souham, who had crossed the bridge of Tordesillas on the 6th, after Wellington's departure from Rueda, and had sent reconnaissances in all directions to look for the Army of the South, whose approach had come to his knowledge not by any dispatch received but only by the vague rumours of the country-side. Meanwhile, he had held back his infantry, being not too sure that Wellington might not have evacuated Rueda only as a trick, to lure him forward : it was possible that he had been joined by Hill, and was waiting a few miles back from the Douro, with the object of falling upon the Army of Portugal with superior strength, as it should be debouching from the bridge of Tordesillas. But the roads were found empty in every direction, and presently Souham's cavalry came in touch with Soult's, and both sides discovered the exact situation.

Soult, Jourdan, and the King agreed that their best policy was to bring every man forward from all the three armies, and to force Wellington to battle, if he could be induced to stand his ground. But matters must not be pressed till the Army of the Centre, which had only started from Madrid on the 6th, should come up into line; and some of the divisions of the Army of the South were still far to the rear, having halted about Villacastin and Arevalo. Accordingly, it was not till the 10th that Wellington saw any serious force accumulating before the Salamanca positions, and even then it was the advanced guard alone of the enemy which had arrived. On the 9th Soult's head-quarters were at Peñaranda, those of the King at Flores de Avila, those of Souham at Villaruela. On the 10th Soult was in person before Alba de Tormes, but had only his cavalry and two infantry divisions in hand ; the rest were still in the rear. The Army of the Centre had its vanguard at Macotera ; that of the Army of Portugal had reached Babilafuente [1]. The troops were much tried by the weather, and those of Soult's army in particular were feeling their privations. They had been almost continually on the march since September,

---

[1] These movements from Jourdan to Clarke, of November 10, and Soult to Clarke of November 12.

having halted but a few days on the borders of Valencia. The bitter November cold of the plateau of Old Castile was felt almost unbearable by men who had been for three years lodged in Andalusia, whose climate is almost sub-tropical and never suffers the extremes that are usual in Northern Spain [1]. Soult's Army, too, had the worst roads during the last days of the advance, and its commissariat arrangements had gone wrong, while little could be gleaned from the country-side. The horses began to fail, and stragglers to drop behind.

On the 10th Soult resolved to see whether Wellington was disposed to hold Alba de Tormes, or whether the detachment there would blow up the bridge and retire when attacked. Operations began by the driving in of the pickets of Long's Light Dragoons, who had been kept as far forward as possible till the last moment. They lost a few men in retiring. Soult then placed three batteries on the hill to the east of the town, and commenced to shell it at about two o'clock in the afternoon; shortly afterwards twelve voltigeur companies of the Fifth Division deployed in long lines, and began to press up towards the place, taking every possible advantage of cover, while the heavy columns of the regiments to which they belonged, and of Daricau's division in support, were visible in the rear.

Alba was held by Howard's brigade of the 2nd Division (1/50th, 1/71st, 1/92nd); on the other side of the water, as a reserve, were Hamilton's Portuguese (2nd, 4th, 10th, and 14th Line) and the batteries of Arriaga and Braun, placed in a position from which they could flank any attacks on the bridge. The town had been prepared for defence, the gaps in its walls having been filled up with rough palisading, and its non-existent gates built up with barricades of stone and timber. Each of the three British regiments held one-third of the circumference of the wall, with half its companies in firing-line and the others in reserve under shelter. From two till five, when dusk fell, Soult continued to batter the town; but 'notwithstanding the shower of shot and shell which plunged and danced about the streets in every direction [2] ' the losses of

---

[1] See the Notes of the Baden officer Riegel (vol. iii. p. 537), who complains bitterly of the piercing north wind, and the lack of wood to build fires.

[2] D'Espinchel (ii. p. 71) says that the voltigeurs got within the walls,

the defenders were quite moderate : they had been given time on the 9th to extemporize good shelter with barricades and traverses, and kept under cover.   Thrice during the afternoon the lines of voltigeurs, who had thrown themselves into the ravines and ditches around the walls, received orders to charge in ; but on each occasion the bickering fire which they had hitherto received burst out into a blaze as they approached the walls, and their losses were so great that they had to run back into cover.   Hamilton reinforced the garrison at dusk with two of Da Costa's Portuguese battalions (of the 2nd and 14th Line).   At nightfall the French had accomplished absolutely nothing.

Next morning at dawn (about 6 o'clock) the cannonade recommenced, and the French skirmishers once more pushed up towards the walls.   Da Costa's light companies were used against them, as well as those of the three British battalions. But the attack was not pressed home, and after a few hours Soult desisted : the guns were drawn off, the infantry retired. The Marshal wrote to King Joseph that it was no use pressing on : he had thrown 1,500 shot into the place without effect : by persisting ' *nous y perdrions du monde sans résultat*[1].' Wellington had to be attacked, but the way to reach him was certainly—as it appeared—not to be over the bridge of Alba. From the 11th to the 14th Howard's and da Costa's brigades held the place without further molestation.   Their modest casualty list, on the afternoon of the 10th and the morning hours of the 11th, had been 21 men killed and 3 officers and 89 men wounded : 8 killed and 36 wounded were Portuguese.   The 1/92nd with 38 men hit was the battalion that suffered most[2]. The French loss had been a little greater—apparently 2 officers killed and 6 wounded[3], with some 150 casualties in the rank

but were expelled on each occasion.   The English narratives deny that they ever closed, or reached the barricades.

[1] Soult to Joseph, 8 a.m. on the 11th, ' bivouac sur la hauteur en arrière d'Alba de Tormes.'

[2] General Hamilton's account of the business (Dispatch to Hill, *Wellington Dispatches*, ix. p. 558) is very clear.   There is also a good account of the Alba fighting in Colonel Gardyne's excellent history of the 92nd.

[3] All their names verifiable from Martinien's admirable lists of ' *Officiers tués et blessés*.'

and file : the 45th Ligne with 5 officers hurt contributed the largest total to the list.

The cannonade at Alba settled nothing : on its second day the French commanders were taking counsel together, Soult, the King, Jourdan, with Souham and Clausel (representing the Army of Portugal) were all riding up and down the eastern bank of the Tormes, and seeking for the facts which must determine their next move [1]. Fortunately for the historian, after the debate, which was long and indecisive, Jourdan and Soult each wrote a formal letter of advice to the King that evening. On one point only were they agreed : it would be mad to attack Wellington on the position of San Cristobal, whose strength was well known to all the officers of the Army of Portugal, and had been increased during the last two days by the throwing up of a chain of redoubts armed with artillery. There remained two plans—Jourdan's was a proposal to force the line of the Tormes between Huerta and Alba, by a frontal attack across the numerous fords which Marmont had used in the campaign of the previous July ; Soult's was a plan for turning Wellington's right by going some distance up-stream south of Alba, and utilizing the fords of the Tormes between Alba and Salvatierra. In the main the question turned on the practicability of the fords, and this was varying from hour to hour. The rain, which had made Hill's retreat and Soult's advance so miserable to the troops, had stopped for the moment, and the river was falling. Of the numerous passages about Huerta, La Encina and Villa Gonzalo, Wellington had considered on the 9th that none were really practicable : on the 10th he wrote to Hill that ' the river has certainly fallen since yesterday evening, but I believe that no infantry soldier can pass yet, even if a cavalry soldier can, and small picquets guarding the fords and charging resolutely the first men who pass, will effectually prevent the passage [2].' Hill was not so certain that the enemy could not force his way over the river, and on the 11th Wellington conceded that some of the fords had certainly become practicable for cavalry, if not for infantry [3].

[1] See Jourdan's *Mémoires*, p. 441, for the meeting.
[2] Wellington to Hill, November 10, 4.30 p.m. (*Dispatches*, ix. p. 549).
[3] Same to same, November 11 (ix. p. 550).

Considering the immense superiority of the French in the mounted arm, it was conceivable that they might attack many fords at once, drive in the inferior cavalry-screen of the Allies, and then throw bridges across and attack the British centre. In that case the army would stand to fight, not behind the river bank but in front of the position of the Arapiles. It would be necessary to close in the flanks for a battle; all or most of the troops on the San Cristobal position would cross the Tormes, just as they had done in July, and at the same time Hill would draw in from Alba and form the southern wing of the line, in the woods which had sheltered Marmont's beaten army on the night of the great victory. But Alba was not to be abandoned[1]: its castle was susceptible of a long defence, and effectually blocked the best passage of the Tormes. Wellington selected a battalion of Galician infantry (Monterey, under Major José Miranda) which was to be placed in the castle, and to hold it as long as possible, even when it should (as was inevitable) be cut off from the allied army by the advance of the French. The position was explained to the Spanish major, who (as we shall see) behaved most admirably, blocked the Alba line of communication for many days, and finally escaped by a sudden sally from what looked like an inevitable surrender.

The two plans which were submitted to King Joseph on the evening of November 11 both presupposed the practicability of the fords of the Tormes. The river must evidently have fallen considerably since Wellington surveyed it on the 9th, and drew his conclusion that it was a barrier not to be crossed by any body of troops, but at most passable by individual horsemen.

Jourdan wrote: ' When we arrived on the heights above the right bank of the Almar, Your Majesty was struck with the advantages that the ground presented. I myself at once conceived the hope of forcing the English Army to a general action which must involve its destruction. Wellington's position is too long—extending from the heights of San Cristobal on the right bank of the Tormes as far as Alba. The Imperial Army could pass the river at almost any spot between Huerta and the point where the Almar flows into the Tormes.

[1] Same to same, pp. 550-1.

The immense plain on the opposite bank would permit the whole of our cavalry to cross and form up in front, to protect the passage of our infantry. After that, the Army would march in mass against the English centre (which appears to be between Calvarisa de Abaxo and Calvarisa de Arriba), and would break through the enemy's line. I do not disguise from myself that the piercing of the hostile centre has its difficulties, but I should think that 80,000 French troops could surmount them. Your Majesty must have remarked that Soult, who at first was all for marching toward the upper Tormes, was struck with the advantages which this ground offered, and came round to my opinion. But subsequently he got talking with General Clausel, about the plan for marching up the river, and returned to his first view, which he induced Clausel to support. Both of them are acquainted with the localities over which they wish to move the armies, which gives weight to their opinion. I do not wish to deny that Soult's proposition is the more prudent, and if we want to fight we ought to do so on ground which Wellington has not chosen, and which is less advantageous to the enemy than that which he now occupies. But I fear that we should not obtain from this movement so much advantage as Soult appears to expect.

'For he seems to think that Wellington will be forced to retreat on Ciudad Rodrigo, while it is quite possible that he may choose to retreat on San Felices, in which case our move-ment to the upper Tormes compels him to retire indeed, but enables him to avoid a battle. For my part I think that our superior numbers make a general action desirable. I conclude, then, that Your Majesty may adopt Soult's proposition so far as the movement up the Tormes goes. If so, I believe that the Army of Portugal must follow the Army of the South. The enemy has all his forces united : it would be too dangerous for us to divide ours [1].'

Soult's letter of the evening of the 12th, to the King, runs as follows :

'The passage which we reconnoitred a little below Villa Gonzalo unites all the qualities which one could desire, and

[1] Jourdan to Joseph, head-quarters at Peñaranda : early on November 12.

I should be in favour of it, were it not for the fact that after debouching on this point we should have to form up for the attack under the fire of the enemy, and should be compelled immediately to assail his whole army, in a position which he knows and has thought out, and where very probably he has entrenched himself. I think, therefore, that it would be more prudent and more advantageous to force him to shift his position, and to commit himself to an action on ground which we and not he will have chosen—or else to retreat[1]. I have sent three officers along the upper Tormes : they have reconnoitred and found practicable three fords between Exeme and Galisancho [1].'

From the comparison of these two interesting dispatches we see that Jourdan desired a battle in the style of Wagram, where the attacking army crosses a river, and breaks through the over-long line of an enemy deployed along heights at some distance from the water's edge. But Soult (to use an anachronism) feared a battle in the style of Fredericksburg, where the assailant, debouching from narrow fords or bridges, attacks in heavy masses a well-prepared position, held by an enemy who has had time to settle down comfortably into it, and to entrench the most suitable points. Soult was eminently justified in his criticism of Jourdan's plan : the most noteworthy remark to be made upon it is that this was the battle which Wellington wanted. He wished to be attacked frontally by the fords between Alba and Huerta, and had made all his arrangements. On the other hand, Jourdan's criticism of Soult was equally cogent. If the French armies, keeping in a mass, crossed the upper Tormes far above Alba, Wellington had the choice between fighting in a new position (e. g. behind the river Zurgain), and absconding, before his flank should be threatened seriously. He could, indeed, move off, practically unmolested, towards Ciudad Rodrigo, and not merely (as Jourdan suggested) by the more northern line toward San Felices and Almeida.

Joseph, as was perhaps natural, gave his final decision in favour of Soult's plan. It was true that he had a marked superiority in numbers, and that a defeat of a crushing sort

[1] Soult to Joseph, night of November 11, from the bivouac behind Alba de Tormes.

inflicted on Wellington would go far to end the Peninsular War. No such army on the French side had ever been in line on a single field before in Spain. Jourdan's estimate of 80,000 men was a decided understatement, even allowing for the fact that Soult's divisions had already many stragglers, and that Souham had left a ' minimum ' garrison at Valladolid. Something much more like the 90,000 men at which Wellington estimated the three united French armies must have been collected [1]. On the other hand there is a dreadful risk taken when an army endeavours to cross a group of fords, supplemented at the best by some hastily constructed bridges, in face of an enemy known to be wary, active, and determined. What might not happen if Wellington fell upon the leading divisions, while the rest were crowding down to their crossing points ? Or who could guarantee that sudden rain in the Sierra de Francia might not cause the Tormes to rise three feet on the battle day, and separate the troops who had crossed from those still on the eastern bank ? Every one at the French head-quarters must have remembered Essling, and the narrow escape from supreme disaster there suffered from the caprice of the Danube.

On the whole, the prospect of the enormous advantage to be got by inflicting a complete disaster on Wellington did not balance the possibility of loss that might follow an unsuccessful frontal attack upon his position. Joseph made his choice in favour of Soult's plan for a flank march to the upper Tormes. This manœuvre would take several days to execute, as the

[1] As the table of the French Armies of Spain for October 15 in the Appendix shows, the Army of the South had on that day 47,000 men under arms (omitting ' sick ' and ' detached '), the Army of the Centre 15,000, the Army of Portugal 45,000 (including Aussenac's brigade and Merlin's cavalry, both attached to it provisionally). This gives a total of 107,000, without sick or detached. The Army of Portugal may have lost 1,000 men in action at Villadrigo and Villa Muriel, &c.: the Army of the South not more than 400 at the Puente Larga, Alba de Tormes, &c. The Army of the Centre had not fought at all. A deduction has to be made for Soult's very large body of men attached to the Artillery Park, and for a smaller number in the Army of Portugal—say 3,000 men for the two together. Souham had left a small garrison at Valladolid—perhaps 1,500 men. If we allow 5,000 men for sick and stragglers between October 20 and November 12 there must still have been a good 90,000 men present. Miot (who was present) calls the total 97,000 (iii. p. 254), making it a little too high, I imagine.

Army of the South had to be moved to its left from all its
cantonments facing Alba, while the Armies of the Centre and
Portugal had to wait till this flank march was finished, in order
to come up and take over the former positions of Soult's divisions. For all the French chiefs were agreed that the armies
must keep closed up, and that no gap must be allowed to come
into existence between them. When the Army of the South
should begin to cross the Tormes, the Army of Portugal must
be in direct support of it, and must make no separate attack of
its own to the north of Alba, in the localities which Jourdan
had found so tempting. The whole of the 12th and 13th November was expended in making this shift of troops southward.
Soult moved his army up-stream and placed his head-quarters
at Anaya, six miles south of Alba, above the fords of Galisancho,
where the crossing was to take place. The King moved to
Valdecarros, a little to Soult's right, with the Army of the Centre.
The Army of Portugal, leaving its cavalry and two infantry
divisions[1] as a rearguard about Huerta, moved the other six
to the heights above Alba, where it was hoped that it might
cross, when Soult's manœuvre should force Hill to abandon
that place and draw back.

The King took two unexpected measures before passing the
Tormes. The first was to supersede Souham as commander of
the Army of Portugal—the excuse used was that he was indisposed, and not up to his task : the real cause was that he was
considered to have shown tardiness and over-caution in his
manœuvres since October 30th.[2] Drouet was taken from the
command of the Army of the Centre, and given the more
important charge of that of Portugal. The other, and more
surprising, order was one which made over—as a temporary
arrangement—the charge of the Army of the Centre to Soult,
who thus had nearly 60,000 men put at his disposition. The
object was, apparently, to give him ample forces for the move
now about to be made at his request, and on his responsibility.

Wellington was evidently somewhat puzzled at the posture
of the French on the 12th–13th November. He could not make

---

[1] Maucune and Gauthier (late Chauvel). See *Wellington Dispatches*,
ix. p. 556.

[2] Souham naturally expressed his indignation. See Miot, iii. p. 252–3.

out any reduction of the French forces between Huerta and
Alba, where indeed the whole Army of Portugal still lay, but
now with an accumulation of forces on its left and a weaker
right. Yet so long as the enemy was still in force at Huerta
he could not evacuate the San Cristobal position, in order
to send reinforcements to Hill. Reconnaissances by French
cavalry above Alba were reported each day by outlying picquets
of Hamilton's Portuguese, who were watching the course of
the upper Tormes [1]. But no solid force was sent to back these
outlying posts : Wellington considered it unsafe to extend his
already lengthy front. The disposition of the troops on his
right wing was still that Hill lay in the woods behind Alba,
with the 3rd and 4th Divisions at Calvarisa de Abaxo as a
reserve for him, while Long's and D'Urban's cavalry carefully
watched the course of the river from Alba to opposite Huerta.
On the north of the Tormes Pack's and Bradford's Portuguese
were on the river-bank at Aldea Lengua and Cabrerizos,
watching the two French divisions at Huerta. The 1st, 5th,
6th, 7th Divisions and the Galicians held the San Cristobal
position, with Anson's, Victor Alten's, and Ponsonby's cavalry
far out in their front. Nothing hostile could be discovered in
this direction nearer than the two divisions of the Army of
Portugal at Huerta. Yet Wellington did not like to weaken
his left flank : at any moment the enemy at Huerta might
come forward, and might prove to be the vanguard of an
advancing army, not the rearguard of one about to go off
southward. This hypothesis seemed all the more possible
because Maucune, on the morning of the 12th, had made a
reconnaissance in force against Pack's Portuguese, at Aldea
Lengua : he deployed three brigades, engaged in a lively
skirmish, and only retreated when British reinforcements began
to come up. On the following day Wellington, wishing to see
whether Maucune was on the move, beat up his quarters with
strong reconnaissances of cavalry, and found him still in

[1] D'Urban reports on November 12th : ' Enemy's troops in continual
movement, and he made a careful reconnaissance of the river from Huerta
to Exeme [above Alba].' On the 13th he writes : ' The enemy moved all
his troops between Huerta and Alba by his left into the woods behind
Exeme on the high road to Avila. From thence he can either go in that
direction or cross the Tormes by fords above Alba bridge.'

position [1]. Till Maucune should leave Huerta, in advance or
retreat, the situation was not clear. For these two days, it
seems, Wellington was still thinking it possible that he might
be attacked either on the San Cristobal position or by the
fords between Huerta and Alba. But he was quite aware that
the other possibility (a flank movement of Soult by the upper
Tormes) existed, and had sent a staff officer with a party of
the 13th Light Dragoons to cross the river at Salvatierra and
ascertain the southernmost point to which the French had
moved [2]. And he had given Hill elaborate orders as to what
should be done if he were turned and driven in. Whether
there would be a battle to follow, or a retreat on Ciudad Rodrigo,
depended on the exact movements of the enemy, and the force
that he brought up to the crucial point. If the French split
themselves into many columns, with long gaps between them,
there was still a chance of administering a second lesson like
that of July 22nd on much the same ground.

On the early morning of the 14th the crisis came. At dawn
Pierre Soult's Light Cavalry crossed the Tormes in force at
three fords between Galisancho and Lucinos, which were
perfectly passable, the water only coming up to the horses'
bellies. The Portuguese picquets beyond the river gave the
alarm, but had to retire at once ; some few were cut off by
the chasseurs. Two divisions of dragoons followed Vinot's
and Avy's light horse, and when they had scoured the west
bank of the Tormes up and down and found no enemy in force,
the infantry began to pass, not only by the fords but by several
trestle bridges which were constructed in haste. As soon as
there were a couple of divisions across the river, they advanced
to a line of heights a couple of miles ahead, where there was a
fair defensive position above the village of Martin Amor. By
the afternoon the whole Army of the South was across the
water, and had taken up a more advanced line towards Mozarbes,

[1] This fact, very important in justification of Wellington's long stay on
San Cristobal, is not mentioned in any of his dispatches. But there is a
full account of the skirmish in the *Mémoire* of Colonel Béchaud of Maucune's
Division, printed in *Études Napoléoniennes*, iii. pp. 98–9.

[2] The reconnaissance was executed by Leith Hay, who found the
French flank at Galisancho and reported its exact position. See his
Narrative, ii. pp. 99–100.

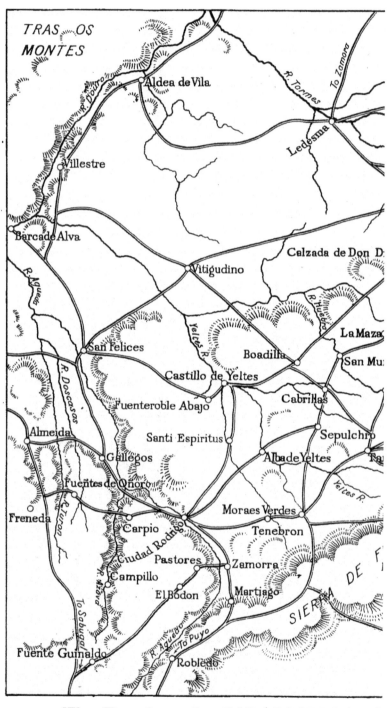

The Roads of the SALAMANCA A
SALAMANCA Retre

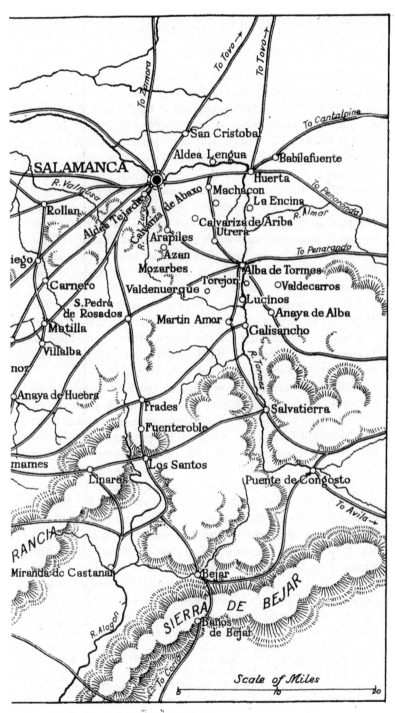

ALMEIDA REGION illustrating the
at of November 1812

while the Army of the Centre was beginning to follow. It had
been hoped that the Army of Portugal would be able to cross
at or near Alba, for Soult supposed it likely that Hill would
evacuate that town, when he saw 40,000 men arrayed behind
his left flank. But though Hill did withdraw Howard's and
da Costa's brigades in the afternoon, he left Miranda's Spanish
battalion in the castle, and blew up the bridge. As the castle
commanded the ruined structure and the ford near it, and
fired furiously on both, there was no chance of passing here or
of repairing the ruined arch. Drouet found that he would have
to march up-stream, and made his crossing at Torrejon, four
miles south of Alba and near the fords that Soult had employed.
He had the bulk of his army over the river by the afternoon,
and his two rear divisions under Maucune, which had arrived
late after a forced march from Huerta, crossed at dusk [1]. The
whole 90,000 men of the French Army were over the Tormes
that night, bivouacking on the heights from Torradillos to
Valdenuerque, in front of Martin Amor. The operation had
been neatly carried out, and was quite successful.

Wellington had early knowledge of the French movement
from two sources—his cavalry told him almost at daybreak
that the French camps above Huerta were empty, and soon
after came Hill's news that Soult had begun to cross the Tormes
in force at Galisancho. Quite early in the morning Wellington
rode out in haste, to take command in person on the threatened
front, after having issued orders that the whole of the troops
on the San Cristobal position should follow him. He himself
pushed on with his staff, met Hill in the wood south of the
Arapiles, and told him to watch the roads from Alba with the
4th Division and Hamilton's Portuguese. Then, taking the
strong 2nd Division—8,000 infantry—and all the cavalry
brigades that had been watching the middle Tormes (Slade's,
Long's, and D'Urban's, and Penne Villemur's Spaniards) he
pushed on to 'contain' and possibly to attack Soult [2]. But on
arriving in front of Mozarbes a little before noon, he saw that

---

[1] Details from Foy's *Vie militaire*, ed. Girod de l'Ain, p. 118, and
Béchaud (quoted above), pp. 99–100.

[2] His original intention to attack is clearly stated in *Dispatches*, ix. p. 559,
and the statement is corroborated by D'Urban.

the enemy had already three or four divisions and 4,000 horse drawn up in line to cover the passage of the Tormes by the rest of his army. He had arrived too late to check Soult's leading columns, and if he sent for Hill and the other troops which lay to his rear, he would, even when they arrived, have only 25,000 men available to attack an enemy who had already as great a force in line, and who was receiving fresh troops every moment from the fords [1]. Nothing could be done till the great reserve from the San Cristobal position came up, and they were not due till late in the day—the last of them indeed did not cross the bridge of Salamanca till the following morning.

At dusk Wellington ordered Hill to fall back with his infantry from the woods in front of Alba to the old position of the Arapiles, but kept his cavalry to the front, to cover his own line of battle as long as possible. Their screen of vedettes was placed in the line of woods from Miranda de Azan to Utrera, south of the heights on which Marmont's army had taken up its position upon July 22nd. Till this cavalry was driven in, the French, on the rising ground above Mozarbes, could not make out the British position.

On the morning of the 15th Wellington had all his troops in hand, though the last divisions from San Cristobal did not come up till some hours after daybreak. But the enemy had also brought up every man to the front, being resolved to sacrifice not even the smallest part of his numerical superiority. Some critics, among them Jourdan [2], hold that Wellington, since he was determined not to fight save at advantage, should have commenced his retreat on Ciudad Rodrigo the moment that he saw the whole of the three hostile armies massed in his

[1] D'Urban, an eye-witness, thinks that Wellington ought to have called up Hill and attacked, despite of all difficulties. 'Lord Wellington arrived upon the ground at about 12 noon, and at first appeared inclined to attack what of the enemy had already passed, with the divisions and cavalry on the spot. The success of such a measure appeared certain, and would have frustrated all the enemy's projects. However, his opinion changed: they were allowed to continue passing unmolested.'

[2] *Mémoires*, p. 448. Cf. also Napier, iv. p. 381, who seems to share the idea. 'Why, it may be asked, did the English commander, having somewhat carelessly suffered Soult to pass the Tormes and turn his position, wait so long on the Arapiles position as to render a dangerous movement (retreat in face of the enemy and to a flank) necessary ? '

front, and before they could begin to débouch from their position on the heights of Mozarbes. And it is probable that if he had directed the troops from San Cristobal to take the roads towards the Agueda, instead of bringing them up to the Arapiles position, and if he had used Hill's corps and all his cavalry as a rearguard only, he would have reached Ciudad Rodrigo with a smaller loss of life than was actually to be spent. The French would have had to start their pursuit from a more distant and a less favourable point.

It seems, however, that Wellington was prepared to risk a battle, even against the superior numbers opposed to him, supposing that the enemy played his game badly. He resolved to take up the excellent position along the Arapiles heights which he had held on July 22nd, and to stand to fight against any frontal assault—the advantage of the ground, with its bold slopes, good cover for reserves, and favourable emplacements for artillery, were evidently in his eyes so great that he was prepared to risk a general engagement with 20,000 men less in line than had his adversaries. As the morning drew on, he had his army formed up from Calvarisa de Arriba to a point not far from Miranda de Azan. The line was longer than in the battle of July 22nd, for the troops were much more numerous. The extreme left wing was formed by the 4th Division holding the heights and village of Calvarisa de Arriba (which had been in Foy's hands on July 22). The 2nd Division and Hamilton's Portuguese were holding both the Arapiles—the French as well as the English—and the ground from thence as far as the village of the same name. Westward of Hill's troops lay the 3rd Division and Morillo's Spaniards. The second line, composed of troops which had come down from San Cristobal, consisted of the Light Division (on the left), Pack and Bradford, the Galicians, and the 5th, 6th, and 7th Divisions. The 1st Division was placed as a somewhat 'refused' right flank protection for the whole army—much as Pakenham and the 3rd Division had been in July. It lay about Aldea Tejada on the Zurgain river, several miles to the right rear of the 3rd Division. The object for which it was detailed to this separate duty was the same as that for which Pakenham had been told off at the earlier crisis—to protect the Ciudad Rodrigo road, and

to be ready to outflank and intercept any attempt which the
French might make to turn the British position in this direction.
The bulk of the cavalry was also placed on the right wing, to
cover the end of the infantry line. Only the Portuguese horse
of D'Urban and Campbell, Penne Villemur's Spaniards, and
Long's brigade were on the left beyond Calvarisa de Arriba. The
rest, five British brigades, lay out in the direction of Miranda
de Azan and in front of Aldea Tejada. Bock's brigade on the
extreme right long remembered their position of this morning
because they were placed on ' Pakenham's Hill ', the spot
where the 3rd Division had fallen upon Thomières in the old
battle. The ground was thickly strewn with the skeletons of
the French who had then fallen, still lying unburied and in a
horrible state of complete preservation : the horses' hoofs
were continually setting the skulls rolling [1]. Behind Bock were
Ponsonby's, Victor Alten's, Anson's, and Slade's brigades, a
formidable mass, yet far less in strength than the innumerable
cavalry of the Armies of the South and Centre, which lay
opposite them 7,000 strong [2]. Nothing was more uncertain
than the move which the French would next make. If it should
turn out to be one which did not fit in with Wellington's plans,
there would be no alternative but a retreat on Ciudad Rodrigo.
Wherefore all the divisions were directed to send off their
baggage half a march to the west, and preparations were made
to destroy so much of the magazines in Salamanca city as could
not be carried off. The commissariat officers were already
packing up all for which transport could be found, and sending
it forward. By an error of judgement on the part of the
Quartermaster-General, James Willoughby Gordon—not the
first of his blunders in this campaign—all this valuable store
was started on the road Salamanca–Rollan–San Felices, which
was the safest by far of all those open to the Army if a retreat
should become necessary, and the farthest from any probable
line of advance that the French could take. But it had the

[1] This horrid reminiscence I found in the unpublished letters of Hodenberg of the 1st Heavy Dragoons K.G.L., which I reprinted in *Blackwood's
Magazine* in the year 1913.

[2] Details about the exact drawing-up of the second line and reserves
seem impossible to discover. I have only accurate notes as to the position
of the front line and some of the cavalry and the 1st Division.

disadvantage of being far away from the other roads by which the Allied Army might have to move, and the unfortunate result followed on the 16th–17th–18th that the food was moving on the northern road, and the troops—starving for want of it—on three other roads parallel to it at a distance of twenty miles to the south. Soldiers must be fed, or they straggle and turn to marauding, and it is of no profit to have food if it be not in the right place at the right moment. These simple facts were to cause dire trouble during the next three days.

Meanwhile, from a comparatively early hour on the 15th it became evident that Soult was not going to play the game that Wellington desired. It was a miserable morning of drifting rain, and reconnaissances had to be pushed far forward to get any clear information. But the reports soon began to come in, to the effect that the enemy was keeping closed up, that he was constructing trenches and *abattis* on the heights of Mozarbes [1], and that he had pushed out an immense force of cavalry on his left wing, under cover of which infantry divisions were clearly to be seen working westward. Evidently Soult was aiming at the roads toward Ciudad Rodrigo; but he was not (like Marmont on July 22) letting his army break up into unconnected sections, and was keeping it in an unbroken line. The entrenchments on the hills showed that he was prepared to receive in position any frontal attack that Wellington might be prepared to direct against him. His motions were slow, not only because of his cautious method of procedure, but from the badness of the country roads, already made deep and miry from the rain, over which he was moving his left wing towards the west. The Army of Portugal was now in line on his right, and its cavalry was feeling its way forward towards Hill's flank. But obviously the danger was not on this side, where the bulk of the French infantry was standing fast in position : it was the other wing, Soult's troops alone, which was in decided motion, and that for a flank march, not for anything approaching a frontal attack.

---

[1] For doing this Jourdan criticized Soult for over-caution, and wasting of time, describing this measure as timid and unnecessary. *Mémoires*, p. 443.

All this was most disappointing : Wellington at once made up his mind that since the enemy was not about to attack his position, and since it would be madness on his part to take the offensive and assail the well-placed array of the French, there was no alternative save instant retreat. It must not be delayed, because, when Soult should have moved his left wing a little farther on, he would be controlling the road that runs from Mozarbes to Tamames and Ciudad Rodrigo, parallel to that via Matilla and San Muñoz to the same destination, over which Wellington's natural line of retreat lay.

At about two o'clock in the afternoon on the 15th the British commander-in-chief made up his mind that he must delay no longer, and ordered his army to march to its right, in the two lines in which it was already arranged. The mass of cavalry in front of Aldea Tejada remained stationary, to cover the movement of the infantry behind its rear : the smaller body of hòrse on the left held its ground about the Arapiles, till all the divisions had passed on, and then followed as a rearguard. The entire army marched in fighting trim : if attacked at any moment it had only to front to its left flank, and then would be in order of battle. The movement had to be slow for the first few miles, since neither the front nor the rear column was on a good track until it reached the river Zurgain, and there fell into one of the three parallel roads which run from Salamanca to Ciudad Rodrigo. Moreover the rain, which had been a mere drizzle in the morning, turned to a heavy torrential downpour just as the army was starting. The country paths became quagmires in a few minutes ; and when the usually insignificant Zurgain came in sight it was already a roaring river, only to be forded with care. The march was toilsome in the extreme, and the troops, who had expected and desired a general action, were sodden and sulky. ' I never saw the men in such a bad humour,' observes one intelligent eye-witness [1]. The march was absolutely unmolested by the French, and the columns, having crossed the Zurgain, fell into the three parallel roads which run side by side for many miles from Salamanca—the southern one to Matilla, the central one to Maza de San Pedro and San Muñoz, the northern one (the so-called Calzada de Don Diego) to Aldehuela

[1] Donaldson of the 94th. *Recollections*, p. 179.

de la Boveda [1]. Of these the second is the regular high road from Salamanca to the frontier, the other two secondary lines of communication. They are extraordinarily convenient for the retreat of an army which must be kept together, the distance between the two side-roads and the central one being seldom over five miles, and often no more than three. The only misfortune was that the train of transport had gone off, by Colonel Gordon's error [2], on an entirely different and divergent route, towards Rollan and San Felices. The army, after falling into the designated roads, pursued its way till after dark and bivouacked in the patches of forest on the farther side of the Valmusa river, about 10 miles from Salamanca. The head-quarters were at the village of Carnero on the central road [3]. The night was miserable, no food was distributed, and though wood was abundant it was hard to light fires, owing to the incessant rain. The troops were tired and footsore, and straggling had once more begun.

Meanwhile there was quite as much discontent in the French ranks as in those of Wellington. There had been a general feeling that since the whole force of the three armies of the South, Centre, and Portugal had been successfully concentrated on the Mozarbes position, and since the enemy was known to be much inferior in numbers, something decisive ought to have happened on the 15th November. That no collision whatever took place must be attributed partly to the bad weather, but

---

[1] The 4th Division formed the infantry rearguard on the southern road, the Light Division that on the central road.

[2] Colonel James Willoughby Gordon seems not to have been a success as quartermaster-general. Very soon after his arrival we get notes in the earlier part of the Salamanca campaign that intelligent officers ' thought he would not stop long with the Army.' Cf. Tomkinson, p. 224 : ' Nothing could equal the bad arrangements of the Quartermaster-General—the cavalry all retired by one road, allowing that of the enemy to follow our infantry ' [of the central column on November 18]—which was not covered, all the horse having gone on the western or left road. Wellington had a worse accusation against him than mere incapacity (of this more will be found in chap. iii of sect. xxxv)—that of sending letters home which revealed military secrets which got into the English papers. In September he made up his mind that Gordon must not see his dispatches, and must be ' kept at as great distance as possible ' (*Supplementary Dispatches*, vii. pp. 427–8). He was sent home before the next campaign.

[3] D'Urban's diary.

much more to the caution of Soult, who was this day determined above all things that he would not suffer the fate of Marmont on this same ground, by allowing any dislocation to take place between the various sections of his army.

At nine o'clock in the morning it had been reported that—so far as the misty rain allowed of certain observation—Wellington was in line of battle on the Arapiles position. Soult continued to move his cavalry forward with caution, and to extend his left towards Azan. A little before noon Joseph and Jourdan joined Soult on the heights above Mozarbes, the Allies being still stationary. Jourdan suggested that the Army of Portugal should move forward on the right and attack that flank of the hostile line which rested on the Arapiles [1] : this was tried in a tentative way, apparently with the object of holding Hill's divisions to their ground, and preventing them from moving off. But it led to no more than some bickering between the caçadores of the 2nd Division and the advanced light cavalry and voltigeurs of the French right, in the woods south of the greater Arapile. The Army of Portugal made no real attempt to close in. A partial attack on Wellington's line would, indeed, have been unwise. The only chance would have been for Soult to march in upon its right while D'Erlon was pressing in with decision against its left. But Soult, though requested by King Joseph to move forward in force, continued his cautious flanking movement to the westward, and did not carry out a precise and definite order to push out his cavalry and drive in the British squadrons which lay in front of Wellington's right. Then came the torrential rain which set in about two o'clock, just as Wellington ordered his army to move off, still preserving its battle order, toward the river Zurgain. His departure was only partially visible, and no attempt was made to incommode it. A cavalry officer of the Army of the South writes : ' The rain falling in deluge soon rendered the whole field of operations one vast and deep quagmire. The smallest

---

[1] See Foy, *Vie militaire*, p. 190. He was a witness to the conversation. And cf. Espinchel, *Mémoires*, ii. p. 73, who gets the hour too late and exaggerates the contact of the armies. He says that 12 of Hill's guns opened on the French light cavalry. Cf. also Joseph to Clarke of December 20.

dips in the ground became dangerous precipices. The darkness, continually growing blacker, soon added to the horror of the scene, and made us absolutely unable to act. The muskets of the infantry were no longer capable of being discharged. The cavalry was not only unable to manœuvre, but even to advance on the slippery, sodden, and slimy soil. . . . We lay down on the field drenched by the rain, with the mud up to our knees [1].'

Jourdan says that it was pitch dark by four o'clock, the gloom of the terrible downpour melting early into the darkness of the night. There was much recrimination between the French leaders. Joseph wrote to the Minister of War that he tried to bring on decisive action between eleven o'clock and two, and failed entirely by the fault of Soult. He accused him of deliberately wasting two hours by vain excuses, and suggested that the real explanation of his sluggishness was that he knew the incapacity of his brother Pierre Soult, commanding the light horse of the left wing, and thought that he would get matters into a mess if he were charged with the duty of pressing Wellington's cavalry in front of him [2]. ' He knows the extent of his brother's capacity, and fears to compromise him. For this reason his light horse is always kept close in to the rest of the army, and never advances without being immediately supported by the remainder of his cavalry, while the Duke of Dalmatia always marches himself in his brother's company.'

Such a theory is, of course, quite insufficient to explain Soult's reluctance to engage on this day. The simple fact was that, after Albuera, he had a wholesome dread of attacking a British army in position, if it could be avoided, and preferred to manœuvre it from its chosen ground, even if he thereby sacrificed the possibility of a great victory, and secured only an illusory advantage.

On finding that Wellington had got off unmolested, and that Soult had made no attempt to drive in the cavalry which was covering his retreat, King Joseph, by Jourdan's advice, issued orders which proved that both he and his mentor thought that the game was up. Instead of setting every man upon the track

---

[1] Espinchel, ii. p. 73.

[2] Joseph to Clarke, in a long dispatch of December 20. Ducasse's *Correspondance du Roi Joseph*, ix. pp. 119–20.

of the allied columns, Joseph ordered the whole Army of Portugal, as well as his own Guard, to march upon the deserted town of Salamanca, while Soult alone was permitted to pursue the retreating foe. Now since the King was as much convinced as either of the Marshals that, if Wellington was to be brought to book, every man of the 90,000 French troops must be ready to attack him, it is clear that the order to the Army of Portugal to desist from the pursuit meant that no general action was now to be hoped for. Jourdan could indulge in the malicious satisfaction of the adviser who, having seen his counsel rejected, is able to say ' I told you so ! ' to his comrade, when bad luck has supervened. He had prophesied that, if Soult were allowed to try his flank move to the upper Tormes, Wellington would get off without harm[1]. This had now happened ; it was judged that a further pursuit by the whole army was useless, and the 40,000 men of the Army of Portugal and the Royal Guards were directed to seize Salamanca and halt there. Clearly if Soult's 50,000 men went on, and Wellington suddenly turned to bay, the pursuers could not dare to bring him to action, since they would be much outnumbered. Evidently, all that could now be hoped was that Soult might worry the rear of the retreating enemy, and pick up stragglers and baggage.

After dark the light cavalry of the Army of Portugal and Foy's infantry division marched on Salamanca, and reached it that night, after much toilsome trudging over inundated paths : ' The plain was under water : for half the way our infantry were walking through water knee deep : if the moon had not risen we should never have found our way there.' The bridge of Salamanca was discovered to be unbroken, and some half-emptied magazines of flour and rum were captured. A rear-guard of British cavalry—half a troop of the 2nd Hussars of the German Legion—evacuated the place on the arrival of the French, covering a mass of stragglers, sutlers, and Spanish refugees, who found their way to Ledesma and from thence to the Portuguese frontier[2]. Foy, following them forty-eight

---

[1] See above, p. 126.

[2] For the curious adventures of Captain v. Stolzenberg commanding this little party, and of the horde which he shepherded, see Schwertfeger's History of the K.G.L., ii. pp. 262–3.

hours later, moved to Ledesma, and then to Zamora, where he took up cantonments. The cavalry of the Army of Portugal, starting earlier, went to feel for Wellington's rear on the road towards Aldehuela de la Boveda, leaving the pursuit on the other two routes to Soult. The rest of the Army remained cantoned at Salamanca, which had been well plundered by the first division that arrived [1]. King Joseph reviewed it, outside the city, on November 17—all in the rain—a melancholy ceremony. The men and officers were alike weary and discontented. 'We had an army stronger by a third than Wellington's, infinitely superior in cavalry and artillery. Confident expectation of victory was in every man's head. The chance had come of beating the English—perhaps of driving them from the Peninsula. This fine opportunity, so splendid, so decisive, with so few adverse chances, has been let slip [2].' So wrote the disappointed Foy. He adds, 'The King does not know how to show to advantage before his troops ; he can speak with effect neither to the officers nor to the rank and file : he got absolutely wet through, rode home, and went to bed.'

[1] *Mémoires* of Béchaud, quoted above, p. 101.
[2] Foy, *Vie militaire*, pp. 189–90.

SECTION XXXIV : CHAPTER VI

FROM THE TORMES TO THE AGUEDA

THE last crisis of the campaign of 1812 was now over, and, but for two unlucky circumstances, the four days of operations which still remained would havē required little notice from the annalist. But these two mishaps, the continuance of the exceptionally severe and tempestuous weather which had set in upon the 15th November, and the misdirection of the supply column, which had got completely separated from the marching troops, were to have most disastrous results. They cost the army 3,000 men, much misery, and some humiliation, and Wellington great vexation of spirit, leading to one of his rare outbursts of violent rage—his angry words committed to paper, and published abroad by misadventure, were always remembered with a grudge by his officers and men.

It must be remembered that there was no really dangerous pursuit. Soult was not strong enough to press Wellington to a general action, and knew it. On the 16th he wrote to King Joseph : ' I think that your Majesty's intention is that the enemy should only be followed up to the frontier. In two days the campaign will probably be at an end in these parts, for if the enemy's army goes behind the Agueda,. I cannot think that it would be at present possible to pursue it any further. I await your orders for the future destination of the Army of the South, which would be unable to stop two days in position for want of bread and forage. I propose to establish it on the upper Tormes, below Salvatierra and El Barco, where I could rest eight or ten days, to allow the men repose and to collect food [1].' Clearly there was no offensive spirit in the Marshal, who only wished to see Wellington upon his way to Rodrigo, and then contemplated turning back to the upper Tormes.

On the 16th there was little to record in the way of military operations. The British Army started at dawn from its wet

[1] Soult to King Joseph, Matilla, 16th November 1812.

bivouacks behind the Valmusa river, having received no distribution of food. The side roads, on which the larger part of the troops were moving, grew worse and worse as the rain continued. The weakly men began to fall behind, the shirkers to slip away into the woods, to look for peasants to plunder and roofs to shelter them from the drenching rain. After the usual mid-day halt the bad news went round that the supply column had gone off on the wrong road—via Ledesma—and that there would again be no distribution of rations that evening. All that the troops got was the carrion-like meat of over-driven bullocks hastily slaughtered, and acorns gathered in the oak woods through which the roads ran. These, we are assured, though bitter and hard, were better than nothing. It was only in the evening, after the infantry had encamped behind the brook that gets its name from the village of Matilla, that the pursuing French cavalry came up on the two southern roads, and engaged in a bickering skirmish with the screen of allied horse covering the rear. The Polish Lancers, 2nd Hussars, and 5th and 27th Chasseurs engaged in an interchange of partial charges with the 14th Light Dragoons and K.G.L. Hussars of Victor Alten's brigade, in front of the camps of the 2nd Division. It was brought to a sudden end by the light company of the 28th and two guns opening fire on the French from under the cover of a woodside, on which the enemy went off, with a loss of some 50 men, mostly wounded prisoners [1]. Alten's brigade suffered much less. The centre column saw very little of the pursuing French—Digeon's Dragoons—who made no attempt to press in. The cavalry of the Army of Portugal acted even more feebly on the northernmost of the three parallel roads. Yet the retreating army lost several hundred 'missing' this day, all stragglers or weakly men captured singly on the road,

---

[1] There is a good account of the skirmish in the *Mémoires* of Espinchel, ii. p. 73, who frankly allows that the French light cavalry were both out-manœuvred and repulsed with loss. The returns of the three French regiments show 22 killed, *no* wounded, and 25 missing—an odd proportion. Apparently the wounded must all have been captured. The 1st Hussars K.G.L. had 7 wounded and 7 missing, the rest of Alten's brigade under 20 casualties. This brigade was now *three* regiments strong instead of two, having had the 2nd Hussars K.G.L. from Hill's Army attached to it at Salamanca.

or in villages at its sides, whither they had betaken themselves
for shelter or marauding. The rearguard cavalry vainly
attempted to whip them all into the tail of the retreating column
—some were really unable to move—others escaped notice in
hiding-places, and were taken by the French when they emerged
for a tardy attempt to follow the army. The camp-followers,
and the unfortunate women and children whom the evil custom
of the time allowed to remain with the regiments, suffered most
of all. Soult in his dispatch to King Joseph of the night of
the 16th says that he had gathered in 600 prisoners this day,
and is very probably correct.

The 17th November was an even worse day—the rain still
continued to fall, and stomachs were still more empty than on
the preceding morning. The march of the retreating army was
still in three columns, but the 2nd Division replaced the 4th
as the rearguard of the southern column (2nd, 3rd, 4th Divisions ; Hamilton's Portuguese ; Morillo's Spaniards), which
marched unmolested from Matilla by Villalba to Anaya on the
Huebra, turning off towards the end of the day from the high
road to Tamames [1], in order not to get too far from the central
column, which was marching on San Muñoz : for Wellington
intended to have his whole army arrayed behind the Huebra,
a good fighting position, that evening. This was a most
miserable journey. ' The effects of hunger and fatigue were
even more visible than on the preceding day. A savage sort
of desperation had taken possession of our minds, and those
who lived on the most friendly terms in happier times now
quarrelled with each other, using the most frightful impreca-
tions, on the slightest offence. A misanthropic spirit was in
possession of every bosom. The streams which fell from the
hills were swelled into rivers, which we had to wade, and
many fell out, including even officers. It was piteous to see
some of the men, who had dragged their limbs after them with
determined spirit, fall down at last among the mud, unable to

---

[1] Napier says that the column went through Tamames, but no 2nd,
3rd, or 4th Division diary mentions that considerable town as passed—
they all speak of solitudes and oak-woods alone. Wellington's orders on
the night of November 16 (*Supplementary Dispatches*, xlv. p. 157) give
' La Neja ' as Hill's destination, and this oddly spelt place is undoubtedly
Anaya de Huebra.

proceed further, and sure of being taken prisoners if they escaped death. Towards night the rain had somewhat abated, but the cold was excessive, and numbers who had resisted the effect of hunger and fatigue with a hardy spirit were now obliged to give way, and sank to the ground praying for death to deliver them from their misery. Some prayed not in vain, for next morning before daylight, in passing from our halting-ground to the road, I stumbled over several who had died in the night [1].'

The only food that the southern marching column got this day was procured from the celebrated raid upon the swine, which so much enraged Wellington. It is recorded in many 3rd and 4th Division diaries. The main wealth of the peasantry of this forest region lay in their pigs, which had been driven into the heart of the woods, to hide them from the passing armies. From some unknown cause a stampede broke out in one vast herd of the creatures, which ran across the road cutting through the middle of the 3rd Division. The starving soldiers opened up a lively fusillade upon them, and whole battalions broke their ranks and pursued them with the bayonet, cutting up the creatures before they were dead, each man going off with a gory limb or rib. Many officers farther to the rear thought from the firing that the French had cut into the head of the column. Later in the day the same or another herd charged the camp of a brigade of the 2nd Division, and gave many a hungry man an unexpected meal [2].

The southern column had no enemy but hunger and cold on the 17th, but the experiences of the centre column were more military. This corps, consisting of the 1st, 6th, 5th, 7th, Light Divisions, moving in that order, had a tiresome alarm before the rearguard had started in the morning from behind the Matilla brook. By some blunder—on the part of Gordon the Quartermaster-General as was said [3]—the covering cavalry

[1] Memoirs of Donaldson of the 94th, pp. 181-2.
[2] See the Memoirs of Grattan of the 88th, and Bell of the 34th.
[3] See Wellington's Marching Orders for the 17th in *Supplementary Dispatches*, xiv. pp. 157–8, for the cavalry. A perverse reading of them might make the cavalry start too early for ' the brook which passes by La Maza and Aldeahuela ', where they are told to be at dawn. They are not actually directed to wait for the infantry rearguard.

marched off before the Light Division, the rear of the infantry column, had left its ground. There was nothing but the picquets from the 95th Rifles between the camp, where the battalions were just getting under arms, and two divisions of French Dragoons, cautiously advancing along the road and with their flanking parties out in the woods. There was barely time to form close column and start off before the enemy were riding in from all sides. They did not attempt to close, but while keeping their main body on the road, at a safe distance, sent out many detached squadrons, along by-paths in the woods, which from time to time came out unexpectedly not only upon the flank of the Light Division, acting as rearguard, but much farther up the line, where the 7th Division, and the 5th in front of them, were moving along the road to San Muñoz. Hardly any of the allied cavalry appeared to curb these incursions—the main body appears to have gone off too much to the south, in the direction of Hill's column. Hence came the extraordinary chance that small bodies of the French got into the interval between the Light Division and the 7th, and even into that between the 7th Division and the 5th, though the troops themselves were all closed up and perfectly safe in their dense columns. Great part of the baggage of the 7th Division was intercepted and plundered by one party. But the most tiresome incident was that a patrol of three men from Vinot's light cavalry captured the one-armed General Edward Paget, the newly-arrived second-in-command of the Army, as he was riding—accompanied by his Spanish servant alone—from the rear brigade of the 5th Division to the front brigade of the 7th, in order to bid the latter close up rapidly. The French pounced on him out of a corner of the wood, and as he could not defend himself, and had no escort, he was hurried off a prisoner, and it was some time before his absence was noted [1]. A good many isolated soldiers were picked up in the same fashion by the French cavalry, before the central column emerged from the woods and found itself above the broad ravine of the Huebra river, and the town of San Muñoz, in the late afternoon [2].

[1] There is a full account of his capture in the memoirs of Espinchel, ii. p. 77, the officer whose men took Paget prisoner.

[2] The movements of this day are made very difficult to follow by the

The whole column had been ordered to encamp on the farther side of the Huebra, on the plateau in front of Boadilla and Cabrillas, and each division as it passed the river made its way to the ground allotted to it. There was wood to be had in abundance, and fires were lit—the rain had abated in the afternoon—but there was little to cook. Again there was no distribution save of beef from the droves of half-starved oxen which accompanied the divisions, and acorns which turned out more palatable when roasted than when eaten raw.

The 7th Division had just crossed the Huebra, and the Light Division and a few squadrons of cavalry alone were on the farther bank, when a new turn was given to the day by the appearance of infantry behind the French Dragoons, who had been following the retreating centre column since dawn. Soult had at last succeeded in getting his leading division, that of Daricau, to the front. Hitherto the bad roads and the fatigue of the long marches had prevented them from picking up the cavalry of the advanced guard. The Marshal by no means intended to commit himself to a general action, but thought that he had the chance of falling upon the rear of Wellington's retreating central column, as it passed the defile of the Huebra. ' I thought,' he wrote that evening to King Joseph, ' that I might bring off a combat of infantry, and a cavalry affair, to advantage, but had to give up the idea, and to limit my efforts to cannonading the masses of the English Army across the Huebra. The enemy showed us 20,000 men in position, including 3,000 horse, and more than 20 guns—we could see other masses debouching across the bridge of Castillejo de Huebra, and the glare of camp fires announced the presence of more divisions on the plateau of Cabrillas [1].'

What happened at this rearguard action, whose details Soult slurs over, was that the Light Division, suddenly attacked by

fact that Wellington in his dispatches (ix. 464–5) calls Hill's column the right, and the Spanish column the left, of the three in which the Army marched. Vere's *Diary of the Marches of the 4th Division* does the same. But these directions are only correct when the army faced about and stopped to check the French. On the march Hill's was the left column, and the Spaniards the right. For this reason I have called them the southern and northern columns respectively.

[1] Soult to Joseph, November 17, from before San Muñoz.

the French infantry as it was about to cross the Huebra, had
to throw out a strong skirmishing line to its rear, while the
main column plunged down the ravine and over the fords.
Three companies of the 43rd and one of the 95th[1] held back
Daricau's voltigeurs till their comrades had waded across the
water, and then had the dangerous task of withdrawing from
the wood-side and rushing down to the fords sharply pursued.
Soult showed at first every sign of desiring to cross the Huebra
in their wake, brought up four batteries to his side of the ravine,
and began to play upon the Light and 7th Divisions, which
had formed up to defend the passage. His skirmishers swarmed
down to the river bank, under cover of the fire of the guns,
engaged in a lively *tiraillade* across the rapid stream, and
would certainly have attempted to cross if the return fire had
not been as strong and rapid as their own. The 7th Division,
drawn up in three lines of brigades on the higher slopes, was
much shelled by the French artillery, and would have suffered
severely but for the fact that the rain-sodden ground ' swallowed
the shot and smothered the shells [2].' It is an extraordinary fact
that after ' four hours of standing up to the ankles in mud and
water, completely exposed, having nothing to shelter us [3] ' the
regiments in the front brigade were hardly touched at all : the
68th had no loss whatever, the 51st had one officer killed and
eight men wounded, and the total casualties in the division were
under 30. Soult's report that ' notre feu d'artillerie a été très
meurtrier pour l'ennemi ' was plausible enough to any French
officer watching the artillery practice, which was good—but
happened to be incorrect.

At dusk the firing ceased, and the French drew off from the
river and encamped in the woods behind them, as did the
Light and 7th Divisions on the opposite bank. The losses on
both sides in this skirmish—sometimes called the combat of
San Muñoz, sometimes the combat of the Huebra—were very
moderate. Daricau's division had 226 casualties (mostly in
the 21st Léger and 100th Line), and the French cavalry a few

[1] So the regimental histories (both good) of these corps. Napier gives
one more company of the 43rd.

[2] Napier, iv. p. 385.

[3] Autobiography of Green of the 68th, p. 127.

more. On the British side the Light and 7th Divisions and
the cavalry of the rearguard lost 365 men—but this included
178 prisoners not taken in action but individually as stragglers
during the long retreat through the woods since dawn [1]. In
the actual fighting the loss was only 2 officers and 9 men
killed, and 4 officers and 90 men wounded in the British
brigades, with 1 officer and 36 men killed and 2 officers and 43
men wounded in the Portuguese—a total of 187. Next morning
it was expected that the French, having now several more
infantry divisions at the front, would make an attempt to force
the line of the Huebra at dawn. Nothing of the kind happened.
' Daylight came at last,' writes the cavalry officer in charge
of the line of vedettes along the river, ' the French drums beat,
and the troops stood to arms. I took my place to observe their
movements, and expected every moment to see the columns
leaving the camp for the different fords. But no ! after having
had a good opportunity to observe their strength, and to see
their cavalry water their horses, I witnessed with no small
satisfaction the whole, after remaining under arms about
two hours, disperse to their respective bivouacks [2].' The
pursuit was over.

Wellington, in short, had offered battle on the Huebra, on
the evening of the 17th, and Soult had refused it, seeing that
the bulk of the allied army was concentrated close behind that
river, while his own infantry divisions were still straggling up
from the rear. Nor had he any intention of following next day
—he wrote to King Joseph that ' I told your Majesty that
seeing the retreat of the enemy upon the Agueda well pro-
nounced, and having no hope of being able to engage him in a
general action before he has terminated his movement, I should
put a limit to my pursuit after passing the Huebra, and should
move off towards the upper Tormes, to enable the army to
collect the food which it lacks.' The regret expressed at being
unable to force on a battle was of course insincere. All that
Soult did was to wait till the British rearguard had abandoned
the line of the Huebra, and then move his advanced cavalry

---

[1] British ' missing ' one officer (General Paget) and 111 men, Portuguese
' missing ' 66 men.

[2] Reminiscences of Hay, 12th Light Dragoons, p. 86.

to Cabrillas, from which some small reconnoitring parties
pushed as far as the Yeltes river [1], and then came back, reporting that it was impossible to pass that flooded stream without
bridges, and that the British were all across it. On the morning
of the 19th the whole French army retired eastward, marching
by Tamames and Linares towards Salvatierra. The truth was
that the French were by now suffering almost as much from
fatigue and want of food as the British. They could not ' live
on the country ', and the diet of acorns, of which several
diarists speak, was as repugnant to the pursuers as to the
pursued.

On the 18th the British Army had an unmolested retreat.
This did not prevent many losses of men who dropped to the
rear and died of fatigue and starvation. The carcasses of dead
horses all along the road had been hacked up for food. One
observer saw thirteen corpses lying round a single fire : another
counted so many as fifty men sitting in a clump, who declared
their absolute incapacity to march a foot farther, and could
not be induced to move. But the stragglers who did not perish
hobbled on to the camps in the evening for the most part.
The cavalry swept up large numbers of them into safety.
That night the column of Hill reached Tenebron and Moras
Verdes : the centre column lodged about Santi Espiritus and
Alba de Yeltes. The Galicians, forming the northern column,
were about Castillo de Yeltes and Fuenteroble. The march
of the centre column was accompanied by the curious case of
insubordination by three divisional generals (those commanding
the 1st, 5th, and 7th Divisions [2]) of which Napier makes such

---

[1] Espinchel commanded that which went farthest, to the bridge in
front of Santi Espiritus : he says that the whole road was lined with
broken-down carts and carriages, and strewn with dead men. About
100 British stragglers were gathered in.

[2] The tale may be found with details, told from Wellington's point of
view, in *Supplementary Dispatches*, vii. p. 494. The chief offender was
W. Stewart, who had succeeded to the command of the 1st Division on
Paget's capture the preceding day. The others Wellington describes as
' new-comers ' so they must have been Oswald and Lord Dalhousie, for
the other divisional commanders in this column, Clinton and C. Alten,
were not in any sense ' new-comers '. I think, therefore, that Mr. Fortescue
is wrong in giving the names of the culprits as Stewart, Dalhousie, and
Clinton.

scathing notice. Their orders gave an itinerary involving a
march over fords in flooded fields ; they consulted together,
judged the route hopeless, and turned off towards the bridge of
Castillo de Yeltes, which they found blocked by the Army of
Galicia. Wellington, failing to find them on the prescribed path,
set out to seek them, and came upon them waiting miserably
in the mud. He is said to have given them no more rebuke than
a sarcastic ' You see, gentlemen, I know my own business best '
and allowed them to cross after the Spaniards, many hours late[1].
The insubordination was inexcusable—yet perhaps it would
not have been beneath Wellington's dignity to have prefaced
his original order with an explanatory note such as ' the main
road by Castillo bridge being reserved for the Spanish divisions.'
But this would not have been in his normal style. Like Stone-
wall Jackson fifty years after, he was not prone to give his
reasons to subordinates, even when his orders would appear to
them very inexplicable.

On the 19th a march of a few miles brought all the columns
within a short distance of Ciudad Rodrigo, and the commissariat transport having reached that place on the preceding
day, quite unmolested, arrangements had already been made
to send out food to meet the approaching columns. ' About
dusk we took up our ground on the face of the hill near Rodrigo
—the weather now changing to a severe frost was intensely cold.
We had not long been halted when the well-known summons of
" turn out for biscuit " rang in our ears. The strongest went
for it, and received two days' rations for every man. It was
customary to make an orderly division, but that night it was
dispensed with, each man eagerly seized what he could get, and
endeavoured to allay the dreadful gnawing which had tormented
us during four days of unexampled cold and fatigue. In a
short time two more rations were delivered, and the inordinate
eating that ensued threatened to do more mischief than the
former want[2].'

On the 20th the army was distributed in quarters around

<hr/>

[1] See Napier, iv. p. 386. But cf. Fitzroy Somerset's version in Greville
Memoirs, i. pp. 136–7.

[2] Donaldson of the 94th, p. 184. Grattan (p. 315) has a story of a
Connaught Ranger who ate, in addition to his rations, six ox-heads on
six successive days, and died of inflammation of the bowels.

and behind Rodrigo—Hill's column about Martiago, Zamorra, Robledo, Cespedosa, and other villages on the Upper Agueda ; the centre column about Gallegos, Carpio, Pastores, El Bodon, Campillo, and other cantonments well known from the long tarrying of the army there in 1811. The Galicians were left out in the direction of San Felices and the Lower Agueda. Every one was now under cover, and food was abundant—almost too abundant at first. Rest, warmth, and regular rations were indeed necessary. ' Scarcely a man had shoes—not that they had not been properly supplied with them before the retreat began, but the state of the roads had been such that as soon as a shoe fell off or stuck in the mud, in place of picking it up, the man kicked its fellow-companion after it. Yet the infantry was still efficient and fit to do its duty. But the cavalry and artillery were in a wretched state : the batteries of the 3rd, 6th, and 7th Divisions, the heavy cavalry, with the 11th and 12th Light Dragoons were nearly a wreck—the artillery of the 3rd Division lost 70 horses between Salamanca and Rodrigo. . . . The cavalry was half dismounted, the artillery without the proper number of horses to draw the guns, much less the ammunition cars—many died from cold and famine under the harness of the artillery and the saddles of the dragoons. . . . The batteries could with difficulty show three horses in place of eight to a gun [1].'

Stragglers continued to come in for several days. Julian Sanchez was sent out with his lancers to search the woods for them, and brought in 800 mounted on the horses of his men. But when the divisional returns were prepared on November 29th, it was found that besides killed and wounded in action and sick in hospital, there was a melancholy deficit of 4921 ' missing ' since October 23rd. The killed and wounded in action, as opposed to the missing, were very few considering the dangers which the Army had gone through : some 160 at Villadrigo, 440 at Villamuriel and Palencia, 70 at the Puente Larga, 113 at Alba de Tormes, 187 at the combat of the Huebra —smaller fights such as the skirmishes at Tordesillas, Aldea Lengua, and Matilla can hardly account for 200 more between them—the total cannot have exceeded 1,200 casualties in

[1] Grattan, pp. 303 and 305–6.

action. But nearly 5,000 missing was a sad record. How
many of them were dead, how many had deserted, and how
many were prisoners in the hands of the French, it is hard to
determine. The losses in missing before Salamanca had been
insignificant—perhaps 500 in each of the two columns of
Wellington and Hill—there had been many drunkards and
malingerers taken both at Torquemada and at Valdemoro.
But the main loss was suffered between the 16th and the 18th
of November, in the woods and mires between Salamanca and
the Yeltes river. Soult, in his daily letters to King Joseph,
claims to have taken 600 prisoners on the 16th, 1,000 to 1,200
on the 17th, and 100 on the 18th. These figures do not appear
incredible, and would allow in addition for well over a thousand
men dead, and some hundreds of deserters. The latter were
certainly numerous in the foreign corps—the Brunswick-Oels
and Chasseurs Britanniques show losses in ' missing ' out of
proportion to all the other regiments [1]. It is noteworthy, when
comparing the lists of the ' missing ' in the various divisions, to
see that the Portuguese units suffered far more severely in
proportion to their numbers than the British. They showed
the total of 2,469 as against 2,477, but this was out of 22,000
men only, while the similar British figure was out of a total of
32,000 or thereabouts—i. e. their loss was about 10·8 per cent.
as against about 8 per cent. Several observers of the retreat
note that the cold and perpetual rain told much more heavily
upon the stamina of the Portuguese, whose native climate is
far more mild than that of the plateaux of Leon. They simply
sank by the wayside, and died, or suffered themselves to be
taken prisoners without attempting to get away. The unit in
the whole army which suffered most heavily in the way of
' missing ' was Bradford's Portuguese brigade, which lost
514 men out of 1,645. In the Light and 3rd Divisions the
Portuguese battalions were little more than a third of the
British in numbers, but had more missing than their comrades
in the proportion of 168 to 92 in one case and 230 to 184 in
the other. The worst divisional records were those of the 5th

[1] Seventeen of the Chasseurs Britanniques were tried all together for
desertion in October 1812 ! They were mostly Italians. And for one man
recaptured and tried, how many got away safely ?

and 7th Divisions, which lost 800 and 600 men respectively :
the best those of the 1st, 6th, and Light Divisions with only
283, 170, and 255.   Individual British regiments differed much :
the most unsatisfactory figures were those of a battalion which
had only landed at Lisbon that summer, and had not been
present at Salamanca. The 1/82nd distinguished itself by leaving
more drunken stragglers at Valdemoro than any other corps,
and had dropped a terrible proportion of its men between
Salamanca and Rodrigo.   Wellington put the colonel under
arrest, and proposed to try him before a court martial for
' gross neglect of duty,' but in the end did not press matters
to a formal prosecution [1].

For the first few days after the arrival of the army at Ciudad
Rodrigo Wellington was not quite certain that the enemy,
after resting on the Tormes for a few days, might not resume
his advance [2].   This was unlikely, owing to the weather
and the obvious difficulty of finding food for 90,000 men in
a devastated country-side.   Still, it was conceivable, and a
further advance on Soult's part would have been very tiresome,
when the allied troops so much required rest, and when some
dangerous cracks seemed to threaten the stability of parts of
the newly repaired sections of the walls of Ciudad Rodrigo [3].
For six days the army was held together, till on November 26th
arrived certain news that Soult was on his way to the province
of Avila, and that the greater part of the Army of Portugal was
leaving Salamanca for the rear, and distributing itself in its
old cantonments in the direction of Toro and Valladolid [4],
while King Joseph with the Army of the Centre was on his
march for Madrid. Since the French were certainly dispersing,
there was no longer any necessity for keeping the allied army
concentrated.   On the 27th Wellington ordered a general
dislocation of the divisions into winter quarters.   Only the
Light Division and Victor Alten's cavalry remained about

[1] See *Dispatches*, ix. pp. 601–2.

[2] See *Dispatches*, ix. pp. 562 and 570.

[3] See the Life of Burgoyne, who was sent to look after the threatening
symptoms, vol. i. p. 246.

[4] The troops of the Army of Portugal began to march east as early as
November 20, long before Soult got back into touch with them.   Jourdan
to Clarke, from Salamanca, November 20.

Ciudad Rodrigo and Almeida. Of the rest of the army, Hill, with his old corps—the 2nd Division, Hamilton's Portuguese and Erskine's cavalry—marched for Coria and Zarza, being directed to canton themselves in the valley of the Alagon with an advanced post at Bejar. Campbell's Portuguese cavalry went to their old haunts about Elvas in the Alemtejo, and Penne Villemur and Morillo, with the Estremaduran Divisions, returned to their native regions. Castaños and the Galician army retired also to their own province, marching through the Tras-os-Montes by way of Braganza. D'Urban's Portuguese horse were cantoned for the winter north of the Douro, but the rest of the allied cavalry (Bock, Ponsonby, and Anson) were sent far to the rear, to look for comfortable quarters in the Mondego valley and the villages south of Oporto. The remaining British infantry divisions (the 1st, 3rd, 4th, 5th, 6th, and 7th) were distributed about the province of Beira, in various quarters from Lamego to Guarda, at distances of thirty or fifty miles from the frontier [1]. The general disposition of the cantonments of the army was not much different from what it had been in the first days of 1812, before the long eleven months' campaign began. Only Hill was no longer on the Guadiana, but north of the Tagus, since there was no enemy left in Andalusia to require his attention.

While the dispersion was in progress Wellington issued (November 28) the *Memorandum to Officers commanding Divisions and Brigades* which caused so many heart-burnings among his subordinates. It was intended to go no further than those officers ; but some of them dispatched copies to the colonels of the regiments under their charge, and so it became public property. Written in a moment of intense irritation, it contained much rebuke that was merited, but was unjust from the sweeping and general character of the blame that it distri-

---

[1] The 1st Division seems to have been quartered about the upper Mondego between Celorico and Mangualde, the 3rd in villages between Moimenta and Lamego, the 4th about São João de Pesqueira, the 5th, Pack and Bradford, in the direction of Lamego, the 6th and 7th on the lower Mondego and the Alva under the Serra da Estrella, as far as I can make out from regimental diaries. There is no general notice as to cantonments in the *Wellington Dispatches* to help. But see General Orders for December 1, 1812, as to the post-towns for each division.

buted to the whole army, and most certainly failed to take
account of the exceptional conditions of the 15th to the 19th
of November. Wellington wrote :

' I am concerned to have to observe that the army under my
command has fallen off in the respect of discipline in the late
campaign, to a greater degree than any army with which I have
ever served, or of which I have ever read. Yet this army has
met with no disaster : it has suffered no privations which but
trifling attention on the part of the officers could not have
prevented, and for which there existed no reason in the nature
of the service. Nor has it suffered any hardships, excepting
those resulting from the necessity of being exposed to the
inclemencies of the weather at a time when they were most
severe. It must be obvious to every officer that from the
moment the troops commenced their retreat from the neighbourhood of Burgos on the one hand, and of Madrid on the
other, the officers lost all control over their men. Irregularities
and outrages were committed with impunity. Yet the necessity for retreat existing, none was ever made on which the
troops had such short marches ; none on which they made
such long and repeated halts ; and none on which the retreating
army was so little pressed on their rear by the enemy. . . . I
have no hesitation in attributing these evils to the habitual
inattention of the officers of the regiments to their duty, as
prescribed by the standing regulations of the service, and the
orders of this army. . . . The commanding officers of regiments
must enforce the order of the army regarding the constant
inspection and superintendence of the officers over the conduct
of the men in their companies, and they must endeavour to
inspire the non-commissioned officers with a sense of their
situation and authority. By these means the frequent and
discreditable resort to the authority of the Provost, and to
punishments by courts martial, will be prevented, and the
soldiers will not dare to commit the offences and outrages of
which there are so many complaints, when they well know
that their officers and non-commissioned officers have their
eyes on them.

' In regard to the food of the soldier, I have frequently
observed and lamented in the late campaign the facility and

celerity with which the French cooked in comparison with our army. The cause of this disadvantage is the same with that of every other—want of attention of the officers to the orders of the army and the conduct of their men. . . . Generals and field officers must get the captains and subalterns of their regiments to understand and perform the duties required of them, as the only mode by which the discipline and efficiency of the army can be restored and maintained during the next campaign.'

There was undoubtedly much to justify the strong language which Wellington used as to the grievous relaxation of discipline in some of the regiments. Unfortunately he made no exceptions to his general statement, and wrote as if the whole army had been guilty of straggling, drunkenness, and marauding in the same degree. There was not the slightest hint that there were many corps which had gone through the retreat with small loss of men and none of credit. But Wellington had seen with his own eyes the disgraceful scenes at Torquemada, had been roused from his uneasy slumbers by the sound of the pig-shooting on the night of November 17, and he had witnessed the devastation of San Muñoz and other villages by men who were tearing whole houses to pieces to get firewood. He had ordered the Provost-Marshal to hang on the spot two soldiers caught red-handed in plunder, and sent three officers whose men had pulled down cottages, when collecting fuel, to be court-martialled [1]. The figures of the 'missing' in some regiments had rightly provoked his indignation. But he might at the same time have noticed that there were not only battalions but whole brigades where their number was insignificant. In one division of 5,000 men there were but 170—in the five British battalions of the Light Division no more than 96. In both these cases the deficiency represented only weakly men who had fallen by the way from fatigue and disease, and cannot afford any margin for stragglers and marauders.

---

[1] Their cases are in General Orders for 1813, pp. 51–3. Each was condemned to six months' suspension, but the members of the court martial petitioned for their pardon, on account of the privations of the time. Wellington grudgingly granted the request ' not concurring in any way in the opinion of the court, that their cases in any way deserved this indulgence.'

The general feeling in the army was that nearly all the loss and mischief had happened in the inclement days of November 15–18, previous disorders having been comparatively insignificant; and as regards those days they questioned the justice of Wellington's indictment of the troops. To say that ' the army had suffered no privations which but trifling attention on the part of the officers could not have prevented ' was simply not true. What ' trifling attention ' on the part of the regimental officers could have made up for the fact that some divisions had received absolutely no distribution of food of any sort for four continuous days, and others in the same four days nothing but two rations of beef, and no biscuit or other food at all ? [1] It was useless to tell them that they had suffered no privations, or that they could by care have avoided them. As an intelligent general officer wrote on November 20 : ' During the whole of this retreat from the 15th inclusive, not only has the weather been dreadfully severe, but the commissariat arrangements having failed, the troops have been mostly without any issue of rations, and have suffered the extremity of privation, having lived upon acorns and hogs killed occasionally in the woods. The natural result of this has been great disorder and confusion, and the roads in the rear of the columns of march are covered with exhausted stragglers left to the enemy. In fact, by some inconceivable blunder, which the Quartermaster-General's department attribute to that of the Commissary-General, and which the latter throw back on the former, the supplies of the army, which were adequate for much larger numbers, on the morning that we broke up from the Arapiles were sent down the Tormes, by Ledesma toward Almeida, while the army marched on Ciudad Rodrigo—*hinc illae lachrymae* [2].'

There is no doubt that sheer lack of food during inclement weather, and in a desolate and thinly peopled forest-country did most of the mischief. As an indignant subaltern writes :

---

[1] Bunbury, aide-de-camp to General Hamilton, referring to Wellington's memorandum, makes solemn asseveration that his troops got no distribution whatever for those four days. The general himself had no bread. Acorns were the sole diet.

[2] Private and unpublished diary of General D'Urban.

' The officers asked each other, and asked themselves, how or in what manner they were to blame for the privations of the retreat. The answer uniformly was—in no way whatever. Their business was to keep the men together, and if possible to keep up with their men themselves—and this was the most difficult duty—many of these officers were young lads badly .clothed, with scarcely a shoe or a boot left—some attacked with dysentery, others with ague, more with a burning fever raging through their system ; they had scarce strength to hobble along in company with their more hardy comrades, the rank and file [1].'

Wellington's memorandum stated that the marches were short in miles, and this was generally true, though on October 23 the infantry had to do 29 miles. But mileage is not the only thing to be considered in calculating the day's work—the time spent on the miry roads, where every step was ankle deep in slime that tore the shoes from the feet, was inordinate : several of the marches were from 4 o'clock, before dawn, to the same hour in the afternoon. This on an empty stomach and with the regulation 60 lb. of weight on the soldier's back was no mean task. And sometimes the journey ended, as for the Light and 7th Divisions on November 17th, in the troops being deployed in battle order in the drifting rain, and kept for some hours more under arms, to resist a possible advance of the French. The strain was too much for many willing men whose constitution was not over robust. It was not only shirkers who fell out and collapsed.

As to the matter of the cooking, one capable subaltern remarked in his diary, ' if *we* were allowed to tear down doors, &c., in every village, as the enemy do, without having to go miles for wood, we could cook in as short a time as they [2].' And another remarks with justice that when the companies had to prepare their food in the vast Flanders cauldrons, carried on mules which dragged at the tail of the regimental baggage train, they could never be sure of getting them up to their bivouacs in good time. There was an immense improvement in 1813, when light tin camp-kettles carried alternately by the men of each squad, were introduced. These were always at hand, and could be got to boil ' without needing a whole tree

[1] Grattan of the 88th, p. 307.   [2] Tomkinson, p. 227.

or half a church door to warm them.' Wellington might have spared this criticism on his soldiers' cooking when he had already, as his dispatches show, asked for the small kettles to be made, precisely because the cauldrons were too heavy, and seldom got up in good time [1]. He did well to lament the slow cooking, but knowing its cause, and having been in command of the army since April 1809, might he not have indented for portable kettles before May 1812 ?

The real truth with regard to much of the objurgatory language of the 'Memorandum' is that, loth though one may be to confess it, the staff officer—commander-in-chief or whatever his rank—who has slept under cover and had adequate food during such awful days as those of November 15 to November 19, 1812, may easily underrate the privations of the man in the ranks, who has faced the weather unsheltered and with no rations at all. This observation does not in the least affect the points on which Wellington did well to be angry —the disgraceful scenes of drunkenness at Torquemada and Valdemoro, the plundering of villages at more points than one, and the excessive straggling from some ill-commanded battalions. And, as we have had occasion to point out before, there was a residuum of bad soldiers in well-nigh every regiment— Colborne estimates it at 50 or 100 men on the average—and exceptional circumstances like the storm of Badajoz or the hardships of the Salamanca retreat brought this ruffianly element to the surface, and led to deplorable incidents. Presumably many corps got rid of the majority of their *mauvais sujets* by straggling and desertion on those wretched November days upon the Valmusa, the Huebra, and the Yeltes.

Here we may leave the main armies at the end of the campaign. It remains only to speak of Suchet and his opponents on the coast of the Mediterranean. After the departure of Soult and King Joseph from Valencia in the middle of October, it might have been supposed that the Duke of Albufera, now left to his own resources, would have been in some danger. For not only had he in front of him the Anglo-Sicilian troops who had landed under Maitland at Alicante, and his old

---

[1] They had been ordered in May 1812, but had not been distributed by November. See *Dispatches*, ix. p. 603.

adversaries of Joseph O'Donnell's Army, but—since there were now no French left in Andalusia—all the Spanish detachments which had formerly watched the eastern flank of that kingdom were available against him. After Soult had occupied Madrid, Elio, Freire, and Bassecourt all came down to Albacete and Chinchilla, to link themselves with the Alicante troops. Leaving out the Empecinado and Duran, who did not move southward from their mountains on the borders of Aragon and Castile, there were still 25,000 Spanish troops of the 'second' and 'third' armies—the old Valencian and Murcian corps, disposable for use against Suchet in November[1]. And what was still more ominous for the French on the East Coast, a second reinforcement was getting together at Palermo to strengthen the Anglo-Sicilian corps at Alicante. General Campbell with about 4,000 men sailed on November 14th; this force consisted of two British battalions[2], a foreign battalion of light companies, 1,500 Italians, and some miscellaneous details. Though the Italians (as their conduct proved next spring[3]) were eminently untrustworthy material, the rest were an appreciable addition to the strength of the expeditionary force, which was now swelled to an army corps rather than a large division. They only came to hand on December 2, however, and the best opportunity for attacking Suchet had passed before their landing, since obviously he was most vulnerable when all the rest of the French armies had passed on to Salamanca, after November 6th, and before King Joseph had come back to Madrid and Soult to Toledo in the early days of December. The four weeks between those dates, however, were wasted by the British and Spanish generals on the East Coast.

Suchet had recognized his danger, and had taken up a defensive position in front of the Xucar, with Harispe's division at Almanza, Fuente la Higuera, and Moxente, Habert's at Albayda

---

[1] The figures may be found on pp. 170-1 of the Statistical 'Ejércitos Españoles' of 1822, referred to in other places.

[2] See Tables in Appendix. The British battalions were 1/27th and a grenadier battalion formed of companies of the regiments left in Sicily. The light battalion was formed of companies from the 3rd, 7th, 8th Line of the K.G.L. and from de Roll and Dillon. The Italians were '2nd Anglo-Italian Levy'. There was a field battery (British), but only 13 cavalry (20th Light Dragoons).   [3] See p. 279, below.

across the high-road from Valencia to Alicante, and Musnier's in reserve, at Alcira and Xativa. Here he waited on events, having lost touch completely with Soult and the King, from whom he received no dispatch for eighty days after their departure from Albacete and Cuenca in October. It was only by way of Saragossa that he learnt, some weeks later, that they had recaptured Madrid and then marched for the Tormes [1]. He had only 15,000 men in line beyond the Xucar, and knew that in front of him there were 7,000 Anglo-Sicilians, 8,000 of Roche and Whittingham's men, and more than that number of the Murcians, all grouped round Alicante, while Elio, Freire, and Bassecourt, with 8,000 or 9,000 men, were coming in from the direction of Madrid, and Villacampa with 3,000 more might appear from Southern Aragon. This was a formidable combination, though the Spanish troops were badly organized, and had a long record of defeat behind them. The disaster of Castalla had shown a few months before the incapacity of the leaders and the unsteadiness of the men of the Murcian army. Yet the number of troops available was large, and the 5,000 English and German Legionary infantry of the Alicante Army provided a nucleus of trustworthy material, such as in firm hands might have accomplished much.

Unity and continuity of command, however, was completely wanting. On September 25th Maitland had fallen sick, and the charge of the troops at Alicante passed to his second-in-command, General Mackenzie. This officer showed signs of wishing to adopt a timid offensive attitude against Suchet. He pushed his own and Whittingham's divisions out as far as Alcoy, opposite Habert's position at Albayda, and contrived some petty naval demonstration against the Valencian coast. Of these the most important was an expedition which tried on October 5th to capture the town of Denia, the southernmost place in the possession of the French. It was composed of a wing of the 1/81st, and a company each of De Roll's regiment and of marines—about 600 men—under General Donkin. These troops, carried on the *Fame* and *Cephalus*, landed near Denia, and drove the small French garrison into the castle. This was found to be a more formidable work than had been

---

[1] See Suchet, *Mémoires*, ii. p. 269.

M 2

expected, and to require battering by heavy guns. Some
cannons were, with difficulty, landed from the ships, and a siege
would have been commenced but for the news that Habert was
sending up a relieving force. Whereupon the little expedition
re-embarked, men and guns being reshipped with much difficulty under the fire of the French on a rocky beach[1]. The loss
was trifling, but the whole plan was obviously feeble and
useless. To have turned Suchet's sea-ward flank with 5,000
men, while threatening his front with the rest of the British
and Spanish troops available might have been a conceivable
operation. But what could 600 men, entirely isolated, hope to
accomplish ?

It must have been long after this fruitless demonstration that
Mackenzie received a formal order from Wellington dated from
before Burgos on October 13th[2], bidding him attack Valencia,
either by land or by sea, if Soult and King Joseph should have
marched their armies against Madrid. He was instructed not
to accept a general action with Suchet, unless he was very
superior in numbers, and to beware of fighting in ground
favourable to cavalry. His own mounted force consisted only
of 230 sabres[3], and 500 belonging to Whittingham and to the
Murcian army were of doubtful efficiency. But it was thought
that Suchet was very weak, and a little while later Wellington
received false information that the Marshal had lent a considerable part of his army to King Joseph for the march on Madrid[4].
He therefore hoped that a bold advance against Valencia might
shake the hold of the French on the Mediterranean coast.

The letter directed to Mackenzie was received not by him
but by General William Clinton (the brother of H. Clinton of
the 6th Division), who had arrived at Alicante and taken
command—superseding Mackenzie—on October 25th. Lord
William Bentinck had sent him out from Palermo on hearing
of Maitland's illness. The change of generals had no good
results—Clinton fell at once into a fierce quarrel with Cruz the
Spanish governor of Alicante. He opined that he ought not

[1] The best account is in Gildea's *History of the 81st Regiment*, pp. 104–8.
[2] *Dispatches*, ix. p. 487.
[3] 161 of the 20th Light Dragoons, and 71 of the ' Foreign Hussars,' a
newly raised corps, mainly German, which did very creditably in 1813.
[4] Wellington to Lord Bathurst. *Dispatches*, ix. p. 535.

to start to attack Suchet without receiving over control of the Alicante forts, and placing them in the charge of a British garrison. The Governor refused to give up the keys, and much friction ensued, causing an angry interchange of letters which wasted many days. Wellington, when he heard of it, declared that Clinton seemed to have been wholly unreasonable in his demand [1]. Meanwhile Clinton drew in Mackenzie's troops from the front, instead of making an advance toward Valencia. Suchet, hearing that there were no red-coated battalions left opposite Habert, resolved to try the effect of a reconnaissance in force, and moved forward against Roche and Whittingham, who still lay at Alcoy. The English and Spanish divisions at once drew back to Xixona, twenty miles nearer to Alicante. Impressed by this activity on the part of the enemy, Clinton wrote to Wellington that Suchet was too strong to be meddled with, and that he dared attempt no offensive move toward Valencia [2]. Yet counting Roche, Whittingham, and the Murcian troops at Alicante, he must have outnumbered the French by nearly two to one. And on November 22 the Governor of Alicante actually surrendered the keys of the citadel—the point on which Clinton had insisted as the necessary preliminary for active operations.

Nothing had yet been done on the East Coast when on December 2 General Campbell landed at Alicante with the 4,000 Sicilian troops already mentioned a few pages back. He was senior to Clinton, and relieved him of the command. Thus in the 70 days since September 23rd there had been four general officers in successive charge of the force which was intended to keep Suchet in check. It would have been difficult to contrive a more inconvenient arrangement—both Clinton and Campbell were new to the army and the district, and each took many days to make out his situation, and arrive at a conclusion as to what could and what could not be done. Campbell, immediately on his arrival, was solicited by Elio to attack Suchet, in combination with his own army, which should strike in from Albacete on the Marshal's flank. He offered to bring up 10,000 men of his own (Freire, Bassecourt, and Villa-

[1] *Dispatches*, ix. p. 545.

[2] See Wellington to H. Clinton (W. Clinton's brother) on December 9 (*Dispatches*, ix. p. 614), and to Lord Bathurst (ibid., p. 616).

campa) and said—apparently without authorization—that
Del Parque would assist, at the head of the Army of Andalusia.
But Campbell refused to stir, and possibly was right, when
such cases as Barrosa and Talavera are taken into consideration.
Yet Wellington, his commander-in-chief, had ordered the offensive to be taken in no hesitating terms, and the force available
was undoubtedly too large to be wasted. As Wellington himself
remarked, most British generals of that day, though bold enough
in action, and capable of acting as efficient lieutenants, seemed
stricken with a mental paralysis when placed in an independent
position, where the responsibility of taking the initiative was
thrown upon them. It was only exceptional men like Craufurd
and Graham who welcomed it. The general effect of the Anglo-
Sicilian expedition was disappointing in the extreme. Suchet
had thought, and with reason, that it would be ruinous to him,
both in July and again in November. It turned out to be a
negligible quantity in the game, except so far as it prevented
the French Army of Valencia from moving any of its 15,000 men
to co-operate with Soult or King Joseph. Wellington had hoped
for much greater profit from the diversion.

After all, a much larger body of French troops than Suchet's
field force in front of Valencia was being at this time kept
completely employed, by enemies who owned a far less numerous
following than Campbell or Elio. The little Army of Catalonia,
not 8,000 strong, was finding employment all through the
autumn and winter for Decaen's 20,000 men ; and Duran and
Villacampa in Aragon—aided occasionally by Mina from the
side of Navarre, and Sarsfield from the side of Catalonia—were
keeping the strong force under Reille, Severoli, and Caffarelli
in constant movement, and occasionally inflicting severe loss
on its flying columns. Their co-operation in the general cause
was useful and effective—that of the Alicante Army was not.
To sum up all the operations on the eastern side of Spain we
may say that there had been practically no change in the
situation of the adversaries since February. The amount of
territory occupied by the French was unchanged—they had
made no progress in the pacification of Aragon or Catalonia ;
but on the other hand Suchet's hold on Valencia still remained
entirely unshaken.

SECTION XXXIV: CHAPTER VII

CRITICAL SUMMARY OF THE CAMPAIGNS OF 1812

THOUGH Wellington's divisions took up in December 1812 almost the same cantonments that they had occupied in December 1811, ere they marched out at mid-winter to the leaguer of Ciudad Rodrigo, the aspect of affairs in the Peninsula had been completely transformed during the intervening twelve months. It was not merely that Andalusia, Estremadura, and Asturias had been freed from the presence of the French armies, who were never to return. Nor was it merely that— to use Wellington's own words [1]—' we have sent to England little less than 20,000 prisoners,[2] have taken and destroyed, or have now ourselves the use of, the enemy's arsenals in Ciudad Rodrigo, Badajoz, Salamanca, Valladolid, Madrid, Astorga, Seville, and the lines before Cadiz, and upon the whole have taken or destroyed, or now possess, little short of 8,000 pieces of their cannon [3].' Nor was it the all-important thing that the Armies of Portugal, the Centre, and the South, Wellington's immediate enemies, were in November weaker by 30,000 men than they had been in March, and this though they had received 10,000 men in drafts since the summer ended. The fact that really counted was that the whole French system in Spain had been shaken to its foundations. It was useless to pretend any longer that King Joseph was a legitimate sovereign, and the

[1] Wellington to Lord Liverpool, *Dispatches*, ix. p. 573.

[2] These figures seem to represent about 1,400 prisoners at Rodrigo, 4,000 at Badajoz, 300 at the Almaraz forts, 600 at the Salamanca forts, 7,000 at the battle of Salamanca, 2,000 at the Retiro, 1,800 at Astorga, 700 at Guadalajara, with 2,000 more taken in smaller affairs, such as the surrenders of Consuegra and Tordesillas, the combat on the Guarena, the pursuit after Salamanca, and Hill's operations in Estremadura.

[3] This looks a large figure, but over 150 guns were taken at Rodrigo, more than that number at Badajoz, several hundred in the Retiro, and infinite numbers in the Cadiz lines and the arsenal of Seville, not to speak of the captures at Astorga, Guadalajara, Almaraz, and in the field at Salamanca, &c.

Cadiz government a mere knot of rebels driven into their last and remotest place of refuge. The dream of complete conquest, which had lingered on down to the moment of Suchet's capture of Valencia, was gone for ever. The prestige of the French arms was shattered : the confidence of the officers in the marshals, that of the men in their officers, had disappeared. As Foy, the most intelligent of the French observers, sums up the matter, what hope was there for the future when the whole available field force of the French armies of Spain, superior in number by a third to Wellington's army, had been collected on a single field, and had allowed the enemy to march away practically unmolested ? 'Wellington goes off unbeaten, with the glory of his laurels of the Arapiles untarnished, after having restored to the Spaniards all the lands south of the Tagus, after having forced us to destroy our own magazines and fortifications, and deprived us of all the resources that resulted from our former conquests and ought to have secured their retention [1].' There was a profound dissatisfaction throughout the French Army ; and as the winter drew on, and the ill news from Russia began slowly to drift in, it became evident that the old remedy for all ills so often suggested in 1810–11—the personal appearance of the Emperor in Spain with large reinforcements—was never likely to come to pass. Indeed, troops would probably be withdrawn from Spain rather than sent thither, and the extra subsidies in money, for which King Joseph was always clamouring, were never likely to be forthcoming from the Imperial Exchequer.

As to the past campaign, belated recriminations continued to fly about : Clarke—the Minister of War at Paris—was the central point round which they revolved, since it was through him that the reports went to the Emperor from Spain, and to him that the rare answers came back from some Russian bivouac, when the master had a moment's leisure from his own troubles. Generally he wrote in a very discouraging strain : 'vous sentez qu'éloigné comme je suis, je ne puis rien faire pour les armées d'Espagne [2].' His occasional comments were scathing—

[1] Foy, *Vie militaire*, p. 198. Napoleon to Clarke, October 19, 1812.

[2] Report of Colonel Desprez to Joseph of his interview with the Emperor at Moscow on October 19th. *Correspondance du Roi Joseph*, ix. p. 178.

Marmont's reports were all lies, he was to be interrogated in a formal series of questions, as to why he had dared to fight at Salamanca. The quarrels of Joseph and Soult were unworthy of serious attention : 'il ne pouvait pas s'occuper de semblables pauvretés dans un moment où il était à la tête de 500,000 hommes, et faisait des choses immenses.' Considering the way in which Soult had wrecked all the plans of the King and Joseph in June–July, by deliberate disobedience to a long series of orders sent by his hierarchic superior, it was poor comfort to Joseph to be told that he must continue to put up with him. 'Le Maréchal Soult est la seule tête militaire qu'il y eût en Espagne : on ne pouvait l'en retirer sans compromettre l'armée [1].' 'Why had the King ever returned to Spain in 1811 ? ' said the Emperor—though a reference to the correspondence between them in that year tends to show that Joseph had offered to abdicate, or take any other step prescribed to him, and that it was his brother who preferred to keep him at Madrid as a figure-head. Napoleon, it is clear, was vexed at being worried by the affairs of the Peninsula at a moment when he required all his time for the contemplation of his own problems, and discharged his wrath, deserved or undeserved, in all directions. It may be doubted whether he ever thought of himself as perhaps the greatest offender of all ; but it was— as we have already shown at great length [2]—precisely his own elaborate orders which led first to the fall of Ciudad Rodrigo and then to that of Badajoz. But for these initial strokes Wellington's task in the later spring would have been far more difficult. And it is certainly the fact that if Marmont had been allowed to follow his own inspiration in February and March, Badajoz at least might have been saved. As to what followed in June and July, Soult must take the main share of the blame. Wellington's game would have been far harder if the Army of the South had obeyed the King's orders, and come up to the Tagus in June. Soult would have had to evacuate Andalusia, it is true ; but he none the less had to abandon it in the end, and it would have made all the difference in the world to the fate of the campaign if he had come northward while Marmont's Army was still intact, and not after it had received the crushing

---

[1] Ibid., p. 179.   [2] See above, vol. v, pp. 194–5.

blow of July 22nd at Salamanca. No rational student of the
events of that summer can fail to recognize that Jourdan and
the King had found the right conclusion, and issued the right
orders, and that Soult's determination to hang on to Andalusia
till the last moment showed as much mental perversity as
military insubordination. His counter-plan for inducing the
King to come to Seville, abandoning Madrid before Marmont
had even tried the fortune of battle, was simply the wild project
of a viceroy loth to abandon his realm, and convinced that
every one else ought to give way for his own personal profit [1].
To surrender Central and Northern Spain to Wellington, and
to allow all communications between Andalusia and France to
be cut would have been insane. The King would only have
brought 15,000 men with him : Soult could not have added a
greater field force than 25,000 men more—as was repeatedly
shown when he tried to concentrate in Estremadura. Their
joint 40,000 would have neither been enough to face Wellington
nor to threaten Portugal. Meanwhile Spain from the Ebro to
the Sierra Morena would have passed into the hands of the
Allies. It is unnecessary to dilate further on the topic.

A more interesting problem, and one into which Napier
went at great length, is the criticism of the campaigns of 1812
from the other point of view, that of Wellington. It is clear
that there is nothing but praise to be bestowed on the masterly
strategical combination of January and March, which brought
about the captures of Ciudad Rodrigo and Badajoz. Each fell
before a blow delivered at the precise moment when it must be
most effective. The position of the enemy had been carefully
calculated, and every adverse possibility taken into consideration. It is obvious that Rodrigo was doomed without fail from
the first, because Wellington had realized and demonstrated
to himself the inability of the French to hinder his enterprise,
after the Imperial orders had sent Montbrun off to the borders
of Valencia. And Badajoz was destined to fall also, unless
Marmont should help Soult at the earliest possible moment

[1] Napier's statement that Napoleon was thinking of this project when
he declared Soult to be the ' only military head in Spain ' is entirely
unjustified by the context from which he is quoting. The Emperor therein
makes no allusion to the Seville project. See Ducasse's *Correspondance*,
ix. pp. 178–9.

and with the greatest possible force. There was in this case
an adverse chance, though not a very great one : that it never
came near to occurring was due to the Emperor's removal of
Marmont's southern divisions from the Tagus valley. But
even if this fortunate intervention of Napoleon had not simplified the task of the Allied Army, it was still improbable that
Marmont would appear in time; and the improbability had
been ascertained by careful study of the state of the magazines
and the distribution of the cantonments of the Army of Portugal. Soult without Marmont could accomplish nothing, and on
this fact Wellington based his plan. If the Duke of Dalmatia
had brought up 10,000 men more than he actually did, his
advance would still have been insufficient to save Badajoz.

As to the details of the siege of that fortress, we have seen
that things by no means went as Wellington desired. He himself
threw the blame on the want of trained sappers, and the
inexpertness of his engineer officers [1]. The engineers' reply was
that they were directed to work ' against time ', and not given
sufficient days or means to carry out their operations according
to the regular methods of their craft. ' The project of attack
adopted would not stand the test of criticism as a scientific
operation, but possessed merit as a bold experiment to reduce
in an unusually short time a considerable fortress, well armed
and well countermined, by the agency of unskilled sappers,
no miners, and insufficient ordnance [2].' Probably the verdict
of the historian must be that the time-problem was the dominating fact, and that had there been no relieving armies in the
field other methods would have been pursued [3]. It is at least
certain that the rapidity with which the place was taken
disconcerted Soult [4], and upset all the plans of the French in
Spain.

After the fall of Badajoz Wellington had his choice between
the invasion of Andalusia and that of the valley of the Douro.
It can hardly be doubted that he was right in choosing the latter,

[1] See his letter quoted above, vol. v, pp. 255–6.
[2] Jones, *Sieges of the Peninsula*, ii. p. 430.
[3] Jones remarks that ' we had to leave it to the valour of the troops to
surmount intermediate obstacles which in a properly conducted siege
would be removed by art and labour (*Sieges*, i. p. 163).
[4] See above, vol. v, p. 270.

not only on the ground which he himself stated, that Marmont's was the 'operating army'[1] and the more dangerous of the two, but because (as Marmont put it) a disaster in the North would compel the French to evacuate the South, while a disaster in the South would have no such effect in the North. The victory of Salamanca liberated Andalusia and Madrid as well as the Douro valley—a similar victory somewhere in front of Seville would have cleared Andalusia, no doubt, but would not have sufficed to deliver the Castiles and Leon. The Northern operation was the most decisive. The well-timed storm of the Almaraz forts secured for that operation a reasonable amount of time, during which it could not be disturbed by the appearance of reinforcements for the Army of Portugal.

The irruption into Leon in June, for which such careful subsidiary operations had been made on all sides—in Andalusia and Catalonia, on the Bay of Biscay and in Navarre—had at first all the results that could have been expected. But it can hardly be denied that a grave mistake was made when no adequate preparations were made for the siege of the Salamanca forts—and this was a mistake that was to be repeated under very similar circumstances before Burgos in September. There was nothing to prevent a proper battering-train from being brought out from Rodrigo or Almeida. Yet a worse slip, most certainly, was made when on June 21st Wellington refused the battle that Marmont most rashly offered. He could have fought with the advantage of numbers, position, and superiority in cavalry, in a measure that he was not to enjoy again during the Salamanca campaign. Why he held back we now know— he thought (and not without good reason) that if he did not attack Marmont, the presumptuous Marshal would attack him. Such a project indeed was in his adversary's mind, and if it had been carried out the result would undoubtedly have been a second Bussaco. But Marmont hesitated—and was saved for the moment. That he was able to retire with an intact army behind the Douro was a terrible disappointment to Wellington; for, during the deadlock that ensued for nearly three weeks, the French Armies of the North, South, and Centre might have spared reinforcements for the Army of Portugal. Soult's per-

---

[1] See above, vol. v, p. 316.

versity, Caffarelli's want of perception of the relative importance
of things, and King Joseph's tardiness prevented these possible
reinforcements from getting up in time. But this Wellington
could not foresee, and he was under the impression that nothing
was more possible than the arrival of Marmont's expected
succours. If the French should play the right game, Wellington
thought it probable that he might have had to evacuate Salamanca and his other recent conquests, and to retire to the Agueda
and the protection of Ciudad Rodrigo. Fortunately there
turned out to be no necessity for this heart-breaking move.
Marmont came forward on July 15th, without having received
any of the assistance that he had expected from the other armies,
and involved himself in the manœuvres that were to end in
complete disaster. By his first movement, the ingenious demonstration on the side of Toro, ending by the passage of the whole
French army over the Douro at the distant Tordesillas, he
distinctly scored a point over his adversary. Wellington was
only prepared to fight a defensive battle at this moment ; and
when the Duke of Ragusa refused, on the Guarena (July 18),
to indulge him in such a fashion, and continued to turn his
right flank on several successive days, he always gave back,
awaiting an opportunity that seemed never about to arrive.
The head-quarters staff of the allied army marvelled at their
leader's caution, on the days (July 19–20) when the two armies
were executing their parallel marches about Vallesa and Cantalapiedra. At any moment a battle on equal terms could have
been brought about, but it was refused. Yet Wellington had
recently acquired the knowledge that King Joseph was just
starting from Madrid to join Marmont with 15,000 men ; and
a victory over the Army of Portugal before it should be reinforced was the only way out of the dangerous situation. He
would not commit himself to the chance of an offensive battle,
and—as his dispatches show—made up his mind to abandon
Salamanca and fall back upon the Agueda, unless his adversary
should oblige him by making some obvious blunder.

The psychology of the moment—as has been shown above—
was that he considered that an indecisive victory, entailing
heavy loss in his own ranks, would have availed him little.
Unless he could put Marmont completely out of action by a

very crushing blow, the Marshal would be joined by the Army of the Centre and other reinforcements, and would still be able to make head against him. At the bottom of his mind, it is clear, lay the consideration that he had in his hands the only field-army that Great Britain possessed, that in risking it he would risk everything—even the loss of Portugal,—and that the total force of the French in the Peninsula was so great that he must not fight save at a marked advantage. His own 50,000 men were the sole hope of the allied cause—Marmont's Army was but one of several bodies whose existence he had to bear in mind. As long as he kept his army intact, the enemy could do no more than push him back to the Agueda : when they had got him thus far, they would have to disperse again, for they could not feed on the country-side, nor invade Portugal with less than 100,000 men. But if he were to wreck his army by suffering a check, or even by winning a bloody and indecisive success, he could not calculate where his retreat might end, or how great the disaster might be.

Wellington's caution was rewarded on the 22nd July, when his adversary at last fell into reckless over-confidence, and invited defeat, by stringing out his army along an arc of six miles opposite the strong and concentrated line of the Allies. The punishment was prompt and crushing—the sudden advance of Wellington was a beautiful piece of tactics, ' a battle in the style of Frederic the Great ' as the sagacious Foy observed, in a fit of enthusiasm wherein the admiration of the skilled soldier prevailed over the national pride of the Frenchman. Marmont's host was not merely beaten, but scattered and demoralized : it was put out of action for some time, and if Carlos de España had only maintained the castle of Alba de Tormes there would have been nothing left worth mentioning of the Army of Portugal. Even as things actually fell out, the victory was absolutely complete, and placed all the valley of the Douro and Central Spain in Wellington's hands.

After Salamanca he had it in his power to choose between thrusting Clausel and the battered Army of Portugal behind the Ebro, and marching on Madrid to deal with King Joseph and Soult. His choice of the second alternative has often been criticized, and ascribed to motives which were far from his mind. The real cause of his turn to the South was his belief that Soult must now evacuate Andalusia, and that he would therefore have all his army concentrated, and no longer frittered away in garrisons, as it had been for the last two years. Instead of being able to collect 25,000 men only for the field, the Duke of Dalmatia would have 50,000 available, and when joined by the King and perhaps by Suchet, he would need to be faced by the whole allied army. Wellington therefore intended that Hill should join him ; together they could deal with the largest block of French troops still left in the Peninsula. His intention was to force matters to a decision in the South, and he thought it likely that he might find Soult already marching upon Toledo with his whole army. In this expectation he was entirely disappointed ; the Marshal—as we have seen—refused for a month to evacuate his viceroyalty, and stayed there so long that Wellington began to think that he would have to go down to Andalusia to evict him. ' I suspect,' he wrote at last on August 18, ' that he will not stir, till I force him out, by a direct movement upon him, and I think of making that movement as soon as I can take the troops to the South without injuring their health.'

This was an unexpected development : ' any other but a modern French Army would now leave the province (Andalusia), as they have absolutely no communication of any kind with France, or with any other French army, and are pressed on all sides,' wrote Wellington. Yet Soult lingered, and meanwhile the Army of Portugal, rallied in a shorter time than could have been expected, returned to Valladolid, and assumed the offensive in the valley of the Douro. The trouble in that direction became so acute that Wellington resolved to march against Clausel, with a force sufficient to drive him back to the Ebro, intending afterwards to return to Madrid to pick up the other half of his own army, to join with Hill, and then to deal with Soult, whose tardy resolve to evacuate Andalusia was only just becoming evident.

The march against Clausel was necessary ; and it seems a misfortune that Wellington left three of his best divisions at Madrid—which was obviously in no danger for the present, and where Hill was expected to arrive ere long. It turned out that the force put in motion against Valladolid and Burgos was too small—even after it had been joined by Clinton and the Galicians—to secure the complete predominance in the North which was necessary. Clausel retreated, but was pursued in a somewhat cautious fashion, and only as far as Burgos. It would appear that if Wellington had brought 10,000 men more with him from Madrid, and if he had invested Burgos with the Galician Army, and followed hard upon Clausel with all his Anglo-Portuguese, he might have driven the French not only beyond the Ebro, but as much farther as he pleased. For Clausel could not have stood for a moment if Wellington's power had been a little greater, and Caffarelli was in September so entirely taken up with the operations of Home Popham, Mina, and Mendizabal that he had not a man to spare.

But Wellington advanced no farther than Burgos, and allowed Clausel to lie opposite him at Briviesca unmolested, till he had drawn great reinforcements from France, and had at last induced Caffarelli to come to his aid with 10,000 men. Meanwhile, he was devoting himself to the siege of Burgos, where, by his own fault, he had no sufficient artillery resources to subdue an improvised fortress of the third class. The fault was exactly the same as that which had been committed before the Salamanca Forts in June. And—as has been demonstrated above—Wellington had been pressed to take more heavy guns with him, both by Sir Home Popham and by officers at Madrid. And if he had called for them, even after the siege began, they could have reached him in time. His own curious comments on the facts are not convincing :

' I see that a disposition exists to blame the Government for the failure of the siege of Burgos. The Government had nothing to say to the siege : it was entirely my own act. In regard to means, there were ample means, both at Madrid and at Santander, for the siege of the strongest fortress. That which was wanting at both places was the means of transporting ordnance and military stores. . . . I could not find means for moving even one gun from Madrid. Popham is a gentleman who picques himself on overcoming all difficulties. He knows the time it took to find transport even for about 100 barrels of powder and a few hundred thousand rounds of musket ammuni-

tion that he sent me. As for the two guns that he endeavoured
to send me, I was obliged to send my own cattle to draw them,
and felt great inconvenience from the want of those cattle in
subsequent movements of the Army [1].'

The answer that must be made to these allegations is that
when matters came to a crisis at Madrid, on Soult's approach,
enough transport was found there to send off to Ciudad Rodrigo
great part of the Retiro stores—though much of the material
there had to be blown up. If there were not draught animals
for even half a dozen guns to be got at Madrid, why did Wellington write on August 31st that ' if the enemy shall advance, all
arrangements must be made for the evacuation of Madrid, such
as sending away sick, *stores*, &c., and eventually for the destruction of what cannot be carried off [2].' Considerable convoys
marched with Hill when the Spanish capital was evacuated,
and it is impossible to believe that the 322 draught mules
which, by Dickson's estimate, were the proper allowance for
a 24-pound battery of six guns with 180 rounds per gun, could
not have been procured at Madrid in September. A requisition
on the batteries and transport train of the four divisions left
round Madrid could have been made to supplement local
resources. But Wellington had made up his mind to risk the
Burgos campaign with no more than Dickson's trifling ' artillery
reserve '—of which the only efficient part was precisely three
iron 18-pounders. As to the allusions to Home Popham,
they must—with all regret—be described as ungrateful. And
they conceal the fact that the two heavy ship-guns which
Popham had sent forward were only brought *from Reynosa* by
Wellington's own draught beasts. Popham got them across
the mountains from Santander by his own exertions, and would
have sent them some weeks earlier but for Wellington's refusal
to ask for them. And it was the ammunition sent by Popham
which alone enabled the siege to go on for as long as it did.

The calculations—miscalculations rather—which kept the
main Army in front of Burgos to such a late day in the season
as October 20th, have been dealt with in a previous chapter.
The united force of Souham and Caffarelli was undervalued ;

---

[1] Wellington to Lord Liverpool, *Dispatches*, ix. p. 574.
[2] Memorandum for Baron Alten, Madrid, 31st August 1812.

it was not till Wellington saw their two armies deployed that he recognized that they had 20,000 men more in hand than he had supposed. And on the other front he relied too much on the strength of the line of the Tagus for defence. We must concede that if the weather had been the same in New Castile as it was in Wellington's own region, if the Tagus had been in flood like the Arlanzon and the Pisuerga, and the desperate rains that prevailed at Burgos had prevailed also at Toledo and Aranjuez, his plan would probably have been successful. But who dares make the weather a fixed point in military calculations ? The season disappointed him, and Soult was lucky enough to find bright days and hard roads and streams half dry as he advanced on Madrid [1], though Wellington was almost embogged and moved among perpetual fogs in the North.

Still, the cardinal fact at the bottom of the unfortunate Burgos campaign was that the Anglo-Portuguese Army was not strong enough for the task in hand, when Soult's whole force, and great part of the Army of the North also, came into the field to aid the armies of Portugal and the Centre. The permanent evacuation of Andalusia and the temporary evacuation of Biscay put into movement 60,000 men who had hitherto been for the most part locked up in the occupation of those regions. When they became an 'operating army' Wellington was hopelessly outnumbered. He himself thought that he might yet have pulled through the crisis, without being compelled to evacuate Madrid and the two Castiles, if only Ballasteros had obeyed orders, and distracted Soult by an irruption into La Mancha against the flank of the advancing enemy. Undoubtedly that General was most perverse and disloyal ; but it seems quite possible that if he had advanced, as ordered, he would only have let himself in for one of those crushing defeats which commanders of his type so often suffered during the war. The fact was that the French armies, when once concentrated, were too numerous to be held in check. Wellington's only real chance of success would have been to concentrate every man either against Souham and Caffarelli on the one side, or against Soult and the King on the other. This was made

[1] The bad weather on the Tagus only began October 30th.

difficult by the initial division of his army into two nearly equal halves—which resulted in his own force being too weak to deal with the French Northern Army, and Hill's similarly too weak to deal with the Southern Army. He had intended, when he left Madrid on August 31st, to return thither with the bulk of his marching force, after disposing of the northern enemy, and (as we have seen) this idea was still in his head even as late as early October. But he failed to carry out his intention, partly because he had allowed himself to get entangled in the siege of Burgos, partly because the French army in front of him proved much stronger than he had originally calculated.

The only occasion on which it was actually in his power for a few days to combine Hill's force and his own for a blow at one of the two hostile armies, while the other was still far off, was on the 3rd–5th of November. He saw the chance, but deliberately refused to take it, for reasons which we have seen set forth [1], and which were perfectly convincing. If he had concentrated against either of the French armies, it might have refused to fight and drawn back, while the other was in a position to cut off his line of communication with Salamanca and Portugal.

He resolved, and at this moment the resolve was wise, not to attempt any such blow, but to fall back on the well-known and formidable positions round Salamanca. Here he thought that he could defend the line of the Tormes, even against a combined force that outnumbered him by 25,000 men. Probably he would have succeeded if the enemy had delivered a frontal attack, as Jourdan and the majority of the French generals desired. But Soult's safe but indecisive policy of refusing to make such an attack, and turning the Allied flank by the fords of the upper Tormes, was adopted. The only counter to this move would have been to assail the French while they were in the midst of their manœuvre, even as Marmont had been assailed at the battle of the Arapiles. But the disparity of numbers was on this occasion too great for such a stroke to be prudent, and Wellington was forced, most unwillingly, to retreat to the frontier of Portugal.

[1] See above, pp. 112–13.

N 2

But for two mishaps—the coming on of absolutely abominable weather and the misdirection of the food-supplies by Colonel Gordon—this retreat would have been uneventful, and would have been attended with little or no loss. For the French pursuit was timid and ineffective, and only carried out by a fraction of the enemy's army—nearly half of it halted at Salamanca, and the remaining part was not strong enough to attack Wellington. As it chanced, Gordon's errors and the plague of immoderate rains not only cost Wellington several thousand men, but produced an impression of disaster both on the minds of those who took part in the miserable march and on those of the captious critics in London. What should have been ' a good clean retreat ' became a rather disastrous affair. But this was not due to the enemy, and the French observers got small comfort from it—as we have already shown by quoting Foy's perspicuous and angry comments on the operations around Salamanca [1]. Wellington got off with ' an army in being,' and if it was tired out, so was that of his opponents. A hundred thousand men had been scraped together from every corner of the Peninsula to overwhelm him, but had failed to do so. Meanwhile he had cleared all Spain south of the Tagus valley from the enemy, had broken their prestige, and had shaken to pieces the pretension of King Joseph to be taken seriously as the monarch of the greatest vassal-kingdom of his brother's empire.

[1] See above, p. 142.

SECTION XXXV

CHAPTER I

WINTER QUARTERS. DECEMBER 1812—JANUARY 1813

WHEN the Anglo-Portuguese Army halted at Ciudad Rodrigo, and came back once more to regular rations and marches that were no longer forced, it was of course in very bad condition. The cold and wet of the last ten days' retreat from Salamanca had caused many a man to drop dead by the way, and had sent thousands of sick to the hospitals, riddled with dysentery and rheumatism. And the hospitals and dépôts were even before this last influx loaded up with convalescents not fit for service, from the casualties of Salamanca and Burgos. The December morning states were enough to fill Wellington with dismay; of his 64 [1] British battalions there were only 30,397 men present with the colours—an average of much less than 500 bayonets to the battalion. There were no less than 18,000 men in hospital—more than a third of the total strength of the infantry arm. Thirteen regiments had more men 'sick' than 'effective'; twelve were down to under 300 strong [2]. The cavalry had not lost so many in proportion—they had 5,700 present under arms to 1,436 sick, but could not mount more than 5,000, owing to the loss of horses during the retreat, and the surviving horses were for the most part in bad condition.

The first thing necessary was to get the troops under cover and well fed: a very long rest was obviously necessary to allow the wayworn and exhausted men time to recover their strength,

---

[1] Not including 2/59th at Cadiz, but including the 1/6th, 20th, and 91st which only landed in November, and the battalions of the 1st Foot Guards which had only just joined during the Burgos retreat.

[2] The Portuguese infantry had suffered quite as heavily—cold being very trying to them, though summer heat affected them less than the British. The 20th Portuguese, starting on the retreat from Madrid with 900 men, only brought 350 to Rodrigo.

and the convalescents to rejoin from the hospitals. With the winter drafts known to be ready and starting from England, to the number of some 5,000 [1], beside one or two more complete battalions promised for the Peninsula, there might be an army in April 1813 no less strong than that which had opened the campaign of 1812. But clearly the only movement to be thought of at present was that of getting the divisions into comfortable winter quarters. Accordingly the army broke up a few days after reaching Ciudad Rodrigo, and spread itself out in dispositions not unlike those of the December previous, save that nothing was left so far to the South as had been the custom in other years. For Soult was no longer in Andalusia, and the right wing of the Allied army had no reason to descend as far as the Guadiana.

By December the 1st Division had distributed itself on the upper Mondego around Guarda and Vizeu [2]; the 3rd Division was farther north, about Moimento de Beira; the 4th, with head-quarters at S. João de Pesquiera, occupied cantonments along the Douro; the 5th was a little lower down the same river in Lamego and the neighbouring villages. The 6th Division lay somewhat farther back on the northern slope of the Serra de Estrella, along the high road parallel with the middle Mondego, with head-quarters at Cea; the 7th at Moimento da Serra and Santa Marinha, also under the Estrella. Pack's and Bradford's Portuguese went north of the Douro, to Penafiel and Villa Real respectively. Only the much-enduring Light Division was left in rather cold and bare quarters on the frontier, occupying familiar billets at Fuentes de Oñoro, Alameda, Gallegos, and other villages between the Coa and the Agueda. The cavalry was all sent back to the rear, even so far as the coast-plain at the mouths of the Vouga and the Mondego, save V. Alten's brigade, which remained on the Agueda in company with the Light Division, and D'Urban's Portuguese, who went back to Braganza, in the far north-east of the Tras-os-Montes, on the Spanish frontier. Any observer noting these dispositions as

---

[1] 4,400 for the infantry, 350 for cavalry, plus drafts for artillery, &c.

[2] Where the new Second Guards Brigade had a dreadful epidemic of fever and dysentery, and buried 700 men. It was so thinned that it could not march even in May, and missed the Vittoria campaign.

a whole could not but conclude that they were most easily explained by an intention to resume in the next spring the old line of the Allied advance of 1812; since all the British troops were conveniently placed for a concentration on the Agueda, and a march on Salamanca. The fact that the three small Portuguese units had been sent north of the Douro would attract little attention. And this no doubt was the impression which Wellington wished to produce on any secret agents of the French who might report the location of his winter quarters.

Meanwhile, as in earlier years, Hill took the old Army of Estremadura, the British 2nd Division, Hamilton's Portuguese division, and Erskine's two cavalry brigades, back to the South, but only as far as the Tagus and the Alagon, not to the Guadiana. He fixed his head-quarters at Coria, and distributed the brigades of the 2nd Division in the mountain villages above, covering the great passes of the Sierra de Francia and the Sierra de Gata, the Puerto de Baños and the Puerto de Perales[1]. Hamilton's division lay inside its own country, at Moraleja, Idanha, and Penamacor. The cavalry head-quarters were at Brozas in the valley of the Tagus, near Alcantara and its Roman bridge. Here Erskine, the cavalry divisional general, committed suicide by jumping out of a high window in a state of frenzy. Wellington had long wanted to get rid of him—though not in this sad way—and for good reason, as is explained by several incidents of 1811 and 1812 which have been noticed in previous volumes. Yet he had never been able to obtain his departure—political influences at home stood in the way. Erskine being thus removed, the Commander-in-Chief at once dissolved the 2nd Cavalry Division, and its two British brigades (Long's and Fane's) ceased to have any other connexion with each other, beyond that of being both attached to Hill's Corps.

The disposition for Hill's winter quarters was obviously intended not merely to cover the great passes between the valleys of the Douro and the Tagus, but also to give the enemy cause to think that Wellington might some day attack on the southern front, either by a sudden advance up the Tagus on

---

[1] Brigades were not always kept together, the regiments being a little scattered. Individual battalions were in Baños, Bejar, Bohoyo, Monte-hermoso, &c.

Talavera and Madrid, or by a blow at Avila across the Puente de Congosto defile. Either operation would be equally possible to a force based on Coria. And repeatedly during the spring rumours ran through the French lines that Hill had advanced to Plasencia or the bridge of Almaraz.

Behind the long front that lay between D'Urban's horse at Braganza and Erskine's horse at Brozas, the British army settled down for a very protracted period of rest and reorganization—it was to be much longer than Wellington had intended, owing to unforeseen chances. The Spanish auxiliary forces which had marched with the Allies in the autumn also dispersed : Castaños led the Army of Galicia back from the Agueda to its own country, by a long march through the Tras-os-Montes. Carlos de España put part of his division as a garrison in Ciudad Rodrigo, and lay with the rest in the mountain villages of the Sierra de Francia. Morillo, sticking close to Hill's side, as he had done all through 1812, went back with him to the South, and wintered once more in Estremadura, at Caçeres and the neighbouring places.

On the other side, King Joseph and Marshal Soult had also to place their armies—as worn out as were those of their enemy—in winter quarters. And the choice of theirs was a much more difficult problem than that which lay before Wellington, since King Joseph had to settle not only a military but a political problem. The whole fabric of the French occupation of Spain had been dashed to pieces in the preceding summer by the loss of Andalusia, the temporary occupation of Madrid by the Allies, and the advance of the Anglo-Portuguese Army as far as Burgos. It had now to be reconstructed—but on what lines ? There was clearly no possibility of reoccupying Andalusia or Estremadura : to do so would have involved a winter campaign—which was unthinkable—and an intolerable dispersion of the army which had been collected with so much difficulty for the repression of Wellington. The real alternatives possible were either (1) to reconstruct King Joseph's Spanish kingdom, as it had existed in the spring of 1812, minus Andalusia, making Madrid the political capital and the military base of operations, or (2) to recognize that the total strength of the French armies no longer sufficed for such an ambitious scheme, and to occupy in strength only Old Castile and Leon, with the provinces beyond the Ebro, making Valladolid both the political and the military centre of operations, and abandoning Madrid altogether, or only holding it as an advanced post towards the south, on the extreme limit of French occupation.

After much debate Joseph and Jourdan chose the former plan, influenced mainly, as the Marshal writes in his Memoirs, by the fact that to give up Madrid as the capital, and to remove to Valladolid, would be a death-blow to the prestige of the Franco-Spanish monarchy. It would matter little whether Madrid were actually abandoned, or held as a precarious outpost : in either case Joseph could no longer pretend to be King of Spain [1]. In addition it must be remembered that to give up New Castile and La Mancha would leave Suchet in a position of isolation at Valencia, far too much advanced, and quite out of touch with the other armies, and also that from the administrative point of view Joseph had always regarded the revenues which he drew from Madrid and New Castile as the only solid part of his very modest and irregular budget. That a great error of choice was made is undoubted ; but its ruinous nature was only to be revealed by circumstances which the King and the Marshal could not possibly have foreseen on November 20, 1812. When they made their decision neither they nor any one at Paris, or elsewhere in Western Europe, had a notion of the awful *débâcle* which was in progress in Russia. Napoleon had evacuated Moscow a month back ; he was now in disastrous retreat from Smolensk toward the Berezina, with an army that was already crumbling under his hands. But that the whole of it was destined to perish during the next few days, and that France was to be left unguarded by any *Grande Armée* when the new year came, seemed an incredible contingency. Joseph and Jourdan expected to draw from the Emperor drafts and reinforcements in 1813, as they had even in 1812. If they had guessed that, instead, he would be drawing drafts and reinforcements from them, they would have adopted a different policy. But the celebrated ' 29th Bulletin ' was published in Paris only on December 3rd, and did not get to Madrid till January 6th,[2]

---

[1] Jourdan, *Memoirs*, p. 449.
[2] See *Correspondance du Roi Joseph*, ix. p. 402.

and even that dismal document did not reveal the full extent of the ruin. It was not, indeed, till private letters from survivors of the Moscow retreat began to drift in, three weeks later, that the French head-quarters in Spain realized what the month of November had meant in Russia.

It was quite natural, then, that King Joseph should have made up his mind, at the end of the Burgos retreat, that he would occupy so much of the regained regions as was possible, and would make Madrid once more his residence and the centre of his operations. He was right in believing that he had at least four months before him for reorganization and reconstruction : Wellington was too hard hit to be able to move before April at the earliest.

It was some weeks before the King was able to spread the three French armies in the final positions which he had chosen for them. He left Salamanca himself at the head of his Guard on November 23rd, and moved on Madrid by way of Peñaranda, Arevalo and the Guadarrama Pass. He reached the capital on December 2nd, to find that it had been occupied a few days after he had left it on his march to Salamanca by the Empecinado and his *partida* [1]. The guerrillero chief had administered the city with the aid of an extemporized junta for more than three weeks [2]. On the approach of the King he retired, taking with him some citizens who had compromised themselves in the patriotic cause. Joseph, however, showed himself particularly gracious on his return, and endeavoured to produce an impression of the restored solidity of his régime, by holding court functions, reopening the theatres, and visiting hospitals and public institutions. The demonstration had little effect, all the more because it was accompanied by increased market-dues and the collection of arrears of taxation. It was impossible to persuade the Madrileños that the King's return was for good, and confidence in his power was never restored.

[1] For a curious narrative of adventures in Madrid, November 4–10, by a party of English prisoners who escaped in the confusion that followed the outmarch of the French, see the Memoirs of Captain Harley of the 47th, ii. pp. 42–50.

[2] Fortunately for themselves most of King Joseph's Spanish partisans, who fled from Madrid in July to Valencia, were still under Suchet's charge and had not returned, or their lot would have been a hard one.

Meanwhile the Army of the Centre reoccupied the provinces of Segovia and Guadalajara with the northern part of that of Toledo. While crossing the Guadarrama a few days after the King, its leading division was caught in a blizzard similar to that which, on the same spot, had impeded Napoleon on December 22nd, 1808, and lost a hundred men frozen or buried in the snow [1]. Soult was directed to place his head-quarters at Toledo, and to occupy that province and Avila, with so much of La Mancha as he thought proper. The Army of Portugal was allotted the provinces of Zamora, Leon, Salamanca, Palencia, and Valladolid, with head-quarters at the last-named city. The front towards Portugal and Galicia was held by one division at Leon, another at Zamora, and two at Salamanca, the rest of the eight divisions of this army being écheloned in reserve at various points in Old Castile. But at the end of December the King determined that there must be a shifting of cantonments, in order to tighten up his connexion with Suchet at Valencia. He ordered Soult to send a division to Cuenca, as a half-way house to the East Coast. To enable him to spare these troops he was relieved of the charge of the province of Avila, which was taken over by Foy, with the 1st Division of the Army of Portugal.

The extent of the French occupation in central and northern Spain at the commencement of the new year, 1813, may best be defined by a list of the Divisional head-quarters of the armies, which were, on January 15, Army of the South, 1st Division (Leval), Toledo [2]; 3rd Division (Villatte), Talavera; 4th Division (Conroux), Madridejos; 5th Division (Pécheux), Daymiel in La Mancha; 6th Division (Daricau), San Clemente in the province of Cuenca. Of the cavalry Pierre Soult's light horse and Digeon's dragoons were in a forward position in La Mancha, Tilly's dragoons in reserve at Toledo. The effective total of Soult's army was on this day 36,000 officers and men effective, beside men in hospital or detached.

Of the Army of the Centre, Darmagnac's Division, as also the Royal Guard, was at Madrid, Cassagne's Division at Arganda

---

[1] *Miot de Melito*, iii. p. 258.

[2] The 2nd Division (see above, p. 90) had been taken from Soult and lent to the Army of the Centre during the operation of November. It was never given back.

(twenty miles farther east), the Franco-Spanish Division of Casapalacios at Segovia, the cavalry dispersed at various points in a circle round Madrid. This army had just lost Palombini's Italian Division, which had served with it during the autumn campaign of 1812. It was on its way to Burgos, to join the Army of the North, to which it properly belonged. With this deduction the Army of the Centre had still 12,000 French troops, plus Joseph's Guards and Spaniards, who must have made up at least 5,000 more.

The Army of Portugal was much more widely dispersed. It showed the 1st Division (Foy) at Avila, 2nd Division (Barbot) at Valladolid, 3rd Division (Sarrut) at Leon, 4th Division (Fririon) at Saldaña, 5th Division (Maucune) and 8th Division (Chauvel) at Salamanca, with detachments at Ledesma and Zamora. The 6th and 7th Divisions, both weak, were in process of being cut up to strengthen the others, as will be explained later, when reorganization is in question. Of the two cavalry divisions of the Army of Portugal both Boyer's dragoons, with head-quarters at Mayorga, and Curto's light horse, with head-quarters at Medina de Rio Seco, were keeping a line of advanced posts on the Esla, to watch the Spanish army of Galicia. The total effective strength, omitting sick, was 42,000 men.

The three armies had thus about 95,000 men under arms to cover the enormous block of territory which they occupied. The distance from Salamanca to San Clemente is 250 miles ; that from Leon to Daymiel 280 miles. It is clear that a concentration on Madrid or Valladolid would be comparatively easy. On the other hand there would be an intolerable distance for the Army of the South to cover, if Salamanca were the point chosen by an enemy for assault, or for the remoter divisions of the Army of Portugal to traverse, if Talavera were selected. But, as was obvious, there was no chance of any such blow being delivered at present, since Wellington could not possibly stir till the spring, while the Spanish regular forces in Andalusia and Murcia were negligible quantities until the Anglo-Portuguese army should be able to move.

All round the position of the French there was at this moment a broad ' no man's land '; for their farthest outposts were nowhere in direct touch with the enemy, but separated from

him by many miles of unoccupied ground, in which neither
party kept permanent posts. Between Astorga—the farthest
advanced post of the Galicians—and the line of the Esla,
between Salamanca and Ciudad Rodrigo, between Avila and
Bejar, between Talavera and Coria, between Daymiel and
San Clemente and the northern foothills of the Sierra Morena,
this broad debatable land was in possession neither of the
French nor of the regular armies of their enemy, but of the
guerrillero bands, under a score of leaders small and great.
And the difficulty of the situation for King Joseph was that,
while Wellington and Castaños and Del Parque and Elio were
quiet perforce at midwinter, the guerrilleros were not. Having
ample spaces of unoccupied border, in which they could take
refuge when pursued, and many mountain recesses, even within
the zone of French occupation, where they could lie safe against
anything less than a considerable flying column, they seemed
to defy extermination. Even in King Joseph's most prosperous
days, when the final triumph of the French seemed probable,
there had always been guerrilleros; but since Wellington's
march to Madrid and Soult's evacuation of Andalusia, it no
longer looked as if the national cause was hopeless. To collect
the army which drove Wellington back to Portugal in November
every district in Spain, from Biscay to La Mancha, had been
stripped for a time of its army of occupation. Regions long
tamed had been out of hand for four or five months, enjoying
an unruly and uncomfortable freedom, in which local juntas
and guerrillero chiefs, who took the pose of military governors,
contended for authority. And when the French came back
they found that their old prestige was gone and that it could
only be restored, if it could be restored at all, by ceaseless acts
of repression of the most drastic sort. For if any town or village
showed any signs of willing submission, the guerrilleros descended
upon it when its garrison was absent, and hung or arrested
' Afrancesados ' : while if the population (as was more usual)
showed ill-will and offered passive resistance, the French
imprisoned or shot the magistrates, and imposed heavy fines
for disloyalty [1].

[1] A good picture of the state of Central Spain in January and February
1813 may be got from the Memoirs of d'Espinchel, of the 2nd Hussars, an

But while the whole of northern and central Spain was full of punitory raids and executions, there was one region where the trouble passed the limit of unrest, and could only be called insurrection, where the French garrisons were practically blockaded in their cantonments, and where the open country was completely out of hand. This was the sub-Pyrenean district comprising Navarre, the three Basque provinces, and the mountainous lands between Santander and Burgos. And from the strategical point of view this was the most important tract in all Spain, since the main communication with France lay through its midst, by the great road from Madrid to Bayonne through Valladolid, Vittoria, and Tolosa. We have seen in earlier pages that trouble had been endemic in these lands ever since Mina's appearance in 1810, and the permanent establishment of those active partisans, Porlier and Longa, on the Cantabrian coast-line. The creation of Reille's ' Army of the Ebro ' in 1811 for the special purpose of making an end of the northern bands had failed in its purpose. But things only came to a crisis in the summer of 1812, when Sir Home Popham's operations on the Biscay coast cleared the French out of most of the smaller ports, and gave the insurgents for the first time free communication with the sea, and the inexhaustible supplies of Britain. We have seen in the last volume [1] how the co-operation of Caffarelli with Marmont in the Salamanca campaign was completely prevented by this diversion, how Longa and Mendizabal retook Santander and for a space Bilbao, and how Mina held the Governor of Pampeluna blockaded in the strongest fortress of northern Spain. Caffarelli had recovered Bilbao in August ; but when Wellington marched on Burgos in September, and the Army of the North was compelled to abandon all other operations, in order to succour the retreating Army of Portugal, the capital of Biscay and all the surrounding district passed back into the power of the Spaniards. In the whole region nothing remained in the hands of the French save the

officer charged with the raising of contributions in La Mancha—a melancholy record of violence and treachery, assassination by guerrilleros and reprisals by the French, of villages plundered and magistrates shot. D'Espinchel had mainly to deal with the bands of El Medico and the Empecinado. See his *Souvenirs militaires*, pp. 86–110.

[1] Vide v. pp. 550–8.

ports of Santoña, Guetaria, and San Sebastian, and a line of fortified posts along the high road from the Bidassoa to the Ebro. And in Navarre Mina held full possession of the open country, raised the taxes, established courts of justice, and (what appears more strange) set up custom-houses on the French frontier, at which he allowed non-military goods to pass into Spain on the payment of regular dues [1]. He had raised his original *partida* to a strength of nine battalions of infantry and two regiments of cavalry, possessed cannon, and had a munition factory working at the head of the Pyrenean valley of Roncal.

Before Wellington commenced his retreat from the Douro to the Portuguese frontier, or the armies of Soult and of Souham had joined, to bring their overpowering force against the Anglo-Portuguese, Souham, as we have already seen, had released the troops of the Army of the North, and sent them back by Burgos to the Ebro, in order that Caffarelli might reoccupy the lost districts, and make safe once more the high road from the Bayonne to Miranda, and the almost equally important route along the Ebro from Miranda to Saragossa, by which he had to keep up his connexion with Suchet and the East Coast. Turning back from Valladolid on November 1st, the commander of the Army of the North spent some time in opening up the high road, on which many convoys were lying blockaded in the garrisons and unable to move, and not till December was come did he clear Bilbao, and drive the coast-land guerrilleros out of all the Biscayan harbour towns save Castro-Urdiales, which had been fortified and was firmly held. Putting off its siege for a time, he then pushed along the coast to relieve Santoña, which had been blockaded for many months by Mendizabal and Longa. He cut his way thither, and threw in a convoy and reinforcements ; but as soon as he was gone the Cantabrians came back and resumed their former positions around the place. By the end of the year Caffarelli had done nothing conclusive—some shadow of occupation had been restored in Biscay, but when this was completed the new garrisons had reduced his troops

[1] See Mina's Life of himself, pp. 39–43. He declares that the French custom-house at Yrun paid him 100 *onzas de oro* (£300) a month, for leave to pass goods across the Bidassoa.

available for active service to a very modest figure. And on January 7 he had to part with the best unit of them—the brigade of the Young Guard under Dumoustier, which had been left in Spain when all the rest of the Guards went off for the Russian campaign in the preceding year. He was also directed to give up to their proper owners three provisional regiments composed of drafts for the armies of Portugal and the South, which had been intercepted on their way to Valladolid, and used to stop gaps in the line of communication. In return for these deductions he was told that he should be given Palombini's Italian Division, taken from the Army of the Centre, three depleted regiments from the Army of Portugal,[1] and one from Soult's Army,[2] which he might fill up with drafts from the Bayonne reserve. But it took some time to move these units northward, and meanwhile Caffarelli was left with no more than 10,000 movable troops—though the Army of the North was theoretically about 40,000 strong. The Bayonne *chaussée* was again out of control—so much so that in January and February there were two complete breaks of some weeks, during which neither convoys nor couriers could get through from Tolosa to Burgos. Bitter complaints about this interruption of communications are to be found in the correspondence of Napoleon and King Joseph. The famous ' 29th Bulletin ' sent off from Paris on December 4th only reached Madrid on January 6th—the Emperor's order for the reorganization of the Spanish armies, dispatched on January 4th, came to hand only on February 16th ; and the reply acknowledging its receipt was not received in Paris till March 18th![3] It had travelled by the circuitous route of Valencia and Barcelona.

This was intolerable to both parties, and they joined in placing the blame for delay on the shoulders of Caffarelli, who was denounced as dilatory and wanting in energy. Jourdan accused him of deliberate disregard of all military obedience. ' He was ostensibly under the orders of the King, but rarely corresponded with Madrid. When he did send a report, he seemed to do so rather as a matter of politeness than as the

---

[1] The remains of Thomières' unlucky division, cut to pieces at Salamanca—the 1st, 65th, and 101st Line.   [2] 64th Line.

[3] *Correspondance du Roi Joseph*, ix. p. 224.

duty of a subordinate towards his hierarchical superior[1].' On January 14th the Emperor ordered him to quit the command of the Army of the North and return to Paris. Transmitting this welcome piece of news to Joseph, the Minister of War remarked that Caffarelli had insufficient numbers, but that ' with more activity, continuity, and method in his operations he might have been much more successful[2].' In his place the Emperor nominated Clausel, who was on sick-leave in France, but was able to rejoin almost at once. This choice was generally approved, as his operations with the Army of Portugal after the battle of Salamanca had won him a well-deserved reputation. But all concerned, from Paris to Madrid, were destined to discover that it was not Caffarelli's incapacity, but the difficulty of the problem, that was responsible for the unsatisfactory condition of affairs in Biscay and Navarre. The capable Clausel made little more of the game than the short-sighted and mediocre officer whom he superseded. But this could hardly have been foreseen at mid-winter ; the fact was not obvious till May, when (as we shall see) Clausel, though he had been lent many thousands of troops much wanted elsewhere, had to confess that his task was not completed, despite of four months of energetic effort, countless marches and counter-marches, and a dozen bloody but inconclusive defeats inflicted on the Northern insurgents.

---

[1] Jourdan, *Mémoires*, p. 452.
[2] Clarke to King Joseph, *Correspondance du Roi*, ix. p. 186.

SECTION XXXV: CHAPTER II

THE TROUBLES OF A GENERALISSIMO. WELLINGTON AT CADIZ AND FRENEDA

HAVING sent his war-worn divisions into winter quarters, where they were to remain with little change of billets till the next April, Wellington could turn to the consideration of many political and military problems for which he had been granted little leisure during the long stress of the autumn campaign. He fixed himself down at his old frontier head-quarters of 1811 and 1812, the village of Freneda near the Coa, between Almeida and Fuentes de Oñoro. It was a small and bleak place: observers often wondered why, with the whole of Portugal before him, he chose it for month-long residence in the worst time of the year. But in the winter of 1812–13 he remained stationary there from the end of November to the latter half of May—save for one rapid excursion to Cadiz and Lisbon, which took him away from December 12th to January 25th— an odd time for cross-country travelling in the Peninsula. Freneda had no amenities of any kind—save indeed that it was in the midst of a good fox-hunting country, a rare thing in Portugal. The Commander-in-Chief, on returning to his old base of operations, picked up his pack of hounds, and treated himself not infrequently to the one sort of field-sport in which he had a real delight. In other respects the village was dull and inconvenient—it could only just house his very small general staff; it was by no means a central point among the cantonments of his army; and its remoteness from Lisbon caused a delay of two or three days in all his correspondence to and from home. The only things to be said in its favour were that it was so close to the front line of the army on the Agueda that there would be no possibility of missing any information as to hostile movements, and that its remoteness and inaccessibility preserved the Commander-in-Chief from many interviews with useless and inconvenient visitors, who would have thronged around him if he had lodged in Lisbon. The intriguer, the man with a grievance, or the man with a job in hand, could not easily get to windy Freneda.

Only a steady perusal of Wellington's Original and Supplementary Dispatches can give the chronicler an idea of the varied nature of his troubles and worries, during the winter that followed the Salamanca campaign. They were not merely those of an ordinary general in command of an army : his political position had now grown so important that not only did all happenings in the Peninsula fall within his sphere, but the Cabinet at home was continually consulting him on questions of general European importance. And in the months after Napoleon's Russian *débâcle* the politics of Europe came to a crisis, such as had never been seen since first he assumed the Imperial crown. His domination was breaking up : his prestige had received a mortal wound : alliances were shifting : the wildest enterprises were advocated. There were those at home who proposed that Wellington should take his Peninsula army to Germany—or to La Vendée—and others who wanted to saddle him with a large Russian auxiliary force to be brought by sea from Reval or Odessa. On every scheme, however wild, he had to give his opinion.

But, placing in order of importance the many worries that beset Head-Quarters at Freneda, it would seem that the most constant and prolific source of trouble was a circumstance which ought rather to have lessened than increased Wellington's military difficulties—if only men had been other than they were. It will be remembered that as early as 1809 the project of making him Generalissimo of all the Spanish armies had been mooted and rejected [1]. He had expressed his opinion that Spanish national pride made it impossible. ' I am much flattered,' he had written to the British Minister, ' by the notion entertained by some of the people in authority at Seville of appointing me to the command of the Spanish Armies. I believe it was considered an object of great importance in England that the Commander-in-Chief of the British troops should have that situation. But it is one more likely to be attained by refraining from pressing it, and leaving it to the

[1] See vol. ii, pp. 465–6.

Spaniards themselves to discover the expediency of the arrangement, than by any suggestion on our parts.'

Much water had flowed under the bridge since 1809. The
appointment had not come after Talavera or Bussaco, nor after
the horrible disasters of Ocaña, the Sierra Morena, and the
surrender of Valencia. But the summer campaign of 1812 had
at last convinced the Cortes that the British general, who had
so often been criticized and accused of selfishness and reluctance
to risk anything for the common cause of the Allies, was the
inevitable man. In the full flush of joy and confidence that
followed the battle of Salamanca and the triumphal entry into
Madrid, a bill was laid before the Assembly to appoint Wellington generalissimo of all the Spanish forces. It was supported
by most of the leading men of the 'Liberal' party, introduced
by the ex-regent Cisgar, and barely opposed by the 'Serviles ',
though one clerical member—Creux, afterwards Archbishop of
Tarragona—raised objections to giving such a command to any
foreigner, and expatiated on the selfish character of British
commercial policy. Despite of such murmurs, the motion was
carried by an immense majority, and the President of the Cortes
was authorized to direct the Council of Regency to make the
offer to Wellington. The form of words ran that considering
the advantages of unity in command, and the urgent necessity
for utilizing to the full the recent glorious triumphs of the allied
arms, it was decreed that as long as the allied forces were
co-operating in the defence of the Peninsula ' Captain-General
the Duke of Ciudad Rodrigo ' should have conferred upon him
the supreme command of all of them, to be exercised in accordance with general orders, his authority to extend over all the
provinces of the Peninsula. And the 'illustrious chief' was
directed to correspond with the National Government through
the Secretary of the War Office [1].

This decree reached Wellington on October 2, while he lay
at Villatoro, conducting the siege of Burgos. He resolved to
take up the long-delayed commission, provided that he should
receive the permission of the Prince Regent to do so, and sent,
through his brother at Cadiz, a letter of conditional acceptance.
His consent to serve was not couched in very enthusiastic

[1] For text see Toreno, iii. p. 149.

terms : being anxious to do all that could be done to support
the legitimate quarrel of the Spanish nation with France, he
had no objection to taking upon himself the additional labour
and responsibility of commanding the Spanish armies. The
delay which must be required, for getting leave from the Prince
Regent to make a formal acceptance of the offer, seemed to him
of secondary importance, because he was already in the habit
of communicating his general views on operations to the
Spanish generals, and of making suggestions to them, which
always received the utmost attention. ' I am convinced they
will continue the same practice, even though I am not invested
with the supreme command.' These phrases look like deliberate
sarcasm, considering Wellington's former relations with Cuesta,
Del Parque, Blake, and Mendizabal. But they probably mean
no more than that the present commanders of the forces which
were actually co-operating with him in 1812, Castaños, Morillo,
and Carlos de España, had been loyal and obliging. Finally,
' he hopes that in the new and prominent situation in which he
is to be placed, he will have not only the full support but the
confidence of the Spanish Government, Cortes, and nation[1].'

The inner meaning of these somewhat double-edged phrases
is explained in a memorandum for Lord Bathurst, the British
Secretary of State for War, which was sent home under the
same cover as the Cadiz document[2]. It was eminently not a
letter to be shown to Spaniards, and contained some of the
most bitter expressions concerning them which Wellington
ever penned. No use could be got out of their armies, he wrote,
unless they were under his control. They had lost nearly all
their guns and cavalry, and generally could not act in bodies
separate from the Allied Army. Their discipline, equipment,
and organization was as bad as ever : yet if put in line with his
own troops they might behave quite well. He would prevent
by good management repetitions of those terrible disasters to individual armies which had so often happened in past years.
But his power over them must be made real, and for that
purpose he intended to apply the financial screw. All subsidies
advanced by the British Government to Spain must for the
future be expended wholly on such Spanish troops as were

---

[1] *Wellington Dispatches*, ix. p. 467.   [2] Ibid., pp. 474–5, October 5.

actually employed in co-operation with the Anglo-Portuguese army, or else those troops would become a fresh burden on the military chest.   And in his letter to Cadiz he had been careful to show that he did not intend to allow the Spanish Government to dictate a military policy to him, because they had placed their troops at his disposition.

These letters, sent off from the camp before Burgos on October 5, got to London on October 20, and the Prince Regent's approbation of Wellington's acceptance of the offer from the Cortes was granted at once [1]. The dispatch conveying it was delivered at Cadiz on the 17th of November, and on the 20th the Cortes confirmed its former decree, and sent off a formal warrant of appointment to the new generalissimo, which reached him at Freneda on December 4th. The confirmation was not made with such general approval as the original appointment—and for good reason. By this time it had become evident that Wellington was not about to drive the French over the Pyrenees : he had raised the siege of Burgos, and when the Cortes repeated their vote, was known to be in full retreat for Salamanca. Hopes from his success were no longer so high as they had been in September, and a nasty jar had been given to the whole arrangement by the mutinous conduct of Ballasteros, who (as has been shown in an earlier chapter) had issued a manifesto against all submission to foreign generals, and had refused to obey Wellington's directions at a critical moment. It is true that Ballasteros had been arrested and imprisoned, without any consequent trouble [2]; but it was known that there were other Spanish generals who were not without sympathy with his views.

Having received his formal nomination as generalissimo, Wellington wrote to Carvajal, the Minister of War, on December 4th, one of the most stringent letters that any secretary of state has ever received. It reminds the reader of one of Napoleon's epistles to Clarke or King Joseph. The Spanish Government, he said, had now a right to expect from him an accurate representation of facts, and he was going to perform this duty. The discipline of the Spanish armies was in the

[1] Bathurst to Wellington, October 21. *Supplementary Dispatches,* vii. p. 462.   [2] See above, pp. 61-2.

very lowest state ; their efficiency was much deteriorated. How could any army be expected to keep order when neither officers nor men had received any pay for months—or even for years ? But it was not financial arrears that explained all defects : even in corps—like those of the Galician and Estremaduran armies—which had recently been reclothed and regularly paid by Wellington's own exertions, insubordination and indiscipline were rife : they were as little to be depended upon in the field as the rest. The officers, with some few exceptions, were absolutely slack and careless : the desertion from the ranks immense. He had hesitated at accepting the command, when he thought of what he had seen of the Spanish troops of late. But having undertaken it, he would not relinquish the task because it was laborious and of doubtful success. There were four demands which he must make as a preliminary condition : the Government must give him power—

(1) To have under his control all promotions and appointments to command ;

(2) To dismiss from the service any officer whom he thought deserving of such punishment ;

(3) To apply the whole war-budget to such services as he might choose ;

(4) To appoint to his head-quarters a Spanish chief-of-the-staff, to whom all military reports from the whole kingdom should be sent : so that nothing should take place without his knowledge. Through this officer he would correspond with the Regency, and send them regular reports.

He then proceeded to definite demands as to administration. The present state of military organization was absurd, burdensome, and expensive. The realm was overrun with unnecessary army-commanders and captain-generals, with immense and useless staffs. ' For example, General Castaños is most usefully employed as commander of the 5th Army, whose territory consists of Estremadura and Castille. But there is a captain-general and a large staff in each of these provinces, though the troops in the former are not enough to make a full garrison for Badajoz, or those in the latter to make a full garrison for Ciudad Rodrigo [1].' The captain-generals and their staffs have nothing

[1] Roughly correct : the joint force of the Castilian and Estremaduran

to administer, are quite useless, and absorb money which should go to the army. In the same way the 2nd (Valencian) and 3rd (Murcian) Armies, together have a strength equivalent to two divisions, yet have each the full military and civil staff of a complete army[1]. So has the 9th (Cantabrian) Army, which is composed entirely of guerrillero bands. Only the Andalusian and Galician troops are sufficiently numerous to be worth calling armies at all.

The first thing to do is to cut down unnecessary commanders-in-chief and staffs. The Galician, Castilian, and Estremaduran commands should be at once amalgamated, and put under Castaños, with one single staff for all three. Probably the same should be done with the Andalusian, Murcian, and Valencian commands. An immense body of superfluous staff-officers must be sent back to Cadiz at once. As a second step he would have to revise the organization of the country into captain-generalships and intendancies. Captain-generals often hampered army-commanders; intendants must probably be put under military authority. This was no doubt wrong in principle. But the civil intendant was powerless, in a country just liberated from the enemy and full of trouble and disorder. He could not exert authority unless he were lent military assistance: yet he would probably fall out with the military chief, because their ends would be divergent[2]. 'When the enemy is still in the country that must be done which tends most directly to drive him out—whatever constitutional principles may be violated in the process[3].'

Finally, Wellington resolved that he must come down to Cadiz in person to urge his schemes of reorganization on the Regency and the Cortes—obviously a most invidious task, since no nation likes to have administrative reforms thrust upon it divisions in October 1812 was 8,000 men with the colours—there were some 7,000 men in dépôts and garrisons.

[1] In November the 3rd Army had about 5,000 men with the colours, 3,000 in dépôt: the 2nd, 7,000, excluding the guerrilleros of the Empecinado and Duran.

[2] Two days later Wellington sent Carvajal a definite instance of this friction. The Civil Intendant of Old Castile had collected a magazine for the benefit of the garrison of Rodrigo. The Captain-General had seized it, and used it to support his own staff. *Dispatches*, ix. p. 623.

[3] Wellington to Carvajal. *Dispatches*, ix. pp. 604-5.

by a foreigner—more especially by a foreigner whose tone is dictatorial and whose phrases seem almost deliberately worded so as to wound national pride.

On December 12th he started out to deal with the Cadiz bureaucrats, planning to cover the whole 300 miles from Freneda in six days. As a matter of fact he took eleven, partly because he was smitten with lumbago, which made riding painful, partly because he was delayed one night in the Pass of Perales, and two at Albuquerque, by floods, which made mountain-streams impassable for many hours. Immediately on reaching the seat of government, where he was received with great state if with little real cordiality, he started on his campaign against the Regency, the Cortes, and the Minister of War. It is much to the credit of the Spaniards that, though many of his demands were unpalatable, the greater part of them were conceded with slight variation of terms. It is curious to note the points on which the Regency proved recalcitrant and started argument. Of the four great preliminary conditions which Wellington exacted, they granted at once that which seemed the most important of all—the creation of a Spanish chief-of-the-staff to be attached to Wellington's head-quarters, and conceded that all military correspondence should pass through his hands. The person selected was General Wimpffen, a Spanish-Swiss officer, of whom we have had to speak occasionally in dealing with Catalonian affairs—he had been Henry O'Donnell's adjutant-general in 1810. He was a non-political soldier of good abilities, and Wellington found him laborious and obliging : there seems never to have been any friction between them. Secondly, the Regency granted the great point that the whole British subsidy should be applied to such military expenses as Wellington should designate : and they afterwards went so far as to order that in the recovered provinces nine-tenths of the taxes raised should be devoted to military purposes. But they haggled on the two conditions dealing with military patronage. Instead of giving the generalissimo power to revise all appointments, they proposed that ' no officer should be promoted to a chief command, or the command of a division, or any extra-ordinary command, except at the recommendation of the general-in-chief. With regard to other promotions the rules of the Spanish service shall be strictly observed.' This left all patronage from the rank of brigadier-general downward in the hands of the Minister of War and the Cortes. And whereas Wellington had proposed, as his second condition, that he should have power to cashier any officer whom he considered deserving of such punishment, the Regents offered him only the right of suspending and sending away from the army in the field officers guilty of grave misconduct [1].

It is clear that these variations on the original proposals had two main objects. The Spaniards evidently thought that if Wellington had every officer down to the lowest under his thumb, liable to be cashiered without any appeal, he might use this tremendous power to stock the whole army with men of one political colour, and make it into a machine quite independent of the Government, and capable of being turned against it. And similarly there was a great difference between the right to send an officer away from the front, and the right to drive him out of the army. To be put on half-pay, or on administrative duty in some office at Cadiz, was a much less terrible fate than cashiering.

It must be remembered that many Spaniards thought Wellington capable of aiming at a military dictatorship, to which he might be helped by generals who were considered Anglophils, such as Castaños, his nephew and chief-of-the-staff Giron, or Morillo. And others believed that British policy secretly desired the seizure of Cadiz and Minorca and the reduction of Spain to a Protectorate. Now if there had been any truth in these absurd suspicions, there is no doubt that the powers which Wellington demanded would have given him the chance of carrying out such designs. And there were an infinite number of Spanish officers, from generals like La Peña down to petty governors and members of provincial staffs, who had come into direct contact with Wellington, and knew his unflattering opinion of them. All these men in disgrace, or disgruntled placemen, thought that the new generalissimo would start his career by a general cashiering of those against whom he had an old grudge.

---

[1] For the exact text of the reply see the Spanish Minister of War's letter. *Supplementary Dispatches*, xiv. pp. 170–1.

Hence pressure was brought to bear upon the Regents and the Cortes from many and diverse quarters, with the common plea that there must be no British military dictatorship, and that Spanish officers must be protected from possible persecution and oppression. The underlying idea was that if the mass of the middle and lower grades in the army were out of Wellington's supervision, it did not matter so much who held the post of army-commander or captain-general. For the chiefs, though in influential posts, were few, and would not be able to carry their subordinates with them in any unpopular movement dictated to them by the generalissimo.

After much discussion, and with reluctance [1], Wellington accepted the modifications—thinking that the other things conceded gave him practically all that he needed. He was to find out his error in the year that followed. He had not guarded himself against seeing officers with whom he was satisfied removed from his field-army under the pretence of promotion, or of transference to other duties, or of political offences. He had forgotten to demand that he should have the power of *retaining* as much as that of *dismissing* generals. In this way he was deprived of the services of Castaños and afterwards of Giron, both of whom he was anxious to keep. Successors technically unobjectionable, whom he had no wish to 'blackball,' were substituted for them, to his deep regret. And another evasion of his intention was that officers whom he had intended to disgrace, and had removed from the front, were given posts elsewhere which could not be called 'divisional' or 'separate' commands, but were quite desirable; and so while the letter of the bargain was kept, the purpose of inflicting punishment on such people was foiled.

Another long controversy was provoked by Wellington's proposal that the small armies should be amalgamated, and that unnecessary captain-generals with their staffs should be got rid of. Much but not all of what he asked was conceded. The Murcian and Valencian armies were consolidated, and given the new name of the 'Second Army'—the Catalan army being still the 'First Army'. But they were not amalgamated with the Andalusian command (now the 'Third Army'),

---

[1] See *Supplementary Dispatches*, vii. pp. 529–30 and 546.

as Wellington suggested. And similarly the Estremaduran, Castilian, and Galician armies, with the outlying Cantabrian division, ceased to be the 5th, 6th, and 7th Armies, and took the new name of the Fourth. And a great reduction of staffs and removal of contending military authorities was procured, by nominating Elio, commander of the new 2nd Army, to be Captain-General of Murcia and Valencia, Del Parque of the 3rd Army to be Captain-General of Granada and Jaen, and Castaños to be Captain-General alike of Estremadura, Galicia, and Castile. This was all to the good, but the Cortes refused Wellington's other proposal, that the civil government in each province should be placed under the control of the army-commanders. Declaring that it was constitutionally impossible to abolish the independence of the civil power, the Cortes yet conceded that the *jefe politico* (or provincial prefect) and the Intendant should obey the Captain-General ' in all matters relating to the Army [1],' also that nine-tenths of the revenue in each province should be allocated to the military budget. This would have worked if all parties concerned had been both willing and competent ; but it remained a melancholy fact throughout the next campaign that the army-commanders could seldom get either money or food from the civil authorities, and that most essential operations were delayed by the absolute impossibility of moving large bodies of men without adequate magazines or a fair supply of money. The only regular income of the army was that drawn from the British subsidy.

But the worst of Wellington's troubles were yet some months ahead. The Regency with which he had made his bargain [2] was displaced in March 1813, and succeeded by another. The Cortes was jealous of the Executive, and had determined to make for itself a supreme authority which should have neither brains nor energy. The subject of quarrel chosen was the old Regency's alleged slackness in carrying out a recent Act which had abolished that moribund abuse the Inquisition [3]. After

---

[1] Wellesley to Castlereagh. *Supplementary Dispatches*, vii. p. 530.

[2] They were the Duke of Infantado, Admiral Villaviciencio, and Señors Ignacio Rivas, Mosquera, and Villamil. The last two were reputed very anti-British.

[3] This Act had been a great demonstration of the ' Liberales ', and they were desirous of punishing certain canons and bishops who had refused

an all-night sitting and a vote of censure, the Regents were dismissed, and replaced by a group appointed under an absurd principle borrowed from the old régime, which was applied because it suited the desires of the assembly for the moment. It was composed of the three senior members of the Council of State—senility and weakness being desired. These were the Cardinal Bourbon—Archbishop of Toledo—an aged scion of the royal house, and the Councillors Pedro Agar and Gabriel Cisgar, who had been Regents before, but had been got rid of for incompetence. Thus all real power went to the Chamber itself—the Regency having become a negligible quantity. Wellington's position was decidedly impaired by the change—largely because a new minister-of-war had come into office, General Juan O'Donoju, of whom he had an evil memory as Cuesta's chief-of-the-staff during the Talavera campaign. This clever, shifty, and contentious Irish-Spanish officer broached the theory that the agreement of December 1812 did not bind the new Regents, because they had never assented to it, and because it was contrary to the spirit of the Constitution that a foreigner should have the power to appoint or dismiss Spanish generals.

When Henry Wellesley at Cadiz, instructed by his brother, turned his heaviest diplomatic batteries [1] upon the Regents, and privately warned the leading members of the Cortes of the awkward results that would follow the repudiation of the agreement, O'Donoju was disavowed but not displaced. He continued to give perpetual trouble through the following summer by his persistent intrigues. Wellington was by no means satisfied with the attempts that were made to propitiate him, by the formal recognition of his status as generalissimo by the new Regents, and the gift of a great estate in Granada, the royal domain of Soto de Roma, which had been usurped by Godoy. He did not want grants but real authority. Of his future troubles we shall have to speak in their proper place.

The most enduring of them was provincial maladministration,

to read it publicly in their cathedrals ; an odd parallel to the case of James II and the Seven Bishops in English history.

[1] Including the presentation of a thundering letter from the British Prince-Regent : see H. Wellesley to Wellington, July 28, *Supplementary Dispatches*, viii. p. 160 and ibid., p. 188.

which rendered so many of his orders futile. For usually when
he directed a division to move, he was informed that it was
destitute of both munitions and transport [1]. And changes of
organization were often made against his protests—e. g. a new
army regulation cut down all regimental formations to a single
battalion of very heavy strength (1,200 bayonets). Wellington
would have preferred a two-battalion formation, in which the
second unit should act as a dépôt and feeder to the first [2]. He
complained that if a regiment was badly cut up in action, there
would be no machinery for keeping it up to a decent average.
The experience of the British army with regard to single-
battalion corps had been conclusive against the system for the
last five years of Peninsular service. But his protests were
vain—internal organization of units did not come within the
wording of his powers as generalissimo, and the new organization
continued, dozens of second battalions being scrapped.

The net result was that, when Wellington took the field in
May 1813, he only had with him two of Castaños's divisions and
three of those of the Army of Galicia—less than 25,000 men.
The Andalusian ' Army of Reserve,' which had been promised
to him, started late for want of organization, moved slowly for
want of magazines, and only reached the front when the battle
of Vittoria had been won and the French had been expelled
from Spain [3]. The Cortes had at least 160,000 men under
arms ; not a sixth part of them were available during the
decisive operations. But of this more in its proper place.

Portugal, as usual, contributed its share to the troubles of
the Commander-in-Chief, though they were but trifling compared to the Spanish problems. The Prince Regent at Rio de
Janeiro was an expensive person, who actually at the worst of
the war drew money out of Portugal from the Braganza private
domains, though he had all the revenues of Brazil to play with [4].

---

[1] See especially below the difficulties with the Galician army as to
ammunition, and the Andalusian reserve as to transport and magazines.

[2] *Dispatches*, x. pp. 211–12.

[3] See *Dispatches*, x. p. 181, when Wellington writes in March : ' There is
not a single battalion or squadron fit to take the field, not in the whole
kingdom of Spain a dépôt of provisions that would keep one battalion
for one day—not a shilling of money in any military chest.'

[4] *Wellington Dispatches*, x. p. 199.

Moreover, he had a tiresome habit of sending incompetent hangers-on to Europe, with a request that berths might be found for them. But he was not actively noxious—the same could not be said of his wife, the Spanish princess Carlotta, who was still harping on her natural claim to be Regent of Spain on behalf of her imprisoned brother Ferdinand, and still interfered from time to time at Cadiz, by ordering the small knot of deputies who depended on her to attack the existing regency, or to vote in incalculable ways on questions of domestic politics. Fortunately she was so great a clerical and reactionary that the ' Liberal ' majority in the Cortes had secretly resolved that she should never get into power. When the old regency was evicted in March 1813, it was suspected that the Cardinal Bourbon was put at the head of the succeeding body mainly because the presence of a prince of the blood in the Executive seemed to make it unnecessary to import another member of the royal house. For this small mercy Henry Wellesley wrote a letter of thanksgiving to his brother at the front. It was fortunate that the Prince Regent himself gave no encouragement to his wife's ambitions, being as indolent as she was active, and very jealous of her secret intrigues with foreigners. At one time during the winter of 1812–13 she showed an intention of departing for Europe, but with the assistance of the British ambassador João succeeded in frustrating her scheme for appearing at Cadiz in person to claim her supposed rights.

Meanwhile the civil government of Portugal continued to be directed by the existing Council of Regency, of whom the majority were honest if not always well-advised. It is true that Wellington's old enemies [1] the Patriarch of Lisbon and the Principal Sousa still remained members of it : the determination to evict them which he had declared in 1810 was never carried out—the one was so powerful from his position in the Church, the other from the influence of the widespread Sousa family, that in the end he left them undisturbed. They

---

[1] See above, vol. iii. pp. 193, 415–17, and iv. p. 71. The best sketch of the personalities of the Portuguese regency is that in Lord Wellesley's *Memorandum respecting Portugal*, in *Wellington Dispatches, Suppl.*, vii. pp. 199–204, a very interesting document.

were perhaps less dangerous in the Regency than out of it, with their hysterical appeals to narrow national sentiment, protests against the doings of their colleagues, and perpetual intrigues. A *frondeur* is partly muzzled when he holds office. And in practical administration they were steadily voted down by the majority of the Regency, consisting of the Marquis of Olhão, the Conde de Redondo [1], Dr. Nogueira, and last but not least the British Minister Sir Charles Stuart, whose presence on the board was perhaps necessary, but certainly very trying to Portuguese *amour-propre*. The three native regents were genuine patriots, and good friends of the alliance, but a little antiquated in their views as to administration and finance. The Secretary of State, Miguel Forjaz, to whom so many of Wellington's letters are addressed, was a much more modern personage with a broader intelligence : indeed, Wellington considered him on the whole the most capable statesman in the Peninsula.

There were two standing sources of friction between the British army and the Portuguese Regency—both inevitable, and both tiresome from the point of view of the necessary *entente* between two allied nations. The more irritating but less important was trouble caused by the daily movement of troops, especially troops in small bodies, or individual officers. A perusal of the records of many scores of courts martial, as well as of the correspondence of Wellington and Beresford, leads to the conclusion that there were grave faults on both sides. Parties of British soldiers on the march, when unaccompanied by an officer, were given to the illegal 'embargoing' of carts or mules, to the extortion of food by force or threats, to mishandling of the peasantry when denied what they asked : occasionally they went so far as acts of murder or arson [2]. And it cannot be denied that individual officers of unsatisfactory type were occasionally guilty of gross misconduct—drunken orgies, wanton disregard of legal authority in requisitions, even acts of insult or assault on local magistrates [3]. On the other hand,

---

[1] Now Marquis de Borba by his father's death in 1812.

[2] See e. g. *Wellington Dispatches*, x. pp. 37 and 106–7.

[3] See e. g. the cases dealt with in *Wellington Dispatches, Suppl.*, vii. pp. 240 and 316.

the provocation was often considerable—there were plenty of
cases established of the denial of legal billets, which kept
parties waiting in the rain for hours, of wanton incivility, of
attempts at extortion in prices, of actual highway robbery [1],
and false accusations brought up to cover neglect of duty.
One of Wellington's main complaints was that he had to waste
time in investigating imaginary outrages, which, on inquiry,
turned out to have been invented to serve as countercharges
against accusations of slackness or misfeasance.   He was
determined that outrages by the army should cease—indeed,
he hanged, first and last, some fifty soldiers for plunder accompanied with violence, an offence which he would never pardon.
But the Portuguese magistrates were prone to make accusations, and then to protest against having to support them by
evidence.   By a curious turn of official pride many of them
refused to testify before courts martial, or even to send
witnesses to appear before such bodies, standing to the theory
that it was beneath the dignity of a magistrate to come with
evidence before a foreign military tribunal [2].   The result of
this was that offenders brought up for trial, and often probably
guilty, had to be acquitted for lack of proof.   On the other
hand, accusations, made and supported, were sometimes found
to be entirely groundless—in one supposed murder case, the
alleged corpse was discovered in perfect health ; in another, a
magistrate who accused a British officer of assault was found to
have been dining with him and frequenting his quarters, long
after the supposed offence [3].

The Portuguese Regency was bound to stand up in defence
of its magistrates—Wellington, though always ready to punish
proved crimes, was determined not to take accusation as
equivalent to conviction, merely because it was preferred by
a constituted authority.   Hence came perpetual friction and
recrimination ; that things were no worse was certainly due to
the fact that the commander-in-chief's iron discipline, and
rigorous dealing with his own people, could not fail to impress

[1] e. g. *Wellington Dispatches*, x. p. 129, and another case accompanied
by the murder of a soldier, x. p. 117.

[2] See *Wellington Dispatches*, x. pp. 131, 191, and 201.

[3] See *Wellington Dispatches*, x. p. 88 and ix. p. 615.

the Portuguese with the fact that he was always trying to be just.

The other and more fundamentally dangerous source of wrangling in Portugal was finance. There could be no disputing the fact that the part of the army which was not directly maintained from the British subsidy was often six months in arrears of pay, and still more often on the edge of starvation. Portuguese paper money, in which many transactions had to take place, and which could be legally used for a certain percentage of all army payments, was not only at a habitual discount of at least 25 per cent., but also fluctuating in exchange-value from day to day. Hence came all manner of illicit speculations by merchants, both British and Portuguese, who were always trying to buy Government paper at under its quotation for the day, and to put it off on others at an exaggerated estimate. The same took place with Commissariat Warrants, which unscrupulous brokers bought from the ignorant peasantry for a mere song, after setting rumours about concerning impending bankruptcy of the state, and then cashed at full face-value in Lisbon or London.

The Regency maintained that all the trouble came from the simple fact that the war had placed upon the back of Portugal, a small country, half of whose territory had been wasted by Soult and Masséna in 1809 and 1810, a much greater burden than could be borne. The armed forces alone—some 50,000 regular troops, and often as many militia in the garrisons—were so many hands taken away from agriculture, the only staple industry of the land. Money was going out of the realm year by year to purchase wheat, because the people could not produce enough to maintain their existence. Prices had risen to heights that terrified those who remembered pre-war days : the pay of the army was enormous compared to the rates before 1808, and much of it was going, under Marshal Beresford's system, to the British officers who were now holding a clear majority of all the senior ranks and commands. All available money went to the army, and the civil administration was starved. The Regency acknowledged the deplorable state of its finances, but could only suggest remedies which had grave inconveniences. Another British loan was asked for ; but considering the heavy subsidy that Portugal was receiving already, the British Government gave little encouragement to such an idea [1]. The Portuguese minister in London (the Conde de Funchal, one of the Sousas) suggested a large measure of confiscation of Church and Crown lands—which could then be sold. But this would involve a quarrel with the Church party in Portugal, who had been loyal supporters of the British alliance, and probably with the Prince Regent also, since he was drawing a private income from the Braganza estates. It might also produce a general shock to national credit, for it would deal a blow to the general stability of society, and terrify all landholders. Moreover, it appeared doubtful if purchasers of Church lands would present themselves : and Crown lands were largely uncultivated and worthless tracts in the Alemtejo [2]. The measure was carried out, indeed, many years later, during the civil wars of Miguel and Maria ; but then it came as a consequence of a purely domestic struggle, in which the Church party had taken the beaten side. The circumstances of 1813 were entirely different. A third expedient suggested was the establishment of a National Bank, after the model of the Bank of England, which should take over the management of the public debt and currency. But credit and guarantees must be at the back of any such association, and unless the British Government were ready to become the guarantor (which was impossible) it was hard to see what new securities could be found.

Wellington's panacea for financial distress was not heroic measures but careful and honest administration of details. He held that there was great slackness and partiality in the raising and collection of taxes, and that the amount received could be very largely increased by the abolition of abuses. In a very long memorandum, addressed to the Prince Regent João in April 1813, he launched out into an indictment of the whole financial system of the realm. ' The great cities and even some of the smaller places of the kingdom have gained by the war : the mercantile class generally has enriched itself by the great disbursements which the army makes in cash : there are individuals in Lisbon and Oporto who have amassed immense

---

[1] See Wellington to Forjaz, *Dispatches*, ix. p. 353.
[2] See Wellington to Bathurst, ibid., ix. pp. 461–2.

sums. The fact is not denied that the " tributes " regularly established at Lisbon and Oporto, and the contribution of ten per cent. on the profits of the mercantile class are not really paid to the state. . . . I have recommended the adoption of methods by which the taxes might be really and actually collected, and merchants and capitalists really pay the tenth of their annual profits as an extraordinary contribution for the war. . . . It remains for the Government to explain to your Royal Highness the reasons why it will not put them in practice—or some other expedient which might render the revenue of the state equal to its expenses.' He then proceeds to urge supervision of a Custom House notorious for letting off powerful importers overlightly, and of the collectors of land-revenue, who were allowed to keep state balances in their hands for months without paying them in to the Treasury [1].

In letters to Charles Stuart [2] as a member of the Regency Wellington let out in much more unguarded terms. The root of corruption was in the mercantile community, who had squared the minor bureaucracy. The army and state would have been ruined long ago, but for his own protests and insistence, by the jobbers of Lisbon, not only Portuguese, Jews, cosmopolitans of all sorts, but 'sharks calling themselves British merchants.' The Government is 'teased into disapprobation of good measures by the merchants, who are interested in their being discontinued. But when it is necessary to carry on an expensive system of war with one-sixth of the money in specie necessary, we must consider questions and adopt measures of this description, and we ought to have the support and confidence of your Government in adopting them.'

Making allowance alike for the difficulties of the Regency, and the irritation of the much-worried general, it seems fair to say that on the one hand Wellington was right in denouncing jobbery and urging administrative reforms, but that on the other hand no such reforms, however sweeping, would have sufficed to make both ends balance in the revenue of the exhausted kingdom of Portugal. The task was too heavy—

---

[1] Wellington to the Prince-Regent of Portugal, *Dispatches*, x. pp. 284–7.
[2] Wellington to Stuart, ibid., x. pp. 342, &c.

but the eighteenth-century slackness and corruption, which still survived in too many corners of the bureaucracy, made it even heavier than it need have been. It is probable that Wellington's palliatives would have failed to make receipts meet expenditure, however hardly the screw might have been turned. But a levy of 10 per cent. on commercial profits does not look very heavy to the taxpayer of 1921 !

This is a military not an economic or a financial history; it is unnecessary to go further into Portuguese problems. The main thing to be remembered is that they bulked large in the correspondence of the harassed chief, who sat writing minutes on all topics, civil no less than strategical, in his desolate headquarters at Freneda.

SECTION XXXV : CHAPTER III

WELLINGTON AND WHITEHALL

THE position which Wellington had won himself by five years of successful campaigning in the Peninsula was such as no British commander since Marlborough had enjoyed. His reputation was now European ; his views, not merely on the Spanish struggle but on the general politics of the Continent, had to be taken into consideration by the Ministry. He was no longer an officer to whom orders could be sent, to be carried out whether he liked them or not. He had become a political personage, whose views must be ascertained before any wide-reaching decision as to the struggle with Napoleon was taken. In 1813 it is not too much to say that he exercised a determining influence not only on the military policy of Britain, but on the whole course of the Great War : as we shall presently see, the triumph of Vittoria had the most marked and direct effect on the action of Russia, Prussia, and Austria. But even before Vittoria he had asserted his will in many ways—he had stopped some projects and approved others. The factious resignation of his brother Lord Wellesley from the Perceval Cabinet had not impaired his position, nor had the coming into office of Lord Liverpool, when Perceval perished by the bullet of a crazy assassin a month after the fall of Badajoz. Wellington's correspondence with the War Minister, Lord Bathurst, in 1813, is as confidential and amicable on both sides as had been the case when the domineering Wellesley had been in power : with the new Prime Minister, Liverpool, there is no trace of any friction whatever—rather every sign of reciprocal respect.

But the position which Wellington had achieved had its drawbacks as well as its advantages. Since it had become habitual for the Cabinet to ask his opinion on high military matters not connected with the Peninsula, an endless vista of troubles was opened up before him, for (as always happens in times of exceptional crisis) the Ministry at home was being plagued with all manner of solicitations from every quarter of Europe, to which answers were required.

While Wellington had been trailing back reluctantly from Burgos to Ciudad Rodrigo, Napoleon had been conducting a retreat of a very different kind from Moscow to the Berezina, a retreat whose character and consequences were not known in London or in Spain for some weeks later. He had left Moscow on October 19th, had dictated the famous 29th Bulletin, acknowledging the wreck of his project and the ruin of his army, at Molodetchno on December 3rd, and had started on his headlong flight to Paris on December 5th, leaving the small remnant of his host to perish in the snow. He reached the Tuileries on the night of December 18th, on the heels of the disastrous bulletin, which his ministers had only received thirty-six hours before, on the preceding day [1]. In London the fact that the Russian expedition had failed was well known by the end of November, but the extent of the failure was only realized when the 29th Bulletin got to Lord Liverpool's hands, by the usual smugglers' route, on December 21st, rather less than five days after its arrival in Paris [2].

The Prime Minister sat down next morning to communicate the fact to Wellington, and to consult him upon the logical consequences. 'There has been,' he wrote, 'no example within the last twenty years, among all the extraordinary events of the French Revolution, of such a change of fortune as Bonaparte has experienced during the last five months. The most formidable army ever collected by Bonaparte has been substantially destroyed. It only remains to be ascertained whether he will succeed in escaping himself—and with what remnant of an army. . . . Under these circumstances the question naturally occurs whether he will leave the French army in Spain ? We have a report that he has already ordered 40,000 men from that country to rejoin him—but it is only a report. I am inclined, however, to be of opinion that he will withdraw the greater part of his forces from Spain. The only efficient French Army at the present moment in existence is

[1] See Meneval's *Mémoires*, iii. p. 317.

[2] It was generally known in London next day. See Sir G. Jackson's *Memoirs*, iii. p. 447.

that under Soult : and whatever it may cost Bonaparte to abandon Spain, I think he will prefer that alternative to the loss of Germany. I may be wrong in this speculation, but give you my reasons, and I am particularly desirous of calling your attention to this view of the subject, in order that you may take the necessary means for obtaining early information of the movements of any French divisions toward the frontier, and that you may consider what measures may be proper to be adopted if my conjecture should be realized [1].'

Thus on the first day after the arrival of the epoch-making bulletin, and before it was known that Napoleon himself had reached Paris, the great strategical question of the winter of 1812–13 was formulated, and put before Wellington. Will the French evacuate Spain ? and, if so, what should be done with the British Army in the Peninsula ? There were three possible contingencies—(1) the Emperor might abandon Spain altogether, in order to have the nucleus of an army ready for the campaign of 1813 in Germany, or (2) he might not evacuate Spain altogether, but might cut down his forces there, and order them to stand on the defensive only, or (3) he might value his prestige so highly that he would take little or nothing in the way of troops from the Peninsula, and endeavour to make head against the Russians with whatever remnant of an army might be left him in the North, with the conscripts of 1813, and the levies of the German States—if the latter should remain obedient to him [2].

At first it seemed as if the third and least likely of these three hypotheses was the correct one. For strange as it might appear, considering what had happened in Russia, Wellington could detect no signs of any great body of French troops being moved towards the Pyrenees. So far was this from being the case, that the cantonments adopted by the enemy in December were so widely spread to the South, that the only possible deduction that could be made was that the whole of the armies of 1812 were being kept in Spain. We now know that the reason for

[1] Liverpool to Wellington. *Supplementary Dispatches*, vii. pp. 502–3.
[2] Lord Liverpool doubted whether Prussia or Austria would move. Prussia might stir, if only she was sure that Austria would support her. But ' the councils of Vienna at this time are abject.'

this was that the communications between Madrid and Paris were so bad, that Napoleon's orders to his brother to draw in towards the North, and send large drafts and detachments to France, only reached their destination in February. For many weeks Wellington could report no such movements as Lord Liverpool had expected.

It was not till March 10th that the much-desired news began to come to hand[1], time having elapsed sufficient to allow of King Joseph beginning to carry out the Emperor's orders. On that day Wellington was able to send Lord Bathurst intelligence which seemed to prove that the second hypothesis, not the third, was going to prove the correct one : i. e. there was about to be a certain deduction from the French armies in Spain, which would make it unlikely that they would take the offensive, but nevertheless the main body of them was still to be left in the Peninsula. Though the enemy had made no move of importance, it was certain that Soult and Caffarelli had been recalled to France—the latter taking with him the troops of the Imperial Guard, which had hitherto formed part of the Army of the North. To replace the latter Palombini's division had been moved from near Madrid to Biscay. A large draft of artillery had been sent back to France, and twelve (it was really twenty-five) picked men for the Imperial Guard from each battalion of the Army of Spain. On the other hand, a body of 4,000 men —probably convalescents or conscripts—had come down from Bayonne to Burgos[2]. Seven days later a more important general move could be detected : not only had Soult gone towards France with a heavy column of drafts, but the French had evacuated La Mancha, the troops formerly there having retired north to the province of Avila[3]. Again, a week later, on March 24th, it became known[4] that the Army of the Centre had moved up towards the Douro, and that King Joseph and

[1] Though on February 17 Wellington heard of the departure northward of the 7th (Polish) Lancers, and some squadrons of Gendarmerie belonging to the Army of the North. But this was too small a move to serve as the base of a deduction. *Dispatches*, x. p. 125.

[2] Wellington to Bathurst. *Dispatches*, x. p. 177.

[3] Ibid., p. 207, March 17.

[4] By an intercepted letter from the King to Reille, dated March 14, now in the ' Scovell Cyphers,' which mentions both facts.

his Court were about to quit Madrid. A little later this move
was found to have taken place : the enemy had evacuated a
broad stretch of territory, and 'concentrated very much
toward the Douro [1].' On the same day an intercepted letter,
from General Lucotte at Paris to King Joseph, let Wellington
into the main secrets of the enemy : the General reported to
his master that the Emperor's affairs were in a bad way, that
there would be no men and very little money for Spain, and
that he must make the best of what resources he had. His
Imperial Majesty was in a captious and petulant mood, blaming
everything done by everybody beyond the Pyrenees, but more
especially his brother's neglect to keep open the communication
with France and to hunt down the northern insurgents [2].

This useful glimpse into the mentality of the enemy made
it abundantly clear that Lord Liverpool's original theory, that
Napoleon would withdraw his whole army from Spain in order
to hold down Germany, was perfectly erroneous. At the same
time, Lucotte's report coincided with all the other indications,
in showing that the enemy had been perceptibly weakened,
could count on no further reinforcements, and must stand on
the defensive during the campaign that was to come.

But while it was still thought in Whitehall that the Emperor
might evacuate Spain altogether, various projects for turning
the Russian *débâcle* to account began to be laid before Wellington. The first was a scheme for fostering a possible insurrection
in Holland, where grave discontent was said to be brewing.
Would it be wise for the Prince of Orange, now serving as an
aide-de-camp on the head-quarters staff, to be sent home, so
that he might put himself at the head of a rising ? Wellington
replied that he no more believed in an immediate insurrection
in Holland than in one in France. 'Unless I should hear of an
insurrection in France or in Holland, or should receive an order
to send him, I shall say nothing on the subject to the Prince [3].'
He was undoubtedly right in his decision : the Dutch required
the news of Leipzig, still nine months ahead, to make them stir :

---

[1] Wellington to Graham, April 7. *Dispatches*, x. p. 270.

[2] In the 'Scovell Cyphers,' like the dispatch quoted above.

[3] Wellington to Bathurst, January 26. *Dispatches*, x. p. 39 ; cf. ibid.,
p. 256.

an expedition to Holland in the early spring would have been hopelessly premature.

A little later came a much more plausible proposition, which met with an equally strong negative from Wellington. The ever-loyal Electorate of Hanover was prepared to rise : to start the movement it would be only necessary to land a nucleus of British-German troops somewhere on the Frisian coast. Could Wellington spare the three cavalry regiments, five infantry battalions, and one battery of the King's German Legion which were serving with him ? After Tettenborn's March raid to Hamburg the insurrection actually broke out, and Bathurst suggested [1] that the time had come to throw a considerable force ashore in the electorate. He asked whether the Hanoverian officers in Spain were beginning to chafe at being kept so far from their homes at the critical moment. Again Wellington put in a strong negative. He had been to consult General Charles Alten, ' by far the best of the Hanoverian officers,' as to the expedience of sending the Legion to Germany. Alten held that ' the best thing for England, for Germany, and the world, is to make the greatest possible effort *here* : ' the services of a few thousand veteran troops would be important in the narrower field in Spain—they would be lost in the multitudes assembling on the Elbe. If a large body of loyal levies were collected in Hanover it might ultimately be well to send a part of the Legion thither : but not at present [2]. This was the policy which the Ministry followed : in the spring they dispatched to North Germany only cadres from the dépôts of the Legion at Bexhill—500 men in all, including some experienced cavalry and artillery officers. In July the 3rd Hussars went across to Stralsund, in August two batteries of Horse Artillery, all from England [3]. But no deduction of units was made from Wellington's Spanish army—only a few officers were permitted to sail, at their own request. The senior of them, General Bock of the Heavy Dragoons, unfortunately perished by shipwreck with his three aides-de-camp off the coast of Brittany in the winter that followed Vittoria.

---

[1] *Supplementary Dispatches*, vii. pp. 601–2, April 7.
[2] Wellington to Bathurst. *Dispatches*, x. p. 307.
[3] For details see Schwertfeger's *History of the K.G.L.*, vol. i, pp. 500–50.

Bathurst was so far right that many of the Hanoverian officers regretted their stay in the Peninsula : on the other hand, Wellington was not merely trying to keep his own army strong, when he refused to listen to the suggestions made him. It was perfectly true that 4,000 good soldiers were an appreciable unit in a Spanish battle—while they would be ' entirely thrown away,' as he put it, in Germany. The margin of strength was so narrow in the Peninsular Army that it was not safe to decrease it.

The same question that arose about the King's German Legion also came up during the spring of 1813 with regard to the Brunswickers. Many officers of the Brunswick-Oels battalion in the 7th Division were fired with the idea of liberating Germany—they wrote to their duke, then in England, begging him to have the battalion ordered home. He replied that he had tried to get the War Office to let him go to the Elbe, even with a small cadre, a few hundred men, but had been refused [1]. It is much more surprising that this corps was not spared from the Peninsula : Wellington had a bad mark against it, for its terrible propensity to desertion, and a worse for the behaviour of one of its companies at Tordesillas in the recent campaign. Probably he thought that, if he surrendered the Brunswickers, he would have to give up the German Legion also.

It is odd to find that among Wellington's troubles were not only the proposed subtraction of troops whom he did not want to lose, but the proposed addition of troops whom he was not at all anxious to see in the Peninsula. The story is one which illustrates the casual methods of Russian officers. In February there came to Freneda a well-known British secret agent, Mackenzie, the man who had organized the successful evasion of La Romana's Spaniards from Denmark in 1808 [2]. He brought letters from Admiral Greig, commanding the Russian Black Sea fleet, to the effect that there was a surplus of troops from Tchitchagoff's Army of the Danube, which could not be utilized in Germany for want of transport and supplies. There were 15,000 men who could be collected at Odessa and shipped

---

[1] See letters in von Wacholz's Diary, pp. 311–12. It is doubtful if the men, largely waifs and prisoners of all nations, felt the same zeal as the officers. [2] See vol. i, pp. 371, &c.

to Spain, to be placed in the Allied Army, if Wellington would accept them. The memory of Russian co-operation in Holland in 1799 was not a very happy one : but it seemed unwise to offend the Tsar, on whose goodwill the future of Europe now depended. Wherefore the answer given was that they might come if the British Cabinet approved, and if the Spanish and Portuguese governments saw no objection. ' One would think that the Emperor had demands enough for his men,' wrote Wellington to Charles Stuart, ' but Mackenzie says that they have more men than they can support in the field, which is not improbable. The admission of Russians into the Peninsula, however, is quite a new feature of the war : and it is absolutely necessary that the allied Governments should consent to the measure [1].' The correspondence with Cadiz and London ended in the most tiresome and ridiculous fashion—the Spanish Regency was at the moment in a state of diplomatic tension with Russia, on some questions of precedence and courtesy. It answered in the most downright fashion that the presence of Russian troops in Spain would be neither helpful nor welcome. The British ambassador at Cadiz was shocked at the language used, which would be most offensive to the Tsar [2]. But the whole project suddenly collapsed on news received from London. Count Lieven, the Russian representative at the Court of St. James's, declared that he had never heard of the offer, that he was sure that no such scheme would be approved by the Tsar, and that there was certainly no Russian corps now available for service in the Mediterranean. Admiral Greig had once communicated to him a scheme for a Russian auxiliary force to be used in Italy—but this was a plan completely out of date, when the whole Russian army was wanted for Germany [3]. Wellington had therefore to explain to the Spanish and Portuguese Governments that his proposals to them had been made under a complete misapprehension : his *amour-propre* was naturally hurt—Greig and Mackenzie had put him in an absurd position.

---

[1] *Supplementary Dispatches*, vii. pp. 449–50.
[2] Henry Wellesley to Wellington. *Supplementary Dispatches*, x. pp. 571–3.
[3] Bathurst to Wellington, *Supplementary Dispatches*, vii. 577, and Castlereagh to Sir Charles Stuart, ibid., p. 586, March 3, 1813.

Prince Lieven's mention of Italy takes us to another of Wellington's worries. It has been mentioned in the preceding volume that Lord William Bentinck, commanding the British Army in Sicily, had already in 1812 been planning descents on Italy, where he rightly thought the French military strength was low, after the departure of the whole of the Viceroy's contingent for the Russian War, and of many of Murat's Neapolitans also. So set had he been on expeditions to Calabria or Tuscany, that he had made great difficulties when ordered to send out the Alicante expedition to favour Wellington's Salamanca campaign [1]. The news of the Russian disaster had filled Bentinck's mind with new Italian schemes—the conditions were even more favourable than in 1812. He was now dreaming of invading Italy with all the men he could muster, and proposed on February 24th to the British War Minister that he should be allowed to withdraw all or some of the Anglo-Sicilian troops from Alicante. He had also seen Admiral Greig, and put in a claim for the hypothetical 15,000 Russians who had caused Wellington so much trouble. Knowing how much importance the latter attached to the Alicante Army, as the real nucleus of resistance to Suchet in Eastern Spain, he had the grace to send copies of his February dispatch to Freneda.

This was a most irritating interruption to Wellington's arrangements for the next campaign : the Alicante force was a valuable piece in the great game which he was working out. To see it taken off the board would disarrange all his plan. Accordingly he made the strongest protest to Lord Bathurst against the Italian expedition being permitted. To make any head in Italy, he said, at least 30,000 or 40,000 men would be needed. No doubt many Italians were discontented with the Napoleonic régime, but they would not commit themselves to rebellion unless a very large force came to their help. If only a small army were landed, they would show passive or even active loyalty to their existing government. They might prefer a British to a French or an Austrian domination in their peninsula, because it would be more liberal and less extortionate. But they would want everything found for them—arms, equipment, a subsidy. Unless the Government were prepared

---

[1] See above, vol. v, pp. 342–7.

to start a new war on a very large scale, to raise, clothe, and equip a great mass of Italian troops, and to persevere to the last in a venture as big as that in Spain, the plan would fail, and any landing force would be compelled to re-embark with loss and disgrace [1].

On the whole Wellington's protest proved successful : Lord William was forced to leave a large body of his Anglo-Sicilians in Spain, though he withdrew 2,000 men from Alicante early in April, when it was most needful that the Allied force on the East Coast should be strong. The remainder, despite (as we shall see) of very bad handling by Sir John Murray, proved sufficient to keep Suchet employed. No Italian expedition was permitted during the campaigning season of 1813, though Lord William sent out a small foreign expeditionary force for a raid on Tuscany, which much terrified the Grand Duchess Eliza [2]. Next year only, when the whole Napoleonic system was crumbling, did he collect a heterogeneous army of doubtful value, invade Liguria, and capture Genoa from a skeleton enemy. But by that time the French were out of Spain, and Wellington's plans could not be ruined by the distraction of troops on such an escapade. In May 1813 the Italian expedition, if permitted, might have wrecked the whole campaign of Vittoria, by leaving Suchet free to join the main French army. How it would have fared may be judged from the fact that the Viceroy Eugène made head all through the autumn against 80,000 men of the Austrian Army of Italy.

So much may suffice to explain Wellington's dealings during the winter and spring of 1813 with the British Cabinet. His advice, as we have seen, was always asked, and generally settled the problem in the way that he desired. So much cannot be said for his dealings with the Commander-in-Chief at the Horse Guards : the Duke of York seems to have been the last person in Whitehall to recognize the commanding intellect of the great general. Though he always wrote with perfect courtesy, he evidently considered that his own views on the organization, personnel, and management of the British

---

[1] Wellington to Bathurst. *Dispatches*, x. pp. 384–5.

[2] For this forgotten raid in December 1813, see *Études Napoléoniennes*, 1914, p. 191. For the Genoa affair see C. T. Atkinson in the *R.U.S.I. Journal*, 1915.

Army were far more important than those of the victor of Salamanca. The correspondence of Wellington with the Duke and his Military Secretary, Colonel Henry Torrens, occupies an enormous number of pages in the volumes of Dispatches and Supplementary Dispatches. Torrens, an obliging man, seems to have tried to make himself a buffer between the two contending wills, and Wellington was conscious of the fact that he was no enemy. The subjects of contention were many.

One of the most important was patronage. Now that he had reached the fifth year of his command in the Peninsula, Wellington considered that he had won the right to choose his own chief subordinates. But still he could not get officers of tried incapacity removed from the front, nor prevent others, against whom he had a bad mark, from being sent out to him. When he asked for removals, he was told of ' the difficulty of setting aside general officers who have creditably risen to high rank' on the mere ground that they have been proved incapable, and unfit for their situations. But it was far worse that when he had requested that certain generals should not be sent out, they came to him nevertheless, despite of his definite protest ; and then, when he requested that they might be removed, he was told that he would incur odium and responsibility for their removal. ' What a situation then is mine ! It is impossible to prevent incapable men from being sent to the army ; and then when I complain that they have been sent, I am to be responsible ! Surely the " odium " ought not to attach to the person who officially represents that they are not capable of filling their situations '—but (the aposiopesis may be filled up) to the Horse Guards for sending them out. Yet Wellington's pen did not add the words which are necessary to complete the sense.

The most tiresome case in 1812–13 was that of Colonel James Willoughby Gordon, who had come out as Quartermaster-General in 1812, when Wellington's first and most trusted quartermaster, George Murray, was removed (quite without his desire) to a post in Ireland. Gordon was sent by the Duke of York's personal choice [1], without any previous consultation

---

[1] See Wellington to Torrens, May 28, 1812. *Dispatches*, ix. p. 182. Yet Wellington, unconsulted though he had been, expresses his thanks to the Duke for fixing upon a successor to Murray.

with the Commander-in-Chief in Spain as to whether he would
be acceptable. The atrocity of this appointment was not only
that Gordon was incapable, but that he was a political intriguer,
who was in close touch with the Whig Opposition at home, and
before he went out had promised to send confidential letters on
the campaign to Lord Grey. This he actually did : the malicious
Creevey had a privileged peep at them, and found that ' his
accounts are of the most desponding cast. He considers our
ultimate discomfiture as a question purely of time, and that
it may happen any day, however early : and that our pecuniary
resources are utterly exhausted. The skill of the French in
recovering from their difficulties is inexhaustible : Lord W.
himself owns that the resurrection of Marmont's broken troops
after Salamanca was an absolute miracle of war. In short,
Gordon considers that Lord W. is in very considerable danger [1].'
The writer was holding the most important post on Wellington's
staff, and using the information that he obtained for the benefit
of the Parliamentary Opposition ; he should have been court-
martialled for the abuse of his position for personal ends.
Wellington at last detected his mischief-making, by the appearance in the Whig papers of definite facts that could only have
been known to three people—Wellington himself, his secretary
Fitzroy Somerset, and the Quartermaster-General. ' I showed
him,' writes Wellington to Bathurst, ' my dispatch to your
Lordship of August 3, as the shortest way of making him
acquainted with the state of affairs. . . . The topics of this
dispatch find their way into the *Morning Chronicle*, distorted
into arguments against the Government. I am quite certain
that the arguments in the *Morning Chronicle* are drawn from
a perusal of my dispatches, and that no one saw them here
excepting the Quartermaster-General and Lord Fitzroy. Even
your Lordship had not yet received this dispatch, when the
topics it contained were used against the Government in the
newspapers. . . . For the future he shall not see what I write—
it would be no great loss to the Army if he were recalled to
England. I cypher part of this letter in the cypher you sent
me to be used for General Maitland [2].'

[1] *Creevey Papers*, i. p. 173.
[2] *Supplementary Dispatches*, vii. pp. 427–8.

It was four months before this traitor was got rid of, though Lord Bathurst had been shocked by the news, and corroborated it by his own observation : he had seen mischievous letters from Gordon to the Horse Guards, and if he wrote such stuff to the Duke it was easy to guess what he might write to Lord Grey or Whitbread. Certain of the newspaper paragraphs *must* have come ' from some intelligent person with you [1].' The strange way in which the removal was accomplished was not by a demand for his degradation for misuse of his office [2], but by a formal report to the Horse Guards that ' Colonel Gordon does not turn his mind to the duties to be performed by the Quartermaster-General of an Army such as this, actively employed in the field : notwithstanding his zeal and acknowledged talent, he has never performed them, and I do not believe he ever will or can perform them. I give this opinion with regret, and I hope His Royal Highness will believe that I have not formed it hastily of an officer respecting whose talents I, equally with His Royal Highness, had entertained a favourable opinion [3].' Three weeks later the Military Secretary at the Horse Guards writes that Wellington shall have back his old Quartermaster-General George Murray—and Gordon is recalled [4]. But why had Gordon ever been sent ? The Duke of York alone could say. The impression which he had left as a soldier upon men at the front, who knew nothing of his political intrigues, was exceedingly poor [5].

This was the worst trick which was played on Wellington from the Horse Guards. Another was the refusal to relieve him of the gallant but muddle-headed and disobedient William Stewart, who despite of his awful error at Albuera was allowed to come out to the Peninsula again in 1812, and committed other terrible blunders : it was he who got the three divisions into a marshy deadlock on the retreat from Salamanca, by deliberate and wilful neglect of directions [6]. ' With the utmost zeal and

---

[1] *Supplementary Dispatches,* vii. p. 457.

[2] Oddly enough, Wellington wanted the Duke of York to take the initiative and odium, by appointing Gordon to a home post. The Duke refused, holding that Wellington must take the responsibility.

[3] *Supplementary Dispatch s,* vii. p. 499.   [4] Ibid., p. 527.

[5] See examples on page 138, above.

[6] See above, pp. 151–2.

good intentions he *cannot* obey an order,' wrote Wellington on December 6, 1812—yet Stewart was still commanding the Second Division in 1814 [1]. In letters sent to the Horse Guards in December 1812 the Commander-in-Chief in Spain petitioned for the departure of five out of his seven cavalry generals— which seems a large clearance—and of ten infantry divisional and brigade commanders. About half of them were ultimately brought home, but several were left with him for another campaign. He had also asked that he might have no more generals who were new to the Peninsula inflicted upon him, because their arrival blocked promotion for deserving colonels, to whom he was anxious to give brigades. ' I hope I shall have no more new Generals : they really do but little good, and they take the places of officers who would be of real use. And then they are all desirous of returning to England [2].' The appeal was in vain—several raw major-generals were sent out for the spring campaign of 1813, and we have letters of Wellington making apologies to Peninsula veterans, to whom he had promised promotion, for the fact that the commands which he had been intending for them had been filled up against his wishes by the nominees of the Horse Guards. Things went a little better after Vittoria, when several undesired officers went home, and several deferred promotions took place—the news of that victory had had its effect even in Whitehall.

It is more difficult to sympathize with Wellington's judge-ment—though not with his grievance—in another matter of high debate during this winter. Like most men he disliked talking about his own coffin, i. e. making elaborate arrange-ments for what was to happen in the event of his becoming a casualty, like Sir John Moore. He loathed the idea of ' seconds in command ', arguing that they were either useless or tiresome. He did not want an officer at his elbow who would have a sort of right to be consulted, as in the bad old days of ' councils of war ' ; nor did he wish to have to find a separate command for such a person to keep him employed [3]. It was true that he often trusted Hill with an independent corps in Estremadura ; but frequently he called in Hill's

---

[1] See Wellington to Torrens, *Supplementary Dispatches*, vii. pp. 494–5.
[2] Ibid., p. 486.   [3] *Wellington Dispatches*, ix. p. 592.

column and it became part of the main army—as on the Caya in 1811, in the Salamanca retreat in 1812, and at Vittoria in 1818. In the winter of 1812–13 a point which might have been of high importance was raised : who would be his successor in case of a regrettable accident ? Wellington decided that Beresford was the proper choice—despite of Albuera. ' All that I can tell you is that the ablest man I have yet seen with the army, and the one having the largest views, is Beresford. They tell me that, when I am not present, he wants decision : and he certainly embarrassed me a little with his doubts when he commanded in Estremadura : but I am quite certain that he is the only person capable of conducting a large concern [1].' He also held that Beresford's position as a marshal in the Portuguese Army gave him a seniority in the Allied Army over British lieutenant-generals.

This judgement of Wellington's is surprising : Beresford was courageous, a good organizer, a terror to shirkers and jobbers, and accustomed to command. Yet one would have thought that his record of 1811, when he displayed almost every possible fault alike of strategy and of morale in Estremadura, would have ruled him out. Wellington thought, as it would appear, that he had a better conception of the war as a whole—' the large concern '— than any of the other generals in the Peninsula, and had every opportunity of knowing. On this most critical point Wellington and the Duke of York fell out at once : it was not that the Duke wanted to rule out Beresford because he was undecided in the field, unpopular with his colleagues, self-assertive or arrogant. He had a simple Horse Guards rule which in his view excluded Beresford from consideration at once. ' According to the general received opinion of the Service no officer in the British Army above the rank of lieutenant-colonel is ever expected to serve under an officer junior to himself, even though he may possess a superior local commission.' He then proceeded to recall the fact that in 1794, when Lord Moira came to Flanders with the local rank of general, Sir Ralph Abercrombie, and a number of other general officers with commissions of senior date, refused to serve under him : in consequence of which Lord Moira had to resign and to return to England.

---

[1] Wellington to Bathurst, *Supplementary Dispatches*, vii. p. 484.

There were many similar examples in the past. The right of officers to refuse to serve under a junior being established, it could not be argued that higher rank acquired by that junior in a foreign service had any weight. Beresford might be a Portuguese field-marshal, but from the British point of view he was junior to Sir Thomas Graham, Sir Stapleton Cotton, and Sir Rowland Hill. If by some deplorable accident Lord Wellington were incapacitated from command at the present moment, Sir Thomas Graham, if with the Army, would succeed. If Sir Thomas were on sick leave, Sir Stapleton Cotton would be the senior officer in the Peninsula, and the command of the Army would automatically devolve on him : if Sir Stapleton were also on leave, it would go to General Hill.

' It appears impossible to expect that British generals senior to Marshal Beresford will submit to serve under him. It appears to the Commander-in-Chief, therefore, that there remains but one of two alternatives—the one to recall Marshal Beresford from the Peninsula in case he should persist in his claim ; the other, in case Lord Wellington still prefers that officer as his second in command, to recall all the British lieutenant-generals senior to him in our own Army [1].'

This was a maddening reply, for though Wellington liked Stapleton Cotton he had no delusions about his intellectual capacity. The best he could say about him during the controversy was that ' he commands our cavalry very well ; I am certain much better than many who might be sent out to us, and who might be supposed much cleverer than he is.' As a matter of fact, Graham was on sick leave, with an affliction of eyesight, which was supposed to be likely to result in permanent incapacity. Cotton was also on short leave to England on ' urgent personal affairs [2],' but expected back shortly. Therefore the Duke's letter was a proposal to consign the fate of the British Army in the Peninsula to a gallant officer with the mental capacity of a cavalry brigadier, who had never commanded a force of all arms, and who was the cause of much

---

[1] Duke of York to Bathurst, *Supplementary Dispatches*, vii. pp. 516–17.

[2] He was bothering Lord Bathurst for a peerage, which he was not yet destined to obtain. *Supplementary Dispatches*, vii. p. 515. He was put off with the colonelcy of a cavalry regiment.

quiet amusement to his comrades, from his ostentatious dress and unconcealed admiration for his own perfections.

Lord Bathurst tried to smooth matters, by asking Graham whether he felt inclined to surrender any claim to take over the Peninsular Army on account of his bad health. Sir Thomas replied that he should decline the responsibility for that reason : that he hoped to cause no difficulties, but that he could not agree that Beresford had any claim, ' his obligation to the service bound him not to sacrifice the rights of British officers from a purely personal spirit of accommodation.' To which Bathurst replied that if he waived his rights as a consequence of his ill health, while making no concession on grounds of principle, perhaps Hill and Cotton might do the same. To this the victor of Barrosa answered that he might consent, on the distinct understanding that no precedent was created, and that the arrangement was temporary [1].

His compliance proved useful : Stapleton Cotton arrived in London shortly after and ' expressed himself decidedly against Sir William Beresford's claims, and with some warmth.' Lord Bathurst explained to him that Graham's consent to the ' temporary arrangement ' must govern his own, and tried to put him off the idea that he himself would undoubtedly become Wellington's destined successor, if Graham refused the post, by hinting that after all Graham might recover his eyesight, and be able to take over the command. After showing much soreness, Cotton reluctantly acquiesced. The War Minister, writing an account of the interview to Wellington, ends with ' I think it necessary to have this explained beforehand, that you might not have any doubt whether you were, after what has passed, to consider Sir Thomas Graham or Sir Stapleton Cotton as the person who was to exercise the command in case of your personal indisposition [2].' So Beresford's nomination was passed, as Wellington desired, and contrary to the Duke of York's views as to the inevitable power of old precedent. But it was only passed by the consent of the other parties concerned, however reluctantly given. Fortunately Wellington preserved his usual splendid health, and the experi-

[1] Bathurst to Wellington, *Supplementary Dispatches*, vii. pp. 538–9.
[2] Ibid., vii. pp. 577–8.

ment of trusting the whole Allied Army in the Peninsula to the victor of Albuera was never made.

On another great controversy which (since Wellington never went off duty for a day) was of more practical importance than that of the right of succession, the Duke of York was partly successful in discomfiting the Commander-in-Chief in Spain. This was a question on which there had been much argument at the end of each Peninsular campaign, but never so much as in 1812–13. The exceptionally heavy casualty lists of the storming of Badajoz, the battle of Salamanca, and the retreat from Burgos had brought a great number of units, both cavalry and infantry, to very low figures. There were (as has been mentioned in a previous chapter) twelve battalions which had at the end of the retreat less than 300 bayonets effective, thirteen which had more sick than men present with the colours. For some of these the difficulty was only a momentary one—there was a large draft on the way to reinforce the unit, or at least a good number of trained recruits in Great Britain ready to be sent out. But this was not the case with all of them : the reason of this was to be sought in the organization of the Army in 1812 : the majority of infantry regiments had two battalions ; if the second unit was on home service, it regularly found drafts for the one at the front. But if the regiment was a single-battalion corps (and there were seven such with Wellington [1]), or if it chanced to have both units abroad and none at home (as was the case with fifteen other corps [2]), there was only a dépôt in Great Britain, and this had to feed two battalions both on active service overseas, and often could not discharge the double task effectively. There were of course regiments so popular, or recruited with such zeal and efficiency, that they succeeded in keeping two units abroad with adequate numbers : but this was exceptional.

What was to be done if a Peninsular battalion had got very low in numbers, had no sister-unit at home to feed it, and had few or no recruits at its British dépôt ready to be sent out ? This was the case in December 1812 with twelve good old batta-

---

[1] The 2nd, 20th, 51st, 68th, 74th, 77th, 94th Regiments.

[2] The 9th, 11th, 24th, 27th, 30th, 34th, 39th, 44th, 47th, 53rd, 58th, 66th, 81st, 83rd, 87th, as also *Chasseurs Britanniques* and Brunswick-Oels.

lions of the Peninsular Army [1]. The Duke of York maintained that since they all showed under 350 effectives present (one was as low as 149 rank and file), and since there was no immediate prospect of working them up to even a low battalion strength of 450 or 500 men, they must come home at once, and take a long turn of British service, in which they could be brought up gradually to their proper establishment. He had carried out this plan in earlier years with some very fine but wasted battalions, such as the 29th and 97th. To replace the depleted veteran corps, there should come out new battalions from home, recently brought up to full strength. The same ought to be done with four or five cavalry regiments, which could show only about 250 horses effective.

But Wellington had other views, and had begun to carry them out on his own responsibility. He held that a well-tried battalion acclimatized to Peninsular service was such a precious thing, and a raw battalion such a comparatively worthless one, that it would be best to combine the wasted units in pairs as 'Provisional Battalions' of 600 or 700 bayonets, each sending home the cadres of four or five companies to its dépôt, and keeping six or five at the front. The returning cadres would work up to full strength by degrees, and could then come out again to join the service companies. On December 6th, 1912, he issued orders to constitute three Provisional Battalions [2]: he intended to carry out the same system for several more pairs of battalions [3], and it was put into practice for the 2/31st and 2/66th as from December 20. So with the cavalry, he intended to reduce four regiments to a two-squadron establishment, sending home the cadres of their other squadrons to be filled up at leisure.

On January 13th the Duke of York sent out a memorandum entirely disapproving of the system. He regretted to differ in principle from the Commander-in-Chief in Spain, but could not possibly concur in the arrangement. All depleted battalions

[1] 2nd, 2/24th, 2/30th, 2/31st, 2/44th, 51st, 2/53rd, 2/58th, 2/66th, 68th, 2/83rd, 94th.
[2] 1st Prov. Bat. = 2/31st and 2/66th ; 2nd = 2nd and 2/53rd ; 3rd = 2/24th and 2/58th ; 4th = 2/30th and 2/44th.
[3] e.g. the 51st and 68th. *Wellington Dispatches*, ix. p. 609.

for which no drafts could be found must come home at once. ' Experience has shown that a skeleton battalion composed of officers, non-commissioned officers, and a certain foundation of old and experienced soldiers can be reformed for any service in a short time : but if a corps reduced in numbers be broken up by the division of its establishment, such an interruption is occasioned in its interior economy and *esprit de corps*, that its speedy recompletion and reorganization for foreign service is effectually prevented. The experiment now suggested has once been tried, and has resulted in a degree of irregularity, contention, and indiscipline in the regiment concerned, which had made necessary the strongest measures.' (Many court martials, and the removal of the whole of the officers into other battalions.) It was justly urged that seasoned men are more valuable than men fresh from England, but for the sake of a present and comparatively trifling advantage the general efficiency of the whole British Army must not be impaired. All the depleted battalions should be sent home at once[1].

Wellington was deeply vexed at this decision. He replied that orders, if definitely given, would of course be obeyed ; but if left to act on his own responsibility, he could only say that the service in America or Sicily or at home was not his concern, and that he was bound to state what was best for the Peninsular Army. One old soldier who has served two years in Spain was more effective than two, or even three, who had not. Raw battalions fill the hospitals, straggle, maraud, and starve. He never would part with the Provisional Battalions as long as it was left to his discretion : and the same with cavalry. He had four depleted cavalry regiments much under-horsed : he would like to have the horses of the four hussar regiments which were being sent to him from England to give to his old Peninsula troopers, rather than the regiments themselves. But orders are orders and must be obeyed [2].

The Duke replied that for his part he had to take into consideration not only the Peninsula but the British service all over the world. Drafting of one corps into another was hurtful to the service and depressed the spirits of corps : it was even

---

[1] The Duke to Wellington, *Supplementary Dispatches*, vii. pp. 524–5.
[2] Wellington to Torrens, *Dispatches*, x. pp. 77–8.

deemed illegal. Though the last person in the world to wish
to diminish the Army in Spain or cripple its general's exertions,
he was compelled to persevere in his direction from necessity [1].

On March 13th Wellington reluctantly carried out the orders
from the Horse Guards as regards his depleted cavalry regiments : the 4th Dragoon Guards, 9th and 11th Light Dragoons,
and 2nd Hussars of the German Legion were ordered to make
over their effective horses to other regiments, and to prepare
to embark at Lisbon. A paragraph in the General Orders
expressed Wellington's regret at losing any of his brave old
troops, and his hope that he might yet see them again at the
front [2].

As to the infantry, the Duke repeating his general precept
that depleted battalions must come home, but not giving
definite orders for them by name and number, a curious compromise took place. Wellington sent back to England the two
weakest units, which were still in April well under 300 bayonets
apiece [3] : he had already drafted a third into the senior
battalion of its own regiment, which was also in the Peninsula.
Four more of the war-worn battalions had been worked up to
about 400 of all ranks, by the return of convalescents and the
arrival of small drafts—Wellington ventured to keep them,
and to report them as efficient battalions, if small ones [4]. The
challenge to Home authority lay with the remaining six [5] :
though five of them were well under 400 strong he nevertheless
stuck to his original plan and formed three provisional battalions
out of them. If the Duke of York wanted them, he must ask
for them by name : he did not, and they kept the field till the
end of the war, and were repeatedly mentioned by Wellington
as among the most efficient units that he owned. Presumably
Vittoria put his arrangements beyond criticism—at any rate,
the controversy was dropped at the Duke's end. The net result
was that Wellington lost three depleted infantry units and
four depleted cavalry units of the old stock—about 2,000

---

[1] The Duke to Wellington, *Supplementary Dispatches*, vii. p. 553,
ebruary 17.

[2] Ibid., vii. pp. 581–3.

[3] The 2/30th and 2/44th.   [4] The 51st, 68th, 2/83rd, and 94th.

[5] 2nd, 2/24th, 2/31st, 2/53rd, 2/58th, 2/66th.

veteran sabres and bayonets. In return he received before or during the campaign of 1813 four new cavalry regiments —all hussars [1]—and six new infantry battalions [2] all much stronger than the units they replaced, and making up about 1,600 sabres and 3,000 bayonets. He would probably have said that his real strength was not appreciably changed by getting 4,500 new hands instead of 2,000 old ones. Certainly, considering the effort that was required from the Peninsula Army in 1813, it is sufficiently surprising that its strength was, on balance, only four infantry units to the good—the cavalry regiments remaining the same in number as in 1812.

There were plenty of small administrative problems to be settled during the winter-rest of 1812–13, which worried Wellington but need not worry the modern student of history, being in themselves trivial. It is well, however, to note that in the spring of 1813 his old complaint about the impossibility of extracting hard cash from the Government, instead of the bank-notes and bills which the Spanish and Portuguese peasantry refused to regard as real money, came practically to an end. By heroic exertions the Chancellor of the Exchequer was scraping together gold enough to send £100,000 a month to Lisbon. A large sum in pagodas had been brought all the way from Madras, and the Mint was busy all the year in melting them down and recoining them as guineas. It was the first time since the ' Suspension of Cash Payments Act ' of 1797 that any gold of this size had been struck and issued. As the whole output went straight to the Peninsula for the Army, the new coin was generally known as the ' military guinea.' Considering that gold was so much sought for in England at the time that a guinea could command 27s. in paper, it was no small feat to procure the Indian gold, and to see that the much wanted commodity went abroad without diminution. Wellington could have done with much more gold—six times as much he once observed—but at least he was no longer in the state of absolute bankruptcy in which he had opened the campaign of the preceding year—nor obliged to depend for a few thousand

[1] 7th, 10th, 15th, 18th Hussars.
[2] 2/59th (from Cadiz), 2/62nd, 76th, 77th (from Lisbon garrison), 2/84th, 85th.

dollars on profits to be made on Egyptian corn which he sold in Lisbon, or impositions of doubtful legality made upon speculators in Commissariat Bonds. The Portuguese troops had their pay still in arrears—but that was not Wellington's responsibility. The muleteers of the transport train were suffering from being paid in *vales*, which they sold to Lisbon sharks, rather than in the *cruzados novos* or Pillar Dollars which they craved, and sometimes deserted in not unnatural disgust. But, at the worst, it could not be denied that finance looked a good deal more promising than it had in 1812 [1].

There had been much reorganization since the end of the Burgos retreat. In uniforms especially the change was greater than in any other year of the war : this was the first campaign in which the British heavy cavalry showed the new brass helmet, discarding the antiquated cocked hat—the light dragoons had gone into shakos, relinquishing the black japanned leather helmet with bearskin crest. Infantry officers for the first time appeared in shakos resembling those of the rank and file—the unwise custom by which they had up till now worn cocked hats, which made them easy marks for the enemy's snipers, being at last officially condemned. Another much needed improvement was the substitution of small tin camp kettles, to be carried by the men, for the large iron Flanders cooking-pots, four to each company and carried on mules, which had hitherto been employed. They had always been a nuisance ; partly because the mules could never be relied upon to keep up with the unit, partly because their capacity was so large that it took much firewood and a long space of time to cook their contents. Nothing is more common in personal diaries of 1808–12 than complaints about rations that had to be eaten half-cooked, or were not eaten at all, because the order to move on arrived before the cauldrons had even begun to get warm.

A more doubtful expedient was that of putting the great-coats of the whole of the infantry into store before the march began. Wellington opined that the weight of coat and blanket combined was more than the soldier could be expected to carry. One or

---

[1] On all this the reader interested in military finance will find excellent commentaries in chap. i of vol. ix of Mr. Fortescue's *History of the British Army*, which appeared three months after this chapter of mine was written.

other must be abandoned, and after much consideration it was
concluded that the blanket was more essential. ' Soldiers while
in exercise during the day seldom wear their great-coats, which
are worn by them only at night, together with the blanket :
but as the Commander of the forces has now caused the army
to be provided with tents, the necessity for the great-coat for
night use is superseded [1].' And tents, as a matter of fact, were
provided for the first time during this campaign. The expedient
worked well enough during the summer and autumn, when the
weather was usually fine, in spite of some spells of rainy weather
in June. But in the Pyrenees, from October onward, the tents
proved inadequate protection both from sudden hurricanes and
from continuous snowfall. And bad though the plight of men
huddled in tents frozen stiff by the north wind might be, it
was nothing to that of the sentry on some mountain defile,
trying to keep a blanket round his shoulders in December
blizzards. Yet the tents, with all their defects, were a decided
boon—it would have been impossible indeed to hold the Pyrenean passes at all, if some shelter had not been provided for the
battalions of the front line. Villages available for billeting were
few and always in the hollows to the rear, not on the crests
where the line of defence lay. It would seem that the experiment of dispensing with the great-coats was dropped, and that
they were brought round by sea to Pasages or St. Sebastian,
for personal diaries mention them as in use again, in at least
some regiments, by December. Oddly enough, there appears
to be no official record of the revocation of the order given in
May.

Another innovation of the period was the introduction of a
new unit into the British Army—called (after the idiotic system
of nomenclature used at the Horse Guards) the ' Staff Corps
Cavalry.' They were really military mounted police, picked
from the best and steadiest men in the cavalry regiments, and
placed under the command of Major Scovell, the cypher-
secretary on Wellington's head-quarters staff, of whose activities
much has been said in the last volume. There were two troops
of them, soon raised to four, with a total strength of about
300 of all ranks [2]. The object of the creation of the corps was

---

[1] See *Supplementary Dispatches*, xiv. p. 212.　　　[2] Ibid., vii. pp. 539–41.

to make more effectual the restraint on marauding, and other crimes with which the Provost-Marshal and his assistants were too few to deal. Wellington had railed with almost exaggerated emphasis on the straggling, disorder, and looting which had distinguished the Burgos retreat, and the Duke of York had licensed the formation of this police-cavalry as the best remedy for the disease. They had plenty to do after Vittoria, when the British Army had the greatest orgy of plunder that ever fell to its lot during the war. Wellington's own view was that the slackness of discipline in certain regiments, rather than privations or casual opportunity, was the main source of all evil. But he welcomed any machinery that would deal with the symptoms of indiscipline, even if it did not strike at the roots of the disease. Over-leniency by courts martial was another cause of misconduct according to his theory—with this he strove to cope by getting from home a civilian Judge-Advocate-General, whose task was to revise the proceedings of such bodies, and disallow illegal proceedings and decisions. The first and only holder of this office, Francis Larpent, has left an interesting and not always discreet account of his busy life at Head-Quarters, which included a strange episode of captivity in the French lines on the Bidassoa [1].

[1] He was captured by a raiding party, while watching the enemy from too short a distance, on August 31.

SECTION XXXV: CHAPTER IV

THE PERPLEXITIES OF KING JOSEPH. FEBRUARY–MARCH 1813

WE have seen, when dealing with the last month of 1812 and the distribution of the French army into winter quarters, that all the arrangements made by King Joseph, Jourdan, and Soult were settled before any knowledge of the meaning of the Moscow Retreat had come to hand. The famous ' 29th Bulletin ' did not reach Madrid till January 6th, 1813 ; this was a long delay : but the Emperor's return to Paris on December 16th, though he arrived at the Tuileries only thirty-six hours after the Bulletin had come to hand, was not known to Joseph or Jourdan till February 14th—which was a vastly longer delay. The road had been blocked between Vittoria and Burgos for over five weeks—and couriers and dispatches were accumulating at both these places—one set unable to get south, the other to get north. The Minister of War at Paris received Joseph's dispatches of the 9th, 20th, and 24th of December all in one delivery on January 29th [1]. The King, still more unlucky, got the Paris dispatches of all the dates between December 18th and January 4th on February 14th to 16th by several couriers who came through almost simultaneously [2]. It was not till Palombini's Italian division—in a series of fights lasting from January 25 to February 13—had cleared away Longa and Mendizabal from the high-road between Burgos and Vittoria, that quicker communication between those cities became possible.

Long as it had taken in 1812 to get a letter from Paris to Madrid, there had never been such a monstrous gap in correspondence as that which took place in January 1813. Hence came the strange fact that when Napoleon had returned to France, and started on his old system of giving strategical orders

---

[1] So Clarke to the King, *Corresp. du Roi Joseph*, vol. ix. p. 189.
[2] Jourdan, *Mémoires*, p. 452.

for the Army of Spain once more, these orders [1]—one on top of another—accumulated at Vittoria, and came in one overwhelming mass, to upset all the plans which Joseph and Jourdan had been carrying out since the New Year.

The King had received the 29th Bulletin on January 6th: he had gathered from it that matters were going badly with the army in Russia, but had no conception of the absolute ruin that had befallen his brother's host. Hence he had kept his troops spread in the wide cantonments taken in December, and had sent Daricau's to the province of Cuenca, to reopen the way to Suchet at Valencia. The great convoy of Spanish and French administrators, courtiers, and refugees, which had been left in Suchet's care, retraced its way to Madrid under escort of some of Daricau's troops in the last days of January. Meanwhile Pierre Soult's cavalry continued to sweep La Mancha, imposing contributions and shooting guerrilleros, and the Army of the Centre cleared the greater part of the country east and north of Madrid of strong parties of the Medico's and the Empecinado's men. Caffarelli, as Jourdan complained, ought to have been making more head in the North—but his dispatches were so infrequent that his position could not be fully judged— it was only certain that he could not keep the Burgos–Bayonne road open for couriers.

There was only one touch during the winter with Wellington's army, whose cantonments, save those of the Light Division, were far back, behind the ' no man's land ' which encircled the French armies. This single contact was due to an adventurous reconnaissance by Foy, who at his head-quarters at Avila had conceived a project for surprising Hill's most outlying detachment, the 50th regiment, which was billeted at Bejar, in the passes in front of Coria. On false news that no good look-out was being kept around Bejar, he started on the 19th February from Piedrahita with a column of three very weak infantry battalions and 80 horse—about 1,500 men in all, and marching day and night fell upon the cantonments of the 50th at dawn on the morning of the 20th. The surprise did not come off. Colonel Harrison of the 50th was a cautious officer, who had barricaded the ruined gates of the town, and patched its crumbling walls—

---

[1] See *Corresp. du Roi Joseph*, ix. p. 187.

He had picquets far out, and was accustomed to keep several
companies under arms from 2 o'clock till daylight every night.
Moreover Hill, thinking the position exposed, had lately
reinforced him with the 6th Caçadores, from Ashworth's
brigade. Foy, charging in on the town in the dusk, dislodged
the outlying picquets after a sharp skirmish; but his advanced
guard of 300 voltigeurs met such a storm of fire from the gate
and walls, which were fully manned, that it swerved off when
30 yards from the entrance. Foy ordered a general retreat,
since he saw the enemy ready for him, and marched off as
quickly as he had come, pursued for some distance by the
Caçadores [1]. He says in his dispatch to Reille that he only lost
two men killed and five wounded, that he could have carried
the town had he pleased, and that he only retired because he
was warned that the 71st and 92nd, the other regiments of
Cadogan's brigade, were marching up from Baños, seven miles
away [2]. This those may believe who please: it is certain that
he made off the moment that he saw that his surprise had
failed, and that he was committed to an attack on a barricaded
town. Hill expected more raids of this sort, but the attempt
was never repeated.

It was on the 14th of February, five days before Foy's
adventure, that King Joseph received his first Paris mail. Its
portentous and appalling contents were far worse than anything
that he had expected. The most illuminating item was a letter
from Colonel Desprez, his aide-de-camp, who had made the
Moscow retreat, and was able to give him the whole truth
concerning Russia. 'We lost prisoners by the tens of thousands
—but, however many the prisoners, the dead are many more.
Every nightly bivouac left hundreds of frozen corpses behind.
The situation may be summed up by saying that the army is
dead. The Young Guard, to which I was attached, quitted
Moscow 8,000 strong; there were 400 left at Wilna. All the
other corps have suffered on the same scale; I am convinced

[1] See account in the Memoirs of Patterson of the 50th, pp. 303–5.
[2] See dispatch in Girod's *Vie militaire du Général Foy*, pp. 386–7. The
whole is written in a boastful and unconvincing style, unworthy of such a
good soldier. Colonel Harrison's report is singularly vague and short.
He only says that the enemy made off, leaving their dead behind.

that not 20,000 men recrossed the Vistula. If your Majesty asks me where the retreat will stop, I can only reply that the Russians will settle that point. I cannot think that the Prussians will resist : the King and his ministers are favourably disposed—not so the people—riots are breaking out in Berlin : crossing Prussia I had evidence that we can hardly count on these allies. And it seems that in the Austrian army the officers are making public demonstrations against continuing the war. This is a sad picture—but I think there is no exaggeration in it. On returning to Paris and thinking all over in cold blood, my judgement on the situation is as gloomy as it was at the theatre of war [1].'

Napoleon had spent several days at the Tuileries, busy with grandiose schemes for the organization of a new *Grande Armée*, to replace that which he had sacrificed in Russia, and with financial and diplomatic problems of absorbing interest, before he found a moment in which to dictate to Clarke his orders for the King of Spain. The note was very short and full of reticences [2] : it left much unsaid that had to be supplied by the recipient's intelligence. 'The King must have received by now the 29th Bulletin, which would show him the state of affairs in the North ; they were absorbing the Emperor's care and attention. Things being as they were, he ought to move his head-quarters to Valladolid, holding Madrid only as the extreme point of occupation of his southern wing. He should turn his attention to the pacification of Biscay and Navarre while the English were inactive. Soult had been sent orders to come back to France—as the King had repeatedly requested ; his Army of the South might be given over to Marshal Jourdan or to Gazan.' If Joseph had owned no independent sources of information such a statement would have left him much in the dark, both as to the actual state of the Emperor's resources, and as to his intentions with regard to Spain. The Emperor did *not* say that he had lost his army and must create another, nor did he intimate how far he intended to give up his Spanish venture. But the order to draw back to Valladolid and hold Madrid lightly, could only be interpreted as a warning that

---

[1] Desprez to Joseph, from Paris, January 3, *Corresp. R. J.* ix. pp. 180–2.
[2] *Nap. Corresp.* xxiv, no. 19411.

there would be no more reinforcements available for Spain, so that the area of occupation would have to be contracted.

The recall of Soult was what Joseph had eagerly petitioned for in 1812, when he had come upon the curious letter in which the Marshal accused him before the Emperor of treason to the French cause [1]. But the Marshal was not brought home in disgrace ; rather he was sent for in the hour of danger, as one who could be useful to the new *Grande Armée*. It must have been irritating to the King to know, from a passage in the already-cited letter of Colonel Desprez, that Napoleon had called the Duke of Dalmatia ' the only military brain in the Peninsula ', that he stigmatized the King's denunciations of him as *des pauvretés* to which he attached no importance, and that he had added that half the generals in Spain had shared Soult's suspicions. The Marshal left, in triumph rather than in disgrace, with a large staff and escort, and a long train of *fourgons* carrying his Andalusian plunder, more especially his splendid gallery of Murillos robbed from Seville churches [2].

Dated one day later than the Emperor's first rough notes, we find the formal dispatch from the war-minister Clarke, which made things a little clearer. Setting forth his master's ideas in a more verbose style, Clarke explained that the affairs of Spain must be subordinated to those of the North. The move to Valladolid would make communication with Paris shorter and safer, and provide a larger force to hold down Northern Spain. Caffarelli was not strong enough both to hunt down the guerrilleros and at the same time to provide garrisons on the great roads and the coast. The King would have to lend him a hand in the task.

There were other dispatches for Joseph and Jourdan dated on the 4th of January, but only one more of importance : this was an order for wholesale drafts to be made from the Army of Spain, for the benefit of the new Army of Germany. But large as they were, the limited scale of them showed that the Emperor had not the least intention of surrendering his hold on the Peninsula, or of drawing back to the line of the Ebro or the Pyrenees, as Lord Liverpool had expected [3]. All the six

[1] See vol. v. pp. 538–9.
[2] Miot de Melito, iii. pp. 263–4.   [3] See above, pp. 215–16.

Armies of Spain—those of the North, Portugal, the Centre, the South, Aragon, and Catalonia—were to continue in existence, and the total number of men to be drawn from any one of them did not amount to a fourth of its numbers. There were still to be 200,000 men left in the Peninsula.

The first demand was for twenty-five picked men from each battalion of infantry or regiment of cavalry, and ten from each battery of artillery, to reconstitute the Imperial Guard, reduced practically to nothing in Russia. Putting aside foreign regiments (Italian, Neapolitan, German, Swiss) there were some 220 French battalions in Spain in January 1813, and some 35 regiments of cavalry. The call was therefore for 5,500 bayonets and 875 sabres—no great amount from an army which had 260,000 men on its rolls, and 212,000 actually under the colours.

But this was only a commencement. It was more important that the Armies of the South and Catalonia were to contribute a large number of cadres to the new *Grande Armée*. Those of Portugal, Aragon, the Centre, and the North were at first less in question, because their regiments were, on the average, not so strong as those of the other two. The Army of the South was specially affected, because its units were (and always had been) very large regiments. In 1812 Soult's infantry corps nearly all had three battalions—a few four. Similarly with the cavalry, many regiments had four squadrons, none less than three. The edict of January 4th ordered that each infantry regiment should send back to France the full cadre of officers and non-commissioned officers for one battalion, with a skeleton cadre of men, cutting down the number of battalions present with the eagle by one, and drafting the surplus rank and file of the subtracted battalion into those remaining in Spain. The cadre was roughly calculated out to 120 of all ranks. When, therefore, the system was applied to the Army of the South, it was cut down from 57 battalions to 36 in its 19 regiments [1]. The 21 cadres took off to France 2,500 officers and men. Similarly 15 cavalry regiments, in 50 squadrons, were to send 12 squadron-cadres to France, some 600 sabres.

[1] Two regiments which had only two battalions in February 1813 got cut down to one apiece.

The small Army of Catalonia was to contribute a battalion-cadre from each of those of its regiments which had three or more battalions—which would give six more cadres for Germany.

The Armies of Portugal, Aragon, and the Centre were mainly composed of regiments having only two battalions—they were therefore for the present left comparatively untouched. The first named was only ordered to give up one battalion-cadre, the second two, the third three (all from Palombini's Italian division). Of cavalry the Army of Portugal only gave up one squadron-cadre, the Army of the Centre three.

In addition, the small number of foreign auxiliary troops still left in Spain were ordered back to France, save the remnant of Palombini's and Severoli's Italians and the Rheinbund units [1] in the Army of the Centre, viz. the 7th Polish Lancers (the last regiment of troops of this nationality left south of the Pyrenees), the Westphalian horse in the Army of the Centre, and the Berg and Westphalian infantry in Catalonia. Moreover, the brigade of the Young Guard in the Army of the North (that of Dumoustier) and the three naval battalions from Cadiz, which had served so long in the Army of the South, were to come home, also four batteries of French horse-artillery and two of Westphalian field artillery. Lastly, cadres being as necessary for the military train as for any other branch of the service, all the armies were to send home every dismounted man of this corps. The same rule was applied to the *Équipages militaires* and the Artillery Park. This whole deduction from the Army of Spain under these heads came to nearly 12,000 soldiers of all arms, over and above these cadres.

There was an elaborate clause as to reorganizing the Army of the North: in return for giving up four provisional regiments of drafts to the Armies of Portugal and the South, it was to get three regiments made over to it from the former, and one from the latter. Napoleon calculated that it would lose nothing in numbers from the exchange, but as a matter of fact it did. The drafts to be returned to their proper corps ran to over 8,000 men. But General Reille, being told to contribute three regiments to the Army of the North, selected the three depleted units which had composed Thomières' unlucky

---

[1] A brigade not a division, since the Hessian regiment perished at Badajoz.

division at the battle of Salamanca (the 1st, 62nd, and 101st), which together did not make up 3,000 bayonets [1], though Gazan chose to make over the 64th, a three-battalion regiment with 1,600 men. The Army of the North, therefore, lost nearly 3,000 men on the balance of the exchange, though the Emperor was aware that it was already too weak for the task set it. But he probably considered that Palombini's Italians, detached (as we have already seen [2]) from the Army of the Centre, would make up the difference.

In addition to the squadron-cadres which he requisitioned on January 4th, the Emperor had a further intention of bringing back to Central Europe some complete units of heavy cavalry, to furnish the host now collecting in Germany with the horse-men in which it was so notoriously deficient. The whole of the dragoon-division of Boyer in the Army of Portugal is marked in the March returns with *ordre de rentrer en France* ; so are several dragoon regiments in the Army of the South. But as a matter of fact hardly one of them had started for the Pyrenees by May [3], so that both in the Army of Portugal and the Army of the South the cavalry total was only a few hundreds smaller at the time of the opening of the campaign of Vittoria than it had been at the New Year—the shrinkage amounting to no more than the squadron-cadres and the few men for the Imperial Guard.

The Emperor's intentions, therefore, as they became known to King Joseph and Jourdan on February 16th, left the three armies opposed to Wellington some 15,000 men smaller than they had been at the time of the Burgos retreat ; but this was a very modest deduction considering their size, and still kept nearly 100,000 men in Castile and Leon, over and above the Army of the North, which might be considered as tied down to its own duty of suppressing the rising in Biscay and Navarre, and incapable of sparing any help to its neighbours. When we reflect on the scale of the Russian disaster, the demand made upon the Army of Spain seems very moderate. But there were

---

[1] He had also later to give up the 22nd, a weak one-battalion regiment of 700 bayonets.   [2] See above, p. 188.

[3] Even the 2nd Dragoons, the first regiment scheduled, though it started in March, shows casualties at Vittoria, so did not get away.

two ominous doubts. Would the Emperor be content with his original requisitions in men and horses from the armies of Spain ? And what exactly did he mean by the phrase that the King would have to lend *appui et secours* to the Army of the North, for the destruction of the rebels beyond the Ebro ? If this signified the distraction of any large body of men from the forces left opposed to Wellington, the situation would be uncomfortable. Both these doubts soon developed into sinister certainties.

On receiving the Emperor's original orders King Joseph hastened to obey, though the removal of his court from Madrid to Valladolid looked to him like the abandonment of his pose as King of Spain. He ordered Soult's successor, Gazan, to evacuate La Mancha, and to draw back to the neighbourhood of Madrid, leaving a small detachment of light troops about Toledo. The Army of the South also took over the province of Avila from the Army of Portugal, and it was intended that it should soon relieve the Army of the Centre in the province of Segovia. For Joseph had made up his mind that any help which he must give against the northern rebels should be furnished by D'Erlon's little army, which he would stretch out from Segovia towards Burgos and the Ebro [1], and so take Mina and the insurgents of Navarre in the rear. Early in March all these movements were in progress, and (as we have seen in the last chapter) were beginning to be reported to Wellington, who made many deductions from them. Joseph himself transferred his head-quarters to Valladolid on March 23rd, by which time the greater part of the other changes had been carried out. The Emperor afterwards criticized his brother's delay of a whole month between the receipt of his orders to decamp and his actual arrival at Valladolid. To this Jourdan made the reply that it was useless to move the head-quarters till the drawing in of the Army of the South had been completed, and that the bringing in of such outlying units as Daricau's division from the province of Cuenca, and the transference of the Army of the Centre northward, took much time [2]. Evacuations cannot be carried out at a day's notice, when they involve the moving of magazines and the calling in of a civil administration.

---

[1] See Joseph to Suchet, *Correspondance*, ix. p. 200.
[2] See *Mémoires du Roi Joseph*, ix. p. 134.

On March 12th, while all the movements were in progress, another batch of orders from Paris came to hand. They contained details which upset the arrangements which the King was carrying out, for the Emperor decided that the succour which was to be given to the Army of the North was to be drawn from Reille's Army, and not from D'Erlon's, so that a new series of counter-marches would have to be carried out. And—what was more ominous for the future—Napoleon had dropped once more into his old habit of sending orders directly to subordinate generals, without passing them through the head-quarters of the Army of Spain. For Clarke, in his dispatch of February 3rd, informed the King that the Emperor had sent Reille directions to detach a division to Navarre at once, ' a disposition which cannot conflict with any orders which your Majesty may give to the Army of Portugal, for the common end of reducing to submission the provinces of the North [1].' Unfortunately this was precisely what such an order did accomplish, for Joseph had sent D'Erlon in the direction to which he now found that Reille had simultaneously detached Barbot's division of the Army of Portugal, without any knowledge that D'Erlon had already been detailed for the job.

The Emperor was falling back into the practice by which he had in the preceding year ruined Marmont—the issuing of detailed orders for the movement of troops, based on information a month old, it being certain that the execution of these orders would take place an additional three weeks after they had been formulated. As we shall presently see, the initial successes of Wellington in his Vittoria campaign were entirely due to the position in which the Army of Portugal had placed itself, in obedience to Napoleon's direct instructions.

Meanwhile Clarke's dispatch of February 2nd, conveying these orders, arrived at the same moment as two others dated ten days later [2], which were most unpleasant reading. The first contained an absolutely insulting message to the King from his brother : ' his Imperial Majesty bids me say,' wrote Clarke, ' with regard to the money for which you have asked in several recent letters, that all funds necessary for the armies of Spain

---

[1] Clarke to Joseph, *Correspondance*, ix. p. 193 (February 2).
[2] Ibid. (February 12), pp. 194–5.

could have been got out of the rich and fertile provinces which
are being devastated by the insurgent bands. By employing
the activity and vigour needed to establish order and tranquillity, the resources which they still possess can be utilized. This
is an additional motive for inducing your Majesty to put an
end to this war in the interior, which troubles peaceful inhabitants, ruins the countryside, exhausts your armies, and deprives
them of the resources which they could enjoy if these fine regions
were in a peaceful state. Aragon and Navarre are to-day under
Mina's law, and maintain this disastrous struggle with their food
and money. It is time to put an end to this state of affairs.'

Written apparently a few hours later than the dispatch
quoted above came another [1], setting forth the policy which was
to be the ruin of the French cause in Spain three months later.
It is composed of a series of wild miscalculations. When the
head-quarters of the Army of Spain should have been moved
to Valladolid, it would be possible to send the whole Army of
Portugal to help the Army of the North beyond the Ebro. ' The
Armies of the Centre and South, occupying Salamanca and
Valladolid, have sufficient strength to keep the English in
check, while waiting on events. Madrid and even Valencia are
of secondary importance. Valladolid and Salamanca have
become the essential points, between which there should be
distributed forces ready to take the offensive against the
English, and to wreck their plans. The Emperor is informed
that they have been reinforced in Portugal, and that they seem
to have two alternative schemes—either to make a push into
Spain, or to send out from the port of Lisbon an expedition
of 25,000 men, partly English, partly Spanish, which is to land
somewhere on the French coast, when the campaign shall
have begun in Germany. To prevent them engaging in this
expedition, you must always be in a position to march forward
and to threaten to overrun Portugal and take Lisbon. At the
same time you must make the communications with France
safe and easy, by using the time of the English inactivity to
subdue Biscay and Navarre. . . . If the French armies in Spain
remain idle, and permit the English to send expeditions against
our coast, the tranquillity of France will be compromised, and
the ruin of our cause in Spain will infallibly follow.'

[1] Clarke to Joseph, February 12. Ibid., pp. 197–9.

A supplementary letter to Jourdan of the same day recapitulates all the above points, adding that the Army of Portugal must send to Clausel, now Caffarelli's successor in the North, as many troops as are needed there, but that the King at the same time must menace Portugal, so that Wellington shall not be able to detach men from his Peninsular Army.

The fundamental error in all this is that, underrating Wellington's strength, Napoleon judged that the Armies of the South and Centre could keep him in check. They were at this moment under 60,000 of all arms : if the Army of Portugal were out of the way, they were absolutely insufficient for the task set them. As to their menacing Lisbon, Wellington would have liked nothing better than an advance by them into Portugal, where he would have outnumbered them hopelessly. The hypothesis that Wellington was about to send 25,000 men by sea for a landing inside the French Empire, on which Napoleon lays so much stress, seems to have been formed on erroneous information from French spies in London, who had heard the rumour that a raid on Holland or Hanover was likely, or perhaps even one aimed at La Vendée. For the royalist *émigrés* in England had certainly been talking of such a plan, and pressing it upon Lord Liverpool, as the dispatches of the latter to Wellington show [1]. The Emperor did not know that all such schemes would be scouted by the British Commander in Spain, and that he now possessed influence enough with the Cabinet to stop them.

It would appear that the Emperor's intelligence from England misled him in other ways : he was duly informed of the departure from Lisbon of the depleted cavalry and infantry units, about which Wellington disputed so much with the Duke of York, and the deduction drawn was that the Peninsular Army was being decreased. The exaggerated impression of the losses in the Burgos retreat, which could be gathered from the Whig newspapers, led to an underrating of the strength that the British Army would have in the spring. Traitors from Cadiz wrote to Madrid that the friction between the Regency and Wellington was so great, that it was doubtful whether the new Generalissimo would have any real control over the Spanish armies. And the sickness in both the British and the Portuguese armies—bad as it was—was exaggerated by spies, so

[1] See above, p. 219.

wildly that the Emperor was under the delusion that Wellington
could not count on more than 30,000 British or 20,000 Portuguese troops in the coming campaign. It may be worth while
to quote at this point the official view at Paris of the British
army in Portugal, though the words were written some time
later, and only just before the news of Wellington's sudden
advance on the Douro had come to hand :

' In the position in which the enemy found himself there was
no reason to fear that he would take the offensive : his remoteness, his lack of transport, his constant and timid caution in
all operations out of the ordinary line, all announced that we
had complete liberty to act as suited us best, without worry or
inconvenience. I may add that the ill feeling between English
and Spaniards, the voyage of Lord Wellington to Cadiz, the
changes in his army, of which many regiments have been sent
back to England, were all favourable circumstances allowing
us to carry out fearlessly every movement that the Emperor's
orders might dictate [1].'

It is only necessary to observe that Wellington was not more
remote from the French than they were from him : that he had
excellent transport—far better than his enemies ever enjoyed :
that timid caution was hardly the policy which stormed
Badajoz or won Salamanca : that his rapid and triumphant
offensive was just starting when the Minister of War wrote the
egregious paragraph which we have just cited. Persistent
undervaluing of the resources and energy of Wellington by
Head-quarters at Paris—i.e. by the Emperor when present, by
the Minister of War in his absence—was at the roots of the
impending disaster.

Leaving the King newly established at Valladolid, the Army
of the South redistributing itself between Madrid and the
Douro, the Army of the Centre turning back from its projected
march to Burgos in order to reoccupy the province of Segovia,
and the Army of Portugal beginning to draw off from in front
of Wellington troops to be sent to the North, we must turn for
a moment to explain the crisis in Navarre and Biscay which was
engrossing so much of Napoleon's attention.

[1] *Correspondance du Roi Joseph,* ix. p. 290, written just before Clarke
got news of Wellington's start.

SECTION XXXV : CHAPTER V

THE NORTHERN INSURRECTION. FEBRUARY–MAY 1813

It has been explained in an earlier chapter that ever since General Caffarelli concentrated all the available troops of the Army of the North, in order to join Souham in driving away Wellington from the siege of Burgos, the three Basque provinces, Navarre, and the coastland of Santander had been out of hand [1]. The outward and visible sign of that fact was the intermittent stoppage of communication between Bayonne and Madrid, which had so much irritated Napoleon on his return from Russia. It was undoubtedly a just cause of anger that important dispatches should be hung up at Tolosa, or Vittoria, or Burgos, because the bands of Mina or Mendizabal or Longa were holding the defile of Salinas—the grave of so many convoy-escorts—or the pass of Pancorbo. It had been calculated in 1811 that it might often require a small column of 250 men to bring an imperial courier safely through either of those perilous narrows. But in the winter of 1812–13 things had grown far worse. ' The insurgents of Guipuzcoa, Navarre, and Aragon,' as Clarke wrote to Jourdan with perfect truth [2], ' have had six months to organize and train themselves : their progress has been prodigious : they have formed many formidable corps, which no longer fear to face our troops when numbers are equal. They have called in the English, and receive every day arms, munitions, and even cannon on the coast. They have actually begun to conduct regular sieges.' Yet it was three months and more since the King had sent back Caffarelli and the field-force of the Army of the North from Valladolid, to restore order in the regions which had slipped out of hand during the great concentration of the French armies in November.

If it be asked why the North had become so far more unquiet

---

[1] See above, pp. 190–91.

[2] Dispatch of February 26, *Correspondance du Roi Joseph*, ix. p. 206.

than it had been in previous years, the answer must be that the
cause was moral and not material.　It was not merely that
many small places had been evacuated for a time by the French
during the Burgos campaign, nor that the British fleet was
throwing in arms and supplies at Castro-Urdiales or Santander.
The important thing was that for the first time since 1808 the
whole people had got a glimpse of hope : the French had been
driven out of Madrid ; they had evacuated Biscay ; Old Castile
and Leon had been in the power of Wellington for several
months.　It was true that Madrid had been recovered, that
Wellington had been forced to retreat.　But it was well known
that the general result of the campaign of 1812 had been to free
all Southern Spain, and that the French had been on the verge
of ruin in the early autumn.　The prestige of the Imperial
armies had received at Salamanca a blow from which it never
recovered.　Wherefore the insurgents of the North put forth
during the winter of 1812–13 an energy such as they had never
before displayed, and the French generals gradually discovered
that they had no longer to do with mere guerrillero bands, half-
armed, half-fed wanderers in the hills, recruited only from the
desperate and the reckless, but with a whole people in arms.
When Caffarelli returned from Burgos, he found that the Spanish
authorities had re-established themselves in every town which
had been left ungarrisoned, that taxes and requisitions were
being levied in a regular fashion, and that new regiments were
being formed and trained in Biscay and Guipuzcoa.　The
nominal Spanish commander in this region was Mendizabal,
theoretically Chief of the ' Seventh Army '—but he was an
officer of little resource and no authority.　The real fighting
man was Longa, originally a guerrillero chief, but now gazetted
a colonel in the regular army.　He was a gunsmith from the
Rioja, a very resolute and persistent man, who had taken to the
hills early, and had outlived most of his rivals and colleagues—
a clear instance of the ' survival of the fittest.'　His useful
co-operation with Sir Home Popham in the last autumn has
been mentioned above : his band, now reorganized as four
infantry battalions, was raised from the mountaineers of the
province of Santander and the region of the upper Ebro.　His
usual beat lay between the sea and Burgos, and he was as

frequently to be found on the Cantabrian coast as at the defile of Pancorbo, where the great Bayonne *chaussée* crosses from the watershed of the Ebro to that of the Douro. His force never much exceeded 3,000 men, but they were tough material—great marchers and (as they proved when serving under Wellington) very staunch fighters on their own ground. West of Longa's hunting grounds were those of Porlier, in the Eastern Asturias : the star of the ' Marquesito,' as he was called, had paled some- what of late, as the reputation of Longa had increased. He had never had again such a stroke of luck as his celebrated surprise of Santander in 1811 [1], and the long French occupation of the Asturias in the days of Bonnet had worn down his band to little over 2,000 men. At this moment he was mainly engaged, under the nominal command of Mendizabal, in keeping Santoña blockaded. To besiege it in form he had neither enough men nor a battering train : but if driven away once and again by Caffarelli, he never allowed himself to be caught, and was back again to stop the roads, the moment that the relieving column had marched off. In Biscay the leading spirit was Jauregui (El Pastor), another old ally of Sir Home Popham, but in addition to his band there was now on foot a new organiza- tion of a more regular sort, three Biscayan and three Guipuzcoan battalions, who had received arms from the English cruisers. They held all the interior of the country, had fortified the old citadel of Castro-Urdiales on the coast, with guns lent them from the fleet, and co-operated with Mendizabal and Longa whenever occasion offered. They had held Bilbao for a time in the autumn, but were chased out of it when Caffarelli returned from Burgos. In January they made another attempt upon it, but were repulsed by General Rouget, in command of the garrison.

Between the fields of operation of the Biscayans and Longa and that of the Navarrese insurgents, there was the line of the great Bayonne *chaussée*, held by a series of French garrisons at Tolosa, Bergara, Mondragon, Vittoria, Miranda del Ebro, and the castle of Pancorbo. This line of fortified places was a sore hindrance to the Spaniards, but on many occasions they crossed it. Mina's raiding battalions from Navarre were

[1] See vol. iv. p. 472.

frequently seen in the Basque provinces. And they had made communication between one garrison and another so dangerous that the post-commanders often refused to risk men on escorts between one place and the next, and had long ceased to attempt requisitions on the countryside. They were fed by convoys pushed up the high road, with heavy forces to guard them, at infrequent intervals. In Navarre, as has been already explained, Mina held the whole countryside, and had set up an orderly form of government. He had at the most 8,000 or 9,000 men, but they spread everywhere, sometimes operating in one column, sometimes in many, seldom to be caught when sought after, and capable of turning on any rash pursuing force and over-whelming it, if its strength was seen to be over-small. Mina's sphere of action extended far into Aragon, as far as Huesca, so that he was as much a plague to Paris, the Governor of Sara-gossa, as to Thouvenot, Governor of Vittoria, or Abbé, Governor of Pampeluna. His strategical purpose, if we may ascribe such a thing to one who was, after all, but a guerrillero of special talent and energy, was to break the line of communication down the Ebro from Miranda to Saragossa, the route by which the King and the Army of the North kept up their touch with Suchet's troops in Aragon. It was a tempting objective, since all down the river there were French garrisons at short distances in Haro, Logroño, Viana, Calahorra, Milagro, Tudela, and other places, none of them very large, and each capable of being isolated, and attacked for some days, before the Governor of Navarre could come to its aid with a strong relieving column. And there were other garrisons, such as those at Tafalla and Huesca, covering outlying road-centres, which were far from succour and liable to surprise-attacks at any moment.

Nor was Mina destitute of the power to call in help for one of his greater raids—he sometimes shifted towards the coast, and got in touch with the Guipuzcoans and Biscayans, while he had also communication with Duran, south of the Ebro, This officer who was theoretically a division-commander in the Valencian Army, was really the leader of a band of four or five thousand irregulars, who hung about the mountains of Soria, and kept the roads from Madrid to Saragossa and the Ebro blocked. And Duran was again in touch with the Empecinado, whose beat lay on the east side of New Castile, and whose main object was to molest the French garrisons of Guadalajara, Segovia, and Alcalà. Temporary combinations of formidable strength could be made, when several of these irregular forces joined for a common raid : but the chiefs generally worked apart, each disliking to move very far from his own district, where he was acquainted with the roads and the inhabitants. For in a country of chaotic sierras, like Northern Spain, local knowledge was all-important : to be aware of exactly what paths and passes were practicable in January snow, or what torrents were fordable in March rain, was the advantage which the guerrillero had over his enemy. It is probable that in March or April 1813 the total force of all the insurgent bands was no greater than that of the French garrisons and movable columns with which they had to contend. But the Army of the North was forced to tie down the larger half of its strength to holding strategical points and long lines of communication, while the guerrilleros could evacuate one whole region for weeks at a time, in order to mass in another. They could be unexpectedly strong in one district, yet lose nothing by temporary abandonment of another. They were admirably served for intelligence, since the whole population was by goodwill or by fear at their service: the French could only depend on *afrancesados* for information, and these were timid and few ; they grew fewer as Mina gradually discovered and hanged traitors. When the French columns had gone by, it was easily to be guessed who had guided them or given them news—and such people perished, or had to migrate to the nearest garrison. But local knowledge was the real strength of the guerrilleros : a French column-commander, guiding his steps from the abominable maps of Lopez—the atlas which was universally used for want of a better—was always finding his enemy escape by a path unindicated on the map, or appear in his rear over some unknown cross-road, which could not have been suspected to exist. Hence the local Spanish traitor was absolutely necessary as a guide, and often he could not be found—treachery having been discovered to be a path that led inevitably to the gallows. The Army of the North had acquired, from old and painful experience of counter-marches, some general knowledge of the cross-roads between the Ebro and the Pyrenees. But when troops from a distance—sections of the Bayonne Reserve, or reinforcements from the Army of Portugal—were turned on to the game of guerrillero-hunting, they found themselves very helpless. As a rule, the most promising march ended in finding the lair still warm, but the quarry invisible.

Napoleon and his mouthpiece, the War Minister Clarke, refused to the end, as Marshal Marmont remarked [1], to see that the War of Spain was unlike any other war that the French armies had waged since 1792. The nearest parallels to it were the fighting in Switzerland in 1798 and against Hofer's Tyrolese in 1809. But both of these earlier insurrectionary wars had been fought on a very limited area, against an enemy of no great numerical strength, practically unhelped from without. In Spain the distances were very great, the mountains—if less high than the Alps—were almost as tiresome, for in the Alps there were vast tracts completely inaccessible to both sides, but the Sierras, if rugged, are less lofty and better furnished with goat-tracks and smugglers' by-ways, where the heavily laden infantryman cannot follow the evasive mountaineer. Moreover, the English cruisers continued to drop in the arms and munitions without which the insurgents could not have kept the field.

There can be no doubt that Napoleon undervalued the power of the Spanish guerrilleros, just as he undervalued the resources and the enterprise of Wellington. From the first moment of his return from Russia he had continued to impress on Joseph and Jourdan the necessity for pacifying the North, before the season for regular campaigning should have arrived, and Wellington should have taken the field. But his theory that the winter was the best time for dealing with the bands was rather specious than correct. For although the short days, the snow in the passes, and the swollen torrents were, no doubt, great hindrances to that freedom of movement which was the main strength of the guerrilleros, they were even greater hindrances to combined operations by bodies of regular troops. Rapid marches are impossible off the high roads in Northern Spain, during the midwinter months; and it was only by

[1] *Mémoires*, iv. p. 202.

combined operations and the use of large forces that the insurgents could be dealt with. Indeed, the country roads were practically impassable for any regular troops in many regions. What officer would risk detachments in upland valleys that might be found to be blocked with snow, or cut off from their usual communication by furious streams that had overflowed the roads and made fords impracticable ? Winter marches in unexplored hills are the most deadly expedients : all the weakly soldiers fall by the way—had not Drouet lost 150 men in passing the Guadarrama during the early days of December— and the Guadarrama was crossed by one of the few great royal roads of Spain ? What would be the losses of columns sent out on cross-roads and caught in blizzards, or in those weeks of continuous rain which are not uncommon in the sub-Pyrenean region ?

The Emperor's view was that Caffarelli had failed in his task from want of resourcefulness. He was always trying to parry blows rather than to strike himself : he allowed the insurgents to take the initiative, and when they had executed some tiresome raid would set out in a pursuit which was seldom useful, since they naturally outran him [1]. He was always marching to deliver or revictual some threatened garrison, anywhere between Santoña and Pampeluna, instead of setting himself to destroy the main agglomeration of hostile forces. Now Caffarelli, it is true, was no great general, and may have been on occasion wanting in vigour. But the best reply to the criticism of him sent from Paris is to observe that his successor, Clausel, universally acknowledged to be the most active officer in Spain, failed in exactly the same way as his predecessor, even when he had been lent 20,000 veteran troops to aid him in his task.

Napoleon wanted a great general movement *pour balayer tout le Nord.* He granted that Caffarelli had not enough troops both to furnish garrisons for every important point, and to hunt down the guerrilleros with a large field-force. Therefore he ordered Reille to furnish Caffarelli's successor with every man

---

[1] ' Au lieu de les poursuivre, de les inquiéter, d'aller au devant de leurs entreprises, on attendait la nouvelle de leurs tentatives sur un point pour s'y porter soi-même : on agissait toujours après l'événement.' Clarke to Clausel, *Correspondance du Roi Joseph*, ix. p. 210.

that he asked for. If necessary, the whole Army of Portugal might be requisitioned, since those of the South and Centre would be enough to keep Wellington in check. The letter of instructions which Clarke was directed to give to Clausel, when the latter took up his appointment, explains the Emperor's views. ' By a continual taking of the offensive it ought to be possible to reach a prompt and happy result. The moment that the reinforcements to be furnished by General Reille arrive (and possibly they have already put themselves at your disposition) in Navarre and Biscay, I am convinced that your usual activity will change the face of affairs. Rapid pursuits, well directed, and above all properly adapted to the topographical configuration of the district ; raids made without warning on the insurgents' dépôts of provisions, their hospitals, their stores of arms, and in general on all their magazines, will infallibly carry confusion into their operations. After you have had some successful engagements with them, it will only require politic measures to complete their disorganization. When you have scattered their juntas, all the young men they have enrolled by compulsion will melt home. If you leave them no rest, and surprise them in their remotest places of refuge, the matter should end by their going wholly to pieces. . . . As to the keeping open your communication with France, one particular device, to whose utility all the generals who have served in that region bear witness, is to establish at regular distances and in well chosen positions, especially where roads meet, small palisaded forts, or blockhouses, which will form a chain of posts and support each other. Owing to the wooded nature of the country they will not cost much to build—the estimate for such a system of blockhouses has been calculated to me at no more than 300,000 francs.

' Santoña and Pampeluna must be held—the latter because its capture is Mina's main ambition, the former because it is a terror to the English, who recently tried to have it besieged : General Caffarelli had to lead an expedition to relieve it. Pampeluna is the more important for the moment : when a division of the Army of Portugal reaches Navarre you ought to be able to make Mina change his tone. Santoña can wait—it may be reprovisioned by sea from the small ports of Biscay.

As General Caffarelli has inconsiderately evacuated most of them, you should reoccupy them all, especially Bermeo and Castro-Urdiales. The latter is said to have been fortified with the help of the English. For the sake of the safety of Santoña all these places must be retaken at once : from the mouth of the Bidassoa to Santander every maritime position should be in French hands. Santander especially is, by the Emperor's express orders, to be permanently occupied by an adequate garrison.

'It is necessary that all these operations should be carried out simultaneously. The pursuit of Mina in Navarre should synchronize with the operations in Biscay. The insurgents should be hunted in the inland, at the same time that they are attacked on the coast. This is the only way to disorganize them, to make them weak and divided at all points. . . . It seems preferable to use every available man for a general simultaneous attack, than to undertake each necessary operation in succession, with a smaller force and more leisure—all the more so because the reinforcements, which are to co-operate in your scheme, may be called elsewhere by some unforeseen development of affairs [1].'

Clausel, in obedience to his instructions, tried to carry out the whole of this scheme, and had small luck therewith. He built the chain of blockhouses from Irun to Burgos, thereby tying up many battalions to sedentary duty. He hunted Mina right and left, drove the insurrectionary Junta of Biscay from its abode, occupied all the little ports from Santander to San Sebastian, stormed the well-fortified Castro-Urdiales, revictualled Pampeluna and Santoña, and at the end of three months had to report that his task was unfinished, that the insurrection was still unsubdued, and that although he had borrowed 20,000 infantry from the Army of Portugal, he must ask for another 20,000 men [where were they to be got ?] in order to finish the campaign. And by this time—the end of May—Wellington was loose, and the King was falling back on the Ebro, vainly calling for the five divisions that his brother had made over to the Army of the North. But we must

---

[1] Clarke to Clausel, March 9, *Correspondance du Roi Joseph*, ix. 209–12— a very long and interesting dispatch, of which this is only a short *précis*.

resume the chronicle of the Northern campaign, before com-
menting on its inadequate and unhappy conclusion.

The operations may be said to have begun in January, when
Palombini's Italian division marched from Old Castile to join the
Army of the North, in order to replace Dumoustier's brigade of
the Young Guard, which was being recalled to France.   After
crossing the Guadarrama Pass in a blizzard, which cost some
lives, they got to Burgos on the 28th, driving away the Cura
Merino and his band, who had been blocking the road from
Valladolid.   From Burgos Palombini marched to Vittoria,
escorting a convoy of drafts returning to France, couriers,
officials, and convalescents.   There he heard that Longa and
Mendizabal had cut in behind him, and had again stopped
communications.   Wherefore he turned back, and swept the
Bureba, where they were reported to be.   Not finding them, he
marched as far as Poza de la Sal, not far from Briviesca, but
some leagues off the great *chaussée*.   In this town his head-
quarters were fixed, while the bulk of his division was sent out
in flying columns to collect food.   He had only 500 men with
him, when on the night of February 10–11 he found himself
surrounded by three Spanish columns, which had slipped
through the intervals of the outlying Italian regiments, and
ran in on the town from different quarters.   The surprise,
contrived by Longa, was complete ; but Palombini, collecting
his men in a clump, held out till daylight, when his battalions
came flocking in to the sound of the musketry and relieved
him.   The Spaniards disappeared, taking with them some
baggage and prisoners captured in the first rush, and were soon
lost to sight in the mountains.

The Italians, lucky to have escaped so cheaply, marched
back to the Ebro by way of Domingo Calzada, where there was
a French garrison in imminent danger of starvation, as it had
long been blockaded by local bands [1].   Palombini took it on
with him, and blew up the castle, as the place was inconveniently
remote from any other French post.   He then returned to
Vittoria by way of Haro (February 18) and next pushed on to
Bilbao, where he relieved Dumoustier's brigade of the Imperial

---

[1] For a long account of the Combat of Poza, see Vacani, vol. vi.
pp. 228–33.

Guard, which was at last able to obey the Emperor's order to return to France (February 21). Caffarelli used this force as his escort back to Bayonne, and returned in some disgrace to Paris. Clausel assumed command in his stead on the next day.

Pampeluna had been declared by the new commander's letter of instructions to be the place of which he should be most careful. But seeing no chance of visiting and relieving it till his reinforcements from the Army of Portugal should have come up, Clausel, while waiting for their arrival, came to Bilbao, where he began to make preparations for the siege of Castro-Urdiales, by far the most important, for the moment, of the ports along the coast which the Emperor had commended to him for destruction.

Meanwhile the Biscayan insurgents collected opposite Bilbao, on the Eastern side, and Mendizabal brought up Longa's troops and some of the smaller bands to threaten it from the West. The idea was to give Clausel so much trouble about his head-quarters that he would be unable to march away against Castro. The days slipped by, and farther East Mina was more active than ever in Navarre. He had at last become the happy possessor of two siege guns, landed at Deba on the Biscay coast, and dragged by incredible exertions across mountain paths to the farthest inland. When they came to hand he set to work to beleaguer the French garrison of Tafalla, an outlying place, but less than thirty miles from Pampeluna. This was a challenge to General Abbé, the Governor of Navarre : a force which has dug trenches and brought up heavy guns is obviously asking for a fight, and not intending to abscond. Abbé marched with 3,000 infantry and 150 chasseurs to raise the siege, and found Mina with four of his battalions and his regiment of cavalry drawn up across the high road, in a mountain position at Tiebas, ten miles north of Tafalla. After a hard day's fighting, Abbé failed to break through, and had to fall back on Pampeluna [1] (February 9). The news of his repulse disheartened the garrison, whose walls were crumbling under the fire of Mina's heavy guns, and they surrendered on Feb-

---

[1] Martinien's lists show casualties in the 3rd, 52nd, and 105th Line and 10th Léger of Abbé's division on this day, so he had clearly gone out in force.

ruary 11th to the number of 11 officers and 317 men—the post-commander and many others had been killed during the siege.

This success of Mina's meant nothing less than that the whole open country of Navarre was at his mercy, since Abbé had been beaten in the field ; wherefore Clausel hastened to dispatch the first reinforcements from the Army of Portugal which reached him—Barbot's division—to this quarter. But the affair created less excitement than an exploit of reckless courage carried out by one of Mina's detachments in the following month. The old castle of Fuenterrabia commands the passage of the Bidassoa, and looks across its estuary into France : on March 11 it was surprised by escalade by a handful of guerrilleros, the garrison taken prisoner, the guns thrown into the water, and the whole building destroyed by fire. The flames were visible far into France—troops hurried up from Irun and Hendaye, but of course found the guerrilleros gone [1].

This exploit was rather spectacular than harmful to the French—quite otherwise was the last event of the month of March. Barbot's division, on entering Navarre, was directed to help Abbé to clear the country between Pampeluna and the Ebro. Having reached Lodosa on March 30, Barbot sent out two battalions to raise requisitions in the neighbouring town of Lerin. The place was being sacked, when the scattered French were suddenly attacked by two of Mina's battalions, while two more and 200 Navarrese lancers cut in between the enemy and Lodosa. The French, thoroughly surprised, lost heavily in the first shock, but rallied and started to cut their way back to their division, only eight miles away. In a running fight they were much mauled, and finally had to form square to receive the cavalry. In this inconvenient formation they were forced to a long musketry fight with the Navarrese, which so shook the square that it finally broke when Mina's lancers charged. The two battalions were annihilated, 28 officers and 635 men taken prisoners—the rest cut down. Gaudin, the colonel commanding the detachment, escaped with a few mounted officers [2]. The

---

[1] The interesting dispatch of Leguia, the captor of Fuenterrabia, will be found in the Appendix to Arteche, vol. xiii.

[2] Mina's claim to have annihilated these unfortunate troops is sustained by Martinien's lists, which show 8 officers killed and 23 wounded in the

extraordinary part of the affair was that its last crisis took
place at only two miles from Lodosa, where Barbot was lying
with his remaining six battalions. The French general never
stirred, but only put himself in a posture of defence, thereby
provoking Mina's surprise [1], for he could have saved the column
by going out to its help. After the disaster he retired to
Pampeluna, with a division reduced to little over 3,000 men.
But not long after Taupin's division of the Army of Portugal
also entered Navarre, and joined Abbé. This gave the latter
a very heavy force—at least 13,000 men, and when Clausel had
finished his own operations in the direction of Bilbao, and
marched from Biscay to encircle Mina on one side, while Abbé
was to hold him on the other, the great guerrillero was in grave
danger. But this was only in late April and May, and before
the chronicle of these weeks is reached we have to turn back
westward for a space.

Napoleon's orders had told Clausel to attack at all points at
once, and to lose no time in setting to work. But it was quite
clear that no general synchronized move could be made, until
the divisions borrowed from Reille had all arrived. What
active operations meant, before the reinforcements had come
up, had been sufficiently proved by Abbé's defeat at Tiebas : and
Clausel's own doings in March were equally discouraging, if not
so disastrous. He had resolved to carry out one of the Emperor's
urgent orders by capturing Castro-Urdiales, the touching-place
of British cruisers and the one fortified port which the Allies
possessed on the Biscay coast. Undervaluing its strength, he
marched out on March 21 with the bulk of Palombini's Italian
division and a single French battalion, intending to take it by
escalade. For he had been told that its ancient walls had been
indifferently repaired, and were almost without guns. When,
however, he had reached the neighbourhood of Castro on the
22nd, he had to own on inspection that the enterprise would be
hopeless—his commanding engineer, the historian Vacani [2]—

25th Léger and 27th Line, at Lerin, March 31. There would not be more
than 40 or 45 officers present with two battalions.

[1] Expressed at some length in the great guerrillero's *Memoirs*.

[2] Who has a long and interesting narrative of the expedition in his
vol. vi. pp. 240–50.

maintained that it would take 6,000 men and a siege train of at least six heavy guns to deal with the place. And, as subsequent events showed, this was quite true. Castro is built on a rocky spit projecting into the sea, with a stout wall 20 feet high drawn across the isthmus which joins the headland to the coast. The narrow front of this wall, from water to water, had been well repaired ; there were some 20 guns mounted, and an old castle on the extreme seaward point of the spit served as a citadel or inner fortification. Mendizabal and his lieutenant, Campillo, had come down from the interior with three or four thousand men, and were visible on the flank, ready to fall upon the Italian column if it should approach the town, through the labyrinth of vineyards and stone fences which covered its outskirts.

Clausel, always venturesome, was inclined at first to go on with his enterprise, when news reached him that Bilbao, which he had left rather weakly garrisoned, was threatened by the guerrillero Jauregui, and the battalions of the volunteers of Biscay and Guipuzcoa. He returned hastily to his head-quarters with his French battalion, but found that the danger had been exaggerated for the moment, so sent out General Rouget with two battalions to join Palombini, who had meanwhile on the 24th fought a severe action with Mendizabal. The Spaniard had tried to surround him in his camp at San Pelayo, with several outflanking columns—the Italian sallied out and drove him off with loss—but suffered himself no less [1]. Clausel, on reaching the front, came to the conclusion that Castro must not be attacked without heavy guns and a larger field-force. He directed Palombini to burn the ladders, fascines, &c., prepared for the assault, and to go off instead to raise the blockade of Santoña, while he himself returned to Bilbao. The Italian division therefore marched westward on Colindres, on the other side of the bay on which Santoña stands, thrusting aside the Spanish blockading forces, and communicated with the governor, General Lameth. A supply of small arms and ammunition,

---

[1] Vacani's statement that the Italian division lost this day only 110 men, is made absurd by the lists in Martinien, which show that the 4th, 6th, and 2nd Ligeros lost that day 3 officers killed and 16 wounded— which implies a total casualty list of at least 350.

money, and food was thrown into the place. On the other hand, Lameth was ordered to get six heavy guns on shipboard, and to be prepared to run them down the coast, when next a French force should appear in front of Castro-Urdiales, along with a provision of round shot, shells, and entrenching tools. Lameth got the siege material ready, but was not asked for it till another full month had gone by, for Clausel had other business pressed upon him.

Palombini thereupon turned back, and regained Bilbao in three forced marches, unmolested by the Spaniards, for they had gone off in the direction of Balmaseda, not expecting him to return so quickly. He had only been in Bilbao for two days when Clausel sent him out again, eastward this time and not westward, with two of his regiments, for a surprise attack on Guernica, the head-quarters of the Biscayan insurgents and the seat of their Junta. A French column of two battalions of the 40th Line from Durango was to co-operate and to assail the enemy in the rear. This expedition was quite in consonance with Napoleon's orders to strike at the enemy's central dépôts in front and rear by unexpected raids. But it also showed the difficulty of carrying out such plans. Palombini reached Guernica, driving before him bands which gave way, but were always growing stronger: behind Guernica they made a stand —the French flanking column failed to appear—having found troubles of its own—and Palombini was repulsed and forced to cut his way back out of the hills. He reported his loss as only 80 men—but it was probably somewhat more [1] (April 2). Having picked up the stray French column, and replenished his ammunition from Bilbao, Palombini, with a laudable perseverance, attacked the Guernica position again on April 5, and this time forced it. Thence pushing east, he tried to drive the enemy before him along the coast road, on which, in the neighbourhood of St. Sebastian, a brigade from the Bayonne reserve had been set to block their flight. But the Biscayans and El Pastor evaded him and slipped south into the hills: the Guipuzcoan battalions, instinctively falling back on their own

---

[1] In Martinien's lists there are five officer-casualties given for this fight, but they do not include all the names of officers mentioned as killed by Vacani in his narrative.

province, were in more danger. But warned in time that the
coast road was stopped, some of them took refuge in the boats
of English warships at Lequeytio and Motrico, and were
shipped off to Castro-Urdiales in safety, while others simply
dispersed. No prisoners were taken, but Palombini captured
the petty magazines of the Guipuzcoans at Aspeytia and
Azcoytia, and thinking that the insurrection was scotched
returned to the Bayonne *chaussée* at Bergara (April 9).

So far was this from ending the campaign, that while Palombini
was devastating Guipuzcoa, the Biscayans and El Pastor had
concerted a new attack on Bilbao with Longa and Mendizabal,
who had been left with no containing force in front of them
when the enemy had retired from before Castro-Urdiales.

Clausel had gone off from Bilbao on March 30, with a large
escort, to join at Vittoria the newly arrived divisions of the
Army of Portugal, those of Taupin and Foy, and was set on
organizing a new attack on Mina. In the absence of both
the Commander-in-Chief and of Palombini, Bilbao was very
weakly garrisoned—not more than 2,000 men were left to
General Rouget to defend a rather extensive system of outworks. On April 10th the Spaniards attacked him on both
sides of the Nervion river, and would probably have broken into
Bilbao but for the incapacity of Mendizabal, whose main body
did not come up in time to assist the attack of the Biscayans
on the other bank of the river. Rouget was still holding out
when Palombini came to his rescue from Bergara via Durango,
in two forced marches. The Spaniards thereupon dispersed,
after their usual fashion, Mendizabal disappearing to the east,
the Biscayans falling back on their old head-quarters at
Guernica. Palombini was strong at the moment, having been
joined by the brigade from Bayonne, under General Aussenac,
which had been blocking the coast road. He therefore tried to
surround the Biscayans with converging columns—but when
he thought that he had cut them off from the inland, and was
about to drive them into the water, the bulk of them were
picked up at Bermeo by English cruisers, and landed farther
down the coast. Only some baggage and a store of munitions
fell into the pursuer's hands (April 14).

On this, Palombini, ' convinced,' says his admiring chronicler

Vacani, ' of the uselessness of trying to envelop or destroy local bands among mountains which they knew too well, when he could only dispose of columns of a few battalions for the pursuit,' resolved to halt at Bilbao, and prepare for the siege of Castro. He put the brigade from Bayonne in charge of the high road to San Sebastian, and waited for the arrival of Foy from Vittoria. For he had been informed that this general, with his division of the Army of Portugal, was to be detailed to help him in the subjection of Biscay. Meanwhile April was half over, the insurgents had been often hunted but never caught, and Wellington might be expected to be on the move any morning : it was strange that he had not been heard of already.

Leaving Biscay to Palombini and Foy, Clausel had collected at Vittoria one of his own divisions, hitherto scattered in small detachments, but relieved by the reinforcements sent him from the Army of Portugal. For beside the four divisions lent for active service, he had taken over the whole Province of Burgos, to which Reille had sent the division of Lamartinière. With his own newly-collected division, under Vandermaesen, and Taupin's of the Army of Portugal, Clausel set out for Navarre on April 11th, to combine his operations with those of Abbé and to hunt down Mina. As he had already sent forward to the Governor of Navarre the division of Barbot, there was now a field-force of 20,000 men available for the chase, without taking into consideration the troops tied down in garrisons. This was more than double the strength that Mina could command, and the next month was one of severe trial for the great guerrillero.

Clausel's first idea was to catch Mina by a sweeping movement of all his four divisions, which he collected at Puente la Reyna in the valley of the Arga (April 24). Mina answered this move by dispersion, and his battalions escaped through intervals in the cordon with no great loss, and cut up more than once small detachments of their pursuers. Clausel perceiving that this system was useless, then tried another, one of those recommended by the Emperor in his letter of instruction of March 9, viz. a resolute stroke at the enemy's magazines and dépôts. Mina kept his hospitals, some rough munition factories

which he had set up, and his store of provisions, in the remote
Pyrenean valley of Roncal, where Navarre and Aragon meet: it
was most inaccessible and far from any high road. Nevertheless
Clausel marched upon it with the divisions of Abbé, Vandermaesen, and Barbot, leaving Taupin alone at Estella to
contain Western Navarre. He calculated that Mina would be
forced to concentrate and fight, in order to save his stores and
arsenal, and that so he might be destroyed. He was partly
correct in his hypothesis—but only partly. Mina left four of
his battalions in Western Navarre, in the valleys of the Amescoas,
to worry Taupin, and hurried with the remaining five to cover
the Roncal. There was heavy fighting in the passes leading to
it on May 12 and 13, which ended in the Navarrese being beaten
and dispersed with the loss of a thousand men. Clausel captured and destroyed the factories and magazines, and made
prisoners of the sick in the hospitals, whom he treated with
unexpected humanity. Some of the broken battalions fled
south by Sanguesa into lower Navarre, others eastward into
Aragon. Among these last was Mina himself with a small party
of cavalry—he tried to fetch a compass round the pursuing
French and to return to his own country, but he was twice headed
off, and finally forced to fly far into Eastern Aragon, as far as
Barbastro. This region was practically open to him for flight,
for the French garrison of Saragossa was too weak to cover the
whole country, or to stop possible bolt-holes. Mina was therefore able to rally part of his men there, and called in the help of
scattered *partidas*. Clausel swept all North-Western Aragon
with his three divisions, making arrests and destroying villages
which had harboured the insurgents. But he did not wish to
pursue Mina to the borders of Catalonia, where he would have
been quite out of his own beat, and inconveniently remote
from Pampeluna and Vittoria.

But meanwhile the division which he had left under Taupin
in Navarre was having much trouble with Mina's four battalions
in the Amescoas, and parties drifting back from the rout in
the Roncal vexed the northern bank of the Ebro, while Longa
and Mendizabal, abandoning their old positions in front of
Bilbao, had descended on to the Bayonne *chaussée*, and executed many raids upon it, from the pass of Salinas above

Vittoria as far as the Ebro (April 25–May 10). The communications between Bayonne and Burgos were once more cut, and
the situation grew so bad that Lamartinière's division of the
Army of Portugal had to be moved eastward, to clear the road
from Burgos to Miranda, Sarrut's to do the same between
Miranda and Bilbao, while Maucune detached a brigade to
relieve Lamartinière at Burgos. Of the whole Army of Portugal
there was left on May 20th only one single infantry brigade at
Palencia which was still at Reille's disposition. Five and a half
divisions had been lent to Clausel, and were dispersed in the
north. And Wellington was now just about to move! The
worst thing of all for the French cause was that the communications of the North were as bad in May as they had been in
January: after Clausel had taken off the main field-army to the
Roncal, and had led it from thence far into Aragon, the roads
behind him were absolutely useless. Only on the line Bayonne–
Vittoria, where the new blockhouses were beginning to arise,
was any regular passing to and fro possible. Clausel himself
was absolutely lost to sight, so far as King Joseph was concerned
—it took a fortnight or twenty days to get a dispatch through
to him.

Meanwhile, before turning to the great campaign of Wellington on the Douro, it is necessary to dispose of the chronicle of
affairs in Biscay. Foy and his division, as we have seen, had
marched from Vittoria to Bilbao and reached the latter place on
April 21st [1]. On the way they had nearly caught Mendizabal at
Orduña, where he chanced to be present with a guard of only
200 men; but, warned just in time, he had the luck to escape,
and went back to pick up his subordinates Longa and Campillo
nearer the coast.

Soon after Foy's arrival at Bilbao he was joined by Sarrut's
division of the Army of Portugal, which had followed him from
Vittoria. He had therefore, counting Palombini's Italians, the
brigade of Aussenac, and the regular garrison of Bilbao, at least
16,000 men—ample for the task that Clausel had commended
to him, the capture of Castro-Urdiales, with its patched-up
mediaeval wall. The only thing presenting any difficulty was

[1] Not the 24th as in Vacani and Belmas. See Girod de l'Ain's *Life of Foy*,
p. 260.

getting a siege train to this remote headland : Lameth, the
Governor of Santoñar, as it will be remembered, had been
ordered to provide one, and there were four heavy guns in Bilbao :
—the roads on both sides, however, were impracticable, and the
artillery had to come by water, running the chance of falling in
with British cruisers.

On April 25th Foy marched out of Bilbao with his own,
Sarrut's, and Palombini's divisions, more than 11,000 men,[1]
leaving Aussenac on the Deba, to guard the road from San
Sebastian, and Rouget in garrison as usual. On the same
evening he reached the environs of Castro, and left Palombini
there to shut in the place, while he went on himself to look for
Mendizabal, who was known to be watching affairs from the
hills, and to be blocking the road to Santoña, as he had so often
done before. Foy then moved on to Cerdigo where he established
his head-quarters for the siege, on a strong position between the
sea and the river Agaera. Mendizabal was reputed to be holding
the line of the Ason, ten miles farther on, but in weak force : he
had only the *partidas* of Campillo and Herrero with him, Longa
being absent in the direction of Vittoria. On the 29th Foy
drove off these bands at Ampuero, and communicated with
Santoña, into which he introduced a drove of 500 oxen and
other victuals. The governor Lameth was ordered to ship the
siege train that he had collected to Islares, under the camp at
Cerdigo, on the first day when he should find the bay clear—
for three English sloops, the *Lyra*, *Royalist*, and *Sparrow*, under
Captain Bloye, were lying off Castro and watching the coast.
Foy then established Sarrut's division to cover the siege at
Trucios, and sent two Italian battalions to Portugalete to guard
the road to Bilbao, keeping his own division and the three other
Italian battalions for the actual trench work. The heavy guns
were the difficulty—those expected from Bilbao were stopped
at the mouth of the Nervion by the English squadron, which
was watching for them—but in the absence of the sloops on this
quest, the governor of Santoña succeeded in running his convoy

---

[1] Figures in Belmas are (in detail) Foy's own division (10 battalions)
5,513 men, Palombini's (5 battalions) 2,474, artillery 409, Sarrut's division
about 4,500. Foy left behind Aussenac's brigade about 1,500, and the
garrison of Bilboa about 2,000.

across the bay on May 4th. The guns from Bilbao were afterwards brought up by land, with much toil.

Foy then commenced three batteries on the high slopes which
dominate the town : two were completed on the 6th, despite
much long-distance fire from the British ships, and from a heavy
gun which Captain Bloye had mounted on the rocky islet of
Santa Anna outside the harbour. On the 7th fire was begun from
two batteries against the mediaeval curtain wall, but was
ineffective—one battery was silenced by the British. On the
10th, however, the third battery—much closer in—was ready,
and opened with devastating results on the 11th, two hours' fire
making a breach 30 feet wide and destroying a large convent
behind it.

The Governor, Pedro Alvarez, one of Longa's colonels, had
a garrison of no more than 1,000 men—all like himself from
Longa's regiments of Iberia ; he made a resolute defence, kept
up a continuous counter-fire, and prepared to hold the breach.
But it was obvious that the old wall was no protection from
modern artillery, and that Foy could blow down as much of it
as he pleased at leisure. On the afternoon of the 11th part of
the civil population went on board the British ships : the
governor made preparations for holding the castle, on the sea-
side of the town projecting into the water, as a last stronghold : but it was only protected by the steepness of the rock on
which it stood—its walls were ruined and worthless. Late in the
day the British took off the heavy gun which they had placed
on the islet—it could not have been removed after the town
had fallen, and the fall was clearly inevitable.

Foy, seeing the curtain-wall continuing to crumble, and
a 60-foot breach established, resolved to storm that night,
and sent in at 7.20 three columns composed of eight French and
eight Italian flank companies for the assault—the former to the
breach, the latter to try to escalade a low angle near the Bilbao
gate. Both attacks succeeded, despite a heavy but ill-aimed
fire from the defenders, and the Spaniards were driven through
the town and into the castle, where they maintained themselves.
Alvarez had made preparations for evacuation—while two
companies held the steep steps which were the only way up to
the castle, the rest of the garrison embarked at its back on the

boats of the British squadron. Some were killed in the water by the French fire, some drowned, but the large majority got off. By three in the morning there were only 100 men left in the castle : Alvarez had detailed them to throw the guns into the sea, and to fire the magazines, both of which duties they accomplished, before the early dawn. When, by means of ladders, the French made their way into an embrasure of the defences, some of this desperate band were killed. But it is surprising to hear that most of them got away by boat from the small jetty at the back of the castle. They probably owed their escape to the fact that the stormers had spent the night in riotous atrocities vying with those of Badajoz on a small scale. Instead of finishing off their job by taking the castle, they had spent the night in rape and plunder in the town [1].

The Spaniards declared that the total loss of their garrison was only 100 men, and the statement is borne out by the dispatch of Captain Bloye of the *Lyra*. Foy wrote to Clausel that the whole business had only cost him fifty men. The two statements seem equally improbable, for the siege had lasted for six days of open trenches, and both sides had fought with great resolution [2].

But the really important thing to note about this little affair is that it absorbed three French divisions for sixteen days in the most critical month of 1813. Eleven thousand men were tied down in a remote corner of Biscay, before a patched-up mediaeval wall, while Longa was running riot in Alava and breaking the line of communication with France—and (what is more important) while Wellington's columns were silently gliding into place for the great stroke on the Douro. Colonel Alvarez could boast that his thousand men had served a very useful and honourable end during the great campaign. He and they were landed by Captain Bloye at Bermeo, and went off over the hills to join Longa : the majority of them must

[1] For horrid details of mishandlings of both sexes see Marcel (of the 6th Léger) in his *Campagnes d'Espagne*, pp. 193-4. Marcel is a *raconteur*, but Belmas bears him out (iv. p. 566).

[2] Napier says the Spanish loss was 180—which seems more probable. The British ships lost one officer and sixteen men wounded, by Bloye's report. As to the French loss, we have the names of 3 officers killed and 6 wounded during the operation—which looks like 150 to 180 casualties.

have been present at the battle of Vittoria, some six weeks after their escape by sea.

Having discharged the first duty set him by Clausel, Foy left the Italians at Castro, to guard the coast and keep up communications with Santoña. He sent Sarrut southward to hunt for Longa, by way of Orduña ; but the Spaniard crossed the Ebro and moved into the province of Burgos, evading pursuit. Then, finding that Lamartinière's division was guarding the great road in this direction, he turned off north-westward, and escaped by Espinosa to the mountains of Santander. Sarrut, having lost him, turned back to Biscay.

Meanwhile Foy himself, after retiring to Bilbao to give a few days of rest to his division, started out again on May 27th for a circular tour in Biscay. His object was to destroy the three Biscayan volunteer battalions which had given his predecessor so much trouble. Two he dispersed, but could not destroy, and they ultimately got together again in somewhat diminished numbers. The third was more unlucky : caught between three converging columns near Lequeytio, it was driven against the seashore and nearly annihilated—360 men were taken, 200 killed, only two companies got off into the hills (May 30th). But to achieve this result Foy had collected three brigades—5,000 men—who would have been better employed that day on the Esla, for Wellington was crossing that river at the moment—and where were the infantry of the Army of Portugal, who should have stood in his way ?

So while the British Army was streaming by tens of thousands into the undefended plains of Leon, Foy and Sarrut were guerrillero-hunting in Biscay, and Taupin and Barbot had just failed in the great chase after Mina in Aragon and Navarre. Such were the results of the Emperor's orders for the pacification of the North.

SECTION XXXV: CHAPTER VI

AN EPISODE ON THE EAST COAST. CASTALLA, APRIL 1813

DURING the winter months, from November to February, affairs had been quiet on the Mediterranean side of the Peninsula. The transient sojourn of the Armies of Soult and King Joseph in the kingdom of Valencia, which had so much troubled the mind of General Maitland, had lasted no more than a few weeks. After they had marched off to retake Madrid, no traces remained of them, in the end of October, save the mass of sick, convalescents, and Spanish refugees which they had left behind —guests most undesired—in charge of Suchet. There was no longer any fear of a siege of Alicante, or of the expulsion of the Anglo-Sicilian expeditionary corps from Spain.

When the shadow of this fear had passed, the Allied forces resumed something like their old position. The Anglo-Sicilians had passed under many commanders since the autumn : Maitland had resigned owing to ill-health before October 1st : he was succeeded for six weeks by John Mackenzie, the senior Major-General at Alicante, who was superseded about November 20th by William Clinton (brother of Henry Clinton of the 6th Division). But Clinton was only in charge of the expeditionary force for twelve days, being out-ranked by James Campbell, Adjutant-General of the Army of Sicily, who turned up with a large body of reinforcements on December 2nd. Campbell, however, only bore rule at Alicante for a period of three months, giving place to Sir John Murray on February 25th. It was therefore on the last-named officer that the stress of co-operating with Wellington in the campaign of 1813 was to fall. The unlucky man was quite unequal to the position, being singularly infirm of purpose and liable to lose his head at critical moments, as he had shown at Oporto on May 12th, 1809 [1]. It is surprising that Wellington, knowing his record, should have acquiesced in the appointment—perhaps he thought that

---

[1] See above, vol. ii. p. 341.

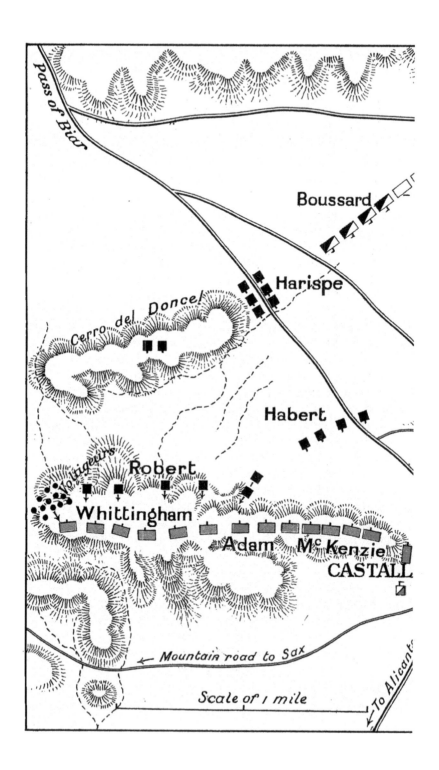

Pass of Biar

Boussard

Harispe

Cerro del Doncel

Habert

Voltigeurs

Robert

Whittingham

Adam   McKenzie

CASTALL

← Mountain road to Sax

To Alicante

Scale of 1 mile

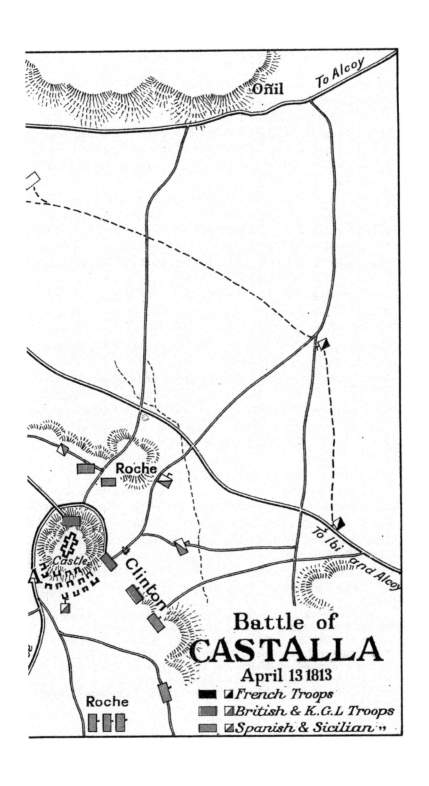

Oñil

To Alcoy

Roche

Castle

Clinton

To Ibi and Alcoy

Roche

Battle of
CASTALLA
April 13 1813

French Troops
British & K.G.L Troops
Spanish & Sicilian "

here at least was a general who would take no risks, and have no dangerous inspirations of initiative.

The strength of the Alicante army had risen by January 1813 to something like 14,000 men, but it remained (as it had been from the first) a most heterogeneous force, consisting in the early spring of 1813 of six British [1], three German [2], and two foreign battalions belonging to the regular forces of the Crown [3], with four Italian units [4] of various sorts. The cavalry consisted of one British and one Sicilian regiment and an odd squadron of 'Foreign Hussars.' The artillery was partly British, partly Sicilian, and partly Portuguese. In addition to these troops the commander at Alicante had complete control over General Whittingham's 'Majorcan division,' a Spanish corps which had been reorganized in the Balearic Islands by that officer, and which had been clothed, armed, and paid from the British subsidy. It consisted of six infantry battalions and two weak cavalry regiments, and was in the spring about 4,500 strong. They were rightly esteemed the best Spanish troops on the Eastern front, and justified their reputation in the subsequent campaign. There was a second Spanish division in the neighbourhood, that of General Roche, which, like Whittingham's, had been taken on to the British subsidy, and reclothed and re-armed. But this unit was not reckoned part of the Alicante force, but belonged theoretically to Elio's Murcian army, in which it was numbered as the 4th Division. It counted only five battalions and was at this time not more than 3,500 strong. But though it was registered as part of the Army of Murcia, it often acted with Murray's Anglo-Sicilian troops, being cantoned alongside of them in the Alicante region. When Wellington became Generalissimo of the Spanish armies, he not infrequently gave orders to Roche to join Murray rather than Elio—apparently conceiving that the fact that the

---

[1] 1/10th, 1/27th, 1/58th, 1/81st, and 2/27th which came in time for Castalla, also a battalion of grenadier companies of units in Sicily.

[2] 4th and 6th Line battalions, and a light battalion composed of the light companies of 3rd, 4th, 6th, 7th, 8th, and of De Roll and Dillon.

[3] Three companies of De Roll and four of Dillon—the whole making up a battalion 800 bayonets and the Calabrees Free Corps.

[4] 1st and 2nd Italian Levy, and two battalions of Sicilian Estero Regiment.

division lived on the British subsidy had placed it on a some-what different footing from the rest of the Murcians.

If we count Whittingham and Roche as attached to the Expeditionary Army at Alicante, the strength of that hetero-geneous host would have been rather over 21,000 men—a total perceptibly greater than Suchet's field-force encamped over against it on the Xucar. And in addition there lay close behind, within the borders of the kingdom of Murcia, Elio and his 'Second Army,' which, even after deducting Roche's division, was a considerable accumulation of troops. But the Murcian army's record was more unhappy than that of any other Spanish unit, and it had been dashed to pieces once more in the preceding July, at the discreditable battle of Castalla. Though it nominally counted 30,000 men in its six divisions, only three of them were available[1], for two were really no more than the old guerrillero bands of the Empecinado and Duran, who hung about in Southern Aragon, and shifted for themselves. They were both remote and disorganized. Since Roche's division was also often out of Elio's control, he really had no more than 13,000 infantry and 2,000 horse in hand.

There were facing Suchet, of allied troops of one sort and another, some 35,000 men, a fact which the Marshal never ceased to utilize in his correspondence with Madrid, when he wished to excuse himself from lending aid to his neighbours. But the Murcian army had still not recovered from the demoraliz-zation caused by the battle of Castalla, and the Alicante army was suffering from two evils which reduced its value as a campaigning force to a very low level. The first was a terrible deficiency of transport. When Lord William Bentinck sent out the first expeditionary force from Sicily, he intended it to equip itself with mules, horses, and carts in Spain. But in the summer of 1812 the Kingdom of Murcia was the only unoccupied region on the east side of the Peninsula, and all its not too copious resources were wanted for its own army. Successive captains-general refused, not unnaturally, to help Maitland or Murray in the task of collecting sumpter-beasts, and suggested that they ought to draw both animals and food from

---

[1] Those of Villacampa, Mijares, and Sarsfield.

Sicily. Food was indeed procured from thence, and even from Algeria and the Levant, so that the army did not starve. But there was insufficient means to move that food from the water's edge. A certain number of mules were collected by paying very heavy hire—not at all to the gratification of the Spanish authorities, who wanted them for their own use. But they were so few that the Army could make no long general marches, and could count on little more than what the men carried in their haversacks. The best that could be done was to move it forward from the immediate neighbourhood of Alicante, so that it could live upon the resources of the inland, where there were many fertile and well-peopled valleys. The main object, indeed, of James Campbell's forward move was to get food for Whittingham's and Roche's divisions, which were (though paid by the British subsidy) dependent for their rations on the Spanish Government, and seldom received them. Local food for these troops had to be sought, as the only possible means of keeping them alive. In February the line of occupation reached as far as Biar, Castalla, and Xixona, all held by Whittingham's division, while Roche and the Anglo-Sicilians were mostly in second line, at Elda, Monforte, and Alicante. But the problem of making the Anglo-Sicilian army a mobile force was not much further advanced in March 1813 than it had been in October 1812.

The second weak point of the Alicante army was the extremely doubtful quality of some of its foreign elements. It is true that the German Legion battalions were as steady as those of the same corps in Wellington's own army. But all the others were crammed with deserters from the enemy's ranks, or prisoners of war who had enlisted in order to escape the miseries of the prison-camp or the hulks. The 'Calabrese Free Corps' was a trifle better than the rest, being mostly composed of genuine exiles. But the only difference between the recent recruits of Dillon's cosmopolitan regiment in the British service and of the 'Italian Levy' and 'Estero regiment' was that the former corps contained more French and Swiss deserters, and the latter pair more Italians. All had the usual sprinkling of Poles, Dutch, Croats, and other miscellaneous adventurers. A lurid light was thrown upon their possibilities on February 11th,

when 86 men of the 2nd Italian Levy deserted to the
French lines, bringing over their officer as a prisoner. It was
discovered that the rest of the battalion were in a plot to betray
Xixona to Suchet, and with it one of Whittingham's Spanish
regiments, which was encamped beside them. There was just
time to march in the 1/27th and a second Spanish battalion,
who surrounded and disarmed the Italians, before a French
column appeared at dawn. It directed itself to the quarters
from which the traitors had just been drawn off, was surprised
to be received with a heavy fire, and rapidly withdrew [1]. Such
an incident was certainly not calculated to inspire a timid
general, like Sir John Murray, with any great craving for a bold
offensive.

On the other hand, Murray had a formidable force on paper,
and when Suchet reflected that there lay close behind him, first
Elio's army in Murcia—at least 13,000 men without counting
the Empecinado's and Duran's bands—and farther back Del
Parque's Andalusian ' 3rd Army,' which had also some 13,000
effectives, he could not but see that 50,000 men might march
against his comparatively weak force in Valencia at any
moment. His strength on the Xucar was very modest—not much
over 15,000 bayonets and sabres : for though he had 60,000 men
of all arms effective, and 75,000 on his rolls, including sick and
detached, yet such a force was not enough to control the
whole of the ancient lands of the Aragonese crown—Aragon
Proper, Catalonia, and Valencia. He was in possession of all
of them save the Catalan inland, where the ' First Army ' still
maintained itself, the extreme southern region of the Valencian
kingdom round Alicante, and the mountains between Aragon
and Castile, which were the hunting ground of the guerrilleros
of Duran and the Empecinado. The garrison was small for
such a widespread occupation, and the only thing that made
the Marshal's position tolerable was the fact that (unlike
Catalonia) Aragon and Valencia had shown themselves very

---

[1] For details see letter of February 22nd in Sir Samuel Whittingham's
Memoirs, pp. 172–4. He says that Colonel Grant, commanding the 2nd
Italian Levy, had made himself cordially detested by his men by ' employing the minute worry of the old British School,' and that Bourke of the
1st Italian Levy had much more control over his men.

' quiet ' regions. Suchet's rule had been severe, but at least orderly ; there had been little of the casual plunder and requisitioning which made French rule detested under other commanders. The coast-plain of Valencia and the broad stretch of the Ebro valley in Central Aragon were districts less suitable for the operations of guerrilleros than almost any other part of Spain. On the Valencian frontier there was only one active *partida,* that of the ' Fraile ' (Agostin Nebot), whose welcome gift of 60 captured French transport mules to the Alicante army is acknowledged in one of Wellington's dispatches. It is true that the sub-Pyrenean parts of Aragon were exposed to Mina's raids, and that the solid block of sierras round Molina and Albaracin was always the refuge of Duran and Villacampa, but these were not essential regions for the maintenance of the hold on the Mediterranean coast. With the exception of these tracts the land was fairly quiet : there was a general submission to the French yoke, and an appreciable proportion of *afrance-sados.* The blow inflicted on public opinion by the fall of Valencia in January 1812 was still a recent thing. Wellington's army had been heard of, but never seen ; and the operations of the Alicante expeditionary force had hitherto served to depress rather than to encourage insurrection. Hence it was possible that 35,000 men could hold the broad lands that lay between Tudela and Saragossa and Lerida on the North, and Denia and Xativa on the South—though Decaen's 28,000 had a much more precarious grip on Catalonia. But the occupation was a *tour de force* after all, and was liable to be upset at any moment by an active and capable enemy. Fortunately for Suchet his opponent on the East Coast during the spring of 1813 was neither active nor capable.

As long as King Joseph kept his head-quarters at Madrid and occupied the province of La Mancha, extending his line eastward to San Clemente, he had been in touch with Suchet's front, and communications were open. Indeed Daricau's division marched to the borders of Valencia in the end of January, and took over from the Marshal the large body of Spanish refugees and convalescents of the Army of the South, who had been under his charge since October. But the whole situation was changed when the orders of the Emperor compelled

Joseph to draw back his head-quarters to Valladolid, and to hold Toledo as his extreme post towards the South.. When this change was made, the touch between Valencia and Madrid was lost—the Spanish cavalry of the Army of Andalusia advanced across the Sierra Morena into La Mancha : Villacampa's division descended from the hills to occupy the more level parts of the province of Cuenca. For the future the King and Suchet could only keep touch with each other by the circuitous route through Saragossa. The situation of the French Army of Valencia was rendered far more isolated and dangerous—it was in a very advanced position, with no communication whatever with any friendly force save through Aragon. And its inland flank was exposed to all manner of possible molestation—if Villacampa, Duran, and the Empecinado had represented a serious fighting force, capable of regular action in the field, Suchet would have been bound to retire at once to the line of the Ebro, on pain of finding himself surrounded and cut off. But these irregular ' divisions ' of the Army of Murcia were, as a matter of fact, good for raids and the cutting of communications, but useless for battle. They were local in their operations, seldom combined, and only obeyed their nominal commander, Elio, when it pleased them. It was very hard for any one of them to move far from its accustomed ' beat,' because they had no magazines, and lived each on their own region.

Suchet accordingly resolved to try the hazardous experiment of preserving his old positions, even when communication with Madrid had been cut off. He left on his inland flank only a flying brigade or two, and the normal garrisons of the small fortified towns of upper Aragon, and kept his main striking force still concentrated on the line of the Xucar, in order to cover the plain of Valencia from the one serious enemy, the Alicante army. The available troops consisted of the three small infantry divisions of Habert, Harispe, and Musnier (this last temporarily under Robert), and the cavalry division of Boussard, the whole amounting to about 12,500 foot and 1,500 horse, or a gross total of all arms of some 15,000 men. They were disposed so as to cover the front of 50 miles from Moxente, at the foot of the Murcian mountains; to the mouth of the Xucar, and were not scattered in small parties, but concentrated in four groups which could easily unite. The right wing was covered by an entrenched camp at Moxente, the centre by another at San Felipe de Xativa. Denia on the sea-coast was held as a cover to the left wing. Cavalry was out in front, and in a rather exposed position a brigade of Habert's division held Alcoy, a considerable town in a fertile upland valley, whose resources Suchet was anxious to retain as long as possible.

Soon after he had taken over command at Alicante on February 25th, Murray obtained accurate local information as to the exact distribution and numbers of the French, and noting the very exposed position of the brigade at Alcoy, made an attempt to cut it off by the concentric advance of four columns. The scheme failed, partly because of the late arrival of the right-hand column (a brigade of Whittingham's division), partly because Murray, having got engaged with the French in front, refused to support his advanced troops until the flanking detachments should appear, and so allowed the enemy to slip away (March 6th) [1]. He then halted, though his movement must obviously have roused Suchet's attention, and rendered a counter-attack possible. But after a week, finding the enemy still passive, he sent forward Whittingham to drive the French outposts from Consentaina, and the pass of Albeyda, in the mountain range which separates the valley of Alcoy from the lowland. This was to ask for trouble, and should only have been done if Murray was proposing to challenge Suchet to a decisive general action : Whittingham indeed thought that this was the object of his commanding officer [2]. At the same time two British battalions under General Donkin made a demonstration against the French right, ten miles farther east, in the direction of Onteniente. Habert, whose whole division was holding the line of hills, gave way after a sharp skirmish, and allowed Whittingham to seize the pass of Albeyda (March 15th). Every one supposed that the Alicante army was now about to attack the French main position between Moxente and Xativa.

[1] Murray to Wellington. *Supplementary Dispatches*, xiv. p. 191.

[2] See his letter of March 19th, written after the skirmish : ' Our army is concentrating itself, and a few days I hope will bring on a general action, in which I hope to play my part ' (*Memoirs*, p. 188).

But Murray's plan was different : having, as he supposed, attracted Suchet's full notice, by his forward movement, he was proposing to send out an expedition by sea, to make a dash at the town of Valencia, which (as he calculated) must be under-garrisoned when heavy fighting was expected on the Xucar. He told off for the purpose Roche's Spanish division, strengthened by the British provisional battalion of grenadier companies and a regiment borrowed from Elio. The orders were to land on the beach south of the city, make a dash for it, and if that failed to seize Cullera at the mouth of the Xucar, or Denia, farther down the coast. The project looked hazardous, for to throw 5,000 men ashore in the enemy's country, far from their own main body, was to risk their being cut up, or forced to a re-embarkation on a bare beach, which could not fail to be costly. Unless Murray at the same moment attacked Suchet, so that he should not be able to send a man to the rear towards Valencia, the force embarked was altogether too small. Murray's calculation was that the Marshal would make a heavy detachment, and that he would then attack the line of the Xucar himself. With this object he invited Elio to co-operate, by turning the French right on the inland on the side of Almanza. The Spanish General, though he had been quarrelling with Murray of late, was now in an obliging frame of mind[1] and so far consented that he brought up one infantry division to Yecla, a place which would make a good starting-point for a flank march round the extreme right of Suchet's positions.

Meanwhile, for ten days after the combat of Albeyda nothing happened on the main front. Whittingham was still left in an advanced position north of Alcoy, while the rest of the Alicante army was concentrated at Castalla fifteen miles farther back. The marvel is that Suchet did not make a pounce upon the isolated Spanish division pushed up so close to his front. He had not yet taken the measure of his opponent, whose failing (as the whole campaign shows) was to start schemes, and then to abandon them from irresolution, at the critical moment when a decisive move became necessary.

Meanwhile, on March 26th Roche's division and the attached British battalion were actually embarking at Alicante, for the

---

[1] Murray to Wellington. *Supplementary Dispatches*, xiv. p. 200.

dash at Valencia, when Murray received a dispatch from Lord
William Bentinck at Palermo, informing him that a political
crisis had broken out in Sicily, that civil strife there had become
probable, and that he was therefore compelled to order the
immediate recall of two regiments of trustworthy troops from
Spain. The fact was that the new Sicilian constitution, proclaimed as the solution of all discontent in the island in 1812,
had failed to achieve its purpose. The old King Ferdinand had
carried out a sort of mild *coup d'état*, and proclaimed his own
restoration to absolute power (March 13th, 1813) : the Neapolitan troops who formed the majority of the armed force in the
island had accepted the position. The Sicilian constitutional
party seemed helpless, and the attitude of the local battalions
under their control was doubtful. Nothing could save the
situation but a display of overpowering force. Wherefore
Bentinck directed Murray to send back to Palermo, without
delay, the 6th Line battalion K.G.L. and the battalion of
grenadier companies belonging to British regiments still
quartered in Sicily. This was not a very large order, so far as
mere numbers went—the force requisitioned being under
2,000 bayonets. But the prospect of the outbreak of civil war
in Sicily scared Murray—if the strife once began, would not
more of his best troops be requisitioned, and the Alicante force
be reduced to a residuum of disloyal foreign levies ? Moreover,
one of the units requisitioned by name was the battalion of
grenadiers just about to sail for Valencia. Perhaps not without
secret satisfaction, for he hated making decisions of any sort,
Murray declared that Bentinck's orders rendered the naval
expedition impossible, and countermanded it. He sent off, on
the transports ready in harbour, the grenadier battalion
ordered to Sicily, and returned the Spanish contingent to its
old cantonments [1]. The K.G.L. battalion was just embarking

[1] Napier blames the British Government for having got things into such
a position of double command that Bentinck could withdraw from Spain
troops which he had sent there, and which had passed under Wellington's
authority (v. p. 54). Wellington seems to have made no objection to this
particular recall (*Dispatches*, vii. p. 260), thinking (I suppose) that the risk
of losing Sicily was much more serious than the deduction of 2,000 men
from the Alicante side-show. He wrote at any rate to Murray to send them
off at once, if he had not done so already. The fault, of course, lay with

when news arrived (April 1st) that the Sicilian crisis was now over, wherefore Murray retained it for a few more days [1].

For the counter-revolution at Palermo had only lasted for four days ! Finding Lord William Bentinck firm, and prepared to use force, King Ferdinand withdrew his proclamation, and resigned the administration into the hands of his eldest son, the Prince Royal. The Queen, whose strong will had set the whole affair on foot, promised to return to her native Austria, and actually sailed for the Levant, to the intense satisfaction of every one save the knot of intriguers in her Court. The scare was soon over—its only result was the abandonment of the raid on Valencia. Murray had now received orders from Wellington to await the arrival of a detailed scheme for the way in which his army was to be employed. Pending the receipt of these [2] directions he lapsed into absolute torpidity— the only record of his doings in the last days of March and early April being that he set the troops concentrated at Castalla to entrenching the hillsides around that formidable position— a clear sign that he had no further intention of taking the offensive on his own account.

Suchet had been much puzzled by the advance of his enemy to Alcoy and Albeyda, followed by subsequent inactivity for a whole month. When he found that even the movement of Elio's troops to Yecla did not foreshadow a general assault upon his lines, he concluded that there must be some unexplained reason for the quiescence of the Allies, and that the opportunity was a good one for a bold blow, while they remained inexplicably waiting in a disjointed and unconcentrated line opposite his positions. The obvious and easy thing would have been to fall upon Whittingham at Alcoy, but probably for that very reason the Marshal tried another scheme. He secretly passed all his available troops to Fuente la Higuera, on his extreme right flank, leaving only a trifling screen in front of Murray's army, and on April 10th marched in two columns against the allied

Bentinck, for denuding Sicily before he was sure of the stability of the new Constitution.

[1] Murray to Wellington, April 2. *Supplementary Dispatches*, vii. p. 605. The 6th K.G.L. was present at Castalla on April 13th.

[2] Wellington, *Dispatches*, x. p. 162.

left. One consisting of six battalions of Harispe's division and two cavalry regiments aimed at the isolated Murcian division at Yecla, the other and larger column four battalions of Habert's division, and seven of Musnier's (under Robert during the absence of its proper chief), with his cuirassier regiment, marched by Caudete on Villena, to cut in between the Spaniards and Murray, and intercept any aid which the latter might send from Castalla towards the Spaniards.

The blow was unexpected and delivered with great vigour : Harispe surprised General Mijares' Murcians at Yecla at dawn ; they were hopelessly outnumbered, only four battalions being present—the fifth unit of the division was at Villena. And there was but a single squadron with them, Elio's cavalry being in its cantonments thirty miles away in the Albacete–Chinchilla country. Mijares, on finding himself assailed by superior numbers, tried to march off towards Jumilla and the mountains. Harispe pursued, and seeing the Spaniards likely to get away, for the retreat was rapid and in good order, flung his hussars and dragoons at them. The Spaniards turned up on to a hillside, and tried a running fight. The two leading battalions of the column made good their escape—the two rear battalions were cut off : they formed square, beat back two charges with resolution, but were broken by the third, and absolutely exterminated : 400 were cut down, about 1,000 captured. Of these two unlucky regiments, 1st of Burgos and Cadiz, hardly a man got away—the other two, Jaen and Cuenca, took little harm [1]. The French lost only 18 killed and 61 wounded, mostly in the two cavalry regiments, for Harispe's infantry were but slightly engaged.

Ill news flies quickly—the fighting had been in the early dawn, by noon mounted fugitives had brought the tidings to Villena, fifteen miles away. Here there chanced to be present both Elio and Sir John Murray, who had ridden over to consult with his colleague on a rumour that Suchet was concentrating at Fuente la Higuera. He had brought with him the 'light

---

[1] The best account of all this from the Spanish point of view is a dispatch written by Colonel Potons y Moxica, Elio's chief of the staff, in the Record Office, 'East Coast of Spain' file. It is equally valuable for the battle of Castalla.

brigade,' under Colonel Adam, which he had recently organized [1], and 400 horse [2]. The Generals soon learned that beside the force which had cut up Mijares, there was a larger column marching on their own position. They were in no condition to offer battle, Elio having with him only a single battalion, Murray about 2,500 men of all arms. They agreed that they must quit Villena and concentrate their troops for a defensive action. Elio sent orders to his cavalry to come in from the North and join the wrecks of Mijares' division, and for the reserves which he had got in the neighbourhood of Murcia to march up to the front [3]. But it would obviously take some days to collect these scattered items. Meanwhile he threw the single battalion that he had with him (Velez Malaga) into the castle of Villena, which had been patched up and put into a state of defence, promising that it should be relieved when his army was concentrated.

Murray, on the other hand, retired towards his main body at Castalla, but ordered Adam's 'light brigade' to defend the pass of Biar for as long as prudence permitted, so as to allow the rest of the army to get into position. Whittingham was directed to fall back from Alcoy, Roche to come up from the rear, and by the next evening the whole Alicante army would be concentrated, in a position which had been partly entrenched during the last three weeks, and was very strong even without fortification. Murray refused (very wisely) to send back Adam to pick up the Spanish battalion left in Villena, which Elio (seized with doubts when it was too late) now wished to withdraw.

Suchet reached Villena on the evening of the 11th, and got in touch with the cavalry screen covering Adam's retreat. Finding the castle held, he started to bombard it with his field artillery, and on the morning of the 12th blew in its gates and

---

[1] Consisting of 2/27th British, Calabrese Free Corps, 1st Italian Levy, and the rifle companies of 3rd and 8th K.G.L.

[2] Two squadrons 20th Light Dragoons, the troop of Foreign Hussars, and some of Whittingham's Spaniards, two squadrons of Olivenza.

[3] I do not know who was commanding this division (3rd of the Murcian army) in April : its divisional general, Sarsfield, was absent. It included Bailen, Badajoz, America, Alpujarras, Corona, and Guadix : O'Ronan had it in the preceding autumn.

offered to storm.   He sent in a *parlementaire* to summon the garrison, and to his surprise it capitulated without firing a shot —a mutiny having broken out among the men [1], who considered that they had been deserted by their General.   Suchet now intended to fall on Murray at Castalla, reckoning that Elio's concentration had been prevented by the blows at Yecla and Villena, and that he would have the Alicante army alone to deal with.   He ordered the troops that were with him to drive in without delay Adam's light brigade, which his cavalry had discovered holding the village of Biar and the pass above it. His other column, that of Harispe, was not far off, being on the march from Yecla.   Finding that it was gone, Mijares cautiously reoccupied that place with his two surviving battalions.

The combat of Biar, which filled the midday hours of April 12th, was one of the most creditable rearguard actions fought during the whole Peninsular War.   Colonel Adam had only one British and two Italian battalions, with two German Legion rifle companies, four mountain guns, and one squadron of the ' Foreign Hussars '—about 2,200 men in all.   He had prepared a series of positions on which he intended to fall back in succession, as each was forced.   At the commencement of the action he occupied Biar village with the Calabrese Free Corps, flanked by the light companies of the 2/27th and 3rd K.G.L.   The rest of the brigade was above, on the hills flanking the pass, with the guns on the high road.   The leading French battalion assaulted the barricaded village, and was repulsed with heavy loss.   Then, as was expected, the enemy turned Biar on both flanks : its garrison retired unharmed, but the turning columns came under the accurate fire of the troops on the slopes above, and the attack was again checked. Suchet, angered at the waste of time, then threw in no less than

---

[1] Potons y Moxica's dispatch says that ' la entrega del castillo provino de una especie de sedicíon en la tropa de Velez Malaga,' which is conclusive. Why Napier (v. 57) calls Velez Malaga ' the finest regiment in the Spanish army ' I cannot conceive.   It was one of O'Donnell's old regiments, cut to pieces at Castalla in the preceding July, and hastily filled up with drafts. I suspect that Napier is paraphrasing Suchet's description of this corps as ' mille hommes de belles troupes.'   Except that they had been recently reclothed from the British subsidy, there was nothing ' fine ' about them.

nine battalions [1] intending to sweep away all opposition, and
turning Adam's left flank with swarms of voltigeurs. The
Light Brigade had, of course, to retire ; but Adam conducted
his retreat with great deliberation and in perfect order, fending
off the turning attack with his German and British light
companies, and making the column on the high road pay very
dearly for each furlong gained. His four mountain guns, on
the crest of the pass, were worked with good effect to the last
moment—two which had each lost a wheel were abandoned
on the ground. When the crest had been passed, Suchet sent
a squadron of cuirassiers to charge down the road on the
retreating infantry. Foreseeing this, when the cavalry had
been noted on the ascent, Adam had hidden three companies
of the 2/27th in rocks where the road made a sharp angle :
the cuirassiers, as they trotted past, received a flank volley at
ten paces distance, which knocked over many, and sent the
rest reeling back in disorder on to their own infantry. After
this the pursuit slackened ; ' the enemy seemed glad to be
rid of us,' and after five hours' fighting the Light Brigade
marched back in perfect order to the position beside Castalla
which had been assigned to it [2]. Its final retirement was
covered by three battalions which Murray had sent out to
meet it, at the exit from the pass [3].

So ended a very pretty fight. Whittingham, who had
witnessed the later phases of it from the hill on the left of
Castalla, describes it as ' a beautiful field-day, by alternate
battalions : the volleys were admirable, and the successive
passage of several ravines conducted with perfect order and
steadiness. From the heights occupied by my troops it was
one of the most delightful panoramas that I ever beheld.' The

---

[1] In his own narrative he says that he sent in the 1st and 3rd Léger,
14th, 114th, and 121st Line—a big deployment of forces.

[2] The best account of the combat of Biar is that of the anonymous officer
of the 2/27th, quoted at length by Trimble in his *History of the Inniskilling
Regiment*, pp. 61–2. See also the less trustworthy Landsheit (of the ' Foreign
Hussars '), ii. pp. 86–9.

[3] De Roll-Dillon, 81st, and one of Whittingham's Spanish battalions.
They had some casualties—the Spaniards 29, De Roll-Dillon probably 25 :
its total casualty list for the days April 12–13 of 34 cannot be divided
between the two actions.

allied loss was about 300 [1], including Colonel Adam wounded
in the arm, yet not so much hurt but that he kept the command
and gave directions to the end. On the ground evacuated
41 ' missing ' and two disabled mountain guns were left in the
enemy's hands. The French must have suffered much the
same casualties—Suchet gives no estimate, but Martinien's
invaluable lists show two officers killed and twelve wounded,
which at the usual rate between officers and men implies about
300 rank and file hit.

On emerging from the pass of Biar in the late afternoon
Suchet could see Murray's army occupying a long front of
high ground as far as the town of Castalla, but could descry
neither its encampment, behind the heights, nor the end of its
right wing, which was thrown back and hidden by the high
conical hill on which the castle and church of Castalla stand.
Seeing the enemy ready, and apparently resolved to fight, the
Marshal put off serious operations to the next day. He had to
wait for Harispe's column, which was still coming up many
miles in his rear.

Murray had long surveyed his ground, and had (as we have
seen) thrown up barricades and entrenchments on the hill of
Castalla and the ground immediately to its right and left.
He had very nearly every available man of his army in hand,
only a minimum garrison having been left in Alicante [2]. The
total cannot have been less than 18,000 men ; he had divided
his own troops into the Light Brigade of Adam, and the two
divisions of Mackenzie and Clinton. The first named had
three and a quarter battalions—not quite 2,000 men after its

---

[1] It is impossible to disentangle the losses of Adam's brigade on April 12
and April 13, given together in Murray's report. But on the second day
the 2/27th regiment was the only unit seriously engaged. The total for
both days was killed 1 officer and 56 men, wounded 10 officers and 231 men,
missing 32 men : or a total of 330. If we *deduct* 40 for assumed losses of
the 2/27th on the second day, and 30 more for casual losses of the other
units on April 13—they were engaged but not seriously—and *add* 29 for
losses in Whittingham's battalion (he gives the figure himself) and 25
(including 9 missing) for those in De Roll-Dillon (which was barely under
fire on the second day and lost 34 altogether), we must conclude that the
total was very close to 300.

[2] The light company 7th K.G.L., two newly arrived squadrons of
Brunswick Hussars, and two batteries.

losses at Biar on the previous afternoon [1]. Mackenzie seems to have had one British, two German Legion, and two Sicilian battalions [2] : Clinton three British, one composite Foreign, and one Italian battalion [3]. Whittingham had six Spanish battalions with him [4]—Roche only five [5]. The cavalry consisted of three squadrons of the 20th Light Dragoons, two of Sicilian cavalry, one of ' Foreign Hussars,' and about 400 of Whittingham's Spanish horse [6], under 1,000 sabres in all. There were two British, two Portuguese, and a Sicilian battery on the ground.

The sierra on the left, known as the heights of Guerra, was held by Whittingham's Spaniards for a mile, next them came Adam's brigade, above a jutting spur which projects from the sierra towards the plain, then Mackenzie's division, which extended as far as the hill on which the castle of Castalla stands : this was occupied by the 1/58th of Clinton's division, and two batteries had been thrown up on the slope. With this hill the sierra ends suddenly ; but a depression and stream running southward furnished a good protection for Murray's right, which was held by the rest of Clinton's division. The stream had been dammed up, and formed a broad morass covering a considerable portion of the front. Behind it Clinton's troops were deployed, with three of Roche's battalions as a reserve in their rear : two batteries were placed on commanding knolls in this part of the line, which was so far thrown back *en potence* that it was almost at right angles to the front occupied by Mackenzie, Adam, and Whittingham. The Spanish and Sicilian cavalry was thrown out as a screen in front of Castalla, with two of Roche's battalions in support. The 20th Light Dragoons were in reserve behind the town. The east end of the sierra, near Castalla, was covered by vineyards in step-cultivation, each en-

---

[1] 2/27th, Calabrese Free Corps, 1st Italian Levy, two light companies K.G.L.

[2] 1/27th, 4th and 6th K.G.L., ' Estero ' regiment (two battalions).

[3] 1/10th, 1/58th, 1/81st British, composite battalion of De Roll-Dillon, 2nd Italian Levy.

[4] Cordoba, Mallorca, Guadalajara, 2nd of Burgos, 2nd of Murcia, 5th Grenadiers.

[5] Chinchilla, Canarias, Alicante, Cazadores de Valencia, Voluntarios de Aragon.

[6] Two squadrons each of Olivenza and Almanza.

closure a few feet higher than the next below it.   Farther west there was only rough hillside, below Whittingham's front.   The whole position was excellent—yet Murray is said by his Quartermaster-General, Donkin, to have felt so uncomfortable that he thrice contemplated issuing orders for a retreat, though he could see the whole French army, and judge that its strength was much less than his own [1].   But he distrusted both himself and many battalions of his miscellaneous army.

Suchet, contrary to his wont, was slow to act.   It is said that he disliked the look of the position, and doubted the wisdom of attacking, but was over-persuaded by some of his generals, who urged that the enemy was a mixed multitude, and that the Spaniards and Sicilians would never stand against a resolute attack.   It was not till noon that the French army moved—the first manœuvre was that the whole of the cavalry rode out eastward, took position opposite the angle *en potence* of Murray's position, and sent exploring parties towards Clinton's front.   Evidently the report was that it was inaccessible.   While this was happening the infantry deployed, and Habert's and Robert's division advanced and occupied a low ridge, called the Cerro del Doncel, in the plain facing Murray's left and left-centre.   Harispe's division, minus a detachment left behind the pass of Biar to watch for any possible appearance of Elio's troops on the road from Sax, formed in reserve.   The whole of Suchet's infantry was only 18 battalions, individually weaker than Murray's 24 ;   he was outnumbered in guns also —24 to 30 apparently—but his 1,250 cavalry were superior in numbers and quality to Murray's.   He had certainly not more than 13,000 men on the ground to the Allies' 18,000.

His game was to leave Clinton's division and Castalla alone, watched only by his cavalry ;   to contain Mackenzie by demonstrations, which were not to be pushed home ;   but to strike heavily with Robert's division at the Spaniards on the left. If he could break down Whittingham's defence, and drive him off the sierra, he would attack the allied centre from flank and front alike—but meanwhile it was not to be pressed.   When, therefore, Habert faced Mackenzie nothing serious happened,

---

[1] Napier, v. 58, quoting Donkin MSS., which are unpublished and unfindable.

the French sent out swarms of tirailleurs, brought up eight
guns and shelled the position with grape. Mackenzie's light
companies and guns replied, ' but there was nothing more than
a skirmish : the columns shifted their ground indeed more
than once, but they did not deploy, and their officers took good
care not to bring them under the fire of our line [1].'

On the left, however, there was hard fighting. Suchet first
sent out five light companies to endeavour to turn the extreme
western end of Whittingham's line, and, when they were far
up the slope, delivered a frontal attack on the heights of Guerra
with six battalions of Robert's division : the 3rd Léger and
114th and 121st Line [2] : of these the left-hand battalions
(belonging to the 121st) came up the projecting spur mentioned
above, and faced the 2/27th on the left of Adam's brigade.
The other four were opposed to the Spaniards.

Whittingham was caught in a rather dangerous position, for
a little while before the attack developed, he had received an
order from head-quarters bidding him execute against Robert's
division precisely the same manœuvre that Suchet was trying
against himself, viz. to send troops to outflank the extreme
French right. He was told by the bearer of the orders, a Sicilian
colonel, that this was preliminary to a general attack downhill
upon the French line, which Murray was intending to carry out.
The Spanish division was to turn its flank, while Adam and
Mackenzie went straight at its front. There is some mystery
here—Murray afterwards denied to Whittingham that he had
given any such order [3], and Donkin, his Chief of the Staff,
maintained that his general was thinking of a retreat all that
morning rather than of an attack. Yet Colonel Catanelli was
a respectable officer, who was thanked in dispatches both by
Murray and Whittingham for his services ! Three hypotheses
suggest themselves : (1) that Murray at one moment meditated
an attack, because he saw Suchet holding back, and then (with
his usual infirmity of purpose) dropped the idea, and denied

---

[1] Landsheit, ii. p. 91.

[2] Suchet says that to support the voltigeurs he sent in only *four* battalions
of the 3rd Léger and 121st—but most undoubtedly the 114th attacked also,
for it lost four officers killed and nine wounded, as many as the 3rd Léger,
and this means 250 casualties at least in the rank and file.

[3] Whittingham, *Memoirs*, p. 197.

having made any such plan to Whittingham, whose position had been gravely imperilled by its execution. This is quite in accordance with his mentality, and he often tampered with the truth—as we shall see when telling the tale of Tarragona. (2) That Donkin and the head-quarters staff, enraged with Murray's timidity, were resolved to commit him to a fight, and gave unauthorized orders which must bring it on. (3) That Catanelli, from lack of a good command of English, misunderstood the General's language, and gave complete misdirections to Whittingham. I must confess that I incline to the first solution [1].

Whatever the source of these orders may have been, Whittingham began to carry them out, though they seemed to him very ill-advised. But noting that if he completely evacuated the heights of Guerra there would be a broad gap in the allied line, he left his picquets in position and two battalions on the crest of the hill [2], with another in support behind [3], while with the remaining three [4] he moved off to the left. The march was executed, out of sight of the enemy, by a mountain path which ran along the rear of the heights.

Whittingham had been moving for some half an hour, and slowly, for the path was steep and narrow, when the sound of musketry on the other side of the crest reached his ears, and soon after a message that the enemy was attacking the whole of the front of his old position. On its left the voltigeur companies had got very near the top of the hill—farther east the assault was only developing. It was lucky that the marching column had not gone far—Whittingham was able to send his hindmost battalion straight up the hill against the voltigeurs, to strengthen his flank—with the other two he counter-marched to the rear of the heights of Guerra, and fed the fighting line which he had left there, as each point needed succour.

The contest all along the heights was protracted and fierce. At several points the French reached the crest, but were never

---

[1] Mr. Fortescue (*British Army*, ix. p. 43) seems rather to lean to the idea that the staff, or at any rate Catanelli, resolved to force Murray to fight despite of himself. This may have been the case.

[2] Cordoba and 2nd of Burgos.   [3] Guadalajara.

[4] Murcia, Majorca, and 5th Grenadiers.

able to maintain themselves there, as Whittingham had always a reserve of a few companies ready for a counterstroke. The troops of the Army of Aragon had never before met with such opposition from Spaniards, and for a long time refused to own themselves beaten. There was still one regiment of Robert's division in reserve [1], but evidently Suchet shrank from committing the last fraction of his right wing to the attack, which was obviously not making any decisive headway.

Meanwhile the easternmost column of the French advance suffered a complete defeat: this body, composed of two battalions of the 121st regiment, had mounted the heights, not at their steepest, but at the point where a long projecting spur falls down from them into the plain. But even so there was a sudden rise in the last stage of the ascent, before the crest was reached. On coming to it the French colonel (Millet by name) began to deploy his leading companies, which found themselves opposite the 2/27th, on the left of Adam's brigade. This manœuvre had always failed when tried against British infantry—notably at Albuera, for deployment at close quarters under the deadly fire of a British line was impracticable, and always led to confusion. There was a pause [2], many casualties, and much wavering; then, seeing the enemy stationary and discouraged, Colonel Reeves flung his battalion at them in a downhill bayonet charge—like Crauford at Bussaco. The effect was instantaneous and conclusive—the French column broke and raced headlong down the slopes, arriving in the valley as a disorganized mob. It had lost 19 officers and probably 350 men in five minutes.

Either in consequence of this rout, or by mere chance at the

---

[1] 1st Léger, in reserve on the Cerro del Doncel.

[2] During which occurred the dramatic duel in front of the line between Captain Waldron and a French Grenadier officer mentioned in Napier, v. p. 59. The picturesqueness of the story induced some critics to doubt it. But there is no getting over the fact that Waldron gave his opponent's weapon, which was a sword of honour presented by the Emperor, to the Quartermaster-General (Donkin), who forwarded it to the Duke of York, and the Commander-in-Chief gazetted Waldron to a brevet-majority in consequence. (See Trimble's *Historical Record of the 27th*, p. 64.) It is extremely odd (as Arteche remarks) that Suchet in his short and insincere account of Castalla tells a story of a *French* officer who killed an English officer in single combat (*Mémoires*, ii. p. 308).

same moment [1], the columns which had been assailing Whittingham so long and ineffectively, also recoiled in disorder before
a charge of the last four companies of the Spanish reserve.
The whole of the French right wing had suffered complete
and disastrous defeat. The left division, Habert's, was still
intact and had never committed itself to any serious approach
to Mackenzie's front. But six of the eighteen French battalions
in the field were in absolute rout at half-past four o'clock, and
Suchet's right wing was completely exposed—his cavalry were
two miles away to the left, and out of reach for the moment.
All eye-witnesses agree that if Murray had ordered an immediate
general advance of the line from Castalla westward, the Marshal
would have been lost, and cut off from his sole line of retreat
on the pass of Biar. Murray, however, refused to move till
he had brought up his unengaged right wing to act as a reserve,
and only when they had filed up through the streets of Castalla,
gave the order for the whole army to descend from the heights
and push forward.

It was far too late : Suchet had retreated from the Cerro del
Doncel the moment that he saw his attack repulsed, Habert's
division and the guns covering Robert's routed wing. The
cavalry came galloping back from the east, and long before
Murray was deployed, Suchet took up a new and narrow front
covering the entry of the pass of Biar. The only touch with
his retreating force was kept by Mackenzie, who (contrary to
Murray's intention) pushed forward with four of his battalions
in front of the main body, and got engaged with Suchet's rearguard. He might probably have beaten it in upon the disordered
troops behind, if he had not received stringent orders to
draw back and fall in to the general front of advance. By the
time that the whole allied army was deployed, the French, save
a long line of guns across the mouth of the pass, with infantry
on the slopes on each side, had got off. Thereupon, after
making a feeble demonstration with some light companies
against the enemy's left flank, Murray halted for the night.
The enemy used the hours of darkness to make a forced march
for Fuente la Higuera, and were invisible next day.

[1] I am inclined to think the latter, as it is doubtful whether, with the
spur between, Adam's fighting-ground was visible from Whittingham's.

Suchet declared that he had lost no more than 800 men in the three combats of Yecla, Biar, and Castalla, an incredible statement, as the French casualty rolls show 65 officers killed and wounded on the 11th–12th–13th of April ; and such a loss implies 1,300 rank and file hit—possibly more, certainly not many less. It is certain that his 800 casualties will not suffice even for Castalla alone, where with 47 officers *hors de combat* he must have lost more probably 950 than 800 men. But the 14 officer-casualties at Biar imply another 280 at the least, and we know from his own narrative that he lost 4 officers and 80 men in destroying Mijares' unfortunate battalions at Yecla[1].

Murray, writing a most magniloquent and insincere dispatch for Wellington's eye, declared that Suchet had lost 2,500 or even 3,000 men, and that he had buried 800 French corpses. But Murray had apparently been taking lessons in the school of Soult and Masséna, those great manipulators of casualty lists ! His dispatch was so absurd that Wellington refused to be impressed, and sent on the document to Lord Bathurst with the most formal request that the attention of the Prince Regent should be drawn to the conduct of the General and his troops, but no word of praise of his own[2]. The allied loss, indeed, was so moderate that Murray's 2,500 French casualties appeared incredible to every one. After we have deducted the heavy losses to Adam's brigade at Biar on the preceding day, we find that Whittingham's Spaniards had 233 casualties, Mackenzie's division 47, Clinton's about 20, Adam's brigade perhaps 70, the cavalry and artillery 10 altogether—the total making some 400 in all[3].

Having discovered that the Alicante army was formidable, if its general was not, Suchet was in some fear that he might find himself pursued and attacked, for the enemy seemed to

---

[1] Taking Murray's casualty list for comparison with Suchet's, we find that he had 4 officers killed and 16 wounded to 649 men at Biar and Castalla, i. e. 1 officer to 32 men. But this was an exceptionally low proportion of officers lost. At such a rate Suchet might have lost 2,000 men ! I take 1,300 as a fair estimate.

[2] Cf. Wellington, *Dispatches*, x. pp. 354–5, in which Wellington asks what sort of a victory was it, if Suchet was able to hold the pass of Biar, only two miles from the battle-field, till nightfall ?

[3] See Appendix on Castalla losses, English and French, at the end of the volume.

be concentrating against him.   Murray advanced once more to Alcoy, Elio brought up his reserve division and his cavalry to join the wrecks of Mijares' column, and extended himself on Murray's left.   Villacampa, called down from the hills, appeared on the Upper Guadalaviar on the side of Requeña. But all this meant nothing—Murray was well satisfied to have won a success capable of being well ' written up ' at Castalla, and covered his want of initiative by complaining that he was short of transport, and weakened in numbers—for after the battle he had sent off the 6th K.G.L. to Sicily, in belated obedience to Bentinck's old orders.   He asked Wellington for more men and more guns, and was given both, for he was told that he might draw the 2 /67th from the garrison of Cartagena[1], and was sent a field battery from Portugal.   But his true purpose was now to wait for the arrival of the promised ' plan of campaign ' from Freneda, and thereby to shirk all personal responsibility.   Anything was better than to risk a check—or a reprimand from the caustic pen of the Commander-in-Chief.

Suchet, then, drew down Pannetier's brigade from Aragon to strengthen his position on the Xucar, and waited, not altogether confidently, for the next move on the part of the enemy. But for a month no such move came.   He had time to recover his equanimity, and to write dispatches to Paris which described his late campaign as a successful attempt to check the enemy's initiative, which had brought him 2,000 Spanish prisoners at Yecla and Villena, and two British guns at the pass of Biar. Castalla was represented as a partial attack by light troops, which had been discontinued when the enemy's full strength had been discovered, and the losses there were unscrupulously minimized.   And, above all, good cause had been shown that the Army of Aragon and Valencia could not spare one man to help King Joseph in the North.

But the ' plan of campaign ' was on its way, and we shall see how, even in Murray's incompetent hands, it gave the Marshal Duke of Albufera full employment for May and June.

---

[1] Six companies of Dillon came from Sicily, to replace the 2/67th at Cartagena.

SECTION XXXVI
THE MARCH TO VITTORIA

CHAPTER I

WELLINGTON'S PLAN OF CAMPAIGN

Good generals are very properly averse to putting on paper, even for the benefit of premiers or war ministers, the plan of their next campaign. Points of leakage are so inscrutable, and so hard to detect, that the less that is written the better is it for the projected enterprise. And Wellington was the most reticent of men—even going to the length of hiding from his own responsible subordinates intentions that they much desired to learn, and of giving orders that seemed eccentric while the secret reason for them was kept concealed. He never wrote autobiographical memoirs—the idea was repulsive to him—nor consented to open up (even to William Napier, who much desired it) his full confidence. For the genesis of the plan of the Vittoria Campaign we are compelled to rely mainly on the careful collection of hints from his contemporary dispatches, supplemented by certain rare confidential letters, and some *obiter dicta* of his later years, which may or may not have been reproduced with perfect accuracy by admirers like Croker or Lord Stanhope.

One thing is clear—he was conscious of the mistakes of 1812, and was not going to see them repeated in 1813. When the Burgos campaign was just over he wrote two short comments [1] on it, for the benefit of persons whom he judged capable of appreciating his difficulties. He owned up to his errors—he acknowledged four. The first was that he had tried to take Burgos by irregular means, without a proper battering train : the second that he had under-estimated the strength of the

[1] Wellington to Dumouriez, *Supplementary Dispatches*, vii. 482–3, and to Cooke, ibid. pp. 477–8.

united French armies of Portugal and the North : the third
that he had kept his army in two equal halves over-long—Hill
should have been called in from Madrid to join the main body
much sooner than he actually was : the fourth and most notable
was that he had entrusted a crucial part of his plan of campaign
to a Spanish general, over whom he had no formal authority—
Ballasteros, who should have advanced from Andalusia to
distract and hinder Soult. ' If the game had been well played
it would have answered my purpose. Had I any reason to
suppose that it would be well played ? Certainly not. I have
never yet known the Spaniards do *anything*, much less do
anything *well*. . . . But I played a game which *might* succeed
(the only one that *could* succeed) and pushed it to the last.
The parts having failed—as I admit was to be expected—I at
least made a handsome retreat to the Agueda, with some
labour and inconvenience but without material loss.'

The interest of these confessions is that we find Wellington
in his next campaign making a clear effort to avoid precisely
these four mistakes. He made elaborate preparations long
beforehand for getting up a battering train : he rather over-
than under-estimated his adversary's numbers by way of
caution : he never divided his army at all during his great
advance of May–June 1813 ; after the first six days it marched
in close parallel columns all in one mass, till Vittoria had been
reached : and, last but not least, he entrusted no important
part of the scheme to any Spanish general, and indeed used
a much smaller proportion of Spanish troops than he need
have done, although he had now become Generalissimo of all
the allied armies, and could command where he could formerly
only give advice.

Immediately after the termination of the Burgos retreat
Wellington's views for the future do not seem to have been
very optimistic. He wrote to the Prime Minister that at
present he could do nothing against an enemy whose numbers
had proved too great for him to contend with [1]. Next spring
he hoped to take the field with a larger force than he had ever
had before, but unless the Spaniards could display a discipline
and efficiency which it seemed impossible to teach them, he

---

[1] Wellington to Liverpool, November 23, 1812. *Dispatches*, ix. p. 572.

saw no prospect of ever obliging the French to quit the Peninsula by force of arms. To Lord Bathurst he wrote in much the same terms—the French, he thought, would canton their army in Old Castile and wait for the arrival of fresh reinforcements from France.

But the whole aspect of affairs was changed when the news of Napoleon's Russian *débâcle* came to hand. It soon became clear that so far from any French reinforcements coming to Spain, it would be King Joseph who would be asked to send reinforcements to Germany. Lord Liverpool's letter, enclosing the 29th Bulletin, reached Wellington at Lisbon on January 18th, and put him in a more cheerful mood. Moreover, he thought that his visit to Cadiz to accept the position of Generalissimo had been a success, and that he would get more help out of the Spaniards now that he had the formal power of issuing orders to their generals, 'though I am not sanguine enough to hope that we shall derive much advantage from Spanish troops *early* in the campaign.' But he intended to start betimes, 'and at least to put myself in Fortune's way [1].' The French would be compelled to stand on the defensive ; if they continued to hold the immense line that they were still occupying in January, they must be weak somewhere, and it was impossible that they should be reinforced.

It is on February 10th [2] that we get the first hint that Wellington's scheme for the campaign of 1813 was going to be a very ambitious one—aiming not at local successes in Castile, or on recovering Madrid, but at driving the French right up to the Pyrenees. On that day he wrote to Lord Bathurst to say that ' the events of the next campaign may render it necessary for the army to undertake one or more sieges in the North of Spain,' wherefore he wished certain heavy guns and munitions to be sent by sea to Corunna, to be at his disposal, as soon as might be convenient, and twice the quantity of each to be prepared in England to be shipped when asked for.

The mention of ' one or more sieges in the North of Spain ' for which guns had better be sent by sea to Corunna, can only

---

[1] Wellington to Graham, January 31. *Dispatches*, x. p. 67.

[2] Wellington to Bathurst. Ibid., p. 104.

mean that Wellington was thinking of Burgos and St. Sebastian
—perhaps also of Santoña and Pampeluna. There were no
other fortresses needing the attention of a heavy battering
train in that direction. It is clear that, even in February,
Wellington's mind was travelling far afield ; and on June 26th,
Vittoria having been now won, he wrote to remind Lord
Bathurst of his demand, and to point out that his forecast
had come true [1].

In March, as was shown in an earlier chapter, Wellington
began to get the news which proved that the French were
making large drafts from Spain for the new Army of Germany,
and that Soult, Caffarelli, and other generals were summoned to
Paris. He knew, a few days later, that the enemy was evacuating
La Mancha, and that the King was moving his head-quarters
from Madrid to Valladolid. Everything indicated conscious
weakness on the part of the enemy—it would be well to take
instant advantage of it : Wellington wrote to his brother on
March 28 that he hoped to start out in force on May 1st [2]—
giving no hint where that force would be employed. At the
same time he expressed his doubt as to whether any of the
Spanish corps which were to join him could be ready by that
date. But he was depending so much on the sole exertions of
the Anglo-Portuguese army, that the tardiness of the Spaniards
would not put a complete stop to his projected operations. Two
other practical hindrances were a late spring, which made green
forage for the horses harder to procure than it normally was in
April, and accidents from bad roads and bad weather to his
pontoon train, which he was secretly bringing up from the
Tagus to the Douro, as it was to play a most essential part in
the commencement of the campaign[3]. These mishaps appear mere
matters of detail, but (as we shall see) there were immense consequences depending upon them—the presence of a large pontoon
train on the Esla and the Douro, when its normal habitat was
on the lower Tagus, was one of the first surprises in the wonderful

---

[1] *Dispatches*, x. p. 464.

[2] Wellington to Henry Wellesley. *Dispatches*, x. p. 239.

[3] Wellington to Stapleton Cotton, ibid., p. 268, and to Bathurst,
ibid. 295, speaking of the extraordinary dry spring. Dickson notes in his
Diary that for two months before April 4 there had been no rain.

campaign of May–June 1813. Starting from Abrantes in the end of April, it did not reach Miranda de Douro till the 20th of May [1].

The first definite revelation as to what Wellington's plan was to be, is contained in a letter to Beresford of April 24th. ' I propose to put the troops in motion in the first days of May : my intention is to make them cross the Douro, in general within the Portuguese frontier, covering the movement of the left by that of the right of the Army toward the Tormes, which right shall then cross the Douro, over the pontoons, in such situation as may be convenient. I then propose to seize Zamora and Toro, which will make all future operations easy to us [2].'

Here the first half of the great movement is accurately set forth, just as it was executed, though owing to the delays spoken of above, the general orders for the marching out of all the allied divisions were issued on May 13th instead of on May 1st–2nd. But in all other respects we have the exact analysis of the scheme : the ' Left '—Graham with the equivalent of six divisions—crossed the Douro far inside Portugal at various points, and was in and about Braganza and Miranda by May 21st–24th: meanwhile the ' Right '—Hill with three divisions—moved forward from the Agueda to the Tormes, attracting the main attention of the French between the 20th and the 26th, till it reached Salamanca, from whence it swerved off to the left, and joined Graham's wing by the bridge of Toro, thus establishing the whole army in one mass north of the Douro, and completely turning the western flank of the entire French front of defence. On May 12 only, three weeks after he had communicated the secret to Beresford, did Wellington divulge it to the Ministers at home : evidently he dreaded leakage somewhere in London, such as he had discovered in the preceding autumn [3]. For Lord Bathurst's benefit he descends a little more into detail :

' I propose to commence our operations by turning the enemy's position on the Douro, by passing the left of our army over that river within the Portuguese frontier. I should cross

---

[1] See *Dispatches*, x. pp. 372–3.
[2] Wellington to Beresford, April 24. *Dispatches*, x. p. 322.
[3] See above, pp. 224–5.

the Right in the same manner, only that I have been obliged to throw the Right very forward during the winter, in order to cover and connect our cantonments, and I could not well draw them back without exposing a good deal of country, and risking a counter-movement on the part of the enemy. I therefore propose to strengthen the Right, and move with it myself across the Tormes, and to establish a bridge on the Douro below Zamora. The two wings of the army will thus be connected, and the enemy's position on the Douro will be turned. The Spanish Army of Galicia will be on the Esla, to the left of our army, at the same time that our army reaches that river.

'Having turned the enemy's position on the Douro, and established our communications across it, our next operation will depend on circumstances. I do not know whether I am now stronger than the enemy, even including the Army of Galicia. But of this I am very certain, that I shall never be stronger throughout the campaign, or more efficient, than I am now : and the enemy will never be weaker. I cannot have a better opportunity for trying the fate of a battle, which if the enemy should be unsuccessful, must oblige him to withdraw entirely. We have been sadly delayed by the pontoon bridge, without which it is obvious we can do nothing[1].'

Neither in the letter to Beresford nor in that to Bathurst does Wellington make a forecast beyond the first stage of his advance—obviously it would be impossible to do so till it was seen how the French would act. If they should be tempted to fight—say in front of Valladolid—when their flank was turned, in order to keep their hold on Castile, Wellington would welcome the decisive engagement. But of course they might refuse to fight, as indeed did they. They retired on Burgos, as we shall see, without taking any risks.

But that Wellington already foresaw the possibility of a victorious march to the Pyrenees is, I think, proved not only by his letter of February 10th concerning the siege of fortresses in Northern Spain, quoted above, but by similar hints on May 6 concerning the absolute necessity for naval co-operation in the North. He asks Lord Bathurst to insist on the presence of a squadron under an admiral in the Bay of Biscay, and for

---

[1] Wellington to Bathurst, *Dispatches*, x. 372.

careful supervision of the whole coast from Bayonne to Corunna, which must absolutely stop French enterprise at sea, and 'simplify arrangements for convoy and naval operations in concert with the army during the ensuing campaign [1].' Taking this in conjunction with the letter of February 10, it seems certain that Wellington was thinking of stores to be landed at Santander, and a battering train to destroy San Sebastian—which was to look forward some way! There was, however, a secondary reason for requiring more naval supervision in the Bay of Biscay: American privateers had been putting in an appearance in these waters, and had captured several small transports.

A plan of campaign that contemplated the driving back of the French to the Pyrenees must, of course, embrace a good deal more than the mere reorganization of the Anglo-Portuguese army for a great push north of the Douro. There were many minor factors to be taken into consideration and utilized. First and foremost came the question as to how far the position of Generalissimo of the Spanish Armies could be turned to account. After his experiences in 1812 Wellington was determined to entrust to his Allies no crucial part of the operations, whose failure could wreck the whole scheme. With his own striking-force he intended to take only one Spanish army, that which was under the sole Spanish general whom he could trust for willing co-operation, even though he knew him to be no great military genius. Castaños had, by his influence at Cadiz, been nominated as Captain-General alike in Galicia, Castile, and Estremadura, and all the troops in those provinces now formed part of the new ' 4th Army.' They included Morillo's division, now cantoned about Caçeres, Carlos de España's in the mountains between Ciudad Rodrigo and the pass of Perales, the lancers of Julian Sanchez—now counted a brigade of regular cavalry and not a *partida*—on the front between the Agueda and the Douro, and the two Galician divisions of Losada and Barcena, with their weak attendant cavalry brigade: to bring this up to strength two extra regiments [2] had filed up the Portuguese frontier during the

---

[1] Wellington to Bathurst, May 6. *Dispatches*, x. p. 361.
[2] Algarve, and Hussars of Estremadura.

winter from Estremadura. All these were in touch with the Anglo-Portuguese army, and were intended to move with it. They made up 18,000 foot and 3,000 horse. In addition there were many other troops theoretically belonging to the 4th Army, but at present cut off from it by the intervening zone of French occupation—viz. Porlier's division in the Eastern Asturias, and Mendizabal's irregular forces in Biscay and Cantabria—the troops of Longa and the Biscayan volunteers with other smaller bands. These scattered units, which could only come under Wellington's real control when he should have beaten the French back to the Ebro, might make up 10,000 or 12,000 men. But they could not be counted upon for the first month of the campaign.

In addition, Castaños had a number of immovable troops— the garrisons of Rodrigo and Badajoz, a dépôt of unhorsed cavalry in Estremadura, and a sedentary unit called the 'Army of Reserve of Galicia,' consisting of all the most depleted corps of the old Galician army : its six battalions only made up 2,000 men, and it stopped at Vigo or Corunna all through the year 1813. Two other Galician battalions [1] had been sent round by sea during the winter, to join the much-tried Army of Catalonia. This small transference of troops had reached the knowledge of the French in an exaggerated shape, and caused much speculation at Madrid.

Beside the 21,000 men of the 4th Army, who marched in the Anglo-Portuguese line under Castaños's nephew General Giron [2], there was only one other Spanish force which Wellington intended to employ in his own operations. This was the so-called 'Army of Reserve of Andalusia,' which had to come up all the way from Seville, and was far too late to join in the campaign of Vittoria : it did not get to the front till July : even later than the Generalissimo expected. The origin of this corps was that, when Soult evacuated Andalusia in September 1812, the best-equipped of the Cadiz garrison troops joined the field-army of Ballasteros, and advanced with him to Granada. This body was in April 1813 known as the 'Third Army' and was

[1] Pontevedra and Principe.

[2] Castaños himself during the campaign acted more as Captain-General than as Army-Commander—stationing himself at Salamanca and reorganizing the districts just recovered from the French.

now commanded by the Duque del Parque, the successor of the cashiered Ballasteros.   But the remainder of the Cadiz garrison, which had not gone to the front, was organized during the winter into a separate unit, under Henry O'Donnell, the Conde d'Abispal.   It was rather a miscellaneous assembly— seven of its fourteen battalions having been regiments which did not march in October 1812 because they were low in numbers or equipment, and three more newly-raised units, formed to replace in the Army List old regiments which had perished in previous campaigns.   However, they were filled up with recruits, re-clothed and re-equipped, and Wellington intended to use them with his own army, as *étape* and blockade troops.   He preferred to take them with him rather than the 3rd Army, which was suspected of having many officers who had been devoted to Ballasteros, and who had resented the appointment of the new British generalissimo [1].   Moreover, O'Donnell was in every way a better officer than Del Parque, and had a good fighting reputation, though he was noted as impetuous and quarrelsome.   The Army of Reserve of Andalusia was 14,000 strong, in two infantry divisions under Generals Echevari and Creagh and a weak cavalry brigade under Freire—late second in command of the Murcian army.   The slow equipment of this corps, its late start, and its frequent halts for want of provisions, formed a perpetual source of dispute between Wellington and the Minister of War at Cadiz.   But as it was not destined to form part of the original striking-force at the opening of the campaign, or to discharge any essential duty in the general scheme, its absence was not much felt.   When it did appear, after Vittoria, it was usefully employed in blockading Pampeluna.

But in the summer campaign of 1813 it must be remembered that Wellington employed no Spanish troops save the original 21,000 Galicians and Estremadurans under Giron, and Longa's 4,000 Cantabrians, who joined in from the North ten days before Vittoria, and took a creditable share in that battle.

---

[1] Apparently not without reason, if we can trust King Joseph's correspondence, which contains notes of a treasonable intrigue in May, between certain officers of the 3rd Army and General Viruez, an *Afrancesado* at Madrid.   See *Correspondance du Roi*, ix. pp. 130 and 466.

It remains to be explained how Wellington intended to get an indirect profit out of the existence of the other Spanish corps—the re-named First, Second, and Third Armies, as well as out of the Anglo-Sicilian expeditionary force at Alicante, whose conduct had given him so many just causes of complaint during the autumn of 1812.

As to the 'First Army,' now commanded by General Copons (the defender of Tarifa), this gallant remnant of the old Catalan levies could not take the field 10,000 strong, was almost destitute of cavalry and artillery, and had no large town or secure fortress in its possession [1]. It held, in a rather precarious fashion, a considerable portion of the mountainous inland of Catalonia—the head-quarters were usually at Vich—but had no safe communications with the sea, or certainty of receiving succours, though it was intermittently in touch with Captain Codrington's cruising squadron. Copons, who took over command in March 1813, though less disliked than his arbitrary and ill-tempered predecessor Lacy, was not popular with the Catalans. They would have liked to see their local hero, the Baron de Eroles, who had been in charge of the principality for some months after Lacy's departure, made captain-general [2]. Weak in numbers as it was, the Army of Catalonia could obviously do no more than detain and keep employed General Decaen's French army of occupation, which had more than double its strength. The garrisons of Barcelona, Tarragona, Figueras, Lerida, and Tortosa absorbed 13,000 of Decaen's men. But he had 15,000 more available for field service, and his flying columns often put Copons in danger, for the Catalan army had to scatter its cantonments far and wide in order to live, and a sudden hostile concentration might easily cut off some fraction of it, when one part was as far north as the Ampurdam and the passes into France, and another as far east as the Aragonese border [3]. Normally the Catalans

[1] Total force a nominal 15,000, but dépôts, hospitals, petty garrisons, &c., absorbed a full third—the cavalry was 441 sabres only.

[2] See Codrington to Wellesley, January 18, in *Supplementary Dispatches*, vii. p. 569.

[3] Sarsfield with one of the two Catalan field divisions was normally operating as a sort of guerrillero on the Aragonese side. Manso generally hung about the Ampurdam with a brigade.

employed themselves in cutting the communications between the great fortresses, with an occasional foray into Roussillon. Wellington thought that they could not be better employed, and that nothing more could be expected of them. He sent them a small reinforcement of 2,000 men from the suppressed third division of the Army of Galicia, and urged that munitions should be thrown in from the side of the sea whenever possible.

There was little to be expected from the exertions of the Catalan army, persevering and meritorious though they were. It remained to be seen, however, whether something could not be done in the Principality with external help. Here came in the main problem of the Eastern Coast : Suchet must be kept employed at all costs, while the main blow was being delivered by Wellington himself on the other side of the Peninsula. Murray's and Elio's futile operations of April had accomplished little : the Marshal, though frightened at first by their movements, and though he had suffered the bloody check of Castalla, had been able to preserve his forward position on the Xucar : he retained complete possession of the Valencian coastland, and his army was intact as a striking force. If, during the forthcoming campaign north of the Douro, he chose to draw off his main force towards Aragon, and to come in to join the King, there was at present nothing on foot that could stop him from such a course. Wellington resolved that this possibility must be averted, by giving the Marshal a problem of his own, which should absorb all his attention, and keep him from thinking of his neighbour's needs. And this was all the more easy because Suchet was notoriously a selfish commander, who thought more of his own viceroyalty and his own military reputation than of the general cause of France : his intercepted dispatches, of which Wellington had a fair selection in his file of cyphers, showed that he was always ready to find plausible excuses for keeping to his own side of the Peninsula.

The plan which Wellington formulated for the use of Sir John Murray, in two dispatches dated on the 14th and 16th of April, was one which depended entirely on the judicious use of naval power. The British fleet being completely dominant in the Mediterranean, and Murray having at his disposition the large squadron of transports which had brought his troops from

Sicily, it was clearly possible to land as many men as the transports could carry, at any point on the immensely long coast-line of Valencia and Catalonia that might be selected. They would have a local superiority on the selected point until the French troops, dispersed in many garrisons and cantonments, could mass in sufficient strength to attack them : and meanwhile the Catalan army would join Murray. If the French should draw together in overwhelming power, the expedition could, if proper precautions were taken, re-embark before its position became dangerous. The farther north that the landing took place, the more inconvenient would it be for Suchet, who would obviously have to draw on his field army in Valencia for numbers that would enable him to deal with the Anglo-Sicilian force. But the moment that Suchet should be forced to deplete his field army in the South, which was already too weak for the task set it, the Spaniards could advance on the line of the Xucar, and make a dash at Valencia during the Marshal's absence. In order to give them an irresistible numerical preponderance over the divisions that Suchet might leave behind him, Del Parque should bring up the Andalusian army to reinforce Elio's Murcians. Between them they would have some 30,000 regular troops, besides the bands of the Empecinado and Duran, who would operate on the side of the mountains against the French rear. It would be hard if such an accumulation of force could not thrust back the thinned line of the enemy on to and beyond Valencia.

Finally, the point at which the expeditionary force was to make its thrust was to be Tarragona, which was known to be in a state of bad repair, and thinly garrisoned, while it had also the advantage of being a very isolated post, and remote both from Decaen's head-quarters at Gerona, and from Suchet's at Valencia. Moreover, it was conveniently placed for communication with the Catalan army, but separated by difficult defiles both from Tortosa southward and Barcelona northward, at which French relieving forces would have to gather.

If the whole plan worked, and Tarragona were to fall in a few days, the Catalan army would once more have a safe debouch to the sea, and the Allies would gain a foothold such as they had never owned north of the Ebro since 1811, while at the same time Valencia ought to fall into the hands of Elio and Del Parque during Suchet's enforced absence. But supposing that Tarragona held out firmly, and Decaen and Suchet united to relieve it, the expeditionary force could get away unharmed, and meanwhile Valencia ought to have been taken. And even if the blow at Valencia failed also, yet at least the whole French army on the East Coast would be occupied for a month or more, and would certainly not be able to spare a single man to help King Joseph or Jourdan.

As we shall see, a long series of blunders, for which Murray was mainly responsible, though Elio and Del Parque each took his share in the muddle, prevented all Wellington's schemes for active profit from coming to a successful end. Nevertheless, the main purpose was achieved—not a Frenchman from the East Coast took any share in the campaign of Vittoria.

To descend to details. Murray was directed to ship off every man of the Alicante army for whom he could find transport, provided that the total of infantry and artillery embarked should not fall short of 10,000 of all ranks. He was to take with him both the Anglo-Sicilians and as many of Whittingham's Spaniards as could be carried : if the ships sufficed, he might take all or some of Roche's Spaniards also. Less than 10,000 men must not sail—the force would then be too small to cause Suchet to detach troops from Valencia. Elio and Del Parque would remain behind, with such (if any) of Roche's and Whittingham's battalions as could not be shipped. They were to keep quiet, till they should learn that Suchet had weakened his forces in Valencia. When it became certain that the French opposite them were much reduced in numbers, they were to advance, always taking care to turn the enemy's positions rather than to make frontal attacks upon them.

If, which was quite possible, Murray should fail to take Tarragona, and should find very large French forces gathering around him, such as he and Copons could not reasonably hope to hold in check, he was to re-embark, and bring the Expeditionary Force back to the kingdom of Valencia, landing it at such a point on the coast as should put him in line with the front reached by Elio and Del Parque in their advance.

There was a subsidiary set of directions for a policy to be

carried out if the transports available at Alicante should be found insufficient to move so many as 10,000 men.   But as the shipping proved enough to carry 14,000, these directions have only an academic interest.   In this case Murray and Elio were to threaten the line of the Xucar frontally, while Del Parque turned it on the side of the mountains of the interior.   Duran and Villacampa were to devote themselves to cutting the line of communications between Suchet and the King.   In this way employment would be found for all the French on the East Coast, for Copons was to receive a reinforcement of 3,000 men, and was to keep Decaen on the move by raids and forays.

Finally, and this clause governed the whole of the instructions, ' the General Officers at the head of the troops must understand that the success of all our endeavours in the ensuing campaign depends on *none of the corps being beaten.* They must not attack the enemy in strong positions : I shall forgive *anything* excepting that one of the corps should be beaten and dispersed.'   Wellington afterwards said that this warning was intended for Elio and Del Parque only, but it had a deleterious effect during the ensuing operations on all the actions of the timid and wavering Murray.   To say to such an officer that it would be a sin not to be forgiven if he let his corps get beaten under any circumstances, was to drive him to a policy of absolute cowardice.   Wellington was an austere master, and the mental effect of such a threat was to make Murray resolve that he would not take even small and pardonable risks. The main idea that he had in his head in May and June 1813 was that he ' must not allow his corps to be beaten and dispersed.' Hence, like the unprofitable servant in the parable, he was resolved to wrap it up in a napkin, and have it ready to return to his master intact—though thereby he might condemn himself to make no worthy use of it whatever while it was in his hands.   The threat of the Commander-in-Chief might have been addressed profitably to Robert Craufurd ; when administered to John Murray it produced terror and a sort of mental paralysis.

It is true that Murray's weakness of will and instability of purpose were so great that he would probably, in any case, have made a very poor game from the splendid cards put into his hand.

But that the Tarragona expedition ended in the discreditable fiasco which we shall have to narrate, was undoubtedly
the result in part of the impression which Wellington's orders
produced on his wavering mind. Yet, contemptible as his
conduct of operations was, still Suchet was kept employed in
the East and gave no help to King Joseph. That much was
secured by Wellington's knowledge of how sea-power can be used.

By the 1st of May everything should have been ready, but
the late spring and the slow-moving pontoons delayed the
start. On the 12th–13th–14th, however, every soldier, British
and Portuguese, was ready to march. Every available unit was
being brought up—there remained behind only the fever-ridden
Guards' brigade at Oporto ; the weak 77th, which provided,
along with one Veteran Battalion, a skeleton garrison for Lisbon ;
three Portuguese line regiments, two in Elvas, one in Abrantes,
and the dismounted dragoons of the same nation, who had not
taken the field for three years : only D'Urban's and Campbell's
squadrons marched in 1813. The infantry consisted of 56
British and 53 Portuguese battalions—making about 67,000
bayonets. The British battalions were of very unequal size—
a few as low as 450 men, a few others as strong as 900 : the
average was 700. The Portuguese battalions were rather weaker,
some of the regiments never having recovered from the privations of the Burgos retreat, and did not exceed on an average
500 bayonets or 550 of all ranks. Of cavalry there were 22
regiments, of which four only were Portuguese—total 8,000
sabres. Of artillery there were 102 guns, in seventeen batteries,
of which three were Portuguese and one belonged to the King's
German Legion [1]. Adding Engineers, Staff Corps, Wagon
Train, &c., the whole represented 81,000 men of all ranks and
all arms.

[1] The H.A. troops were 'A' Ross, 'D' Bean, 'E' Gardiner, 'F'
Webber-Smith, and 'I' Ramsay. The foot companies were those of
Dubourdieu (1st Division), Maxwell (2nd Division), Douglas (3rd Division),
Sympher K.G.L. (4th Division), Lawson (5th Division), Brandreth (6th
Division), Cairnes (7th Division). Tulloh's Portuguese company was
attached to the 2nd Division, Da Cunha's to Silveira's division. The
reserve was composed of Webber-Smith's H.A. troop, Arriaga's Portuguese
heavy 18-pounders, and Parker's foot company. See Colonel Leslie's
edition of the *Dickson Papers*, ii. p. 719.

OPERATIONS OF HILL'S COLUMN: MAY 22—JUNE 3

THE concentration of the southern wing of Wellington's army for the great advance was in some ways a more difficult, in others an easier, problem than the concentration of the northern wing.

On the one hand, the distances from which the various elements of Hill's force were to be drawn were in many cases shorter than those of Graham's force; the roads were well known to all the troops, who had used them repeatedly in their moves up and down the Spanish-Portuguese frontier in 1811–12; and, though poor enough, they were on the whole better than those of the Tras-os-Montes, which the northern column had to employ. No part of the British army had tried these latter routes since the pursuit of Soult in 1809, and few remembered how bad they were. But, on the other hand, the concentration of the southern column was from points more remote from each other than those of the northern: the divisions of the latter had all been collected in the Douro country during the course of the spring, and started on their final march from a single area: moreover, they were moving well inside Portugal, by routes very remote from the enemy. But the larger half of the southern force had to be brought up from a region far distant from that where the smaller half was cantoned in May. For Hill's two divisions, the British 2nd and the Portuguese independent division (so long commanded by Hamilton, but now under Silveira, the Conde de Amarante), had been sent back to the borders of Estremadura at the end of the Burgos campaign, and were lying, much scattered, at points so remote from each other as Coria, Plasencia, Bejar, Bohoyo, and Brozas. Morillo's Spanish division, so often associated before with Hill, was even farther off, south of the Tagus, in the Caçeres-Alcantara country. All these troops would have to move up, in order to join Wellington, by routes not very remote from the French

division at Avila, which (as it will be remembered) had tried
to beat up Hill's winter-quarters as late as the preceding
February. And there was a chance that, if the enemy were
alert and well-informed, he might try to block Hill's march, by
coming out from the Puente de Congosto or some such point.
If Wellington had only known it, the French higher command
had actually been fearing that Hill might make a stroke at
Avila by some of the passes leading from the upper Tormes to
the upper Adaja, and was nervous about this line of country.

The plan for the concentration of the southern force was that
Hill should unite the 2nd Division, Morillo's Spaniards, and
Long's Cavalry [1] at Bejar, and then march by the pass through
the Sierra de Francia to Miranda de Castanar and Tamames.
Silveira, with the independent Portuguese division, was to take
a parallel route farther west, by the pass of Perales, Peñaparda,
and Moras Verdes, to the same point [2]. These troops on arriving
near Tamames would find themselves in touch with another
column, which was already on the ground where operations
were to begin. It consisted of the Light Division, which had
been cantoned on the Coa and Agueda during the winter, and
Victor Alten's, Fane's, and Robert Hill's cavalry brigades—the
last-named a unit new to the army, and lately arrived from
Lisbon : it consisted of six squadrons from the three regiments
of Household Cavalry. To join these British troops came Julian
Sanchez's Castilian lancers—now reckoned regular cavalry
and not a *partida*—and Carlos de España's Castilian division,
which had been wintering in the valleys above Ciudad Rodrigo.
When united, the whole strength of the southern wing of
Wellington's army would be about 30,000 sabres and bayonets,
including only five brigades of British infantry, the equivalent
of four brigades of Portuguese, and two Spanish divisions.
The cavalry was very strong in proportion—this was intentional,
as Wellington intended to keep out in his front such a strong

[1] Long was now in charge of Hill's cavalry *vice* Erskine, a general whose
acts have so often required criticism. This unfortunate officer had committed suicide at Brozas during the winter, by leaping out of a lofty window
while *non compos mentis*. The moment he was removed Wellington
abolished the ' 2nd Cavalry Division ', and threw its two brigades into the
general stock under Stapleton Cotton for the campaign of 1813.

[2] Wellington to Hill, *Supplementary Dispatches*, xiv. pp. 206 and 216.

cavalry screen that the enemy should have no chance of discovering for some time that the column was not the main Anglo-Portuguese army, but in fact a demonstrating force. The real strength of his army, six of his old eight divisions, was marching under Graham to turn the line of the Douro, far to the north.

On the 22nd Wellington abandoned his head-quarters at Freneda, where he had stopped ever since his return from Cadiz in January, and rode out to Ciudad Rodrigo ; the Light Division and three cavalry brigades had preceded him to Santi Espiritus, ten miles in front, where they were in touch with Silveira's Portuguese, who formed Hill's left-hand column, and had reached Tamames. Hill himself with the 2nd Division was a march behind Silveira : Morillo's Spaniards keeping more to the right, on the road along the mountains, was moving from Los Santos and Fuenteroble, by the track which leads straight to Salamanca from the direct south. Far out on the left Julian Sanchez's lancers were feeling their way towards Ledesma and watching the western flank.

On the 24th the union of the forces was complete, and the news that came from all quarters was satisfactory. Villatte was in Salamanca, with no more than his own infantry division and one regiment of cavalry [1] : he had small detachments on his flanks at Ledesma and Alba de Tormes, but no friends nearer than Daricau at Zamora ; and for Daricau full employment was about to be found, since Graham's great column was marching straight upon him. It was pretty certain that King Joseph had not yet ordered the general concentration which was the only thing that could save him from destruction. The French division at Avila had not moved : Madrid was being held, and as late as the 20th Maransin's brigade had been at Toledo, and some of the Avila division at Monbeltran on the borders of Estremadura. The map showed, therefore, that the Army of the South could not possibly meet on the Tormes in time to succour Villatte, who would have either to retreat or to be destroyed. And Villatte being driven off eastward on Cantalpino, or northward on Toro, the junction of the two wings of Wellington's army at or near Zamora was certain.

---

[1] 12th Dragoons, of Digeon's division.

But haste was necessary, wherefore the army advanced by very long marches, through the devastated country over which it had passed in such different conditions seven months back. On the 25th, head-quarters were at Matilla, with the infantry advancing in three parallel columns, the Light Division on the high road to Salamanca, Hill and Silveira to the right, Morillo still farther out, making for Alba de Tormes. The satisfactory news came in that Villatte had withdrawn his detachment from Ledesma, which indicated that he did not intend to keep touch with Daricau at Zamora, so that the passage of the Douro would be simplified [1]. A very long march on the 26th brought matters to a crisis. Victor Alten's cavalry pushing for Salamanca bridge, and Fane's for the fords which lie above the town, found that Villatte had just evacuated it, after barricading and obstructing its exits, but was visible on the heights above the fords of Santa Marta (one of Wellington's old positions of June 1812) in line of battle. His delay in retreating is censured equally by Jourdan and by Wellington—apparently he wished to be certain that he was not being imposed upon by a mere cavalry demonstration, and had a serious force opposite him : moreover, he was waiting to pick up his detachment from Alba de Tormes, which he had only just ordered to join him, when he heard that Long's cavalry and Morillo were moving on that place.

On seeing the French in position the British cavalry pushed on with all speed, Alten through Salamanca city, Fane by the fords above, leaving the infantry far behind them, but hoping to detain the enemy long enough to assure his destruction. Realizing over-late his danger, Villatte moved off eastward when he recognized that heavy forces were concentrating upon him, and threatening his retreat. He marched not for Toro, but due east by roads parallel with the Tormes. ' It is rather extraordinary,' wrote Wellington that evening, ' that he should have marched by Cabrerizos and the ravine, which we used to think so bad for even a horse, and thence by Aldea Lengua [2].' At any rate the two cavalry brigades caught him up not far

---

[1] This is Wellington's own observation, *Dispatches* x. 397, to Graham from Matilla.

[2] Wellington to Graham, *Dispatches*, x. 401.

from Aldea Lengua, and, after scattering his rear-guard of dragoons, rode in upon his infantry, which were marching hard in close column.   The tactical conditions were exactly the same as those which had been seen during the retreat of Picton and the 3rd Division from El Bodon to Fuente Grimaldo in September 1811.   The brigadiers, after trying some partial and ineffective charges [1], judged it useless to attack steady and unbroken infantry in solid order, and contented themselves with following the column at a cautious distance and picking up stragglers—just as Montbrun had done in 1811 on the way to Fuente Grimaldo.   Fane's horse-artillery battery got up, and put in some damaging shots on the rear battalions, but they closed up and hurried on.   The day was hot, many of the French fell out of the ranks exhausted and were gleaned up on the way.   Their divisional ammunition train got jammed in a hollow road and was captured—the leading caisson had been overturned and blocked the exit of the rest.   But the main body of the infantry held on its way in a solid mass, and after five miles, Wellington, who had just ridden up, ordered Fane and Alten to desist from the pursuit.   Villatte, therefore, got off, leaving behind him a couple of hundred prisoners, and some scores of men who had fallen dead from sunstroke and over-exertion, or had been knocked over by the round-shot of Gardiner's H.A. battery [2]. This was one more example of the incapacity of cavalry unsupported to deal with unbroken infantry, of which we have had to give so many previous instances.   The only exception to the rule was the extraordinary achievement of Bock's heavy German dragoons at Garcia Hernandes on the day after the battle of Salamanca.   Clearly Villatte waited too long, and should never have allowed himself to be caught so near Salamanca.   He got off better than he deserved [3], and picked up his

---

[1] That the charges were not pushed home is shown by the casualties—10 wounded in the Royals, 1 killed no wounded in the 1st Hussars K.G.L.

[2] Creditable as was the conduct of Villatte's infantry, it is hyperbole to say with Napier (v. p. 98) that ' the dauntless survivors won their way in the face of 30,000 enemies ! '   For only 1,600 British horsemen were up, and the nearest allied infantry was 6 or 8 miles away.

[3] Jourdan (Mémoires, p. 464) holds that Villatte was to blame, and ' engagea le combat mal à propos,' but considers that he was ' faiblement suivi ' by Fane and Alten.   He acknowledges the loss of some of Villatte's guns, probably in error, for Wellington speaks of captured caissons only

detachment from Alba, which came in upon him from the right a few miles farther on, beyond Babila Fuente, cautiously pursued by Long's Light Dragoons. The column went out of sight, retreating on Cantalpino, not on Toro—one more proof to Wellington that the enemy was not going to attempt to strengthen the line of the Douro, but to concentrate somewhere about Medina del Campo or Valladolid.

The various infantry columns reached the neighbourhood of Salamanca on the evening of the 26th, and crossed the Tormes, some by the bridge, some by fords, next day. They were ordered to take up the position facing north and east on the heights beyond the city which Wellington had held against Marmont in June 1812. The Light Division was on the left, the 2nd Division in the centre, Silveira's Portuguese on the right at Cabrerizos, Morillo on the upper Tormes at Machacon with a detachment in Alba. The cavalry patrolled towards Zamora, Toro, the fords of Fresno on the Douro, and also eastward toward the Guarena. Hill now halted for six days—it was Wellington's intention, now that he had displayed himself in force at Salamanca, and set all the lines of French intelligence quivering, that the enemy should conclude that his great attack was to be delivered between the Douro and the Tormes, and he hoped that they would attempt to parry it by a concentration in the region of Valladolid—Toro for the defence of the line of the Douro, or perhaps (but this was less likely) by a counter-offensive south of the Douro from the direction of Medina del Campo, so as to take him in flank and prevent his further progress northward. Either of these moves would fall in with his desires, since his real intention was to turn the line of the Douro much lower down, in the direction of Zamora, by means of Graham's corps, which was about to start from Braganza and Miranda on the very day of the occupation of Salamanca, and was due to arrive on the Esla, behind Zamora, on the 30th. It pleased him well that Villatte should have retreated due east, that the cavalry found no hostile forces south of the Douro in the direction of either Zamora or Toro, and that it was reported that there was only one French infantry division holding those towns.

in his report of the affair. Martinien's list of casualties shows hardly any officer-casualties on this day in Villatte's division.

Having allowed time for the enemy to get full knowledge of his presence at Salamanca, and to act upon it—it was inevitable that they should regard the place where he had shown himself as the base of his future operations—Wellington made ready to transfer himself rapidly and secretly to the other and stronger wing of his army, which Graham was now conducting against the extreme western flank of the French line. On May 28th he handed over the command of the southern wing to Hill, and announced his own departure. The orders given to Sir Rowland were that he was, unless the unexpected happened, to make ready to march on the Douro at Zamora the moment that he should receive news that Graham had crossed the Esla [1]. Bridges should be ready for him, and the fortunate disappearance of the enemy's horse from the region of Ledesma made the rapid transmission of information between the two wings certain.

There was one possibility to be considered. Though Wellington was convinced that the French would concentrate north of the Douro, in the direction of Valladolid and Medina de Rio Seco, it was just conceivable that they might take the other course of concentrating south of the river, round Medina del Campo, and marching straight on Salamanca with all the troops that could be hastily drawn together. It was impossible for them to gather their whole force in the few days that would be at their disposition ; but conceivably they might think it worth while to make a counterstroke with such divisions as could be got together in haste. It is interesting to know that such an idea did flash through Jourdan's mind for a moment, only to be rejected by King Joseph on the advice of the other generals [2]. Should the French march on the Tormes, a grave responsibility would be placed on Hill's head. He was told to give them battle ' if he was strong enough '—i. e. to judge their force according to the best information to be had, not an easy thing, but Hill was pre-eminently clear-headed and averse to unnecessary risks. Should they be too numerous, he was not to retire on Rodrigo by the route by which Wellington had come, but to throw up his communication with that fortress, and move off

---

[1] See the elaborate dispatch of June 28 (to Hill, *Dispatches*, x. pp. 402–4).
[2] See Jourdan's *Mémoires*, p. 466.

in the direction of Zamora, carrying out at all costs the plan for the junction of the two wings of the army [1]. Nothing was to remain behind to cover the Ciudad Rodrigo road and the Portuguese frontier but the single Spanish division of Carlos de España : all convoys on the march from Salamanca were to be turned off towards Ledesma and Zamora. It might look perilous to leave Central Portugal unprotected, but Wellington was sure that the enemy would be so distracted by his great movement north of the Douro, that they would not dare to advance on Ciudad Rodrigo and Almeida, to strike at his old line of communications. Moreover, it would not matter if they did, for his new line of communication was now entirely north of the Douro, and Oporto, not Lisbon, would be his base.

On the 29th at dawn Wellington rode off to the north-west, almost unattended, and Hill's responsibility began. It was not to turn out a heavy one, since (as his chief had foreseen) the enemy was not in the least thinking of taking up the offensive, but was rather expecting a continuation of the British advance from Salamanca. It did not come, and before the French had made up their minds as to what the halt of the southern column might mean, they were attacked on the 30th by the northern column, whose existence had hitherto been hidden from them. Hill therefore had only to wait for Wellington's directions to march northward, when the date and route should be given. These orders did not come till the 2nd of June, so that the southern corps had to remain for a week in its own cantonments round Salamanca, doing nothing more than watch the French, north and east, by means of cavalry reconnaissances.

We must now turn to the operations of the more important northern corps, which crossed the Portuguese frontier on the 26th, four days after Wellington had started out in person from Ciudad Rodrigo.

[1] For all this see Wellington to Hill, *Dispatches*, x. pp. 402–4.

SECTION XXXVI: CHAPTER III

OPERATIONS OF GRAHAM'S COLUMN: MAY 26—JUNE 3

On May 18th Wellington had issued his final orders for the advance of the great turning force under Graham, all of whose troops were due to converge on the remote corner of Portugal between Braganza and Miranda de Douro between the 21st and 27th of the month. Many of them came from long distances, and had to start early—the 1st Division from Vizeu as early as May 13th; and left behind it, as hopelessly inefficient from sickness, Howard's brigade of the Guards, reduced to a strength of 800 bayonets by the fever which had ravaged its ranks during the spring. Shifted from Vizeu to Oporto for the benefit of the milder climate, this brigade could not be moved for another month, and missed the campaign of Vittoria. The 5th, 6th, and 7th Divisions left their winter quarters in the Beira on the 14th, the 3rd and 4th, who were close to the Douro or actually on it, at Moimenta and St. João de Pesqueira, could afford not to move till the 16th. To secure a rapid movement for the columns which had farthest to go, and to save any congestion of traffic at the usual ferries of passage on the Douro—bridges there were none—Wellington had collected a large number of barges and river boats at Peso de Regoa, St. João de Pesqueira, and the Barca of Poçinho near the confluence of the Coa and the Douro.

The arrangement of the marches was calculated to allow the heavy infantry columns to make use as far as possible of the only two good roads in the Tras-os-Montes, of which the one goes from the Douro to Braganza, the other to Miranda. The 1st and 5th Divisions crossed by the much-used ferry of Peso de Regoa near Lamego, and marched by Villa Real and Mirandella on two separate routes to the neighbourhood of Braganza [1].

---

[1] There are some slips either in the original or the copy of the Marching Orders printed in *Supplementary Dispatches*, xiv. pp. 215–16. For Carazedo, given on the itinerary of the 1st Division, is many miles from it,

The 3rd Division crossed the ferry at St. João de Pesqueira and went by Villaflor and Vinhas to Vimioso, half-way between Braganza and Miranda. All these columns had some cross-road marching to do, where they were forced to cut across from one *chaussée* to another. The third column, the 4th, 6th, and 7th Divisions, more fortunate, was on the high road nearly all the way : after crossing the Douro at the ferry of Poçinho, they marched from Torre de Moncorvo by the great *chaussée* to the frontier town of Miranda and the neighbouring village of Malhadas, where they were due to arrive on three successive days (24th, 25th, 26th May). This column was followed by the all-important pontoon-train, and by the reserve of siege artillery—Portuguese 18-pounders under Major Ariaga[1]—as well as by the main ammunition train.

The three British cavalry brigades which Wellington had allotted to the great turning movement, those of Anson, Bock, and Ponsonby, had been cantoned in the winter months in the lower Beira, along the coast, and in the valley of the Vouga. Before the infantry had moved, they had all three been brought north of the Douro about May 1, through Oporto, and billeted in Braga, Guimaraens, San Tyrso, and neighbouring villages. On May 12th orders set them moving eastward to the Braganza country—their march was much more fatiguing than that of the infantry divisions, for there are no high roads of any value going directly from the Braga country to the direction of Miranda and Braganza—all run north and south, not east and west. Though allotted short daily stages of only three or four leagues, the cavalry found the route fatiguing—the mountain cross-roads were more like staircases than paths—the horse artillery accompanying the brigades had in some cases to swerve off from its itinerary and take circuitous turns[2] : in others it had to be

though it *is* on the proper line of the 5th Division, which was going to Outeiro and not to Braganza. Limão on the itinerary of the 3rd Division should be Vinhas, if I am not mistaken.

[1] Another odd error in Marching Orders given in *Wellington Dispatches*, x. p. 368, had turned the Portuguese heavy guns into infantry ' 18th Portuguese Brigade ' which should read ' Portuguese 18-pounder brigade.' There was no higher numbered Portuguese infantry brigade than the 10th. This misprint has misled many historians.

[2] See Tomkinson, p. 232, for the road by Chaves and Monforte.

man-handled down precipitous tracks.   The only horsemen
who had an easy job were the Portuguese brigade of D'Urban,
who had been wintering at Braganza, and had only to advance
a few miles to the frontier, and Grant's newly-arrived Hussar
Brigade which, coming from the south, followed the infantry
column that went by Torre de Moncorvo to Miranda, along
the high road all the way.

Pack's and Bradford's Portuguese infantry, who (like
D'Urban's dragoons) had wintered north of the Douro, at
Penafiel and Villa Real respectively, had a short way to go, and
were timed to arrive at Braganza before the heavy columns
from the south came up.

Portugal and Spain, as is well known, turn their backs on
each other for the greater part of their long frontier, and though
there were decent *chaussées* from the Douro to Braganza and
Miranda they stopped short at the boundary line.   From thence
onward there were no good roads till Zamora was reached, and
those bad ones which existed were country tracks, only useful
for operations in the summer.   That they could be so used, for
all arms, in May and June, was one of Wellington's secrets,
which he trusted that the French would never guess.   For both
parties during the war had left alone this remote corner of the
Peninsula.   The only operations seen near it had been Soult's
spring campaign of 1809, and the forays of Silveira's militia
when they occasionally raided towards Zamora.

Country roads, however, existed between the Sierra de
Culebra and the bend of the Douro between Zamora and
Miranda, and the whole detail of Graham's march depended on
their practicability : Wellington had caused the whole region
as far as the Esla to be explored by his intelligence officers, and
the report had been that the movement of all arms was possible
in the summer.   The permanent bridges of the Esla, from
Benavente down to its confluence with the Douro, had been
broken long ago ; but there was a certain number of fords,
and convenient places for the laying of temporary bridges.   By
the end of May it was calculated that the spring floods due to
the melting of snows in the Galician and Asturian mountains
would be over, and that the river would be down to its normal
low summer level.   On these facts depended the success of the

operation, which must be a rapid one, in order that the French might have no time for concentration. But Wellington's provident mind had taken into consideration the possibility of unexpected high-water, and as a matter of precaution he had ordered up his main pontoon-train from the Tagus. To get the cumbrous pontoons, 33 of them, from Abrantes to Miranda de Douro by land was no small matter. They travelled slowly on specially constructed wheeled trucks [1] by Castello Branco, Sabugal, and Pinhel, crossed the Douro at Villa Nova de Foscoa, and were then brought up on the Miranda high road as far as Villa Velha, where they were halted for a short time, as Wellington was not quite certain whether he would not lay them at Espadacinta on the middle Douro, rather than farther up, beyond Miranda. For across the pontoons he intended to lay the main line of communication between Graham's and Hill's wings of the army, and if the latter failed to get forward on the Tormes and to open up touch with Graham via Zamora, it might be necessary to throw the bridge at some lower point, such as Espadacinta [2]. On the 20th he made up his mind that 14 pontoons should be sent to Espadacinta, while the remaining 19 should proceed to Miranda, and from thence follow the course of the Douro to the point where they would be laid—probably the ferry of Villa al Campo, a mile below the confluence of the Esla and the Douro. The nineteen all-important trucks with their burdens reached Miranda safely, and moved close behind the right-hand column of Graham's army during its advance.

Down to May 26 all the British troops had been kept behind the Portuguese frontier, nothing having been sent beyond it save D'Urban's Portuguese dragoons, who formed a screen some little way on the Spanish side. Their appearance would, in the event of a French cavalry raid from Zamora, create no suspicion of there being in the rear anything more than the usual Tras-os-Montes militia. Nor could spies draw any deduction from their presence.

But on the 26th the whole of Graham's army [3] started out in three columns arranged as follows :

1. From Braganza marched, as the northern column, Anson's

---

[1] Improvised by dismantling artillery carriages. Wellington to Bathurst, *Dispatches*, x. 388.   [2] Wellington to Graham, *Dispatches*, x. p. 392.

[3] Minus Grant's hussars, who only arrived on the 27th.

light and Ponsonby's heavy dragoon brigades, preceding the
1st Infantry division and Pack's Portuguese independent
brigade. Crossing the frontier river, the Manzanas, at fords by
Nuez, they were ordered to move on Tabara in four marches,
by the country road through Sesnande.

2. From Outeiro and Vimioso marched, as the central column,
following D'Urban's Portuguese light horse (who were already
over the border), Bock's heavy German dragoons accompanied
by the 3rd and 5th Divisions and Bradford's independent
Portuguese brigade. They were directed to move by Alcanizas
in four marches on Losilla, five miles south of Tabara.

3. From Miranda de Douro marched, as the right column,
close to the river, the 4th, 6th, and 7th Divisions ; their cavalry,
Grant's hussar brigade, overtook them on the second day.
Having a shorter distance to cover than the other two columns,
their van was to reach Carvajales on the 28th, in three marches.
On the 30th the pontoons, which followed in their rear, were
to reach the ferry of Villa al Campo, where it was intended that
they should be laid down across the Douro.

The left-hand or northern column was to get into touch with
the Army of Galicia—Barcena's and Losada's divisions and
Penne Villemur's cavalry, about 12,000 strong, who, marching
from Astorga on the 26th, were to be at the broken bridge of
Benavente on the Esla on the 29th–30th.

It will be seen that Graham's force was marching on a very
compact front, the central column being not more than five or
six miles distant from each of the flanking ones, so that the
whole could be assembled for action, in the unlikely event of
opposition being met, in a very few hours. The cavalry screen
of five brigades was so strong that it was impossible for any
French horse which might be in the Zamora direction to pierce
it, or discover what was behind. The whole army counted not
less than 42,000 sabres and bayonets, exclusive of the Galicians—
as strong an Anglo-Portuguese force as that with which Wellington had fought the battle of Salamanca, and outnumbering
considerably the other wing of Wellington's army, which was
marching south of the Douro.

By an extraordinary piece of luck the attention of the French
higher command was completely distracted at the moment

from the Esla front, as a result of the last authentic reports received from that direction. For as late as May 20th Reille had sent Boyer's division of dragoons across the Esla at Benavente, to make a sweep to the north and west in the direction of La Baneza and the road to Puebla Senabria. They had gone almost as far as Astorga without meeting troops of any kind ; and reported that some of the Galician army were at Astorga, but that they had heard of no British save two or three commissaries, who had been buying up barley and wheat in the valley of the Tera, which were to be sent back into Portugal [1]. Reille drew the natural deduction, that there was nothing stirring in this part of the world, and Boyer, after thoroughly destroying the bridge of Castro Gonzalo outside Benavente, went back to his former cantonments east of the Esla. If the raid had been made a week later, he could not have failed to bring news of the advance of the Galicians, and would probably have heard of Graham's movements from Braganza and Miranda de Douro. But by the 27th all the attention of the French generals was already distracted to Wellington's march against Salamanca, at the head of Hill's column, and the Esla front received little notice. There remained opposite the advancing troops of Graham only Daricau's infantry division of the Army of the South, with a brigade each at Zamora and Toro, and three regiments of Digeon's dragoons watching the Esla from San Cebrian to its juncture with the Douro, and at the same time keeping a look-out southward towards Salamanca. For the cavalry of Hill's column was already on the 27th–28th pushing out northward towards Zamora as well as eastward towards the Guarena. On the 28th this danger began to prey so much on Daricau's mind that he withdrew all his infantry save four companies from Zamora, leaving Digeon's dragoons practically unsupported to watch rather than to defend the line of the Esla. Urgent requests were sent to the cavalry of the

---

[1] Jourdan's *Mémoires*, p. 464. Note that Napier (v. 102) has got this expedition a week too late—May 29–30. His statement that the French cavalry got in touch with the northern wing of Graham's army and was closely followed by British scouting parties, is contradicted by the absolute silence about any touch with the French in the diary of Tomkinson, whose regiment was at Tabara and must have been the one which Boyer would have met.

Army of Portugal, farther north along that river, to keep touch with Digeon and help him if necessary.

The cavalry at the head of Graham's three columns reached their destinations—Tabara, Losilla, Carvajales, on May 28th—the infantry on the 29th. No French parties were found on the hither side of the Esla, and though the peasantry reported that there were vedettes on the farther bank, none were seen. Exploration of the course of the Esla, however, led to the vexatious discovery that the river was very high, owing to torrential rain on the night of the 28th–29th, and that some of the fords intended for use were probably impracticable for cavalry, most certainly so for infantry. Graham, though vexed at the delay, refused to push across the water with horsemen alone, and waited for the pontoon-train—due on the 30th—to come up, resolving to lay it across the Esla, and not across the Douro as had been at first intended. Meanwhile the French showed no signs of life on the 30th—it had been feared that Daricau might come out of Zamora, only eight miles away, with infantry and guns, to oppose the passage. But, as we have seen, he had really departed on the 28th, and there was nothing opposite Graham but a cavalry screen. The main attack seemed to the French generals to be on the side of Salamanca, where Wellington was known to have been present on May 27th. Digeon had discovered on the 29th that there were British troops on the opposite bank of the Esla, but had no notion of their strength or purpose [1].

But if Wellington's presence marked the danger-point, it was now suddenly displaced. On the morning of the 29th the British Commander-in-Chief had gone off on one of his not unusual lightning rides. Starting early from Salamanca, he rode by Ledesma to the Douro opposite Miranda—over 50 miles—before dark. Facing Miranda there is no road on the Spanish side, the river descends fiercely in something like cataracts, with

---

[1] Digeon's own report, which chanced to be entirely inaccurate, was that on the 29th his reconnaissance reported that there were signs of intentions to throw trestle bridges across the Esla opposite the ford of Morellas, the lowest ford on the Esla toward the Douro, and at Santa Enferina opposite San Cebrian, where Spanish troops were visible. Also that at Almendra there was a post of British hussars. Only the third item was correct. (*Archives Nationaux*—copy lent me by Mr. Fortescue.)

high rocks on its eastern bank. The only communication from shore to shore was by a rope and basket contrivance, worked by a windlass, and stretched high above the water. By this strange method Wellington crossed the Douro—what would have been the results of the campaign of 1813 if the ropes had been rotten ? He slept at Miranda, started off at dawn on the 30th and was at Carvajales—20 miles away—by the afternoon, not so tired but that he could write dispatches to Hill and Giron that night, and settle with Graham the dispositions for next morning.

Wellington's first decision was that the pontoons, which had come up on the 30th, should be laid not on the Douro at Villa al Campo, but on the Esla opposite Almendra, where the high road from Puebla Senabria to Zamora crossed the river. But at the same time attempts were to be made to get cavalry (and infantry if possible) across the water at other points.

At dawn on the 31st Grant's hussar brigade entered the ford of Almendra, where it was intended that the bridge should be laid ; each man of the leading squadron had an infantry soldier of the 7th Division hanging on to his stirrup. At the same time Bock's German dragoons and D'Urban's Portuguese essayed the ford at Pallomilla, opposite Montemarta, four miles up-stream. The hussars crossed with great trouble—the bottom was stony, the water had risen in the night, some horses lost their footing— many of the infantry stepped into holes, or stumbled and were carried away. The majority were saved, but ten of the 51st and rather more of the Brunswickers were swept right down-stream and drowned. Yet, despite mishaps, the hussars got over, and, advancing rapidly, surprised the French cavalry picquet at the village of Val de Perdrices, a little way up-stream, taking it whole—an officer and 32 men. This was certainly about the most extraordinary instance of carelessness on the part of outposts during the war, and reflects as much discredit on Digeon, whose dragoons were supposed to be watching the lower Esla, as on the wretched officer in charge of the picquet. How was it possible that such a large body as a brigade could approach in daylight the best-known ford of the neighbourhood, at a spot where the course of the high road showed the convenience of the passage, without finding a single vedette on the bank ? And why was such an important point watched (or not watched) by a half-troop, instead of by a force which could have offered at least a momentary opposition, and have passed the alarm to its regiment, which, as Digeon's report shows, was at Iniesta, only four miles to the rear ?

Meanwhile Bock's Germans and D'Urban's Portuguese dragoons had an equally difficult, though equally unopposed, passage at the ford of Palomilla, four miles up-stream. The river was running furiously, and seven or eight horses and three or four men were washed away and drowned. Anson's light dragoons at the head of the third column had an even worse experience at San Vincente del Barco, opposite San Cebrian : the ford was found utterly impracticable, and the brigade was ordered back toward Tabara : on its way it was turned off to a second projected crossing-spot farther south. This was also discovered to be hopeless, and finally the whole northern column was ordered to cross at Almendra, behind the southern column. After a day's profitless countermarching[1], it came down thither, to find the pontoons laid, the infantry of the southern column all across the river, and well forward, while that of the centre column was crossing rapidly. In the end all Graham's troops save the leading cavalry brigades had to use the bridge.

Meanwhile Grant's hussars, advancing on Zamora, found that the French had evacuated it in haste on the first news of the crossing of the Esla. Digeon, with his two regiments of dragoons, his half-battery of horse artillery, and the four companies of voltigeurs, had gone off to Toro. Wellington therefore was able to occupy Zamora without opposition on the night following the passage of the fords[2], and moved his head-quarters thither next day. The moment that he knew that Daricau and Digeon had absconded, he sent orders to Hill to march not on Zamora, or the ford of Villa al Campo, as he had at first intended, but directly on Toro, which would save twenty miles

---

[1] Tomkinson says that his regiment, the 16th Light Dragoons, was 20 hours on horseback this day, continually hurried off and counter-marching (p. 235).

[2] Julian Sanchez's lancers, from Hill's wing, moving from Penauseude, got in the same night to Zamora.

marching for the right wing. For it was clear that Digeon and Daricau could not hold Toro with some 6,000 men against Graham's 40,000, now across the Esla and in close pursuit of them. And there was no great body of French available to reinforce them within a couple of days' march—at most Reille's horse and one infantry division could have come up. On June 1st the signs were that the enemy would not stand—Digeon's dragoons were falling back on the Toro road—Reille's cavalry, heard of at Belver in the morning, had gone off eastward towards Medina del Rio Seco in haste. Wherefore Wellington pushed on fast on that day, sending on Graham's columns by the two roads Zamora–Toro and Zamora–Rio Seco, which do not diverge sufficiently to make it impossible to concentrate the troops on them in a few hours. But caution proved unnecessary. The French evacuated Toro in the afternoon, so that the junction-point with Hill was safely secured, and Graham's divisions were present in full force next morning, to cover the passage of the southern wing across the Douro.

Wellington moved his head-quarters to Toro on the morning of June 2nd, and sent out his cavalry on all the roads which branch out from it : Anson's and Bock's brigades going north-east occupied Vezdemarben. Grant's hussars pushing along the river-road toward Tordesillas came up with Digeon's rear at Morales, six miles outside Toro, and fell upon it vigorously. The French dragoons—two regiments—were drawn up in a defensive position, with a swamp in front and bridge over a ravine behind. Grant charging furiously with the 10th Hussars and the 18th in support on the flank, broke the front regiment, whereupon the enemy went to the rear in disorder, and was chased for two miles, prisoners being captured in considerable numbers. At last pursuers and pursued ran in on the rear brigade of Daricau's infantry, drawn up in good order, with a battery across the road, on the heights of Pedroso del Rey. Grant had therefore to call off his men, and to wait for the enemy to retire, which they presently did in good order. Two officers and 208 men, all of the 16th Dragoons, were captured [1],

---

[1] Digeon has an elaborate and unconvincing account of this affair in the long dispatch quoted above. He says that he had two regiments (16th and 21st Dragoons) drawn up in front of a bridge and ravine, awaiting

about a hundred of them wounded [1]; the rest were mainly taken owing to the bad condition of their mounts, ' raw-boned horses with evident marks of bad provender, escort duties, and counter-marches—nearly the whole of them had horrible sore backs.' The 10th Hussars had only 16 casualties—one of them an officer who had pursued incautiously and ridden into the French infantry, by whom he was wounded and taken prisoner. This was a good day's record for the 10th Hussars, who started their first Peninsular service—they had only landed in February —with a very handsome success.

During the day of the combat of Morales Hill's infantry had started off from their billets in the villages ten miles north of Salamanca to move on Toro. A forced march of over twenty miles, through Fuentesauco, across a very bare and desolate country, brought the head of the column down to the Douro, where they encamped among well-watered fields and vegetable gardens. ' Officers and men, after the long sultry day, devoured with zest and relish the raw cabbages, onions, and melons.' Next morning (June 3rd) the whole column began to cross the river at Toro, the artillery and baggage by a ford no more than knee-deep, the infantry by the fine but broken bridge. Only one arch of it had been blown up, and a resourceful engineer, Lieutenant Pringle, had contrived an easy method of utilizing it. A row of long ladders had been laid against each side of the gap in the roadway : their feet inclined together and united in

the return of a reconnaissance sent to Toro : that the detachment arrived hotly pursued by British hussars, whereupon he resolved to retire, and told the brigade to file across the ravine. But the 16th Dragoons charged without orders, in order to save the flying party, and got engaged against fourfold numbers, while the 21st was retiring. They did wonders : killed or wounded 100 hussars, captured an officer and 13 men, and retired fighting on the battery and infantry at Pedroso, losing only 100 men.

[1] Two officers of the 16th were taken : the lists in Martinien show only one more officer wounded—from which we should gather that the resistance must have been poor. For a regiment fighting strongly should have had more officer-casualties than three to 208 other ranks. The 16th Dragoons must have been pretty well destroyed—with 1 officer and 108 men unwounded prisoners, 1 officer and 100 men wounded prisoners, and 1 officer and an unknown number of other ranks wounded but not captured. This was the same regiment which had lost the 1 officer and 32 men taken by their own carelessness at Val de Perdices on the 31st. It had been less than 400 strong by its last preserved morning-state.

the shallow water below. Long and stout planks had then been
laid across, resting at each end on the rungs of each pair of
corresponding ladders, and making a sort of platform. The
men went down the upper rungs of one set of ladders, walked
a few steps over the planks, and ascended by the rungs of the
ladders on the other side. This was rather tedious for the
passage of four divisions, and took the whole day and the following morning. But by noon on June 4 the entire army was
concentrated in the vicinity of Toro on the north bank. Its
cavalry was many miles in advance, at Pedroso del Rey on the
Tordesillas road, Almaraz and Villavelid on the Rio Seco road.
Parties sent out northward had got in touch with Giron's
Galician army, which had passed Benavente on June 1 and
reached Villalpando on the 3rd, with Penne Villemur's squadrons
out in its front.

Thus every man of Wellington's striking force, 80,000 sabres
and bayonets, was concentrated north of Toro on the night of
June 3—all the British in a single mass, the Galicians some
18 miles off on the flank, but easily available. Nothing was now
south of the Douro save Carlos de España's Spanish division,
left to garrison Salamanca, and Julian Sanchez's horse, who
were searching the roads south of the river, and had just captured
a large French cavalry patrol at Castro Nuño, near Pollos. It
seemed to Wellington incredible that the enemy would reply to
his stroke at their communications by a similar stroke at his on
the Salamanca–Rodrigo line. Indeed, all reports showed them
moving north, in order to form opposite him on the north bank
of the Douro. Moreover, it was clear that they would have the
greatest difficulty in concentrating a sufficient force to fight him,
for the possession of Valladolid and the defence of the great
northern *chaussée*. The first stage of his plan had been completed with entire success.

SECTION XXXVI: CHAPTER IV

AT the moment when Wellington launched his two great columns into Spain, the French head-quarters staff was in a condition of nervous expectation. The spring was so far advanced that it had been expected that the Allies would have been already on the move, and their long quiescence was supposed, very reasonably, to cover some new plan which it was impossible to divine. The position of the French armies was very unfavourable, entirely owing to the continued absence from the front of the whole infantry of the Army of Portugal, which, by Napoleon's desire and by the detailed instructions of the Minister of War at Paris, had been lent to the Army of the North, and sent backward into Biscay, Navarre, and Aragon to hunt the guerrilleros. Five and a half out of the six divisions of Reille's command were still occupied on these marches and countermarches in the rear, when May was far spent, and when the offensive of the Allies must be expected at every moment.

The French army, available for immediate operations, was therefore short of one-third of its strength, and Jourdan and King Joseph disliked the situation. Jourdan confesses in his Memoirs that he and his master ought to have ordered Clausel to suspend his operations, however incomplete they might be, and to send back all the borrowed infantry to the valley of the Douro. But the minister's letters kept repeating so often that the campaign north of the Ebro must be completed at all costs, that the King considered that he could do no more than transmit to Paris the warnings that he was receiving, urging on the minister that it was time to suspend those operations, and that General Clausel should be ordered to come back in haste towards Burgos [1]. This self-exculpation of Jourdan shows clearly enough the miserable consequences of the system of

[1] Jourdan, *Mémoires*, p. 463.

double-command which Napoleon had always kept up in Spain. The habit of sending orders direct from Paris to fractions of the Army of Spain was so deeply ingrained, that the titular Commander-in-Chief and his Chief of the Staff dared not issue instructions of primary importance to one of the generals under them without obtaining leave from the Emperor ! And at this moment the Emperor was not even at Paris—he had long been at the front in Germany, and had fought the battle of Lützen on May 2. What came from Paris was not even the orders of Napoleon, but the orders of Clarke, transmitting his impression of the imperial will from dispatches already many days old, which would be doubly out of date before they reached Valladolid. The supreme master must take the responsibility of the fact that on May 15 or May 18 his representatives in Spain were asking for leave to modify his arrangements, by petitions which could receive no reply—for mere reasons of space and time—till the crisis which they were fearing had burst upon them. The whole system was ruinous—in 1813 as it had been in 1812. The only rational method would have been to turn over the whole conduct of affairs in Spain to some local authority, supreme in everything and responsible for everything. Yet stronger men than Joseph and Jourdan would perhaps have taken the risk of offending their master, and have issued peremptory orders, which Clausel, Foy, and the other outlying generals would probably have obeyed.

On May 20 the distribution of the Army of Spain was as follows: King Joseph and the 2,500 men of his guards, horse and foot, lay at general head-quarters at Valladolid. Of the two infantry divisions of D'Erlon's Army of the Centre, one, that of Darmagnac, had been lent to Reille, when all the infantry of the Army of Portugal had been borrowed from him, and was lying at Medina de Rio Seco, in the rear of Reille's cavalry, who were watching from a discreet distance the Army of Galicia and the roads in the direction of Astorga and Leon. It will be remembered that on May 20 Reille, hearing vague rumours of allied movements beyond the Esla, had executed a great sweep with Boyer's dragoons across the bridge of Benavente, and for five leagues beyond it, had found nothing, and had reported that there were no British troops in the direction, and no Spaniards nearer than Astorga [1].

The other division of the Army of the Centre, that of Cassagne, was at Segovia, far south of the Douro, keeping touch with the large garrison still left in Madrid, which, as long as it was maintained there, could not be left in a state of absolute isolation.

Of the Army of the South, Gazan had his head-quarters at Arevalo, not very far from the King at Valladolid, but retained with him only Tilly's cavalry division. The rest of his troops were wofully dispersed. Daricau's division and Digeon's dragoons lay at Zamora and Toro—nearly 100 miles from head-quarters—maintaining a loose touch with Reille's cavalry. Villatte—with one detached regiment of Digeon's dragoons to keep watch for him—was at Salamanca—fifty miles from Daricau. Conroux, with a third division, was at Avila, with a whole block of mountains between him and Villatte. He was supposed to be watching Hill, and had detachments as far out as Monbeltran on the borders of Estremadura. He was also separated from the force at Madrid by several sierras and the formidable pass of the Guadarrama. In the capital itself lay Leval with one more division, while the independent brigade of Maransin [2], had been intermittently holding Toledo, and was actually there on the 20th, in company with a brigade of light cavalry under Pierre Soult [3]. The extreme outer flanks of the Army of the South were as far apart therefore as Zamora and Toledo—160 miles as the crow flies—and a Spanish crow has rough country to fly over—and each of them was some 90 miles by road from the head-quarters in the centre.

As to the infantry of the Army of Portugal, the only element of it which lay anywhere near head-quarters was a brigade of Maucune's at Palencia on the Carrion, which was guarding a large dépôt of stores and transport. The other brigade of Maucune's was at Burgos. Lamartinière's division (late that commanded for so long by Bonnet) was watching the great

---

[1] See above, p. 327.   [2] 45th Ligne and 12th Léger.

[3] 2nd Hussars, 5th and 10th *Chasseurs à Cheval*. For an interesting narrative of Maransin's and P. Soult's manœuvres about Toledo, see the book of Wellington's intelligence officer, Leith Hay, who was then a prisoner with them, having been captured while scouting (vol. ii. pp. 142–55).

chaussée from Burgos by Briviesca to Miranda del Ebro, in order to keep touch with Clausel in Navarre. Similarly Sarrut's division, after its long and fruitless chase of Longa, was keeping safe the roads from Bilbao to Miranda, in order to link Foy with the main army. Foy himself was on the shores of the Bay of Biscay, where he had stormed Castro-Urdiales on May 12, and was trying to make an end of the local guerrilleros. The other two divisions of Reille's infantry were lost to sight in the mountains of Navarre, where they were marching and counter-marching with Clausel, in pursuit of the elusive Mina. These were the divisions of Taupin and of Barbot : the troops which were working along with them were the two ' active ' divisions of the Army of the North, those of Abbé and Vandermaesen. Clausel's great flying column, of 15,000 men or more, was so con-tinually on the move through regions where cross-communication was impossible, owing to the insurrection, that it could not be located with certainty on any given date, or receive instruction without a delay that might run to eight or ten days.

Obviously it would take the French army a week to concen-trate on Valladolid or Arevalo, if Wellington should be aiming at Salamanca and the Central Douro. But if he were about to attack one of the extreme wings, at Zamora or Madrid, the time required would be much greater. And Joseph and Jourdan were not at all sure that the secret plan of Wellington might not be a thrust, with Hill's force as the spear-head, at Madrid. One of the many false rumours sent to head-quarters was that forage had been ordered for Long's cavalry at Escalona on the Tietar, many miles in front of Talavera.   While another report truly chronicled the concentration of Hill's brigades at Bejar, and the gathering of stores there, but interpreted their meaning as preparation for a march on Avila by the Puente de Congosto.

Uncertain as to what was Wellington's plan, the French Higher Command finally resolved to await its manifestation before giving the final orders—a system which was certain to lead to some initial loss of territory at the opening of the campaign, since the enemy would have a week in hand, before he could be opposed by a sufficient mass on the line which he might select. On May 18th Jourdan ordered Gazan to push exploring reconnaissances towards the Portuguese frontier,

356.6   z

and, if Wellington should be met advancing, to order Leval to
evacuate Madrid, to send forward all his cavalry to support
Villatte at Salamanca, and, when the latter should be driven in,
to have his whole army ready to receive him behind the line of
the Trabancos river, except Daricau's division, which should
remain at Toro. Reille was to bring forward Darmagnac's
infantry from Rio Seco to support his cavalry on the Esla, and
to unite Maucune's scattered force by calling up his rear brigade
from Burgos, so as to provide a reserve for Darmagnac. If
Wellington should advance, as was thought most probable,
from Ciudad Rodrigo, marching on Salamanca in full strength,
and driving in Villatte, it was intended to bring in all the troops
of Gazan and D'Erlon to the north bank of the Douro, and to
defend the course of that river from Toro to Tordesillas, as
Marmont had done in June 1812. If the British showed strength
on the Esla, which was thought unlikely, Reille would reinforce
Daricau and Digeon with all his cavalry and the divisions of
Darmagnac and Maucune. But no definite orders were sent
either to Clausel [1] or to Foy, Sarrut, and Lamartinière—the
directions to be given them would depend on the strength
which the British displayed, and the front on which they
appeared. Thus a week or more after Wellington should have
shown his hand, the two armies of the South and Centre, with
the cavalry and one infantry division of the Army of Portugal,
ought to be concentrated on the required points north of the
Douro, with the possibility of bringing up later the five missing
divisions of the Army of Portugal, and Clausel's two disposable
divisions from the Army of the North. But these last might
take a very long time to appear, and meanwhile there would
only be 45,000 infantry and 10,000 cavalry in hand opposite
Wellington [2]. Considering the latter's estimated numerical
superiority, it seemed that he might be brought to a stand,
but hardly beaten, by the forces which the King could collect.

---

[1] Clausel was sent a dispatch on May 27 *not* ordering him to come
south at once, but requesting him to send back Barbot, Taupin, and Foy
if his operations were now completed in Navarre ! *Mémoires du Roi Joseph*,
ix. 280.

[2] Viz. four and a half divisions of the Army of the South, two of the
Army of the Centre, one of the Army of Portugal, the King's French
Guards, and his trifling Spanish auxiliary force.

A defensive campaign on the Douro was really Jourdan's forecast of the game; it might perhaps be turned into an offensive, when the missing divisions of the Army of Portugal and Clausel should come up, with some 30,000 men of reinforcements.

It is a nervous business to wait for the move which finally betrays the enemy's intention, as every one knows who remembers August 1914. It was probably with some feeling of relief that Gazan at Arevalo and King Joseph at Palencia heard, on the 24th, that Wellington had passed the Agueda on the 22nd, and was apparently marching on Salamanca in great strength. Conroux sent in news that Hill was at the same time marching up from Bejar northward—not turning east. The campaign therefore, as it appeared, was to take the form which had seemed most probable, and the hypothetical orders for concentration which had been issued to the generals on the 18th became valid. But Gazan lost a day in evacuating Madrid, by riding over from Arevalo to Valladolid and formally requesting the King's authorization for the retreat of Leval from the capital. So the aide-de-camp bearing the dispatch of recall only started from Valladolid on the morning of the 25th, instead of from Arevalo on the afternoon of the 24th : it was clear therefore that Leval would be late at the concentration point.

The other parts of the French scheme were carried out according to plan between the 25th and the 29th. When Villatte found himself attacked at Salamanca, and got away with some loss eastward on the 26th, he fell back on Medina del Campo, and found waiting for him there on the 28th Conroux's division from Avila and the division of cavalry which Gazan had been keeping at his head-quarters at Arevalo— Tilly's dragoons. D'Erlon was in march from Segovia with Cassagne's division and Treillard's horse, and had reached Olmedo, only fifteen miles from Medina, so that he would be available next day. The whole made up a force of 16,000 foot and 4,000 horse. But Leval was late, and would not be up for three days more, nor had Maucune's brigade yet come down from Burgos, while Daricau and Digeon began to look uncomfortably remote in their position at Toro and Zamora, where only Reille could reach them.

z 2

Joseph and Jourdan had intended to take position behind
the Zapardiel on the 30th, there to demonstrate against Wellington, who ought by this time to be coming down upon them. It
was necessary to hold him in check till Leval should have got
in from Madrid to join the main body, and then all would
retire beyond the Douro, to the intended defensive position.
But this day two disquieting facts became notable : one was
that Wellington was not advancing from Salamanca : the
troops that he had brought thither had not moved since the
26th. The other was that Digeon sent word that there were
allied forces approaching the lower Esla from the direction of
Braganza, although Reille had reported ten days back that
there were absolutely no signs of allied movement from this
direction—their numbers were as yet incalculable. The
suspicion, then for the first time, arose that the Salamanca
advance might be a mere feint, despite of Wellington's personal
appearance in that direction.

On the morning of June 1st suspicion became certainty.
Digeon reported that the British had crossed the Esla in
great force, by several fords, and that he and Daricau
were retiring on Toro at once. Joseph would have liked to
go behind the Douro without delay, but could not possibly do
so until Leval, Maransin, and Pierre Soult should have come
up from the south. And the Madrid column was not due on
the Douro for two more days, owing to its late start—no fault
of its own, but due to Gazan's dilatory conduct on May 24th.

Leval had only got the order to evacuate the capital on the
20th. Luckily for him Maransin had come in with his flying
column from Toledo on the 21st, so that there was no need to
wait to pick up this detachment. The garrison was directed to
be under arms for marching at daybreak on the 27th, and with
them went a considerable train of *Afrancesado* refugees, for
many of Joseph's ministers and courtiers had refused to start
by the earlier convoys, which had gone to Valladolid in March
and April, hoping that emigration might never again become
necessary. The remembrance of the miserable march to
Valencia in July 1812 weighed on their minds, and made them
unwilling to face a second *hegira* of the same sort. Now all had
to go ; and quantities of carriages, carts, wagons, and mules

belonging to civilians were mixed with, or trailed behind, the columns of Leval's infantry. The convoy could not travel very fast ; it only reached the foot of the mountains on the night of the 27th, crossed the Guadarrama pass on the 28th, and reached Espinar on the northern descent on the 29th. Here Leval turned off the baggage and refugees on to the road of Segovia, under charge of an escort commanded by General Hugo, late Governor of Madrid. He himself with the fighting men went on to Arevalo by the great *chaussée*, reached the Douro on the 2nd of June, and joined Gazan at Tordesillas. The latter had crossed the river on May 31st, the moment that it became clear that the Madrid column was not going to be intercepted by any British force from the Salamanca direction. D'Erlon passed the Douro only on June 2, the same day as Leval, having waited behind to cover the arrival of the column of refugees and transport from Madrid, which had been directed on Segovia and Cuellar.

On June 2nd therefore the south bank of the Douro had been at last evacuated by all the French forces, but Jourdan's and Joseph's plan for defending the northern bank was obviously out of date and impossible. For Wellington was already at Toro with Graham's 40,000 men, and there was no means of preventing Hill's 30,000 and the Galicians from joining him north of the river. The Salamanca column, if only the French had known it, was already marching north, to fall in alongside of the other and larger mass of the allied army, and was due at Toro next day (June 3rd).

This last fact was, of course, unknown at French headquarters on the afternoon of June 2nd—all that had transpired was that Wellington was at Toro with a very large force, and the Galicians close by his flank on the Benavente road. The exact position of the imperial army was that Gazan, with four and a half infantry divisions of the Army of the South and all the cavalry of Digeon, Tilly, and Pierre Soult, was concentrated on a ten-mile front between Tordesillas and Torrelobaton : Reille, with Darmagnac's division and Boyer's cavalry, was at Medina de Rio Seco, twelve miles farther north. D'Erlon, with Cassagne's division and Treillard's dragoons, was at Valladolid, fifteen miles behind Tordesillas ; the King and his Guards at Cigales, ten miles north of D'Erlon, twelve miles east of Reille. Maucune's two brigades had at last concentrated at Palencia—some 25 miles north of Valladolid. There was now a very solid mass of troops, which could be united at one spot— Torrelobaton for example—by a concentric march, taking up one day, or could on the other hand string itself out in a well closed-up front behind the Carrion and Pisuerga rivers, from Palencia to Simancas, to defend the line of those streams. The force was formidable—over 40,000 bayonets, quite 10,000 sabres. It was physically possible either to mass and offer Wellington a battle, or to stand fast to defend the line of the Pisuerga. But would either course be prudent, considering that Hill could join Wellington with ease at Toro, so that the entire Anglo-Portuguese army could be concentrated for a general action, not to speak of the Galicians of Giron on his flank ? Exact calculations as to the allied strength were impossible—but it would certainly exceed 70,000 men : some of the French generals put it at 90,000. To engage in an open battle west of the Pisuerga against such superior numbers would be insane. But what of the idea of taking up a defensive line east of that river, in the hope of rallying Foy, Clausel, and other outlying forces within a week or ten days ? Marmont had done well with his position behind a river in July 1812, and had only been ruined at Salamanca because he had left his strong line and attacked with insufficient numbers.

There was much debate at head-quarters on the afternoon of June 2. Several policies were discussed, even, as it would appear, a desperate suggestion of Jourdan's to bring the whole army back southward across the Douro, to Medina del Campo and Olmedo, and defy Wellington to cross its front so as to cut the Burgos road and the communication with France. ' It is doubtful whether Wellington would have dared to continue his march to the Carrion, and to abandon his line of connexion with Portugal,' writes Jourdan ; ' more probably he would have repassed the Douro, to follow the French army, which could then have retired up-stream to Aranda, and from thence either on Burgos or on Saragossa. Time would have been gained— Clausel would have come up, and we could have fought on ground more suitable for cavalry [1].' This most hazardous

[1] Jourdan, *Mémoires*, p. 466.

plan would have commenced by abandoning to the enemy all
Old Castile and Biscay, with the French forces scattered in
them ; for even if Wellington had followed the King with his
Anglo-Portuguese army, Giron's Galicians and the insurgents
of the North—Longa, Porlier, El Pastor, and the rest—would
have been left free to clear the whole country up to the Pyrenees.
The French detachments in the North must have retired on
Bayonne.   King Joseph and the generals rejected the scheme
at once, on the ground that Napoleon's orders had always
insisted on the retention of the direct road to France, by
Burgos and Vittoria, as the most important of all considerations.
This was undoubtedly a correct decision.   Not only was the road
along the south bank of the Douro to Aranda a very bad one,
through an exhausted country, but it is clear that, if they took
it, the French would never have got back again on to the Burgos
line, but would have been forced to take the Saragossa line.
The way from Aranda by Soria to Saragossa was through
a rough country infested by Duran, the Empecinado, and other
active guerrillero leaders.   It could never have served as the
main artery of communication for an army of the size of King
Joseph's.   But supposing that the King should have reached
Saragossa, his only touch with France would be through
Barcelona and Roussillon, for there is no decent carriage road
from Saragossa across the Central Pyrenees—the difficult pass
by Jaca having often been tried and found wanting, save for
small and unencumbered detachments.   To base the whole
army of Spain on Perpignan instead of Bayonne would have
been hopelessly impracticable.

The question as to whether the line along the Pisuerga, from
Palencia to opposite Simancas, could not be held was the
really hard problem.   It was 35 miles long, well marked, but with
local faults ; the water was low ; there were points where the
west bank commanded the east ; from near Palencia to Cabezon
the only good road was on the western side of the river, and so
out of control ; while the bad path on the eastern side was cut up
by three streams coming in from the high plateaux of the province
of Burgos.   In the rear there was the defile of Torquemada,
where the road and the Pisuerga itself came out of the upland.
After pondering over the question, Joseph decided that the

Pisuerga was too dangerous a line to hold, that he was still too weak in numbers, and that he had better fall back on Burgos, and wait in position there, on ground much more defensible than the broad plains of the Pisuerga and the Carrion, for the arrival of the missing divisions of the Army of Portugal and of Clausel.

On the evening of the 2nd orders were issued that all the *impedimenta* of the Army of Spain should move off northward at once. The Grand Park and other transport, the Spanish refugees with all their carriages and lumber, the French civil administrators, the King's ministers with his private baggage and treasure, and much miscellaneous stuff from the royal palaces—pictures, books, and antiquities—were to start off at once on the road to Burgos. One great convoy was dispatched that night, a second and still larger one the following morning. Escort was found for them from the King's Spanish troops, the so-called 'division' of Casa Palacios, and other detachments, making up 4,000 men in all. On the afternoon of the 3rd the army executed a general movement of retreat, leaving only a cavalry screen behind, to observe Wellington's advance. The Army of the South came back through Valladolid, after blowing up all the bridges on the lower Pisuerga and the neighbouring streams, and then marched up its western bank to Cabezon. Reille evacuated Medina de Rio Seco and fell back on Palencia, where he picked up Maucune. Head-quarters and the King's guard moved to Magaz, just south of Palencia. D'Erlon marched from Valladolid to Dueñas, ten miles farther south than Magaz, and made ready to blow up the bridge there and cross to the other side of the Pisuerga. The whole army was collected in a space of 15 miles, and halted for two days, in a safe position for retreat on Burgos, when it should be pressed. For Joseph and Jourdan naturally wished to gain time—every day that passed made it more likely that the missing divisions from the North would be heard of, or even be reported as approaching. Yet it would seem that even yet no direct and peremptory orders had been sent to Clausel, for Jourdan writes in his Memoirs that ' the King suspended the retrograde movement because he thought to gain time, *and hoped that the Minister of War would have given orders to General Clauzel to come down on Burgos* [1].' Again the wretched system of double-command and constant reference to Paris was working! If it be remembered that it was only on the 18th of May that the King had made his final appeal to the minister to let loose Clausel from the northern operations, and that the news of Wellington's actual advance had only been sent to France on the 24th, when could it be expected that the directions from Paris would reach the scattered columns lost in the mountains of Navarre? And was there any certainty that Clarke would visualize the full danger of the position, and give at once the kind of orders that the King desired? He might send instead a lecture on the Emperor's intentions, if past experience was to be trusted, and some suggestions which the events of the last ten days would have put completely out of date.

[1] Jourdan, *Mémoires*, p. 467.

SECTION XXXVI: CHAPTER V

THE OPERATIONS AROUND BURGOS : JUNE 4–14

ON June 3rd Wellington had halted the infantry of Graham's column at Toro, in order to allow the whole of Hill's column to cross the bridge and fords, and to complete the junction of the army. He gave as his reasons that he expected to meet Gazan, D'Erlon, and the King, on the Hormija river, when he should have debouched from Toro, and that he intended to fight them with his whole force, not with the northern column only. ' I do not think,' he wrote, ' that we are so close up or so well concentrated as we ought to be, to meet the enemy in the strength in which he will appear on the Hormija, probably to-morrow ; and therefore I propose to halt the heads of the different columns to-morrow, and close up the rear of each, moving Hill in this direction preparatory to our further movement [1].' Only the cavalry continued to press forward on the 3rd ; they found no signs of resistance, but only vedettes, which retired cautiously on their approach. Wellington was so far right in his apprehension, that the idea of fighting in front of Valladolid had been one of the three plans which the French Head-quarters Staff had considered on June 2. But, as we have already seen, that scheme had been rejected as rash, and during Wellington's halt upon June 3 the enemy were evacuating Valladolid and all its neighbourhood, and commencing their retreat behind the Pisuerga. By eight o'clock on the evening of that day the cavalry reports, all along the front, showed that the enemy was retiring on every road, and it appeared certain that they did not intend to fight ; the army therefore advanced in three main columns, Wellington himself with the 3rd, 4th, 6th, and 7th Divisions, followed by Hill, by the high road on Valladolid through La Mota : Graham with the 1st and 5th Divisions, Pack and Bradford, by the more northern parallel road, by Villavelid and Villar de Frades, on Medina de Rio Seco. The

[1] Wellington to Graham, *Dispatches*, x. p. 411.

Galicians were converging on the same point as Graham, by the high road from Villalpando and Villafrechos, but were directed not to approach too close to Medina till further notice. The reason for their delay was a curious one—Giron had just written on the previous day to say that he had no reserve of infantry cartridges, and only 60 rounds a man in the soldiers' pouches. He wanted to borrow a supply from the British army. Wellington replied in considerable heat : when he was on the move he could not give away his own reserve ammunition : no doubt Giron was not personally to blame—nor his men—but the administration in Galicia. Yet the unfortunate result would be that the Galicians must never be put in a position where there would be a heavy consumption of cartridges, i. e. must be held in reserve, or used for subsidiary operations only. Giron was directed to make small regimental reserves, by taking away a proportion of the cartridges from each man and carrying them on mules. The general got off easily—but Wellington thundered that night on the War Minister O'Donoju, ' Here is an army which is clothed, armed, and disciplined, but cannot be brought into action with the enemy : I am obliged to keep it in the rear. How can troops march without provisions, or fight without ammunition ? The cause of the country may be lost unless the Government establish in the provinces some authority to which the people will pay obedience, and which will insure their resources for the purposes of the war [1].' It will be noted that all through the rest of the campaign Giron's corps was used for flanking movements, and never put in the forefront of the fighting—though the other Spanish troops with the army, Morillo's and later Longa's divisions, were used freely.

On the 4th June Wellington moved with the ' Head-Quarters Column ' as far as La Mota, Hill getting no farther than Morales. At La Mota the information received showed that the French were in general retreat—the cavalry advance got into Valladolid and found some undestroyed stores of ammunition there. Julian Sanchez, scouting far towards the south, discovered a considerable magazine of grain at Arevalo, where Gazan's head-quarters had been. In view of the new situation it was

[1] Wellington to Giron, *Dispatches*, x. 413 and 414, and to O'Donoju, x. pp. 414–15.

necessary to recast the movements of the army—there was to be
no fight on the Hormija, or for the possession of Valladolid.
The initial strategical success of the passage of the Esla had
settled the event of the first phase of the campaign, and cleared
the French not only out of New Castile, but out of the kingdom
of Leon and great part of Old Castile.   The fact that the enemy
had abandoned Valladolid and the lower crossings of the
Pisuerga, would seem to show that he intended to fall back on
the Burgos country : he could hardly be intending to defend
a position behind the middle Pisuerga and the Carrion, since he
had surrendered the passages at and about Valladolid, by which
the southern flank of such a position could be turned.

Now nine months ago Wellington had been in these same
regions, with the army of Clausel retreating before him from
Valladolid on Burgos.   On that occasion he had followed the
enemy in a straightforward pursuit along the great high road,
by Cabezon and Torquemada.   On this occasion his strategy
was entirely different.   Leaving only a cavalry screen between
himself and the enemy, he proceeded to move his whole army
towards the north-west by secondary roads, marching in four
parallel columns not on Burgos but on the upper Pisuerga
north-west of that fortress, so as to turn entirely any position
that the enemy might take up on the Hormaza, the Arlanzon,
or the Urbel.   It can hardly be doubted that he had already in
his mind the great manœuvre which he was to accomplish
during the next fortnight—that of outflanking the French
right wing by a wide sweeping movement, which would not only
force Joseph and Jourdan to evacuate Burgos and its neighbourhood, but would cut them off from the royal road to Bayonne
and their main communication with France. . The first order
in his dispatch book which definitely reveals this intention does
not appear till June 10 [1], but the facts which it contains prove
that the plan must have been laid long ere Wellington started
from Portugal.

This plan was no less a scheme than the transference of the
base of the British army from the port of Lisbon to the Bay of
Biscay, so that when, in its wide turning movement, it should

---

[1] Viz. Wellington to Colonel Bourke from Melgar, June 10, *Dispatches*,
x. p. 429.

have passed the Ebro and neared the Cantabrian coast, it should find stores and munitions awaiting it, and be no longer tied to the long line of communication with Portugal, which it had always used hitherto. It was an astonishing example of the strategical use of sea-power, to which there had hitherto been no parallel in the Napoleonic wars. The only manœuvre at all resembling it was that by which Sir John Moore in December 1808 had changed his line of communication from Lisbon to Corunna. But this was for a sudden hasty retreat, made by a small army—a very different thing from an advance made by a large army. For Moore had only wanted transports on which to abscond from the Peninsula ; Wellington had planned the arrival of a fleet of supply vessels, on whose contents he was to rely for the future sustenance of his army during a long campaign.

Their existence was his second great secret in 1813—the first had been his plan for the crossing of the Esla. But the latter might have been guessed at as a possibility by any intelligent French general : the former, it is safe to say, had never been dreamed of as a conceivable move. Santander is so remote from Portugal, and the French were so firmly rooted in Northern Spain in the spring of 1813, that it could never enter into the head of any of Napoleon's subordinates that the British Commander-in-Chief was planning such an elaborate surprise. They were bound to believe that all Wellington's operations would be founded on, and circumscribed by, the basic fact that his line of communication was on Lisbon. A manœuvre which presupposed the complete abandonment of that line was not conceivable by officers reared in Continental campaigns, and unused to contemplating the correlation of land operations and naval strategy. Yet the fact that the supply fleet had been gathered at Corunna long weeks before, and kept there till the conquest of Northern Spain was well on its way to completion, is conclusive evidence as to Wellington's intentions. The crucial dispatch of June 10 ran as follows—it was addressed to Colonel Bourke in charge of the British dépôts in Galicia :

'There are at Corunna certain ships loaded with biscuit and flour, and certain others loaded with a train of heavy artillery and its ammunition, and some with musket ammunition, and I shall be much obliged if you will request any officer of the navy who may be at Corunna, when you receive this letter, to take under his convoy all the vessels loaded as above mentioned, and to proceed with them to Santander. If he should find Santander occupied by the enemy, I beg him to remain off the port till the operations of this army have obliged the enemy to abandon it.

'If the enemy is not occupying Santander, I beg him to enter the port, but to be in readiness to quit it again if the enemy should approach the place, until I shall communicate with him [1]'.

It should be noted that Wellington had carefully avoided calling attention to the accumulation of ships and stores at Corunna, even in his letters to the ministers at home [2]. Their existence there was plausibly explained by the need for supplying the Spanish army of Galicia—which had indeed received much material during the spring. The provision of heavy artillery shows that he was contemplating as a probability the siege of San Sebastian and the other northern fortresses. He had failed at Burgos in 1812 for lack of the 24-pounders which Home Popham had vainly offered to send him from Santander : now he was quite ready to receive them from that port. As things stood on the Pisuerga, at the moment that he sent this prescient dispatch to Bourke, it was certainly a bold prophecy to write that he was about to clear the Cantabrian coast by his next move. The French were still unbeaten, and he was more than a hundred miles from the Bay of Biscay, from which he was separated by a most rough and complicated land of mountains. But he had already taken his measure of the capacity of the hostile commanders, and his hopes were high.

The great flank movement's initial stages can be best traced by following on the map Wellington's nightly head-quarters. They were La Mota on the 4th, Castromonte on the 5th, Ampudia on the 6th—all these carefully avoid the neighbourhood of the Pisuerga, though the cavalry pushed on to feel the lines of the French along the river. But the army, instead

---

[1] Wellington to Bourke from Melgar, June 10, *Dispatches*, x. 429.

[2] As, for example, in the letter to Bathurst about ships. *Dispatches*, x. 416.

of making for the crossings at Valladolid, Cabezon, or Dueñas, kept steadily on in four parallel columns, on roads far from the river. Hill, still as always on the right, went by Torrelobaton, Mucientes, and Dueñas ; Graham, on the left, by Medina de Rio Seco and Grixota; 'the Head-Quarters Column' under Wellington himself, by Castromonte and Ampudia—while, far off, the Galician army on the north moved by Villaramiel and Villoldo on Aguilar de Campos. The flanking cavalry kept up a continual bickering along the Pisuerga with French outposts ; on the 6th those at the head of the advance had a distant glimpse of a great review of the Army of the Centre, which King Joseph was holding outside Palencia, from the heights which overlook that city from the west. In front of Dueñas there was an exchange of letters under a flag of truce between Wellington and Gazan—a most odd proceeding at such a moment—from which both parties thought they had derived useful information [1]. The British *parlementaire* reported to the Commander-in-Chief that Dueñas was still held by French infantry—which was good to know : the French, on the other hand, got a reply to Gazan's letter to Wellington within four hours—which proved that British Head-Quarters must be a very short way from them—which was equally a valuable scrap of knowledge.

The King had now waited three days in the temporary position behind the Pisuerga, without being attacked, though he was in the close neighbourhood of the enemy. The quiescence of such an adversary made him uncomfortable, and at last he guessed part of what was going on opposite him. The British must be pushing up northward parallel to his line, and preparing to turn his right flank (which extended no farther than Palencia) by way of Amusco and the upper Carrion. Whereupon Joseph on the 7th hastily resumed his retreat, and got behind the defile of Torquemada. There was danger in waiting—nothing had been heard of Clausel, but news were to hand that Lamartinière, with one of the missing divisions of the Army of Portugal, was

---

[1] These sort of courtesies were most misplaced. The subject of discussion was the exchange of the British officer captured at Morales (see above, p. 332) for a French officer whom Gazan was anxious to get back. See *Dispatches*, x. 421, Wellington to Gazan ; Jourdan's *Mémoires*, p. 467 ; and the narrative of the flag-bearer in Maxwell's *Peninsular Sketches*, ii. pp. 97–8.

nearing Burgos from the north. The main body took post on the Arlanzon—but Reille with his two divisions at Castroxeriz on the Odra. Jourdan went forward to report on the condition of Burgos, where important new works had been commenced in the spring, and to choose good defensible positions in its neighbourhood. It was expected that the British army would follow in pursuit, up the great *chaussée* from Palencia to Torquemada.

And at first it looked as if this might be the case : entering Palencia on the same day that the King had left it, Wellington pushed up the *chaussée* part of Hill's column—Grant's and Ponsonby's cavalry brigades and the Light Division, which kept in touch with the enemy's rear. The rest of the right column had got no farther forward than Palencia. But the main body of the army continued its north-westerly turning movement, Graham's infantry that day reached Grixota, five miles north of Palencia ; the Galicians were up parallel with Graham farther west, somewhere near Becceril. The movements of June 8 and 9, however, were the decisive revelations of Wellington's intentions. He moved his head-quarters not up the Torquemada road, but to Amusco on the Carrion river, and continued to urge his columns straight northward—Graham to San Cebrian and Peña on the 8th and Osorno on the 9th, the main body of Hill's column to Amusco and Tamara, the Galicians to Carrion. He was thus getting his army well north of any positions which the enemy would be likely to take up in the neighbourhood of Burgos, giving it very long marches, but still keeping it closely concentrated.

On the 10th he judged that he had got sufficiently round the enemy, and turned all his columns due east towards the upper Pisuerga—Graham's and Wellington's own divisions crossing it at Zarzosa and Melgar, Hill at Astudillo, some miles farther south. Head-quarters were fixed that night at Melgar. With the passage of the Pisuerga ended the long march through the great flat corn-bearing plainland of Northern Spain, the Tierra de Campos. The next ten days were to be spent among rougher paths. The triumphant and almost unopposed advance from the Esla to the Pisuerga, executed in one sweep and at high speed, was an episode which those who were engaged in it never forgot.

' From the time of our crossing the Esla up to this period,' wrote one diarist, ' we have been marching through one continuous cornfield. The land is of the richest quality, and produces the finest crops with the least possible labour. It is generally wheat, with a fair proportion of barley, and now and then a crop of vetches or clover. The horses fed on green barley nearly the whole march, and got fat. The army has trampled down twenty yards of corn on each side of the roads by which the several columns have passed—in many places much more, from the baggage going on the side of the columns, and so spreading farther into the wheat. But they must not mind their corn if we get the enemy out of their country ! . . . The country gives bread and corn, and hitherto these have not failed, and this is a region that has been plundered and devastated for five years by the enemy ! It was said before our march that until the harvest came in, not a pound of bread by way of supplies for the army could be procured [1].'

A Light Division diarist writes in a more romantic frame of mind : ' The country was beautifully diversified, studded with castles of Moorish architecture, recalling the chivalric days of Ferdinand and Isabella. The sun shone brilliantly, the sky was heavenly blue, and clouds of dust marked the line of march of the glittering columns. The joyous peasantry hailed our approach and came dancing to meet us, singing, and beating time on their small tambourines ; and when we passed through the principal street of Palencia, the nuns, from the upper windows of a convent, showered down rose-leaves upon our dusty heads [2].'

The dry comment of the Commander-in-chief, in his report to the War Minister at home, contrasts oddly with this enthusiasm : ' I enclose the last weekly and daily states. We keep up our strength, and the army are very healthy and in better order than I have ever known them. God knows how long that will last. It depends entirely upon the officers [3].'

While Wellington's columns were hurrying northward, the French remained for two days (June 7–9) in position behind the Pisuerga—Reille on the right at Castroxeriz, the rest of the

---

[1] Tomkinson's *Diary* (16th Light Dragoons), pp. 239–40.
[2] Maxwell's *Peninsular Sketches*, ii. 37.   [3] *Dispatches*, x. 437.

army holding the heights down to Villadiego and the Arlanza river. Only British cavalry scouts appeared in front of them. ' The position was excellent,' says Jourdan, ' and it was hoped to hold it for some days. But the generals commanding the armies represented to the King that the troops lacked bread, and that they dared not send out large detachments far afield to requisition food from the peasantry, wherefore the whole force retired on Burgos.' No doubt the country was bare ; and, when the enemy is known to be near, it is unsafe to make large detachments : but it may be suspected that the real cause for retreat was the continuous uncertainty as to Wellington's northward movement. Yet it is clear that the French Head-Quarters had no suspicion how far that movement was going.

For on the 9th, when they retreated, they took up position on a very short line north and south of Burgos. Reille's two divisions lay behind the Hormaza river, ten miles west of the fortress—with the right opposite Hormaza village, the left at Estepar—forming a front line. The Army of the South was on both banks of the Arlanzon, five miles behind Reille—right wing behind the Urbel river, left wing behind the Arcos river. The Army of the Centre and the King's Guards were in reserve, billeted in Burgos itself. But already Wellington's columns were aiming at points far north of Reille's position. That day the northernmost divisions of Graham's infantry [1] were at Osorno, next day (June 10th) at Zarzosa, beyond the Pisuerga, a point from which they could easily march round the Hormaza position, and on June 11th, at Sotresgudo, where they halted for a day [2]. The centre [3], with Wellington himself, on the same day had reached Castroxeriz on the Odra river, while Hill was close by at Barrio de Santa Maria and Valbases. Nothing had been sent south of the Arlanzon save Julian Sanchez's lancers, who were scouring the country in the direction of Lerma, on the look-out for belated French convoys or detachments. The Galician army, keeping (as always) far out on the left wing, had reached the Pisuerga at Herrera, ten miles north of Graham's extreme flank. They were now within two marches of the

[1] 1st and 5th with Bradford's Portuguese.
[2] Food having run low, owing to the mule-transport falling behind.
[3] 3rd, 4th, 6th, 7th Divisions and Pack's Portuguese.

upper Ebro, and there was absolutely no enemy in front of them for scores of miles—the nearest Frenchmen in that direction were the columns with which Foy was scouring the roads of Biscay, after his capture of Castro-Urdiales.

The halt of the French army in the neighbourhood of Burgos was not to mark the end of its retreat, and the commencement of offensive operations, as King Joseph had hoped. The only cheering features in the general outlook were that Lamartinière's division of the Army of Portugal was now in touch—it was reported coming up from Briviesca—and that a bulletin of the Grand Army was received from Germany, telling of the victory of the Emperor at Bautzen. But the discouraging news was appalling—the first instalment of it was that Jourdan reported, after investigating the fortifications of Burgos, that he considered the place untenable. During the spring building and demolition had been taken in hand, for the purpose of linking up the old castle, which had given so much trouble to Wellington in 1812, with the high-lying ' Hornwork of St. Miguel ' on the rising ground above. The scheme was wholly unfinished—the only result achieved was that St. Miguel, as reconstructed, commanded the castle, and that the alterations started in the *enceinte* of the latter, with the object of linking it up with the former, had rendered it, in the marshal's opinion, incapable of holding out for a day. Yet this would not have mattered so much if the army had been about to resume the offensive, or to put up a stable defence in the Burgos region.

But it was declared that this was impossible—the governor reported that the immense convoys which had been passing through Burgos of late, and the recent stay of considerable bodies of troops in the place [1], had brought his magazines to such a low ebb that he could not feed an army of 50,000 men for more than a few days. The town was still crammed with the last great horde of Spanish and French refugees, who had come on from Madrid, Segovia, and Valladolid, and all the King's private train. They were sent on at once towards Vittoria, under escort of Lamartinière's division—which thus no sooner became available than it was lost again. No news

[1] Presumably Maucune's brigade, which had been there some time, as well as the convoy escorts.

had arrived either from Foy or from Clausel: but Sarrut's division of the Army of Portugal had been located north of the Ebro, and would be coming in ere very long. The news that Clausel was undiscoverable brought King Joseph to such a pitch of excitement that he took, on June 9th, a step which he should have taken a fortnight before, and threw over all his fears of offending the minister at Paris or the Emperor in Saxony. He sent direct peremptory orders to Clausel to join him at once, and told off a column of 1,500 men to escort the aide-de-camp who bore them : it went off by Domingo Calzada and Logroño. As a matter of fact the order reached the general in six days—but it might have taken longer for all that Joseph could guess. And the King came to the conclusion that if he were at all pushed by Wellington within the next few days, he must abandon Burgos and retire behind the Ebro. He might even have to go without hostile persuasion, on the mere question of food-supplies.

But on June 12 the pressure was applied. Wellington had now got all his forces over the Pisuerga, and his two southern columns were concentrated between Castroxeriz and Villadiego : Graham was farther off, but not out of reach. Having reconnoitred the advanced position of Reille on the Hormaza river, and found that his supports were far behind, he resolved to attack him in front and flank that morning. Only the southern column—Hill's troops—was employed, the centre divisions being halted in a position from which they might be brought in on the enemy's rear, if the King reinforced Reille, but not if the French showed no signs of standing. But the push against the Army of Portugal, made by the 2nd Division, Silveira's Portuguese, and Morillo's Spaniards, was sufficient to dislodge the enemy : for while they were deploying against the French front, the cavalry brigades of Grant and Ponsonby, supported by the Light Division, appeared behind Reille's right flank. The enemy at once gave way, before infantry fighting had begun, and retreating hastily southward got behind the Urbel river, where the Army of the South was already in line. Reille then crossed the Arlanzon by the bridge of Buniel and took post south of Burgos. The French loss was small—the retreat was made in good order and with great speed, before the British infantry could arrive. Grant's and Ponsonby's horse, already out-flanking the rearguard, got in close, but did not deliver a general attack—by Wellington's own orders as it is said [1] : for (despite of Garcia Hernandez) he held to his firm belief that cavalry cannot break intact infantry. A half troop of the 14th Light Dragoons, under Lieut. Southwell, charged and captured an isolated French gun, which had fallen behind the rearguard; but this was the only contact between the armies that day. Jourdan says that Reille lost about fifteen men only —an exaggeration no doubt, but not a very great one.

The result, however, was to determine King Joseph to retreat at once, and to abandon Burgos, before his obviously out-flanked right wing should be entirely circumvented. That night desperate measures were taken—everything that could travel on wheels was sent off by the high road towards the Ebro : the infantry followed, using such side roads as were available. At dawn only cavalry rearguards were covering Burgos. Jourdan explains the haste of the retreat as follows. ' It was easy to foresee that next morning that part of the Army of the South which lay behind the Urbel river would be attacked, and that being separated by the Arlanzon from the bulk of the army, which lay on the south bank, it would be compromised. Three choices lay open—first, to bring the whole army across the Arlanzon and to fight on the Urbel ; but this would have brought on the general action which it had been determined to avoid, ever since the King had made up his mind to call in Clausel. Second—to bring the whole army across to the south bank of the Arlanzon, where there was a good position : but this move would have allowed the enemy to cut the great road and our communications with France—and the same motives which had caused the rejection of the scheme to retire south of the Douro on June 2 caused this alternative to be disapproved on June 12. Third—to fall back by the great road to the Ebro, and so secure the earliest possible concentration of all the armies of Spain. This was the scheme adopted [2].'

[1] ' Grant begged Lord Wellington to allow him to attack the retiring infantry, but in spite of his pressing solicitations was not permitted.' Maxwell's *Peninsular Sketches*, ii. 99.

[2] Jourdan, *Mémoires*, p. 469.

It is said that Gazan was for fighting on the Urbel [1], while Reille and D'Erlon opted for the second choice—that of abandoning the high road to France, going south of the Arlanzon, and retreating by the bad track to Domingo Calzada and Logroño, because Clausel, being certainly somewhere in Navarre, would be picked up much sooner at Logroño than at Miranda or other points higher up the Ebro. But the Emperor's orders that the direct communication with France must be kept up at all costs, were adduced against them, and settled the question.

Before leaving, the French made arrangements to blow up the castle which had served them so well in the preceding October, and to destroy a great store of powder and munitions for which no transport could be procured. According to Jourdan the disaster which followed was due to the professional ignorance of General d'Aboville, the director-general of artillery, who maintained that shells would do no great harm if they were exploded, not in a great mass but placed in small groups, at distances one from another. He had 6,000 of them laid in parcels on the ground in the castle square, and connected with the mines which were placed under the donjon keep. Orders were given that the fuses were only to be lit when the last troops should have left, and the inhabitants were told that if they would keep to their houses they would incur no danger. But the mines by some error were fired before seven o'clock in the morning, and the effects of the explosion had been so badly calculated, that not only were many houses in the city injured, all the glass blown out of the splendid cathedral, and its roof broken in several places, but a hail of shells fell all over the surrounding quarter, and killed 100 men of Villatte's division, who were halted in the Plaza Mayor, and a few of Digeon's dragoons who were crossing the bridge [2]. There were casualties also, of course, among the unfortunate citizens. When the smoke

---

[1] Cf. Miot de Melito in Ducasse, ix. p. 468.

[2] Cf. Jourdan's *Mémoires*, p. 470 ; *Wellington Dispatches*, x. pp. 436-7 ; Digeon's Report, and the Appendix in Arteche, xiii. p. 486. Toreno (iii. p. 230) says that the citizens held that the French had intended the mine to work when they were gone, and to destroy the city and the incoming allied troops, but leans to the view that ignorance of the power of explosives explains all.

cleared away, and the fire had gone out, it was found that the destruction of the donjon keep and upper works of the castle had been complete, but that most of the outer wall was standing—as indeed it is to this day. Wellington remarked that it was quite capable of restoration, if the fortunes of the war made it necessary [1]. They did not ; and the skeleton of the castle still remains ruined and riven on its mound, to surprise the observer by its moderate size. Those who go round it can only marvel that such a small fortress should have held all Wellington's army at bay during so many eventful days in 1812.

The British general, hearing at Castroxeriz, on the early morning of June 13, that the French had evacuated Burgos and blown up its works, did not even enter the town, and sent nothing more than cavalry scouts to follow the retreating enemy, but ordered the instant resumption of the north-westward march of the whole army. It was now his intention to turn the line of the Ebro, in the same fashion that he had turned the line of the Douro on May 31—by passing it so far to the westward that any position which the enemy might adopt would be outflanked, even before it was fully taken up. And he was aiming not only at turning the Ebro line, but at cutting Joseph's communication with France : he was already taking Vittoria, far behind the Ebro, as the goal for which he was making.

We have Wellington's own word for the fact that it was the collapse of the French opposition in front of Burgos which finally induced him to develop his original plan of campaign, spoken of above, into the more ambitious scheme for driving the French completely out of the Peninsula, which he now took in hand. Unfortunately his statement was taken down many years after the event, and his memory of details was not all that it might have been in his old age. But the story is so interesting and fits into the psychology of the moment so well that it must not be omitted.

' When I heard and saw the explosion (I was within a few miles, and the effect was tremendous) I made a sudden resolution forthwith—to cross the Ebro *instanter*, and to endeavour to push the French to the Pyrenees. We had heard of the battles

---

[1] *Dispatches*, x. p. 436.

of Lützen and Bautzen, and of the Armistice, and the affairs of
the Allies looked very ill. Some of my officers remonstrated with
me about the imprudence of crossing the Ebro, and advised me
to "take up the line of the Ebro", &c. I asked them what they
meant by "taking up the line of the Ebro",—a river 300 miles
long, and what good I was to do along that line ? In short
I would not listen to that advice, and that evening (or the very
next morning) I crossed the river and pushed the French till
I afterwards beat them at Vittoria. And lucky it was that
I did ! For the battle of Vittoria induced the Allies to denounce
the Armistice—then followed Leipzig and all the rest.

' All my staff were against my crossing the Ebro : they
represented that we had done enough, that we ought not to
risk the army and all that we had obtained, that the Armistice
would enable Bonaparte to reinforce his army in Spain, and we
therefore should look for a defensive system. I thought
differently—I knew that the Armistice could not affect in the
way of quick reinforcement so distant an army as that of Spain.
I thought that if I could not *hustle* them out of Spain before they
were reinforced, I should not be able to hold any position in
Spain after they should be. Above all I calculated on the effect
that a victory might have on the Armistice itself, so I crossed
the Ebro and fought the battle of Vittoria.'

How far is this curious confidence, made to Croker in January
1837, and taken down by him in two separate drafts (*Croker
Papers*, ii. p. 309, and iii. pp. 336–7), a blurred impression,
coloured by after events ? It is quite true that the Burgos explosion took place early on the morning of June 13, that the
orders dictated at Villadiego that day (*Suppl. Disp.* vii, p. 637)
give a sudden new direction to the army, and that next evening
(June 14) the heads of the columns were over the Ebro. But
Wellington's own dispatches seem to show that he did not know
anything of the Armistice on June 13, for he wrote to his brother
Henry that day, ' I have no news from England. The French
have a bulletin of May 24th, when Napoleon was at Dresden—
they talk of successes, but as he was still at Dresden on the
24th, having arrived there on the 8th, they cannot have been
very important.' Now the Armistice of Pläswitz was signed
on June 4, and on the 13th Wellington's latest news was of

May 24. But on the 17th, when he had been two days across the Ebro, he did at last hear something. Again he writes to his brother :

'I have got, by Corunna, English papers of the 3rd. There were several actions in the neighbourhood of Bautzen on the 20th–22nd May. . . . Bonaparte turned then, and they retired. The Allies have lost ground but are unhurt. He has offered (before the battle) to consent to a congress at Prague. . . . An armistice is to commence when the ministers shall arrive at Prague. . . . I do not think that the Russians and Prussians can agree to the armistice, unless they submit entirely' (*Disp.* p. x. 443).

Clearly, then, Wellington on the 13th knew nothing of any armistice, since he introduces the proposal, not the accomplishment, of it to his most trusted correspondent on the 17th, as the last news to hand. He was committed to the advance on Vittoria long before he could know of its subsequent political effects. And thus in his old age he underrated his own prescience. But the fact that his officers doubted the wisdom of the advance, and that he swept their objections away, is probably correct. That he had considered the possibility of an advance far beyond the Ebro seems, as has been said before (pp. 301–3), to be proved by orders given in the spring, before the campaign began.

On the evening of the 13th head-quarters were at Villadiego, while the columns were all heading northward on parallel routes. The Galicians were moving from Aguilar on the bridge of Rocamonde [1], the highest on the Ebro save that at its source near Reynosa. The bulk of Graham's column was marching by La Piedra on the bridge of San Martin, a few miles lower down than Rocamonde, though some of its flanking cavalry crossed at the latter passage, ahead of the Galicians. The Head-Quarters divisions and Hill's column moved, using all available secondary roads, from their position opposite the lower Urbel, by Villadiego and Montorio respectively, on the bridge of Puente Arenas, some fifteen miles below that of San Martin. All three columns had on the 13th–14th–15th very hard marches, of four long Spanish leagues on three successive days, across upland roads

---

[1] Sometimes called the bridge of Policutes, from the name of the village on the opposite bank.

where artillery had never been seen before. The move would only have been practicable at mid-summer. But the columns were absolutely unopposed, and the upper Ebro country had been entirely neglected by the French, as Wellington had foreseen. 'One division could have stopped the whole column at the bridge of San Martin,' wrote an intelligent observer, 'or the other at Rocamonde, where some of our column likewise crossed—the enemy cannot be aware of our movement [1].' Graham was all across the Ebro by noon on the 14th, Hill by the morning of the 16th. Wellington who had fixed his head-quarters at the lost village of Masa in the hills, was able to declare with confidence that the whole army would be over the river by the night—' and then the French must either fight, or retire out of Spain altogether.'

The Ebro country was a surprise to the British observers who had spent so many years in the uplands of Portugal or the rolling plains of the Tierra de Campos. ' Winding suddenly out of a narrow pass, we found ourselves in the river valley, which extended some distance on our right. The beauty of the scenery was beyond description : the rocks rose perpendicularly on every side, without any visible opening to convey an idea of an outlet. This enchanting valley is studded with picturesque hamlets and fruitful gardens producing every description of vegetation. At the Puente Arenas we met a number of sturdy women loaded with fresh butter from the mountains of the Asturias. We had not tasted that commodity for *two years*, therefore it will be unnecessary to describe how readily we made a purchase, nibbling by the way at such a luxury [2].' Northern or Pyrenean Spain is a very different country from the dusty wind-swept central plateaux : above all the lack of water, which is the curse of Castile, ceased at last to be the bane of marching columns.

After crossing the Ebro on the 14th Graham's column made another four-league march on the 15th to the large town of Villarcayo, while the Galicians got to Soncillo on the main road from Santander to Burgos ; thus Wellington was certain of the new naval base to which he had bid the Corunna transports sail only five days before. Hill's troops, who had a longer march

[1] Tomkinson's *Diary*, p. 341. [2] Maxwell's *Peninsular Sketches*, ii. p. 38.

during the last two days than the other columns, were not so far forward, but nearing the river had occupied the heights on the southern side of the Puente de Arenas. The three columns forming the Anglo-Portuguese army were, as a glance at the map shows, in close touch with each other, and in a position where the whole 80,000 men could be concentrated by a single march. Undoubtedly the most surprising features of the advance is that Wellington's commissariat was able to feed such a mass of troops in such a limited area, after they had left the plains of Castile and plunged into the thinly inhabited mountains. The local supplies obtainable must have been very limited. Several diarists speak of biscuit being short [1], though meat was not. But somehow or other the commissaries generally contrived to find more or less food for the army—the well-organized mule trains were not far behind the infantry columns, and the long and difficult movement was never checked—as earlier marches had been in 1809 and 1811 [2]—by the mere question of provisions, though many brigades got but scanty meals.

[1] e. g. Wachholz of Brunswick-Oels, attached to the 4th Division, p. 314.
[2] See, for example, vol. ii. p. 586 and vol. iv. p. 159.

AFTER evacuating Burgos the French army had retired, at a rather leisurely rate, down the high road which leads by Briviesca and the defile of Pancorbo to the valley of the Ebro. The rearguard, as we have seen, had left Burgos on the morning of the 13th, and halted for great part of the day at Gamonal, a few miles east of the city, on the spot where Napoleon had won his easy victory over the Conde de Belveder on November 10, 1808. It was only followed by Spanish irregular horse—some of Julian Sanchez's ubiquitous lancers. Head-quarters that night and the next (June 14) were at Briviesca, and remained there for forty-eight hours : on the 15th they were moved on to Pancorbo, an admirable position with a high-lying fort in the centre, while the road is flanked for miles by steep slopes, on which an advantageous rearguard action might have been fought. But no pursuing enemy came in sight : this fact began to worry the French Head-quarters Staff. ' What could have become of Lord Wellington ? The French Army, in full retreat, was permitted to move leisurely along the great route, without being harassed or urged forward, not a carriage of any description being lost. It appeared inexplicable [1].' The French retreat was leisurely for two reasons—the first was that King Joseph wished to gain time for the immense convoys lumbering in front of him to reach Miranda and Vittoria without being hustled. The second was that he thought that every day gained gave more time for Clausel to come up : at the slow rate at which he was proceeding he might almost hope to find the missing divisions of the Army of Portugal converging on Miranda, at the moment when he should arrive there himself. The Council of War at Burgos had decided that Wellington

---

[1] These were the words of Colonel Arnaud, senior aide-de-camp to Gazan, conversing (most incautiously) with his prisoner Leith Hay, whose diary is most interesting for these days. See Leith Hay, ii. p. 176.

must inevitably pursue by the great *chaussée*. The routes from the Burgos region to the upper Ebro had been reported both by French officers who claimed to know the country, and by local *Afrancesados*, as presenting insuperable difficulties to a large army. There was, it is true, the high road Burgos–Santander by Santijanez, Pedrosa, and Reynosa—but this led north-west in an eccentric direction, not towards Miranda or Vittoria. That the danger lay on the rough mountain ways a little farther east, which fall down to San Martin and Puente de Arenas, seems not to have been suspected. Yet it was disquieting to find no pursuit in progress : could the Allied Army possibly have been forced to halt at Burgos for want of supplies ?

On the 16th the French army descended from the defile of Pancorbo to the Ebro, and proceeded to distribute itself in the region round Miranda, in cantonments which permitted of rapid concentration when it should become necessary. Nothing was yet to be heard of Clausel—but on the other hand Lamartinière's division was again picked up—it handed over the duty of escorting the convoys toward Vittoria to Joseph's Spanish contingent, the small division of Casapalacios. Sarrut's division also came in from Biscay, and reported that it had been lately in touch with Foy, who was successfully hunting the local guerrilleros in the coast-land. But neither Foy himself, nor the troops of the Army of the North which had been co-operating with him of late, were anywhere near. Strange as it may appear, that very capable officer had wholly failed to understand the general situation : though apprised ere now of the evacuation of Madrid and Valladolid, he had nothing in his mind save his wholly secondary operations against the Biscay bands. His dispatches of this period show him occupied entirely with the safety of Bilbao, and the necessity for guarding the high road from Bergara and Tolosa to France. There were 20,000 troops in Biscay, but they were entirely dispersed on petty expeditions and convoy work. On June 19, when he got from head-quarters the first dispatch that caused him to think of concentrating and joining the main army, Foy had only one battalion with him at the moment at Bergara. A column of 1,000 men was moving to reinforce the garrison of Bilbao, a brigade was at Villafranca escorting towards France the large body of prisoners whom he had captured in his recent operations—another brigade was waiting on the road between Vittoria and Mondragon, to pick up a large convoy which, as he had been warned, would be coming up the Royal Road and would require to be protected as far as San Sebastian. He was making efforts to send provisions by sea to Bilbao and Castro-Urdiales—a task in which he was being worried by British cruisers off the coast—and was preparing to go to Bilbao himself [1].

No doubt the main blame for this untimely dispersion of forces lay with General Head-Quarters. Jourdan and Joseph ought to have sent orders to Foy, after the evacuation of Madrid, ordering him to cease all secondary operations, to leave minimum garrisons at a few essential points, abandon all the rest, and collect as strong a field-force as possible, with which to join the main army. But they had written to the minister at Paris suggesting such moves, instead of dispatching direct orders to that effect to the general himself. Foy had been sent information, not orders, and had failed to realize the full meaning of the information—absorbed as he was in his own particular Biscayan problems. Events were marching very quickly : it was hard to realize that Wellington, who had been on the Esla on May 31, would have been across the upper Ebro with 70,000 men on June 15. It had taken little more than a fortnight for him to overrun half of Northern Spain. The fact remained that of all the French troops operating in Biscay in June, only Sarrut's division, from Orduña, joined the King in time for the battle of Vittoria. Yet Foy had under his orders not only his own division but the Italian brigade of St. Pol, and the mobile brigade of Berlier from the Army of the North, in addition to 10,000 men of the garrisons of the various posts and fortresses of the North and the littoral. And he had no enemy save the great partisan Longa in the western mountains, and the scattered remains of the local insurgents under El Pastor and others, whom he had defeated in April and May, and whom he was at present harrying from hill to coast and from coast to hill. We are once more forced to remember that the French armies in Spain were armies of occupation as

---

[1] Foy to Jourdan, Bergara, June 19.

well as armies of operation, and that one of their functions was often fatal to the other.

But to return to the moment when the King's army came back to the Ebro. Head-quarters were, of course, established at Miranda, where the royal Guard served as their escort. The Army of the South sent three divisions across to the north bank of the river ; they were cantoned on the lower Zadorra about Arminion ; but Gazan kept three brigades on the south bank as a rearguard for the present, but (as the King hoped) to form a vanguard for a counter-advance, if only Clausel should come up soon, and an offensive campaign become possible. A small observing force was left at Pancorbo, into whose castle a garrison was thrown. Cavalry exploring parties, pushed out from this point, sought for Wellington's approaching columns as far as Poza de la Sal on the right, Briviesca on the high road, and Cerezo on the left ; but to no effect. They came in touch with nothing but detachments of Julian Sanchez's Lancers. D'Erlon, with the Army of the Centre, went ten miles down the Ebro to Haro : he had now recovered his missing division, Darmagnac's, which had been lent to Reille for the last two months. For the Army of Portugal having now three infantry divisions collected—Maucune's, Sarrut's, and Lamartinière's—was ordered to give back the borrowed unit to its proper commander. Reille took the right of the Ebro position, having Maucune's division at Frias, Sarrut's at Espejo, and Lamartinière's at the Puente Lara. He was ordered to use his cavalry to search for signs of the enemy along the upper Ebro. The King had thus an army which, by the junction of Sarrut and Lamartinière, had risen to over 50,000 infantry and nearly 10,000 cavalry, concentrated on a short front of 25 miles from Frias to Haro, covering the main road to France by Vittoria, and also the side roads to Orduña and Bilbao on the one flank, and Logroño and Saragossa on the other. His retreat, though dispiriting, had not yet been costly—it is doubtful whether he had lost 1,000 casualties in the operations of the last six weeks. With the exception of the combats at Salamanca on May 26 and Morales on June 2, there had been no engagements of any importance. The army was angry at the long-continued retreat ; the officers were criticizing the generalship of their commanders in the most outspoken fashion, but there was no demoralization—the troops were clamouring for a general action.

But on June 17, when the French armies settled down into their new position, with no detected enemy in their neighbourhood, their fate was already determined—the Ebro line had been turned before it was even taken up. For on this same day Wellington had not only got his whole army north of the Ebro, but was marching rapidly eastward, by the mountain roads twenty miles north of the river, into the rear of Reille's cantonments. Of all his troops only Julian Sanchez and Carlos de Españas' infantry division were left in Castile.

The movements of the Allied Army on the 15th–16th–17th June had been carried out with surprising celerity. The Galician infantry, who had crossed the river first, at Rocamonde, the bridge highest up on its course, on the 13th were hurrying northward, by cross roads not marked on the map, and obviously impracticable for guns, to Soncillo (15th), Quintanilla de Pienza (16th), Villasana (17th), and Valmaseda in Biscay (18th). When they had reached the last-named town they were threatening Bilbao, and almost at its gates. This was the great demonstration, intended to throw confusion among all the French detachments on the northern coast. Several of the stages exceeded thirty miles in the day.

Meanwhile the three great columns of the Anglo-Portuguese army were executing a turning movement almost as wide as that of Giron's Galicians. Converging from different bridges of the Ebro—Rocamonde (where some of Graham's cavalry passed), San Martin de Lines (where the bulk of Graham's force debouched northward on the 14th), and Puente Arenas (used by the Head-quarters column on the 15th and by Hill's column on the 16th[1])—the whole army came in by successive masses on to the two neighbouring towns of Villarcayo and Medina de Pomar. At the latter place Longa turned up with his hard-marching Cantabrian division, and joined the army. These considerable towns are the road-centres of the whole rugged district between the Ebro and the Cantabrian mountains.

---

[1] Some of Hill's troops used the bridge of Rampalares also, a few miles west of Puente Arenas.

From them fork out the very few decent roads which exist in the land—those northward over the great sierras to Santander, Santoña, and Valmaseda–Bilbao : those eastward across their foot-hills to Orduña–Vittoria and to Frias–Miranda.   These five roads are the only ones practicable for artillery and transport : there are, however, minor tracks which can take infantry in good summer weather.

From his head-quarters at Quintana, near the bridge of Puente Arenas, Wellington dictated on the 15th the marching orders which governed the next stage of the campaign.   With the exception of the Galicians, already starting on their circular sweep towards Bilbao, all his columns were directed to utilize the road parallel to the Ebro, but twenty miles north of it, which runs from Medina de Pomar to Osma, Orduña, and Vittoria.   He deliberately avoided employing the other high road, which runs closer to the river from Medina de Pomar to Frias and Miranda, even for a side-column or a flying corps : only cavalry scouts were sent along it.   The reason why the whole army was thrown on to a single road—a thing generally to be avoided, especially when time is precious—was partly that the appearance of British troops before Frias, where the enemy was known to have a detachment, would give him early warning of the move.   But the more important object was to strike at the French line of communication with Bayonne as far behind the known position of King Joseph's army as possible.   If the line Frias–Miranda had been chosen, the enemy would have had many miles less to march, when once the alarm was given, if he wished to cover his proper line of retreat.   If a fight was coming, it had better be at or about Vittoria, rather than at or about Miranda.   Moreover, the high road, for a few miles east of Frias, passes to the south bank of the Ebro, which it recrosses at the Puente Lara—there is only a bad track north of the river from Frias to that bridge.   It would be absurd to direct any part of the army to cross and recross the Ebro at passages which might be defended.

So the whole force was committed to the Medina–Osma road, except that the infantry occasionally took cross-cuts by local tracks, in order to leave the all-important main line, as far as possible, to the guns and transport.   The three corps in which the army had marched from the Pisuerga fell in behind each other, in the order in which they had crossed the Ebro—Graham leading—the Head-Quarters column following—Hill bringing up the rear. Longa's Cantabrians went on as a sort of flying vanguard in front of Graham, not being burdened with artillery[1]. The road was one which could only have been used for such a large force in summer—it hugged the foot-hills of the Cantabrian sierras, crossing successively the head-waters of several small rivers running south to the Ebro, each in its own valley. The country was thinly peopled and bare, so that little food could be got to supplement the mule-borne rations. For this reason, as also with the object of granting the French as little time as possible after the first alarm should be given, the pace had to be forced. The marches were long : on the 15th the head of Graham's infantry was at Villarcayo : on the 16th at La Cerca (five miles beyond Medina de Pomar) : on the 17th at the mountain villages of San Martin de Loza and Lastres de Teza: on the 18th it was due at Osma and at Berberena—a few miles up the Osma–Orduña road. The Head-Quarters column having no exploration to do, since the way was reported clear in front, covered the same distance in three marches instead of four, and was expected to reach the neighbourhood of Osma on the 18th. Hill's column had also to hurry—its leading division was on that same day expected to be at Venta de Membligo, a posting station six miles short of Osma, so that its head would be just behind the tail of the preceding corps. But Hill's rear would be strung out for many miles behind. However, all the fighting army was again in one mass—with a single exception. Wellington had ordered the 6th division, commanded temporarily by his own brother-in-law Pakenham, to halt at Medina de Pomar. The reason which he gives in his dispatch [2] for depriving himself, now that the day of crisis was at hand, of a good division of 7,000 men, is that he left it ' to cover the march of our magazines and stores.' This is almost as puzzling a business as his leaving of Colville's corps at Hal on the day of the battle of Waterloo— the only similar incident in the long record of his campaigns.

---

[1] But did not follow the main road to Osma, going off by a by-path north of the sierras to Orduña.

[2] *Dispatches*, x. p. 450.

If this was his sole reason, why should not a smaller unit—Pack's or Bradford's independent brigade—or both of them—have been left behind ? For that purpose such a force would have sufficed. We are not informed that the 6th Division was more afflicted with sickness than any other, or that it was more way-worn. The only supposition that suggests itself is that Wellington may have considered the possibility of Giron's raid into Biscay failing, and bringing down on his rear some unsuspected mass of French troops from Bilbao. If this idea entered his head, he may easily have thought it worth while to leave behind a solid reserve, on which Giron might fall back, and so to cover the rear of his main army while he was striking at the great road to France. But it must be confessed that this is a mere hypothesis, and that the detachment of Pakenham's division seems inexplicable from the information before us. It was ordered to follow when the whole of the transport should be clear, if no further developments had happened to complicate the situation. Carrying out this direction literally, Pakenham waited three days at Medina de Pomar, and so only got to the front twenty-four hours after the battle of Vittoria.[1]

The orders which Wellington issued upon the 17th[2] brought the head of his columns into touch with the enemy. They directed that Graham, with the 1st and 5th Division, Pack and Bradford, should move past Osma on to Orduña, by the two alternative routes available between those places, while the Head-Quarters column should not turn north toward Orduña on reaching Osma, but pursue the roads south-eastward by Espejo and Carcamo, which lead to Vittoria by a more southerly line. The result contemplated was very much that which was worked out in the battle of the 21st—a frontal attack by the main body, with an outflanking move by Graham's corps, which would bring it into the rear of the enemy. But the

[1] Pakenham's *Private Correspondence* (ed. Lord Longford, 1914) gives no help. He only writes on June 24th, ' Lord W. left me to protect his rear : I executed my duty, but have lost my laurel. . . . I have satisfied myself, and I hope my master ' (p. 211).

[2] In *Supplementary Dispatches*, vii. the two papers on pp. 641 and 644 should be read together, the first giving the moves for Graham and the Light and 4th Divisions, the second for Hill and the 3rd and 7th Divisions.

route via Orduña was not the one which the northern column was actually destined to take, as the events of the 18th distracted it into a shorter but rougher road to the same destination (Murguia), which it would have reached by a much longer turn on the high road via Orduña.

But all the columns were not moving on the main track from Medina de Pomar to Osma this day, for Wellington had directed the Light Division to drop its artillery to the care of the 4th Division, and cut across the hills south of the high road, by a country path which goes by La Boveda, San Millan, and Villanan to a point, a few miles south of Osma, in the same valley of the Omecillo in which that town lies. And Hill, still far to the rear, was told to detach two brigades of the 2nd Division, and send them to follow the Light Division along the same line : if Alten should send back word that the route was practicable for guns, Hill was to attach his Portuguese field battery to this advance-column.

It was, apparently, on the morning of the 17th June only that the French got definite indications of the direction in which the British army might be looked for. Maucune reported from Frias, not long after his arrival there, that hostile cavalry were across the Ebro in the direction of Puente Arenas, and that other troops in uncertain strength were behind them. It was clearly necessary to take new measures, in view of the fact that the enemy was beyond the Ebro, in a place where he had not been expected. How much did the move imply ? After consideration Joseph and Jourdan concluded, quite correctly, that since the main body of Wellington's army had been invisible for so many days—it had last been seen on the Hormaza on June 12th—it was probably continuing its old policy of circular marches to turn the French right. This was correct, but they credited Wellington with intending to get round them not by the shorter routes Osma–Vittoria, but by the much longer route by Valmaseda and Bilbao, which would cut into the high road to France at Bergara, far behind Vittoria.

With this idea in their heads the King and the Marshal issued orders of a lamentably unpractical scope, considering the position occupied by Wellington's leading divisions on June 17th. Reille was ordered to collect his three infantry divisions at

Osma, and to hurry across the mountains by Valmaseda, to cover Bilbao from the west, by taking up a position somewhere about Miravalles. He would find the Biscayan capital already held by St. Pol's Italians, and Rouget's brigade of the Army of the North. Foy, who was believed to be at Tolosa, was instructed to bring up his division to the same point. Thus a force of some 25,000 men would be collected at Bilbao. Meanwhile Reille's original positions at Frias and the Puente Lara would be taken over by Gazan, who would march up the Ebro from Arminion with two divisions of infantry and one of cavalry, to watch the north bank of the Ebro. 'These dispositions,' remarks Jourdan, 'were intended to retard the advance of the enemy in this mountainous region, and so to gain time for the arrival of the reinforcements we were expecting [i. e. Clausel]. But it was too late ![1]'

No worse orders could have been given. If Wellington had struck twenty-four hours later than he did, and Reille had been able to carry out his first day's appointed move, and to get forward towards Bilbao, the result would have been to split the French army in two, with the main range of the Cantabrian sierras between them : since Reille and Foy would have joined at Bilbao—three days' forced marches away from the King. Meanwhile Joseph, deprived of the whole Army of Portugal, would have had Wellington striking in on his flank by Osma, and would have been forced to fight something resembling the battle of Vittoria with 10,000 men less in hand than he actually owned on June 21. Either he would have suffered an even worse defeat than was his lot at Vittoria, or he would have been compelled to retreat without fighting, down the Ebro, or towards Pampeluna. In either case he would have lost the line of communication with France ; and while he was driven far east, Foy and Reille would have had to hurry back on Bayonne, with some risk of being intercepted and cut off on the way.

As a matter of fact, Reille was checked and turned back upon the first day of his northward march. He had sent orders to Maucune to join him from Frias, either by the road along the Ebro by Puente Lara, or by the mountain track which

---

[1] Jourdan, *Mémoires*, p. 472.

goes directly from Frias to Espejo. Then, without waiting for
Maucune, he started from Espejo to march on Osma. He had
gone only a few miles when he discovered a British column
debouching on Osma, by the road from Berberena [1] and the
north-west, which he had been intending to take himself.
Seeing his path blocked, but being loth to give way before
what might be no more than a detachment, he drew up his
two divisions on the hillside a mile south of Osma and appeared
ready to offer battle. Moreover, he was expecting the arrival
of Maucune, and judged that if he made off without delaying
the enemy in front of him, the column from Frias might be
intercepted and encircled.

The troops which Reille had met were Graham's main column
—the 1st and 5th divisions with Bradford's Portuguese and
Anson's Light Dragoons, on their march towards Orduña.
Graham prepared to attack, sent forward the German Legion
light battalions of the 1st Division, and pushed out Norman
Ramsay's horse artillery, with a cavalry escort, to the right of
Osma, forming the rest of his force for a general advance
across the Bilbao road. After estimating the strength of the
British, Reille appeared at first inclined to fight, or at least to
show an intention of fighting. But a new enemy suddenly
came up—the 4th Division appeared on a side road, descending
from the hills on the right of Graham's line. It had just time
to throw out its light companies to skirmish [2] when Reille, seeing
himself obviously outnumbered and outflanked, retreated
hastily on Espejo; the 5th Division followed him on the left,
with some tiraillade, the 4th Division on the right, but he was
not caught. 'Considerable fire on both sides but little done,'
remarked an observer on the hillside [3]. Reille's loss was
probably about 120 men, nearly all in Sarrut's division [4] : that
of the British some 50 or 60.

Meanwhile there had been a much more lively fight, with
heavier casualties, a few miles farther south among the moun-

---

[1] Not Barbacena as in Napier : the latter place is in Portugal.
[2] They lost 1 officer and 1 man wounded only.
[3] Tomkinson's *Diary*, p. 242.
[4] At least Martinien's lists show one officer killed and five wounded—
all but one in Sarrut's regiments—which at the usual rate would mean
120 casualties.

tains nearer the Ebro. Maucune had started before dawn from
Frias, intending to join Reille by a short cut through the hills,
instead of sticking to the better road along the river-bank by
the Puente Lara. He only sent his guns with a cavalry escort
by that route. He was marching with his two brigades at a
considerable distance from each other, the rear one being
hampered by the charge of the divisional transport and baggage.

The leading brigade had reached the hamlet of San Millan
and was resting there by a brook, when British cavalry scouts
came in upon them—these were German Legion Hussars, at
the head of the Light Division, which Wellington had sent by
the cross-path over the hills by La Boveda. The approaching
column had been marching along a narrow road, shrouded
by overhanging rocks and high banks, in which it could neither
see nor be seen. On getting the alarm the four French battalions
formed up to fight, in the small open space about the village,
while the head of the British column, Vandaleur's brigade,
deployed as fast as it could opposite them, and attacked ; the
2 /95th and 3rd Caçadores in front line, the 52nd in support.
Maucune was forced to make a stand, because his rear brigade
was coming up, unseen by his enemies, and would have been
cut off from him if he had retreated at once. But when the head
of Kempt's brigade of the Light Division appeared, and began
to deploy to the left of Vandaleur's, he saw that he was outnumbered, and gave ground perforce. He had been driven
through the village, and was making off along the road, with
the Rifle battalions in hot pursuit, when his second brigade,
with the baggage in its rear, came on the scene—most unexpected by the British, for the track by which it emerged issued
out between two perpendicular rocks and had not been noticed.
Perceiving the trap into which they had fallen, the belated
French turned off the road, and made for the hillside to their
right, while Kempt's brigade started in pursuit, scrambling
over the rocky slopes to catch them up. The line of flight
of the French took them past the ground over which Vandaleur's men were chasing their comrades of the leading brigade,
and the odd result followed that they came in upon the rear
of the 52nd, and, though pursued, seemed to be themselves
pursuing. The Oxfordshire battalion thereupon performed the

extraordinary feat of bringing up its left shoulder, forming line facing to the rear at a run, and charging backward. They encountered the enemy at the top of a slope, but the French, seeing themselves between two fires, for Kempt's men were following hotly behind them, avoided the collision, struck off diagonally, and scattering and throwing away their packs went off in disorder eastward, still keeping up a running fight. The large majority escaped, and joined Gazan's troops at Miranda. Meanwhile the first brigade, pursued by the Rifles and Caçadores, got away in much better order, and reached Reille's main body at Espejo. The transport which had come out of the narrow road too late to follow the regiments, was captured whole, after a desperate resistance by the baggage-guard. Maucune got off easily, all things considered, with the loss of three hundred prisoners, many of them wounded, and all his impedimenta[1]. The fight was no discredit to the general or to his men, who saved themselves by presence of mind, when caught at every disadvantage—inferior troops would have laid down their arms *en masse* when they found themselves between two fires in rough and unknown ground[2]. The total British loss in the two simultaneous combats of Osma and San Millan was 27 killed and 153 wounded.

Reille, having picked up Maucune's first brigade at Espejo, continued his retreat, and got behind the Bayas river at Subijana that night. The report which he had to send to head-quarters upset all the plans of Jourdan and the King, and forced them to reconsider their position, which was obviously most uncomfortable, as their line of defence along the Ebro was taken in flank, and the proposed succour to Bilbao made impossible. At least four British divisions had been detected by Reille, but where were the rest, and where

[1] Most of these details are from the excellent account by an officer of the 43rd in Maxwell's *Peninsular Sketches*, ii. pp. 39–40. This narrative was evidently seen by Napier, who reproduces many of its actual words, as I have done myself. It must have been lent him long before it was printed in 1845.

[2] Martinien's lists show only 1 officer killed and 5 wounded this day in Maucune's division—this means about 120–50 casualties, but of course does not include the unwounded prisoners from the baggage-guard. Jourdan says that the division had ' une perte assez considérable.'

were the Spaniards, who were known to be in some strength
with Wellington ? Was the whole Allied host behind the force
which had driven in the Army of Portugal, or was there some
great unseen column executing some further inscrutable
movement ?

There was hot discussion at Miranda that night. Reille
repeated the proposition which had already been made at
Burgos six days back, that in consideration of the fact that
the army was hopelessly outflanked, and that its retreat by the
high road to Vittoria and Bayonne was threatened by the
presence of Wellington on the Bayas, it should abandon that
line of communication altogether, march down the Ebro, and
take up the line of Pampeluna and Saragossa, rallying Clausel
and, if possible, Suchet, for a general concentration, by which
the British army could be driven back as it had been from
Burgos in 1812. Foy and the Biscay garrisons would have to
take care of themselves—it was unlikely that Wellington would
be able to fall upon them, when the whole of the rest of the
French armies of Spain were on his flank, and taking the
offensive against him.

Joseph, for the third time, refused to consider this scheme,
alleging, as before, the Emperor's strict orders to keep to the
Bayonne base, and to hold on to the great royal *chaussée*. But,
as is clear, his refusal was affected by another consideration
which in his eyes had almost equally decisive weight. Vittoria
was crammed with the great convoys of French and Spanish
refugees which had accumulated there, along with all the
plunder of Madrid, and the military material representing the
' grand train ' of the whole army of Spain—not to speak of
his own immense private baggage. There had also arrived,
within the last few days, a large consignment of hard cash—the
belated arrears of the allowance which the Emperor had
consented to give to the Army of Spain. One of Foy's brigades
had escorted these fourgons of treasure to Vittoria, and dropped
them there, returning to Bergara with a section of the refugees
in charge, to be passed on to Bayonne.[1] The amount delivered
was not less than five million francs—bitterly needed by the
troops, who were in long arrears. All this accumulation at

[1] See *Vie militaire du Général Foy*, pp. 206–7.

Vittoria was in large measure due to the King's reluctance during the retreat to order a general shift of all his officials and impedimenta over the border into France. As long as his ministers, and all the plant of royalty, remained on the south side of the Pyrenees, he still seemed a king. And he had hoped to maintain himself first on the Douro, then about Burgos, then on the Ebro. It was only when this last line was forced that he made up his mind to surrender his theoretical status, and think of military considerations alone. The lateness of his decision was to prove most fatal to his adherents.

Having resolved to order a general retreat on Vittoria, Joseph and Jourdan took such precautions as seemed possible. Reiterated orders for haste were sent to Foy and Clausel : the latter was told to march on Vittoria not on Miranda. Unfortunately he had received the dispatch sent from Burgos on June 15th, which gave him Miranda as the concentration-point, and had already gathered his divisions at Pampeluna on June 18, and started to march by Estella and Logroño and along the north bank of the Ebro. This gave him two sides of a triangle to cover, while if he had been assigned the route Pampeluna–Salvatierra–Vittoria, he would have been saved eighty miles of road. But on June 9th, when the original orders were issued, no one could have foreseen, save Wellington, that the critical day of the campaign would have found the French army far north of the Ebro. And the new dispatch, sent off on the night of the 18th–19th, started far too late to reach Pampeluna in time to stop Clausel's departure southward. Indeed, it did not catch him up till the battle of Vittoria had been fought, and the King was a fugitive on the way to France. Foy received orders a little earlier, though not apparently those sent directly by the King, but a copy of a dispatch to Thouvenot, governor of Vittoria, in which the latter was instructed ' that if General Foy and his division are in your neighbourhood, you are to bid him give up his march on Bilbao, and draw in towards Vittoria, unless his presence is absolutely necessary at the point where he may be at present [1].' This unhappy piece of

[1] *Vie militaire du Général Foy*, p. 206. The editor, Girod de l'Ain, seems to prove that Foy got no other dispatch, though Jourdan declares that several had been sent to him.

wording gave Foy a choice, which he interpreted as authorizing him to remain at Bergara, so as to cover the high road to France, a task which he held to be ' absolutely necessary.'

As to the troops already on the spot, Reille was ordered to defend the line of the Bayas river, until the armies of the South and Centre should have had time to get past his rear and reach Vittoria. Gazan was ordered to collect the whole of the Army of the South at Arminion, behind Miranda, drawing in at once the considerable detachment which he had left beyond the Ebro. In this position he was to wait till D'Erlon, with the Army of the Centre, who had to move up from Haro, ten miles to the south, should have arrived and have got on to the great *chaussée*. He was then to follow him, acting as rearguard of the whole force. Between Arminion and Vittoria the road passes for two miles through the very narrow defile of Puebla, the bottle-neck through which the Zadorra river cuts its way from the upland plain of Vittoria to the lower level of the Ebro valley.

D'Erlon, starting at dawn from Haro, reached Arminion at 10 o'clock in the morning of the 19th, and pushed up the defile : the head of his column was just emerging from its northern end when a heavy cannonade began to be heard in the west. It continued all the time that the Army of the South was pressing up the defile, and grew nearer. This, of course, marked the approach of Wellington, driving the covering force under Reille before him toward the Zadorra. The British commander-in-chief had slept the night at Berberena near Osma, and had there drafted a set of orders which considerably modified his original scheme : probably the change was due to topographical information, newly garnered up from the countryside. Instead of sending Graham's column via Orduña, to cut in on the flank of the *chaussée* behind Vittoria, he had resolved to send it by a shorter route, a mere country road which goes by Luna, Santa Eulalia, and Jocano to Murguia—the village which it had been ordered on the previous day to reach via Orduña and the high road. Presumably it had been discovered that this would save time,—the advantage of using a first-rate track being more than counterbalanced by the fact that the Orduña road was not only ten miles longer but crossed and recrossed by steep slopes the main sierra, which forms the watershed between Biscay and Alava. Or possibly it was only the discovery that the Luna–Jocano route could be taken by artillery that settled the matter : if it had been reported useless for wheeled traffic the old orders might have stood. At any rate, the turning movement, which was to take Graham into the rear of Vittoria, was made south of the main mountain chain, and not north of it [1].

Meanwhile, though Graham diverged north-eastward, the rest of the Army moved straight forward from the valley of the Omecillo to that of the Bayas in four columns, all parallel to each other, and all moving by country roads. The 3rd Division was ordered from Berberena to Carcamo—the 7th followed behind it. The 4th Division with D'Urban's cavalry in front, and the Light Division with V. Alten's hussars in front, were directed on Subijana and Pobes, keeping in close and constant communication with each other. Behind them came the cavalry reserve—R. Hill's, Grant's, and Ponsonby's brigades—also the heavy artillery. Hill's column, which had now come up into touch with the leading divisions, kept to the high road from Osma and Espejo towards the Puente Lara and the Ebro. But only cavalry reconnaissances went as far as the river—the mass of the corps turned off eastward when it had passed Espejo, and moved by Salinas de Anaña, so as to come out into the valley of the Bayas south of the route of the Light Division. It thus became the right wing of the army which was deploying for the frontal attack.

It has been mentioned above that a local Spanish force from the Cantabrian mountains had joined Wellington at Medina de Pomar ; this was the so-called 'division', some 3,500 bayonets, of the great guerrillero of the coast-land, Longa, now no more an irregular but a titular colonel, while his *partida* had been reorganized as four battalions of light infantry. Longa was a tough and persistent fighter—a case of the 'survival

---

[1] It would appear, however, that though the 1st and 5th Divisions and Anson's cavalry never went near Orduña, yet Bradford and Pack's Portuguese (without artillery) had got so near it on the preceding day that Wellington let them go through it, bringing them back to the main body via Unza by a mountain path. See *Supplementary Dispatches*, vii. p. 647.

of the fittest ' among many insurgent chiefs who had perished. His men were veteran mountaineers, indefatigable marchers, and skilled skirmishers, if rudimentary in their drill and equipment. Wellington during the ensuing campaign gave more work to them than to any other Spanish troops that were at his disposal—save the Estremaduran division of Morillo, old comrades of Hill's corps, to which they had always been attached since 1811. The use which Wellington now made of Longa's men was to employ them as a light covering shield for Graham's turning force. They had been sent across the hills from Quincoces [1] on the 17th to occupy Orduña—from thence they descended on the 19th on to Murguia, thus placing themselves at the head of the turning column. The object of the arrangement was that, if the enemy should detect the column, he would imagine it to be a Spanish demonstration, and not suspect that a heavy British force lay hid behind the familiar guerrilleros. While Longa was thus brought in sideways, to form the head of Graham's column, the other Spanish force which Wellington was employing was also deflected to join the main army. Giron's Galicians, as has been mentioned above, had been sent by a long sweep through the sierras to demonstrate against Bilbao. They had reached Valmaseda on the 18th, and their approach had alarmed all the French garrisons of Biscay. Now, having put themselves in evidence in the north, they were suddenly recalled, ordered to march by Amurrio on Orduña and Murguia, and so to fall into the rear of Graham's column. The distances were considerable, the roads steep, and Giron only came up with the Anglo-Portuguese army on the afternoon of the battle of Vittoria, in which (unlike Longa) he was too late to take any part. Somewhere on his march from Aguilar to Valmaseda he picked up a reinforcement, the very small Asturian division of Porlier—three battalions or 2,400 men—which Mendizabal had sent to join him from the blockade of Santoña. This raised the Galician Army to a total of some 14,000 bayonets.

The 19th June was a very critical day, as no one knew better than Wellington. The problem was whether, starting with the heads of his column facing the line of the Bayas, where Reille

---

[1] Probably by Angulo, and the valley of the Gordajuela.

had rallied his three divisions and was standing at bay, he could drive in the detaining force, and cross the Zadorra in pursuit of it, fast enough to surprise some part of the French army still in its march up from the south. And, as an equally important problem, there was the question whether Graham, marching on Murguia, could reach the upper Zadorra and cut the great road north of Vittoria, before the French were in position to cover it. If these operations could be carried out, there would be a scrambling fight scattered over much ground, rather than a regular pitched battle. If they could not, there would be a formal general action on the 20th or 21st against an enemy established in position—unless indeed King Joseph should choose to continue his retreat without fighting, which Wellington thought quite possible [1].

Wellington is censured by some critics, including Napier [2], for not making a swifter advance on the 19th. It is said that a little more haste would have enabled him to get to Vittoria as soon as the enemy, and to force him to fight in dislocated disorder on ground which he had not chosen. This seems unjustifiable. The distance between the camps of the Allied Army, in front of Osma and Espejo, and Vittoria is some twenty miles—difficult ground, with the Bayas river flowing through the midst of it and a formidable position held by 15,000 French behind that stream. As Reille, conscious how much depended on his gaining time for the King to retreat from Miranda, was determined to detain the Allied Army as long as he could, it would have been useless to try to drive him away by a light attack. The rear of each of Wellington's columns was trailing many miles behind the leading brigade. It was necessary to bring up against Reille a force sufficient to make serious resistance impossible, and this Wellington did, pushing forward not only the 4th and Light Divisions, but Hill's column in support, on the southern flank. It took time to get them deployed, and the attack was opened by a cannonade. By the time that a general advance was ordered Reille had begun to retire—he did so very neatly, and crossed the Zadorra by the

---

[1] He says so in his letter to the Conde d'Abispal, *Dispatches*, x. pp. 445–6.
' Je les attaquerai demain, *s'ils ne font pas la retraite dans la nuit*.'
[2] Napier, v. p. 114.

four nearest bridges without any appreciable loss. By this
time the afternoon had arrived, the rest of the French army
had passed the defile of Puebla, and Wellington judged the
hour too late for the commencement of a pitched battle [1].
Moreover, he did not intend to fight without the co-operation
of Graham's column, and the latter was not where he would
have wished it to be. The day had been very rainy, the cross
roads were bad, and by some error of staff-work the head of
the column had not received the counter-marching orders
directing it to march direct on Murguia, but had started in
accordance with the earlier plan on to the Orduña road ; the
1st and 5th Divisions had gone some way upon it before they
were recalled and counter-marched into the right path [2].
Owing to blocks and bad weather they only reached Jocano,
some six or eight miles east of Osma, by six in the evening.
Murguia was still nine miles ahead, the rain was still falling in
torrents, and Graham ordered the divisions to halt and encamp
for the night. The fate of the campaign was not to be fought
out that day, nor on the next, but on the third morning—that
of June 21st, 1813.

    [1] There is a good account of the skirmish on the Bayas in Wachholz,
p. 314. He remarks on the abominable weather, ' incredible for the time
of year—continuous unbearable cold and rain—the sun visible only for
short intervals. Very bad roads.'
    [2] For all this see Tomkinson's *Diary*, p. 243. His statement that the
column went off on the Orduña road by *mistake* and was at once set right,
seems to me conclusive against Napier's views.

SECTION XXXVI : CHAPTER VII

THE BATTLE OF VITTORIA. JUNE 21, 1813

(A) THE FIRST STAGE

THE plain of Vittoria, into which the French army debouched on the afternoon of June 19th, is a plain only by comparison with the high hills which surround it on all sides, being an oval expanse of rolling ground drained by the swift and narrow Zadorra river, which runs on its north-eastern side. Only in its northern section, near the city, does it show really flat ground. It is about twelve miles long from north-east to south-west, and varies from six to eight miles in breadth. The Zadorra is one of those mountain streams which twist in numberless loops and bends of alternate shallows and deep pools, in order to get round rocks or spurs which stand in the way of their direct course [1]. At one point seven miles down-stream from Vittoria it indulges in a complete 'hairpin-bend' in which are the bridges of Tres Puentes and Villodas, as it circles round a precipitous knoll. At several other spots it executes minor loops in its tortuous course. The little city of Vittoria stands on an isolated rising ground at its northern end, very visible from all directions, and dominating the whole upland with two prominent church spires at its highest point. The great road from France enters the plain of Vittoria and the valley of the Zadorra three miles north-east of the city, descending from the defile of Salinas, a long and difficult pass in which Mina and other guerrilleros had executed some of their most daring raids on French convoys. After passing Vittoria the road keeps to the middle of the upland in a westerly direction, and issues from it by the defile of La Puebla, where the Zadorra cuts its way through the Sierra de Andia in order to join the Ebro. There is not much more than room for road and river in the gorge, which is dominated by the heights of La Puebla, a spur of the

---

[1] An English eye-witness calls it 'nowhere fordable': a French eye-witness 'fordable everywhere'; both are wrong. Cf. Fortescue, ix. p. 152.

Andia, on the east, and by a corresponding but lower range, the end of the heights of Morillas on the west.

But the Bayonne *chaussée* is by no means the only road in the Vittoria upland. The city is the meeting point of a number of second-class and third-class routes, debouching from various subsidiary valleys of the Pyrenees and leading to various towns in Navarre or Biscay. Of these the chief were (1) the Salvatierra–Pampeluna road, running due east, and then crossing from the valley of the Zadorra to the upper waters of the Araquil, by which it descends into Navarre. This was a route practicable for artillery or transport, but narrow, ill repaired, and steep—eminently not a line to be taken by a large force in a hurry; (2) the main road to Bilbao by Villareal and Durango, a coach road, but very tortuous, and ascending high mountains by long curves and twists; (3) the alternative coach route to Bilbao by Murguia and Orduña, easier than the Villareal road in its first section, but forced to cross the main chain of the Pyrenees by difficult gradients before descending into Biscay; (4) a bad side road to the central Ebro, going due south by Trevino and La Guardia to Logroño; (5) a similar route, running due east from Subijana on the Bayas to the bridges of Nanclares three miles up-stream from the defile of Puebla. At the opening of the battle of Vittoria Graham's column was already across the Murguia–Bilbao road, and in its earliest advance blocked the Durango–Bilbao road also. Thus the only route beside the great *chaussée* available for the French was that to Salvatierra and Pampeluna. The road to Trevino and Logroño was useless, as leading in an undesired direction.

In addition to these five coach roads there were several country tracks running from various points on the Bayas river to minor bridges on the Zadorra, across the lofty Monte Arrato, the watershed between the two streams. It was these fifth-rate tracks which Wellington used on the battle-day for the advance of some of his central columns, while Hill on the right was forcing the defile of La Puebla, and Graham on the left was descending from Murguia on to the bridges of the upper Zadorra north-east of Vittoria.

Having their troops safely concentrated east of the Zadorra on the evening of June 19, Joseph and Jourdan made up their

minds to stand on the position behind that river, even though
Clausel had not yet come up, nor sent any intelligence as to the
route by which he was arriving. Aides-de-camp were searching
for him in all directions—but nothing had yet been ascertained,
beyond the fact that he had started from Pampeluna on
June 15th, marching on Logroño [1]. There was a high chance
that some one of many missives would reach him, and turn him
on to Vittoria. But the idea that Clausel must now be very
near at hand was less operative in compelling Joseph to fight
than the idea that he must at all cost save the vast convoys
accumulated around him, his treasure, his military train, his
ministers, and his refugees. He was getting them off northward by the high road as fast as he could : one convoy marched
on the 20th, under the charge of the troops of the Army of the
North who had formed the garrison of Vittoria, another and
a larger at dawn on the 21st, escorted by the whole of Maucune's
division. It had with it many of the Old Masters stolen from
the royal palace at Madrid—the pictures of Titian, Rafael, and
Velasquez, which had been the pride of the old dynasty—with
the pick of the royal armoury and cabinet of Natural History [2].
It is almost as difficult to make out how Joseph, already unequal
in numbers to his enemy, dared to deprive himself of Maucune's
division of the Army of Portugal, as to discover why Wellington
left the 6th Division at Medina de Pomar. It does not seem
that the morale of the unit had been shaken by its rude experience at San Millan on the 18th, for it fought excellently in
subsequent operations : nor had it suffered any disabling losses
in that fight. A more obvious escort might have been found in
Casapalacios' Spanish auxiliaries, who had already been utilized
for similar purposes between Madrid and Vittoria, or in the
scraps of the Army of the North which had lately joined the
retreating host. But they remained for the battle, while
Maucune marched north, with the cannon sounding behind
him all day.

When Jourdan and Joseph first arrayed their host for the
expected battle, it would seem, from the line which they took
up, that they imagined that Wellington would attack them
only from the direction of the Bayas, and paid no attention to

---

[1] Jourdan's *Mémoires*, p. 474.   [2] See Toreno, iii. pp. 233–6.

Graham's flanking movement, though afterwards they wrote
dispatches to prove that they had not ignored it. For they
drew up the Army of the South on a short front, from the exit
of the defile of Puebla on the south to the bridge of Villodas on
the north, a front of three miles, with D'Erlon's two divisions in
second line on each side of the village of Gomecha, two miles
farther back, and the Army of Portugal and the King's Guards
as a third line in reserve about Zuazo, not far in front of Vittoria,
along with the bulk of the cavalry. This order of battle, as
a glance at the map shows, presupposed a frontal attack from
the line of the Bayas, where Wellington was known to be. It
was ill-suited to face an attack from the north-west on the line
of the Zadorra above Villodas, and still more so an attack from
the due north by the roads from Orduña and Murguia. On the
morning of the 20th cavalry reconnaissances went out to look
for the Allied Army—they reported that the camps along the
Bayas above Subijana Morillos did not seem very large, and
that on the Murguia road they had fallen in with and pushed
back Longa's irregulars, obviously a Spanish demonstration [1].
' No indication being available of the details of a projected
attack, and further information being unprocurable, only conjectures could be made [2].'

It is interesting to know from the narrative of Jourdan
himself what these conjectures were. ' Wellington,' he writes,
' had shown himself since the start of the campaign more disposed to manœuvre his opponents out of their positions, by
constantly turning their right wing, than to attack them
frontally and force on a battle. It was thought probable that,
pursuing this system, he would march on Bilbao by Orduña, and
from thence on Durango, so as to force them to fall back
promptly on Mondragon [3], in order to retain their communications with France. He might even hope to force them to
evacuate Spain by this move, because it would be impossible to
feed a great army on that section of the Pyrenees. The King,

[1] There is an account of this skirmish in Digeon's report, and in Hay's
Reminiscences under Wellington, pp. 107–8.

[2] Jourdan, p. 473.

[3] The fortified position north of the defile of Salinas, where the road
from Bilbao to France joins the great *chaussée*.

knowing that Clausel was on the move, had little fear of the results of a march on Bilbao, for on receiving Clausel's corps he would be strong enough to take the offensive himself, and would strike at Wellington's communications. It did not escape him that if the enemy, instead of wasting more time on flank movements, should attack him before the arrival of Clausel, he was in a perilous position. For there was little chance of getting the better of an adversary who had about double numbers, and a lost battle would cut off the army from the road to France, and force it to retire on Pampeluna by a road difficult, if not impracticable, for the train and artillery of a great host. To avoid the risk of an instant attack from Wellington, ought we to fall back and take up the position above the pass of Salinas ? [1] But to do this was to sacrifice the junction with Clausel, who was expected on the 21st at latest. And how could the army have been fed in the passes ? The greater part of the cavalry and the artillery horses would have had to be sent back to France at once—famine would have forced the infantry to follow. Then the King would have been accused of cowardice, for evacuating Spain without trying the fortune of battle. To justify such a retreat we should have had to be *certain* that we were to be attacked before the 22nd, and we considered that, if Wellington did decide to fight, it would be unlikely that he could do so before the 22nd, because of the difficulty of the roads which he had taken. After mature consideration of the circumstance the King resolved to stand fast at Vittoria.'

Putting aside the gross over-estimate of Wellington's strength —he fought with a superiority of 75,000[2] to 57,000, not with two to one—the main point to note in this curious and interesting argument is its defective psychology. Because Wellington had hitherto avoided frontal attacks, when flank movements suited him better, was it safe to conclude that he would do so *ad infinitum* ? That he was capable of a sudden onslaught was obvious to every one who remembered the battle of Salamanca. Why, if he were about to repeat his previous encircling policy, should he go by Orduña, Bilbao, and Durango, rather than by

---

[1] i. e. the position above the northern exit from the plain of Vittoria.
[2] Not counting Pakenham and Givon, but including Longa and Morillo.

the shorter turn Osma–Murguia–Vittoria ?   Apparently the French staff underrated the possibilities of that road, and took the presence of Longa upon it as a sign that it was only to be used for a Spanish demonstration [1]. Should not the speed with which Wellington had traversed the detestable country paths between the Arlanzon and the Ebro have served as a warning that, if he chose to push hard, he could cover at a very rapid rate the rather less formidable tracks north of the Zadorra ? In short, the old marshal committed the not uncommon fault of making false deductions from an imperfect set of premises.   It is much more difficult to say what should have been his actual course under the existing circumstances of June 20. Napier holds that he might still have adopted Reille's old plan of June 12 and June 18, i.e. that he should have thrown up the line of communication with France by the high road, have made ready to retreat on Pampeluna instead of on Bayonne, and have looked forward to making Saragossa his base.   After having picked up first Clausel and then so much of the Army of Aragon as could be collected, he might have got 100,000 men together and have started an offensive campaign [2]. This over-looks the impossibility of getting the convoys and train safely along the bad road from Vittoria to Pampeluna, and the difficulty of making Saragossa, where there were no great accumulations of stores and munitions, the base of an army of the size projected. All communication with France would have been thrown on the hopelessly long and circuitous route from Saragossa to Perpignan, for the pass by Jaca was impracticable for wheeled traffic. Certainly Joseph would have had to destroy, as a preliminary measure to a retreat via Salvatierra or Pampe-luna, the greater part of his train.   And what would have become of his wretched horde of refugees ?

Another school of critics—among them Belmas—urge that while it was perfectly correct to cling as a primary necessity to the great road to France, Vittoria was not the right point at which to defend it, but the pass of Salinas. Jourdan's objection that the cavalry would be useless in the mountains is declared

---

[1] Digeon in his report insists that he thought there was something more behind Longa. But this is *ex post facto* allegation.

[2] Napier, v. p. 134.

to have little weight, and his dread of famine to be groundless. For Wellington could not have remained for many days in front of the passes—he must have attacked at once a very formidable position, or Foy and the other troops in Biscay would have had time to join the King ; and with 15,000 extra bayonets the French would have been hard to dislodge. The danger to Clausel would have been not very great, since Wellington would not have dared to detach a force sufficient to crush him, while the main French army was in his front, intact and ready to resume the offensive. And on the other flank Biscay, no doubt, would have been exposèd to an invasion by Giron's Galicians, when Foy had withdrawn its garrisons to join the main army. But it is improbable that this movement would have been backed by any large section of the Anglo-Portuguese force ; for Wellington, as his previous action showed, was intending to keep all his own old divisions in one body. He would not have risked any of his own troops between the Pyrenees and the sea, by trying to thrust them in on the back of the French position, to Durango or Mondragon. And if Giron alone went to Bilbao and Durango, his presence in that direction, and any threats which he might make on the King's rear, would be tiresome rather than dangerous.

Be this as it may, whatever the general policy of Jourdan and Joseph should have been, their particular dispositions for occupying the Vittoria position were very faulty. It was as well known to every practical soldier then as it is now, that a normal river-position cannot be held by a continuous line of troops placed at the water's edge. For there will be loops and bends at which the ground on one's own side is commanded and enfiladed by higher ground on the enemy's side. If troops are pushed forward into such bends, they will be crushed by artillery fire, or run danger of being cut off by attacks on the neck of the loop in their rear [1]. Unless the general who has to defend a river front is favoured with a stream in front of him absolutely straight, and with all the commanding ground on his own side (an unusual chance), he must rather look to arranging his army in such a fashion as to hold as strong points all the favourable sections of the front, while the unfavourable

[1] Cf. events in the Nimy–Obourg Salient at Mons on August 22, 1914.

ones must be watched from suitable positions drawn back from the water's edge. By judicious disposition of artillery, the occupation and preparation of villages, woods, or other cover, and (if necessary) the throwing up of trenches, the enemy, though he cannot be prevented from crossing the river at certain points, can be kept from debouching out of the sections of the hither bank which he has mastered. And if he loads up the captured ground with heavy masses of troops which cannot get forward, he will suffer terribly from artillery fire, while if he does not hold them strongly, he will be liable to counter-attacks, which will throw the troops who have crossed back into the river. The most elementary precaution for the general on the defensive to take is, of course, to blow up all bridges, and to place artillery to command all fords, also to have local reserves ready at a proper distance behind every section where a passage is likely to be tried [1].

We may excuse Joseph and Jourdan for not entrenching all the weak sections of their front—hasty field works were little used in the Peninsular War ; indeed the trenches which Welling-ton threw up on the second day of Fuentes de Oñoro were an almost unique instance of such an expedient. But the other precautions to be taken were commonplaces of contemporary tactics. And they were entirely neglected. The front liable to attack was very long for the size of the defending army : whole sections of it were neglected. Bridges and fords were numerous on the Zadorra : incredible as it may seem, not one of eleven bridges between Durana to the north and Nanclares to the south was blown up. The numerous fords seem not to have been known accurately to either the attacking or the defending generals, but some of the most obvious of them were ignored in Joseph's original disposition of his troops. Several alike of bridges and fords were lightly watched by cavalry only, with no further precaution taken. What is most astonishing is to find that bridges which were actually used by French exploring

---

[1] The classical instance of the proper defence of a river front is (I suppose) Lee's defence of the Rappahannock at the battle of Fredericksburg. For the ruinous fate of an army which gets across at one or two points of a long front, and is counter-attacked, cf. the battle of the Katzbach, fought two months after Vittoria.

parties on June 20th, so that their existence was thoroughly realized, were found intact and in some cases unguarded on the 21st [1]. The fact would seem to be that the King's head-quarters staff was dominated by a false idea : that Wellington's attack would be delivered on the south part of the river front, from the defile of Puebla to the bridge of Villodas ; and that the troops discovered on the Murguia road were Longa's irregulars only, bound on a demonstration. An acute British observer remarked that the French position had two main defects—the more important one was that it faced the wrong way [2] : this was quite true.

The final arrangement, as taken up on the morning of June 20 was that the Army of the South arrayed itself so as to block the debouches from the defile of La Puebla and the bridges immediately up-stream from it—those of Nanclares and Villodas. Gazan did not occupy the entrance of the defile of La Puebla—to do so he must have stretched his line farther south and east than his numbers permitted. But he held its exits, with some voltigeur companies from Maransin's brigade, perched high up on the culminating ground immediately above the river.

From this lofty point on the heights of Puebla his first line stretched north-eastward along a line of low hills, past the villages of Subijana (low down and not far from the Puebla heights) and Ariñez (on the high road, at the spot where it crosses the position), a dominating point on the sky-line. The right wing nearly reached to the Zadorra at the spot where it makes the ' hairpin bend ' alluded to above. But the solid occupation by formed troops did not extend so far : there were only a cavalry regiment and three guns watching the bridge of Mendoza [3], and a single company of voltigeurs watching that of Villodas. The disposition of the units was, counting from the French left, first Maransin's brigade occupying Subijana, next Conroux's division in a single line on the slopes to the north of the village of Zumelzu, with a battalion holding a wood in front

[1] Especially the bridges of Tres Puentes and Nanclares by which a reconnaissance was made on June 20, and that of Mendoza up-stream. See Jourdan, p. 473.

[2] Blakiston's *Twelve Years of Military Adventure*, ii. p. 207.

[3] And this not belonging to the Army of the South, but to d'Erlon—Avy's 27th Chasseurs.

on lower ground. Then came Daricau's division, one brigade in front line across the high road, the other brigade (St. Pol's) in reserve north of the road, and in rear of Leval's division, which was deployed on the prominent height in front of the village of Ariñez, which formed the end of the main position. Between Leval and the Zadorra there was only Avy's few squadrons of light horse, watching the bridge of Mendoza. Nearly a mile to the rear of the main line Villatte's division stood in reserve, on the heights on the other side of Ariñez, and with it Pierre Soult's cavalry. The position was heavily gunned, as artillery support went in those days. Each of the three front-line divisions had its battery with it—a fourth belonging to Pierre Soult's cavalry was placed on a knoll in front of the position, from which it could sweep the approaches from the bridge of Nanclares. In reserve behind Ariñez was not only Villatte's battery, but two others drawn from the general artillery park, and during the early stage of the battle another pair of batteries, belonging to the Army of Portugal, were sent to join Leval's divisional guns on the north end of the position. Gazan had therefore some 54 pieces in hand, without counting the half-battery of horse artillery belonging to Digeon's dragoons, which was absent far to his extreme right, by the banks of the upper Zadorra.

Three-quarters of a mile behind Gazan's reserves, the whole Army of the Centre was deployed on each side of the high road, Darmagnac's division north of it in front of Zuazo, Cassagne's division south of it, level with Gomecha. Treillard's dragoons were behind Cassagne ; Avy's chasseurs (as has been mentioned above) were watching the Zadorra on the right.

In the original order of battle of the 20th the Army of Portugal had been in third line, a mile behind the Army of the Centre, on a level with the villages of Ali and Armentia. But when Digeon's dragoons reported in the afternoon that they had discovered Longa's column on the Murguia road, it was decided that a flank guard must be thrown out in that direction, to cover Vittoria and the high road to France from possible raids. Wherefore Reille was told that it would be his duty to provide against this danger. He took out Menne's brigade of Sarrut's division from the line, pushed it over the Zadorra, and established it in a position level with Aranguiz on the Murguia road, a mile and more beyond the river. Late at night, apparently on a report from a deserter that there were British troops behind Longa [1]—(indeed the man said that Wellington himself was on the Bilbao road)—Reille took off the other brigade of Sarrut's division in the same direction, and sent it with Curto's regiments of light horse to join Menne. There remained in front of Vittoria of infantry only Lamartinière's division, and the King's Guards ; but there was a very large body of cavalry in reserve—Tilly's and Digeon's dragoon divisions of the Army of the South, the King's two Guard regiments of lancers, and the bulk of the horse of the Army of Portugal, Boyer's dragoons and Mermet's chasseurs : there must have been 5,000 sabres or more in hand.

One further precaution was taken—lest the enemy might be moving against the high road to France from points even more to the north than Murguia, a trifling force was sent to cover the exit of the *chaussée* from the pass of Salinas ; this was the Spanish ' division ' of Casapalacios belonging to the Army of the Centre, strengthened by some scraps of the French troops of the Army of the North, which had come in from minor garrisons during the recent retreat. Casapalacios' *Afrancesados*, nominally three regiments strong, were under 2,000 bayonets—they had with them five weak squadrons of their own nation, a half-battery, also Spanish, and an uncertain (but small) French auxiliary force, which included a battalion of the 3rd Line, part of the 15th Chasseurs, and a section of guns equipped from the artillery dépôt of the Army of the North, which had long been established at Vittoria and had not been sent to the rear [2]. Casapalacios took post at Durana, covering

---

[1] This story is given by Gazan in his report, as a proof that Jourdan had ample warning that there was danger from the north as well as from the east.

[2] These troops were ' nobody's children ' and get ignored in Gazan's and Reille's reports. But we hear of the 3rd Line defending Gamarra Menor in one French report, a fact corroborated by its showing two officer-casualties in Martinien's lists—the guns are mentioned in Tirlet's artillery report. Cavalry of the Army of the North is vaguely mentioned—its presence seems established by an officer-casualty of the 15th Chasseurs in Martinien. I suspect the presence of part of the 10th Léger, which has an officer-casualty, Vittoria *22nd* June, presumably a misprint for 21st.

the bridge of that village, the most northerly one on the
Zadorra : the French battalion was at Gamarra Menor on the
other side of the water.

Wellington spent the 20th in arranging for the general attack,
which he had determined to deliver if Joseph stood his ground.
The plan was ambitious, for the battlefield was far larger than
any on which the Anglo-Portuguese Army had ever fought
before, and the numbers available were 30,000 more than they
had been at Salamanca or Bussaco, and more than double those
of Fuentes de Oñoro.   Moreover, he intended to operate with
a great detached turning force against the enemy's flank and
rear, a thing that he had only once done before—at Salamanca—
and then only with a single division.   The battle plan was
essentially a time-problem : he had to arrange for the simultaneous appearance of four separate masses in front of the
French position.   All started from parallel points in the valley
of the Bayas, but the obstacles in front of them were of very
varying difficulty, and the distances to be covered were very
different.

(1) Hill, with the large 2nd Division (four brigades), Silveira's
Portuguese division, Morillo's Spaniards, and V. Alten's and
Fane's light dragoons, 20,000 sabres and bayonets in all, was
to cross the Zadorra completely outside the extreme French
left wing, to storm the heights of Puebla, which formed the end
of Gazan's line, and then, advancing from the defile, to strike at
Subijana de Alava with his main body, while continuing to
thrust his flank along the heights above, which dominated the
whole region, and extended far behind the enemy's left wing.

(2) Two parallel columns were to march from the camps on
the Bayas ; one consisting of the 4th and Light Divisions,
R. Hill's, Grant's, and Ponsonby's cavalry brigades, and
D'Urban's Portuguese horse, was to advance by the country
road from Subijana Morillas to the two bridges of Nanclares.
Opposite those passages and the neighbouring ones it was to
deploy, and to attack the French centre, when Hill should have
got a footing on the Puebla heights and in the plain by Subijana.
The second column, consisting of the 3rd and 7th Divisions,
was to move from Zuazo and Anda on the Bayas across the high
mountain called Monte Arrato by a country track, and to

descend into the valley of the Zadorra at Las Guetas, opposite
the bridge of Mendoza, up-stream from the ' hairpin bend '.
In this position it would be almost in the rear of Gazan's right
wing above Villodas : it was to attack at once on reaching its
ground, if the progress of Hill on the south was seen to be
satisfactory. ' The movement to be regulated from the **right** :
although these columns are to make such movements in advance
as may be evidently necessary to favour the progress of the two
columns on their right, they are not to descend into the low
ground toward Vittoria or the great road.' The total strength
of the four divisions and cavalry of this section of the army was
about 30,000 sabres and bayonets.

(3) Graham's column-head was at Olano, three miles in front
of Murguia, and six from the Zadorra. He had in front Longa's
Spanish infantry, with whom Anson's light dragoons were to
join up when operations should begin. Behind were the 1st and
5th Divisions, Pack's and Bradford's Portuguese brigades, and
Bock's heavy dragoons. The total force was about 20,000 men
of all nations. As an afterthought on the 20th Wellington
directed Giron, who was to reach Orduña that day, to come
down to the upper Bayas in Graham's rear, where he would act
as a support if necessary. The object of this order is not quite
obvious. Giron came down too late for the battle, arriving at
Murguia only in the afternoon. It is known from his own
dispatches that Wellington over-estimated Reille's force, which
Graham had to fight, not knowing of Maucune's departure [1],
and Giron may have been intended to add weight to the attack
in this quarter. His troops would, apparently, have been more
usefully placed if they had been sent from Murguia to attack
the unguarded upper fords of the Zadorra.

The orders issued to Graham gave him a rather perplexing
choice of action. He was (like the 3rd and 7th Divisions) to
guide himself by what was going on upon his right : he must
get in touch at once with the centre columns ; he might attack
if it was obviously profitable to the main advance, but he was

---

[1] *Dispatches*, x. p. 449, says that Reille had two *divisions* in reserve (they
were only two *brigades*) in addition to his front line holding the bridges :
and cf. x. p. 450, which says directly that four divisions of Reille's army
were present.

to avoid letting his whole corps be drawn into close action in front of Vittoria, for his main object must be to turn the enemy's position, by getting round its right wing and cutting the great road to France. The lack of precise direction in this order is, no doubt, a testimony to Wellington's confidence in Graham's judgement. But it cast a grave responsibility on him : if he had been told simply that he was to turn the French right and seize the great *chaussée*, matters would have been simple. But he is given leave to attack frontally if circumstances farther down the line seem to make such a policy desirable : yet he must not attack so heavily as to make his great turning movement impossible. It must be confessed that the difficult problem was not well solved that day by the gallant old general.

The whole day of the 20th was spent in getting the columns into order, and the arrangements for the attacks synchronized. Wellington took a survey of all the routes in person, as his wont was. It was not till late in the afternoon that he became certain from the dispositions of the enemy that an eleventh hour retreat was not contemplated by the King [1]. The timing was that Hill, who had a few miles to march, should attack at eight in the morning, that both Graham and the column consisting of the 3rd and 7th Divisions should get into position by the same hour, and make ready to attack, when it was clear that the flank movement of Hill had already begun and was making good progress. Meanwhile the other central column, the Light and 4th Divisions, should cross when Hill had won the defile of Puebla and room to debouch beyond it, but not before. The rather late hour fixed, in a month when dawn comes at 4 a.m., was dictated by the fact that Hill had a river to cross, and the 3rd and 7th Divisions mountain tracks to follow, which neither

---

[1] Here comes in a curious incident, illustrating the extraordinary carelessness of the French Staff. Gazan was very anxious to get restored to him an artillery officer, a Captain Cheville, then a prisoner. As an exchange for him he sent into the British lines on the 20th, Captain Leith Hay, a captured British intelligence officer, who had been with the Army of the South for a month, and had witnessed the whole retreat, during which he had been freely in intercourse with General Maransin and many staff officers. On his release he was able to tell Wellington that the French were definitely halted, and expected to fight. Why exchange such a prisoner on such a day ? See Leith Hay, ii. p. 190. Cf. *Wellington Dispatches*, x. p. 443, which corroborates Hay's story.

could have negotiated in the dark. Some hours of daylight were
needed to get them into position. Even so the brigades of the
left-centre column were several hours late at their rendezvous.

The French commanders, as we have seen, made no move on
the 20th, save to hurry off convoys and to throw back Reille on
the north-west flank of Vittoria, to protect the royal *chaussée*
and the two Bilbao roads. Jourdan wrote to Clarke that evening
a perfectly sensible dispatch as to the difficulties of the situation,
but one which showed that he was wholly unaware that he might
be forced to a general action within the next twelve hours. All
depended, he said, on Clausel's prompt arrival : if he should
come up on the 21st there was no danger : if he delayed, the
army might have to choose between two tiresome alternatives—
a retreat on the pass of Salinas and one on Pampeluna. If
Wellington, as he suspected, was making a great turning movement by Orduña and Durango, the army would be forced to
take the wretched road Salvatierra–Pampeluna. 'The King
does not yet know what decision he will have to make : if
General Clausel delays his junction much longer, he will be
forced to choose the retreat into Navarre.' Of any idea that
Wellington was about to attack next morning the dispatch
shows no sign.

Jourdan had been indisposed all that day—he was laid up in
bed with a feverish attack. This caused the postponement of
a general reconnaissance of the position, which he and his King
had intended to carry out together. They rode forth, however,
at 6 a.m. on the 21st. ' No intelligence had come to hand,'
writes Jourdan in his memoirs, ' which could cause us to foresee
an instant attack. We arrived at the position by Zuazo, from
which Count Reille had been recently moved, and stopped to
examine it. Its left rested on the mountain-chain in the
direction of Berostigueta, its right came down to the Zadorra
behind La Hermandad and Crispijana. It is dominating, yet not
over steep, and has all along it good artillery emplacement for
many batteries. It connected itself much better than does the
Ariñez position with the ground about Aranguiz now occupied
by Reille, which might be heavily attacked. Struck with the
advantages of this position, the King appeared inclined to
bring back the Army of the South to occupy it, and to place the

Army of the Centre between it and the Army of Portugal. The three armies would have been closer together, and more able to give each other rapid assistance ; and the eye of the Commander-in-Chief could have swept around the whole of this more concentrated field in one glance. This change of dispositions would probably have been carried out on the 20th if Marshal Jourdan had not been indisposed, and might perhaps have prevented the catastrophe that was to come. But the officer sent to call General Gazan to confer with the King came back to say that the general could not leave his troops, as an attack on him was developing. It was judged too late to change position. Riding to the front of Ariñez, to a long hill occupied by Leval's division, on the right of the Army of the South, the King saw that in fact the enemy was on the move. About eight o'clock the posts on the mountain reported that the Allies had passed the Zadorra above La Puebla : a strong column was coming up the high road and the defile, a smaller one had diverged to its right and was climbing the mountain itself. General Avy, sent on reconnaissance beyond the Zadorra on the side of Mendoza, reported at the same time that a large corps was coming in on Tres Puentes behind the rear of General Leval. And he could see signs in the woods opposite, which seemed to indicate the march of other troops in the direction of the bridge of Nanclares. No news had yet come in from Reille, but we prepared ourselves to hear ere long that he, too, was attacked [1]'.

It is unnecessary to comment on the character of a Headquarters where a passing indisposition of the Chief of the Staff causes all movements to be postponed for eighteen hours, at a moment when a general action is obviously possible. But it is necessary to point out that the existing dislocation of the troops left three miles of the Zadorra front between Reille's left and Gazan's right unguarded when the battle began, and that this had been the case throughout the preceding day. And during that day who was responsible for the fact that not a single one of the eleven bridges between the defile of La Puebla and Durana had been ruined and only three obstructed [2] ? Gazan must take a good deal of responsibility, no less than Jourdan.

[1] Jourdan, *Mémoires*, p. 475.
[2] Digeon had obstructed the bridges of Arriaga and Gamarra. The

At eight o'clock on the morning of the 21st the action commenced, on a most beautiful clear day, contrasting wonderfully with the heavy rain of the 19th and intermittent showers on the 20th. Every hill-crest road and village for twenty miles was visible with surprising sharpness, so much so that incidents occurring at a great distance were easily to be followed by the naked eye, still more easily by the staff officer's telescope.

The clash began, as Wellington had intended, on the extreme right. Here Hill's columns crossed the Zadorra, where it broadened out below the defile of La Puebla, far outside the French line. The 2nd Division led up the high road, with Cadogan's brigade heading the column; but before they entered the narrows, Morillo's Spaniards were pushed forward on their right, through a wood which covered the lower slopes, to seize the spur of the Puebla heights immediately above the road. Till this was cleared, it would be impossible to move the 2nd Division forward. Eye-witnesses describe the deploying of the Spanish column as clearly visible from the high ground on the Monte Arrato heights: the first brigade appeared emerging from the woods below, then came stiffer ground, ' so steep that while moving up it they looked as if they were lying on their faces or crawling [1].' Then the smoke of the French skirmishing fire began to be visible on the crest, while Morillo's second brigade, deployed behind the first, went up the heights in support. The enemy, who was not in great strength at first, gave way, and the Estremadurans won the sky-line, formed there, and began to drive up from the first summit to the next above it. This also they won, but then came to stand—Gazan had pushed up first one and then the other of the two regiments of Maransin's brigade from his left, on the main position, to support the voltigeur companies which had been the only troops originally placed on this lofty ground. Hill, seeing the advance on the mountain stop, sent up, to help Morillo, Colonel Cadogan, with his own regiment the 71st, and all the light companies of Cadogan's and Byng's brigades. This turned the fight, and after a stiff struggle for the second summit, in which

bridge of Villodas, below Gazan's extreme right, had been partly barricaded. Not so Nanclares, Mendoza, and the bridge immediately below Tres Puentes.

[1] Diary of the 43rd officer, in Maxwell, ii. p. 40.

Morillo was severely wounded, Maransin's brigade was turned back and flung down hill : it halted and reformed low down on the slope, losing the crest completely.

Having his flank now reasonably safe, Hill turned off the other two battalions of Cadogan's brigade to follow the 71st, and then pushed his second British brigade (O'Callaghan's) up the defile of La Puebla, and deployed it on the open ground opposite the village of Subijana de Alava, which lay near the high road, and was the first obstacle to be carried if the whole corps was to issue forth and attack the French left. One battery moved up with the brigade, and got into action on a slope to its right. The rest of the 2nd Division and Silveira's Portuguese issued from the defile, ready to act as reserve either to Morillo on the heights or O'Callaghan in the open ground. Meanwhile the enemy could be seen dispatching troops from his reserves, to attack the spurs of the mountain which had been won by Morillo and Cadogan. For the heights of Puebla commanded all the left flank of the main French position, and, if Allied troops pushed along them any further, Gazan's line would be completely turned. Jourdan says that his orders were that Maransin's brigade should have attacked, with a whole division in support, but that Gazan took upon him the responsibility of sending in Maransin alone, and only later, when the latter had been beaten down from the crest, first Rey's brigade of Conroux's division and then St. Pol's reserve brigade of Daricau's division, from the hill on the right behind Leval. It would seem that Daricau's two regiments took post on the slopes behind Subijana, where there was a gap in the line, owing to Maransin's departure, while Rey and his brigade went up the Puebla heights, to try to head off Morillo's and Cadogan's attack.

In this it was wholly unsuccessful : after a severe struggle on the crest, in which Cadogan was mortally wounded [1], the French reinforcements were checked and routed : the Allied troops began to push forward again on the heights, and were

[1] There is a good account of the heroic death of Cadogan, a much-loved colonel of the 71st, in the diary of his quarter-master, William Gavin, of the same regiment. When aware that he was mortally hit, Cadogan refused to be moved from the field, and had himself propped up against two knapsacks, on a point from which his dying eyes could survey the whole field, and watched the fight to the bitter end.

getting right round the flank of Gazan's left wing, while Maransin's troops on the lower slopes were being contained by the
92nd and 50th, the rear regiments of Cadogan's brigade,
and Daricau's were hotly engaged with O'Callaghan's three
battalions, which occupied Subijana and then attacked the
hillside above it, but failed for some time to secure a lodgement there.

Jourdan was by this time growing anxious, and not without
reason, at the rapid progress of the Allies on the Puebla heights.
He ordered Gazan to send up at once his only remaining reserve,
Villatte's division from the height behind Ariñez, to gain the
crest at a point farther east than any that the enemy could
reach, and to attack in mass along it.   In order that he might
not be forestalled on the summit, Villatte was told to march
by a long détour, through the village of Esquivel far to the east,
where there was a country road debouching from the *chaussée*.
Indeed so perturbed was the Marshal by the threat to his left,
that he suspected further turning movements in this quarter,
and sent orders for Tilly's dragoons, from the cavalry reserve,
to ride out by Berostigueta to the Trevino road, to see if there
were no British columns pressing in from that quarter.   He
also directed D'Erlon to move one of his two infantry divisions,
Cassagne's, in the same direction, to support Tilly if necessary.
Gazan, if we may credit his long and contentious report on the
battle, suggested to Jourdan that it was dangerous to disgarnish
his centre, and to push so many troops to his left, while it was
still uncertain whether Wellington's column-heads, visible on
the other side of the Zadorra, were not about to move.   Might
not Hill's attack be a feint, intended to draw off the French
reserves in an eccentric direction ?   The Marshal, says Gazan,
then declared in a loud voice, so that all around could hear,
' that the enemy's movements opposite our right are mere
demonstrations, to which no attention should be paid, and
that if the battle were lost it would be because the heights on
the left of Subijana remained in the enemy's power [1].'   There
lay the real danger.

---

[1] From Gazan's report in the French Archives, written at St. Jean-
Pied-du-Port in July—very much *ex post facto*.   It was lent me by
Mr. Fortescue, along with several other Vittorian documents.

Orders were given that when Villatte should have got on the crest of the mountain, and should be delivering his attack, a simultaneous move forward was to be made by Conroux, and the brigades of Maransin and St. Pol, to cast the enemy out of Subijana, as well as off the heights of Puebla. It is interesting to note that Hill had as yet only engaged two British brigades, and one small Spanish division, and had succeeded in attracting against himself a much larger force—the whole of Conroux's and Villatte's divisions, and the two brigades of Maransin and St. Pol. In the French centre and right there remained now only Leval's division and the remaining brigade of Daricau's, and in reserve there was only one of D'Erlon's divisions, since the other had gone off on a wild goose chase toward the Trevino road. Wellington could have wished for nothing better.

But by the time that the French counter-attack on Hill's corps was developing, matters were beginning to look lively all along the line of the Zadorra, and the combat on the heights was growing into a general action. It was now about eleven o'clock, and Wellington had been for some time established on a high bank above the river, facing the centre of the French position, to the left of the village and bridges of Nanclares, from which he could sweep with his glass the whole landscape from the heights of La Puebla to the bridge of Mendoza. To his left and right the Light and 4th Divisions lay in two masses, a mile or more back from the river, and hidden very carefully in folds of the Monte Arrato, the battalions in contiguous close column lying down in hollow roads or behind outcrops of rock, and showing as little as possible. The great mass of cavalry in reserve, four brigades, had not been brought over the sky-line yet, and lay some distance to the rear. Only Grant's hussars were near the Light Division, dismounted and standing to their horses in covered ground. The French lines were perfectly visible, ' unmasked, without a bush to prevent the sweeping of their artillery, the charging of their cavalry, or the fire of their musketry acting with full effect on those who should attempt to cross the bridges in their front, which it was necessary to carry before we could begin the attack on their centre [1],' King

---

[1] Diary of Cooke of the 43rd in Maxwell's *Peninsular Sketches*, ii. 42.

Joseph and his staff were conspicuous on the round hill before Ariñez.

Hill's advance having begun, and made good progress, Wellington was watching for the two other movements which ought to have coincided with the attempt to cross the river at Nanclares for the frontal attack. They had neither of them developed as yet : at least nothing was to be seen of the 3rd and 7th Divisions on the down-slope of the lofty Monte Arrato, and there had not yet been any heavy burst of cannonading from the upper Zadorra (which was not visible from the spot where the Commander-in-Chief had placed himself), to tell that Graham was engaged.

The reason for the comparative silence in this quarter was undoubtedly the wording of Wellington's orders to Graham, which left so much to the judgement of the commander of the great turning column. He had been placed, almost from the start of his march, in the presence of a secondary problem. Reille, as we have seen, had been given on the 20th the charge of the upper Zadorra and the great road to France. Hoping that he had only Longa's Spaniards in front of him, and judging that it would be well to keep them as far from the road and the river as possible, the commander of the Army of Portugal had placed Sarrut's division and a brigade of Mermet's light horse in an advanced position a mile and more in front of the river, on a ridge flanking the main Bilbao road, above the village of Aranguiz. Lamartinière's division and Boyer's and Digeon's dragoons had been left on the nearer bank. When therefore Graham, marching down from Olano, neared Aranguiz, he found a considerable French force blocking the way. Remembering his orders to look to the right, to adapt his movements to those of the troops in that direction, and not to be drawn into unnecessary fighting, he halted for some time, to see how matters were going on the critical wing, and meanwhile deployed alongside of Longa's men in his front, Pack's Portuguese brigade and Anson's light dragoons, with the 5th Division in support, before Sarrut's position. He also detached Bradford's Portuguese to his right, with the idea of getting in touch with the troops in that direction. Reille, who was present in person with his advanced guard, saw with dismay the depth of the column descending upon him, and recognized that he must fall back and hold the line of the Zadorra, the only possible front on which he could oppose such an enemy. About midday or a little later Graham ' thought himself justified in advancing, in order to draw the enemy's attention to his right, and so assist the progress of the army from the side of Miranda (i. e. Hill's column), where the enemy seemed to be making an obstinate resistance in the successive strong positions which the country afforded [1].' The very moment that Graham sent forth Longa and Pack to advance, the French retired by order, not without some skirmishing, in which the 4th Caçadores stormed the hill just above Aranguiz. But neither side had any appreciable losses.

Graham could now advance to within a mile of the Zadorra, and was in command of the plain-ground as far as the villages of Abechuco, and Gamarra Mayor and Menor. All three are on the northern or right bank of the river, and Reille had determined to hold them as *têtes de pont* covering the bridges. They had been hastily barricaded, and the artillery of the Army of Portugal had been placed on the opposite bank in a line of batteries, ready to sweep the open ground over which an assault on the villages must be launched. Graham had therefore to deploy for a formal attack on the new position. He sent Longa up-stream and over the hills, to attack Gamarra Menor and Durana, placed Oswald and the 5th Division, with a section of Lawson's battery, over against Gamarra Mayor, and drew out the 1st Division and the two Portuguese brigades opposite Abechuco, which would have to be taken before the bridge of Arriaga could be attacked. Keeping in mind Wellington's main purpose, indicated in his orders, of cutting the great road to France, he told Longa and Oswald on the flank that they might push hard, while he seems to have acted in a much more leisurely way in front of Abechuco, where no attack was launched till actual orders had been received from head-quarters bidding him press harder. But meanwhile Longa took Gamarra Menor from the French battalion of the 3rd Line, and then, pushing on, came into collision at Durana bridge with his renegade compatriots the Franco-Spanish division of

---

[1] Graham's Report, *Wellington Supplementary Dispatches*, viii. 7–8.

Casapalacios. As the great road to Bayonne actually passes through Durana, and was now under fire from Longa's skirmishers, it may be said to have been blocked for all practical purposes at this early stage of the battle. It was not till the afternoon, however, that Longa succeeded in storming the bridge and occupying the village, thus formally breaking the enemy's main line of communication with France—to save which King Joseph had risked his all. Apparently he was hampered by having no artillery, while the Franco-Spaniards had some four or five guns with them, bearing on the bridge.

Meanwhile Robinson's brigade of the 5th Division had stormed Gamarra Mayor, defended by the French 118th and 119th—Gauthier's brigade of Lamartinière's division. This was a brilliant and costly affair—it being no light matter to attack in column of battalions the barricaded streets of a compact village. The British, however, burst in—Colonel Brooke with the 1/4th being the first to force an entrance : the French abandoned three guns which had been placed in the barricades, and fell back in disorder across the bridge. General Robinson endeavoured to improve the success by instant pursuit, but the French had guns bearing on the bridge, which swept away the first platoons that tried to cross it. Very few men reached the other side, and they were shot down before they could establish a lodgement on the farther bank. It was necessary to halt, reform, and bring up more artillery before the attack could be repeated.

It was now past two o'clock, and the noise of Graham's attack was sufficiently audible all down the British line, and was carrying dismay to French head-quarters. But what of the other column, that of the 3rd and 7th Divisions, which was to appear on the middle Zadorra opposite Gazan's almost unguarded flank, in the direction of the bridge of Mendoza ? It was overdue, now that both the large flanking corps were seriously engaged, and the attention of the enemy attracted toward them. But before the missing column came into action, there had been an unexpected modification of the position in the right centre. At 11.30 Wellington appeared before the Light Division, and told Alten to move it more to the left, so as to be over and above the bridge of Villodas, which it would have to attack at the moment of general advance, leaving the two bridges by Nanclares to the 4th Division and the cavalry. So rough and wooded was the ground that the division, moving in a hollow way, was established less than 300 yards from the brink of the Zadorra and the French line, without attracting the notice of the enemy. An officer of the 43rd writes : ' I felt anxious to obtain a view, and walking leisurely between the trees found myself at the edge of the wood, in clear sight of the enemy's cannon, planted with lighted matches and ready to apply them [1]. Had our attack begun here, the French could never have stood to their guns, so near were they to the thicket —our Riflemen would have annihilated them.' The British bank of the Zadorra here completely commanded the bridge and the French bank, which accounts for the fact that the enemy's artillery did not detect the approach of such a large body of troops as the Light Division. But after a time a bickering fire across the river between skirmishers on both sides broke out at several points, and some voltigeurs even pressed across Villodas bridge, and had to be cast back again by the skirmishers of the 2/95th.

There was to be, however, no attempt to pass this bridge as yet by the British. While Wellington was still with the Light Division, a peasant came up to him with the astounding intelligence that the bridge of Tres Puentes, the one at the extreme point of the ' hairpin-bend ' of the Zadorra, was not only unoccupied but unwatched by the enemy : he offered to guide any troops sent to it. The Commander-in-Chief made up his mind at once to seize this crossing, which would outflank the French position at Villodas, and told the peasant to lead Kempt's brigade of the Light Division to the unwatched point, about a mile and a half to the left. ' The brigade moved off by threes at a rapid pace, along a very uneven and circuitous path, concealed from the observation of the French by high rocks, and reached the narrow bridge, which crossed the river to the hamlet of Yruna (part of the scattered village of Tres Puentes). The 1st Rifles led the way, and the whole brigade following

---

[1] Cooke, the 43rd officer in Maxwell's *Peninsular Sketches*, ii. 44. The guns were undoubtedly the Horse Artillery battery on the high-road in front of Gazan's centre.

passed at a run, with firelocks and rifles ready cocked, and
ascended a steep road of fifty yards, at the top of which was an
old chapel. We had no sooner cleared it than we observed
a heavy column of the French on the principal hill, and commanding a bird's eye view of us. However, fortunately, a con-
vex bank formed a sort of *tête de pont*, behind which the
regiments formed at full speed, without any word of command.
Two round shots now came among us : the second severed the
head from the body of our bold guide, the Spanish peasant.
The brigade was so well covered that the enemy soon ceased
firing. Our post was extraordinary—we were in the elbow
of the French position, and isolated from the rest of the army,
within 100 yards of the enemy [1] and absolutely occupying part
of his position, without any attempt having been made to
dislodge us. . . . Sir James Kempt expressed much wonder at
our critical position, without being molested, and sent his
aide-de-camp at speed across the river for the 15th Hussars,
who came up singly and at a gallop along the steep path, and
dismounted in rear of our centre. Some French dragoons,
coolly and at a slow pace, came up to within 50 yards of us, to
examine, if possible, our strength, but a few shots from the
Rifles caused them to decamp. We could see three bridges
within a quarter of a mile of each other, in the elbow of the
enemy's position. We had crossed the centre one (Tres Puentes),
while the other two, right and left (Villodas and Mendoza), were
still covered by French artillery [2].'

   Expecting to be instantly attacked, and to have to fight hard
for the chapel-knoll on which they had aligned themselves,
Kempt's brigade spent ' half an hour of awkward suspense.'
The immunity with which they had been allowed to hold their
position was suddenly explained by a movement which they
had not been able to observe. The missing column of Wellington's army had at last come up, and was plunging with headlong
speed into the rear of the troops which were facing Kempt, so

   [1] Of course, Cooke is understating the distance, which was about
a quarter of a mile.

   [2] This interesting narrative of Captain Cooke of the 43rd must have
been in Napier's hands before it was printed by Maxwell, as several
phrases from it are repeated in Napier, vol. v, p. 121. Sir William himself was in England that day.

that the French had no attention to spare for the side-issue in the hairpin-bend of the Zadorra. Instead of being attacked the brigade was about to become at once an attacking force.

A word is necessary as to the leading of this column. It had been placed by Wellington under Lord Dalhousie, now commanding the 7th Division. This was an extraordinary choice, as this officer had been only a few months in the Peninsula, and had no experience of the higher responsibilities—though he had commanded a brigade in the Walcheren expedition [1]. But being as Lieutenant-General slightly senior to Picton (though they had been gazetted major-generals on the same day in 1808), he was entitled to take the command over the head of the war-worn and experienced leader of the 3rd Division. The latter had been directing one of the great marching columns during the early stages of the advance, and was not unnaturally sulky at being displaced. Common report in the army held that he was in disfavour at Head-Quarters, for intemperate letters complaining of the starving of his division during the recent march beyond the Ebro [2]. Be this as it may, Picton was during the forenoon hours of June 21st in one of his not infrequent rages. For though his column had started early, and the 3rd Division had reached Las Guetas, the villages on the south side of the Monte Arrato, which were to be its starting-point for the attack on the line of the Zadorra, Lord Dalhousie refused to advance farther than the edge of the hills, using apparently his discretion in interpreting the orders given him ' to regulate his action from what was going on to his right ', and only to move when it should be ' evidently necessary ' to favour the progress of the columns in that direction. He was obviously worried by the fact that the two rear brigades of his own division, Barnes's and Le Cor's, had been hindered by an artillery breakdown in the steep road

---

[1] He was, along with Stewart and Oswald, one of the three divisional generals who committed the gross breach of orders during the Burgos retreat mentioned above, p. 152.

[2] Cf. Burgoyne, *Life and Letters*, i. 263 (June 23, 1813), with Picton's letters in *Wellington Supplementary Dispatches*, xiv. 225, about ' the 3rd Division being kept in the background, for Sir T. P. is by no means a favourite with Lord W.' Cairnes (in Dickson, ed. Leslie) puts the change down as ' most mortifying to Picton '.

behind, and were not yet up, though Cairnes's battery, which had delayed them, ultimately overtook the leading brigade[1]. Hence he used his discretion to wait for formal orders from Head-Quarters, and to do nothing. Picton, who could note the advance of Hill's column, and could see that the French were utterly unprepared for an attack on the middle Zadorra, chafed bitterly at the delay.

We have an interesting picture of him on that morning from eye-witnesses. He was a strange figure—suffering from inflammation of the eyes, he had put on not his cocked hat but a broad-brimmed and tall civilian top-hat—the same that may be seen to-day in the United Service Museum. ' During the struggle on the right the centre was inactive. General Picton was impatient, he inquired of every aide-de-camp whether they had any orders for him. As the day wore on, and the fight waxed louder on the right, he became furious, and observed to the communicator of these particulars, ' D—n it ! Lord Wellington must have forgotten us.' It was near noon, and the men were getting discontented. Picton's blood was boiling, his stick was beating with rapid strokes upon the mane of his cob. He rode backward and forward looking in every direction for the arrival of an aide-de-camp, until at last one galloped up from Lord Wellington. He was looking for Lord Dalhousie—the 7th Division had not yet arrived, having to move over difficult ground. The aide-de-camp checked his horse and asked the general whether he had seen Lord Dalhousie. Picton was disappointed ; he had expected that he might at least move now, and in a voice which did not gain softness from his feelings, answered in a sharp tone, ' No, Sir : I have *not* seen his Lordship, but have you any orders for *me*.' ' None,' replied the aide-de-camp. ' Then, pray Sir, what are the orders that you *do* bring ? ' ' Why,' answered the officer, ' that as soon as Lord D. shall commence an attack on that bridge,' pointing to the one on the left (Mendoza), the 4th and Light are to support him.' Picton could not understand the idea of any other division fighting in his front, and drawing himself up to his full height said to the astonished aide-de-camp, ' You may tell

Lord Wellington from me, Sir, that the 3rd Division, under my command, shall in less than ten minutes attack that bridge and carry it, and the 4th and Light may support if they choose.' Having thus expressed his intention, he turned from the aide-de-camp and put himself at the head of his men, who were quickly in motion toward the bridge, encouraging them with the bland appellation of ' Come on, ye rascals ! Come on, ye fighting villains [1].'

Ten minutes as the time required to plunge down from the hillside to a bridge two miles away seems a short estimate. But there is no doubt that the advance of the 3rd Division was fast and furious—an eye-witness describes it as shooting like a meteor across the front of the still-halted column-head of the 7th Division. The military purist may opine that Picton should have waited till he got formal orders via Lord Dalhousie to advance. But the moments were precious—Kempt was across the Zadorra close by, in an obviously dangerous state of isolation : the French in a few minutes might be sending infantry to block the bridge of Mendoza, which they had so strangely neglected. The 7th Division was short of two brigades, and not ready to attack. Wellington's orders were known, and the situation on the right was now such as to justify the permissible advance which they authorized. Neither Wellington nor Dalhousie in their dispatches give any hint that Picton's action was disapproved—complete success justified it.

Picton had directed Brisbane's brigade of the 3rd Division straight upon the bridge of Mendoza, Colville's upon a ford 300 yards farther up-stream. Both crossed safely and almost unopposed. The only French troops watching the stream here were Avy's weak brigade of cavalry—under 500 sabres—and their three horse-artillery guns commanding the bridge. But the latter hardly got into action, for on Picton's rapid approach becoming visible, General Kempt threw out some companies of the 1/95th under Andrew Barnard, from his point of vantage on the knoll of Yruna, who opened such a biting fire upon the half battery that the officer in command limbered up and galloped off. Avy's chasseurs hovered about in an undecided way—but were not capable either of defending a bridge or of

[1] Narrative of one of Picton's staff in Robinson's *Life of Picton*, ii. 195–6.

attacking a brigade in position upon a steep hill. Wherefore Picton got across with small loss, and formed his two British brigades on the south side of the river. Power's Portuguese rapidly followed Brisbane, as did a little later Grant's brigade of the 7th Division—Lord Dalhousie's other two brigades (as we have already noted) were not yet on the ground. On seeing Picton safely established on the left bank Kempt advanced from his knoll, and formed on the right-rear of the 3rd Division. The trifling French detachment at the bridge of Villodas—only a voltigeur company—wisely absconded at full speed on seeing Kempt on the move. The passage there was left completely free for Vandeleur's brigade of the Light Division, who had long been waiting on the opposite steep bank.

The British were across the Zadorra in force, and the critical stage of the action was about to commence : the hour being between 2 and 3 in the afternoon.

SECTION XXXVI: CHAPTER VIII

BATTLE OF VITTORIA. ROUT OF THE FRENCH

WHEN Picton and the 3rd Division, followed by the one available brigade of the 7th Division, came pouring across the Zadorra on the side of Mendoza, while Kempt debouched from the knoll of Yruna, and Vandeleur crossed the bridge of Villodas, the position of Leval's division became desperate. It was about to be attacked in flank by four brigades and in front by two more, and being one of the weaker divisions of the Army of the South, only 4,500 bayonets, was outnumbered threefold. Its original reserve (half Daricau's division) had gone off to the Puebla heights hours before : the general army-reserve (Villatte's division) had been sent away in the same direction by Jourdan's last orders. The nearest disposable and intact French troops were Darmagnac's division of the Army of the Centre—two miles to the rear, in position by Zuazo : the other divisions of that army had (as we have seen) gone off on a wholly unnecessary excursion to watch the Trevino road. The left wing and centre of the Army of the South was absorbed in the task of keeping back Hill, and had just begun the counter-attack upon him which Jourdan had ordered an hour before.

The sudden change in the situation, caused by the very rapid advance of Picton and the brigades that helped him, was all too evident to King Joseph and his chief of the staff, as they stood on the hill of Ariñez. The whole force of the 3rd division struck diagonally across the short space between the river and Leval's position—Brisbane's brigade and Power's Portuguese making for the French flank, while Colville, higher up the stream, made for the rear of the hill, in the direction of the village of Margarita. Kempt followed Brisbane in second line, Grant's brigade of the 7th Division, when it crossed at Mendoza, came on behind Colville. So did Vandeleur, from Villodas, after he had pulled down the obstructions and got his men over the narrow bridge. Nor was this all—the 4th Division, so long halted on the scrubby hillside opposite the left-hand of the two Nanclares bridges, suddenly started to descend the slope at the double-quick, Stubbs's Portuguese brigade leading.

Jourdan had to make a 'lightning change' in all his dispositions. Leval, obviously doomed if he did not retire quickly, was told to evacuate his hill and fall back past Ariñez, into which he threw a regiment to cover his retreat, on to the heights behind it. The two brigades of Daricau and Conroux, which had stood on the other side of the high road from Leval, were to make a parallel movement back to the same line of heights. The other brigades of Daricau and Conroux, with Maransin— now deeply engaged some with O'Callaghan and others with the 50th and 92nd—were to abandon the attack which they had just begun, and which had somewhat pushed back the British advance. They too must go back to the slopes behind Ariñez. It would take longer to recall Villatte, who was now far up on the crest of the mountain to the left, engaged with Morillo's Spaniards and the 71st. But this attack also must be broken off. Lastly, to fill the gap between Leval's new position and the Zadorra, the Army of the Centre must come forward and hold Margarita, or if that was impossible, the hill and village of La Hermandad behind it. But only Darmagnac's division was immediately available for this task, Cassagne's having to be brought back from the eccentric counter-march toward the Trevino road, to which it had been committed an hour before. In this way a new line of battle would be formed, reaching from the Zadorra near Margarita across the high road at Gomecha, to the heights above Zumelzu on the left. It was at best a hazardous business to order a fighting-line more than two miles long, and bitterly engaged with the enemy at several points, to withdraw to an unsurveyed position a mile in its rear, where there was practically no reserve waiting to receive it. For on the slopes above Ariñez there was at that moment nothing but Pierre Soult's light horse, and Treillard's dragoons, with two batteries of artillery [1]. The new front had to be

---

[1] The third battery originally at Ariñez was Villatte's divisional battery, which had gone off with him to the Puebla heights. Neither P. Soult nor Treillard had guns with them.

constructed from troops falling back in haste and closely pursued by the enemy, combining with other troops coming in from various directions, viz. the two divisions of the Army of the Centre. And when the line should be reformed, what was to prevent its left from being turned once more by the Allied troops on the Puebla heights, or its right by columns crossing the middle Zadorra behind it [1]. For there would still be a gap of two miles between Margarita village and the nearest troops of the Army of Portugal, who were now engaged with Graham at Abechuco and Arriaga.

To speak plainly, the second French line was never properly formed, especially on its left; but a better front was made, and a stronger stand, than might perhaps have been expected, though the confusion caused by hasty and imperfect alignment was destined in the end to be fatal.

On the extreme left Villatte had been caught by the order of recall at the moment when he was delivering his attack on Morillo and the British 71st. He had reached the crest as ordered, had formed up across it, and then had marched on a narrow front against the Allies. Both British and Spanish were in some disorder when he came in upon them—they had now been fighting for four hours, and in successive engagements had driven first Maransin's and then St. Pol's brigades for two miles over very steep and rocky ground. At the moment when Villatte came upon the scene, the Allied advance had just reached a broad dip in the crest, which it would have to cross if its progress were to be continued. The Spaniards were on the right and the 71st and light companies on the left, or northern, part of the ridge. It would have been a suitable moment to halt, and reform the line before continuing to press forward over dangerous ground. But the officer who had succeeded Cadogan in command [2] was set on 'keeping the

---

[1] Such turning *might* have been done either by the two belated brigades of the 7th Division or by troops detached by Graham, who had several brigades to spare, which he never used, but might have sent to pass the Zadorra at the bridge of Yurre or the fords west of it, both well behind the new French line.

[2] Who was this officer? *Not* Brevet Lieut.-Colonel Cother of the 71st nor Brevet Lieut.-Colonel Harrison of the 50th. Hope of the 92nd, in his rather detailed narrative of this fight, calls him ' Colonel R——.' I cannot

French upon the run,' and recklessly ordered the tired troops
to plunge down the steep side of the declivity and carry the
opposite slope. He was apparently ignorant that fresh French
troops were just coming to the front—several eye-witnesses
say that a column in light-coloured overcoats with white shako-
covers, which had been noticed on the right, was taken for a
Spanish detachment [1]. At any rate, the 71st crossed the
dip—four companies in its centre, the remainder at its upper
end—and was suddenly met not only by a charging column
in front, but by an attack in flank and almost in rear. The first
volley brought down 200 men—the shattered battalion recoiled,
and remounted its own slope in utter disorder, leaving some
forty prisoners in the hands of the enemy. These were the
only British soldiers who fell into the hands of the French
that day [2]. Fortunately the 50th, coming up from the rear,
was just in time to form up along the edge of the dip and cover
the retreat, and was joined soon after by the 92nd, who had
been facing another separate French unit lower down the slopes
and to the left flank. Seeing their opponents move off for no
visible reason (they had received no doubt the general order
to retire), the Highland regiment had pushed up on to the crest
and joined the 50th and the Spaniards.

Villatte, still ignorant that the whole French army was
falling back, tried to improve his success over the 71st into a
general repulse of the Allied force upon the crest, and ordered
his leading regiment to cross the dip and attack the troops
upon the opposite sky-line. They suffered the same fate as
the 71st and from the same cause : the climb was steep among
stones and furze, they were received with two devastating

identify him. Conceivably, it may have been Colonel Rooke, the senior
officer of Hill's staff who *may* have been sent up the heights, and *may*
have taken over command on Cadogan's being mortally wounded.

[1] So says the anonymous but invaluable ' T. S.' of the 71st. Leith Hay,
a prisoner with the French in this campaign, remarks that they were all
in their summer wear of long linen overcoats, with the cross-belts put on
above.

[2] They were released at Pampeluna on the surrender of that fortress
three months later, in a state of semi-starvation, having been carried on
with Villatte's division during the French retreat. They described to
Gavin of the 71st, who happened to be present at the surrender, their
unhappy fortunes. See his diary, p. 25.

volleys when they neared the top of the declivity, and then charged by the 50th and 92nd—the column broke, rolled down hill, and went to the rear. A second but less vigorous attack was made by another French regiment, and repulsed with the same ease—the wrecks of the 71st joining in the defence this time. Villatte then brought up a third regiment, but this was only a feint—the attack never developed, and while it was hanging fire the whole division swung round to the rear and went off—Jourdan's general order to retreat had at last been received, and Villatte was falling back to the new line [1]. Cameron of the 92nd, now in command on the heights, followed him up, as did the Spaniards. But there was to be no more serious fighting upon the Puebla mountain: the French gave way whenever they were pressed [2].

Long before Villatte's fight on the high ground had come to an end, the engagement at the other end of the French line had taken an unfavourable turn. The battle in this direction fell into three separate sections. Close to the Zadorra, Colville, with the left-hand brigade of the 3rd Division, was pushing up towards Margarita, while Darmagnac, from the heights of Zuazo, was making for it from the other side. It had taken some time to file Colville's battalions across the ford, and deploy them for the advance, and the French brigade of Darmagnac's division got into the village first, and made a

[1] Gazan's most unconvincing account of all this engagement is that 'General Villatte attacked the enemy with his usual vigour: nothing could resist the shock of his division. The position, whose recapture ought to have assured us the victory, was retaken, as well as the height in front of Subijana. The enemy was routed at every point. Such was the position of the Army of the South, when news came to the King that our troops by the Zadorra were attacked, and could not maintain themselves. I was told to break off my attack and retire to a position further back.'

[2] The 71st lost, beside their well-loved colonel—the only man mentioned in Wellington's private letter of next morning to his brother Henry (*Dispatches*, x. p. 454)—44 killed, 272 wounded, and nearly 40 prisoners : half the battalion. The 50th lost only 7 officers and 97 men ; the 92nd no more than 20 men. If Villatte gave correct figures, his total loss was only 2 officers and 289 men—including 22 prisoners. Of these the 63rd, obviously the leading regiment, was responsible for 135 casualties, the 95th for 94. The other two regiments had practically no losses. These figures are very low, but seem to be corroborated by Martinien.

strong defence there, while the German brigade occupied
La Hermandad in its rear. Colville was held in check, suffered
heavily, and could not get forward. But after half an hour's
deadly fighting the enemy gave way, not only because of the
frontal pressure, but because the troops on his left (Leval's
division of the Army of the South) had been defeated by Picton
and were retiring, thereby exposing the flank of Darmagnac's
line. D'Erlon drew back Chassé's much thinned brigade half a
mile, to the better defensive ground formed by the village of La
Hermandad and the height above it, where his German brigade
was already in position : this was an integral part of the new
line on which Jourdan had determined to fight, while Margarita
was on low ground, and too far to the front. Colville's brigade,
like its adversaries much maltreated [1], was replaced by
Grant's brigade of the 7th Division in front line [2], while Vandeleur's of the Light Division followed in support. They had
now in front of them not only Darmagnac's but Cassagne's
division, which had come back from its fruitless excursion to
the Trevino road, and had joined the other section of the
Army of the Centre [3], taking up ground in second line.

Meanwhile the really decisive blow of the whole battle was
being delivered by Picton, a thousand yards farther to the
south, in and above Ariñez. The striking force here consisted
of Power's Portuguese brigade on the left, and of Brisbane's
British brigade on the right, opposite the village. Kempt's
half of the Light Division had followed Picton faithfully in his
diagonal movement across the slopes, and was close behind
Brisbane. Farther to the right the new front of attack of
Wellington's army was only beginning to form itself—the
4th Division had deployed after crossing the upper bridge of

[1] Its heavy loss of 33 officers and 515 men out of about 2,200 present
was nearly all, I believe, suffered at this point. The 2/87th with 244
casualties out of about 600 present lost 40 per cent. of its strength. Chassé's
French brigade, the immediate opponents, had 800 casualties, nearly all
at this moment.

[2] Why did not Dalhousie support Colville more promptly ? He had a
bridge to cross, and some way to go, but was evidently late.

[3] These details come mainly out of the *Mémoire sur la Retraite des
Armées françaises* in the French Archives, lent me by Mr. Fortescue.
Internal evidence shows it written by some member of D'Erlon's staff.
Tiriet's report is also useful.

Nanclares, and was now coming on in an échelon of brigades—Stubbs's Portuguese in the front échelon, then W. Anson, last Skerrett. They extended from the high road southwards, and were getting into touch with Hill's column, which after the French evacuated the height behind Subijana had also deployed for the advance—the 2nd division having now thrown forward Byng's brigade on its left, with O'Callaghan's next it, and Ashworth's Portuguese in second line. Silveira's division remained in reserve. The cavalry of the centre column had crossed after the infantry—R. Hill, Ponsonby, Victor Alten, and Grant by the upper bridge of Nanclares, D'Urban's Portuguese by the lower. They deployed on each side of the high road east of the river, behind the 4th Division, ground suitable for horsemen being nowhere else visible. On the heights of Puebla there still remained Cadogan's brigade (now under Cameron of the 92nd) and Morillo's Spaniards. This detached force, which was hard in pursuit of Villatte's retreating column, was decidedly ahead of the rest of the army, and well placed for striking at the new French flank, but it was tired and had fought hard already for many hours.

When the 4th Division had passed the upper bridge of Nanclares, and before the cavalry began to cross the Zadorra, Colonel Dickson had by Wellington's orders commenced to bring forward the reserve artillery. Very few British batteries had yet come into action, the broken nature of the ground preventing them from keeping close to their divisions. Hence it came to pass that there was by this time an accumulation of guns in the centre : during the rest of the battle it was employed in mass, many divisional batteries joining the artillery reserve, and a formidable line of guns being presently developed along the heights which had been the original position of Gazan's centre and right. Some of them were to the north of the high road, on Leval's hill : some to the south, where Daricau's front brigade had stood when the action commenced. As soon as they had come up, they began to pound the French infantry on the opposite hill. Here General Tirlet had a still more powerful artillery force in action—all the guns of the front line had got back in safety save one belonging to the horse artillery battery which had been placed opposite the bridge of Nanclares [1], and three batteries from the reserve were already in position. The cannonade on both sides was fierce—but it was the infantry which had to settle the matter, and the disadvantage to the French was that their troops, much hustled and disarranged while retreating into the new position, never properly settled down into it— especially Conroux's and Daricau's divisions, which had been divided into separate brigades by the way in which Gazan had dealt with them at the commencement of the action, never got into regular divisional order again, and fought piecemeal by regiments.

The decisive point was on the ground at and above Ariñez, which was held by Leval's division, with one regiment of Daricau's (103rd Line) on their left. The village, low down on the slope, was held by Mocquery's brigade—Morgan's was in support with the guns, higher up and more to the right. Picton attacked with Power's Portuguese on his left, Brisbane's brigade on his right, and Kempt's brigade of the Light Division in support, except that some companies of the 1/95th had been thrown out in front of Brisbane's line, and led the whole attack. The Riflemen rushed at the village, penetrated into it, and were evicted after a fierce tussle, by a French battalion charging in mass down the street. But immediately behind came the 88th and 74th. The former, attacking to their right of the village [2],

---

[1] Captured by skirmishers of the 1/95th, as it was retreating up the high road and was nearing Ariñez. The French infantry recovered it for a moment by a counter-stroke, but as the Riflemen had cut the traces and shot or removed the horses, they could not get the gun away. Tirlet says the battery lost only *one* gun, which is corroborated by Costello of the 95th, present on the spot. Kincaid and other Riflemen say three.

[2] There is a curious problem connected with a correspondence (*Dispatches*, x. pp. 329–31) between Picton and Wellington on July 16—three weeks after the battle. Wellington apparently thought that Picton blamed the 88th for losing Ariñez in the first assault, while it was really only two companies of the 1/95th which had entered that village and been driven out. He says that he had seen the 88th coming into action in a very ragged line, and had himself halted them and dressed their front, before he let them go on : after this he did not notice what became of them, but saw them again after the fighting formed on the other side of the village.

What Wellington did not witness is chronicled by Costello of the 1/95th : after describing the repulse of the Riflemen, he notes their pleasure at seeing ' our favourite third division ' coming down the road. Ariñez was promptly

completely smashed the French regiment which came down to meet them in a close-fire combat, and drove them in disorder up the hill, while the latter carried Ariñez itself and swept onward through it. The 45th, farther to the right, attacked and drove off the regiment of Daricau's division which was flanking Leval. Power's Portuguese would seem to have got engaged with Morgan's brigade, on the left of the village ; it gave way before them, when the 74th had stormed Ariñez and the Connaught Rangers had broken the neighbouring column. Leval's routed troops appear to have swept to the rear rather in a southerly direction, and to their left of the high road, so as to leave the beginnings of a gap between them and Cassagne's division of the Army of the Centre, which was coming up to occupy the ridge north of Gomecha, in the new position.

The complete breach in the French centre made by Picton's

---

retaken and the advance recommenced. ' I noticed a regiment, which by its yellow facings was the Connaught Rangers, marching in close column of companies to attack a French regiment drawn up in line on the verge of the hill, with a small village [Gomecha ?] in its rear. The 88th, although under a heavy cannonade from the enemy's artillery, continued advancing gallantly, while we skirmishers took ground to the left, close to the road, in order to allow them to oppose this line in front. Though we were hotly engaged I watched their movements. The 88th next deployed into line, advancing all the time towards their opponents, who seemed to wait very coolly for them. When they had approached within 300 yards the French poured in a volley, or I should rather say a running fire from right to left. As soon as the British regiment recovered the first shock, and closed their files on the gap that had been made, they commenced advancing at double time till within fifty yards nearer to the enemy, when they halted and in turn gave a running fire from the whole line, and then without a moment's pause, cheered and charged up the hill against them. The French meanwhile were attempting to reload. But they were hard pressed by the British, who gave them no time for a second volley. They went immediately to the right about, making the best of their way to the village behind.'

From this it is clear that the 88th fought on open ground, to the right of Ariñez and the high road. It was the centre regiment of the brigade : the 45th, therefore, must have been more to the right and well south of the road ; the 74th on the high road were the actual takers of Ariñez. We have unluckily no description of Power's Portuguese at the moment—but they lost heavily—the casualties being 25 officers and 386 men. They *must* have been engaged with Leval's 2nd Brigade, which had been stationed about and to the north of Gomecha, while the 1st Brigade held the village of Ariñez and the hill behind.

capture of Ariñez, and the driving of Leval out of his position
above it, had the immediate effect of compelling Darmagnac's
division to conform to the retreat, by falling back from Margarita
on to La Hermandad and the hills behind it on the one wing,
while the confused line of Daricau's, Conroux's, and Maransin's
troops, on the other hand, had to retire to the level of Gomecha,
though the 4th and 2nd Divisions were not yet far enough
forward to be able to press them. Nearly all the French guns
appear to have been carried back to the new position, which
may roughly be described as extending from Hermandad on
the Zadorra by Zuazo and Gomecha to the hills in front of
Esquivel. It was quite as good as the Margarita–Ariñez–
Zumelzu line which had just been forced by Picton's central
attack.

It took some little time for Wellington to organize his next
advance; the troops which had forced the Ariñez position had
to be re-formed, and it was necessary to allow the 4th and 2nd
Divisions to come up level with them, and to bring forward
Dickson's mass of artillery to a more advanced line, to batter
the enemy before the next infantry assault was let loose. The
only point where close fighting seems to have continued during
this interval was on the extreme left, where Lord Dalhousie,
after the French had left Margarita, was pressing forward
Grant's brigade of his own division, supported by Vandeleur's
brigade of the Light Division, against D'Erlon's new position,
where Neuenstein's brigade of five German battalions lay
in and about La Hermandad, with Chassé's dilapidated regiments in reserve behind. There was a very bitter struggle
at this point, rendered costly to the advancing British by the
superiority of the French artillery—D'Erlon had now at least
two batteries in action—Dalhousie only his own six divisional
guns, those of Cairnes. Grant's brigade, after advancing some
300 yards under a very heavy fire, came to a stand, and took cover
in a deep broad ditch only 200 yards from the French front.
According to an eye-witness Dalhousie hesitated for a moment
as to whether a further advance was possible [1], and had the

---

[1] The amusing story told of this storm by Harry Smith in his autobiography (i. pp. 97–8) is too good to be omitted. ' My brigade was sent
to support the 7th Division, which was hotly engaged. I was sent forward

matter settled for him by the sudden charge of Vandeleur's
brigade, which came up at full speed, carried the 7th Division
battalions in the ditch along with it in its impetus, and stormed
La Hermandad in ten minutes. The German defenders—
Baden, Nassau, and Frankfurt battalions—reeled back in
disorder, and retreated to the crest of the heights behind, where
Cassagne's division, hitherto not engaged, picked them up.
D'Erlon succeeded in forming some sort of a new line from
Crispijana near the Zadorra to Zuazo, where his left should
have joined the right of the Army of the South. It is curious
to note that while Grant's brigade lost heavily in this combat
(330 casualties), Vandeleur's, which carried on the attack to
success, suffered hardly at all (38 casualties). Their German
opponents were very badly punished, having lost 620 men,

to report to Lord Dalhousie, who commanded. I found his lordship and
his Q.M.G. Drake in deep conversation. I reported pretty quick, and
asked for orders (the head of the brigade was just getting under fire).
I repeated the question, "What orders, my lord?" Drake became
somewhat animated, and I heard his lordship say, "Better take the
village." I roared out, "Certainly, my lord," and off I galloped, both
calling to me to come back, but "none are so deaf as those who won't
hear." I told General Vandeleur we were immediately to take the village.
The 52nd deployed into line, our Riflemen were sent out in every direction,
keeping up a fire nothing could resist.... The 52nd in line and the swarm
of Riflemen rushed at the village, and though the ground was intersected
by gardens and ditches nothing ever checked us, until we reached the rear
of it. There was never a more impetuous onset—nothing could resist such
a burst of determination.' Smith's addition that the brigade took twelve
guns in this charge seems (as Mr. Fortescue remarks) to be of more doubtful
value.

Naturally there is nothing of this in Dalhousie's dispatch—a most
disappointing paper. It is mostly in a self-exculpatory tone, to justify
his lateness and the absence of his two rear brigades. He *says* that they
came up at the same time as Vandeleur, which is certainly untrue, as
neither of them had a single casualty all day. And they could not have
failed to catch a shell or two if they had been anywhere near the fighting-
line during the subsequent capture of Crispijana and Zuazo. Mr. Fortescue's note that Captain Cairnes's letter in the *Dickson Papers*, p. 916,
proves that Barnes's brigade had arrived by this time, is a misdeduction
from Cairnes's carelessness in talking of Grant's brigade as 'our first
brigade,' meaning thereby our leading brigade, not the brigade officially
numbered 1. When Cairnes says that the 'first brigade' and the guns
were 'in their place,' while the rest arrived very late in the action, we
need only contrast the casualty lists—1st Brigade *nil*, 2nd Brigade
330 casualties, 3rd Brigade *nil*, to see what he means.

including 250 prisoners, in defending La Hermandad against the two British brigades [1].

While Wellington, after the first breaking of the French line, was preparing under cover of the cannonade of Dickson's guns for the assault on their new position in front of Zuazo and Gomecha, General Graham was developing his attack on the Army of Portugal and the French line of retreat, but not with the energy that might have been expected from the victor of Barrosa.

He had, as it will be remembered, sent Oswald and the 5th Division against the bridge of Gamarra Mayor, and Longa's Spaniards against that of Durana, while he himself remained with the 1st Division, Pack's and Bradford's Portuguese, and

---

[1] It will be noticed that I put La Hermandad as the village where the heavy fighting took place, and which Vandeleur's brigade stormed. All historians up to now have followed Napier in making Margarita the important place. A glance at the map will show that the latter village is too far forward to have been held for any time, after Leval had evacuated his original position on the great knoll facing Tres Puentes and Villodas. I have to point out that neither Wellington nor Lord Dalhousie in the two contemporary dispatches (*Dispatches*, x. p. 451, and *Supplementary Dispatches*, viii. pp. 4–6) mention either place by name—only speaking of 'a village.' D'Erlon's staff-officer in the report of the Army of the Centre says that Margarita was held for some time but was rendered untenable by Leval's retreat—so that Darmagnac had to go back to the heights behind. Gazan's report says that the British were masters of Margarita before he took up his position on the heights above Ariñez, and that the *heights behind Margarita* were the fighting position of D'Erlon. Of the diarists or chroniclers who issued their books *before the fifth volume of Napier came out*, and who were present on this part of the field, Green (68th), Wheeler (51st), Captain Wood (82nd), mention no village names, nor do Lord Gough's and Captain Cairnes's contemporary letters, nor Geo. Simmons' contemporary diary. Nor does Sir Harry Smith's amusing account of his dealings with Lord Dalhousie before 'the village' which Vandeleur took (*Autobiography*, i. pp. 97–8) quoted in the preceding note. After Napier's book stated that the Light Division battalions took Margarita, and Gough with the 2/87th La Hermandad (a reversal of the real time and facts as I think), most later writers accepted these statements as gospel. But the report of Kruse, commanding the Nassau regiment, absolutely proves that Napier is wrong. Moreover, the rough map, annexed to D'Erlon's original report of the battle in the French Archives, gives Hermandad as the position of Darmagnac, with his march thither *from* Gomecha and *to* Zuazo indicated by arrows. Kruse's report may be found at length in the Nassau volume of Saussez's *Les Allemands sous les Aigles*, pp. 340–1.

the bulk of his cavalry on the high road, facing the bridge of
Arriaga and its outlying bulwark the village of Abechuco.
We should have expected that the main attack would be
delivered at this point, but nothing of the sort took place.
When the noise of Oswald's heavy fighting at Gamarra Mayor
had begun to grow loud, Graham directed the two Light Battalions of the German Legion (under Colonel Halkett) to clear
the French out of Abechuco. This they did with trifling loss—
1 officer and 51 men, capturing several guns in the village[1].
But Graham made no subsequent attempt to improve his
success by forcing the bridge behind—as is sufficiently witnessed
by the fact that of his remaining battalions the Guards' Brigade
had no casualties that day, and the three Line battalions of
the K.G.L. one killed and one wounded. Before drawing up
in front of Arriaga he had sent Bradford's Portuguese, for a
short time, to demonstrate to his right, toward the bridge of
Yurre; but he called them back after a space, and placed
them to the right of Abechuco, continuing the general line of
the First Division. Bradford's battalions lost precisely 4 men
killed and 9 wounded. It is clear, therefore, that Graham
never attacked the Arriaga position at all. Why he massed
4,000 British and 4,000 Portuguese infantry on this front—not
to speak of two brigades of cavalry—and then never used them,
it is hard to make out.

We know, it is true, that not only Graham but Wellington
himself over-estimated the strength of Reille's force. They
did not know that Maucune had gone away in the dark, in
charge of the great convoy, and thought that Foy's and Taupin's
divisions were the only troops of the Army of Portugal which
had not rejoined. Arguing that he had four infantry divisions
in front of him (though they were really only two), Graham no
doubt did well to be cautious—but he was much more than that.
It was at least his duty to detain and engage as many of the
enemy's troops as was possible—and he certainly did not do so.

There was opposite him at Arriaga one single infantry
division—Sarrut's, and he did so little to employ it that Reille
dared—after observing the British movements for some time—

---

[1] This British claim is corroborated by the narrative of the French
surgeon Fée, present at Abechuco that day.

to take away Sarrut's second brigade (that of Fririon) for use
as a central reserve, which he posted at Betonio a mile back
from the river, leaving Menne's brigade alone—not much
over 2,000 bayonets—opposed to the whole 1st Division,
Bradford, and Pack. It is true that Menne had heavy cavalry
supports—Digeon's dragoons and Curto's brigade of Mermet's
light horse—on one flank, and Boyer's dragoons not far away
on the other. But cavalry in 1813 were not troops which could
defend a bridge or the line of a river. There was also a good
deal of French artillery present—a more important fact under
the existing circumstances. For Reille had still twenty guns
ranged along the river [1], beside those which were detached on
the flank with Casapalacios' Spaniards. But Graham had almost
as many—the three batteries of Lawson, Ramsay, and Dubourdieu—and of these the two last, ranged opposite Arriaga bridge,
and pounding the village behind it, quite held their own against
the opposing guns.

It can only be supposed that Graham, in refraining from any
serious attack along the high road, was obeying in too literal
a fashion Wellington's orders not to commit himself to close
fighting in the low ground, and to regulate his movements by
those of the columns on his right (Picton's and Dalhousie's
divisions). When these had worked their way up the Zadorra
to his neighbourhood he *did* advance. But it was then so late
that the enemy in front of him was able to get away, without
any very disastrous losses.

While Graham kept quiet on the high road, Oswald was
engaged in a very different style at Gamarra Mayor, where after
his first capture of the village, he made at least three desperate
attempts to force the bridge, held most obstinately by Lamartinière's division. The passage was taken and retaken, but no
lodgement on the southern bank could be made. After Robinson's brigade had exhausted itself, Oswald put in the 3/1st
from Hay's brigade and some of his Portuguese [2]. But no

---

[1] Though he had lost several when La Martinière was driven out of
Gamarra Mayor (see above, p. 425) and Abechuco.

[2] The other regiments of Hay's brigade were evidently kept in reserve,
for the casualties of the 1/38th were eight only, and those of the 1/9th 25.
The 8th Caçadores of Spry's brigade lost 40 men, the Portuguese Line
battalions only 41 between the four of them.

success was obtained, though both sides suffered heavily. The
casualty rolls of the 5th Division show a loss of 38 officers and 515
men—those of their French opponents 38 officers and 558 men.
Practically all on both sides fell in the murderous fighting up
and down Gamarra bridge. The forces were so equally balanced
—each about 6,000 bayonets and one divisional battery—that
on such a narrow front decision was impossible when both
fought their best. The only way of attacking the bridge was
by pushing straight down the narrow street of the village from
the British side, and across an open field from the French. Both
parties had guns trained upon its ends, which blew to pieces
any column-head that debouched. There were no fords anywhere near, and the banks for some distance up-stream and
down-stream were lined by the skirmishers of both sides, taking
what cover they could find, and doing their best to keep down
each other's fire. ' It plainly appeared this day that the enemy
had formed a sort of determination not to be beat : we never
saw them stand so vigorous before,' writes a diarist from the
ranks, in Robinson's brigade [1].

There was an absolute deadlock at Gamarra Mayor till nearly
five o'clock in the afternoon. At Durana things went otherwise : Longa, though hampered by his lack of guns, ended
by pushing the Franco-Spanish brigade across the bridge, and
then for some way down the south side of the Zadorra. The
retreating party then made a stand behind a ravine and brook
some half-mile farther on, where they were flanked by a
brigade of Mermet's light cavalry, as well as by their own five
squadrons, and supported by the French battalion of the
3rd Line which had been in their quarter of the field from the
first. Longa was unable to push them farther—probably for
fear of lending his flank to cavalry charges, and gained no
further ground till the general retreat of the French army
began. But he had effectively cut King Joseph's communication with France by seizing Durana—and this was the governing factor of the whole fight, since the enemy had now only
the Pampeluna road by which he could retreat. If Joseph had

---

[1] Sergeant James Hale of the 1/9th, who has left us the only good
detailed account of the fighting at Gamarra with which I am acquainted
(pp. 105–6).

owned some infantry reserves, he could (no doubt) have driven
Longa away; but he had not a man to spare in any part of the
field, and things were going so badly with the Army of the
South that he had no attention to spare for the Army of
Portugal.

It must have been about four o'clock before Wellington,
having rearranged his line and brought up his artillery, determined to renew the general attack on the French right and
centre. Joseph had brought up to the new position (extending
from Crispijana on the left by Zuazo to the heights in front
of Esquivel) the whole of the infantry of the Armies of the
South and Centre, which now formed one rather irregular line.
The only infantry reserve was the six weak battalions of the
Royal Guard—perhaps 2,500 bayonets [1], placed on the high road
in front of Vittoria—there was also a mass of cavalry in reserve,
but this was of as little use for the defence of a hill-position as
was Wellington's for the assault on it. There were now in line
Tilly's division of dragoons which had been brought back from
its useless excursion on the Logroño road, and Pierre Soult's
light horse, both of Gazan's army, with Treillard's dragoons,
Avy's Chasseurs, and the two cavalry regiments of the Royal
Guard, all from the Army of the Centre—in all some 4,500 sabres.

The artillery, however, was very strong, and—deployed in a
long line on both sides of the high road—was already sweeping
all the slopes in front. There were present 46 guns of the Army
of the South (all that it owned save one piece lost at Ariñez
and three absent with Digeon's dragoons), twelve guns of the
Army of the Centre, and 18 from the reserve of the Army of
Portugal—76 in all [2]. Dickson would appear to have brought
up against them very nearly the same number: 54 British,
18 Portuguese, and 3 Spanish guns, when the last of the reserve
batteries had got across the Zadorra and come forward into
line—a total of 75 pieces [3]. The cannonade was the fiercest ever

[1] Numbers impossible to determine, as they are never borne in the
muster rolls of the Army of the Centre. But as they were 2,019 strong on
July 16, when Soult reorganized the whole Army of Spain, they were
probably 2,500 strong before the battle.

[2] So Tirlet, making allowances for the lost pieces.

[3] Viz. the divisional batteries of the 2nd Division (one British, one
Portuguese), 3rd, 4th, 7th, Light, and Silveira's Divisions, two H. A.

known in the Peninsula—each side was mainly trying to pound the enemy's infantry—a task more easy for the French than the Allied gunners, since the assailant had to come up the open hillside, and the assailed was partly screened by woods (especially in front of Gomecha) and dips in the rough ground which he was holding.

The French line was now formed by Cassagne's division on the extreme right, with one regiment (the 16th Léger) in Crispijana, and the others extending to meet Darmagnac's much depleted battalions which were in and about Zuazo. Leval ought to have been in touch with Darmagnac, but obviously was not, the ground on each side of the high road being held by guns only, with cavalry in support some way behind. For after losing Ariñez Leval's infantry had inclined much to their left. But on the other flank Villatte had, as it seems, inclined somewhat to the right, for having lost the heights of La Puebla, he could not prevent Cameron and Morillo from pressing along their crest and getting behind his new position : they were edging past his flank all through this period of the action.

The long front of the British advance started with Colville's brigade—now once more in front line—opposite Crispijana, and was continued southward by those of Grant, Power, Brisbane, Stubbs, Byng, and O'Callaghan, while Vandeleur, Kempt, W. Anson, Skerrett, and Ashworth were formed in support, with Silveira's division and the cavalry in third line. The missing brigades of the 7th Division were not yet on the field, possibly not even across the Zadorra, for neither of them lost a man that day. The advance of the line was a splendid spectacle, recorded with notes of admiration by many who witnessed it from the hill of Ariñez or the heights of La Puebla.

The French artillery fire was heavy, and in some sections of the line very murderous—Power's and Stubbs's Portuguese brigades were special sufferers. But the infantry defence was not resolute : on many parts of the front it was obviously very weak. The enemy was already a beaten army, he had been turned out of two positions, the news had got round that

batteries attached to the cavalry, two British and one Portuguese batteries of the reserve, and three Spanish guns belonging to Morillo.

the road to France had been cut, and that Reille's small force
was in grave danger of losing the line of the Zadorra—in which
case the whole army would find itself attacked in the rear. It
is clear from the French narratives that the infantry did not
support the guns in front line as they should. The reports of
the Army of the Centre speak of being turned on their right
by a column which kept near the river and took Crispijana—
obviously Colville's brigade. As the 16th Léger in that village
only suffered a loss that day of one officer and 26 men, its
resistance cannot have been very serious. But D'Erlon's
divisions were also outflanked on their left—by clouds of
skirmishers drifting in by the wood and broken ground about
Gomecha, who turned on the line of artillery, and began
shooting down the gunners from flank and rear[1]. Obviously
there was a gap along the high road, by which these light
troops must have penetrated, and as obviously it was caused
by Leval having sheered off to the south. For the artillery
report of Gazan's army also speaks of being turned on its right
wing—' enveloped by skirmishers who had got into Gomecha
and were in rear of the position, which was being also attacked
frontally.' Nor is this all, ' the mass on the mountain (Cameron
and Morillo) descended on the left flank and rear of the Army
of the South before it had time to form again : the artillery
found itself without support.' If so, where were the four and
a half divisions of infantry which should have been protecting it ?

The only possible deduction from all our narratives is that
Gazan's army made no real stand on the Gomecha–Esquivel
position, and retired the moment that the attack drew near.
And the person mainly responsible for the retreat was the
Army-Commander himself, whose very unconvincing account
of this phase of the action is that ' the right flank of the line
was continually being outflanked : I received no further orders
about the taking up of the position of which the King had
spoken ; the enemy was getting near the gates of Vittoria (!),
and so I had to continue my movement toward that town,
after having taken up a position by Zuazo, with the intention

[1] These notes are partly from Tirlet's very interesting artillery report,
partly from the narrative of the staff-officer of the Army of the Centre,
already often quoted above.

of covering with my right-hand division and my guns the retreat of the rest of the army, which without this help would have been hopelessly compromised. At this time I had only lost four guns, abandoned on the extreme left of the line : the artillery was intact, and the army had suffered no greater loss than it had inflicted on the enemy.'

Reading this artful narrative, we note that (1) Gazan evacuated on his own responsibility a position that the King had definitely ordered him to take up—because he had ' no further orders ' ; (2) the continued ' turning of his right ' could only have resulted from the defeat of his own troops on and about the high road—which was in his sector, not in D'Erlon's, Leval was across it when the last phase of the battle began ; (3) D'Erlon held Zuazo and complained that there was nothing on his left, which was completely turned on the side where Leval *ought* to have been but was not ; (4) Gazan retreated without any serious loss having compelled him to do so. This is obviously the fact. Villatte's whole division had less than 300 casualties, Leval's under 800, Daricau's under 850 : the only troops hard hit were Maransin's brigade, Rey's brigade of Conroux's division, and the 103rd Line in Daricau's. Moreover, the 4th and 2nd British Divisions, the troops immediately opposed to Gazan's main line, had insignificant losses in this part of the action, Byng's brigade under 150, Ashworth's just 23, Anson's 90, Skerrett's 22 ; the only appreciable loss had been that of Stubbs's Portuguese—about 240. For the heavy casualty lists of O'Callaghan's, Cadogan's, and Brisbane's battalions had all been suffered in the earlier phases of the fight [1].

The fact is that Gazan went off without orders, and left the King and D'Erlon in the lurch. Jourdan is telling the exact truth when he says that ' General Gazan, instead of conducting his divisions to the position indicated, swerved strongly to the right, marching in retreat, so as to link up with Villatte ; he continued to draw away, following the foothills of the mountain [of Puebla], leaving the high road and Vittoria far to his left, and a vast gap between himself and Count D'Erlon ' [2].

No doubt the breach made in the French centre when Picton

---

[1] See tables of losses in Appendices, nos. xi and xii.
[2] *Memoirs*, p. 479.

stormed the heights behind Ariñez had been irreparable from
the first ; and no doubt also the flanking movement of Morillo
and Cameron on the mountain must have dislodged the Army
of the South, if it had waited to come into frontal action with
Cole and Hill.   But Gazan showed complete disregard of all
interests save his own, and went off in comparatively good
condition, without orders, leaving the King, D'Erlon, and Reille
to get out of the mess as best they might.

Some of the British narratives tend to show that many parts
of Gazan's line had never properly settled down into the
Gomecha–Esquivel position, having reached it in such bad
order that they would have required more time than was
granted them to re-form.   An officer present with the skirmishing line of the 4th Division writes in his absolutely contemporary
diary : 'From the time when our guns began to open, and to
throw shells almost into the rear of the enemy's height, we saw
him begin to fall back in haste from his position.   We [4th
Division] marched on at a great pace in column.   From that
moment the affair became a mere hunt.   Our rapid advance
almost cut off four or five French battalions—they made some
resistance at first, but soon dissolved and ran pell-mell, like
a swarm of bees, up the steep hill, from which they began to
fire down on us.   We disregarded their fire, and kept on
advancing—in order to carry out our main object : broken
troops are easy game.   When we found the enemy in this
second position there was heavy artillery fire.   Since his left
wing was somewhat refused, we advanced in échelon from
the right.   When we got within musketry range, we found
he had gone off out of sight.   After that we drove him out of
one position after another till at last we were near the gates
of Vittoria [1].'   Several other 4th Division and 2nd Division
narratives agree in stating that after the storming of Ariñez
the French never made anything like a solid stand on the
Gomecha–Esquivel heights.   But (as has been said above) the
best proof of it is the British casualty list, which shows that
the reserve line was hardly under fire, and that the front line
had very moderate losses, except at one or two points.

[1] *Diary* of Wachholz, attached with a Brunswick light company to the
4th Division, pp. 315–16.

D'Erlon made a more creditable resistance on the French right, but he was obviously doomed if he should linger long after Gazan had gone off.   After losing Crispijana and Zuazo he made a last stand on the slopes a mile in front of Vittoria, between Ali and Armentia, to which the whole of his own artillery and that of the reserve, and perhaps also some guns of the Army of the South, retired in time to take up a final position [1].   For some short space they maintained a furious fire on the 3rd Division troops which were following them up, so as to allow their infantry to re-form.   But it was but for a few minutes—the column near the Zadorra (Grant, Colville, and Vandeleur) got round the flank of the village of Ali, and the line of guns was obviously in danger if it remained any longer in action.   Just at this moment D'Erlon received the King's orders for a general retreat by the route of Salvatierra.   The high road to France had ceased to be available since Longa got across it in the earlier afternoon.   Any attempt to force it open would obviously have taken much time, and might well have failed, since the French were everywhere closely pressed by the pursuing British.   Jourdan judged the idea of reopening the passage to be hopelessly impracticable, and ordered the retreat on Pampeluna as the only possible policy, though (as his report owns) he was aware of the badness of the Salvatierra road, and doubted his power to carry off his guns, transport, and convoy of refugees by such a second-rate track.   But it was the only one open, and there was no choice.

The orders issued were that the Train and Park should get off at once, that the Army of the South should retreat by the country paths south of Vittoria, the Army of the Centre by those north of it.   The Army of Portugal was to hang on to its position till D'Erlon's troops had passed its rear, and then follow them as best it could.   All the cross-tracks indicated to the three armies ended by converging on the Salvatierra road east of Vittoria, so that a hopeless confusion was assured for the moment when three separate streams of retreating troops should meet, and struggle for the use of one narrow and inadequate thoroughfare.   But as a matter of fact the chaos began

---

[1] Thirty guns according to Garbé's report—40 according to that of D'Erlon's staff-officer, quoted above.

long before that time was reached, for the road was blocked
or ever the three armies got near it. The order for the retreat
of the Park and convoys had been issued far too late—Gazan
says that he had advised Jourdan to give it two hours before,
when the first positions had been abandoned. But the Marshal
had apparently high confidence in his power to hold the
Hermandad–Gomecha–Esquivel line ; at any rate, he had given
no such command. The noise of battle rolling ever closer to
Vittoria had warned the mixed multitude of civil and military
hangers-on of the army who were waiting by their carriages,
carts, pack-mules, and fourgons, in the open fields east of
Vittoria, that the French army was being driven in. Many of
those who were not under military discipline had begun to
push ahead on the Salvatierra road, the moment that the
alarming news flew around that the great *chaussée* leading to
France had been blocked. The Park, however—which all day
long had been sending up reserve ammunition to the front, and
even one or two improvised sections of guns—had naturally
remained waiting for orders. So had the immense accumulation
of divisional and regimental baggage, the convoy of treasure
which had arrived from Bayonne on the 19th, and the heavy
carriages of the King's personal caravan, stuffed with the plate
and pictures of the palace at Madrid. And of the miscellaneous
French and Spanish hangers-on of the Court—ministers,
courtiers, clerks, commissaries, contractors, and the ladies who
in legitimate or illegitimate capacities followed them—few had
dared to go off unescorted on an early start. There was a vast
accumulation of distracted womenfolk—*nous étions un bordel
ambulant*, said one French eye-witness—some crammed together
in travelling coaches with children and servants, others riding
the spare horses or mules of the men to whom they belonged.
When the orders for general retreat were shouted around,
among the fields where the multitude had been waiting, three
thousand vehicles of one sort and another tried simultaneously
to get into one or another of the five field-paths which go east
from Vittoria, all of which ultimately debouch into the single
narrow Salvatierra road. A dozen blocks and upsets had
occurred before the first ten minutes were over, and chaos
supervened. Many carriages and waggons never got off on a

road at all. Into the rear of this confusion there came charging, a few minutes later, batteries of artillery going at high speed, and strings of caissons, which had been horsed up and had started away early from the Park. Of course they could not get through—but the thrust which they delivered, before they came to an enforced stop, jammed the crowd of vehicles in front of them into a still more hopeless block. Dozens of carriages broke down—whereupon light-fingered fugitives began to help themselves to all that was spilt. Of course camp followers began the game, but Jourdan says that a large proportion of the French prisoners that day were soldiers who *s'amusaient à piller* in and about Vittoria ; one of the official reports from the Army of Portugal remarks that the retreating cavalry joined in the ' general pillage of the valuables of the army,' and other narrators mention that the treasure-fourgons had already been broken into long before the English came upon the scene [1]. Be this as it may, there was no long delay before the terrors of the stampede culminated with the arrival of several squadrons of Grant's hussars, who had penetrated by the gap between D'Erlon's and Gazan's lines of retreat, and had made a short cut through the suburbs of the town. Of the chaos that followed the firing of the first pistol shots which heralded the charge of the British light cavalry, we must not speak till we have dealt with the last fight of the Army of Portugal, on the extreme French right.

Till Grant's and Colville's brigades broke into Crispijana and Ali, the line of Reille's gallant defence along the Zadorra had remained intact. Only artillery fire was going on opposite the bridge of Arriaga, where the 1st Division and the two Portuguese brigades had halted by Graham's orders at some distance from the river, and had never advanced. The two cavalry brigades were behind them. At Gamarra Mayor the 5th Division had failed to force a passage, though it had inflicted on Lamartinière's troops as heavy a loss as it suffered. Longa was held up half a mile beyond Durana, though he had success-fully cut the Bayonne *chaussée*. There was considerable cannonade and skirmishing fire going on, upon a front of three miles, but no further progress reported. The whole scene,

[1] Blaze, p. 244.

F f 2

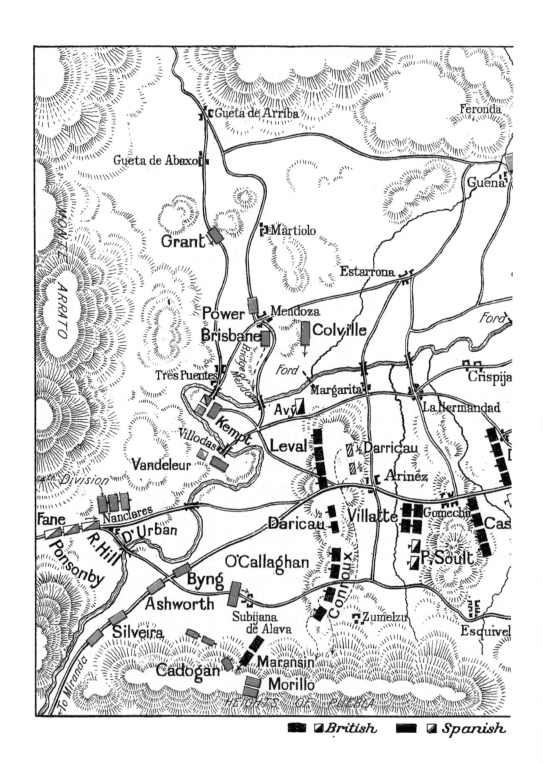

Feronda

Gueta de Arriba

Gueta de Abaxo

Guena

MONTE ARRATO

Martiolo

Grant

Estarrona

Power
Brisbane

Mendoza

Colville

Ford

Très Puentes

Bridge of Mendoza

Ford

Crispija

Margarita

La Hermandad

Avy

Kempt

Villodas

Leval

Darricau

Vandeleur

Arinéz

Division

Fane

Nanclares

Daricau

Villatte

Gomecha

Cas

D'Urban

Ponsonby

R. Hill

O'Callaghan

P. Soult

Byng

Ashworth

Subijana
de Alava

Conroux

Zumelzu

Esquivel

Silveira

To Miranda

Cadogan

Maransin

Morillo

HEIGHTS OF PUEBLA

British   Spanish

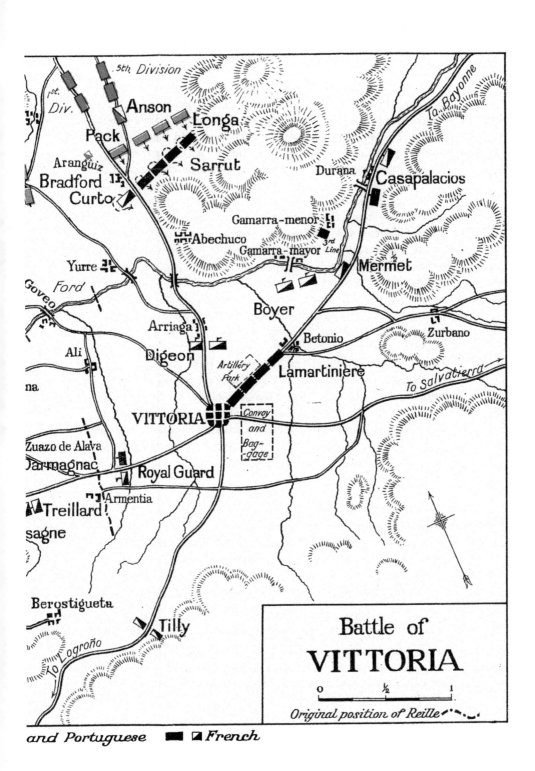

5th. Division

1st. Div.

Anson

Pack

Longa

Aranguiz

Sarrut

Durana

Casapalacios

Bradford
Curto

Gamarra-menor

3rd
Line

Yurre

Abechuco

Gamarra-mayor

Mermet

Goveo

Ford

Boyer

Arriaga

Betonio

Zurbano

Ali

Digeon

Artillery
Park

Lamartiniere

na

To Salvatierra

VITTORIA

Convoy
and
Bag-
gage

Zuazo de Alava
Darmagnac

Royal Guard

Treillard
sagne

Armentia

Berostigueta

To Logroño

Tilly

Battle of

VITTORIA

0   ½   1

Original position of Reille

and Portuguese   ▪ ◪ French

however, was changed from the moment when Grant's and
Colville's brigades, turning the flank of D'Erlon's line close to
the Zadorra, came sweeping over the hills by Ali into the very
rear of Reille's line. The Army of Portugal had been directed
to hold the bridges and keep back Graham, until the rest of the
French host had got off. But the danger now came not from
the front but from the rear. In half an hour more the advancing
British columns would be level with the bridge of Arriaga and
surrounding the infantry that held it. Reille determined on
instant retreat, the only course open to him : so far as was
possible it was covered by the very ample provision of cavalry
which he had in hand. Digeon, who has left a good account
of the crisis, made several desperate charges, to hold back the
advancing British while Menne's brigade was escaping from
Arriaga. One was against infantry, which formed square and
beat off the dragoons with no difficulty [1]—the other against
hussars, apparently two squadrons of the 15th, which had
turned northward from the suburbs of Vittoria and tried to
ride in and cut off the retreat of Menne's battalions [2]. They
were beaten back, and the infantry scrambled off, leaving behind
them Sarrut, their divisional general, mortally wounded as
the retreat began. Moreover, all the guns in and about Arriaga
had to be abandoned in the fields, where they could make no
rapid progress. The gunners unhitched the horses, and escaped
as best they could.

Reille had drawn up in front of Betonio the small infantry
reserve (Fririon's brigade) which he had wisely provided for
himself, flanked by Boyer's dragoons and Curto's brigade of
light cavalry. The object of this stand was not only to give
Menne's and Digeon's troops a nucleus on which they could

---

[1] What regiment was this ? Obviously one of Colville's or Grant's—as
obviously not the 51st, 68th, 82nd, 87th, 94th, from all of which we have
narratives of the battle, which do not mention their being charged by cavalry
or forming square. There remain the *Chasseurs Britanniques*, 1/5th, 2/83rd
—it may have been any of these.

[2] Tomkinson of the 16th, fighting not far off, says that these squadrons
' got into a scrape ' by charging about 2,000 French cavalry (p. 249).
They lost 2 officers and 57 men. This was obviously the affair of which
Digeon speaks. His 12th Dragoons, which charged the square, lost 22
casualties.

rally, but to gain time for Lamartinière to draw off from in front of Gamarra Mayor bridge, where he was still hotly engaged with Oswald's division. This infantry got away in better order than most French troops on that day, and even brought off its divisional battery, though that of the cavalry which had been co-operating with it had to be left behind not far from the river-bank; having got into a marshy bottom where it stuck fast. The Franco-Spaniards of Casapalacios and their attendant cavalry escaped over the hills east of Durana, pursued by Longa, who took many prisoners from them.

When Lamartinière's division had come in, Reille made a rapid retreat to the woods of Zurbano, a mile and a half behind Betonio, which promised good cover. He was now being pursued by the whole of Graham's corps, which had crossed the Zadorra when the bridges were abandoned. Pack's brigade, followed by the 1st Division and Bradford, advanced on Arriaga; they were somewhat late owing to slow filing over the bridge. At Gamarra Oswald sent in the pursuit of Lamartinière two squadrons of light dragoons [1] which had been attached to his column ; these were followed by the rest of their brigade, which Graham sent up from the main road to join them, and also by Bock's German dragoons. The object of using the smaller and more remote bridge was that cavalry crossing by it had a better chance of getting into Reille's rear than they would have secured by passing at Arriaga. The much exhausted 5th Division followed the cavalry.

Having reached the edge of the woods, Reille ordered the bulk of his troops to push on hard, by the two parallel roads which traverse them, keeping Fririon's brigade in hand as a fighting rearguard. The rather disordered columns were emerging on the east side of the woods, and streaming into and past the village of Zurbano, when the leading squadrons of the 12th and 16th Light Dragoons came in upon them. These squadrons had avoided entangling themselves in the trees till the French rearguard had passed on, but prepared to charge the moment they got into open ground, though the main body of the brigade had not come up. They found opposed to them a regiment of Boyer's dragoons, supported by another of

[1] One each of the 12th and 16th.

hussars, which they charged but did not break [1]. But on the coming up of the rear squadrons, the attack was renewed with success. The French cavalry gave way, but only to clear the front of the 36th Line of Fririon's brigade, which was in square outside Zurbano. The British light dragoons swept down on the square, but were completely repulsed by its steady fire. This gained time for the rest of Reille's troops to make off, and the pursuit slackened. But the bulk of the French went off in such haste that they abandoned four guns of Lamartinière's artillery, and took away with them only the remaining two—the sole pieces that escaped that day of the immense train of Joseph's three armies. Some hundreds of stragglers were taken, but no single unit of the retiring force was cut off or captured whole. Reille wisely kept his army, so long as was possible, on the side-paths by Arbulo and Oreytia, before debouching into the main Salvatierra road, which was seething over with the wrecks of the other armies and the convoys. Hence he succeeded in escaping the utter confusion into which the rest fell, and, finally, when he turned into the main track, was able to constitute himself a rearguard to the whole. Graham's pursuit of him seems to have been slow and cautious —no troops indeed ever came near the retreating columns except the two light dragoon regiments, the Caçador battalions of Pack and Bradford, and some of Longa's skirmishers, who (as Reille mentions) followed him along the hills on his left, shooting down into the retreating masses, but not attempting to break in. The 5th Division appears to have followed not much farther than the open ground beyond the woods of Zurbano, where it halted and encamped after eight o'clock in some bean-fields. Nor does it seem that the 1st Division got

---

[1] The best account of all this is in the invaluable Tomkinson's *Diary* (pp. 250–1). There is also an interesting narrative by Dallas, who took part in the charge, though he had no business there (pp. 92–3). The French cavalry were the 15th Dragoons and 3rd Hussars. They suffered heavily—the former regiment losing 4 officers and 53 men, the latter 4 officers and 36 men. The British dragoons got off lightly, all things considered, with 1 officer and 11 men hit in the 12th, and 1 officer and 20 men in the 16th. Tomkinson much praises the French infantry. ' I never saw men more steady and exact to the word of command. I rode within a yard of them, they had their arms at the port, and not a man attempted to fire till we began to retire.'

more than a league or so beyond the Zadorra [1]. The Caçadores and cavalry, however, did not halt till they reached El Burgo, four or five miles farther on.

The scene was very different on the other side of Vittoria, where D'Erlon's army was pushing its way, in utter disorder, through the fields and by-paths over which the Parks and convoy were trying in vain to get off, and Gazan's (farther to the south) was making a dash over ground of the most tiresome sort. For in the rugged tract east of Esquivel and Armentia such paths as there were mostly ran in the wrong direction— north and south instead of east and west—and it was necessary to disregard them and to strike across country. Six successive ravines lay in the way—marshy bottoms in which ran trifling brooks descending toward the Zadorra—and several woods on the ridges between the ravines. Hill's and Cole's skirmishers were pressing in the rear, and above, on the heights of Puebla, Morillo's and Cameron's troops could be seen hurrying along with the intention of getting ahead of the retreating masses. The confusion growing worse every moment—for companies and battalions each struck out for the easiest line of retreat without regard for their neighbours—Gazan gave orders to abandon all the artillery, which was getting embogged, battery after battery, in the ravines, and gave leave for every unit to shift for itself—general *sauve-qui-peut*. The horses were un- hitched from the guns and caissons, many of the infantry threw off their packs, and the army went off broadcast, some in the direction of Metauco and Arbulo, others by village paths more to the south. The general stream finally flowed into the Salvatierra road, where it was covered by the Army of Portugal, which was making a much more orderly retreat [2]. English eye-witnesses of this part of the battle complain bitterly that

---

[1] Cf. the reports of the Army of Portugal, Tomkinson, Hale of the 1/9th, and Graham's very sketchy dispatch, which says that the infantry was much delayed at the bridges, but that ' the greatest eagerness was mani- fested by all the corps. The Caçador battalions of both Portuguese brigades followed with the cavalry. . . . The enemy's flight, however, was so rapid that no material impression could be made on them, though more than once charged by squadrons of General Anson's brigade.' (*Supple- mentary Dispatches*, viii. p. 9.)

[2] Gazan says in his report that he only abandoned the guns because he

no horsemen ever came up to assist the wearied 2nd Division infantry in the pursuit, and maintain that thousands of prisoners might have been taken by a few squadrons[1]. But all the cavalry seems to have been directed on Vittoria by the high road, and save Grant's hussar brigade none of it came into action. This is sufficiently proved by its casualty lists—in R. Hill's, Ponsonby's, Long's, Victor Alten's, and Fane's brigades that day the total losses were one man killed and eleven wounded! Only Anson's Light Dragoons in Graham's corps and Grant's regiments in the centre got into the fighting at all. The rugged ground, it is true, was unfavourable for cavalry action in regular order, but it was almost as unfavourable for disordered infantry escaping over ravines and ditches. Something was wrong here in the general direction of the mounted arm—perhaps it suffered from the want of a responsible cavalry leader—the brigadiers dared not act for themselves, and Bock (the senior cavalry officer) was not only short-sighted in the extreme, but absent from the main battle all day in Graham's corps. One cannot but suspect that Wellington's thunderings in previous years, against reckless cavalry action, were always present in the minds of colonels and brigadiers who had a chance before them. And possibly, in the end, there was more gained by the avoidance of mistakes of rashness than lost by the missing of opportunities, if we take the war as a whole. But at Vittoria it would most certainly appear that the great mass of British cavalry might as well have been on the other side of the Ebro for all the good that it accomplished.

It only remains to speak of the chaos in the fields and roads east of Vittoria. When the general *débâcle* began King Joseph and Jourdan took their post on a low hill half a mile east of the town, and endeavoured to organize the departure of the Park and convoys—a hopeless task, for the roads were blocked, and no one listened to orders. It was in vain that aides-de-camp and orderlies were sent in all directions. Presently a flood of

found the roads south of Vittoria blocked by fugitive vehicles from Vittoria.

[1] L'Estrange of the 31st says that some of the French, moving almost in the middle of advancing British brigades, were mistaken for Spaniards, and allowed to get off unharmed. Surtees of the 2/95th tells a similar story.

fugitives were driven in upon the staff, by the approach of
British cavalry in full career. These were Grant's 10th and
18th Hussars, who had turned the town on its left, and galloped
down on the prey before them. Joseph had only with him the
two squadrons of his Lancers of the Guard, which had been
acting as head-quarters escort all day. It would appear that
the Guard Hussars came up to join them about this time. At
any rate, these two small regiments made a valiant attempt to
hold off the hussars—they were of course beaten, being hopelessly outnumbered [1]. The King and staff had to fly as best
they could, and were much scattered, galloping over fields and
marshy ravines, mixed with military and civil fugitives of all
sorts. Some of the British hussars followed the throng, taking
a good many prisoners by the way : more, it is to be feared,
stopped behind to gather the not too creditable first-fruits of
victory, by plundering the royal carriages, which lay behind the
scene of their charge. The French stragglers had already shown
them the way.

Wellington, on reaching Vittoria, set Robert Hill's brigade of
the Household Cavalry to guard the town from plunder, and
sent on the rest of the horse, and the infantry as they came up,
in pursuit of the enemy. The French, however, had by now a
good start, and troops in order cannot keep up with troops in
disorder, who have got rid of their impedimenta, and scattered
themselves. The country, moreover, was unfavourable for
cavalry, as has been said above, and the infantry divisions
were tired out. The chase ended five miles beyond Vittoria—
the enemy, when last seen, being still on the run, with no formed
rearguard except on the side road where the Army of Portugal
was retreating.

If the prisoners were fewer than might have been expected,
the material captured was such as no European army had ever
laid hands on before, since Alexander's Macedonians plundered
the camp of the Persian king after the battle of Issus. The

---

[1] The lancers are shown in Martinien's lists to have lost six officers, the
hussars four. The casualties of the 18th Hussars (3 officers and 37 men)
and of the 10th (16 men) were certainly got in this affair, which was
evidently hot while it lasted. The best account of Joseph's last half-hour
on the battlefield is in the *Memoires* of Miot de Melito (iii. pp. 280–1), who
was at the King's side and shared his wild ride.

military trophies compared well even with those of Leipzig and Waterloo—151 guns, 415 caissons, 100 artillery waggons. Probably no other army ever left *all* its artillery save two solitary pieces in the enemy's hands [1]. There was but one flag captured, and that was only the standard of a battalion of the 100th Line which had been reduced in May, and had not been actually borne in the battle [2]. The baton of Jourdan, as Marshal of the Empire, was an interesting souvenir, which delighted the Prince Regent when it arrived in London [3], but only bore witness to the fact that his personal baggage, like that of his King, had been captured. A few thousand extra prisoners—the total taken was only about 2,000—would have been more acceptable tokens of victory.

But non-military spoil was enormous—almost incredible. It represented the exploitation of Spain for six long years by its conquerors. ' To the accumulated plunder of Andalusia were added the collections made by the other French armies— the personal baggage of the King—fourgons having inscribed on them in large letters " *Domaine extérieur de S.M. l'Empereur* " —the military chest containing the millions recently received from France for the payment of the Army, and not yet distri- buted—jewels, pictures, embroidery, silks, all manner of things costly and portable had been assiduously transported thus far. Removed from their frames and rolled up carefully, were the finest Italian pictures from the royal collections of Madrid : they were found in the " imperials " of Joseph's own carriages. All this mixed with cannon, overturned coaches, broken-down waggons, forsaken tumbrils, wounded soldiers, French and Spanish civilians, women and children, dead horses and mules, absolutely covered the face of the country, extending over the

---

[1] Of the artillery Tirlet's report shows that 104 were field guns actually used in the battle. The remaining 47 were partly the reserve guns of the Army of the North, left stacked at Vittoria when Clausel took his divisions to hunt for Mina, and partly guns of position from the garrisons of Burgos, Vittoria, Miranda, &c.

[2] There is a report of the regiment in the *Archives Nationales* setting forth that it did not lose its eagle, but the flag of the battalion reduced by Imperial orders in the spring, which was in the regimental fourgon.

[3] It inspired him with the idea of designing a British marshal's baton, on which lions were substituted for eagles. Wellington naturally got the first ever made.

surface of a flat containing many hundred acres [1].' The
miserable crowd was guessed by an eye-witness to have numbered
nearly 20,000 persons. Spanish and French camp-followers and
military stragglers had already started plunder—on them
supervened English and Portuguese civil and military vultures
of the same sort—servants and muleteers by the thousand,
bad soldiers by the hundred : for while the good men marched on,
the bad ones melted out of the ranks and flew to the spoil,
evading the officers who tried to urge them on. In such a chaos
evasion was easy. Nor were the commissioned ranks altogether
without their unobtrusive seekers after gain—as witness the
subjoined narrative by one whom a companion in a contemporary letter describes as a ' graceless youth.'

' As L. and I rode out of Vittoria, we came to the camp in
less than a mile. On the left-hand side of the road was a
heap of ransacked waggons already broken up and dismantled.
There arose a shout from a number of persons among the
waggons, and we found that they had discovered one yet
unopened. We cantered up and found some men using all
possible force to break open three iron clasps secured with
padlocks. On the side of the fourgon was painted " Le Lieu-
tenant-Général Villatte." The hasps gave way, and a shout
followed. The whole surface of the waggon was packed with
church plate, mixed with bags of dollars. A man who thrust
his arm down said that the bottom was full of loose dollars
and boxes. L. and I were the only ones on horseback, and
pushed close to the waggon. He swung out a large chalice,
and buckling it to his holster-strap cantered off. As the people
were crowding to lay hold of the plate, I noted a mahogany box
about eighteen inches by two feet, with brass clasps. I picked
out four men, told them that the box was the real thing, and if
they would fetch it out we would see what it held. They caught
the idea : the box was very heavy. I led the way through the
standing corn, six or seven feet high, to a small shed, where we
put it down and tried to get it open. After several devices had
failed, two men found a large stone, and, lifting it as high as
they could, dropped it on the box. It withstood several blows,

[1] All this from Leith Hay (always an interesting narrator), vol. ii.
pp. 203 and 208.

but at length gave way. Gold doubloons and smaller pieces filled the whole box, in which were mixed some bags with trinkets. Just then an Ordnance store-keeper came up, and said there was no time to count shares : he would go round and give a handfull in turn to each. He first poured a double handfull into my holster. The second round was a smaller handfull. By this time I was reflecting that I was the only officer present, and in rather an awkward position. I said they might have the rest of my share,—there was first a look of surprise, and then a burst of laughter, and I trotted away. I rode eight or ten miles to the bivouack and found the officers in an ancient church—housed à la Cromwell. On the 23rd, before we left our quarters, I and —— went up into the belfry, and counted out the gold—the doubloons alone made nearly £400. I remitted £250 to my father, and purchased another horse with part of the balance [1].'

General Villatte, no doubt, had special facilities in Andalusia —but every fourgon and carriage contained something that had been worth carrying off. The amount of hard cash discovered was almost incredible. Men and officers who had been self-respecting enough to avoid the unseemly rush at the waggons, had wonderful bargains at a sort of impromptu fair or auction which was held among the débris of the convoy that night. Good mules were going for three guineas—horses for ten. Every one wished to get rid of the heavy duros and five-franc pieces, which constituted the greater part of the plunder ; six and eight dollars respectively were offered and taken for a gold twenty-franc piece or a guinea. ' The camp was turned into a fair—it was lighted up, the cars, &c., made into stands, upon which the things taken were exposed for sale. Many soldiers, to add to the absurdity of the scene, dressed themselves up in uniforms found in the chests. All the Portuguese boys belonging to some divisions are dressed in the uniforms of French officers—many of generals [2].'

[1] Oddly enough, two contemporary diaries mention Mr. D.'s luck. He got by no means the biggest haul. Sergeant Costello of the 1/95th says that he got over £1,000. A private of the 23rd carried off 1,000 dollars in silver—a vast load ! Green of the 68th records that two of his comrades got respectively 180 doubloons, and nearly 1,000 dollars (p. 165).
[2] Tomkinson, p. 254.

Wellington had hoped to secure the five million francs of the French subsidy which had just arrived at Vittoria before the battle. His expectations were deceived; only one-twentieth of the sum was recovered, though an inquisitorial search was made a few days later in suspected quarters. One regiment, which had notoriously prospered, was made to stack its knapsacks on the 23rd, and they were gone through in detail by an assistant provost-marshal—but little was found : the men had stowed away their gains in belts and secret pockets; or deposited them with quartermasters and commissaries who were known to be honest and silent.

The only feature in this discreditable scene that gives the historian some satisfaction is to know that there was no mishandling of prisoners—not even of prominent Spanish traitors. The only person recorded to have been killed in the chaos was M. Thiébault, the King's treasurer, who fought to defend his private strong-box containing 100,000 dollars, and got shot [1]. The women were particularly well treated—the Countess Gazan, wife of the Commander of the Army of the South, was sent by Wellington's orders in her own carriage to join her husband— a courtesy acknowledged by several French diarists [2]. The same leave was given later to many others, and the Commander-in-Chief wrote to the Spanish Ministry to beg that no vengeance might be taken on the captured *afrancesados*, and seems to have secured his end in the main.

The French loss in the battle, according to the definitive report made from the head-quarters of the three armies after they had got back into France, was 42 officers and 716 men killed, 226 officers and 4,210 men wounded, and 23 officers and 2,825 prisoners or missing—a total of 8,091. It is known that of the 'missing' some hundreds were stragglers who rejoined later, and some other hundreds dead men, who had not got into the list of killed. The total number of prisoners did not really exceed 2,000. But on the other hand the official returns are incomplete, not giving any figures for the artillery or train of the Armies of Portugal and the Centre, or for the Royal

[1] Miot de Melito, iii. p. 279.
[2] There are amusing accounts of the conversation of this lively lady in the narratives of Leith Hay and Dr. McGrigor, who took care of her.

Guards (which lost 11 officers and therefore probably 150 to 200 men), or for the General Staff (which had 35 casualties), or for the stray troops of the Army of the North present in the battle. Probably the real total, therefore, was very much about the 8,000 men given by the official return.

The Allied casualties were just over 5,000—of whom 3,672 were British, 921 Portuguese, and 552 Spaniards. A glance at the table in the Appendix will show how unequally they were distributed. Seven-tenths of the whole loss fell on the 2nd and 3rd Divisions, with Grant's brigade of the 7th, Robinson's of the 5th, and Stubbs's Portuguese in the 4th. These troops furnished over 3,500 of the total loss of 5,158. The 1st Division (54 casualties), the British brigades of the 4th Division (125 casualties), Hay's and Spry's brigades of the 5th (200 casualties), Barnes' and Lecor's of the 7th (no casualties [1]), the Light Division (132 casualties), Silveira's Division (10 casualties), the cavalry (155 casualties) had no losses of importance. The 266 men marked as missing were all either dead or absent marauding, save 40 of the 71st whom the French took prisoners to Pampeluna. The Spanish loss of 14 officers and 524 men was entirely in Morillo's and Longa's Divisions, and much heavier among the Estremadurans, who fought so well on the heights of La Puebla, than among the Cantabrians who skirmished all day at Durana. Giron's Galicians were never engaged, having only arrived in the rear of Graham's column just as the fighting north of the Zadorra was over. They encamped round Arriaga at the end of the day.

That the battle of Vittoria was the crowning-point of a very brilliant strategic campaign is obvious. That in tactical details it was not by any means so brilliant an example of what Wellington and his army could accomplish, is equally obvious. Was the General's plan to blame ? or was a well-framed scheme wrecked by the faults of subordinates ? It is always a dangerous matter to criticize Wellington's arrangements—so much seems clear to the historian that could not possibly have been known to the soldier on the morning of June 21st.

---

[1] But Lecor had a straggler or two out of one of his line-battalions—no doubt men who had gone off marauding, like most of the missing in the British list.

It is obvious to us now that there was a fair chance not only
of beating the French army, and of cutting off its retreat on
Bayonne, but of surrounding and destroying at least a considerable portion of it. Wellington's orders are always extremely
reticent in stating his final aims, and give a list of things to be
done by each division, rather than a general appreciation of
what he intends the army to accomplish. But reading his
directions to Graham, Hill, and Dalhousie, and looking at the
way on which they work out on the map, and the allocation
of forces in each column, it would seem that in view of the
distribution of the French troops on the afternoon of June 20th,
he planned a complete encircling scheme, which should not
only accomplish what he actually did accomplish, but much
more. Graham, with his 20,000 men, must have been intended
not only to force the line of the Zadorra and cut the Royal
Road, but to fall upon the rear of the whole French army,
which on the afternoon of the 20th had been seen to have a
most inadequate flank-guard towards the north-east. Hill's
20,000 men were not, as Jourdan thought, the only main
attack, nor as Gazan (equally in error) thought, a mere demonstration. They were intended to make an encircling movement
to the south, as strong as Graham's similar movement to the
north. But obviously both the flanking columns, Hill's far more
than Graham's, were in danger of being repulsed, if the French
could turn large unemployed reserves upon them. Wherefore the
central attacks, by the 4th and Light Divisions on the Nanclares
side, and by the 3rd and 7th Divisions on the Mendoza side, were
necessary in order to contain any troops which Jourdan might
have sent off to overwhelm Hill or Graham.

And here comes the weak point of the whole scheme—all the
movements had to be made through defiles and over rough
country : Hill had to debouch from the narrow pass of Puebla,
Graham had a long mountain road from Murguia, and, worst of
all, Dalhousie, with the 3rd and 7th Divisions, had to cross the
watershed of a very considerable mountain by mere peasants'
tracks. Only the column which marched from the Bayas to
Nanclares had decent going on a second-rate road. There was,
therefore, a considerable danger that some part of the complicated scheme might miscarry. And any failure at one point

imperilled the whole, since the Nanclares column was not to
act till Hill was well forward, and the Mendoza column was
ordered to get into touch with the troops to its right, and regulate its movements by them ; while Graham, still farther off,
was also to guide himself by what was going on upon his right,
to correct himself with the Mendoza column, and only to attack
on the Bilbao road when it should be seen that an attack would
be obviously useful to the main advance.

Hill discharged his part of the scheme to admiration, as he
always did anything committed to him, and took up the
attention of the main part of the Army of the South. But the
central and left attacks did not proceed as Wellington had
desired. Graham got to his destined position within the time
allotted to him, but when he had reached it, was slow and
unenterprising in his action. He was seeking for Dalhousie's
column, with which he had been directed to co-ordinate his
operations : he sent out cavalry scouts and Bradford's Portuguese to his right, but could find nothing. This, I think,
explains but does not wholly excuse his caution at noon. But
it neither explains nor excuses at all his tactics after he had
received, at two o'clock, Wellington's orders telling him to press
the enemy hard, and make his power felt. With his two
British divisions, the Portuguese of Pack and Bradford, and
two cavalry brigades, he only made a genuine attack at one
point, and did not put into serious action (as the casualty lists
show) more than four battalions—those used at Gamarra
Mayor. The whole left column was contained by little more
than half of its number of French troops. Graham says in his
dispatch to Wellington that ' in face of such force as the enemy
showed it was evidently impossible to push a column across
the river by Gamarra bridge.' He does not explain his inactivity at other points, except by mentioning that the enemy
had ' at least two divisions in reserve on strong ground behind
the river [1].' There was really only one brigade in reserve, and
so far from being compelled to attack at Gamarra only, Graham
had besides Arriaga bridge on the main road, two other bridges
open to assault (those of Goveo and Yurre), besides at least one
and probably three fords. All these more southern passages

---

[1] *Supplementary Dispatches*, viii. p. 8.

were watched by cavalry only, without infantry or guns. It is clear that Graham could have got across the Zadorra somewhere, if he had tried. Very probably his quiescence was due to his failing eyesight, which had been noticed very clearly by those about him during this campaign[1]. The only part of his corps which did really useful work was Longa's Spanish division, which at least cut the Bayonne road at the proper place and time.

But if Graham's tactics cannot be praised, Lord Dalhousie was even more responsible for the imperfect consequence of the victory. Why Wellington put this fussy and occasionally disobedient officer in charge of the left-centre column, instead of Picton, passes understanding. The non-arrival of the 7th Division, which was to lead the attack, was due to incompetent work by him or his staff. He says in his dispatch that he was delayed by several accidents to his artillery (Cairnes's battery). But from his own narrative we see that the guns got up almost as soon as his leading infantry brigade (Grant's), while his two rear brigades (Barnes and Le Cor) never reached the front in time to fire a shot. What really happened was that for want of staff guidance, for which the divisional commander was responsible, these troops did not take the path assigned to them, and went right over, instead of skirting, the summit of Monte Arrato, making an apparently short (and precipitous) cut, which turned out to be a very long one[2]. So when Dalhousie did arrive, with one brigade and his guns, Picton had long been waiting by Las Guetas in a state of justifiable irritation. Finally, Dalhousie (lacking the greater part of his division) did not attack till he got peremptory orders to do so from the Commander-in-Chief. Hence the extreme delay, which caused grave risk to Hill's wing, so long engaged without support. It is fair to add that the delay had one good effect—since it led Jourdan to think that his right was not going to be attacked, and therefore to send off Villatte's and Cassagne's

[1] See e. g. Swabey's note on his dangerous ride with Graham along the Esla, at the end of May, ' whether the General is blind or mad I have not decided—he must have been one or the other to ride in cold blood over those rocks and precipices '. Swabey's *Diary*, p. 595.

[2] Cairnes's *Diary*, p. 926.

divisions to the far left. If Dalhousie had advanced an hour earlier, these divisions would have been near enough to support Leval. But this is no justification for the late arrival and long hesitations of the commander of the 7th Division. Undoubtedly a part of the responsibility devolves on Wellington himself, for putting an untried officer in charge of a crucial part of the day's operations, when he had in Picton an old and experienced tactician ready to hand.

The strategical plan was so good that minor faults of execution could not mar its general success. Yet it must be remembered that, if all had worked out with minute accuracy, the French army would have been destroyed, instead of merely losing its artillery and train. And the fact that 55,000 men escaped to France, even if in sorry condition, made the later campaign of the Pyrenees possible. There would have been no combats of Maya and Roncesvalles, no battles of Sorauren and St. Marcial, if the eight French divisions present at Vittoria had been annihilated, instead of being driven in disorder on to an eccentric line of retreat.

SECTION XXXVII

EXPULSION OF THE FRENCH FROM SPAIN

CHAPTER I

THE PURSUIT OF CLAUSEL

At ten o'clock on the morning of June 22nd Wellington moved out from Vittoria in pursuit of the French. Touch with them had been lost on the preceding night, as the divisions which had fought the battle had ceased to move on after dark, and had settled into bivouacs four or five miles beyond the city. The enemy, on the other hand, had continued his flight in the darkness, till sheer exhaustion compelled each man to throw himself down where he was, all order having been lost in most units, and only Reille's rearguard of the Army of Portugal having kept its ranks. About midnight the majority had run to a standstill, and the hills along the Salvatierra road began to be covered with thousands of little fires, round which small groups were cooking the scanty rations that they had saved in their haversacks. ' The impromptu illumination had a very pretty effect : if the enemy had seen it he might have thought that we had rallied and were in order. But it was only next morning that the regiments began to coalesce, and reorganization was not complete till we got back to France. Generals were seeking their divisions, colonels their regiments, officers their companies. They found them later—but one thing was never found again—the crown of Spain, fallen for ever from the brow on which it was not to be replaced[1].' King Joseph himself, pushing on ahead of the rout, reached Salvatierra, sixteen miles from the field, before he dismounted, and shared a meagre and melancholy supper with D'Erlon and two ministers, the Irish-Spaniard O'Farrill and the Frenchman Miot de Melito.

---

[1] Fée, *Souvenirs de la guerre d'Espagne*, pp. 249–50.

To them entered later Jourdan, who had been separated from the rest of the staff in the flight. He flung himself down to the table, saying, ' Well, gentlemen, they *would* have a battle, and it is a lost battle,' after which no one said anything more. This was the old marshal's reflection on the generals who, all through the retreat, had been urging that it was shameful to evacuate Spain without risking a general action. After three hours' halt, sleep for some, but the wakefulness of exhaustion for others, the King's party got to horse at dawn, and rode on toward Pampeluna, the army straggling behind them. It was a miserable rainy day with occasional thunderstorms: every one, from Joseph to the meanest camp-follower, was in the same state of mental and physical exhaustion. But the one thing which should have finished the whole game was wanting— there was practically no pursuit.

Of Wellington's nine brigades of cavalry only two, those of Grant and Anson, had been seriously engaged on the 21st, and had suffered appreciable losses. The other seven were intact, and had not been in action. It is obvious that they could not have been used to effect in the darkness of the night, and over rough ground and an unknown track. But why an early pursuit at dawn was not taken in hand it is difficult to make out. Even the same promptness which had been shown after Salamanca, and which had been rewarded by the lucky gleanings of Garcia Hernandez, was wanting on this occasion. There was no excuse for the late start of the cavalry, and in consequence it rode as far as Salvatierra without picking up more than a few wounded stragglers and worn-out horses and mules. The French had gone off at dawn, and were many miles ahead.

The infantry followed slowly ; not only were the men tired by the late marches and their legitimate exertions in the battle, but many thousands had spent the hours of darkness in a surreptitious visit to the field of the convoy, and had come back to the regimental bivouac with plunder of all kinds bought at the cost of a sleepless night. Many had not come back at all, but were lying drunk or snoring among the débris of the French camps. Wellington wrote in high wrath to Bathurst, the Minister for War: ' We started with the army in the highest order, and up to the day of the battle nothing could get on better. But that event has (as usual)[1] annihilated all discipline. The soldiers of the army have got among them about a million sterling in money, with the exception of about 100,000 dollars, which were got for the military chest.   They are incapable of marching in pursuit of the enemy, and are totally knocked up.   Rain has come and increased the fatigue, and I am quite sure that we have now out of the ranks double the amount of our loss in the battle, and that we have more stragglers in the pursuit than the enemy have, and never in one day make more than an ordinary march.   This is the consequence of the state of discipline in the British army.   We may gain the greatest victories, but we shall do no good till we so far alter our system as to force all ranks to do their duty.   The new regiments are as usual worst of all.   The —— are a disgrace to the name of soldier, in action as elsewhere : I shall take their horses from them, and send the men back to England, if I cannot get the better of them in any other manner [2].'

This, of course, is one of Wellington's periodical explosions of general indiscriminating rage against the army which, as he confessed on other occasions, had brought him out of many a dangerous scrape by its sheer hard fighting.   He went on a few days later with language that can hardly be forgiven : ' We have in the Service the scum of the earth as common soldiers, and of late years have been doing everything in our power, both by law and by publication, to relax the discipline by which alone such men can be kept in order.   The officers of the lower ranks will not perform the duty required from them to keep the soldiers in order.   The non-commissioned officers are (as I have repeatedly stated) as bad as the men.   It is really a disgrace to have anything to say to such men as some of our soldiers are [3].'   The Commander-in-Chief's own panacea was more shooting, and much more flogging.   All this language is comprehensible in a moment of irritation, but was cruelly unjust to many corps which kept their discipline intact, never straggled, and needed no cat-o'-nine-tails : there were battalions

---

[1] He is thinking of the nights after the storms of Rodrigo and Badajoz.

[2] *Dispatches*, xii. p. 473.. The regiment named is a newly arrived cavalry unit, which attracted the Commander-in-Chief's special notice by its prominence in plundering.

[3] Wellington to Bathurst, *Dispatches*, xii. p. 496.

where the lash was unknown for months at a time. But Wellington usually ignored the moral side of things : he seldom spoke to his men about honour or patriotism or *esprit de corps,* and long years afterwards officially informed a Royal Commission on the Army that ' he had no idea of any great effect being produced on British soldiers by anything but the immediate fear of corporal punishment.' It is sad to find such mentality in a man of strict honour and high military genius. On this particular occasion he, no doubt, did well to be angry : but were there no regiments which could have marched at dawn to keep up the pursuit ? Undoubtedly there were many : Ponsonby's heavy dragoons had ridden through the chaos of plunder without a man leaving the ranks, and had bivouacked five miles to the front of Vittoria. There were several infantry brigades which had been so far to the left or the right in the action that they never came near the temptation, and only remembered the night of the 21st as one of short commons and hard lying [1]. Perhaps the sight of the disgraceful confusion in and about Vittoria gave the Commander-in-Chief an exaggerated impression of the general condition of the army. And undoubtedly he had an absorbing night's task before him, when he sat down to work out the entire recasting of his operations which the victory had made necessary.

His main design, as expressed in the order for the 22nd, was to send Giron and Longa into Biscay by the great Bayonne *chaussée,* to pursue Maucune's convoy and to cut off, if possible, Foy and the garrison of Bilbao, while the Anglo-Portuguese army marched in pursuit of the French main army on Pampeluna. Clausel had been heard of in the direction of Logroño ; a zealous and patriotic innkeeper had ridden 40 miles on the night of the 20th to report to Wellington the position of the head of his column ; and it was the knowledge that he was more than a full day's march from Vittoria which had enabled the arrangements for the battle to be made with complete security against any intervention on his part [2]. But, though it was

---

[1] Personal diaries seem to show that this was the case with Cadogan's brigade on the right, and the whole 5th Division on the left.

[2] This interesting fact is recorded in a conversation of Wellington with Croker, which contains some curious notes on the battle (Croker, ii. p. 232),

most probable that he would have heard of the disaster to the King's army, and have turned back to Pampeluna or Saragossa, there was a chance that the news might not have reached him. If so, he could be at Vittoria by the afternoon of the 22nd, and his appearance there might prove very tiresome, as the British hospitals and the whole spoil of the battle would have been at his mercy. Wherefore Wellington, who somewhat underrated Clausel's strength [1], left behind at Vittoria the 5th Division and R. Hill's cavalry brigade to guard the place : the 6th Division was due to arrive at noon, or not much later, from Medina de Pomar, so that 12,000 men would be available if the possible but improbable event of a raid on Vittoria should come to pass.

These precautions having been taken, the army marched off at ten o'clock, in three columns, the ' Centre Column ' of previous days with head-quarters and the bulk of the cavalry sticking to the main Salvatierra–Pampeluna road, while Hill and Graham kept to side-tracks [2], which were available so long as the march lay in the plain of Vittoria, but converged on Salvatierra, where the watershed comes, and the mountains of Navarre block the way. Here all the roads met, and there was a steep rise and a defile, before the headwaters of the Araquil, the main river of north-western Navarre, were reached.

That afternoon Wellington's quartermaster-general, George Murray—about the only man who ever dared to make a suggestion to his chief—asked him whether it might not be worth while to send a detachment northward, by the mountain road which goes from Salvatierra to Villafranca on the great Bayonne *chaussée*. For Giron and Longa might have been detained by the French forts at the defile of Salinas, at Mondragon and elsewhere, and so have failed to get forward in their pursuit of Maucune's convoy and the Bilbao garrison. But a force sent across the hills from Salvatierra would cut in to the *chaussée* behind the fortified posts ; and, if the convoy

[1] Thinking that he had only his own two divisions of the Army of the North, and Taupin's of the Army of Portugal, while really Barbot's division was also with him.

[2] The former going by El Burgo and Alegria, the latter by Arzubiaga and Audicana.

were moving slowly, might catch it as it passed through Villa-franca, or at any rate intercept other stray bodies of French troops [1]. Wellington approved the idea at once, and ordered Graham to take the greater part of his own column—the 1st Division, Pack's, and Bradford's Portuguese, and Anson's cavalry brigade,—to leave the pursuit of the King's army, and to march to co-operate with the Spanish troops who had already been detached to press the retreat of the French garrisons of Biscay. The road Salvatierra–Villafranca turned out practicable for all arms, but very trying both to cavalry and artillery, its first stage being a long uphill pull, over a road of the most stony kind—on the watershed at the Puerto de San Adrian it was taken through a tunnel cut in the solid rock. The diversion of Graham's column being an afterthought—the orders for it were only issued at 3 p.m.—there was some delay in finding the troops in an afternoon of blinding rain, and turning them on to the new direction. The general himself, as his dispatch shows, was not reached by Wellington's orders till next morning [2]. Only the light brigade of the German Legion got well forward on the 22nd,—the rest of the 1st Division and Bradford's Portuguese hardly got started. Anson's Light Dragoons and Pack's Portuguese, like Graham himself, never received their orders at all that night, having pushed on beyond Salvatierra for two leagues or more, where the officers sent in search of them failed to catch them up. They had actually gone forward some miles farther towards Navarre, on the morning of the 23rd, before they were found and set right. This caused a tiresome countermarch of some miles to get back to Salvatierra and the cross-roads. Wellington was much vexed with the bad staff-work, but vented his wrath, unfortunately, not on his own aides-de-camp but on a meritorious officer whom they had failed to find or warn. Captain Norman Ramsay, the hero of the 'artillery charge' at Fuentes de Oñoro [3], was attached with his battery to Anson's cavalry brigade. He was still moving eastward, on the night of the 22nd, when the Commander-in-Chief chanced to come upon him. Wellington

[1] Murray to Wellington, *Supplementary Dispatches*, viii. pp. 3–4.
[2] See his dispatch to Wellington dated from Tolosa on June 26th.
[3] See vol. iv. p. 327.

at once ordered him to halt, billet his men in a neighbouring
village, and wait for new directions. According to Ramsay's
version of the words used, they were that ' if there were any
orders for the troop in the course of the night, he would send
them [1].' But Wellington was under the impression that the
phrase used was that Ramsay was not to move until he had
direct orders from Head-Quarters as to his route. Next morning
about 6 a.m. an assistant quartermaster-general (Captain
Campbell) came to the village, and asked Ramsay if he had yet
received his directions. On hearing that he had not, the staff-
officer told him to follow Anson's brigade, who (as Ramsay
supposed) were still moving eastward ; for no hint of the change
of route had been given him on the previous night. The
battery was started off again on the road towards Pampeluna,
and its commander rode on ahead to seek for the cavalry to
whom he was attached. At this moment Wellington came up,
expressed high wrath at finding the guns on the move in the
wrong direction, and asked for Ramsay, who was not forthcoming for some time. Whereupon the angry general ordered
him to be put under arrest for flagrant disobedience, and spoke
of trying him by court martial. His version of the offence was
that ' Captain Ramsay disobeyed a positive order given him
verbally by me, in expectation of a circumstance which occurred,
namely that he might receive orders, from some one else to move
as I did not wish him to move [2].' It is easy to see how the
vagueness in the wording of the order, or even a misconception
of the stress laid upon one of its clauses, brought about Ramsay's
mistake. He understood that he was to halt till he got orders,
and took Campbell's message to be the orders meant. It is
pretty clear from Wellington's own language that Ramsay was
not warned that he might receive orders not directly proceeding
from G.H.Q., which he was to disregard entirely. Explanation
of that kind would not have been in the Wellingtonian manner.

The unfortunate battery-commander, who had done splendid
service on the 21st, and had a brilliant record behind him,
gained the sympathy of the whole army, and such senior officers

---

[1] See Colonel Frazer's account in his *Peninsular Letters*, p. 186.

[2] See, for this statement of the Duke's, Fortescue's *British Army*, vol. ix.
p. 199.

as dared continued to make intercession for his pardon. After keeping him for some weeks under arrest, Wellington resolved not to try him, and to send him back to his battery. But he was cut out of the reward which he had earned at Vittoria, and did not receive the brevet advance in rank or the decorations given to the other battery-commanders, so that he practically lost ground in comparison with his equals and fell to the bottom of the list. This was a deadly blow to Ramsay, who was sensitive and full of professional pride : he kept silence—not so his comrades, who filed the incident as another flagrant example of Wellington's dislike for and injustice to the artillery arm [1]. He fell, still only a battery-commander, at Waterloo.

The result of the miscarriage of orders on the night of the 22nd and the morning of the 23rd was that Graham's turning column was late in its movement. The general himself was one of the last to get the new direction—the cavalry which should have been at the head of the march was at its tail. The German Light Battalions were very far ahead of all the other units, and had to hold back in order to let the rest come up. Hence the attack on Villafranca was not delivered on the evening of the 23rd, as it might have been, but on the afternoon of the 24th, and in the intervening twenty-four hours the greater part of the French troops whom Graham might have cut off filed through Villafranca on their way to Tolosa and the frontier, and only a flank-guard was brought to action. Of this more in its proper place.

The rest of the troops under Wellington's immediate eye, the ' Centre Column ' and Hill's corps, pursued their way on the 23rd along the Salvatierra–Pampeluna road—only Victor Alten's hussars got in touch with the tail of King Joseph's fugitive host, which was moving at a great pace and had a long start. There was now a proper rearguard—Cassagne's division of the Army of the Centre, which had lost only 250 men at Vittoria, and had been more shaken than hurt, having replaced the much-tried Army of Portugal as the covering force. King Joseph halted for some hours at Yrurzun, and there gave orders

---

[1] See Duncan's *History of the Royal Artillery*, vol. ii. pp. 356–60, an indictment of Wellington's whole policy to the corps, and especially of his famous Waterloo letter on their conduct in 1815.

for Reille to diverge from the main line of retreat, and to take his two divisions, a cavalry brigade, and all the teams of his lost artillery by the route of Santesteban and the valley of the Bastan, back to the French frontier on the lower Bidassoa[1]. Finding himself so feebly pursued, he had jumped to the conclusion that Wellington might have marched with the bulk of his force on the great *chaussée*, making directly for Irun and Bayonne. There being nothing to stop him save the scattered detachments under Foy, an invasion of France was possible. Hence Reille was directed to join Foy in haste, and cover the line of the Bidassoa. Thus Graham and Reille were now moving parallel to each other, both in a direct northerly direction, but separated by many a mile of impracticable mountains. The Armies of the South and Centre continued their retreat on Pampeluna.

Meanwhile Wellington on the morning of the 23rd received some important news from Vittoria. The unexpected had happened : Clausel having failed to hear of the King's defeat— as chance would have it—was marching on the city by the Trevino road. Pakenham had already arrived there, but the 5th Division had gone forward to join the tail of Graham's column on being relieved by the 6th, nothing having yet been heard of the French till midday. The force on the spot, therefore, was rather weak, if Clausel had meant mischief. But he did not, and was becoming aware of the danger of his own position. He had heard on the 20th, when he was in march along the Ebro from Logroño on Haro, that the King had evacuated Miranda that day, and was drawing back to Vittoria. It was obviously dangerous to seek to join him by the road near the river, and Clausel on the 21st, the day of the battle, was trying to recover touch with the main army by taking the route La Guardia–Trevino. This détour removed him out of striking distance during all the critical hours. By some strange chance he neither met any of the King's aides-de-camp, who were hunting for him on all sides, nor fell in with any of the fugitives from the routed army either on the night of the 21st nor on the morning of the 22nd. He resumed his march

---

[1] Reille reported that the straggling was so portentous that only 4,200 infantry were with the eagles on July 24th. See Vidal de la Blache, i. p. 79.

from La Guardia, and reached Trevino in the afternoon. There he heard from *afrancesados* the news that there had been a disastrous battle on the previous day, but could get no details. He therefore detached some squadrons to explore along the mountain road from Trevino to Vittoria—they made their way as far as the crest of the heights of Puebla, above Berrostigueta, driving in first some Spanish irregulars, and then picquets of British cavalry ; from the watershed they could see allied troops getting into order, but not their numbers. Pakenham, on being warned by the guerrilleros, had occupied Vittoria town with two Portuguese battalions, drawn up the rest of his troops for a fight, and sent to warn Oswald and the 5th Division, as well as Giron's Spaniards, who had not gone many miles yet, that trouble was at hand. Both of these forces halted and prepared to turn back.

But on hearing the report of his horsemen Clausel had no thought of a raid on Vittoria : his only idea was to get out of danger, and rejoin the main army as quickly as possible. That Joseph and Jourdan had been beaten, he was now aware ; but details were wanting : he did not know whether the rout had been complete, or whether the King's army was capable of rallying and making head at Pampeluna. If he had understood that all the artillery had been lost, and that a retreat into France was imminent, he might probably have given up the idea of a junction, and have set out in haste to retire on Saragossa, by way of the main road down the Ebro by Logroño and Tudela. But not knowing this, his first plan was to march for Salvatierra by the mountainous road which goes from Viana on the Ebro to the upper valley of the Ega. On the 23rd he marched from Trevino to Viana, on the 24th he started out from that place and went 20 miles as far as Santa Cruz de Campero, where he heard that Mina and all his bands were on his flank, and that an English column was coming down upon him from Salvatierra. The latter rumour was false, but induced Clausel to abandon any idea of taking a short cut to join the King. It would seem also that he had picked up some news as to the crushing effect of Vittoria on the French army, and knew that it must have fallen back on Pampeluna. He hurriedly retraced his steps, picked up the garrison of Logroño and set out to move on Pampeluna by the Mendavia–Puente la Reyna road late on the 25th. His vanguard had got as far as Sesma when he heard that Mina had dropped down from Estella to Lerin, blocking this road also. It might have been possible to attack and beat him, but renewed reports that the British were also approaching disturbed Clausel, and he swerved back to the Ebro by cross-roads and crossed it at Lodosa on the 26th.

This move, which placed him on the high road from Logroño to Saragossa, implied the abandonment of all hope of reaching Pampeluna and joining the King. He had resolved to fall back on Aragon and seek refuge with Suchet's troops in that direction. But he had lost much time in his countermarches, and was on the 27th in greater danger than he knew, since Wellington was now coming down from the north, in the hope of heading him off and cutting his line of retreat. And if Clausel had lost as much time in the next five days as he had in the last, his position would have been most desperate, for Wellington had ascertained his whereabouts, and was marching upon him in great strength, with a good hope of intercepting him, if he were still adhering to his original plan of making for Pampeluna and rejoining the King.

The idea that Clausel might be caught and destroyed had come to the British general's mind on the 26th, when he had reached the environs of Pampeluna, and had made sure that the whole of King Joseph's armies were well on the road for France. The pursuit had been little more fruitful on the 24th–25th than it had been on the 22nd–23rd. But at least closer contact had been secured with the enemy: on the afternoon of the 24th the leading British troops had brought D'Erlon's rearguard to action at the passage of the Araquil, in front of the cross-roads at Yrurzun. This combat, in which the 1st German Hussars, the 1st and 3rd battalions of the 95th, and Ross's battery were engaged against Darmagnac's division of the Army of the Centre[1] cost the enemy about 100 casualties[2], and one of the only two guns which he had brought off from Vittoria. It was a running fight, in which the rearguard all the

---

[1] Which had relieved Cassagne's division, the rearguard on the 23rd.
[2] The regiment of Nassau alone returned 76 casualties that day.

way from Yrurzun to Berrioplano was being turned and driven in. But no large captures were made.

While this skirmish was in progress, on the afternoon of the 24th, the main body of the French army was already on the march past Pampeluna towards France. The troops were not allowed to enter the fortress, where only the King, his General Staff, and his courtiers lodged on the night of the 24th. It was feared that the famished soldiery might plunder the stores if they got access to them, so they were taken round by suburban roads, which did not pass through the city. Gazan with the Army of the South started on the evening of the 24th, taking the route by Zubiri and the Pass of Roncesvalles to St. Jean-Pied-de-Port. D'Erlon set out nine hours later, at dawn on the 25th, using the better road by the Col de Velate and the Pass of Maya, which took him to the Bastan, whither Reille had gone before him. But while the Army of Portugal passed on to the lower Bidassoa, the Army of the Centre was ordered to halt in the Bastan and hold its ground if possible.

Only three or four hours after D'Erlon's column had left the suburbs of Pampeluna the first English vedettes showed themselves on the Salvatierra road. These came from Victor Alten's light cavalry; they coasted round the city on the south, and picqueted the Puente la Reyna and Tafalla roads, by either of which Clausel might conceivably be on the move to join the King. But no trace of the French could be found, save that of the retiring rearguard of the Army of the Centre. Of British infantry only the Light Division appeared in front of the fortress, on the side of Berrioplano, though the 4th and Grant's hussars were close behind it. Picton and Dalhousie with the 3rd and 7th Divisions were still farther back on the Salvatierra road, and Hill's whole corps was told to halt until their predecessors should have cleared the way in front of them. The 5th Division, having received the alarm about Clausel's raid on Vittoria, had turned back on the 23rd and was a full march behind Hill. The 6th Division had now passed out of Pakenham's hands into those of Clinton, its normal commander, who had just come up from Lisbon [1]. It remained at Vittoria when all danger from

[1] And took over command on the night of the 22nd; see *Pakenham Letters*, June 26, 1813.

Clausel was over, and had originally been intended to come in on the rear of the 5th Division at Salvatierra, leaving the hospitals and spoils under the guard of some details [1]. But other orders were soon to reach it.

During the night of the 25th Wellington got the news from Mina that Clausel's column, which he had supposed to be making a hasty retreat down the Ebro, ever since its vain appearance in front of Vittoria on the evening of the 22nd, was much less far off than he had supposed. Owing to its countermarches on the 23rd–24th it had only just got back to Logroño, and had started off from that town on the 25th by the road north of the Ebro via Mendavia and Sesma, apparently heading for Pampeluna. If this were Clausel's game, he might be intercepted and caught, and allied columns might thrust themselves between him and his escape towards Saragossa or Jaca. The nearer he got to Pampeluna the better, since the French main army was no longer there, but in rapid march for its native soil.

The orders which Wellington had issued upon the afternoon of the 25th for the movements of the army on the 26th, had contemplated nothing more than the investment of Pampeluna by the 3rd and 7th Divisions on the north side, and the Light and 4th Divisions on the south side of the Arga. But the news which had come in from Mina caused a complete change in his plans : the morning orders of the 26th direct Cole, with the 4th and Light Divisions, not to linger near Pampeluna, but to move off as far as the men could go on the Tudela road—to Mendavil, half-way to Tafalla, if possible : Grant's hussar brigade was to push ahead in front of the infantry, and discover whether Clausel was to be heard of on this road, or perhaps on the Estella–Puente la Reyna road, which was an alternative (if less likely) track for him to take if marching on Pampeluna. Hill was ordered to hurry up from the rear, and replace in the blockade not only the troops of Cole, but those of Picton and Dalhousie. For the 3rd and 7th Divisions were to get ready to follow Cole's column the moment that they were relieved : they were to concentrate meanwhile at the

---

[1] Whose riotous and undisciplined conduct so irritated Wellington that he directed that all the officers in charge should miss their next step in regimental promotion, by being passed over by their juniors.

village of Sielvas, south of the Arga, and to march southward as soon as Hill came up. But it was calculated that they would not be able to move till dawn on the 27th, as Hill had a long way to come. Ponsonby's cavalry brigade would attach itself to them when the move should begin. Meanwhile, four divisions being set in motion to head off Clausel from this side, another column was ordered to strike across the mountains and fall in on his rear if possible. The 6th Division was still at Vittoria on the 25th, as was R. Hill's brigade of heavy cavalry. Clinton (now commanding his old division in lieu of Pakenham) received orders to start off with all speed on the Logroño road, taking the Household Cavalry with him, and to endeavour to catch up the retreating French. He made forced marches via Trevino and Peñacerrada, and reached Logroño on the 27th, where he picked up six abandoned French guns, but learned that Clausel had been gone for two days, and had crossed the Ebro at Lodosa instead of continuing on the Pampeluna road. There was little chance of catching him up, when he had a start of two marches, but Clinton continued the pursuit as far as Lerin on the Miranda-de-Arga road, where he gave it up. The Household Cavalry returned to Logroño, where it was directed to go into billets, as horsemen would not be wanted in the Pyrenees, while the 6th Division marched at leisure from Lerin to Pampeluna [1].

---

[1] I have only mentioned the movement of the 6th Division and R. Hill's cavalry above : there is no doubt as to what they did, and on the 30th they are both at Lerin, according to the location given by *Supplementary Dispatches*, viii. p. 39. But there is a puzzle about Oswald's 5th Division on the 26th–30th, which I was long unable to solve. Wellington in his dispatch to Bathurst of July 3 (*Dispatches*, x. p. 501) says that he moved not only Clinton from Vittoria but Oswald from Salvatierra towards Logroño, on the march to intercept Clausel. He ought to have known if any one did ! But I was not able to find any trace of the 5th Division having actually gone to Logroño : to march back from Salvatierra to Vittoria, and thence to follow Clinton to Logroño and Lerin would have been a very long business. Now regimental diaries of the 3/1st and 1/9th prove that the division was at Salvatierra on the 25th, and marched back to Vittoria on the 26th. But the best of them (Hale of the 1/9th) says that from Vittoria the division was turned back towards Pampeluna, and reached a spot within two leagues of it on the third day. At this point it was turned off northward and marched by Tolosa to join Graham's column and assist at the siege of St. Sebastian. All accounts agree that it reached the neighbourhood of that fortress on July 5th–6th. Allowing six days

The only real chance of catching Clausel was to head him off at Tudela, by means of the four divisions which were descending upon him down the Tafalla road. But a glance at the map will show that he could only have been intercepted if he had displayed uncommon torpidity. For having crossed the Ebro at Lodosa on the 26th he was only 35 miles from Tudela on a good road : and marching hard he reached the town on the afternoon of the 27th, when the advanced cavalry of the column sent to intercept him had only got to Olite, 25 miles to the north, and the Light Division at the head of the infantry column was 10 miles behind at Barasoain. Clausel did not halt more than a few hours at Tudela : there was no need for the intervention of the treacherous alcalde—who figures in legends of the time—to bid him press on hard for Saragossa. For the design, attributed to him by some of the contemporary British diarists, of marching up from Tudela along the Aragon river, with the object of reaching France and joining the King by way of Sanguesa was never really in his mind. Ever since he had crossed the bridge of Lodosa his only desire was to get to Saragossa in the shortest possible time. Starting off again at dawn on the 28th, with his force increased by the garrison of Tudela, he marched that day twenty miles to Mallen, and on the 29th a similar distance to Alagon. On the 30th a shorter stage of 15 miles brought him to Saragossa, where he found General Paris, the Governor of Aragon, still completely ignorant of the battle of Vittoria, though it had taken place nine days back.

Since the 26th Clausel had been practically out of danger, for he had the Ebro, whose bridges at Lodosa and Tudela he had destroyed, between him and Wellington's columns. There was no force which could have stopped him, for there are 20 miles less of road between Lodosa and Tudela than between Pampeluna and Tudela. Wellington had hoped for a moment

for the march Vittoria–St. Sebastian, we have only the 27th, 28th, 29th, 30th June for the supposed march Salvatierra–Vittoria–Logroño, and return. The solution at last came to hand in General Shadwell's Life of Colin Campbell of the 1/9th (Lord Clyde). Here it is mentioned, apparently on some record of Campbell's, that his brigade only got to La Guardia, one march beyond Trevino, and was then turned back and sent north (*Life of Campbell*, i. p. 18). This is no doubt correct.

that Mina might have intercepted the French column at Tudela, and have held it in check long enough to allow the British to come up. But though Mina was, so far as mere distances went, capable of striking at Tudela, two things prevented him from being able to do so—the first was the obstacle of the Ebro, the second the fact that Tudela was a fortified place with a competent garrison. Even if the great guerrillero had got his men across the river, he certainly could not have captured Tudela, and equally certainly would have been beaten by Clausel, when the French column—double his available force in numbers—came up, if he had dared to offer battle in the open near the town.

During the night of the 27th Wellington heard that Clausel had slipped past Tudela in haste, and that Mina, quite unable to stop him, was only able to follow him with his cavalry—to which Julian Sanchez's Lancers had joined themselves. At a very early hour on the 28th—before 5 o'clock in the morning—the British Commander-in-Chief issued a fresh set of orders in view of this untoward news [1]. They are a little difficult to understand, but internal evidence seems to show that Wellington must have received some sort of report tending to make him think it possible that Clausel, instead of falling back on Saragossa and joining Suchet's army, might march across country by the road Tauste–Exea–Un Castillo–Jaca, or the alternative road Exea–Luna–Murillo–Jaca, in order to cross the Pyrenees by the pass of Canfranc and join the King's army in Bearn. Or he might march through Saragossa in haste, and make for Jaca by the Gallego river [2]. There was a bare possibility of intercepting him by turning the whole pursuing column eastward, and taking it into the valley of the river Aragon, from which it would march by Sanguesa and Berdun on Jaca. The weak point of the scheme was that there was no certainty that

<hr/>

[1] *Supplementary Dispatches*, viii. p. 33.

[2] Wellington's letters to Hill, Copons, and Castaños in *Dispatches*, x. pp. 470–1, all state very shortly that he hopes to cut off Clausel if he tries to get back into France by Jaca. All that is said is, ' I do not think we shall be able to do much against Clausel. He has passed Tudela on the way to Saragossa. I propose to try for him on the road to Jaca ' (to Hill). The letters to the Spanish generals do not speak of Clausel's going through Saragossa, but of his marching across Aragon to Jaca.

Clausel would march on Jaca at all : he might stop in Aragon and combine his operations with those of Suchet. Or even if he did start for Jaca, when he heard that his road was intercepted by British troops, he would naturally turn back and cast in his lot with the French Army of Aragon, rather than with the King.

It is therefore rather surprising to find that Wellington imposed two days of heavy marching on his left wing, on the bare possibility that Clausel might be intercepted at or near Jaca. The orders for the 28th June were for the cavalry at the head of the column to make the long march Olite-Caparrosa-Caseda, by the good but circuitous road along the valley of the Aragon, taking in charge the artillery belonging to the infantry divisions. The latter were to cut across from the Pampeluna to the Sanguesa roads by country tracks in the hills—the Light Division by Olite-Beyre-Gallipienzo, the 4th Division by Tafalla-St. Martin de Unx-Gallipienzo. The 3rd and 7th Divisions, farther behind, went from Mendavil by Olleta to Caseda. This move concentrated 30,000 men in a solid body on a decent road—but left a very long gap between them and the troops blockading Pampeluna—and the gap would grow longer each day that the marching force pushed north-eastward up the course of the Aragon on its way to Jaca [1].

On the following day (June 29th) the column, now with the 3rd Division at its head and the 4th Division at its tail, had moved along the river till its head reached Sanguesa, when Wellington suddenly made up his mind to relinquish the scheme, which (as he himself owned) had never been a very promising one. He wrote to Castaños that Clausel, having passed Tudela marching hard for Saragossa, had got too long a start, and could not be caught. The plan of intercepting him at Jaca had been given up, firstly because it would probably have failed, and secondly because, if it had succeeded, it would only have forced Clausel to join Suchet—which was not a thing to be desired [2]. A third reason, which he did not cite to Castaños but reserved

---

[1] See 'Dispositions for the 28th June,' *Supplementary Dispatches*, viii. p. 33.

[2] Wellington to Castaños, Monreal, June 30, *Dispatches*, x. p. 477, and to Bathurst, x. p. 496 and ibid. 501.

for Lord Bathurst's private eye, was that the Army was marching very badly, with many stragglers, and many marauders. 'The British on the 17th June were 41,547 rank and file : on the 29th, 35,650 rank and file—diminution, 5,897. Now the loss in the battle was 3,164—so that the diminution from irregularities, straggling, &c., for plunder, is 2,733.' The Portuguese before the battle were 25,489—their present strength is 23,044. As they lost only 1,022 in the battle, they show an extra diminution of another 1,423 rank and file, from the same causes as the British. 'There are only 160 men in the hospital which I established—the others are plundering the country in different directions.' The truth was, that the Army was sulky—the men had not got over the effects of the looting at Vittoria, the weather had been bad, and the hunt after Clausel had been regarded by officers and men alike as a wild-goose chase.

The French General gave his men three days' rest at Saragossa (June 30–July 2) and then started to march up the Gallego river to Jaca, where the head of his column arrived on July 6th : he then halted his divisions for some days, stopping in a position where he could either cross the pass of Canfranc into France, for he had no field-guns or wheeled transport with him, to impede his passage by that steep defile, or else return into the plains of Aragon. If Suchet should come to Saragossa with the Army of Valencia, he could drop back to meet him. But on the 11th arrived the news that Saragossa had been evacuated on the preceding day, after some indecisive fighting between General Paris's garrison and the bands of Mina and Duran, who had beset the city on both sides of the Ebro. All chance of a junction with Suchet having vanished, Clausel crossed the Pyrenees next day, after leaving a garrison in Jaca. He came down into the Val d'Aspe on the French side, with 11,000 infantry, 500 horse, and six mountain guns packed on mules—his sole artillery. He had lost somewhere about 1,500 men in his long march—some broken-down stragglers, others sick left in hospital at Tudela and Saragossa. All these fell into the hands of Mina, but the casualties in actual fighting had been practically *nil*. By July 15th the whole column, marching over the Pyrenean foot-hills, had reached St. Jean-Pied-de-Port, and come into touch with the Armies of the South and Centre, who had so long and vainly desired to see Clausel.

Meanwhile Wellington, having stopped his eastward march on June 29th, had given his troops one day's rest, and then drawn them back toward Pampeluna by the road through Monreal. He was now about to take up the pursuit of the King's troops, which had been abandoned on the 25th while he went off on his fruitless hunt after Clausel—an enterprise which would have been far better left to Mina and the guerrilleros, for there never had been much probability of its succeeding. But the new move required several days of preparation, since four divisions had to be brought back from the valley of the Aragon, and one more, the 6th, to come up from Lerin via Puente La Reyna. And it was necessary to provide a considerable force for the blockade of Pampeluna. The instructions for July 1 were that Hill was to make the first move, by marching northward with the 2nd Division, handing over the investment of Pampeluna to Silveira's Portuguese and Morillo's Spaniards [1], to whose assistance there would come up in 24 hours the 7th Division, and a little later the 3rd Division. Hill was to march by the Col de Velate and Santesteban into the Bastan, from which it was intended that he should drive out D'Erlon's divisions.

But these operations belong to the fighting of July, and before dealing with them it is necessary to go back to June 22nd, in order to follow the fortunes of the other large French force, which might have been present at the battle of Vittoria, but was not.

---

[1] Elaborate dispositions for their distribution round the fortress are given in the Order dated June 30 (*Supplementary Dispatches*, viii. pp. 34–6).

SECTION XXXVII: CHAPTER II

THE PURSUIT OF FOY

WE left General Foy at the decisive momènt when he received the dispatch forwarded by Thouvenot from Vittoria, which informed him of the King's retreat beyond the Ebro, and suggested that he might come in to join the main army, but left him the fatal choice of deciding whether his own immediate operations were or were not of such paramount importance that they could not be abandoned [1]. Foy decided, and many other generals have made a similar error in all ages, that his own job was the really important thing. The dispatch reached him on the 19th, when he had his division concentrated at Bergara, and could have brought it to Vittoria in time for the battle. Probably the brigade of Berlier, belonging to the Army of the North, which was under his orders, could also have been brought in from Villafranca to Vittoria by the 21st.

But on the very eve of the decisive engagement, and with Jourdan's dispatch advising him ' de se rapprocher de Vittoria ' before his eyes, Foy decided that the petty affairs of the Biscay garrisons were of more importance than the fate of the King's Army. Instead of bringing down his own and Berlier's troops to Vittoria, where 5,000 bayonets would have been most welcome to the depleted Army of Portugal, he proceeded to disperse them. He sent, on the 20th, two battalions to El Orrio to facilitate the retreat of the garrison of Bilbao, dispatched two others to Deba, on the coast, to guard against a rumoured British demonstration against that port, and remained at Bergara with the 6th Léger alone. Orders were forwarded to

[1] See above, p. 378. For all the narrative which follows Foy's well-written dispatches, printed in full in his life by Girod de l'Ain, are a primary authority. But I think that historians have given him a little more credit than he deserves—he is a very engaging witness. As to his own strength, that of his enemies, and the losses on both sides, he is no more trustworthy than Soult or Masséna. It may suffice to say that he makes the British 4th and 5th Divisions present at Tolosa, and gives Longa 6,000 men.

Berlier to stand fast at Villafranca, and to the troops expected
from Bilbao to make the best pace that they could, as the
Army of Galicia would soon be upon them [1]. Giron's demonstration on the Balmaseda road had convinced Foy that the
Spanish 4th Army was aiming at Bilbao—he could not know
that Wellington had brought the Galicians down by Orduña
to join his main body.

On the evening of the 21st the division of Maucune, escorting
the convoy which had started from Vittoria at dawn, came
through the pass of Salinas unmolested. Its general met Foy,
and told him that he had heard heavy cannonading for many
hours behind him, but had no notion of what was going on
upon the Zadorra. The column bivouacked between Mondragon
and Bergara, and started off again before daybreak. It had
not gone more than a league when fugitives began to drop in
from Vittoria, bringing news of the disaster. The King's army
had been routed—his artillery abandoned : he had been pushed
aside on to the Pampeluna road, and Allied columns were
coming up the great *chaussée* making for Bergara and Durango.
On hearing these depressing news the commandants of the forts
which guarded the passes—those of Arlaban, Mondragon, and
Salinas—spiked their guns, and fell back without orders to join
Foy at Bergara.

The news was only too true. On the night of the battle
Wellington had issued orders for Longa's Division to set out
at dawn on the 22nd to force the passes, and, if possible, to
overtake Maucune's unwieldy convoy. Giron was to follow,
when his men, who had suffered dreadful fatigue in their forced
march from Orduña, were capable of movement. As the
Galicians were terribly under-gunned—there appear to have
been only six pieces with the 12,000 infantry—Wellington lent
them two batteries from the British artillery reserve [2]. Giron
started from the neighbourhood of Vittoria at 3 o'clock in the
afternoon, and had gone only some six miles when the news
of Clausel's raid was sent to him by Pakenham. The whole
army halted and began to retrace its steps, with the object of

[1] Foy to Jourdan, 20 June, in Girod de l'Ain's appendix, pp. 393–4.
[2] Batteries of Smith and Arriaga. Julius Hartmann, commanding
Artillery Reserve, accompanied them ; see *Dickson Papers*, June 22.

joining the 6th Division and fending off this unexpected attack. But the return march had hardly begun when the message arrived that Clausel's cavalry had retreated in haste, and that there was no danger on the side of Vittoria. Giron therefore resumed his original advance, but only reached Escoriaza, a hamlet half-way between Salinas and Mondragon after dark [1]. His troops were worn out, and had not received any regular rations that day.

It thus chanced that only Longa's Division continued the advance along the Bayonne *chaussée* on the 22nd, and that all day the Cantabrians were far ahead of, and quite out of touch with, the Army of Galicia. It was with this small force alone that Foy had to deal. The French General had been prepared for trouble by the ominous news that Maucune had given him on the previous day, and conceived that it was his duty to hold the passes as long as was prudent, in order to gain time for the convoy to get on its way, and for the garrison of Bilbao to come in from the right rear. Accordingly he was much vexed to find that the officers commanding the Mondragon forts had evacuated them, and had fallen back on Bergara. He resolved to hold the defile if possible, and marched back toward it, taking with him the only two battalions of his division which he had at hand [2], and the garrisons of the three forts.

The fort of Mondragon was found empty—there were no enemies visible save some local guerilleros who fled. But on advancing a little farther, Foy came on the head of Longa's column, descending from the defile of Salinas. He spent the whole afternoon in a series of rearguard actions, making his men fall back by alternate battalions, and defending each turn of the road. The French troops behaved with great steadiness, and Longa was cautious, having received false news that the Bilbao garrison had joined Foy. He contented himself with turning each successive position that the enemy took up, and at nightfall had only got about two miles beyond Mondragon.

---

[1] From the journal of operations of General Giron's Army, lent me by Colonel Arzadun.

[2] In his *Diary* (Girod de l'Ain, p. 210) Foy says that he had only *one* battalion of the 6th Léger, in his formal dispatch to Clarke (ibid. 395) he says that he had two.

Here he halted, having occupied the fort (where he found six spiked guns) and taken 53 prisoners. Foy had lost about 200 men in all in the long bickering, and had been himself slightly wounded in the shoulder, though he was not disabled : the Spaniards probably somewhat less [1].

During the evening hours three more battalions of Foy's own division arrived at Bergara, but the garrison of Bilbao and St. Pol's Italians had not yet been heard of. Having now 3,000 men in hand, the French general resolved to hold Longa up, until the missing troops should have passed behind him and got into a safe position. He waited opposite the Cantabrians all the morning, but was not attacked : a reconnaissance sent out reported that the enemy was quiescent at Mondragon. The fact was that Longa had heard that the French had received reinforcements, and was waiting for Giron to come up with the three Galician divisions. They arrived by noon, much fatigued and drenched by heavy rain, and Giron contented himself with making arrangements for an attack on Bergara on the next morning.

But this attack was never delivered, for Foy having at last picked up the missing brigades, retreated on Villareal during the afternoon, using St. Pol's Italians as his rearguard. He says in his dispatch that he had deduced from Longa's strange quiescence the idea (quite correct in itself) that the Spaniards were refraining from pushing him, because they were hoping that he would linger long enough at Bergara to be cut off by some other column, coming from Salvatierra on to Tolosa far in his rear. And Graham's force had actually been detached for this very purpose that afternoon—but Giron did not know it, and was really detained only by the exhaustion of his troops. It was not till evening that he got a dispatch from Wellington directing him to press hard upon Foy and delay his march, because an Anglo-Portuguese force was moving by the Puerto de San Adrian to intercept his retreat [2]. But Foy, having guessed what plans might be brewing for his discomfiture, had

---

[1] In reporting to Giron Longa mentions his 53 prisoners, and says that his own losses were 'inconsiderable.' *Journal of the Army of Galicia*, June 22.

[2] *Journal of the Army of Galicia*, June 23.

not only retreated betimes, but ordered Maucune, who was now
a day's march in front of him with the convoy, to drop the
impedimenta and bring all his fighting force back to Villafranca, to block the road from Salvatierra until he and his
8,000 men should have got past the point of danger.   This
order Maucune executed on the morning of the 24th, turning
the convoy into Tolosa, and turning back to hold the junction
of the roads, with one of his brigades in Villafranca town, and
the other thrown forward across to the river Oria to Olaverria
and Beassayn on the south bank.   News had by this time come
to hand that the march of a British column from Salvatierra
across the hills had been verified, and that the peril was a real
one.   Wherefore Foy pressed his retreat, and sent Maucune
orders to hold on at all costs till the column from Bergara
should have passed his rear.

Now Wellington's orders to Graham to cut in by the Puerto
de San Adrian with the 1st Division, Pack's and Bradford's
Portuguese, and Anson's Light Dragoons, had been issued late
on the 22nd, but had only reached the General and the greater
part of his troops on the morning of the 23rd.   Of all the column
only the two Light Battalions of the King's German Legion and
Bradford's Portuguese had turned off that night.   Consequently
on the 23rd, the critical day, Graham and the bulk of his
command were toiling up the pass in heavy rain, and had not
crossed the watershed, only Bradford and the two German
battalions having reached the village of Segura.   It was not
till dawn on the 24th that Anson's cavalry and Pack's Portuguese got to the front ; the rest of the infantry was still far off.
Graham then advanced on Villafranca, and soon came into
collision with Maucune, who was already in position covering
the cross-roads.   The head of Foy's column, coming in from
the West, was clearly visible on the other side of the Oria
in the act of passing behind the screen formed by Maucune's
covering force.   He had started from Villareal before dawn,
and got clear away before Longa and Giron were on the move,
or able to delay him.

Graham attacked at once, in the hope of driving in Maucune
before Foy could get past. Bradford's Portuguese, endeavouring
to turn the French flank, pushed to the right ; Halkett's

Germans, supported by the grenadier and light companies of
Pack's brigade, made for Beassayn on the left wing. Bradford's leading unit, the 5th Caçadores, attacking recklessly on
unexplored ground, was thrown back at its first assault ; but
the Brigadier, extending other battalions farther to his right,
ended by taking the village of Olaverria and pushing his
immediate opponents across the river. The German light
battalions carried Beassayn at their first rush. But Maucune,
retiring to a new position on high ground immediately above
Villafranca, continued his resistance, trying to gain time at all
risks. In this he was successful : Foy, hurrying past his rear,
got well forward on the Tolosa road with his two leading
brigades—the other two he dropped behind the town, to support
Maucune or relieve him when he should be driven in.

Owing to the early hour—three in the morning—at which
Foy had started on his retreat from Villareal, the bulk of
Giron's army was never able to catch him up. Only Longa's
Cantabrians, leading the advance as usual, came into contact
with his rear brigade—St. Pol's Italians—at the defile of
La Descarga west of Villafranca. Failing to force a passage
by a frontal attack, Longa turned the position ; but the delay
permitted St. Pol to get off with small loss and to catch up the
rest of Foy's column.

By three in the afternoon Graham was beginning to outflank
Maucune's line about Villafranca, with Bradford's brigade on
his right and Pack's on his left, while Longa had come in sight
upon the *chaussée*. Thereupon the French General, having
held his ground for the necessary space of time, made a prompt
retreat along the Tolosa road, pursued but not much harmed
by the Portuguese.

This ended a rather unsatisfactory day—the French had lost
more men than the Allies [1], but the trap to catch them had
failed completely. It is clear that if Graham's column could
have crossed the Puerto de San Adrian twelve hours earlier,
or if Giron had pressed Foy hard and delayed his movements

---

[1] Maucune reported 200 casualties (Foy, ed. Girod de l'Ain, p. 333),
Graham 93, mostly in the 5th Caçadores. St. Pol's Italians had beaten off
Longa without losing more than 100 men—Giron does not give Longa's
loss, which was probably a little more.

either on the 23rd or on the 24th, the scheme would have
worked. Bad staff work was apparently responsible in some
measure for both of these failures, though the extreme incle-
mency of the weather was a secondary cause. Foy's conduct
of the operations on the 22nd–23rd appears a little rash—he
might have been caught but for his good luck. But till he had
picked up the troops from Bilbao, at noon on the 23rd, he was
constrained to wait at Bergara ; and after he had once received
them he marched hard, and so escaped, thanks to his wise
precaution in sending Maucune to Villafranca.

After the combat of the morning Graham moved forward
a few miles as far as Ichasondo and neighbouring villages on
the Tolosa road, while Giron came up in the evening, and
billeted his army in Villafranca, Beassayn, and other places
on the Oria. As the missing brigades of the 1st Division
appeared that night, there were now some 10,000 Anglo-
Portuguese [1] and 16,000 Spaniards [2] massed along the *chaussée* ;
Foy, having picked up the garrisons of Tolosa and some smaller
places, and having been joined by a stray brigade from the
Army of the North, had also as many as 16,000 men in hand [3],
so that the opposing forces on both sides had swollen to a considerable strength.

Graham having failed (through no fault of his own) to intercept the enemy's retreat at Villafranca, and regarding extreme
haste as no longer necessary, since the scheme had miscarried,
set himself to carry out Wellington's orders to drive back the
enemy to the Bidassoa without any great hurry. He was
much hampered by the fact that Giron's army had outmarched
its train, and was therefore suffering for want of supplies, which
could not be procured in the mountains of Guipuzcoa. On
the 25th he brought the whole of the allied forces up to Alegria,
half-way to Tolosa, driving out Maucune's division, which

---

[1] 1st Division about 4,500 bayonets, Pack and Bradford 4,500, Anson's
cavalry 650.

[2] Giron's two Galician divisions 11,000, Porlier 2,500, Longa 3,000.

[3] His own division and Maucune's about 3,000 each, St. Pol's Italians
1,500, garrisons from Bilbao, Durango, and other western places about
3,000, De Conchy's brigade of Army of the North [64th (2 battalions),
22nd (1 battalion), 1st Line (2 companies), and 34th (4 companies)] 2,000,
garrisons of Tolosa and other places in Guipuzcoa about 2,500.

Foy had left there as a rearguard. It was then discovered that
the enemy had taken up a long and extensive position on each
side of Tolosa, and showed no disposition to give ground. It
was clear that he must be driven off by force.

Foy, as he explains in his dispatch of June 28th [1], had resolved
to make a stand at the junction of roads in Tolosa, because he
was obsessed by a theory (less accurate than that which he had
formed as to Graham's march two days before) to the effect
that King Joseph might have dispatched part or the whole of
his army, by the road which leads from Yrurzun on the Araquil
to Tolosa across the mountains, in order to transfer it to the
lower Bidassoa and the Bayonne road. He was still ignorant
of the full effects of the battle of Vittoria, and having heard
cannonading far to the south-west on the 23rd [2] had jumped
to the conclusion that the main army might be moving up to
join him at Tolosa. As a matter of fact King Joseph *had*
turned a detachment off the Pampeluna road at Yrurzun—
Reille's two divisions—but they had been sent not by the
more westerly road to Tolosa, but by the Col de Velate route
to Santesteban, on which they travelled fast because they had
no guns or transport.

But to cover the imaginary movement Foy disposed his
troops in front of the junction of roads. Tolosa town lies in
a narrow defile, through which pass the Oria river and the
great *chaussée*. It had been prepared long before for serious
defence, as it was one of the chief halting-places on the great
road from Bayonne to Madrid. The old walls had been
strengthened with blockhouses, the gates were palisaded outside and had guns mounted by them. The town blocks the
defile completely, but is commanded by steep hills on either
side.

Foy sent on the great convoy which Maucune had escorted,
under charge of four battalions commanded by General Berlier.
The rest of his troops he disposed for defence. De Conchy's
brigade held the fortified town. On the south-east Bonté's
brigade and St. Pol's Italians were placed on the heights above

[1] Girod de l'Ain, p. 400.
[2] This was merely the noise of the rearguard action of Cassagne with
Wellington's advance, near Yrurzun, on the afternoon of that day.

the Lizarza torrent, a forward position in which they protected the Pampeluna road. The second brigade of Foy's own division was placed on the hill of Jagoz, on the same flank but nearer the town. On the other or western bank of the Oria Rouget's brigade (the troops from Bilbao) were on commanding ground, flanking the town and blocking two mountain paths which came down on to it from Azpeytia in the valley of the Uroli. Maucune's division was in reserve behind Tolosa, massed on the *chaussée*. As Foy very truly observes in his dispatch, the position was strong against frontal attack, and could only be turned by very wide détours by any troops arriving from the south.

This was as evident to Graham as to Foy, and the British General prepared for a long day's work. His intention was to outflank the position, even though it should take many hours. In the centre the bulk of the 1st Division, followed by Pack's Portuguese and Giron's Galicians, advanced up the *chaussée* on the left bank of the river Oria, and halted a considerable distance from Tolosa. But Longa's Cantabrians and Porlier's small Asturian division were sent off to make a very circuitous march over the mountains on the right by Alzo and Gastolu with the object of cutting into the Pampeluna road many miles east of Tolosa, and then taking the town in the rear. A less wide curve was made by a column consisting of Bradford's Portuguese brigade, with the three Line-battalions of the King's German Legion in support, who were also to operate to the east of the *chaussée* and of the river Oria, and were directed to cross the Lizarza ravine and carry the hill behind it, from whence they were to push forward to the Pampeluna road and then turn inwards against the town. A smaller column, consisting of one battalion of Pack's brigade and the light companies of Giron's 3rd Division, was to make a corresponding movement to the west, and to endeavour to get on to the hill dominating Tolosa on that side. Nor was this all : information came to hand that Mendizabal had brought to Aspeytia what remained of the Biscayan irregulars whom Foy had routed and dispersed a month back [1]. Graham wrote to beg him to demonstrate with these bands against the Bayonne

---

[1] See above, p. 274.

chaussée north of Tolosa, and to get on to that road if possible and block it.

The main column halted while the flanking operations were pursuing their slow course. The only fighting which took place in the morning was an attack by Bradford's brigade on the heights occupied by Bonté, opposite Aleon and beyond the Lizarza torrent. The French Brigadier had neglected to guard the passages of the ravine, and allowed the Portuguese to get on to the ridge of his position without much difficulty [1]. He then counter-attacked them, first with his own brigade, then with St. Pol's Italians also, but was unable to cast them down from the hill : nor could Bradford get forward. All the hours of the early afternoon were spent in an indecisive *tiraillade* on this front. It is curious to note that both the commanders-in-chief write in sharp criticism of their subordinates : Foy says that Bonté was careless and disobeyed orders ; Graham that Bradford's men, after a good start, fought in a confused and disorderly fashion [2]. On the other flank the Spanish-Portuguese detachment, sent to try to gain a footing on the hills to the west of Tolosa, reported that they had come up against an absolute precipice, and could do nothing.

So matters wore on till about six o'clock in the afternoon, when distant firing in the rear of the French position announced that both Longa on the right and Mendizabal on the left were in touch with the enemy. Graham then ordered a general attack, the three German Line-battalions, hitherto in reserve behind Bradford, being ordered to strike at the Pampeluna road ; meanwhile the main column, which had so long waited opposite Tolosa, deployed the two light German battalions in its front, with the Guards Brigade and Giron's 3rd Division

---

[1] The column was led—for reasons which are not given—not by its own Caçador battalion, but by three companies of the 4th Caçadores and two of the 1st Line, borrowed from the neighbouring brigade of Pack. Graham praises the conduct of this detachment.

[2] Foy (Girod de l'Ain, p. 400) says that if his orders had been obeyed there would have been a battalion and not a detachment holding the access to the hill. Graham (*Wellington Supplementary Dispatches*, viii. p. 44) declares that though many of Bradford's men fought well, ' the officers did not seem to understand what they were about, or how to keep their men in the proper place,' and a good many hung back.

supporting, and advanced against the south face of the town.
The detachment to the extreme left, which had failed to get
up the precipices in its front, was directed to turn inward to
attack the west side of Tolosa.

These orders brought on very heavy fighting, for Foy had
held his forward positions so long that he had great difficulty
in withdrawing his troops from them, when he found that he
was outflanked, and even attacked in the rear. At the south
end of the field, along the *chaussée*, the allied attack failed
entirely, the strength of the fortifications of the town having
been under-estimated. When the leading battalion (1st Light
Battalion K.G.L.) approached the gate, it came into a cross-fire
from the blockhouses, and still heavier frontal musketry from
the well-lined ramparts, which proved wholly inaccessible.
Scaling ladders would have been required to mount them.
The line broke, but the men did not retire, but threw themselves down behind walls and in ditches and tried to answer
the fire from such cover as they could find. Many took refuge
in the courtyard of a convent not far outside the Vittoria gate,
from which their colonel, Ompteda, led out a second assault,
which melted away under the fire as the first had done. In
truth, the attempt was a misjudged one on Graham's part—
possibly his bad eyesight had failed to note the strength of the
defences. The 1st Light Battalion lost five officers and 58 men
killed and wounded in a quarter of an hour [1], and had to keep
under shelter as best it could ; the supporting troops were
halted and ordered to lie down, while guns were brought up
from the rear to batter the gate. This should obviously have
been done before, and not after, the assault. The check was
unnecessary, as was shown a little later when the artillery
smashed the gate by a few shots, and cleared the neighbouring
walls.

Meanwhile there had been fierce fighting on the eastern side
of the town, where Bradford's Portuguese, and the three German
line-battalions, with Longa's men on their northern flank, had
fallen upon the three French brigades lying outside the town.

[1] Very different figures from those of Foy's dispatch, which stated that
eight minutes of terrible fire laid low 500 of the assailants ! (Girod de l'Ain,
p. 402).

Bonté's and St. Pol's battalions, still frontally engaged against Bradford, suddenly realized the danger of their position, when the Germans attacked their left flank, and Longa appeared almost in their rear. They retreated in haste towards Tolosa, and got jammed outside the Pampeluna gate, which had been blocked for defence and could not readily be entered. To avoid being crushed against the walls, they massed themselves for a counter-stroke, and thrusting back the Germans for a moment, raced along the river-bank, past the foot of the ramparts, till they got under the cover of Foy's second brigade on the hill of Jagoz, and escaped beyond the north end of the town. The Germans, though in great disorder, made an attack on the Pampeluna gate, which failed for the same reason that had wrecked that on the Vittoria gate—the impossibility of escalading a well-defended rampart.

Meanwhile there was heavy skirmishing going on to the north-west of Tolosa : Mendizabal's bands had appeared on the mountain road from Aspeytia, and had engaged Rouget's brigade, which was covering Foy's right flank. The French general's dispatch confesses that the troops from the Bilbao garrison, which included some conscript battalions from the Bayonne reserve, behaved badly, lost ground, and had to be rallied by their general's personal exertions. They were apparently thrown into a panic by an attack delivered on their flank, by the small Spanish-Portuguese detachment which Graham had sent out on his left : it had worked up by the narrow space between the walls of Tolosa and the precipice above, and came up very opportunely to aid Mendizabal. Rouget held on till dark, but with difficulty, and the knowledge that his route of retreat was threatened added to Foy's anxiety, for Longa was also pushing behind the town on the other side. Accordingly he ordered Deconchy's brigade to evacuate Tolosa at once, just as the sun was setting, and prepared for a general retreat.

If the order had been given half an hour later, the garrison of Tolosa would probably have been captured whole, for Graham's guns had just blown the defences of the Vittoria gate to pieces, and the German light battalions burst in with ease at the point where they had been checked before. There was

some confused fighting in the streets, but the French got off
with no great loss under cover of the darkness, and fell in
with the rear of their main column, which went off down the
chaussée at great speed.   Mendizabal made some prisoners
from Rouget's brigade, as it fell back to join the rest across
the slopes, and Longa caught some fugitives on the other
flank [1].

Foy says that he lost some 400 men in the fight, which
would seem a low estimate, as the Allies could show 200 prisoners,
and Bonté's and Rouget's brigades had been very roughly
handled.   Graham reports 58 killed, 316 wounded, and 45
missing—the last all from Bradford's brigade.   Of the Spaniards
Longa and Mendizabal only were engaged : Giron's report
(as so often occurs with Spanish documents) gives no figures,
only remarking that some of Longa's 1st battalion of Iberia
' perished by reason of their rash courage, but had a great
share in deciding the day '—presumably by pushing far ahead
in the turning movement which caused Foy to order a general
retreat.   If we allow 200 Spanish killed and wounded, we shall
probably not be far out of our reckoning.   Had Graham with-
held his unlucky assault on the Vittoria gate till it had been
well battered, and trusted entirely to his turning movements,
he would have got off with a much smaller casualty list.   His
original design of manœuvring Foy out of Tolosa was the right
game, considering the strength of the position.   The French
general could plead in defence of his risky tactics that he had
held up a superior force for a whole day—but at that particular
moment time did not happen to matter—as Graham's leisurely
pursuit on the subsequent days sufficiently shows.   He was
only set on getting Foy across the Bidassoa ; and nothing in
the general course of the campaign depended on whether he
did so a day sooner or a day later.   On the other hand, by

---

[1] There is one paragraph of Foy's dispatch which I cannot make out.
He says that two British regiments tried to storm the hill of Jagoz, and
were repulsed by the voltigeur companies alone of the brigade which held it.
I cannot fit this in to any British narrative—the only red-coated battalions
in that part of the field were the line battalions of the K.G.L., and they had
certainly been engaged against Bonté and the Italians, and afterwards
tried to storm the Pampeluna Gate.   Longa's men only were opposite
the Jagoz position, as far as I can make out.

standing too long at Tolosa Foy nearly lost three brigades, and might indeed have lost his whole force.

The remainder of this side-campaign displays none of the interest of its four first days. Foy retired to Andoain on the night of the combat of Tolosa, where he was joined by the battalions of the 40th and 101st under General Berlier, which had escorted Maucune's convoy to the frontier, and by the 62nd and a Spanish 'Juramentado' regiment withdrawn from Biscay garrisons. This, despite of his recent losses, gave him a force of 16,000 infantry, 400 sabres, and 10 guns. Graham did not press him, his troops being much fatigued : only the indefatigable Longa appeared with his Cantabrians in front of the position. On the 27th the whole French force retired unmolested to Hernani.

It was of course all-important to Foy to know what were the situation and intentions of the King. Nothing could be heard of the main army at Andoain or Hernani, so he detached Berlier's brigade to seek for news in the Bastan, along the upper Bidassoa. On the 28th Berlier discovered Reille and two divisions of the Army of Portugal at Vera. They were in bad order, without guns and much under strength, though stragglers were rejoining in considerable numbers. Reille had been as ignorant of Foy's whereabouts as Foy had been of that of the main army. He was rejoiced to hear that all the Biscay garrisons had been saved, and that there was a solid force ready to co-operate with him in the defence of the line of the Bidassoa. His own troops were not yet fit for fighting. Accordingly he sent Foy orders to evacuate Hernani and come back to the frontier, though he need not actually cross the Bidassoa unless he were compelled to do so. By stopping at Oyarzun he could keep up communication with St. Sebastian, which must be needing attention.

The condition of that fortress, indeed, had already been troubling the mind of Foy on his last day of independent command. It lay so near the French border, and had been for years so far from any enemy—Guipuzcoan guerrilleros excepted—that it had been much neglected. When General Rey, named as Governor by King Joseph two days before the battle of Vittoria, arrived with orders to put it in a state of defence, he found it garrisoned only by 500 gendarmes, a battalion of recruits on the way to join the 120th Line, and two weak companies of pioneers and sappers—1,200 men in all. The stores of food were low, the glacis was cumbered with huts and sheds, there was no provision of gabions, fascines, or timber. Moreover, the town was full of Spanish and French fugitives who had preceded the King on his retreat—there were (it is said) as many as 7,000 of them, lingering in Spain till the last moment, in the hope that Wellington might be stopped on the Ebro. The news of Vittoria arrived on the 23rd, and caused hopeless consternation—the place was not ready to stand a siege—the garrison so small that it could not even spare a battalion to escort the tiresome mass of refugees to Bayonne. Rey began in feverish haste to clear the glacis, palisade the outworks, and rearrange the cannons on the walls, but he had too few hands for work, and was in a state resembling despair when on the 28th Foy turned up for a flying visit, saw and acknowledged the nakedness of the land, and promised to do all that he could to help—though it was less than the Governor required. He took away the old garrison—the recruits were not too trustworthy, the gendarmes not siege troops : to replace them he threw in the whole of Deconchy's brigade—four battalions, about 2,000 infantry—and all the gunners that he could spare. As the garrison of Guetaria, 450 strong, escaped by sea to San Sebastian two days later, and a number of stragglers dropped into the place before the siege began, the gross total of the garrison was raised to some 3,000 men. Rey asked for 4,000, but Foy would not grant him another battalion —and was justified by the course of the siege, for the place was very small and, if it could be held at all, was defensible by the lesser number. The only doubt was whether there would be time to get it in order before the Allies appeared [1]. But perhaps the best service that Foy did for Rey was that he removed, at two hours' notice, the whole mass of refugees. They marched, much lamenting, for Bayonne, under the escort of the old outgoing garrison. On the 29th Reille ordered Foy to evacuate Oyarzun and fall back to the Bidassoa, and before

[1] For all this see Rey's letter in the *Pièces justificatives* of Belmas's History of Sieges in Spain, iv. p. 662.

he had been gone three hours Mendizabal's Guipuzcoan irregulars, 3,000 strong, appeared in front of the fortress and cut its communication with France. They were an unorganized band, without artillery, but effective enough for stopping the highway.

Graham, seeing that the French had escaped him, and had a clear retreat to the frontier, had made no serious attempt to press them. He was quite content that they should go at their own pace, and was determined not to harass the 1st Division, who, as he wrote to Wellington, were in a state of great exhaustion. To have hurried Foy out of Spain two days earlier would have cost men, and would have had no beneficial effect on the general course of the campaign; for Wellington and the main army were far away in Navarre, and if Graham had reached the Bidassoa on the 26th or 28th, with his own and Giron's 25,000 men, they could have done nothing, since they had in front of them the fortress of Bayonne, with Foy's 16,000 men, the 7,000 whom Reille had brought up from Santesteban, and the remains of the general reserve—for though Rouget's battalions and other detachments had been lent from Bayonne already, there were still a few thousand men in hand. In all, Reille would have had an army as large as Graham's own, and though some of it was rather demoralized, the fortress, and the strong positions in front of it along the Bidassoa, Nive, and Nivelle, counterbalanced this disadvantage. If Wellington had chosen to march on Bayonne with his main body, the day after Vittoria, the problem would have been a very different one. But since he had preferred to move in pursuit first of King Joseph and then of Clausel, there was nothing more which the commander of a detached corps like that of Graham could accomplish. He did all that his chief required of him, when he pushed Foy out of Spain and laid siege to St. Sebastian. That the project for cutting off the French detachments at Villafranca came to nothing was no fault of Graham's—being due partly to bad staff-work at Head-Quarters, partly to the chances of rough weather, and partly to Foy's laudable caution and celerity.

The side-show in Guipuzcoa came to a tame end twenty-four hours after the blockade of St. Sebastian had been formed.

On the 30th Reille ordered all the troops on the south bank of the lower Bidassoa to retire into France. Foy's and Maucune's divisions crossed the bridge of Behobie, under the protection of four battalions of the Bayonne reserve, which remained on the heights by the hermitage of St. Marcial, and marched to Urogne and other villages down-stream. Lamartinière's division remained at Vera, Fririon's (late Sarrut's) at Hendaye.

Late on the same afternoon the advance-guard of Graham's army came in sight of the Bidassoa—it consisted as usual of Longa's untiring Cantabrians only, the 1st Division and the Portuguese having been halted near St. Sebastian, the bulk of the Galicians at Hernani and Renteria. Longa, keeping to the coast, surprised and captured the French garrison of Passages (150 men), which was too late in obeying Reille's order to retreat on France while the bridge of Behobie was still available. He then came in contact with the covering force on the heights of San Marcial[1], which was at the same time menaced by Castañon with a brigade of the 4th Galician Division, who had come up the high road from Renteria.

The French brigadier evacuated the position at once. Reille had told him that he was only placed there to protect the retreat of Foy. He crossed the Bidassoa, leaving only a detachment of sixty men in the *tête de pont* which covered the south or Spanish end of the bridge of Behobie ; it consisted of a stone blockhouse surrounded with palisades. The further or French end of the long bridge was blocked by the fortified village of Hendaye.

Next morning Graham resolved that the *tête de pont* must be taken or destroyed, so that the enemy should have no open road by which he might return to Spain. While some Spanish infantry exchanged a vague fusillade across the river with the French in Hendaye, ten guns[2] were turned on the blockhouse. The garrison tried to blow it up and to retreat, but their mine failed, their commanding-officer was killed, and they were about to surrender when Foy sent two fresh companies over

---

[1] Under General Deconchy, who got a new brigade when his old one was thrown into San Sebastian.

[2] Dubourdieu's battery belonging to the British 1st Division, and four guns of Giron's own small artillery equipment.

the bridge to bring them off. This was done, at the cost of
four officers and 64 men, killed and wounded while crossing
the much-exposed bridge. Foy then ordered the structure to
be set on fire ; and as its floor was composed of wood this was
easily done : the four arches nearest France were burnt out
by the following morning (July 1).

This evacuation, without any attempt at defence, of the
bridge-head on the Bidassoa angered the Minister of War at
Paris, and still more Napoleon, when the news reached him
at Wittenberg nine days later. Foy and Reille had men enough
to have held the heights of San Marcial, against anything short
of an attack by the whole of Graham's and Giron's infantry.
And it is certain that Graham would not have delivered any
such assault, but would have halted in front of them, and waited
for orders from Wellington. The Emperor, who—as we shall
presently see—was set on a counter-offensive from the moment
when the news of Vittoria reached him, was wild with wrath
at the abandonment of the foothold in Spain. ' It was insane,'
he wrote to Clarke, ' to recross the Bidassoa : they all show
themselves as timid as women [1].'

But whether it would have been possible for the French to
hold the Irun–Behobie–San Marcial *tête de pont*, when Wellington had come up in person from the south, is another matter.
Probably he would have decided that the enemy must be thrust
back across the Bidassoa, before he dared to sit down to
beleaguer San Sebastian. And undoubtedly he had men enough
to carry out that operation. But this was no excuse for Reille's
evacuation of the position, one of the highest strategical value,
before he was compelled to do so by force. The fact was that
Reille, like most of the other French generals, was demoralized
at the moment by the recent disaster of Vittoria, and had lost
confidence both in himself and in his troops.

[1] Lecestre's *Lettres inédites de Napoléon*, ii. p. 265.

SECTION XXXVII: CHAPTER III

THE EAST COAST. MURRAY AT TARRAGONA

[N.B.—For Map of Catalonia and Plan of Tarragona see Vol. IV, pp. 538 and 524]

THERE are certain episodes of the Peninsular War which the British historian has to narrate with a feeling of some humiliation, but which have to be set forth in full detail, if only for the purpose of illustrating the manifold difficulties with which Wellington had to cope. Of these by far the most distressing is the story of General Sir John Murray at Tarragona.

It will be remembered that a diversion on the East Coast formed an essential part of Wellington's great scheme for the expulsion of the French from Spain, and that he had devoted much care to instructing Murray in the manner in which it was to be carried out. If sufficient shipping to embark 10,000 men could be procured at Alicante, the bulk of the Anglo-Sicilian army was to be transported to Catalonia, and to strike at Tarragona, getting what aid it could from the local Spanish forces under the Captain-General Copons. If, as was to be expected, Suchet should fly northward from Valencia with all his available field-army, to rescue Tarragona, the two Spanish units in the kingdom of Murcia, Elio's and Del Parque's armies, were to take the offensive against the detachments which the French Marshal would have to leave behind him to hold down his southern conquests. Murray might fail in Catalonia, if Suchet were rapid and lucky in his combinations; but in that case Elio and Del Parque ought to get possession of the city of Valencia and all its fertile plainland. Or, on the other hand, Suchet might be loth to abandon his advanced position, might hold it in force, and might order Decaen and the Army of Catalonia to make head against the Anglo-Sicilian expeditionary force. If this should happen, the Spanish generals might be held in check, but Murray would have a free hand at Tarragona. With the aid of Copons he ought to be able to take the place, and to throw all the French occupation of Catalonia into disorder. In the end, Suchet would have to evacuate Valencia, in order to save Decaen and the Catalan garrisons. At the worst the expedition of the Anglo-Sicilian army ought at least to have the effect of giving Suchet so much to think about, that he would have no attention to spare for the perils of King Joseph and the fate of Castile.

This last minimum result was all that was achieved. Suchet, it is true, had an anxious time during the critical days of Wellington's march to Vittoria, and sent no help to the King. But neither was Tarragona taken by the Anglo-Sicilians, nor Valencia by the armies of Elio and Del Parque. Both of those forces endured humiliating checks, from an enemy over whom they had every strategical advantage. And the story of Murray's operations about Tarragona is not the story of an honest and excusable failure, but one which provokes bitter irritation over the doings of a British general who showed himself not only timid and incompetent, but shifty, mendacious, and treacherous to his allies. There is nothing in the whole history of the Peninsular War which produces such an unpleasant impression as the facts revealed by the minutes of Murray's court-martial, supplemented by certain documents which ought to have been forthcoming at that trial, but unfortunately were not.

But to proceed to the details of this unhappy campaign. In obedience to Wellington's orders, Murray began to draw his army in to Alicante between the 25th and 27th of May, the forward positions which the Anglo-Sicilians had held being handed over to Elio's troops, while those of Del Parque, who had at last been brought up from the borders of Andalusia, took post on Elio's left, about Yecla and Chinchilla. Both these armies were to move forward, as soon as Suchet should be detected in the act of detaching divisions northward to deal with Murray's oncoming invasion. The appearance of the Spaniards on ground hitherto held by British outposts gave the Marshal warning that some new plan was developing. A raid by sea was an obvious possibility, but he could not tell whether it might not be directed on a point as far south as Valencia or as far north as Rosas. Till Murray showed his hand only precautionary movements could be made. Suchet was at this

moment stronger than he had been at the time of the battle
of Castalla. Warned of his danger by the results of that fight,
he had strengthened his troops on the littoral at the expense of
the garrisons inland.   Severoli's Italian division had been
ordered down from Saragossa to Valencia [1]. This heavy draft
on the northern section of his army was rendered possible by
the fact that Clausel had come far forward into Aragon in
pursuit of Mina, so that Saragossa and its region could be held
with smaller numbers than usual. The Spanish irregular forces
in this direction had full occupation found for them, by the raid
of the Army of Portugal into their sphere of operations. And
this suited well with Wellington's general plan—the more that
French troops were drawn down to the Mediterranean, the less
would there be of them available for service in Castile, when his
own blow came to be delivered.

Murray had at his disposal in the harbour of Alicante transports sufficient to carry much more than the force of 10,000 men,
which Wellington had named as the minimum with which a raid
on Catalonia might be attempted. He was able to embark the
whole of his own army, with the exception of the regiment of
Sicilian cavalry (he was short of horse-transports), and in
addition nearly the whole of Whittingham's Spaniards—all
indeed save one battalion [2] and the attached squadrons. This
made up a force of 14,000 infantry, 800 cavalry, and 800
artillery, with 24 field-guns and the battering train which had
been sent round from Portugal. The British contingent was
a little stronger than at the time of the battle of Castalla, for if
one battalion of the King's German Legion had been sent back
to Sicily since that fight, Wellington had permitted Murray
to draw in the 2/67th, long in garrison at Cartagena, and had
sent him a Portuguese and a British company of artillery to
man his battering train [3]. Moreover, two squadrons of Brunswick Hussars had arrived direct from England.

---

[1] Severoli reached Valencia on May 2 (Vacani, vi. p. 207), so was not
drawn down in consequence of Murray's move of May 25, as Mr. Fortescue
seems to imply in *British Army*, ix. p. 49. He had with him two battalions
each of the 1st Line and 1st Ligero, with a weak cavalry regiment.

[2] 2nd of Burgos, detached by Wellington's order. See Murray's *Court
Martial*, p. 371.

[3] These changes of units had caused some re-brigading. Murray had

The whole force, having been swiftly embarked at Alicante, sailed on May 31st; and being favoured with a strong south-west wind came in sight of the high-lying Tarragona on June 2nd. The fleet of transports ran into the bay sheltered by Cape Salou, eight miles south of its goal. There would have been no object in risking a more difficult disembarkation on the long open beaches at the mouth of the Francoli river, closer to Tarragona. Before landing his main body Murray shipped off two battalions (2/67th and De Roll-Dillon) under Colonel Prevost, to seize the defile of the Col de Balaguer, the point twenty miles to the south of Tarragona where the coast-road from Tortosa curves round a steep headland between a precipice and the sea. There was a small French fort, San Felipe de Balaguer, blocking the Col, and Prevost was ordered to take it if he could. But its fall was not an absolutely essential condition to the success of the siege, for the road could be cut, blasted away, or blocked with entrenchments north of the fort, at several points where a thousand men could stop a whole army corps. It was desirable to take this precaution, because the Col de Balaguer road was the only route by which succours coming from Valencia could reach the plain of Tarragona, without taking an immense détour inland, by paths impracticable for artillery.

On hearing of the arrival of the British fleet off Cape Salou, General Copons, Captain-General of Catalonia, rode down from his head-quarters at Reus, ten miles away, to report to Murray that he had received Wellington's instructions, and had done his best to carry them out. The Spanish Army of Catalonia consisted of no more than 15,000 men, even after it had received the two battalions which Wellington had sent to it by sea during the winter[1]. Over 5,500 of them were locked up in garrisons in the interior; many of these were untrained recruits, and none were available for the field. Of the remainder, Copons had brought down twelve battalions to the neighbour-

transferred the 4th K.G.L. and the Sicilian 'Estero' regiment to Clinton's division, but taken away from the latter and given to Mackenzie the 2nd Italian Levy, the 1/10th and the 1/81st. But Clinton was given charge over Whittingham's Spaniards, and authorized to use them as part of his division, so that his total command was now much larger than Mackenzie's.

[1] Pontevedra and Principe.

hood of Tarragona, leaving only two under his second-in-command, Eroles, to watch the French garrisons in the north [1]. He had also with him his handful of cavalry—370 sabres ; field-guns the army had none. Altogether there were 7,000 men ready to join Murray at once : 1,500 more might be brought in, if the French of the northern garrisons should move down to join General Decaen at Barcelona. Copons had certainly done all that was in his power to aid Wellington's scheme. Murray asked him to lend two battalions to join the brigade that was to strike at Fort San Felipe and to block the Col de Balaguer, and to arrange the rest so as to cover at a distance the disembarkation of the Anglo-Sicilian army. Copons consented, and on the next morning the whole force came ashore, Prevost's brigade in a creek near the Col de Balaguer, where it found the two Spanish battalions already arrived, the rest of the army at Salou Bay. The expeditionary force was little cumbered with transport, and had but a small allowance of horses and mules : the infantry and some of the field-guns with the greater part of the cavalry were ashore by the early afternoon, and marched that same night on Tarragona, which was invested from sea to sea, Mackenzie and Adam taking up their position by the mouth of the Francoli, Clinton occupying the Olivo heights, and Whittingham extending down to the shore east of the city. The French garrison kept quiet—being of no strength sufficient to justify the showing of a man outside the walls.

General Bertoletti had with him two battalions, one French and one Italian [2], a company of Juramentados, two companies of artillery, and the armed crews of three small vessels which were blockaded in the port—they were turned on to act as auxiliary gunners. The whole did not exceed 1,600 men. This was an entirely inadequate force, and the defences were in an unsatisfactory condition. After Suchet had captured the city in 1811, he had no intention of leaving locked up behind him a garrison of the size required for such a large fortress. The

---

[1] It is interesting to compare the May 31 morning state of the Army of Catalonia with the list of battalions which Murray reports as having been brought down to the neighbourhood of Tarragona. All are there save two (Fernando 7th and Ausona) left at Vich under Eroles (see Table in Appendix), twelve battalions were with Copons.

[2] One of the 20th Line, one of the 7th Italian Line.

outer enceinte had been left in the condition of ruin consequent on the siege [1], and only the Upper City on its high cliff was occupied. Its western front, where the breaches had been, was repaired ; but the Lower City and its fortifications remained practically untouched. All that had been done was to patch up two isolated strong-points, the so-called Fort Royal and Bastion of St. Carlos. These had been cut off from the mass of the ruins, and closed in at the rear : each was armed with one gun. The object of this was merely to prevent British ships from entering Tarragona roadstead and mooring there. These two outlying posts, dangerously remote from the city above, were held by no more than a company each. Bertoletti thought for a moment of abandoning them, since he dared not detach reinforcements from his inadequate garrison, and his communication with the forts was across half a mile of exposed ground : nothing was more likely than that the enemy would slip detachments among the ruined houses and walls of the Lower City, and dig himself in between the Upper City and the weak outlying posts, which must inevitably fall. But reflecting on the advantage of keeping the harbour unusable, he resolved to hold on to them till the last minute. And his policy turned out to be justified, for had they been evacuated, even the torpid and timorous Murray could hardly have avoided the temptation of closing in on the Upper City, which was in no condition to hold out for the space of nine days during which the Anglo-Sicilian army lay in front of it.

From the first moment of his landing Murray seems to have been obsessed with the idea that every disposable French soldier in Catalonia and Valencia would be on his back within a very few days. As his evidence during his court martial shows, he had a notion that Suchet would practically evacuate Valencia, and march against him with three-quarters of his available men, while at the same time Decaen would abandon all Catalonia save the largest towns and bring an even greater force to Tarragona from the north. He had made elaborate,

---

[1] Not only was the whole of the enceinte of the lower city abandoned, but the outer enceinte of the upper city on its east and north sides, from the bastion of El Rey to that of La Reyna (see map of Tarragona, p. 524 of vol. iv).

and in part correct, calculations as to the gross force of the
two French armies, by which he made out that the enemy
might conceivably concentrate 25,000 men against him. For
the fact that such a force would have to be scraped together
from very remote points, between which communication must
be very difficult, he made insufficient allowance. Still less did
he calculate out the handicap on the enemy caused by the fact
that Suchet and Decaen were out of touch with each other, and
would obviously look upon the problem presented to them
from different points of view,—all the former's action being
influenced by his wish to hold on to Valencia, all the latter's by
his anxiety not to have his communication with France cut off.
Murray assumed that all roads marked on his map would be
practicable to the enemy, that Suchet's information would always
be correct, that his troops would march every day the possible
maximum, and that they would have no difficulties concerned
with food, water, or weather. Every conceivable hazard of
war was to fall luckily for the enemy, unluckily for himself. At
his trial in 1814 he explained that he was never sanguine of
success, and that he did not expect when he sailed that he could
take Tarragona [1]. He chose to regard himself as the blind and
unwilling instrument of Wellington's orders, which he would
carry out, so far as he could, with an expectation that they
would lead to failure. And he observed that the dominating
motive which influenced all his doings was that Wellington had
written that ' he would forgive everything excepting that the
corps should be beaten or dispersed ' [2]. Deducing from this
phrase the general policy that he must pursue, Murray came
to the conclusion ' the first principle is the army's safety '. He
started intending to subordinate all chances of success to the
remotest risk of defeat. His mind obsessed with this miserable
prepossession, he was, in fact, defeated before he had ever set
sail. Yet he hid his resolve from his generals, even from the
senior officer, Clinton, who would have succeeded to the command if he had fallen sick or received a chance bullet. They

[1] *Court Martial Proceedings*, p. 228. He adds that his only chance (as he
thought) was that conceivably he might find Tarragona so ill-fortified
that he might risk an immediate assault on unfinished defences.
[2] Ibid., p. 292.

all complained that he never gave them any hint of what were his intentions, or showed them Wellington's orders which it was his duty to carry out. 'We were totally uninformed,' said Clinton at the court martial, 'of the instructions which the Commander of the forces might have for his guidance [1]. The first that we knew of these instructions of the Commander of the forces, and then partially only, was when he produced them at a Council of War on June 17th,' after the siege of Tarragona was over. Clinton, Mackenzie, and Adam, the three commanders of units, were all very confident in their men : ' they were in the highest state of discipline and equipment [2],' said Mackenzie, and spoiling for a fight. Hence their entire amazement as they discovered that Murray was intending to avoid all offensive operations : it even led to an infraction of discipline, when Mackenzie, Adam, and General Donkin [3] called together on their commander to urge on him a more active policy [4], and were chased out of the room with the words ' it will not do '— a decision which, as Mackenzie remarked, ' was unanswerable '. For any further urging of the point would have amounted to military disobedience. From the moment when the army landed at Cape Salou on June 3rd, down to the day of its ignominious flight on June 12th, Murray was thinking of nothing but horrible possibilities—he was what the French call a *catastrophard.*

Probably his most disastrous resolve of all was that which he came to when first he surveyed Tarragona, on the evening of his disembarkation. Though he noted the half-ruinous condition of the two outworks, on which the enemy was working to the last moment, their isolated position, and the fact that they were surrounded by all sorts of cover easily to be seized, he resolved to lay formal siege to them, as if they were the solid front of a regular line of defence. As Napier remarks with perfect good sense, they should have been dealt with as Wellington dealt with the Redoute Renaud at Rodrigo, or Hill with the forts of Almaraz, which were far more formidable works than the Fuerte Real or San Carlos [5].

[1] *Court Martial Proceedings*, p. 183.
[2] Ibid., p. 165.
[3] The Quartermaster-General of the Army.
[4] *Proceedings*, p. 168.
[5] Note, Napier, v. p. 147.

They should have been taken by force, escaladed, on the night of the formation of the blockade. And being incomplete, ill-flanked, and without palisades or ditch, and under-manned, they undoubtedly could have been rushed. But Murray, instead of trying to gain time for the prompt attack on the main fortress and its badly-stopped breaches, proceeded to lay out approaches and commence batteries on the low ground by the mouth of the Francoli river, with the object of reducing the two outworks by regular operations. On June 4th one battery was commenced near the sea, 600 yards from San Carlos, another farther inland, 900 yards from the Fuerte Real. Their construction was covered by a naval bombardment: Admiral Hallowell moved into the roadstead a brig, three bomb-vessels, and two gunboats, which shelled the Upper City freely, in order to distract the attention of the garrison from the work on the batteries by the Francoli. The fire was kept up from dusk till dawn on the 4th–5th, and repeated on the 6th–7th during the same hours—throughout the day the workers in the trenches kept low. This bombardment had the desired result of permitting the batteries to be finished without molestation, but inflicted no great damage on the city, though it set fire to some houses, and caused casualties both among the garrison and the inhabitants. But unaimed night-fire had of course no effect on the walls of the enceinte.

By dawn on the 6th the two batteries were ready and opened on the outworks with six guns: they kept up the fire all day, and with some effect, suffering themselves very little from the distant counter-fire of the Upper City. At dark, according to the French narrative of the defence, parties of skirmishers came out of the trenches, took cover in the ruins of the lower city and kept up a persistent *tiraillade* against the outworks [1]. It was expected that they would try to rush them at some chosen hour—and this would undoubtedly have been the right policy. But nothing of the kind happened; the British parties withdrew at dawn, and Bertoletti began to ask himself whether the whole of these feeble operations were not a mere demonstra-

---

[1] All this from Vacani (vi. p. 321), the only full French source: I can find no mention of this abortive demonstration from the British side.

tion, intended to draw the French armies of Valencia and Catalonia toward Tarragona, while the real blow was being delivered in some other quarter.

During the second night of naval bombardment, that of the 6th-7th, Murray had ordered a third breaching battery to be built, near the bridge of the Francoli, 300 yards closer to the Fuerte Real than the original battery, No. 2. On the morning of the 7th all three batteries were hard at work, and with good effect ; the gorge of the Fuerte Real was blown to bits by flank fire from the new battery, its one gun silenced, its parapet levelled for a long space : the garrison had to keep under cover. At dusk Major Thackeray, the senior engineer of the army, reported that the work could be stormed at any moment. According to Murray's narrative Thackeray made at the same moment the curious comment, that if the fort were escaladed and occupied, the ground gained would be of no immediate use for the attack on the Upper City, whose most accessible front— the bastions of San Juan and San Pablo—might be much more easily battered from the slopes of the Olivo hill, farther inland, than from the low-lying site of the Fuerte Real. To storm the outworks would cost men—to build new advanced batteries on or near them would cost many more, since they were completely commanded by the Upper City. ' As the state of the fort was now such that it could be taken whenever convenient,' wrote Murray, ' I consented to defer the attack, and directed that the fire upon it should continue only sufficiently to prevent its being re-established [1].'

The decision seems of more than doubtful wisdom. It was from ground near the Fuerte Real that Suchet had pushed forward his approaches in the siege of 1811, and his batteries in the lower town had proved effective. To resolve, after four days spent on battering the outworks, that it was better to attack from a new front, was equivalent to sacrificing the whole of the exertions of those four days, and starting the siege anew. But Murray accepted Thackeray's scheme, though the engineer warned him that he should require fourteen days more of open trenches to reduce the Upper City. This would relegate the crisis of the final assault to July 21st, and meanwhile Suchet

---

[1] *Court Martial Proceedings*, p. 49.

and Decaen would have had three weeks to concentrate, instead of one. The time-problem looked very unsatisfactory.

However the new plan was taken up—more artillery and engineer-stores and more guns were landed on the beach west of the mouth of the Francoli, as were also the remainder of the horses of the cavalry and the field-guns. The disembarkation was not always easy, as the surf on the beach grew dangerous whenever the wind was high. On several days communication with the shore had to be given up for many hours on end. Murray complained that the foreign troops worked slowly and unwillingly, and that he had to replace them with British parties, in order to get up the ammunition from the boats to the batteries [1].

However, progress was made, and in the four days between the 7th and the 10th of June two heavy batteries were thrown up on the high-lying slopes of the Olivo hill, in positions from which they could bring an enfilading as well as a frontal fire to bear upon the three corner bastions of the Upper City, including the roughly repaired breaches in the curtain, by which Suchet had made his entry in 1811. On the 9th and again on the 10th Admiral Hallowell sent his available vessels in-shore to resume the bombardment ; and late on the latter day the batteries on the Olivo began their fire, which they continued on the following morning : it was very effective, all the attacked bastions and the curtain between them being much damaged. Meanwhile the old batteries by the Francoli overwhelmed the Fuerte Real and San Carlos forts with renewed fire, destroying such repairs as the garrisons had been able to carry out. The Governor, Bertoletti, made up his mind that there would be a general assault both on the forts and on the Upper City on the night of the 11th, and made such preparations as he could to receive it. But the prospect was gloomy—the garrison was worn out, the walls were crumbling, and there seemed no hope of succour from without.

Meanwhile, harassed as the Governor might be, Murray was in an even greater state of depression. He had never believed, as he acknowledged at his court martial, that he could succeed. The only gleam of hope which ever entered his mind was when

---

[1] Murray's evidence at the Court Martial, p. 50.

on the morning of the 8th he received news that the fort of Balaguer had been taken, so that the road by which Suchet could most easily arrive was completely blocked. At any rate there would be a day or two gained, since the army of Valencia would have to take difficult and circuitous roads, instead of a short and direct one, when it came up.

The siege of the Fort of San Felipe de Balaguer had lasted four days. The place was small, only sixty yards square; it mounted twelve guns, but was held by only a single company. It was in a rocky and inaccessible position, and when Colonel Prevost had landed with his brigade, and had reconnoitred the place on the 3rd, he found that it must be battered by heavy guns. Shelling it with field pieces proved unavailing. Accordingly aid was sought from the fleet, and with great difficulty the sailors of the *Invincible* got two 12-pounders and a howitzer ashore, to a spot 700 yards from the fort. But the ground was so steep and rocky that it was difficult to construct a battery, and when the fire was opened it proved not very effective. It was only when more guns had been hoisted up the rocks, to a position only 300 yards from the fort, that anything was accomplished. On the evening of the 7th a lucky bomb from a mortar exploded one of the French magazines, and the commandant surrendered [1]. It was thought that he might have held out longer, as his main magazine was intact—but nearly a third of his garrison of 150 men had been hurt, and their morale was low. With the capture of Fort San Felipe the coast road became absolutely blocked to any troops coming from Suchet's direction, and Murray, as he confessed, ' entertained a ray of hope, not so much of the capture of Tarragona itself, but that the expedition might prove, as Lord Wellington wished it to prove, an effective diversion in favour of the allied army in Valencia [2].' It was this success, as he explained, which encouraged him to remain two days longer in front of Tarragona than he would otherwise have done, since the loss of the coast-road would add two marches to the distance which Suchet had to cover in order to join Decaen.

---

[1] Prevost's very moderate loss was 1 officer and 4 men killed, 1 sergeant and 38 men wounded. This includes Spaniards.

[2] *Court Martial*, Murray's defence, p. 228.

For already this downhearted general was obsessed with panic fears that the enemy might be upon him at any moment. He was gleaning in every rumour of the near approach of Suchet and Decaen, however incredible. On the 4th he had received an express from Prevost, with a message that the Marshal had reached Tortosa and might be at the Col de Balaguer on the 5th. On the 7th there was a report that a heavy French column was at Amposta, near the mouth of the Ebro, marching north. And on the other side Decaen was said to be in movement—' Could I ever have expected,' said Murray, a year later, ' that his army would not be united, that his movable column would have remained divided at Gerona, Figueras, and Barcelona [1] ? ' Accordingly he wrote that night to Wellington, ' I am much afraid we have undertaken more than we are able to perform. But to execute your Lordship's orders I shall persevere as long as prudence will permit. I have as yet no certain information of Suchet's movements, nor of Decaen to the eastward. But there are reports of both, and if they prove true, in five or six days I may be attacked by a force infinitely superior, without the hope of a retreat in case of misfortune. I calculate that Suchet can bring into the field 24,000 or 25,000 men without difficulty [2].' There is not a thought in Murray's brain of the chance that one of the enemy's columns might be late, and that it might be possible from his central position to fall upon the other, with his own forces and those of Copons united.

As a matter of fact things were working out most favourably for him. Suchet had seen the great transport-fleet pass the coast of Valencia on the 31st May ; but he was wholly in doubt whether the expedition might be intending to strike at Tortosa or Tarragona, at Barcelona or Rosas. The Marshal had to make up his mind to act, before he knew his enemy's objective or his exact numbers. After many searchings of heart he resolved to keep the bulk of his forces in the kingdom of Valencia, which he was most unwilling to give up, and to march with a column of moderate strength to reinforce the Army of Catalonia. He left Harispe in command in the South, with his own division,

---

[1] *Murray's Defence*, p. 232.
[2] Murray to Wellington, *Supplementary Dispatches*, vii. p. 467.

that of Habert, Severoli's Italians, and the bulk of his cavalry,
and resolved to move on Tortosa with Musnier's division, his
hussar regiment, three batteries of artillery, and an improvised
brigade under General Pannetier, composed of four battalions
borrowed some time back from the Army of Catalonia, one
battalion of his own, and an odd squadron of Westphalian
light horse belonging to the Army of the Centre. The whole
made up about 8,000 men [1], a force so weak that it was clear
that he dared not attack Murray till he should be joined by the
troops of Decaen. Pannetier's brigade had a long start, as it
was about Castellon and Segorbe when the order to march
arrived : it reached Tortosa on June 8th, and Perello on the
Balaguer road on the 10th. Then the news came in that the
fort of San Felipe had capitulated two days before. Pannetier
halted, and sent back the information to Suchet, who had
reached Tortosa on the 9th, escorted by a squadron of dragoons.
But Musnier's division had taken some time to assemble, only
left Valencia on the 7th, and was far behind. Suchet was in no
small perplexity this day. The coast-road was blocked : it was
the only one by which guns and transport could move directly
on Tarragona. No news whatever had been received of Decaen
and the Army of Catalonia. Musnier could not reach Tortosa
till the 11th. Should he recall Pannetier, wait for the arrival of
the rest of his column, and then march with his whole force by
the circuitous inland road along the Ebro, by Ginestar, Tivisa,
and Momblanch, so as to reach the plain of Tarragona from the
north ? This would lead to insufferable delays—the country
was desolate and waterless, and when the column reached its
goal the Army of Copons, with help perchance from Murray,
would be in the way. Ten days might easily be wasted, and
meanwhile Tarragona would probably have fallen. Information must at all costs be got, and the Marshal finally ordered
Pannetier to drop all his impedimenta, and push with his

---

[1] Musnier's division had 4,100 men present, by its return of June 15th.
Pannetier's column consisted of two battalions each of the 3rd Léger and
20th Line and one of the 5th Léger and a squadron of Westphalians—by
the return of the same date 2,600 in all. The hussars were 650 sabres—
adding the squadron of dragoons (200), the gunners of three batteries,
train, &c. ; the whole may have made just under 8,000 of all arms. See
Tables in Appendix, p. 755.

infantry alone by mountain paths from Perello to Monroig, on the edge of the hills overlooking the plain of Tarragona. This was to take a dangerous risk—a brigade of 2,500 bayonets might easily be surrounded by the Catalans and cut off. But the attention of Copons was at this moment distracted to the other direction. Pannetier reached the slopes above Monroig on the night of the 11th-12th, and could get no information there— the people had fled up into the mountains. The only fact that came to his notice was that no cannonading could be heard next morning from the direction of Tarragona : the most natural deduction was that the place had fallen. But in case it might still be resisting, Pannetier ordered a row of bonfires to be lighted along the hill-sides, which he thought would be visible to the beleaguered garrison, and would show that succour was at hand. He then drew off again by the same rough paths by which he had come, and returned to Valdellos, half-way back to Perello. From thence he could only send a report of a nega- tive kind to Suchet, who was left none the wiser for this risky reconnaissance. Meanwhile Musnier's division had at last come up, but there had also arrived the news that Del Parque and Elio were on the move in Valencia, and were pushing back Harispe's advanced troops. On the 12th-13th-14th the Marshal remained stationary, waiting vainly for news, and fearing the worst. Murray, if he had but known it, had nothing to fear from this quarter.

On the other flank also things were working out in the best possible fashion for the besieger of Tarragona. There was a long delay before the Army of Catalonia could prepare a field force which could dare to face the Anglo-Sicilians. Decaen himself was at Gerona, far away to the North, and got the news of Murray's landing on June 5th, by a dispatch sent him by Maurice Mathieu, Governor of Barcelona. He had no troops under his hand save the four battalions of Beurmann's brigade of Lamarque's division ; he could only collect more men by cutting down the garrisons of Figueras and Puycerda, and calling in two brigades (those of Petit and Espert) which were acting as flying columns at the moment, and were out of touch, in the sub-Pyrenaean foot-hills. The news that a very large disembarkation had taken place near Tarragona struck him at

first with such dismay that he replied to Maurice Mathieu that
they could not hope to resist such a force, and that it might
even be necessary to evacuate Barcelona [1]. However, resolving
to do what he could, he ordered Beurmann's brigade to march
on Barcelona (June 8), and sent orders around for a general
shifting of the northern garrisons, so that he hoped to collect
another 4,000 men at Gerona in the course of a week, if the
flying columns could be discovered and brought in. With this
reserve he intended to come down to join the rest of the field
force about the 14th or 15th. Meanwhile he ordered Maurice
Mathieu to demonstrate against the enemy, without risking
anything, or quitting the valley of the Llobregat and the vicinity
of Barcelona.

Maurice Mathieu was the only one of the generals in Catalonia,
French or allied, who deserves any credit for his conduct in this
campaign of blunders. He resolved that the one thing necessary
was to take the offensive, and to threaten the besiegers of Tarragona, even if he dared not venture to attack them. Beurmann's
brigade having arrived on June 10th, he marched next day with
it and four battalions of his own to Villafranca, half-way
between Barcelona and Tarragona, and drove in Copons' outposts—leaving his base-fortress occupied by a very inadequate
garrison. He had only 6,000 infantry and 300 horse with him,
so that he was wholly incapable of facing Murray's expeditionary
force if it should show fight. Meanwhile he sent letters to
Decaen, telling him that the honour of the Army of Catalonia
was at stake, and that it was necessary for him to come down
from Gerona without delay, and with every available man. But
the Commander-in-Chief did not appear—he was detained by
a naval demonstration in the Bay of Rosas. For Sir Edward
Pellew, then in command of the Mediterranean Fleet, had run
down from his usual cruising ground opposite Toulon, and concentrated a numerous squadron off the coast of the Ampurdam.
He came close in-shore, made a great display of boats, and even
landed a few hundred marines on June 8th. The news of this
disembarkation filled Decaen with the idea that the Tarragona
expedition was only a snare, intended to make him draw off all
his forces southward, and that the true blow would be struck at

---

[1] Decaen to M. Mathieu, 5th June : see Vidal de la Blache, i. 353.

Rosas. He concentrated his scattered troops with the object of parrying it, and was so long in detecting his mistake that it was only on June 15th that he set out from Gerona, with four battalions and one squadron, to join Maurice Mathieu, having at last discovered that Pellew could do no real mischief.

The Governor of Barcelona, therefore, had never more than 6,000 men at his disposition during the critical days of the campaign—June 11th–12th–13th–14th. He had, as has been mentioned above, reached Villafranca on the first-named day. There he received what had been longed for in vain up till now, a detailed dispatch from Suchet, setting forth his intentions. But it was no less than twelve days old, having been written at Valencia on May 31st, before the Marshal had any knowledge of Murray's strength, objective, or intentions. It stated that he was intending to march via Tortosa, and that he hoped that Decaen with all his disposable field force would come down to meet him at Reus, unless indeed the Anglo-Sicilians were aiming at some more northern point, in which case he would have to follow them to Upper Catalonia. But he added that it was possible that the whole naval expedition might be a mere feint, intended to lure him northward beyond the Ebro; the fleet might turn back again and re-land the whole of Murray's force near Valencia [1].

The dispatch was hopelessly out of date, and Maurice Mathieu had no means of knowing whether Suchet had carried out his original intentions. But his first impression was that he must seek for the Marshal at Reus, according to the directions given. Accordingly on June 12 he pushed his vanguard as far as Arbos, six miles in advance of Villafranca, and some 24 miles from Tarragona. But nothing could be heard of the Marshal's approach, and Copons' troops were gathering in from all sides to block the road, while Murray was only one march away. Seized with sudden misgivings at finding himself close to 20,000 enemies with such a trifling force, Mathieu made up his mind that it would be madness to push on. At 10 o'clock on the night of the 12th–13th [2] he evacuated both Arbos and

---

[1] Suchet to Decaen, Valencia, May 31. See Vidal de la Blache, i. p. 352.

[2] Report of Brigadier Llauder, commanding Copons' left wing, to Murray, *Proceedings*, p. 190. Llauder adds that he had discovered that Mathieu's column was only 5,500 strong.

Villafranca, and retreated in haste to Barcelona, to await the arrival of Decaen and the reserve.

Murray's miserable timidity now intervened, to save Tarragona, just when both the French forces had found themselves foiled, and had given up the relief of the fortress as impossible. The story reads like the plot of a stupid theatrical farce, where every character does the wrong thing, in order to produce absurd complications in the situation. On the 12th Pannetier, on the hills above Monroig, heard no bombardment, because the bombardment had ceased. And Maurice Mathieu on the night of that same day was running away from an enemy who had already absconded that very afternoon. So, after coming within 35 miles of each other, the two French generals had turned back in despair and given up the game. But Murray had given it up also.

The bombardment had gone on very successfully throughout the 11th June, and the engineers reported at noon that the Fuerte Real could be stormed at any moment, and that the works of the Upper City were crumbling in many places. Orders were issued that Mackenzie's division should storm the Fuerte Real at 10 p.m., while Clinton's was to make a demonstration against the Upper City. All arrangements were made, and after dark the troops designated for the assault filed into the advanced trenches : the signal was to be by a flight of rockets [1]. But the rockets never went up.

For some days Murray had been in a state of agonized indecision. On the 9th he had received information from a trusted secret agent in Valencia that Suchet had marched for Tortosa on the 7th with 9,000 men—this was absolutely certain and showed that all the previous rumours from the South had been false. On the same day a dispatch came in from Eroles at Vich to say that a French column (Beurmann's brigade) had left Gerona on the 8th, marching for Barcelona, and that he intended to follow it with his own detachment, and would join Copons before the enemy could concentrate. The French then were on the move on both flanks—but still far off. On the night of the 10th General Manso, commanding on Copons' right flank,

---

[1] See especially Clinton's evidence on pp. 180–2 of Murray s *Court Martial*.

reported the approaching departure of Maurice Mathieu from
Barcelona, but overrated his force at 10,000 men. He undertook
to detain them in the defiles beyond Villafranca for at least one
day. This news was corroborated next evening by an officer of
Whittingham's staff, who had seen the column, estimated it at
7,000 to 8,000 infantry, and reported that it had entered
Villafranca at 4 p.m. on the 11th [1]. But it was the movements
of Suchet which gave Murray the greater alarm : by ingenious
miscalculations [2] he had arrived at the statistical conclusion
that the Marshal had got 12,000 or 13,000 men of all arms with
him, instead of the real 8,000 [3]. And when the arrival of
Pannetier's brigade at Perello on the 10th was reported to him
on the following day, he proceeded to assume that the French
column was all closed up : ' the Marshal with 13,000 men was
within two long marches of Tarragona [4].' Many generals would
have asked for no better opportunity than that of being placed
in a central position with some 28,000 men—the Anglo-Sicilian
troops and those of Copons exceeded that figure—while two
hostile columns, one of 13,000 men and the other of 10,000,
35 miles apart, were trying to join each other across a difficult
country by bad roads. (As a matter of fact, of course, the
French force was much smaller—no more than 8,000 men on
the West, and 6,000 on the East, though Murray must not be
too much blamed for the over-estimate.) But the two governing
ideas that ruled in the brain of the unfortunate general were
firstly the memory of Wellington's warning that ' the one thing
that could not be forgiven would be that the corps should be
beaten or dispersed ', and secondly the fact that his army was
composed of heterogeneous material, some of which might be
found wanting at a crisis. But he concealed his downhearted-

---

[1] See Manso's letter and Guillot's report on pp. 275–6 of the *Court
Martial Proceedings*.

[2] For which see *Court Martial Proceedings*, pp. 282–3.

[3] His main blunder was that he took Pannetier's brigade to be a separate
item of 3,000 men, over and above the 9,000 men coming from Valencia
of whom his emissary had written. He also doubled Suchet's cavalry, by
supposing that the 9th *bis* of Hussars and the 12th Hussars were two
separate regiments. But they were the same unit, the number having
recently been changed by order from Paris.

[4] *Court Martial Proceedings*, p. 285.

ness till the last moment, both from his own lieutenants and from the Spaniards. On the 10th he rode out to meet General Copons at Torre dem Barra, to which place the Catalan head-quarters had just been moved, and agreed with him to defend the line of the Gaya river against the column coming from Barcelona. He promised to send up all his cavalry, 8,000 infantry, and two field batteries to join the Spanish army, which was now concentrated across the two roads by which Tarragona could be approached from Villafranca. Five battalions were on the northern road, by the Col de Santa Cristina, four and the three squadrons of horse on the southern route, nearer the sea. Warnings were issued to Clinton's and Whittingham's divisions, and also to Lord Frederick Bentinck, the cavalry brigadier, to be ready to march to the line of the Gaya [1]. This looked like business, and the spirits of the Anglo-Sicilians were high that night.

On the morning of the 11th, while the bombardment of Tarragona was going on in a very satisfactory way, Murray rode out again, met Copons at Vendrils, behind the Gaya, and spent much time in inspecting the chosen positions. He disliked them ; the river was fordable in many places, and a very long front would have to be guarded : it was considered that the French might break through by one of the roads before the troops guarding the other could arrive. However, adhering to his promise of the 10th, Murray ordered up Bentinck with two squadrons of hussars and two guns to the mouth of the Gaya, where they took over the outposts on the coast-road. The infantry was not brought up—as the assault on Tarragona was to take place that evening. The only news from the front received in the afternoon were rumours that Maurice Mathieu had actually reached Villafranca [2].

At seven o'clock Murray started home, and reached his head-quarters before Tarragona two hours later. There he found a batch of reports awaiting him, which finally broke down his resolution to fight, and drove him to the ignominious flight

---

[1] See evidence of Bentinck, p. 175, and Clinton, p. 180, of *Court Martial Proceedings*.

[2] Evidence of Captain Milner, ibid., p. 397. This was not true at the moment, early in the morning.

which he had already contemplated on more than one day during the preceding week. Two Spanish officers had come in from the Col de Santa Cristina, to report that the Barcelona column had certainly occupied Villafranca, and was apparently pushing on beyond it : this was discouraging. But the document which Murray regarded as all-important was a note from his adjutant-general, Donkin, to the effect that peasants, who had just come in from Perello, reported that Suchet's column had continued its advance : ' This corps of infantry may be at Reus to-morrow, if they think proper to march by Perello *without artillery.* And Decaen (i. e. Mathieu), if he marched this day to Villafranca, can also reach Reus to-morrow. This possibility may, perhaps, make some change in your arrangements [1].' As a matter of fact, we have already seen that it was only Pannetier's brigade which had gone across the hills from Perello towards Monroig, and that this was a mere reconnaissance.

But Donkin's picture of Suchet and the Barcelona column joining at Reus, in his rear, on the 12th, with forces which Murray's imagination raised to 25,000 men, was so much in consonance with the fears which had been obsessing the brains of the Commander-in-Chief throughout the last ten days, that he felt that his nightmare was coming true. There could be no doubt that he was on the brink of a disaster like the Ostend catastrophe of 1798 [2]. Of course Suchet's active brain had planned his complete destruction. He tells us in his defence [3] that he asked himself whether it was probable that an officer of the Marshal's activity and reputation would have left a man more than he could help in Valencia. ' Was it the character of a French general to act with inadequate means when ample means were within his reach ? Was it probable that he would have brought a small force only from the Xucar by the fatiguing march to Tortosa ? Would he have left a man idle in the south when in danger of losing his communication with France ? Every disposable corps, many more than what might be calcu-

---

[1] Donkin to Murray, 3 p.m. 11th June. *Court Martial Proceedings*, p. 360.
[2] He recalls this forgotten disaster in his defence (p. 300). A landing force cut off by storms from its transports had to surrender whole.
[3] *Court Martial Proceedings*, pp. 285–6.

lated to be fairly disposable, must be with the Marshal.' He
might have not 13,000 men but many more. And the Barcelona
column might be not 10,000 men but 13,000.

Rather than take the risk of waiting one day longer in his
present position, Murray resolved to abscond by sea, while the
enemy was still twenty miles away from Tarragona. By
9.30 p.m. he had sent his staff officers with messages to his
divisional generals to stop the projected assault, to order all
guns, horses, and stores to be got on ship-board, and the
infantry after them. He calculated, in his panic, that he had
only eighteen hours in hand : the re-embarkation must be over
by dusk on the 12th. But the most disgraceful part of his
scheme was that he had resolved to leave Copons and the
Catalans to their fate, after having brought them to the Gaya
by definite promises of assistance, without which they would
never have taken up their fighting position, and this though
he had renewed his pledges that same morning. He sent no
warning of his real intentions to his colleague, but only told
him that recent information had made it necessary for him to
re-embark his battering train ; but six Anglo-Sicilian battalions
should be sent out next morning, to strengthen the force behind
the Gaya.

There followed a night and a morning of confusion. No one
in the expeditionary force had hitherto suspected Murray's
wavering confidence, except Admiral Hallowell, to whom he had
on June 9th made the remark that he imagined that they ought
to be thinking about getting away in safety rather than about
prolonging the siege, and the Quarter-Master-General, Donkin,
to whom on the same day Murray had said that he suspected
that they would have ere long to depart, whereupon that officer
had drawn up a secret scheme for the details of re-embarkation[1].
But since nothing more had been heard about such a move on the
10th or the 11th, Hallowell and Donkin had supposed that the
idea was abandoned. Clinton and the other senior officers had
been kept entirely in the dark, till the sudden orders of 9.30 p.m.
were delivered to them. At midnight Admiral Hallowell came
in to Murray's quarters to protest against the hasty departure,
which would cause all manner of confusion and ensure the loss

[1] Donkin's evidence, *Court Martial Proceedings*, p. 448.

of much valuable material : they parted after an angry alterca-
tion.   Colonel Williamson (commanding the artillery) also
appeared, to say that in the time given him he could get off the
guns in the batteries near the shore, but not those on the distant
Olivo.   He understood the general to reply that he might be
granted some extra hours, and that the Olivo guns might be
brought down after dark on the 12th [1].

But in the morning Murray's apprehension grew progressively
worse.   He had at first intended to do something to cover
Copons' inevitable retreat, and ordered Clinton to throw out six
battalions towards the Gaya.   But he soon cancelled this order,
and directed Bentinck to bring back his cavalry and guns from
Altafulla without delay.   At 9 a.m. a message was sent to
Williamson, to say that the guns on the Olivo must be spiked or
destroyed, as it would be perilous to wait till night [2].   Half an
hour later Murray's notions of retreat flickered round to a new
scheme—the troops on the shore should embark there ; but
those on the northern heights—the divisions of Clinton and
Whittingham—should march to the Col de Balaguer via Constanti, and take ship in the much better harbourage behind
Cape Salou.   Half an hour later he abandoned this scheme, and
ordered them down to the beach by the Francoli, there to
embark without delay.

This dispatch reduced Clinton to a state of cold rage : at the
court martial in 1814 he produced seven separate orders which
he had received between dawn and 1.30 that day : they were all
contradictory, and deserve record as showing Murray's state of
mind during the critical hours.   (1) The first, received early,
directed him to take six battalions towards the Gaya, to cover
the retreat of Copons from Altafulla.   (2) The second, sent off
at 9 o'clock, told him not to execute this march, but to wait till
the Spaniards had cleared off, and then to move, not with six
battalions but with the whole of his own and Whittingham's
divisions, to Constanti [3].   (3) The third was to the effect that

[1] Williamson's evidence, *Proceedings*, p. 124.
[2] Williamson's evidence, ibid., p. 125.
[3] Mr. Fortescue has, I think, misinterpreted this order, when he says
that it told Clinton to march to the same spot as the first (*British Army*,
ix. p. 63), for Constanti is not in the direction of the Gaya, but on the
opposite flank, west of the Francali river.

the baggage should be sent to the Col de Balaguer, to which the whole army would now proceed[1]. (4) Half an hour later Clinton was told to cancel the last two dispatches, and to come down to head-quarters on the nearest beach. (5) A supplementary verbal order directed that the guns in the Olivo batteries should be spiked. (6) Twenty minutes later Clinton was told that the guns might still be saved : Whittingham's Spaniards should remain on the Olivo and guard them till dusk, when the artillery would try to get them down to the shore. (7) Lastly, at 1.30, the final order cancelled the sixth, it directed (once more) that Whittingham's troops must follow Clinton's for instant embarkation, and that the guns should be spiked without delay. This was done, to the intense disgust of the gunners, who had been getting everything ready for an orderly retreat after dusk. Seventeen heavy pieces in good condition, and one more which had been disabled, were spiked and left in the Olivo batteries, while the infantry hurried down to the shore.

The momentary wavering in Murray's orders during the early morning, when he seemed inclined to risk a longer stay, and to march Clinton's division and the baggage by land to the anchorage by the Col de Balaguer, was apparently caused partly by new remonstrances from Hallowell, partly by an interview with some of his subordinates, somewhere between 8 and 9 a.m., Mackenzie, Adam, Donkin, and Thackeray, the chief engineer, entered the house of the Commander-in-Chief together, and Adam, as their spokesman, urged him with great heat not to embark, but to advance, join Copons, and attack the French on the Gaya with every available man. Murray replied that if he did so, the French would refuse to fight and give back toward Barcelona ; while Suchet, coming from the other direction, would cut him off from the fleet and relieve Tarragona. But if, on the other hand, he were to march against Suchet, and stop him, then the Barcelona column would relieve Tarragona and get the expeditionary force separated from its transports. Either course would be equally ruinous. He also said that Wellington had told him 'not to commit the army'. The generals withdrew—further insistence would have amounted to

---

[1] A queer misprint in this dispatch makes it say ' the enemy will march.'

military insubordination. The final hurry-scurry order, to destroy the guns and embark pell-mell, was caused by news from Copons that the French at Villafranca had advanced as far as Arbos, only ten miles from the Gaya, and seemed still to be coming on.

During the night and the morning that followed all the guns from the lower batteries, much valuable material, some of the cavalry, and the infantry of Adam, were got aboard. The shipment of artillery stores was still proceeding at 10 o'clock, when Murray ordered that nothing but men should now be embarked—all else must be abandoned. Admiral Hallowell, who was superintending the work on the beach in person, was much incensed with this resolve, and took it upon himself to direct the sailors in the boats to refuse infantry, and to go on lading stores. Then came a deadlock—Hallowell said that there was plenty of time to take off everything : Donkin, coming down from Murray's quarters, maintained that the French were only two and a half hours' march away, and that the infantry must be got off at all costs : horses and mules might have to be shot, and food and ammunition abandoned [1]. There was much disputing, but the naval men, obeying the admiral, continued to embark horses and artillery material till midday, when Mackenzie's infantry began to pour down to the beaches, followed by Clinton's and Whittingham's battalions [2]. All through the afternoon the shipping off of troops continued without any interruption, till only a rearguard of 500 of Clinton's men was left on shore. No news of the French coming to hand, there was a relaxation of the wild hurry which had prevailed between 9 a.m. and 2 p.m. Murray permitted Bentinck to take that part of the cavalry which had not yet embarked round to the anchorage by the Col de Balaguer by land [3], and sent on behind them twelve field-guns escorted by a half battalion of the 2/27th. Meanwhile, the troops having all got off, the boats began to load again with transport mules, entrenching tools,

---

[1] Evidence of Captains Withers and Bathurst, R.N., *Court Martial Proceedings*, pp. 86 and 95.

[2] Mackenzie in his evidence says his men began at 2 p.m. to get into the boats.

[3] Evidence of Bentinck, ibid., p. 176. The cavalry went off at 3 p.m.

spare shot, platform timbers, sand bags, and biscuit. The rear
guard was not taken off till late at night ; and, even after it was
gone and dawn had come, the sailors continued to find and take
off various valuable leavings [1]. No molestation whatever was
suffered from the garrison, who regarded the whole movement
as inexplicable, and only crept out with caution after the last
British troops had disappeared, to find 18 spiked guns and some
artillery stores in the Olivo batteries, and a certain amount of
flour and beef barrels left on the shore. The most distressing
part of the chronicle of this wretched day's work is Murray's
dealings with Copons. He had induced the Captain-General to
bring his army to the line of the Gaya, by the promise of supporting him with 8,000 men, renewed on the morning of the 11th.
At dawn on the 12th the message was sent that six battalions
only could be spared. An hour or two later Copons received
the crushing news that the whole expeditionary army was
about to re-embark, abandoning him to his own resources. If
Murray's view of the situation had been correct, the Spaniards
must have been caught between Suchet advancing on Reus and
Mathieu converging on the same point from Villafranca. His
moral guilt, therefore, was very great. But, as a matter of fact,
nothing disastrous happened.   On hearing that he had been
left in the lurch, Copons withdrew the troops which he had at
Altafulla on the coast-road, to join those at the Col de Santa
Cristina, leaving the way to Tarragona open to Maurice Mathieu,
and preparing to retreat into the mountains if necessary. He
kept a close look-out upon the French column, and was astonished
on the morning of the 13th to learn that, after sending a vanguard to Arbos on the previous day, six miles down the southern
road, it had turned back at ten o'clock at night, and was now
in full retreat on Barcelona. The crisis was over for the
moment. Copons returned to his old head-quarters at Reus,
threw out a slight screen of troops to the line of Gaya, and
reoccupied Villafranca with a few cavalry. He was quite ready

---

[1] The hours of this belated work are stated very differently by various
naval witnesses, some of whom say that they worked till 1 a.m., others
till 4 a.m., others till 7 ; one thinks that embarkations continued till
well into the forenoon of the 13th—say 11 o'clock. At any rate, the hour
must have been long after daylight had come—which was at 4.15, as is
recorded by one witness.

to retreat into the mountains once more if any untoward developments should supervene.

On June 13th Murray had all his army on ship-board,[1] save Prevost's two battalions at the Col de Balaguer, and the guns and cavalry with Bentinck, which had marched by land to that same pass. Wellington's orders told him that if he failed at Tarragona he was to return to Valencia, join Elio and Del Parque, and fall upon the diminished French force on the Xucar before Suchet could get back. It was his obvious duty to pick up Prevost's and Bentinck's detachments, and to depart at once. He did nothing of the kind, but proceeded to employ himself for several days in minor operations, in the vain hope of redeeming the disgrace of June 12th.

On the morning of the 13th Murray received news from Colonel Prevost at San Felipe to the effect that the French column in front of him (Pannetier's brigade), about 3,000 strong, had marched from Perello by mountain paths eastward, but had not been followed by Suchet's main body. Prevost thought that it might be intending to cut him off from the rest of the army by dropping down into the coast-road in his rear. Pannetier's movement was also reported by Bentinck, whose flank patrols had run against similar parties of the French while on their way to the Col de Balaguer. It was necessary to bring off Prevost, the cavalry, and the guns by sea, if the French were trying to get round them. So Murray asked Admiral Hallowell to send ships inshore to the Col, and with them part of Mackenzie's division [2], to act as a covering force for the re-embarkation of Prevost's detachment. These troops—apparently three battalions—were landed near the fort late on the evening of the 13th.

---

[1] The total loss of Murray's Army during the Tarragona operations was :

	Killed.	Wounded.	Missing.	Total.
British, Germans, Calabrese, Italian Levy	14	60	5	
Sicilians	—	15	—	102
Whittingham's Spaniards . . .	1	7	—	

Bertoletti's garrison lost 13 killed and 85 wounded = 98. The enemies did each other little harm !

[2] Not apparently the whole division, for Mackenzie calls it ' a small body of infantry.'

Now during that day Pannetier, conscious that he was too far away from his chief, and quite ' in the air,' had drawn back from near Monroig to Valdellos, ten miles nearer to Perello. The same idea had occurred to Suchet, who simultaneously brought up his main body from Tortosa to Perello, though he knew that the coast-road was blocked by the British force holding Fort San Felipe. But on the morning of the 14th the Marshal, exploring toward the Col, sighted not only Mackenzie's infantry on shore, but the whole transport fleet lying off the coast from opposite the fort as far as Cape Salou—180 ships small and great, as he counted. A frigate and two brigs took a number of long shots at the Marshal and his large escort, which had to retire in haste. Suchet saw the whole expeditionary force before him, and recognized that he was too weak to tackle it. Wherefore he sent orders to Pannetier to fall back and rejoin him—and came to a halt. Early on the morning of the 15th he wrote to Decaen :

' The loss of the Col de Balaguer has foiled all my plans. The English fleet fired more than a thousand shot at us. Menaced by forces of four times my own strength, I wish to know what you propose to do. The enemy [Del Parque] has attacked my lines on the Xucar [1].'

This last fact, at the moment, was worrying Suchet even more than the unknown fate of Tarragona, for Harispe had just reported that the two Spanish armies in Valencia had advanced against him in force, and on a long front. Now, while the Marshal halted in indecision, Murray was seized with a spasmodic fit of energy—he knew that Maurice Mathieu was for the moment out of the game ; he saw that Suchet was blocked, and that Pannetier was in a dangerously advanced position. He conceived the idea that he might land more troops at the Col, and strike in between the French main body and the brigade at Valdellos. To the astonishment of his subordinates he ordered the rest of Mackenzie's troops and all Clinton's to be landed, as also the remainder of the cavalry, and instructed Mackenzie to make a forced march on Valdellos and beat up Pannetier's camp. The General did so, but arrived only just in time to see the French rearguard absconding on

[1] Suchet, *Mémoires*, ii. p. 315.

the 15th [1]. This demonstration of energy having failed, as it was pretty certain to do (for events like the surprise of Arroyo dos Molinos are not common), Murray had another inspiration. On the evening of the 15th [2] he suggested to Admiral Hallowell that the garrison of Tarragona must now be quite off their guard, that they had not been strengthened, and that it might be possible to re-embark 5,000 men secretly at Fort Balaguer, land them at Cambrils, and make a sudden dash at Tarragona by escalade or surprise. The Admiral answered that as Murray had not felt himself equal to storming Tarragona when the whole army was with him, and the batteries playing on the place, he (Hallowell) did not think him equal to it now with 5,000 men [3]. The idea was dropped : it was not without its merits, but though Picton or Craufurd might have succeeded in such a desperate stroke, Murray would certainly have failed from lack of nerve at the decisive moment, as the Admiral meant to insinuate.

This wretched campaign was now nearing its end—but still reserved two extraordinary surprises for its last days. On the 16th Suchet, much impressed with the strength which Murray had shown, judging from the stroke at Valdellos that he was thinking of taking the offensive, and harassed by fresh news of Del Parque's advance on Valencia, retired from Perello, and took his main body back across the Ebro to Amposta, which he reached on the 17th. He left only Pannetier's brigade and the hussar regiment to watch Murray. Thus the Anglo-Sicilians had opposite them on the south only 3,000 men, from whom no possible danger could be apprehended. But their General had no idea as yet that only a rearguard lay before him, and imagined that the Marshal and his main body were close in Pannetier's rear.

The second surprise took place on the other front. Maurice Mathieu had got back to Barcelona by a forced march on the 13th. On the next day spies brought him the news that

[1] Date stated by some as the 16th, but the earlier day seems correct. See Mackenzie's evidence, pp. 152–3 : he was uncertain as to the date.

[2] Hallowell says on the evening of the 14th or the 15th, he forgets which. But the latter date must be the true one.

[3] Hallowell's speech, p. 554 of the *Court Martial Proceedings*.

Murray had raised the siege of Tarragona, and gone away with his whole army by sea. There was nothing to prevent him from relieving Bertoletti's garrison, save Copons' troops holding the line of the Gaya. Therefore, although Decaen had not yet arrived from the North, and indeed had written that he could not start from Gerona until the 17th, Mathieu resolved to make a second attempt to reach Tarragona. He could still count on no greater force than the 6,000 men with which he had made his first fruitless expedition, but he thought this sufficient to deal with the Catalans. He moved once more upon Villafranca early on the 15th, and reached that place the same night. Next day a forced march of twenty-four miles brought him to Tarragona unopposed ; for Copons would not fight when unsupported by Murray, and had withdrawn his troops to Valls. At Tarragona Mathieu learned that the Anglo-Sicilians had not disappeared entirely from Catalonia, as he had hitherto believed, but were concentrated at and about the Col de Balaguer. Though no news had been received from Suchet, it might be conjectured that Murray had landed at the Col in order to hold back the Marshal, who could not be very far off. On the morning of the 17th Mathieu resolved to take the risky step of advancing by the coast-road to feel for Murray's rear, and marched out to Cambrils six miles west of Tarragona, hoping to hear that Suchet was simultaneously attacking the front of the Anglo-Sicilians. He was thereby exposing himself to fearful danger, for Murray had his whole 15,000 men in hand, and quite disposable, since Suchet had withdrawn southward on the 16th. And Copons at Valls was in a position to cut in upon the rear of the Barcelona column with 6,000 men more : each of them was only ten miles from Cambrils, and they were in full communication with each other. Indeed, Murray had sent to Copons late on the 16th, imploring him to fall upon the flank of the enemy, though he spoilt the effect of the appeal by explaining that he was going to be attacked by Suchet and the Barcelona column simultaneously, and expected to be outnumbered—the Marshal had 24,000 men (!), while 8,000 men were coming via Tarragona against his rear. Startled by these astounding figures, the Spanish General did not actually attack Maurice Mathieu, but contented himself with bringing

forward his infantry to La Selva and feeling for the French
column by cavalry patrols sent out from Reus.

The 17th June was a day as full of ridiculous cross-purposes
as the 12th. Suchet's main body was in full march for Amposta
and the road to Valencia [1], just as Maurice Mathieu was at last
coming to look for it. Murray in the centre was expecting to
be attacked on both sides of the Col de Balaguer, believing
that the reckless advance of the Barcelona column was timed
to coincide with a desperate assault on the Col by Suchet and
his whole army. Mathieu was advancing in ignorance into a
death-trap, if he had only known it, expecting every moment
to hear guns in his front, or to get news of Suchet by spies or
patrols. Copons was hanging back on Mathieu's flank, deterred
from pressing in by Murray's ridiculous overstatement of the
total French force. If Murray had marched from the Col that
morning early with 10,000 men and had met the French column
at Cambrils, while the Catalans closed in on its rear, no possible
chance could have saved it from complete destruction.

But Murray was doing something very different; after
having made his urgent appeal to Copons to take part in a
general action on the 17th, it occurred to him that a general
action might perhaps be avoided by the simple method of
absconding once more by sea—and again leaving the Catalans
to shift for themselves. Mackenzie was back from Valdellos,
and the whole force was concentrated in the pass, with the
immense transport fleet at its elbow, and several decent
embarkation places. In the morning he called a council of war
—which, as the old military proverb goes, ' never fights '—
though he had assured Admiral Hallowell on the preceding
night that he had chosen his positions, and intended to stand
and receive the enemy's attack [2]. The council of war voted,
by a large majority, for embarkation—probably as has been
acutely observed [3], because none of the generals liked the idea
of being commanded in action by Murray, after their recent
experience of his methods. The preparations for departure

---

[1] Pannetier's rearguard followed on the 17th. See letter of the Alcalde
of Perello, *Court Martial*, p. 361.

[2] Hallowell's speech, *Court Martial Proceedings*, p. 556.

[3] By Mr. Fortescue, *History of the British Army*, ix. 67.

were begun on the afternoon of the 17th, but no notice of them
was sent to Copons.

Meanwhile Maurice Mathieu had halted at Cambrils : he
could get no news of Suchet, and no firing could be heard in
front. On the other hand, British warships ran close inshore,
and began to cannonade his column, as it defiled along the
coast-road. And his cavalry patrols discovered those of Copons
in front of Reus, and afterwards got in touch with the Spanish
infantry behind them. The situation was getting unpleasant ;
and realizing that he had better draw back, Mathieu turned
the head of his column inland to Reus, for he was determined
not to expose it a second time to the fire of the British ships,
which swept the coast-road at many points. Marching in the
night of the 17th–18th he almost surprised Copons, who had
brought his infantry up to Reus in order to fall in with Murray's
plan for attacking the enemy in flank. But the Spaniard was
warned in time, and escaped to La Selva, from whence he
wrote to Murray, to complain that the British had not kept
their part of the bargain, nor even sent him news of Mathieu's
retirement from their front.

At Reus the French General picked up the spy to whom
Suchet had entrusted his despairing note of June 15, which
avowed his impotence and asked what the Army of Catalonia
could do [1]. Seeing that he must hope for no help from the
Marshal, Mathieu retreated by the inland road to Constanti,
two miles from Tarragona (June 18), where he halted for a day,
after sending on Suchet's letter to his chief Decaen, and
renewing his former petitions that the reserves from the North
should get to Barcelona as soon as possible. It was clear that
the Army of Catalonia must save itself, without any aid from
the Army of Valencia.

While Maurice Mathieu stood doubting at Cambrils, and all
through the night hours while he was marching on Reus, there
had been a rapid shifting of scenes at the Col de Balaguer.
Murray's orders for re-embarkation were just drawn up when
a formidable fleet of men-of-war became visible on the horizon,
and presently ran close inshore. This was Sir Edward Pellew
with the Toulon blockading squadron, twelve line of battle ships,

---

[1] See above, p. 515.

besides smaller craft. They had run down from the Bay of
Rosas, after picking up at Port Mahon a vessel from Sicily, on
which was Lord William Bentinck, who had at last arrived to
assume command of the Anglo-Sicilian army. He had torn
himself away with some reluctance from his plans for raising
a general insurrection in Italy against Napoleon, having
satisfied himself that there was no risk of Murat's invading Sicily
in his absence, and that the local politics of Palermo were
deplorable but not dangerous [1]. When the signal was made
from Pelew's flagship that Lord William had arrived, Admiral
Hallowell answered with the counter-signal, ' We are all
delighted,' which was sincere and accurate, but not officially
correct. It was remembered against him afterwards, as an
improper ebullition of misplaced humour.

Bentinck landed at San Felipe without a moment's delay,
took over the command from Murray, and heard his report.
He also talked with Hallowell and the senior land-officers. He
made up his mind very promptly : the embarkation which had
begun was to continue, and the Army was to be taken back to
Valencia at once, in strict consonance with Wellington's original
orders. He explained in his next dispatch home that he was
aware that he might have chased Maurice Mathieu, and probably have compelled him to throw himself into Tarragona.
But he conceived that a second siege of that fortress would
take many days, and would not be so profitable to the general
cause as an unexpected return to Valencia to join Del Parque
and Elio. The Army, as he wrote to Wellington, was in the
best spirits, but most dissatisfied as to what had happened
before Tarragona, ' concerning which, from motives of delicacy,
he would refrain from saying anything [2].' But there had been
much material lost, the horses and mules were in a bad way,
from having been so often landed and re-shipped, and it was
better to return to Alicante and reorganize everything than to
start another Catalan campaign.

The troops were got on board very rapidly, and the whole
transport fleet set sail southward on the 18th. The fort of
San Felipe was blown up, as Bentinck was not willing to

[1] *Supplementary Dispatches,* viii. pp. 18–19, June 23.
[2] Ibid., p. 20.

leave any troops behind to garrison it. Unfortunately, the
good weather which had been granted to Murray at the starting
of the expedition was denied to Bentinck during its return.
A furious north-east wind was blowing, which scattered the
ships, and drove no less than fourteen of them ashore on the
projecting sands at the estuary of the Ebro. Ten were got off
when the storm moderated, but four had to be burned, after
the crews and troops had been taken off. Bentinck, after
four days at sea, got into Alicante on the 22nd June, ahead of
the great majority of the transports, which continued to drop
in, some much disabled, for three or four days after. This
caused a tiresome delay in the reorganization of the army, as
odd companies of every regiment were missing, and the units
could not be reformed and marched inland for some time. The
delay gave Bentinck time to write long dispatches to the
Secretary for War and to Wellington. These went off on the
23rd by special messenger, and along with them lengthy screeds
from Murray and Admiral Hallowell. The two officers wrote most
bitterly of each other to the Commander-in-Chief—the Admiral
detailing all the General's hesitations and tergiversations with
caustic irony, while the General wrote that 'if I had only
allowed the Admiral to command the army you would never
have been troubled with the long letter which accompanies
this. . . . He thinks that prejudice against him led me to act
as I did. These are the real grounds of all his outcry [1].'
Murray's long dispatch was not only very disingenuous in
suppression of facts, but so vague concerning all necessary
dates and figures, that Wellington, when it came to hand,
showed profound dissatisfaction. He observed that it 'left
him entirely ignorant of what had occurred,' and administered
a searching interrogatory of eleven questions, answers to which
were necessary before a judgement could be formed by himself
or the Home Government on what had really happened in
Catalonia [2]. Murray's replies were as unconvincing as his
original dispatches, and the matter ended in a long-deferred
and lengthy court martial at Winchester in 1814, after the
war had come to an end. To describe it here would interrupt

---

[1] *Supplementary Dispatches*, viii. p. 22.
[2] Wellington to Murray, July 1, *Dispatches*, x. p. 487.

unseasonably the narrative of the summer campaign of 1813. But it may suffice to say that he did not get his deserts. He was only convicted of an error of judgement, and not of the ' disobedience to orders and neglect of duty, highly to the prejudice of the service, and detrimental to the British military character ' for which he was put on trial. He was never even indicted for his worst offence—the callous betrayal of the Spanish colleague who had done his best to serve him.

SECTION XXXVII: CHAPTER IV

WELLINGTON ON THE BIDASSOA

On July 1st the last of Foy's troops on the sea-coast front had recrossed the lower Bidassoa, leaving Graham and Giron in complete possession of the Spanish bank, and free to commence the siege of St. Sebastian. They had 25,000 men in line, without counting Mendizabal's Biscayan irregulars, who were observing the fortress, and the 5th British Division, which was now on its march from Vittoria to the frontier, and was due to arrive on the 5th or 6th. These forces were amply sufficient to hold in check Reille, Foy, and the Bayonne Reserve.

On July 1st also Wellington began to arrange his march northward from Pampeluna, which might have begun on the 26th June if he had not taken off so many divisions for the fruitless pursuit of Clausel. The five days' respite granted to the enemy had been very useful to him. If the King had been followed up without delay, at the moment when he had split his army into the three columns, which marched the first by Yrurzun and Santesteban (Reille), the second by the Col de Velate (D'Erlon), and the third by the Pass of Roncesvalles (Gazan), it is hard to say where or how he could have rallied or offered any effective resistance. Wellington had preferred to take the doubtful chance of intercepting and destroying a secondary force, rather than to devote himself to the relentless pursuit of the demoralized main body of the enemy. But it must be remembered that a resolve to push the chase after the flying King would have involved an instant invasion of France. And though on general military grounds a defeated enemy should be kept on the run and destroyed in detail—like Brunswick's army after Jena—there were in June–July 1813 the strongest political reasons to deter Wellington from crossing the frontier. It was not merely that he had outmarched his transport, and had not yet got into touch with his new bases of supply at Santander and on the Biscay coast, so that for the moment he was a little short of ammunition, and also living on the country, a practice which he disliked on principle and wished to end as soon as possible [1]. Nor was his hindrance the fact that his army was tired and sulky, and that many of his stragglers had not yet rejoined—though both of these vexations had their weight [2]. Nor was the political consideration that held him back the deplorable news from Cadiz, received at Caseda on June 28th, to the effect that the Regency had deposed Castaños from his office as Captain-General of Galicia, Estremadura, and both the Castiles, and had superseded his nephew General Giron in the command of the Fourth Army [3]. This was indeed a serious blow—not so much because Wellington could always rely on Castaños, and had found Giron more obedient than most Spanish officers, but because it looked as if the Cadiz Government was aiming at an open repudiation of the bargain that had been made in January, by which they had agreed not to make or revoke appointments of the military sort without giving notice, and receiving approval. The excuses given for the changes were paltry and unconvincing—Castaños was wanted to take his seat in the Council of State—Giron was to be sent, with large reinforcements, to serve with Copons as second in command of the Army of Catalonia. Wellington concluded, and rightly, that the real causes of these attacks on his friends were petty political intrigues—the 'Liberal' party in Cadiz was trying to secure its own domination by evicting those who might be considered 'Serviles' or even 'Moderates' from positions of power [4]. He had resolved not to bring the relations between himself and the Regency to a crisis, by making a formal demand for the restoration of Castaños and Giron to their posts. He wrote indeed to the Minister of War to say that he considered that he had been 'most unworthily treated'

[1] *Dispatches*, x. p. 495, to Lord Bathurst, July 2.

[2] To the same, *Dispatches*, x. p. 496.

[3] To O'Donoju, Minister of War, *Dispatches*, x. pp. 492–3 ; to Castaños, x. p. 475 ; to Lord Bathurst, x. pp. 473–4.

[4] 'We and the powers of Europe are interested in the success of the War in the Peninsula. But the creatures who govern at Cadiz appear to feel no such interest. All that they care about really is the praise of their foolish Constitution. . . . As long as Spain shall be governed by the Cortes, acting upon Republican principles, we cannot hope for any permanent amelioration.' *Dispatches*, x. p. 474, Wellington to Bathurst, June 29.

and that there were limits to his forbearance, but he avoided
an open rupture, and waited for the Regency to take the next
step. He wrote, however, to his brother, the Ambassador at
Cadiz, that he ought to call together in private all the more
sensible and sound members of the Cortes, and to warn them
of the pernicious effects of this last move : unless they wished
to see him resign the position of Generalissimo, given him only
six months back, they must bring pressure on their government
—' they have it in their power to interfere if they still wish
that I should retain the command [1].'

But this political trouble, ominous though it might be of
friction in the near future, was not the cause of Wellington's
failure to exploit to the utmost the effects of the battle of
Vittoria. The real hindrance was not the state of Spanish
politics, but the posture of affairs in Central Europe. The
Armistice of Plässwitz had been signed on June 4, and till it
came to an end on August 11 there was a possibility of peace
between Napoleon and his Russian and Prussian enemies,
on terms which Great Britain would be unable to accept.
Wellington was sent frequent dispatches by Lord Bathurst, to
keep him abreast of the latest developments in the Conferences,
but inevitably it took a very long time for news from Saxony
to reach London and be transmitted to Spain. Now if Napoleon
should succeed in making a separate peace with the Allies, his
first care would be to evict the British Army, if it should have
entered France in successful pursuit of King Joseph and his
demoralized host. Even if it should have taken Bayonne,
crushed the enemy's field force, and made good way towards
Bordeaux, it would have no chance of standing against the
enormous reserves that could be drawn from Germany, with
the Emperor himself at their head. Therefore it would be
better to take up a good position on the line of the Pyrenees,
secured by capturing St. Sebastian and Pampeluna, than to
make an irruption into France, however brilliant the immediate
results of such a move might be. Still ignorant on July 12 of
the tendency of the conferences at Dresden, Wellington wrote
to the Secretary for War : ' My future operations will depend
a good deal upon what passes in the North of Europe : and if

[1] Wellington to Henry Wellesley, *Dispatches*, x. p. 491.

operations should recommence there, on the strength and
description of the reinforcement which the enemy may get on
, our front. . . . I think I can hold the Pyrenees as easily as I
can Portugal. I am quite certain that I can hold the position
which I have got more easily than the Ebro, or any other line
in Spain [1].' In another letter he explains that he is giving his
army a few days of much needed rest, by the end of which he
hopes not only to have heard of the fall of St. Sebastian, but
of the results of the negotiations in Germany [2]. In a third he
puts the matter in the clearest terms : ' Much depends upon
the state of affairs in the North of Europe. If the war should
be renewed, I should do most good by moving forward into
France, and I should probably be able to establish myself there.
If it is not renewed, I should only go into France to be driven
out again. So I shall do my best to confine myself to securing
what I have gained [3].' In a fourth he complains that many
people, even officers at the front, seem to think that after
driving the French from the frontiers of Portugal to the Pyrenees, he ought to invade France immediately. ' Some expect
that we shall be at Paris in a month.' But though he entertained no doubt that he could enter France to-morrow, and
establish the Army on the Adour, he could go no farther. For
if peace were made by the Allies, he must necessarily withdraw
into Spain, and the retreat, though short, would be through a
difficult country and a hostile population. So from what he
could gather about the progress of negotiations in Germany,
he had determined that it would be unsafe to think of anything
in the way of an invasion of France [4].

Everything therefore at present, and for many weeks to
follow, depended on the news concerning the Armistice. And
the happy intelligence that it had come to an end, and that
the war was renewed, with the Austrians added to the Allied
forces, only reached Wellington on September 7th. The actual
declaration of war by Austria took place on August 11, by

---

[1] *Dispatches*, x. pp. 523–4.   [2] Ibid., x. p. 521.
[3] Ibid., x. pp. 553–4. When this letter was written to Lord William
Bentinck, Wellington had received no London dispatch for twenty days,
mainly owing to bad weather in the Bay of Biscay.
[4] Ibid., x. pp. 613–14, to Lord Bathurst.

which time the situation on the Spanish frontier had suffered many vicissitudes, for in the last fortnight during which the Armistice endured, there had taken place Soult's desperate invasion of Spain, and all the bloody fighting known as the Battles of the Pyrenees.

Meanwhile we must return to July 1st, on which day Wellington had already made up his mind that his present programme should be confined to bringing up his army to the Bidassoa and the Pyrenean passes, and undertaking the siege of St. Sebastian and the blockade of Pampeluna. He was still not quite happy about the intentions of Clausel—he trusted that the French General and his 15,000 men would retire to France by the pass above Jaca [1]. If he were to remain at Saragossa, and Suchet were there to join him, a tiresome complication would be created on his right rear—wherefore he kept sending letters to William Bentinck, ordering him to keep Suchet busy at all costs, by whatever means might seem best to him [2]. It was not till July 16th that news came that this danger had ended in the desired fashion, by Clausel's crossing the passes [3]. But whatever might happen in that direction, there was still one point that had to be settled, before it could be considered that the allied army was established on a satisfactory line for defending the Spanish frontier and covering the sieges of St. Sebastian and Pampeluna. The French were still in possession of the Bastan, the high-lying valley of the Upper Bidassoa, through which runs the main road from Pampeluna to Bayonne, by the Col de Velate, and the pass of Maya. This last corner of Spain must be cleared of the invaders, or the crest of the Pyrenees was not yet secure. Accordingly arrangements were made for marching the main body of the British Army to its destined positions through the Bastan, in order to sweep out the lingering enemy.

A sufficient corps must be left to blockade Pampeluna : during the operations against Clausel this duty had been discharged by Hill's and Silveira's and Morillo's troops. As these units had enjoyed five days' rest, while the remainder of the divisions had been marching hard in eastern Navarre, it was

---

[1] Ibid., x. p. 478, to Bentinck.
[2] Ibid., x. pp. 477–9.   [3] Ibid., x. p. 531.

arranged that they should give over the service of the blockade by sections to the returning columns as each came up. Wellington intended to transfer the whole affair in the end to a Spanish force, the 'Army of Reserve of Andalusia' under Henry O'Donnell, which had been occupied for the last week in the siege of the forts of Pancorbo, after its very tardy arrival in the zone of operations. King Joseph, when lying at Burgos, had thrown a garrison of 700 men into these forts, which command the high road to the Ebro, in the vain hope of incommoding Wellington's advance. But as the allied army did not march by the Camino Real at all, but cut across by side routes to Medina del Pomar, the precaution was useless, and cost the enemy a battalion. However, it was necessary to clear the defile, in order to open the easiest line of communication with Madrid, and O'Donnell was directed to capture the forts on his way north to join the main army. He invested them on June 25, and stormed the lower and weaker fort of Santa Marta on the 28th. The upper fort of Santa Engracia was a veritable eagle's nest, on a most inaccessible position : O'Donnell succeeded with great difficulty in getting six guns up to a point on which they could bear on the work. But the reason why such a strong post surrendered by capitulation two days later was not the artillery fire, but mainly lack of water, the castle well having run nearly dry, and partly the news of Vittoria. A small party of fugitives who had escaped from the field by an incredible détour, corroborated the claims made by the Spanish general when he summoned the place, and the commandant (Major Durand of the 55th Line) surrendered with 650 men, 24 guns, and a good stock of ammunition on June 30th [1].

On getting these news Wellington, on July 2, ordered O'Donnell to come up at once, and take over the blockade of Pampeluna, for which his whole force of 11,000 men would not be too great. For the fortress was large and strongly garrisoned. The King had brought up the number of troops left to the

---

[1] Full details in O'Donnell's report to Wellington of July 1, 1813. *Dispatches*, p. 503. Toreno makes an odd mistake in calling the French commander de Ceva : this was the name of the junior officer who drew up the capitulation.

Governor-General Cassan [1] to 3,600 men before leaving the place, and there were over eighty guns mounted on the walls, though two outlying forts in the plain had been abandoned. Wellington allowed nine days for the orders to reach O'Donnell, and for the Army of Reserve to make the long march from Pancorbo to Pampeluna : as a matter of fact it took eleven. Meanwhile the fortress had to be contained by troops from the main army, till the Andalusians should come up—they were due on July 12th. The scheme adopted was that Hill should collect the 2nd Division and Silveira's Portuguese [2]—their usual contingent of auxiliaries—on the north side of Pampeluna on July 1st, and march on July 2 ; the ground which he had held being taken over by the Light 3rd and 7th Divisions, returning from the chase of Clausel. On the 3rd the 7th Division was to be relieved by the 4th, and to follow Hill. On the 5th the 6th Division (Clinton) would arrive, and relieve the Light Division which would follow the 7th. The greater part of the cavalry was to be left behind in the plains, being obviously useless in the Pyrenees except in small parties for exploration ; but each of the marching divisions had a regiment attached to it.

The result of these arrangements was to leave three divisions (3rd, 4th, 6th), and nearly all the cavalry, for the blockade of Pampeluna—a rather larger force than might have been expected [3]. Four divisions (2nd, Light, 7th, and Silveira's Portuguese) moved out to clear the Bastan, and to establish communications with Graham's corps on the Lower Bidassoa. If the French had been in good fighting trim, four divisions would have been none too many for the task, more especially when it is remembered that they were advancing in three échelons, each separated from the next by a long day's march. But Wellington reckoned that, although he had all Gazan's and D'Erlon's troops in front of him—the presence of Reille's on the Lower Bidassoa had been reported by Graham—they

---

[1] Not to be confounded with General Cassagne, who long commanded a division in the Army of Andalusia.

[2] Late Hamilton's division in 1810–11–12.

[3] Lord Dalhousie was left in command—a great slight to Picton—all the more so after what had happened at Vittoria. See *Supplementary Dispatches*, viii. p. 249.

would have no artillery (since it had been lost at Vittoria), would be low in numbers, because they had not yet gathered in their stragglers, and lower still in morale. His estimate was on the whole justified, for the operation was successfully carried out ; but it did not go off quite so easily as had been expected. It should be mentioned that, on the bare chance that the French might make a movement from St. Jean-Pied-du-Port to disturb the blockade of Pampeluna—an unlikely possibility—the 2nd Division had detached Byng's brigade to hold the pass of Roncesvalles, in conjunction with Morillo's Spanish division. Hill therefore, leading the march towards the Bastan, had only three of his four brigades with him— Cameron's [1], O'Callaghan's [2], and Ashworth's Portuguese. The total of the marching column, from front to rear, was about 22,000 men.

To understand the task set before Hill's corps it is necessary to go back to the arrangements—if arrangements they can be called, for they were largely involuntary—made by the French Head-quarters Staff during the preceding week. After Reille's divisions had turned off towards the Bidassoa, and D'Erlon's had retreated into the Bastan, the main body of the French Army—the four and a half infantry divisions of the Army of the South, with its own cavalry and the bulk of that of the Army of Portugal [3]—had taken the route of the Pass of Roncesvalles, and reached St. Jean-Pied-du-Port, in a state of complete confusion (June 27), preceded by a vanguard of marauders several thousands strong, who swept the countryside of cattle and corn just as freely after they had reached France as while they were still in Navarre. Behind the troops who had kept to their eagles followed a rearguard of footsore stragglers and slightly wounded men, harassed till they came to the frontier by bands of local guerrilleros. The whole mass was in a state of demoralization : the French peasantry had to flee to the hills with what they could carry—every house was plundered save those in which a general or other officer of high rank had

[1] Late Cadogan's.

[2] Pringle arrived and took command of this brigade a fortnight later. Meanwhile the senior battalion commander led it.

[3] Reille had only two chasseur regiments with him.

quartered himself[1]. St.Jean-Pied-du-Port was a small third-class fortress, garrisoned by a battalion of National Guards, not an arsenal or a dépôt. It was impossible to reorganize an army there, or even to feed it for a few days. The Army of the South rolled back on June 29th to the valleys of the Nivelle and Nive, so as to be near the great magazines of Bayonne, which had always been the base from which the French forces in Spain were supplied. There alone would it be possible to reform it, and to re-equip it with all the guns and transport necessary to replace the losses of Vittoria. Gazan left one division—that of Conroux—at St. Jean, to block the pass of Roncesvalles : with the other three and a half divisions he arrived on July 1st at Ustaritz, St. Pée and Espellette in the valleys of the Nive and Nivelle, only twelve or fifteen miles from Bayonne. The cavalry was sent back still farther to the line of the Adour.

Soon after this there was a great reduction made in the mounted arm. Orders arrived from Germany that only the cavalry of the Army of the South was to remain on the frontier. Boyer's dragoons of the Army of Portugal, Treillard's dragoons of the Army of the Centre, and seven light cavalry regiments of the Armies of Portugal and the North were to start off at once [2]. Napoleon in his Saxon campaign had been suffering bitterly from a want of good cavalry, and had directed the King to send these veteran regiments across France with all speed, whatever might be the state of affairs in Spain.

It is quite clear that if Wellington had chosen, on June 26th, to follow Gazan across the Pyrenees, instead of turning aside to chase Clausel, he could have done anything that he pleased with the enemy. But this, for the reasons that we have detailed above—was not his game for the moment. Hence the shattered Army of Spain had a few days in which to commence reorganization. The easiest thing was the replacement of the 151 cannon lost at Vittoria. Bayonne was a great artillery storehouse, and the French gunners had brought away their teams, if they had

[1] See the indignant letters of French officials quoted in Vidal de la Blache, i. pp. 69 and 165-7.

[2] For the Army of Portugal only two chasseur regiments were left : for the Army of the North only one : for the Army of the Centre only the weak Nassau squadrons. But 13 out of the 14 cavalry regiments of the Army of the South remained behind.

left all their pieces behind them. On July 6th General Tirlet, the officer commanding the artillery of the united armies, could report to the King that he had already served out 80 guns— 33 each to the Armies of Gazan and Reille, 10 to the Army of the Centre, and 4 to the mobile division of the Bayonne Reserve. By the end of the month he promised to have 120 or even 150 pieces ready, which would give every division its battery, as well as a good reserve. And these pledges were fulfilled—with help from the arsenals of Toulouse, Blaye, and La Rochelle. But the supply of caissons was for some time very low, and the wheeled transport for the train was much more difficult to procure, requisitions on the Pyrenean departments being difficult to enforce, and slow to collect. As to food supply, the main difficulty was that although there was a considerable accumulation of stores at Bayonne, no one had ever contemplated the chance that 60,000 starving men would be thrown on the resources of the dépôt in one mass. Much flour was there, but not enough ovens to bake it, or wagons to carry it to the troops lying fifteen or twenty miles out, on the Bidassoa or the Nive. And these troops had lost all their own carts and fourgons. Even as much as a month later the army, reorganized in other respects, had not got enough transport to carry more than a few days' food, as Marshal Soult was to find.

King Joseph had left Pampeluna long before his troops, and taking a short cut had reached St. Jean de Luz on June 28th, and set up his last head-quarters there. He was painfully aware of the fact that his great brother would in all probability visit upon his head all his inevitable wrath for the results of the late campaign ; but to the final moment of his command he strove to exercise his authority, and busied himself with the details of projected operations. He was at this moment somewhat estranged from Marshal Jourdan, who had taken to his bed, and kept complaining that the generals would neither give him information nor take his orders, but confined themselves to making ill-natured comments on the battle of Vittoria. The King, instead of relying on his advice, asked council on all sides, and hovered between many opinions.

It is a sufficient proof of the incoherence of both Jourdan's and Joseph's military ideas, that at this moment they were thinking

seriously of resuming the offensive and re-entering Spain.
When he received Clausel's dispatches announcing his safe
arrival at Saragossa, and the possibility of his junction with
Suchet, the King was fascinated for the moment with the idea
of bringing Wellington to a stand, by attacking his flank and
rear in Aragon.   This could only be done by sending large
reinforcements to Clausel, and so weakening the main army.
The real objection to this plan was that the troops were in no
condition to march, or indeed to fight, till they should have had
time for rest and reorganization.   Jourdan, however, drew up
on July 5—the very day on which Wellington was beginning
to drive Gazan out of the Bastan—as we shall presently see—
a memoir for the King's consideration, which laid out three
possible policies.   One was to advance with every unit that
could move, against Graham, who was wrongly supposed to
have only one British division with him.   The second was to
march to relieve Pampeluna by Roncesvalles, after first calling
in Clausel to help.   The third was to accept the idea which lay
at the base of Clausel's last dispatch, to leave 15,000 men on
the Bidassoa to detain Graham, and to move the rest of the
army by the Jaca passes into Aragon.   It was conceded that
artillery could not go that way, and that Clausel had none with
him—but some guns might be picked up at Saragossa and from
Suchet, and a very large body of troops would be placed on
Wellington's flank.   It is difficult to say which of the three
schemes was more impracticable for the moment, as a policy
for the starving and demoralized Army of Spain.

A more serious project, and one for which there would have
been much to say, if the French Army had been at this moment
in a condition to feed itself, or to manœuvre, or to commit itself
to an action which would involve the expenditure of more
ammunition than the infantry could carry in their pouches,
was one for strengthening the front in the Bastan.   While this
long valley was still retained, direct communication between
Wellington's main body about Pampeluna and the large
detachment under Graham on the Bidassoa was blocked.   But
the Bastan was occupied by the weakest section of the French
forces, D'Erlon's Army of the Centre, one of whose infantry
divisions (Darmagnac's) had been ruined at the battle of

Vittoria, where it lost more men in proportion to its strength than any other unit [1], while another—Casapalacios' Spanish division—was disappearing rapidly by desertion.   There were only left, in a condition to fight, the Royal Guards—a little over 2,000 men—and Cassagne's division, which had suffered no serious casualties in the recent campaign.   Clearly the Bastan and the numerous passes which descend into it could not be held by 10,000 infantry, some of them in very bad order, even though they might get some guns from the Bayonne arsenal.   Wherefore Joseph ordered D'Erlon to make over the defence of the Bastan to the Army of the South, and to fall back to the line of the Nivelle, where he should join Reille. Gazan was directed to take over charge of this important salient, with the whole of his army, save Conroux's division left at St. Jean-Pied-du-Port [2] (July 3).

Gazan, who had only reached the Nive two days before, whose troops had not yet recovered from the starvation which they had suffered in the march from Pampeluna to Ustaritz and Espellette, who had lost his transport, and who had not yet received the 33 guns which had been sent him from Bayonne (though he was told that they were just coming up), made objections very rational in themselves to these orders.   He said that his troops must have food and guns, or they could not be expected to maintain their positions.   He also remarked that it was exasperating that he had not been told to march straight from St. Jean-Pied-du-Port to the Bastan by the direct pass at Ispegui, instead of being brought back two days' march to the Nive, and then sent south again to the Maya pass, only twelve miles from his starting-point [3].

Gazan started out, unwillingly and with many protests, from his cantonments on the Nive on the morning of July 3, sending

[1] Chassé's brigade lost 850 men of 1,700 present, and the Nassau regiment in the German brigade had similar casualties, though the Baden regiment got off more lightly.

[2] It should be noted that Daricau's 6th Division was now led by Maransin—its old commander having been badly wounded at Vittoria. Maransin's late brigade, still extra-divisional as at Vittoria, had been made over to Gruardet.

[3] Jourdan answered that it *was* a false movement, but that on June 29th he could not possibly foresee that the King would change his mind as to the destination of the Army of the South.   See Vidal de la Blache, i. p. 103.

one of his divisions, Leval's, by the inferior mountain road from Sarre on the Nivelle to Etchalar and Santesteban in the western Bastan, the rest by the Maya pass to Elizondo, the chief road-centre in the eastern or upper Bastan. From these points they were to spread themselves out, and take over all the passes south and west from D'Erlon's troops. The commander of the Army of the Centre began to clear out his reserves north-wards, and to arrange for the rapid departure of each advanced section, as it should be relieved by the arrival of Gazan's divisions. He met his colleague on the way, handed over the charge to him, and then rode down to make his report to Jourdan at St. Pée (July 5), where he dropped the cheering remark that if the Army of the South did not receive very heavy convoys of food at once, it would go to pieces of its own accord and quit the Bastan within a few days, as his own army had eaten up the valley and no troops could live there [1].

Darmagnac's division and the Royal Guard had been relieved by Leval, while Cassagne's first brigade was marching north by Elizondo, though his second was still blocking the Col de Velate till Gazan's troops should arrive, when Welling-ton's attack was delivered—at the most opportune of moments. Nothing could have been better for him than that the enemy should have been caught in the middle of an uncompleted exchange of troops, before the incoming army had gained any knowledge of the ground. Moreover, though Gazan had double as many men with him as D'Erlon, they had not enjoyed the comparative rest which the Army of the Centre had gained since June 26th, but had been countermarching all the time, and were in a very dilapidated condition. Otherwise there would have been much greater difficulty in driving them out of the Bastan with the very moderate force that Wellington actually used. For he was able to finish the business with four brigades—the three of the 2nd Division and one of Silveira's—which formed the head of his column. Of the rear échelons, the 7th Division, which started from Pampeluna on the 4th, got up only in time to see the very end of the game, and the Light Division were never engaged at all.

[1] See Vidal de la Blache, i. pp. 103–4.

At noon on July 4th Cameron's Brigade [1], forming the advanced guard of the 2nd Division, crossed the highest point of the Col de Velate, and ran into half a battalion of the 16th Léger. This was the rearguard of Braun's brigade of Cassagne's division, which was holding the village of Berrueta, a few miles down the northern slope of the pass, waiting till it should be relieved by Maransin's division from Gazan's army. This detachment was evicted from Berrueta and Aniz, and fell back on Ziga, where the other battalion of its regiment was in position. That village also was cleared, but Hill's leading brigade then found itself in front of Maransin's division marching rapidly up the road, with other troops visible in a long column behind. Hill, seeing that he was about to be involved in a serious fight with heavy numbers, began to deploy the rear brigades of the 2nd Division behind the ravine in front of Aniz, as each came up, abandoning the recently taken Ziga. The French, in the same fashion, gradually formed a long line on their side of the ravine, extending it eastward from the village and showing two brigades in front line and two in reserve on the heights of Irurita some way behind.

Hill appears to have felt the French front in several places, but to have desisted on discovering its strength. Skirmishing of a bloodless sort went on all the afternoon, each side waiting for its reserves to come up. Before dusk Gazan had drawn in all Villatte's division, which had reached Santesteban earlier in the day, and the non-divisional brigade of Gruardet, so that by night he had two complete divisions and two extra brigades concentrated—at least 13,000 men [2]. Behind Hill there was only Da Costa's brigade of Silveira's division, which was a full march to the rear : for Wellington had ordered A. Campbell's brigade—the other half of the Portuguese division—to take a different route, that up the Arga river by Zubiri to Eugui, which goes by a bad pass (Col de Urtiaga) into the French valley of the Alduides.

Hill's position was a distinctly unpleasant one, since he had

---

[1] Under Cameron of the 92nd as senior colonel—Cadogan who fell at Vittoria not having yet been replaced.

[2] Viz. Villatte's and Maransin's divisions, and Gruardet's brigade of his own army, and Braun's brigade of the Army of the Centre.

only three brigades up in line, with another out of any reasonable supporting distance, if the enemy should think fit to press in upon him. The 7th Division was two marches away, while the Light Division was still before Pampeluna; both were altogether out of reach. Owing to heavy losses at Vittoria, the three second division brigades can hardly have numbered 6,000 bayonets [1]. Their commander very wisely waited for the arrival of Wellington from the rear. Head-quarters that day had been at Lanz, on the road from Pampeluna to the Col de Velate.

The Commander-in-Chief came up at about midday on the 5th, following in the wake of Da Costa's Portuguese, who were bringing up with them two batteries of artillery—the first guns that either side had shown in the Bastan. After looking at the French positions Wellington resolved to push on—this was a purely psychological resolve, for his numbers did not justify any such a move; he relied on his estimate of the morale of Gazan, and that estimate turned out to be perfectly correct.

Hill's operations, till Wellington took over charge of the field, had been limited to cautious reconnaissances of the enemy's flanks. But with the change in command decisive action began : Cameron's brigade was sent out by the steep hill-sides on the right to turn Gazan's left flank ; O'Callaghan's, with Ashworth's Portuguese in support, crossed the ravine in front of Aniz, and deployed on each side of the road to attack his centre. If Gazan had stood to fight, and brought up all his reserves, it is hard to see how he could have been moved : indeed he ought to have scored a big success if he had dared to counter-attack—for Wellington had no reserves save Da Costa's Portuguese brigade. But, like Murray at Tarragona, the French general had been making himself dreadful pictures of the strength that might conceivably be in front of him. Three prisoners taken at Ziga on the preceding day had told him that they belonged to Hill's corps—he presumed it complete in front of him, with all its six brigades, instead of the actual three. Then a heavy column had come up at noon—Da Costa's brigade—Gazan judged it

---

[1] On May 1 the three 2nd Division brigades had shown 7,200 bayonets— they had lost 900 men in action at Vittoria. If we allow for sick and stragglers and other casual losses, they cannot possibly have had 6,000 men in line on July 5.

356·6   N n

to be some fresh division from Pampeluna. In addition he had
received a cry of alarm from Conroux at St. Jean-Pied-du-Port—
that officer reported that on July 4 a Spanish corps was threatening his flank from the Val Carlos—this was no more than a reconnaissance thrown out by Morillo. Also he got news from the
Alduides valley of the arrival of A. Campbell's Portuguese
brigade at Eugui—he deduced from this information, joined to
the report about Morillo, a turning movement against his left
flank, by forces of unknown but probably considerable strength.
Lastly, by drawing in Villatte's division to his main body, he
had left open a gap on his right, between his own positions in
front of Elizondo and those of Leval at Santesteban. He was
seized with a panic fear lest another British column might pour
into this gap, by the mountain roads leading from Lanz and
Almandoz into the middle Bastan [1]. And, indeed, Wellington
had started the 7th Division on one of these passes, the Puerto
de Arraiz—but it was still 20 miles away.

   Already on the night of the 4th Gazan had written to the
King that he must ask for leave to make his stand at the Maya
pass, rather than to hold all the minor defiles which converge
into the Bastan—a complicated system of tracks whose defence
involved a terrible dissemination of forces. By noon on the 5th,
having seen Wellington's arrival with Da Costa's brigade, he
made up his mind that if the enemy attacked him frontally it
must be to engage his attention, while encircling columns
closed in upon his flanks and rear, from the Alduides on the one
side and the western passes on the other. When the movement
against his front began, his troops in the position by Ziga
retired, without waiting to receive the attack, and took cover
behind Villatte's division, drawn up on the heights of Irurita.
Hill had to spend time in re-forming his lines before he could
resume the offensive ; but when he did so against Villatte's
troops, they gave way in turn, and retired behind Maransin's
division, which was now placed above the village of Elizondo.
In this way the enemy continued to retire by échelons, without
allowing the pursuers to close, until by dusk he stood still at
last at the Col de Maya, where he offered battle. Gazan was

----

[1] All these absurd theories are to be found in Gazan's reports to Jourdan
of July 4 and 5. See Vidal de la Blache, i. pp. 106–7.

extremely well satisfied with himself, and considered that he had made a masterly retreat in face of overwhelming hostile forces. As a matter of fact he had been giving way, time after time, to mere demonstrations by a force of little more than half his own strength—four weak brigades were pushing back his six. But he never made a long enough stand to enable him to discover the very moderate strength of the pursuers. The whole business was a field day exercise—the total casualties only reached a few scores on each side. Gazan's elaborate narrative about the various occasions on which British van-guards were surprised to run into heavy fire, suffered heavily, and had to halt, find its best comment in the fact that the total loss of English and Portuguese during three days of petty combats was only 5 officers and 119 men, and that this day, July 5, was the least bloody of the three.

Well satisfied to have manœuvred the enemy out of the Bastan without any appreciable loss to himself, Wellington accepted the challenge which the Army of the South offered him by halting on the Maya positions. But he waited for the 7th Division to come up, rightly thinking that the two British and two Portuguese brigades hitherto employed were too weak a force, now that the enemy showed signs of making his final stand. The 7th Division, acting under the senior brigadier, Barnes, for Lord Dalhousie had been left behind to conduct the blockade of Pampeluna, had marched on the 4th, the day when Hill was commencing to push the French north of the Col de Velate. Wellington had intended from the first that it should take a route which would enable it to turn Gazan's right: it went north from Marcalain, where it had concentrated on giving up its blockading work, by Lizaso, to the pass of Arraiz, by which it descended into the Bastan on the 6th. It then occupied Santesteban, from which Leval's division had been withdrawn by Gazan at the same moment at which he fell back himself on to the pass of Maya. Pending its arrival Wellington remained halted in front of the French positions for the whole of the 6th, filling the enemy with various unjustifiable fears; for they over-valued his strength, and credited him with much more ambitious projects than those which he really entertained. This halt on the 6th seemed to them to cover some elaborate snare, while its real purpose was only to allow him to make his next move with 14,000 instead of with 8,000 men. The plan for the morning of the 7th was that Hill's column should attack the Maya positions in front, while the 7th Division should cross the Bidassoa at Santesteban, and take a mountain road which would bring it out upon the flank of Gazan's line, which rested on the Peak of Atchiola. This would be a hard day's march by a rough track, along interminable crests and dips. Meanwhile, on July 8th, another British unit would come up : the Light Division was relieved at Pampeluna by the 4th Division on the 5th, and following in the track of Barnes, Charles Alten was to be at Santesteban on the night of the 7th, and at the fighting front by the next morning.

The halt which Wellington imposed on his leading column upon July 6th gave time for the French Higher Command to make an astounding series of blunders. To discriminate between true and false reports is one of the most difficult tasks for any general, and the faculty of making a correct decision after receiving a number of contradictory data is undoubtedly one of the best tests of military ability. All men may err—but greater errors have seldom been made in a day than those of Jourdan and King Joseph on July 6th. They started, perhaps naturally, with the leading idea that Wellington was about to undertake the invasion of France on a grand scale. Where would the blow fall ? Graham had been quiescent for some days on the Bidassoa, and it was obvious that the troops on his front were mainly Spaniards—the Army of Galicia and Longa's Cantabrians were alone visible. Gazan, though making constant complaints that he was outnumbered and oppressed by a ' triple force ', had not as yet accounted for anything but Hill's corps as present in his front. Where, then, was the rest of Wellington's army ? The concentration of troops in front of Pampeluna had been ascertained—what had become of them ? Now Conroux at St. Jean-Pied-du-Port kept sending in messages of alarm. Morillo's reconnaissances had induced him to push most of his division forward to watch the passes in his front, and he reported Byng's brigade at Roncesvalles as a considerable accumulation of British troops. Then came the news that A. Campbell's Portuguese brigade had entered the Alduides valley, by descending which it could cut in between Conroux and the rest of the army. Probably it was the over-emphasis of Conroux's cries of warning which set the King and Jourdan wrong—but whatever the cause, they jumped to the conclusion that the serious invasion was to come on the inland flank— that Byng and Campbell were the forerunners of a great force marching to turn their left, by Roncesvalles and the eastern passes. Acting on this utterly erroneous hypothesis, they issued a series of orders for the hasty transference of great bodies of troops towards St. Jean-Pied-du-Port. Leval's division of the Army of the South—which had retired to Echalar after evacuating Santesteban—Cassagne's and Darmagnac's divisions of the Army of the Centre—which had handed over the Bastan to Gazan and retired to St. Pée—and Thouvenot's provisional division of troops of the Army of the North[1], from the Lower Bidassoa, were all started off by forced marches to join Conroux at St. Jean-Pied-du-Port. Only Reille with the four divisions of the Army of Portugal was left to face Graham [2], and Gazan was directed to hold the Maya positions with Maransin's and Villatte's divisions and Gruardet's brigade alone. Thus, while Wellington was about to deliver his rather leisurely blow at the French centre, all the enemy's reserves were sent off to their extreme left. Nothing could have been more convenient to the British general, if he had attacked one or two days later on the Maya front, when the troops on the move would all have got past him on their way south-eastward. But as he made his assault the day after the King's orders were issued, it resulted that the marching columns were passing just behind the part of the enemy's line at which he was aiming, so that Gazan had more supports at hand than might have been expected. But this was neither to the credit of the King, who had not intended to provide them, nor to the discredit of Wellington, who could not possibly have foreseen such strategical errors as those in which his enemy was indulging.

[1] The troops of the Army of the North which Foy had collected from the Biscay garrisons, the brigades of Deconchy, Rouget, and Berlier of which we have heard so much in a previous chapter.

[2] Foy, Lamartinière, Maucune and Fririon (late Sarrut). There were behind them the King's Spaniards and the raw Bayonne reserve.

On the morning of July 7th Gazan was in battle order at Maya, with Maransin's division and Gruardet's brigade holding the pass, and the heights on each side of it from the hill of Alcorrunz on the west to the rock of Aretesque on the east. Villatte's division (commanded on this day by its senior brigadier, Rignoux, for Villatte was sick) formed the reserve, on the high road to Urdax, behind the main crest. Wellington's simple form of attack was to send O'Callaghan's brigade to turn the French left by a mountain road, Cameron's brigade to seize the peak of Atchiola beyond his extreme right, so as to outflank Gazan on that side, to demonstrate with the Portuguese and his two batteries in the centre, and to wait for the crucial moment when the 7th Division, on the march since the morning by the hill road from Santesteban to Urdax, should appear in the enemy's rear. Then a general assault would take place.

The scheme did not work out accurately. The Portuguese demonstrated, as was ordered. O'Callaghan's brigade accomplished its turning movement, and got into contact with Remond's brigade of Maransin's division, on the extreme French left at the rock of Aretesque. Cameron's brigade took the hill of Alcorrunz without difficulty, but was then held up by the bulk of Villatte's division, which came up from the rear and held the crest of the Atchiola with six battalions; it could not be dislodged. So far so good—the enemy was engaged all along the line and had used up three-fourths of his reserve. But early in the afternoon a dense fog set in, and the 7th Division never appeared in the enemy's rear. It had got involved in the darkness, lost its way, and wandered helpless. Wherefore the other attacks were never pressed. ' If the 7th Division had arrived in time, and the sea fog had held off for an hour or two, we should have made a good thing of it,' wrote Wellington to Graham [1]. ' Our loss is about 60 wounded—on the other days (4th and 5th) there was a good deal of firing, but we sustained no loss at all.'

Early on the morning of July 8 Gazan, after having written a most insincere report concerning the skirmish of the preceding day, *combat des plus opiniâtres*, in which he had checked the

---

[1] *Dispatches*, x. p. 512. The total losses having been 124 on all three days, Wellington's ' no loss ' means, of course, practically no loss.

enemy with loss, abandoned the Maya positions before he was
again attacked. He had the impudence to write to Jourdan
that he had only recoiled because Head-Quarters refused to
send him any supports [1]. As a matter of fact the King had
checked the progress of the troops marching to St. Jean-Pied-du-
Port, and was sending them straight to Urdax and Ainhoue,
where all the four divisions arrived on the 8th, early in the day.
If Gazan had chosen to hold on to the pass he would have had
15,000 men added to his strength by the evening. But he went
off at 6 a.m., and Hill occupied the crest an hour later. Wellington was so far from intending any further advance that he wrote
that afternoon to Graham that he was now at leisure to take
a look at the whole line of the Bidassoa down to the sea, and
intended to pay his lieutenant a visit. A day later he told
Lord Bathurst that ' the whole of our right being now established on the frontier, I am proceeding to the left to superintend
the operations there '—which meant in the main the siege of
St. Sebastian. The troops which had been brought up to the
Bastan took up permanent quarters—the Light Division at
Santesteban, the 7th at Elizondo, Hill's two British brigades
at the Maya positions, to which artillery was brought up, while
Ashworth's and Da Costa's Portuguese were set to guard the
minor eastern passes which open from the Bastan into the
Alduides, or Val de Baygorri—the Col d'Ispegui and the Col de
Berderis. They connected themselves with A. Campbell's
Portuguese brigade, which watched the southern exit from that
long French valley. Campbell, for his part, had to keep touch
along the frontier with Byng and Morillo in the Roncesvalles
country. The 3rd, 4th, and 6th Divisions still lay round
Pampeluna, anxiously expecting to be relieved by the Army of
Reserve of Andalusia. But Henry O'Donnell, though due on
the 12th, did not appear and take over the blockade till the
16th–17th. This delay began to worry Wellington a few days

---

[1] The clearest proof of Gazan's resolute resolve not to stand, and of the
complete mendacity of his dispatches concerning his heavy fighting on
the 4th–5th and 7th, is that he returned the total of his losses at 35 killed
and 309 wounded. As he had six brigades, or 13,000 men at least, engaged,
it is clear that there was no serious fighting at all—a fact borne out by
Hill's corresponding return of 8 killed, 119 wounded, and 2 missing in the
whole petty campaign.

later, but on the 8th–9th he was still content with the position of affairs, rightly judging that the enemy was in no condition to make a push in any direction, till he should have got his troops rested, his artillery replaced, and his transport reorganized.

Otherwise he could not have taken so lightly the fact that opposite the Maya positions the enemy had now accumulated six and a half divisions, expecting to be attacked by columns descending from the Bastan within the next few days. Joseph and Jourdan spent an immense amount of unnecessary pains in the hurried shifting of troops, during the short space that intervened before the thunderbolt which was coming from Germany fell on their unlucky heads. But who, in their position, could have guessed that a mainly political consideration was intervening, to prevent Wellington from undertaking that invasion of France which seemed his obvious military duty ?

One last measure of precaution on their adversary's part modified the front at the end of the petty campaign of the Bastan—but by that time Joseph and Jourdan were gone. On July 15th Wellington made up his mind that the defensive position on the lower Bidassoa, by which he was covering the siege of St. Sebastian, was not safe on its inland flank, where the French were still in possession of the town of Vera, at the gorge of the Bidassoa, where it emerges from its high upland course in the Bastan. Vera and its bridge presented an obvious point of concentration for a force intending to trouble the right wing of Graham's corps. Wherefore it was necessary to clear the enemy out of this point of vantage, and to shorten the line between Hill in the Bastan and Giron on the lower Bidassoa. Uncertain as to whether the French would make a serious stand or not, Wellington ordered up large forces—the 7th Division and the newly-arrived Light Division from Santesteban, Longa, and one brigade of Giron's Galicians from the covering troops. But the enemy—Lamartinière's division of Reille's army— offered only a rearguard action, and withdrew to the other side of the hills which separate the Bastan from the coast region— abandoning the ' Puertos ' or passes of Vera and Echalar. They feared that the advance of the allied left centre might be

King Joseph at Mortefontaine
from the portrait by Girardet

the prelude to a general attack, and began to make preparations
to receive it.   But their anxiety disappeared when it became
clear that Wellington only wanted Vera and its defile, and had
no further offensive purpose.   The Light Division occupied
Vera : the 7th, extending to the right, took over the pass of
Echalar and got into touch with Hill's advanced guard at Maya.

SECTION XXXVII: CHAPTER V

EXIT KING JOSEPH

WHILE Wellington was pressing his victorious advance to the
Ebro, the Emperor Napoleon had been so entirely engrossed
in the management of his own great campaign in Saxony that
he had little or no time to spare for considering the affairs of
Spain. King Joseph had continued to receive dispatches from
Paris, which purported to set forth his brother's orders and
commands. But, as he well knew, they were really the compo-
sitions of the War-Minister Clarke, who, from the general directions which the Emperor had left when departing for Germany,
and such curt comments as intermittently came back from
Dresden or Wittenberg, used to construct lectures or critical
essays, which he tried to make appropriate to the last news
that came up from Spain. The original instructions were
completely out of date, and no new general scheme of operations
could be got out of Napoleon, who could only find time to make
commentaries of a caustic kind on any correspondence that
came from beyond the Pyrenees [1]. Clarke's dispatches to the
King were quite useless, and they were often offensive in tone—
it is clear that the minister took a personal pleasure in making
sarcastic observations on the conduct of the war in Spain, which
he could foist on King Joseph as his brother's composition.
They generally arrived at moments which made them particularly absurd reading—what could be more annoying to the
King than to be told that Wellington's Army was a wreck, and
that there was little chance of the Allies taking the offensive,
at the very moment when the French Head-Quarters was moving
ever northward, pushed on by what seemed in the eyes of Joseph
and Jourdan to be overwhelming numbers ? It was absurd
to be given hints on the defence of the Douro when the retreat-

---

[1] Cf. Lecestre, *Lettres inédites*, ii. p. 1037, where the Emperor says on
July 3 that he cannot make out what is happening ; and that Joseph and
Jourdan are incapables.

ing host was already on the Ebro, or lectures on the advantages of the line of the Ebro, when the Pyrenees had already been crossed. The habit of Clarke, however, which most irritated the King, was that of corresponding directly with the minor army-commanders in Spain, over the head of the nominal commander-in-chief [1]. Joseph held very strongly to the opinion that a main part of his disasters was due to Clarke's dispatches to Clausel and Suchet, which gave those generals excellent excuses for ignoring orders from Head-Quarters, and carrying out their own designs, under pretence that they were more consonant with the Emperor's intentions than the directions which came to them from Madrid, Valladolid, or Burgos.

But the Emperor's attention was at last attracted to Spain by a disaster which could not be overlooked, or ignored as a passing worry. The news of Vittoria reached him at Dresden on July 1—nine days after the battle had been lost—forwarded by Clarke with imperfect details. For the minister could only transmit a second-hand narrative written by Foy, who had not been present at the battle, and Joseph's first short note from Yrurzun, dated July 23rd, which concealed much and told little. There was, however, enough information to rouse the Emperor to wild rage. He had three weeks before (June 4) concluded the armistice of Plässwitz with the allied sovereigns, so that he was not entirely absorbed in the details of his own strategy, and could at last find time to devote some attention to the affairs of Spain, whose consideration he had been putting off from week to week all through the last two months. His own situation was still perilous enough—he was uncertain whether he could come to terms with Russia and Prussia, despite of his recent victories. And the idea that Austria might be meaning mischief, and not merely playing for the enviable position of general arbitrator between the belligerents, was already present. But at least he was not wholly occupied by the strategical and tactical needs of each day, and could turn to contemplate the Spanish campaign as part of the European crisis. The exasperating thing was not so much that the Imperial arms had suffered a hideous affront, though this was a not unimportant consideration, which might encourage

[1] See, e. g., Joseph to Clarke, p. 336 of vol. ix of his *Correspondance*.

Alexander and Frederick William III to renew the war. It was rather that the position of Spain, as a counter in the negotiations which were going on at Prague, was completely changed. On May 25th the Franco-Spanish kingdom of Joseph Bonaparte made an imposing appearance—Madrid was still occupied, and a solid block of territory from the Esla to the Guadalviar—more than half the Peninsula—showed on the map as part of the Napoleonic empire. On July 1 it was known that the King was a fugitive on the French border, that the Castiles, Leon, Navarre, and Biscay had all been lost, that Valencia would certainly, and Aragon probably, go the same way within a week or two. The pretence that Joseph was King of Spain had suddenly become absurd. In continuing the hagglings at Prague for a new European settlement, it would be ludicrous to insist on the restoration to Madrid of a king whose only possessions beyond the Pyrenees were a few scattered fortresses. For Catalonia, it must be remembered, did not count as part of Joseph's kingdom ; it had been formally annexed to France by the iniquitous decree of February 1812 [1].

It was a bitter blow to the new Charlemagne to see the largest of his vassal-kingdoms suddenly torn from him, by a stroke dealt by an enemy whom he affected to despise, while his attention had been distracted for the moment to the Elbe and the Oder. The unexampled rapidity of the campaign of Vittoria was astounding—there was nothing to compare with it in recent military history, save his own overrunning of the Prussian monarchy in the autumn of 1806. Wellington's army had crossed the Tormes on May 26th—by June 26th King Joseph was a fugitive in France, and the main French Army of Spain was pouring back as a disorganized rabble across the passes of the Pyrenees. The whole affair seemed incredible—even ludicrous [2]—the armies of King Joseph still appeared on the imperial muster-rolls as well over 100,000 strong, not including Suchet's forces on the East Coast. It was only a month or so back that the Emperor had been comforting himself with the idea that Wellington could not put 40,000 British troops in

---

[1] See vol. v, p. 97.

[2] ' Les malheurs de l'Espagne sont d'autant plus grands qu'ils sont ridicules.' Napoleon to Savary, Dresden, 20 July : Lecestre, *Lettres inédites*, ii.

the field, and was no longer a serious danger [1]. Obviously the
only explanation of the disaster must be colossal incapacity in
the French Higher Command in Spain, amounting to criminal
negligence. That there might be another explanation, viz.
that a war could not be successfully conducted in those pre-
telegraphic days by orders sent from five hundred miles away,
by dispatches liable to constant delay or loss, and by a commander-in-chief much distracted by other business, hardly
occurred to him [2]. His own system of managing the affairs of
Spain, as has been set forth in many earlier pages of this book[3],
was really the source of all evil. His nominal transference of the
supreme command to King Joseph had been a solemn farce,
because he still permitted interference by the minister at Paris,
acting in his name, tolerated private reports from army-
commanders, which were concealed from the King, and refused
to allow of the punishment of flagrant instances of disobedience
to his vicegerent's commands.

This perhaps the Emperor could hardly be expected to see.
The news of Vittoria having arrived, a culprit had to be sought,
and the culprit was obviously King Joseph, who with a magnifi-
cent army at his disposal, and a good military situation, had
allowed himself to be turned out of Spain by a contemptible
enemy. It went for nothing that the unfortunate monarch had
repeatedly asked for leave to abdicate, and had demonstrated
again and again that he was not allowed the real authority of
a commander-in-chief. The blame must be laid on his shoulders,
and he must be disgraced at once—not with too great public
scandal, for after all he was the Emperor's brother—but in the
manner which would prove most wounding to his own feelings.
' All the fault was his . . . if there was one man wanting in the
army it was a real general, and if there was one man too many
with the army it was the King [4].' Clarke was told to write to
him a dispatch which not only superseded him in command,
and deprived him of even the services of his own Royal Guard,

---

[1] Even that he was withdrawing the British Army from Portugal.
Lecestre, ii. 998, May 5.

[2] Though he did once make the observation that ' on ne conduit pas
des campagnes à 500 lieues de distance,' in a lucid interval.

[3] See v. pp. 194–6.

[4] Napoleon to Cambacérès, Lecestre, ii. 1055.

but put him under a sort of arrest. He was on no account to go to Paris. 'The importance of the interests that are at stake in the North, and the effect that your Majesty's appearance could not fail to produce on public opinion—both in Europe at large and more especially in France—are so great, that the Emperor is constrained to issue his formal orders that your Majesty should stop at Pampeluna or St. Sebastian, or at least come no further than Bayonne. . . . Extraordinary precautions have been taken to prevent the newspapers from mentioning either the event of June 21st [the battle of Vittoria], or the Emperor's decision concerning your Majesty. . . . It is at Bayonne, where the Emperor foresees that your Majesty has probably arrived, that his further intentions will be signified, when he has acquired full information as to the recent events. It is his definite order that your Majesty should come no further into France, nor most especially to Paris, under any pretext whatever. For the same reasons no officer of your Majesty's suite, and none of the Spanish exiles, must come beyond the Garonne. They may be directed to establish themselves at Auch.'

But though this was bad enough, the greatest insult in King Joseph's eyes was that he was directed to hand over the command of the army and his own Guards to his old enemy Soult, whose expulsion from Spain he had procured with so much difficulty, and whom he had denounced to the Emperor as selfish, disloyal, disobedient, and perjured, 'the author of that infamous letter found at Valencia [1]' which had accused the King of conspiring with the Cadiz Cortes against the interests of his own brother. When Soult had returned from Spain the Emperor had decided that all the accusations against him were frivolous, 'des petitesses.' He might not be an amiable character—how many of the marshals were ?—but he had 'the only military brain in the Peninsula '. He was not given the command of any of the army corps in Saxony, nor any administrative post of importance, but kept at Head-Quarters, at the Emperor's disposition, for two whole months. Apparently even before the news of Vittoria arrived, his master had thought of sending him back to Spain, but had postponed

---

[1] See above, p. 88.

the scheme, because he did not desire an open breach with his brother. But when Joseph's *débâcle* was announced, the Marshal received orders to leave Dresden at a few hours' notice, to call upon Clarke at Paris on the way, in order to pick up the latest military information, and then to assume the command at Bayonne at the earliest possible moment. He was posted up in all the Emperor's latest political and military schemes—even, as it seems, entrusted with the secret that if matters went very badly it might be necessary to open secret negotiations with the Cadiz Regency, on the base that the Emperor might restore Ferdinand VII to his subjects, and withdraw all his troops from Spain, if the Cortes could be persuaded to make a separate peace, and to repudiate the British alliance [1]. It seems to have escaped Napoleon's observation that the return of the ultra-conservative and narrow-minded Ferdinand would be the last thing desired by the Liberal party now dominant in the Cortes. But all the disappointments of the treaty of Valençay were still in the far future.

Among the instructions entrusted to Soult, for use if they should prove necessary, was a warrant authorizing him to put Joseph under arrest, if he should openly flout his brother's orders to halt at Bayonne, and should show any intention of setting out for Paris. This warrant had actually to be employed —the most maddening insult of all in the eyes of the King—it made his treacherous enemy into his jailer, as he complained.

Joseph received the first notice of his supersession from the mouth of the Senator Roederer, who had been sent off by Clarke a few hours in advance of Soult, in order that there might not be any scandalous scene, such as might have occurred if the Marshal had presented himself in person to inform the King of his fate. Roederer had served under Joseph as King of Naples, was friendly to him, and broke the unpleasant tidings as tactfully as he could. The results were what might have been expected—the unfortunate monarch said that he had realized that he must go, that he was already drafting another act of abdication. But it was an insult to send Soult to take over the command, after all the proofs of the Marshal's perversity and disloyalty which he had forwarded to the Emperor.

---

[1] See the very interesting pages of Vidal de la Blache, i. pp. 142–3.

He did not object to being deposed, or imprisoned, or put on his trial for treason, but he did object to being made the prisoner of Soult. ' As often as he got on this topic his Majesty grew quite frantic [1].'

But when Soult presented himself next morning there was no scene. The King handed him over his papers and dispatches, and said that he intended to establish himself in a country house just outside the gates of Bayonne (July 12). Three days later, however, he made a sudden and secret departure, and was well on the way to Bagnères de Bigorre before his escape was discovered. He had to be pursued, stopped by force, and shown the imperial warrant which authorized Soult to put him under arrest. For eight days he was a prisoner at the Château of Poyanne, when a dispatch arrived from Dresden, in which the Emperor said that he might be allowed to retire to his own estate of Mortefontaine, on condition that he saw no one, and never visited Paris [July 24]. If he should make himself a centre of intrigues, and should fail to realize that he was in disgrace, the Minister of Police had orders to imprison him [2].

And thus Joseph disappears from the purview of students of the Peninsular War, though he was to have one more short moment of notoriety in the following spring, when he was made the nominal head of the Council of Regency, which purported to govern France for a few weeks, before the Northern Allies forced their way into the French capital. He did not shine in that capacity, and would have done better to content himself with escaping the notice of the world in the semi-captivity to which his brother had condemned him in July 1813. But Joseph, however much he might deny the impeachment, loved a prominent place, however incapable he might be of filling it in a competent fashion.

This, indeed, is the secret of his whole unfortunate career. The chance which made him the brother of Napoleon put within his grasp ambitions with which his very moderate talents could not cope. He was by no means a bad man : the Spaniards would gladly have drawn him as a tyrant or

---

[1] See Roederer's account of the interview in Vidal de la Blache, i. pp. 132–3. Napoleon had suggested him as the best person for the errand.

[2] Napoleon to Cambacérès, Lecestre, *Lettres inédites*, ii. 1055.

a monster, if it had been possible to do so ; but had to content themselves with representing him as a ludicrous and contemptible character, ' Pepe Botellas ' [1], a comic-opera king, too much addicted to wine and women, and tricked by his courtiers and mistresses.   There seems no reason to suppose that the charge of inebriety had any particular foundation ; but Joseph— long separated from his wife by the chances of war—undoubtedly sought consolations in more than one other quarter at Madrid.   His amatory epistles and souvenirs, captured in his carriage at Vittoria, provoked a smile and a caustic remark from Wellington.   As to the taunt that he was continually cheated and exploited by those about him, there is no doubt that the unfortunate King was possessed of the delusion that his personal charm and affable manners won all hearts ; he wasted much time in cajoling every person of any importance with whom he came in contact, and had many sad moments of disillusion, when he discovered that supposed friends had failed him.   His most persistent and dangerous error was that he imagined that he could win over the Spaniards to his cause, by generous treatment and emotional speeches.   For years he went on enlisting in his ' national army ' every prisoner who was willing to save himself a tramp to a French prison, by taking an easy oath of allegiance.   When given arms and uniforms they deserted : first and last Joseph enlisted 60,000 Spaniards in his leaky regiments—about 1,500 crossed the Bidassoa with him at the moment of his fall.   With those above the rank and file he was a little more successful, because officers and politicians were marked men, when once they had risked their necks by forswearing their allegiance to Ferdinand VII.   They knew that there would be no such easy pardon for them as was granted to the common soldier.   There had been moments of intense depression for the Spanish cause, such as those following the capture of Madrid in December 1808, and the invasion of Andalusia in 1810, at which many timid or selfish souls had despaired of the game, and had taken service with the adversary.   Having once done so it was impossible to go back—hence the King, when his star began to wane, was overloaded with hundreds, and even thousands, of downhearted and pessimistic

---

[1] ' Joey Bottles ' is the English equivalent.

dependants, who had no faith in his ultimate triumph, yet still hung on to his skirts, and petitioned for the doles which he was no longer able to give them. Few served him zealously—those who did were in the main adventurers as destitute of morality as of national feeling, who strove for their own profit rather than their master's—his prefects and intendants had villainous reputations for the most part.

Though vain and self-confident, Joseph was entirely lacking in backbone—he endured all the Emperor's insults and taunts without any real feeling of resentment, though he protested loudly enough. Unlike his brothers, Lucien and Louis, he never dared to set his will against Napoleon's—his threatened abdications never became realities. He pretended that his submission was the result of loyalty and brotherly affection—in reality he had an insufficient sense of righteous indignation and self-respect, and an exaggerated love of royalty—even of its shadow. An intelligent French observer summed up his character in the following curious phrases :

' The King's most striking characteristic is his easy temper. It does not come from a generous heart or a real magnanimity, but from a facile disposition and a total absence of decision. He has not the courage to refuse to do things which his own reason condemns, and is often guilty of acts which he himself acknowledges to be unwise. At bottom he is an honest man, but he has not the firmness to maintain his principles if he is pressed and harried. Tiresome solicitation may induce him to cast aside principle and act like a rogue. His greatest hobby is a belief in his own *finesse*—a great perspicacity in discovering the secret and selfish motives of those about him. He often gives them credit for more Machiavellian ingenuity than they really possess. He does not always withdraw his favour from those whom he has discovered cheating him, but rejoices in making them feel that he has found out their private designs. He is incapable of owning that he has done an injustice : when he discovers that he has wronged one of his followers, he shirks meeting him, and tries to get rid of him by circuitous methods. Hence he often persists in acts of injustice, because he is ashamed of confessing himself to have been mistaken.'

The natural result of this lack of moral backbone was that

Joseph was systematically disobeyed and cheated. Very little was to be feared from his anger, much could be got by threatening or worrying him. It is true that he was much handicapped by the constant interference of the Emperor, and even of the French Minister of War, in all his attempts to create a Spanish administration, and to co-ordinate the efforts of the various armies in the Peninsula. Nevertheless there was much truth in his brother's savage comments on his character—'he cannot get himself obeyed '—' he has neither military talent nor administrative ability '—' he does not know how to draw up accounts '—he ' cannot command an army himself, but he can prevent other and more competent people from doing so '— ' the greatest moral error is to take up a profession which one does not understand : that the King was not a professional soldier was not his fault, but he was responsible for trying to be one [1].' To this last and perfectly just remark Joseph could have made an unanswerable reply, by asking who was responsible for the promotion of a person who was not, and never could be, a professional soldier, to the post of Commander-in-Chief of all the Armies of Spain.

It is only fair to concede to this unlucky prince his good qualities : he was never cruel—no usurper ever shed so little blood : he was a good master to many ungrateful servants : he was courteous and considerate, liberal so far as his scanty means allowed, and interested in literature and art. Unfortunately his artistic tastes brought him only ridicule. He was greatly given to pulling down slums and eyesores in Madrid, but never had the money to replace them by the stately buildings which he had designed—his good intentions were only shown by empty spaces—whence the people called him *El rey Plazuelos*. This was rather to his credit than otherwise—less so the interest in art shown by his eleventh-hour pilfering of the best pictures of the Madrid Galleries, of which Wellington recaptured a selection at Vittoria. To sum him up in a single phrase, Joseph Bonaparte was the mildest mannered man who ever stole a crown—or rather acted as receiver of a crown stolen by his ruthless brother.

---

[1] See especially the caustic paragraphs in Lecestre, ii. 1045, 1047, 1055, to Clarke and Cambacérès.

With King Joseph his Chief-of-the-Staff went into the depths of disgrace. Napoleon wrote that he never wanted to hear of Jourdan again. He must go into complete retirement at his estate of Coudray near Orleans. He was cut down to the strictest minimum of retired pay—not over 20,000 francs a year [1], which left him in miserable straits—for he had a large family, and he was honest, and had never feathered his nest like other marshals. The only notice to be taken of him was that he was to be ordered to draw up a memorandum explaining how the battle of Vittoria had been fought and lost—if any explanation were possible [2]. But Napoleon, when he pardoned Joseph a few months later, pardoned Jourdan also. He was given the command of the Rouen Military District, where he did competent administrative work in the spring of 1814, so far as his broken health permitted. It is surprising to find that, with all his ailments, this worthy old officer—the Cassandra of the great drama of 1812–13—survived till 1833, when he died, after having been for many years Governor of the Invalides. His military memoirs, first published in a scattered and incomplete form in Ducasse's *Life and Correspondence of Joseph Bonaparte*, and afterwards in a better shape so late as 1908, form one of the best critical commentaries on the Peninsular War. As a purveyor of hard truths concerning his imperial master, and the marshals who were his colleagues in Spain, Jourdan has no rival.

[1] So Jourdan's *Mémoires*, p. viii. Vidal de la Blache, i. p. 140, says 5,000 francs only, which seems an impossibly small sum for Marshal's half pay.

[2] Napoleon to Cambacérès, Lecestre, ii. 1045.

SECTION XXXVIII

THE BATTLES OF THE PYRENEES

CHAPTER I

THE SIEGE OF ST. SEBASTIAN. FIRST PERIOD

HAVING pushed his whole front line up to the French border, from Giron at Irun, hard by the ocean, to Byng, far inland on the watershed of the historic Pass of Roncesvalles, Wellington turned his attention to the siege of St. Sebastian, on which he intended to press hard and rapidly, while Pampeluna was to be left for the present to the slower process of blockade and starvation. He had no intention of pushing forward into France till the result of the negotiations in Germany should be known. He was kept informed of the doings at Dresden from time to time, but occasionally bad weather in the Bay of Biscay delayed the courier from Downing Street, and there was an interval of many days, during which the absence of political information began to cause him anxiety. On the whole, as he was informed, it was probable that the war would be renewed ; but the intentions of Austria were still suspect, and the danger of a separate peace in the North never ceased to disturb him until hostilities actually recommenced in the middle of August. On July 10th he had still many weeks to wait, before the news arrived that Metternich had broken with Napoleon—after a certain famous and stormy interview—and that Austria had come into the Grand Alliance. Meanwhile he intended to make his defensive position on the Pyrenean frontier sure, by the capture of the fortresses. It is curious to note that Napoleon understood and approved from the military point of view of this policy. On Aug. 5 he wrote to his minister Maret from Dresden, ' it is certain that Lord Wellington had a very sensible scheme : he wished to take St. Sebastian and Pampeluna before the French Army could be reorganized. He supposed that it had suffered more heavily than was actually the case, and thought that more than a month would be required to refurnish it with artillery [1].' This was a guess that came very near the truth, though the Emperor could not know that the cause of the British general's delay was mainly political and not military.

It was fortunate for Wellington that the astounding triumph of Vittoria had put him in a position to dictate his own policy to the Ministry at home. For Lord Bathurst and Lord Liverpool had been sending him suggestions which filled him with grave apprehensions. Before the news of Vittoria reached London, the War Minister had ' thrown out for consideration ' two most inept projects. If the French in Spain had been driven beyond the Ebro, would it not be possible to ' contain ' them for the future by Spanish and Portuguese armies, and to bring round Wellington himself and the bulk of his British troops to Germany, leaving only a small nucleus to serve as a backbone for the native levies of the Peninsula ? The appearance of Wellington with 40,000 of his veterans on the Elbe would probably induce the Allies to appoint him Generalissimo against Napoleon, and if Great Britain had the chief command in Germany she could dictate the policy of the Coalition. But supposing that the war was not resumed in Central Europe, and that a general peace was negotiated, would it be possible or expedient to allow the Emperor to retain the boundary of the Ebro for the French Empire, on condition that he yielded to the demands of the Allies in other parts of the Continent ? Or would Wellington guarantee that in the event of a Peace from which Great Britain stood out, he would be able to maintain himself in Spain and Portugal, as in 1810 and 1811, even though Napoleon had no other enemies left, and could send what reinforcements he pleased across the Pyrenees ? [2]

Even after the great event of June 21st had become known in London, we find the Prime Minister repeating some of Lord Bathurst's most absurd suggestions. He wrote in a tentative

[1] Napoleon to Maret, No. 28 in *Lettres de Napoléon non insérées dans la Correspondance, Aug.–Sept.–Oct. 1813.* Paris, 1907.

[2] Bathurst to Wellington, June 23, *Supplementary Dispatches*, viii. pp. 17–18.

and deferential style, to set forth the hypothesis that it might be possible to so fortify the Spanish frontier that it might be held by a small British force aided by Spanish levies, ' applying the principle upon which the Lines before Lisbon were formed to the passes of the Pyrenees '; and he inquired whether the warlike Navarrese and Biscayans could not defend this new Torres Vedras, if backed by a small force—20,000 or at most 30,000—veteran Anglo-Portuguese troops [1]. If this could be done Lord Liverpool obviously hoped great things from the effect of the appearance of Wellington, with his new prestige and the bulk of his victorious battalions, in Central Europe.

The recipient of these ill-advised suggestions would have nothing to do with them. When on July 12th he got Bathurst's dispatch of June 23rd, he replied that, being the servant of the State, he must obey any orders given him by the Prince Regent and the Ministry, but that he saw no profit in going to Germany, which he did not know, and where he was not known, whereas in Spain he had a unique advantage in ' the confidence that everybody feels that what I do is right '. ' Nobody could enjoy that same advantage here—while I should be no better than another in Germany. If any British army should be left in the Peninsula, therefore, it is best that I should remain with it.' As to making any general peace which left the French the line of the Ebro as a frontier, that problem had been settled by the battle of Vittoria. ' I recommend you not to give up an inch of Spanish territory ; I think I can hold the Pyrenees as easily as I can Portugal.' It would really be better to have Joseph Bonaparte as King of Spain (considering how ready all Bonapartes are to break away from their brother), than to have Ferdinand back with the Ebro as his frontier. ' In the latter case Spain would inevitably belong to the French [2].'

As to the ridiculous idea of fortifying the Pyrenean passes in the style of the Lines of Torres Vedras, Wellington speaks with no uncertain sound. ' I do not think we could successfully apply to the frontier of Spain the system on which we fortified the country between Lisbon and the sea. That line was a short

---

[1] Liverpool to Wellington, *Supplementary Dispatches*, viii. pp. 64–5, dated July 7.

[2] Wellington to Bathurst, July 12, from Hernani. *Dispatches*, x. p. 524.

one, and the communications easiest and shortest on our side. The Pyrenees are a very long line ; there are not fewer than *seventy* passes through these mountains, and the better communications, so far as I have been able to learn, are on the side of the enemy. We may facilitate defence by fortifying some of the passes : but we can never make in the Pyrenees what we made between the Tagus and the sea [1].'

It looks as if Lord Liverpool, in serene ignorance of local geography, imagined the Pyrenees to be a simple line of precipices, pierced by a limited number of passes, which could be sealed up with walls, in the style in which Alexander the Great in the mediaeval romance dealt with the ' Caucasian Gates '. For we cannot suppose that even the most unmilitary of politicians could have conceived it possible to build something like the Great Wall of China for several hundred miles, along the whole frontier from Fuenterrabia to Figueras. Yet this is what his proposal, if taken literally, would have meant ; and Wellington, to show its absurdity, gave the total number of passes available for mules or pedestrians between the Bay of Biscay and the Mediterranean. Those by which guns or wheeled transport could pass were (of course) no more than five or six— but there would be no finality in sealing up these few : for the enemy could turn the flanks of any of them with infantry scrambling up accessible slopes—as Soult indeed did during the battles of the Pyrenees, only a month after Lord Liverpool had made his egregious suggestion—or as Napoleon had done at the Somosierra in the winter of 1808.

Lastly, as to the Prime Minister's proposal to hand over the defence of the Pyrenees to Spanish armies backed by a mere 20,000 Anglo-Portuguese, Wellington replied that the Spanish Government had shown itself most consistently unable to feed, pay, and clothe its armies, or to provide the transport which would make them mobile. In June 1813 there were 160,000 men on the Spanish muster rolls, but only a third of that number at the front and actively engaged with the French, even when all troops in the Pyrenees, Aragon, and Catalonia were reckoned up. To trust the defence of the frontier to a government which

[1] Wellington to Lord Liverpool, July 23, from Lesaca, ibid., x. p. 568. Cf. same to same, x. p. 596.

could not move or feed more than a third of its own troops, would be to invite disaster. The best way to help the Spaniards was not to ask for more men, but to improve their finances, so that they should be able to employ a greater proportion of their already existing troops. As things stood at present, it would be insane to request them to take over the main burden of the war. 'It is my opinion that you ought not to have less than 60,000 British troops in the field, let the Spaniards have what numbers they may [1].'

Wellington had by this time established himself in such a commanding position that the ministers had to accept his decision—however much they would have liked to move him round to Germany, and to press for his appointment to the unenviable position which Prince Schwarzenberg occupied during the second campaign of 1813. The best proof of the wisdom of his determination to remain in the Peninsula was that the French, far from adopting a defensive policy, resumed the offensive under Soult within a few weeks. It would be an unprofitable, as also a dismal, task to consider what would have happened during the battles of the Pyrenees had Soult been opposed, not by Wellington and his old army, but by a Spanish host under O'Donnell or Freire, backed by two or three Anglo-Portuguese divisions.

Controversy with Lord Bathurst on general principles was only one of Wellington's distractions during the middle weeks of July : he was at the same time carrying on an acrimonious correspondence with the Spanish Minister of War, concerning the removal of Castaños and Giron from their posts, and enduring many controversial letters from Sir John Murray regarding the Tarragona fiasco. Murray had realized the disgust which his wretched policy had roused, alike in the army and in the British public, and was endeavouring to justify himself to his commander-in-chief by long argumentative epistles. Wellington refused to commit himself to any judgement, and agreed with the ministers at home that a court martial would be required [2]. He suggested to the authorities at the Horse Guards that Murray should be charged firstly with making no

---

[1] *Dispatches*, x. p. 570.
[2] See Wellington to Torrens, *Dispatches*, x. p. 616.

proper arrangements to raise the siege of Tarragona or to bring off his guns, secondly with having disobeyed the clause of his instructions which bade him return at once to Alicante if he failed in Catalonia, and thirdly with having betrayed General Copons, by bringing him down to the coast and then absconding without giving any proper warning of his departure [1]. After mature reflection, however, he advised that the third charge should be dropped, not because it was unjustified, but because there would be great inconvenience in bringing Copons or his representatives to bear witness at a British court martial, when they were wanted in Catalonia.

But all this correspondence, and much more on less important subjects, did not prevent Wellington from paying his promised visit to General Graham, to inspect in person the allied positions on the lower Bidassoa, and to supervise the arrangements for the siege of St. Sebastian, which indeed required supervision, for already it was evident that things were not going so well as might have been hoped in this direction (July 12).

The first impression made on the observer by the fortress of St. Sebastian is that it is an extremely small place. This is true—though it is also true that its effect is somewhat dwarfed by its immense surroundings—the limitless expanse of the Ocean on one side, and the high and fantastic peaks of the Jaizquibel, the Peña de la Haya, and the Four Crowns, which have just been passed by the traveller coming from the side of Bayonne. The fortress consists of a lofty sandstone rock, as steep as Edinburgh Castle and 400 ft. high, beaten on three sides by the sea, and united to the land by a low sandy isthmus about 900 yards long. There was an old castle called La Mota, on the summit of the rock, which is named Monte Urgull, with three modern batteries on its southern or landward face [2], which is very steep and only accessible at two points by winding roads. But these were not the main defences of the place, which lay lower down. The town of St. Sebastian

---

[1] See Wellington to Bathurst, *Dispatches*, x. p. 599, and other epistles on same topic.

[2] Called the Mirador ('look-out'), Queen's, and Principe batteries : there were others facing seaward, which were of no account in this siege, as no attack from the water-side took place.

was built on the lower ground below the rock, extending from sea to sea and occupying about a third of the isthmus, the rest of which was broken sandy ground about 400 yards broad. At the southern neck of the isthmus was a hill crowned by the large monastery of San Bartolomé, which the French held as an outwork at the beginning of the siege. The space between this hill and the wall of the town, now thickly packed with the hotels and avenues of a fashionable seaside resort, was in 1813 waste ground dotted with a few isolated houses and gardens, which the governor was busily engaged in levelling when the blockading force arrived. At two points there was a sufficient accumulation of buildings to form a small suburb. One group was at the head of the bridge across the river Urumea, which joined the peninsula to the eastern mainland ; this was named Santa Catalina, from a chapel of that saint which lay in it. The other, called (for a similar reason) San Martin, was immediately at the foot of the hill of San Bartolomé. The bridge had been blown up by the French when the Spaniards first appeared, and the suburbs set on fire, but their roofless and partly fallen houses still gave a good deal of cover.

The land-front of St. Sebastian was very formidable ; it was only 400 yards broad and was composed of a very high curtain from which projected one large bastion in the centre and two demi-bastions overhanging the water on each flank, that of San Juan, above the estuary of the Urumea, that of Santiago on the western side nearest the harbour. In front of the bastions was a very broad hornwork, having outside it the usual counterscarp, covered-way, and glacis. Specialists, wise after the event, criticized the whole land-front : they found its trace defective, considered that the scarp of the hornwork ought to have been more than 23 feet high, and pointed out that in the rear line the two demi-bastions did not well protect the flanks, since they were not themselves covered by the hornwork, and had no ditch or glacis, because the salt water came up to their foot at high tide [1].

But as the land-front was never attacked, these objections were of comparatively little importance. The weak side of St. Sebastian was really its eastern water-front. The western

[1] See Jones's *Sieges of the Peninsula*, ii. p. 94.

water-front on the open bay was inaccessible ; but on the opposite side, where the town wall ran along the estuary of the river Urumea, the conditions were peculiar. The Urumea is a tidal river—at high water it washes right up to the foot of the walls, but at low tide it recedes into a narrow channel and leaves exposed an expanse of rock and sand, ranging in breadth from 50 to 150 yards, all along the water-wall for a length of some 400 yards—half the east side of the town. The rampart here was a plain curtain, not very high and only 8 feet thick : of course it could have no ditch or other outer fittings, since the salt water reached right up to it for half the day. Its only salients, from which flank fire could be used, were one small bastion (St. Elmo) and two ancient round towers called Los Hornos and Amezqueta, which projected slightly from the straight curtain.

At high tide this water-front was unapproachable—at low tide it was weak and accessible, for the Urumea was fordable in many places, and shrank into a channel only 50 yards broad, meandering through a waste of shingle, rocks, and mud. On its eastern bank were rolling sandhills of some height, which commanded the isthmus and the southern half of the town, from a distance of no more than 700 or 800 yards. To the right of the sandhills, called Los Chofres, was a steep hill, the Monte Olia, facing the castle of St. Sebastian across the broader part of the estuary, and by no means out of gunshot of it, since not more than 1,000 or 1,100 yards of water lies between them.

Since it had been rebuilt as a fortress of the Vauban-Cohorn style in the last years of the seventeenth century, St. Sebastian had only once been besieged : for during the Revolutionary War of 1792–5 it surrendered without any resistance to the Jacobin armies, while in 1808 Napoleon had seized it by treachery and not by force. The one formal attack made on it was by the Duke of Berwick in 1719, when the armies of the Regent Orleans crossed the Bidassoa, in the short war provoked by the ambitions of Elizabeth Farnese and Cardinal Alberoni. Berwick had established his siege-batteries not on the isthmus, to batter the land-front, but on the Chofres sandhills, from whence he pounded the eastern sea-front to pieces. Several breaches having been made in it, and trenches on the isthmus having been pushed as far as the glacis of the hornwork, the governor very tamely surrendered, without waiting for an assault [1]. Unwarned by this revelation of the weakness of the defences along the Urumea, the engineers of Philip V made no improvements in them when they were reconstructed after the war, and the fortress was in 1813 little different from what it had been in 1719.

The easy success of Marshal Berwick turned out a very unhappy thing for the British army ; for the history of the last siege being well remembered, Major Charles Smith, the senior engineer with Graham's column, reported that Berwick's plan was the right one [2], when the first survey of the place was made. And when the head-quarters staff came up, his superior officer, Sir Richard Fletcher, agreed with him, as did Colonel Dickson commanding the artillery.   They all forgot that to make a breach with ease is not necessarily the same thing as to capture a fortress, and that the eighteenth-century slackness of the governor, who capitulated when his walls were once breached, gave no indication of what might be done by a very resourceful and resolute French officer, who had in his mind Napoleon's edict of 1811 that every commandant who hauled down his flag before standing at least one assault should be sent before a court martial.   Nor is there any doubt that Wellington himself must take his share of the responsibility, as he went round the place on July 12th and had a good look at it, in company with Charles Smith and Dickson, from Monte Olia and the Chofres sandhills.   Dickson summed up the results of their discussion as follows :—' The project is to effect a breach in the uncovered sea-wall forming an angle on the left of the land-front, between two towers [Los Hornos and Amezqueta], being the same spot the Duke of Berwick breached in 1719, when he took St. Sebastian.   The convent of San Bartolomé, which the French have fortified and occupied in force, is absolutely necessary to take first, in order to be able to advance on the isthmus in support of our breaching operations from the

---

[1] The governor surrendered the town on August 1, but retired into the castle of La Mota, where he capitulated a few days later, just as Rey did in 1813.

[2] Jones's *Sieges of the Peninsula*, ii. p. 14

Chofres. The plan of attack was the proposition of Major Smith [1].'

This, of course, was not the regular and orthodox way to attack such a fortress—as it involved the making of breaches only accessible at low tide, in a part of the wall to which no trenches could draw near, since its lower courses were six feet under water for half the hours of the day. There would have to be a long advance from the nearest dry ground on which approaches could be dug, across the tidal waste, in order to reach the spot selected for breaching. And this would undoubtedly be a very bloody business for the exposed storming troops. The advantages to be gained were rapid action and a quick end, without the necessity which an orthodox scheme would have involved of sapping up to the hornwork, storming it, and then tackling the lofty bastion behind it. The British engineer who wrote the history of the siege considered that ' the operations against San Sebastian afford a most impressive lesson on the advantage of due attention to science and rule in the attack of fortified places : the effort then made to overcome and trample on such restrictions caused an easy and certain operation of eighteen or twenty days to extend over sixty days, and to cost the besiegers 3,500 men killed, wounded, or taken, bearing strong testimony to the truth of the maxim laid down by Marshal Vauban, that hurry in sieges does not lead to an early success, often delays it, and always makes it very bloody [2].'

St. Sebastian had been abandoned to its own resources on June 28, when, after the departure of Foy's troops from Oyarzun, the Spaniards had closed in on the place, and established a blockade. The force employed was four battalions of Biscayan volunteers under Mendizabal, the remains of the bands which Foy had beaten in May, and which had taken part on June 26 along with the British 1st Division in the combat of Tolosa [3]. They were very irregular troops, and their indiscipline and incompetence shocked General Graham when he came to visit their lines on July 6th [4]. They had no notion of guarding

[1] Dickson's diary, July 12, 1813, p. 960 of Colonel John Leslie's edition of the *Dickson Papers*.   [2] Jones, ii. p. 97.   [3] See above, p. 478.
[4] See Graham to Wellington, *Supplementary Dispatches*, viii. p. 62. The K.G.L. brigade of the 1st Division was present for a few days.

themselves, and had suffered severely, first from an attempt to storm San Bartolomé on June 28th, and later from a French sortie on July 3, when Rey sent out two columns of 700 men from the Convent, which surprised their camp, took many prisoners, and drove them back for nearly two miles. Graham recommended that they should be replaced at once by solid troops, and at Wellington's suggestion told off the British 5th Division and the unattached Portuguese brigade of Bradford for the siege [1]. Mendizabal's men were sent off to join in the blockade of Santoña [2]. On July 7th the siege-troops arrived ; the independent brigade established itself on the Chofres, the 5th Division—still under Oswald as at Vittoria—took post on the heights of Ayete, facing the hill and convent of San Bartolomé. From this moment the serious operations may be considered to have begun. A blockade of the sea-side had been established, in a rather intermittent fashion, four days earlier, when Sir George Collier appeared in the bay with a frigate, the *Surveillante*, a corvette, and two brigs, all the force that he could collect for the moment in response to Wellington's appeals to the Admiralty. The amount was wholly inadequate, even when supplemented by some local fishing craft and pinnaces, which were manned by the battalion of marines from Giron's Galician army. All through the siege French *trincadores* and luggers from Bayonne and St. Jean de Luz ran the blockade at night, bringing in food, munitions, and reinforcements. For Rey having asked for more gunners, he was sent several detachments of them, who all arrived in safety, while he got rid of many of his wounded by the returning vessels. Wellington was full of justifiable wrath at the miserable help given him—his objurgations brought from Lord Melville an unsatisfactory reply, to the effect that the operations in the Baltic and the American War absorbed many of the British light craft which would have been available in earlier years, and that the Admiralty had not been warned in the spring that any large fighting force would be wanted on the Biscay coast in July. ' Neither from you, nor from any other person at your suggestion, did we ever receive the slightest intimation that more was expected than

---

[1] Wellington to Graham, *Dispatches*, x. p. 512.
[2] *Wellington Dispatches*, x. p. 525.

the protection of your convoys, till the actual arrival of Sir Thomas Graham on the coast after the battle of Vittoria.' Melville then proceeded to write lengthy observations on the dangerous nature of the coast of Northern Spain, ' where ships cannot anchor without extreme risk, and are exposed to almost certain destruction in a gale, when from its direction they can neither haul off shore nor run for shelter into a port. If you will ensure the ships a continuance of east winds, they could remain with you, but not otherwise. All the small craft in the British navy could not prevent the occasional entry of small boats by night into San Sebastian's, though it may be rendered more difficult and uncertain.' Melville then proceeded to tax Wellington with grave professional irregularity, for having written to Sir George Collier, and other naval officers, letters taxing the Admiralty with neglect and incompetence. ' Appeals to subordinate officers against their superiors are not customary in any branch of the service, and must be injurious to the public interest [1].'

It was not so much the arguments used by Melville as his offensive tone which Wellington resented. The victor of Salamanca was naturally irritated at finding himself treated *de haut en bas* by a personage of such complete insignificance, who had not even the equivocal reputation of his father (the devisor of so many unlucky expeditions, the impeached minister of 1806) to lend weight to his lectures. He replied in a very short letter that he was not desirous of getting into discussions, that his demands for more naval assistance had begun in the winter of 1812–13, and that after reading over again his letters to naval officers he could see nothing to find fault with—save that he had once sent to Sir George Collier an extract of a dispatch to Lord Bathurst, instead of a separate communication on the same topic addressed to Collier personally— a trifling subject on which to start a controversy [2]. Meanwhile he considered, as a dozen letters show, that he was being poorly served by the Admiralty, and ' formed private opinions on the subject—which private opinions may not perhaps deserve much attention,' as he sardonically observed.

[1] Melville to Wellington, *Supplementary Dispatches*, viii. pp. 224–5.
[2] Wellington to Melville, *Dispatches*, xi. p. 115.

One thing, however, the Admiralty had contrived to carry out according to Wellington's request—the stores and battering train, which he had accumulated at Corunna in the spring, had come round to the Biscay coast as soon as could have been expected ; they had been sent to Santander, as he directed, and arrived in that harbour on the very day (June 29) on which Major Frazer, sent off four days after Vittoria, came from Head-Quarters to inquire for them [1]. The orders were to land them at Deba in Guipuzcon, fifteen miles west of St. Sebastian ; but just as the disembarkation was commencing (July 3), a change of destination was made—everything was to be put ashore at Passages, a much more convenient place, only a couple of miles from the blockaded fortress. This is a most astonishing little harbour, the safest port on the coast, for it is absolutely land-locked ; its entrance is so narrow that the circular basin looks like a lake without an issue, till the eye has with some difficulty discovered its exit. It pays for its security, however, by being hard to enter in time of storm, when very careful navigation is required. But a besieging army has seldom been granted a base so near to its field of operations—it was only two and a half miles from the water's edge at Passages to the Chofres sand-hills, where the chief batteries were to be constructed, though four miles to the head of the isthmus where the left attack was to be made. And the fording of the Urumea, whose bridge the French had burned, was sometimes dangerous—more than one gun was lost in the quicksands [2].

By the time that Wellington had worked out the scheme of assault with Charles Smith, the guns were already arriving, not only the battering train from Corunna, which had begun to come ashore on July 7, but the heavy artillery reserve of the army, which had traversed all the weary miles of road from Ciudad Rodrigo. The total of pieces available was twenty-eight from the convoy, six from the heavy battery of the army reserve, and six lent by Sir George Collier from the main deck of his ship, the *Surveillante*—or forty in all [3]—a very different

---

[1] See the interesting account of his cross-country ride on June 25-9 in his *Letters from the Peninsula*, pp. 167-74.   [2] See Frazer, p. 195.

[3] In detail Jones gives them as twenty 24-pounders, six 18-pounders, four 68-pound cannonades, six 8-inch howitzers, and four mortars.

train from the miserable four guns which had battered Burgos in the preceding autumn.

Before any regular siege work could begin, it was obviously necessary to clear the French out of the monastery of San Bartolomé, on its hill at the neck of the isthmus : till this should be taken, it was impossible to get forward on the shore from which the assault was to be delivered. Under-estimating the.strength of the post Graham and the engineers, contrary to the advice of Major Hartmann of the K.G.L., the senior artillery officer present before Dickson's arrival [1], had tried to reduce it on July 7th by the fire of a Portuguese field battery belonging to the artillery reserve ; but the walls proved too solid for 8-pounders to damage, and some firing with red hot shot failed to set fire to the roof. It was clear that it would be necessary to wait for the heavy guns to come up. Meanwhile the French continued to strengthen San Bartolomé, throwing up an earthwork in its cemetery and loopholing and barricading the ruined houses near it, as well as those in the burnt-out suburb of San Martin, which lay at its foot. They also commenced a redoubt on the isthmus, half-way between the outlying convent and the hornwork in front of the city wall.

While the siege train was being got ashore, the engineers made ready the emplacements for the guns—they started with throwing up two batteries on the Ayete heights to play on the convent of San Bartolomé [2], three on the Chofres sand-hills [3] to act against the sea-wall where the main breach was to be formed, and one on the lofty Monte Olia, for long-distance fire against all the fortifications, including those of the rock of Monte Urgull [4]. But on the 14th, when the battering began, the only guns used were those on the left attack opposite the convent, as it was considered unwise to molest the city fortifications before there was any way of getting near them : approach was impossible as long as the isthmus was all in the enemy's hands.

Two days' battering (July 14–15) brought down the roof and part of the walls of San Bartolomé, and damaged the subsidiary works around it severely. But General Rey was determined to

---

[1] See Hartmann's *Life*, pp. 153–4.　　[2] Nos. 4, 5 in map.

[3] Nos. 1, 2, 3 in map.　　[4] No. 6 in the map.

hold on to his outer defences as long as possible : the best part of two battalions was told off to hold the ruins and the suburb of San Martin behind them. On the afternoon of the 15th General Oswald, judging from the dilapidation of the buildings that they were untenable, sent in the 8th Caçadores from his Portuguese brigade to storm them ; but the French had dug themselves well in, a furious fire broke out against the assailants, and the attack was turned back with the loss of 65 men[1]. It was obvious that more battering was required to evict the gallant garrison, so the fire was resumed on the 16th, with the aid of a field battery playing across the Urumea to enfilade the defences, and to pound the ruined houses of San Martin, where the French reserves were sheltering.

The fire was very effective : the inner woodwork of the monastery blazed up, its porch was levelled to the ground, great gaps appeared in the walls, and the earthwork in the cemetery was much damaged. At 10 a.m. on the 17th a second storm was tried, with forces much larger than those used at the first— not one battalion, but the equivalent of three : Oswald drew upon Bradford's independent brigade from across the Urumea for 700 Portuguese volunteers. Two columns were launched against the French position, each consisting of a screen of Caçadores, a support of Portuguese Line troops, and a reserve of British companies from the first brigade of the 5th Division[2]. The right column aimed at the cemetery earthwork and the fortified houses—the left at the main buildings of the convent, which were still smouldering from the fire. Both achieved their purpose without any very serious loss, and the garrison was driven down hill into the suburb of San Martin, pursued by the

---

[1] Why does Belmas, who was very well informed, and used Jones's book, call the stormers ' les Anglais ' and say that they lost 150 men ? (*Sièges*, iv. p. 608). He knew from Jones that they were Caçadores only (Jones, ii. p. 21), and that their loss was under 70.

[2] Right column, to attack the cemetery and fortified houses—150 of 5th Caçadores, 150 13th Portuguese Line, three companies 1/9th Foot, three companies 3/1st Foot (Royal Scots) all under Hay, Brigadier of the 5th Division. Left column : 200 of 5th Caçadores, 200 of 13th Portuguese Line, three companies 1/9th Foot—all under Bradford commanding Portuguese independent brigade. Why did not Oswald use his own Portuguese brigade, but draw on Bradford ? Possibly because Spry's brigade were discouraged by the failure of their Caçador battalion on the 15th.

stormers. Here the French reserves intervened, and for a moment the attack was turned back ; but the companies of the 1/9th which formed the British supports re-established the fight, and the enemy retired in disorder towards the town. Unfortunately the victors pursued recklessly, and came under the fire of the French guns in the hornwork and the bastion behind it, whence many unnecessary casualties. For it had never been intended that the troops should advance on to the isthmus, where of course they could do nothing against an intact front of fortifications. The total losses of the assailants were 207 killed and wounded—the 1/9th which had headed the rush on to the bare ground suffering most, with 70 casualties. The French had 40 killed and 200 wounded.

It was now possible to commence the subsidiary attack on the side of the isthmus, as the French held nothing outside the walls save the recently constructed redoubt in front of the hornwork [1]. Two batteries were thrown up on the San Bartolomé hill, and on the 18th the guns with which the convent had been breached were moved down into them [2]. The main object of these batteries was to enfilade the stretch of sea-wall, on which the greater weight of metal on the Chofres downs was to play from the front. Two additional batteries were thrown up, more to the right, which, while aiding the enfilading fire, were also intended to shell the land-front, and keep down the fire from the bastion and hornwork [3]. Finally, the Chofres attack was strengthened with two more batteries [4]. On the night of the 19th sixteen guns in all were in place on the isthmus front, or left attack, twenty-three on the right attack to the east of the Urumea, including six on the summit of the lofty Monte Olia, on the extreme flank [5]. Meanwhile the approaches, by which the troops would have to move out to assault the breaches when made, were not nearly so far forward as could have been desired : little more had been done than to push a zig-zag down the slope of San Bartolomé into the ruins of San Martin—

---

[1] Generally in British narratives called the Cask Redoubt, because wine-casks had been used to revet the shifting sand of which the soil was there composed.

[2] Batteries 8 and 7 in the map.   [3] Batteries 13 and 14 in the map.
[4] Batteries 12 and 11 in the map.   [5] No. 6 in the map.

further advance was made difficult by the fact that the French were still holding the forward position of the redoubt in the centre of the isthmus. It was only on the night between the 19th and 20th that they evacuated this post [1]. Moreover the fire of the defence was as yet intact, since the British heavy batteries had not begun their work : hence the sap-head was a decidedly unhealthy place.

At 8 a.m. on the morning of July 20 nine of the eleven siege batteries opened—all but the two new ones on San Bartolomé, where the work was a little belated. The effect of the first day's work was fairly satisfactory—the parapet of the sea-wall began to crumble, the enemy's guns *en barbette* on the land-front were partly silenced, and the high trajectory fire from the lofty Monte Olia battery searched the streets, the back of the bastion, and the interior of the hornwork. The enemy concentrated all his attention on the largest British battery upon the Chofres dunes, the eleven guns which were farthest forward (No. 3) and were doing much damage to the sea-wall. The counterfire here was severe—one gun was split by a ball striking its muzzle, others had wheels broken, three had to stop firing because their embrasures, badly built with sand, fell in and could not be kept clear [2]. By evening only six of the eleven guns were still at work.

An afternoon of wind and showers, which had made accurate aim difficult, was followed on the night of the 20th–21st by a torrential rain, which much impeded the special work which had been set aside for the dark hours. Seven hundred men from Spry's Portuguese brigades had been told off to open a parallel right across the isthmus, starting from the lodgment already established in the ruined houses of San Martin. ' In the perfect deluge the working parties sneaked away by degrees into houses and holes and corners. After numerous difficulties and exertions only about 150 could be collected and set to work

[1] There is a curious contradiction between Jones and Belmas as to the fate of the Cask Redoubt. The latter says that the British took it—the former that the garrison abandoned it, though not attacked.

[2] ' From the looseness of the sand in which the battery was constructed, it was found impossible to keep the soles of the embrasures sufficiently clear to use the three short 24-pounders mounted on ship carriages—after a few rounds they had to cease firing. Jones, ii. p. 28.

at 11 p.m. The party was not discovered, and the soil being light soon got under cover. . . . But the parallel finished was for only about one-third of the extent required [1].'

On the next morning Sir Thomas Graham sent out a *parlementaire* to summon the governor to surrender—rather prematurely as it would seem, for no real breach had yet been formed, nor had the fire of the defence been subdued. General Rey having made the answer that might be expected from a resolute officer [2], the battering recommenced, and was continued on the 21st–22nd–23rd–24th July. It was quite effective : on the 23rd fifty yards of the curtain, between the towers of Los Hornos and Amezqueta, fell outward on to the strand that was exposed at low water—appearing to present a practicable breach. But partly to make things sure, and partly because the trenches on the isthmus were still remote from the point which it was intended to reach, the battering was continued for two days longer. Not only was more of the wall thrown down near the tower of Los Hornos, but at Graham's desire a second and minor breach was made, some distance farther north in the sea-wall than the first [3]. The temptation to make it was that Spanish refugees brought intelligence that the ramparts here were very thin—which proved to be the case, as one day's battering brought down a broad patch of stones. On the other hand the specialists are said to have warned Graham that the second breach would be rather useless, because the space of shore below it exposed at low tide was very narrow—under 50 feet wide—and could only be reached by skirting along for 300 yards below the walls and past the foot of the first breach. However, the creation of a second point of attack would certainly distract part of the attention of the garrison from the real place of danger, and if the small breach could be carried, the flank of the defenders of the great breach would be effectually turned.

It was a thousand pities that the formation of the first breach

---

[1] Burgoyne's *Life and Correspondence*, i. p. 267.

[2] Burgoyne, who took out the flag of truce, says that the French officer who met him on the glacis used very angry words (ibid.).

[3] See *Dickson Papers*, ed. Col. Leslie, p. 970. The second breach is marked as ' Lesser Breach ' on the map.

on July 23rd was not followed by an immediate attempt to
storm, as the enemy was given two whole days to perfect his
inner defences. But an assault was impossible till the approaches should have got close to the walls, and owing to the
initial delays they were not ready till two days later. On
the night of the 22nd–23rd the parallel reaching right across the
isthmus was begun and half completed, with the French ' Cask
Redoubt' at its left extremity. Digging close to this spot, the
working parties found a large drain or channel 4 feet high and
3 feet wide, which belonged to the aqueduct which supplied
the town with water. It was empty, as the Spaniards had cut
it off at its source when they first blockaded the town. Lieutenant Reid of the Engineers volunteered to explore it, and
crawling 230 yards forward, found that he was under the
west corner of the counterscarp of the hornwork, where the
French had cut off the channel and blocked it with a door.
This discovery suggested to the engineers that the channel might
be used as a mine ; if its farther end were filled with powder,
and then built up with sandbags, the explosion might bring
down the counterscarp and fill the ditch, so that the hornwork
might be stormed across the débris. Unfortunately there was
complete uncertainty as to whether the plan would work : quite
conceivably it might result in the door being blown open, and
the force of the powder might be spent in sending a local blast
along the ditch, without much damaging the superincumbent
earth. However, the experiment was tried ; layers of sandbags
were placed against the door, then thirty barrels of powder
were inserted, standing on end but not tamped in, for foul air
greatly troubled the miners, so that there was much empty
space above and between the barrels. The near end was then
built up with more sandbags and a train laid to the mouth of
the channel in the trenches [1].

[1] Burgoyne, whose diary of the siege is one of the primary authorities,
says that in his opinion the mine could have been much more useful than
it was. ' On the discovery of the drain, I should have immediately have
altered the whole plan of attack. I would have made a " globe of com-
pression " to blow in the counterscarp and the crest of the glacis, and then
at low water have threatened an attack on the breaches, exploded the
mine, and have made the real assault on the hornwork, which not being
threatened had few people in it, and would undoubtedly have been carried

During the day of the 23rd and the following night the parallel was completed, and good communications made from it to the base, the hill of San Bartolomé. The greater part of the enemy's visible guns were silenced, and the enfilading fire from the two last-erected batteries on the isthmus set ablaze the quarter of the town immediately behind the two breaches. This last achievement turned out to be anything but an advantage.

For arrangements for the assault having been made for daybreak on the 24th, and the storming party and supports having been brought down to the trenches after midnight, to wait till half low-tide, it was found that the whole of the streets adjacent to the great breach were blazing so fiercely that it was thought that any entry into the town would be impossible. Graham therefore countermanded the storm—this was probably necessary ; but Rey thereby gained another day for perfecting his internal defences.

These were most elaborate and excellent, surpassing by far even the very competent arrangements made by Philippon at Badajoz. The peculiar part of them was that Rey had to depend almost entirely on engineering work—his artillery having been completely crushed during the preliminary battering. Such guns as he contrived to use on this day were either very remote— on the rock and its slopes—or else pieces that had been withdrawn and kept under cover till the critical moment should arrive. The British artillery officers, whose telescopes were always busy, discovered some of them, but informed Graham that they undertook to crush them when they should be brought out, provided that light and atmospheric conditions were satisfactory [1].

But the main defence which Rey had prepared depended on fortification, not on artillery fire. His chief advantage was that at both breaches the stones had fallen outward, and the back of the ramparts was intact. All along the sea-wall there was

easily.' There was, he says, good cover in the hornwork, which would have been easily connected with the parallel, and used as the base for attacking the main front, with breaching batteries in its terre-plein and the crest of the glacis. Burgoyne, i. p. 271. But this is wisdom after the event.

[1] Jones, ii. p. 36.

a drop of 15 to 20 feet from the rampart-walk into the street behind : this still existed, as the core of the wall was still standing, though the facing had given way. To descend from the lip of the breach into the town, therefore, was more than a feasible leap : it could not be done without ladders. Rey had demolished some houses which had been built with their back to the ramparts, and had cut away all stairs leading up to them. He had blocked with stone barricades all streets opening towards the breaches, and had loopholed all buildings commanding a view of them. When the fire in the quarter that had been ablaze on the 24th died down, he reoccupied the ruined houses, making shelters in the débris. He had cut off the rampart-walk on each side of the breaches by building a succession of stone traverses across it, so that troops who had mounted to the top could not push out sideways. As it was clear that the storming columns would have to advance for 300 yards parallel with the eastern *faussebraye* of the hornwork, and close to it, because of the water on their right, he told off a large number of picked marksmen to line this flank, and ranged live shells along it, which could be rolled down on to the strand while the enemy were passing.

The preparation for a storm on the 24th, and its countermand because of the conflagration, had been noted by the governor, who understood the cause of the delay. Obviously the attack would come on the following morning, so the reserved guns were got into position after midnight—two in the casemates of the high curtain, two others in the ditch below it, one in the eastern face of the hornwork, two in the south front of the bastion of St. Elmo : into the towers of Los Hornos and Amezqueta, on each side of the main breach, three pieces were hoisted not without difficulty, since the towers, though still standing, were in bad order. Even in the distant and lofty Mirador battery, on top of the rock, some guns were trained on the point of danger [1]. Having made all possible preparations Rey waited for the assault, which came just as he had expected.

The exact share of responsibility for the details of the storm of July 25th, which fell respectively on the engineers who had settled the scheme of attack, on Graham who designated the

[1] For all these details see Belmas, iv. pp. 620-1.

hour, on Oswald who arranged the order of the troops, and on the artillery officers who had undertaken to keep down the enemy's fire, is not easy to determine. All apparently have to take their portion ; but that of Charles Smith, who devised, and Sir Richard Fletcher, who approved, the choice of the sea-wall for the breach-spot would seem to be the heaviest, and that of the gunners the least.

The troops were to sally out from the eastern end of the long parallel across the isthmus, when there should be a sufficient breadth of strand exposed for them to rush straight for the breaches, passing between the hornwork on their left and the receding tidal water on their right. Unfortunately the hour of low tide and the hour of daybreak were not conveniently correlated : the ideal combination would have been that the four hours during which there was good access across the exposed flats should have been from 5.30 a.m. till 9.30 a.m. : daybreak falling at about 5.20 a.m. But as it chanced the extreme of low tide that day was at 6 a.m., and the practicable hours were from 4 a.m. onward. In order to lose none of the limited time available, Graham determined that the rush should be made at 5 o'clock sharp, before it was full daylight ; and this choice had one unlucky effect. The engineers settled that the signal for assault should be the blowing up of the mine in the aqueduct [1] ; but they had so little confidence in its effect, that the only arrangements made to utilize it were that supposing it should do much damage and blow down scarp and counterscarp (which was hardly expected), the Portuguese companies which held the extreme left of the parallel should make a rush at the west flank of the hornwork, and enter over the débris. This was a very half-hearted scheme. For the real assault General Oswald seems to have made a very faulty disposition of his troops. The opening made in the parallel was so narrow that not more than two or three men could issue abreast. The troops, therefore, had to start in a sort of narrow file or procession, and took an unconscionable time in trickling

---

[1] Burgoyne says (i. 369) that the engineers on the 24th settled that the mine was no more than a signal ' with a chance of alarming them '. On the 25th it would seem that a little more attention, but not nearly enough, was given to this useful subsidiary operation.

out from the trench. The head of the column was composed
of the right wing of the 3/1st (Royal Scots) ; then came a ladder
party from all three regiments of Hay's brigade ; then the left
wing of the Royal Scots : all these were to strike for the main
breach. ˙Next were the 1/38th, who were directed to pass
between the leading troops and the water's edge, and to make
for the lesser breach, along the ever-narrowing strip of exposed
beach. Last came the 1/9th, the third battalion of the brigade,
with orders to support wherever it could make itself most
useful. Some picked shots from the 8th Caçadores of Spry's
brigade were placed along the front of the parallel, and in
a ditch which had been scraped during the night a few yards in
advance of it, with orders to try to keep down the enemy's
musketry from the eastern flank of the hornwork.

At 5 o'clock, or perhaps a little earlier [1], the mine was fired,
and did much more damage than was expected, blowing down
the counterscarp of the western flank of the hornwork, injuring
the scarp, and filling the ditch with earth. The Portuguese
troops in the opposite trench made an assault, according to
their orders, swept over the covered way and into the ditch,
and tried to enter the work. They failed with loss, because no
proper preparations had been made to utilize the opportunity [2],
which indeed had hardly been taken into consideration. They
might have got in, for the French garrison flinched at first,
terrified by the explosion.

On the side of the main attack the Royal Scots led out of the
parallel immediately that the explosion was heard, and pushed
forward in almost complete darkness on to the strand. It was
found to consist in many places of hard rock overgrown with
slippery seaweed, and interspersed with deep pools. The men
stumbled over, and into, many traps which might have been
avoided by daylight, and all order was lost. But for the first
few minutes there was little fire bearing on them, and the
platoons at the head of the column reached the main breach.

---

[1] Burgoyne says at 4.30.

[2] This is slurred over in the British narratives except *Dickson's Diary*,
p. 973. Belmas gives some account of it, however, though he calls the
assailants British instead of Portuguese (iv. p. 623). They were some
companies of the 8th Caçadores.

The conducting engineer, Lieutenant Harry Jones, and Major Fraser, commanding the wing of the Royal Scots, had actually got to the lip of the breach, with the leading men of the storming party, before the enemy really opened. That the crowning of the breach was not followed by a rush into the town was due to Rey's precautions—there was a sudden drop of twenty feet between the top of the wall and the street below, and no means to descend, as all stairs and ramps had been cut away. There were some ladders with the column, but not at its head—they were being carried in the rear of the right wing of the Royal Scots. As the leading company came to a halt the French began to shoot hard from behind traverses on the rampart-walk, barricades, and loopholed houses, and the guns in the two flanking towers played on the breach with grape. The head of the column began to wither away ; Fraser and Jones were both wounded—the former mortally—and so was every man who had reached the summit. The survivors on the breach threw themselves down among the stones and began to return the enemy's fire—the first impetus being lost, and any chance of success with it.

But it was only about the equivalent of a company which had advanced so far ; the rear of the right wing of the Royal Scots were still passing along the flank of the hornwork, in a straggling file, when the enemy's fire began to be serious. It came most fiercely from an entrenchment which Rey had thrown up across the main ditch between the hornwork and the high front of the demi-bastion behind it. It seems, from the narrative of an officer who took a prominent part in the storm— Colin Campbell of the 1/9th, who was with the ladder party— that many of the Royal Scots, arriving in the darkness at this opening into the main ditch, mistook it for a passage by which they might force their way into the place, or even for the great breach itself. At any rate they turned in toward it, and on meeting with strenuous resistance began to fire upon the enemy. The men following gathered in upon the first comers, and a crowd accumulated at this point, which checked the ladder party and the left wing of the Royal Scots as they came up. Hardly any one pressed on to join the head of the column on the slope of the breach. Meanwhile the tail of the column was blocked, as it tried to press on past the hornwork. The French, standing above, rolled down the shells which had been laid ready upon the British below, and kept up a vigorous discharge of musketry. With great exertions individual company officers succeeded in collecting parties of their own men, and leading them out of the crowd, so as to pass on to the great breach. But the attack there had already come to nothing : the stones all up the slope were strewn with dead and wounded—a few survivors were keeping up an ineffectual return fire upon the well-concealed enemy. Three or perhaps four attempts to mount again were made by small parties of the rear companies of the Royal Scots, but there were never more than 80 or 90 men acting together, and the officers and leading men were always shot down on the crest. At last the senior captain surviving, seeing the impossibility of getting forward, ordered the stormers to retire, which they did—only half an hour or less after the assault commenced—though the time had seemed much longer, as was natural, to those involved in the bloody business. The larger body of men engaged farther back, opposite the main ditch and under the demi-bastion of St. Juan, gave way also when the head of the column fell back among them : they had themselves suffered heavily, and of course had made no progress. Just as the whole body rolled back along the beach they came into collision with the front of the 1/38th, who had only just finished filing out of the parallel, so slow was the process of emerging from its narrow exit. Their commanding officer, Colonel Greville, had halted them for a short time to let their rear close up, and to prevent them from dribbling forward in a thin string of small parties, as the Royal Scots had done. Just as they came parallel with the north end of the hornwork the broken mass of men from the front ran in upon them ; all order was lost at once, and after some vain attempts to get forward the 38th fell back along with the rest over the slippery shore[1]. The disordered crowd suffered heavily from the French grape and musketry—they were a mark impossible to miss, and strewed the rocks and pools with dead. The 1/9th, who were

---

[1] Most of this narrative is from Colin Campbell's long and interesting letter to Sir J. Cameron, printed on pp. 25–30 of his *Life* by General Shadwell.

just beginning to file out of the parallel, were of course ordered back at once—' but had lost almost as many heads as they showed [1].'

So quickly was the whole affair over that the artillerymen, standing by their guns on the opposite side of the Urumea, ready to co-operate as soon as dawn should come, believed at first that there had been a feint or a false attack. It was only when the growing light showed them the breach strewn from lip to foot with red coats, and the strand below thickly dotted with them also, that they realized that the assault had been made and had failed [2], without their being given the chance to intervene as they had promised.

The loss had, of course, been very heavy—out of 571 casualties of all ranks [3] more than 330 belonged to the unfortunate Royal Scots, whose right wing companies were almost exterminated. Six officers and 118 men, almost all wounded, fell into the hands of the enemy. It should be remembered to the credit of the garrison that, the moment that the storm was over, they collected from the foot of the breach and the neighbouring strand many officers and men who would otherwise have been drowned by the returning tide [4]. When it was seen that this was the task of the French who were seen busy on the beach, a flag of truce was hoisted, and all firing ceased for an hour. The prisoners, one of whom, the engineer Harry Jones, has left an interesting account of his experiences during the next six weeks [5], were very well treated. The extremely moderate loss of the garrison was 18 killed and 49 wounded—all by musketry fire, since by the abominable misarrangement of the assault the British artillery had no chance of acting.

Two comments by eye-witnesses on this woful business are worth giving. Colin Campbell wrote :

' One main cause of failure was the narrow front and consequent length and thinness of the column in which we advanced.

[1] Gomm, p. 312.
[2] Frazer's *Letters from the Peninsula*, p. 205.
[3] The 38th lost 53 men, the 9th 25, the Portuguese 138 in the side-attack. Why need Belmas, who had Jones's book before him, give the total of British losses as 2,000 ? (*Sièges*, iv. 625).
[4] Though Jones says that he saw some wounded bayoneted.
[5] Printed in Maxwell's *Peninsular Sketches*, vol. ii.

This necessarily became more loosened and disjointed by the difficult nature of the ground it had to pass over in the dark. It reached the breach in driblets and never in such body or number as to give the mind of the soldier anything like confidence in success. If some means had been devised of starting the Royals in one big honest lump, which might have been contrived without much difficulty or danger, so that they could have started in some dense form, with the 38th well packed up in a front of fours in readiness to start immediately behind after them, the stoppage at the demi-bastion would never have occurred, and some 200 men at least of the Royals would have reached the breach in a compact body. Such a number would have forced bodily through all opposition. Even under all the disadvantages of bad arrangements, I firmly believe that if we had moved forward by daylight, when an officer could have seen, and been seen by, his men, when the example of the former would have animated the exertions of the latter, the Royals would have gone over the breach on July 25th [1].

Campbell's blame, therefore, would fall mainly on Oswald, who, though he had protested against the points chosen for attack, had actually arranged the troops, and failed to remember that men should go 'over the top' on a broad front, and on Graham, who fixed the ' Zero ' point half an hour before dawn. Gomm, of the 1/9th, also a most distinguished and capable officer, goes for other game—the officers of the scientific services :

' I am afraid our success at Ciudad Rodrigo and Badajoz, owing to the almost miraculous efforts of the troops, has stopped the progress of science among our engineers, and perhaps done more ; for it seems to have inspired them with a contempt for so much of it as they had attained before. Our soldiers have on all occasions stood fire so well that our artillery have become as summary in their processes as our engineers. Provided that they have made a hole in the wall, by which we can claw up, they care not about destroying defences. In fact, we have been called upon hitherto to ensure the success of our sieges by the sacrifice of lives. Our Chief Engineers and Commandants of Artillery remind me of Burke's " Revolutionary Philosophers " and their " dispositions which make them indifferent to the

---

[1] Campbell's letter quoted above in his *Life*, i. p. 30.

cause of humanity ; they think no more of men than of mice in an air pump ". We came before the place well equipped with all the means necessary for attacking it *en règle,* and I saw no reason for attacking it otherwise. I may dwell longer than I ought to do on this subject. But it is, at least, pardonable in us, who are most nearly concerned, to become tedious in passing our censure upon the methods of those whom we cannot but consider as the authors of our calamity ; which, as it *was* foreseen by others, and *might* have been by them, could have been avoided.'

The narrative of the assault seems to show that both Campbell and Gomm had reason for their complaints, though they chose different points to criticize. But of the various errors made, undoubtedly the most fatal of all was attempting to storm breaches that could only be approached by a long defile along the flank of the hornwork, which was intact and well garrisoned. And for this the engineers have to take the responsibility. Camp rumour very cruelly put the blame on the troops[1], alleging that there had been a panic : this was a monstrous injustice. Everything that mismanagement could accomplish had been done to discourage them ; but it was not poor spirit, but physical incapacity to finish a task impossible under the conditions set, that caused them to retire.

Wellington had, on the 24th, received disquieting news about movements on the French front, and was very anxious to hear of the fall of St. Sebastian before he might be committed to another campaign in the field. He stopped at his head-quarters at Lesaca on the morning of the 25th, lest more definite and threatening information might come to hand. During the hours of dawn he was standing about in Lesaca churchyard listening to the guns, and speculating on the cause of their cessation at 6 o'clock, when the armistice to recover the wounded was made. At 11 came a messenger, Colonel de Burgh, to say that the assault had failed with loss. This was a severe and rather unexpected blow ; Wellington had counted on success as

---

[1] 'The men, panic stricken, turned and could never be rallied,' writes Frazer next day (p. 204). 'One party, I believe of the 9th and 38th, went up to the breach and then turned and ran away,' says Larpent (p. 200). Neither saw the actual assault in the dark.

probable [1]. Taking the chance of more news coming in from the Pyrenees during his absence, he rode over in haste to St. Sebastian and inspected the scene of the disaster. He declared that the siege must continue, that the Hornwork and the demi-bastion of San Juan must be battered to pieces, and that the engineers had better draw up an alternative scheme for an attack *en règle* on the land front. More guns and ammunition were expected from England ; the latter was much needed, for the reserve was low after the rapid firing on the 22nd–24th. There would probably be some delay before a second storm could be tried [2].

While riding back to Lesaca after his flying visit to the trenches, Wellington was met on the road by messengers of evil. The threats of the preceding day had turned into imminent dangers. Heavy firing had been heard since noon from the side of the Bastan, seeming to show that Hill's divisions at the Pass of Maya were being attacked. And just as he reached his head-quarters a messenger came up from Cole, at the extreme southern end of the line, to say that he had been assailed in the Pass of Roncesvalles by the enemy in overwhelming strength, and had been fighting hard since dawn—results were still uncertain [3].

Without further information it was, of course, impossible to take more than preliminary measures for parrying the French thrust. Wellington speculated on the situation : one of its meanings might be that the enemy was demonstrating at Roncesvalles and Maya, in order to cover a thrust on the side of the Bidassoa, with the object of raising the siege of St. Sebastian. He wrote at once to Graham that he must expect to be attacked in force, telling him to ship his siege-guns at Passages [4], to leave a minimum of troops to continue the blockade, and to concentrate for the defence of the line of the Bidassoa. It is clear that Wellington was thinking of the scandal caused by the loss

---

[1] So at least he wrote to Castaños on the 24th : 'j'espère que cette affaire est finie.' *Dispatches*, x. p. 564.

[2] See Frazer, p. 206, and Burgoyne, i. p. 269.

[3] See Wellington to Graham, night of the 25th, *Dispatches*, x. p. 566.

[4] Permission was given to leave four guns behind in the main breaching batteries and two on Monte Olia, to keep up a semblance of continued attack. *Dispatches*, x. p. 566.

Attack of S.^T SEBASTIAN

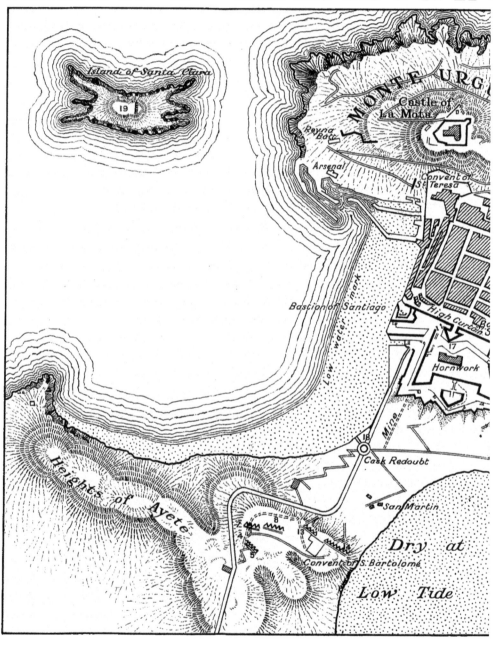

Island of Santa Clara

19

MONTE URGU

Castle of
La Mota

Reyna
Batt.

Arsenal

Convent of
St Teresa

Bastion of Santiago

High Curtain S.

17

Hornwork

Mine

18

Cask Redoubt

San Martin

Heights of Ayete

Convent of S. Bartolomé

Dry   at

Low Tide

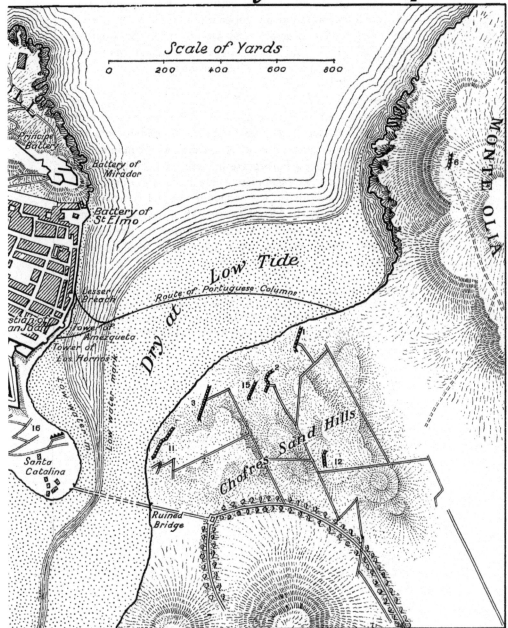

between 11ᵗʰ July & 9ᵗʰ Sept 1813

Scale of Yards

0   200   400   600   800

MONTE OLIA

Principe Battery

Battery of Mirador

Battery of St Elmo

Low Tide

Dry at

Route of Portuguese Columns

Lesser Breach

stian of anJoan

Tower of Amezqueta

Tower of Los Hornos

Low water mark

Chofres Sand Hills

16

Santa Catalina

Ruined Bridge

of Murray's guns at Tarragona, and was determined that his own siege train should be afloat betimes. After the guns were safe other stores were put on shipboard.

So ended the first siege of St. Sebastian—a depressing failure not creditable to any one engaged in it. As if the tale of disaster was not complete, a disgraceful incident happened on the night of the 26th–27th. Rey had noted the disarmament of the batteries proceeding all day, and the departure of troops ; he resolved to try a sortie at night, to see if the besiegers were all absconding. Before dawn five companies emerging from the Hornwork swept along the parallel, guarded at the moment by detachments of Spry's Portuguese brigade. Such a bad watch was kept that they were completely surprised, three officers and 198 men were captured : the remainder of the trench-guard fled back to the suburb of San Martin. When the reserves came up and made for the parallel, it was found that the French had retired with their prisoners, after doing some inconsiderable damage to the works [1].

---

[1] The British officer in command in the trenches, Major O'Halloran, was court martialled, but acquitted. It was proved that he had given the correct orders to the Portuguese captains of the companies on guard, who had not obeyed them. All the prisoners except 30 were Portuguese.

SECTION XXXVIII: CHAPTER II

SOULT TAKES THE OFFENSIVE IN NAVARRE

The Duke of Dalmatia had arrived at Bayonne on the afternoon of July 11th : on the morning of the following day he had
taken over from the hands of King Joseph the command of the
armies of Spain, after a short and formal interview, at which
each said little and thought much. When the King had
departed to his enforced retirement, the Marshal called together
the senior officers of all the four armies, and informed them that
by the Emperor's orders he had to carry out a general reorganization, which would affect the positions of many of them. There
would for the future be one Army of Spain—the separate staffs
would disappear : so would many divisional commands,
administrative offices, and departmental posts. He had been
entrusted by the Emperor with full authority to carry out the
changes on his own responsibility.

This was a great moment for Soult : he had at last achieved
his ambition, and received that full power over all the armies of
Spain which he had coveted since 1808, and had never attained,
either while the Emperor pretended to direct in person the war
in the Peninsula, or while King Joseph held the nominal post of
commander-in-chief. It is true that the long-desired position
came to him in consequence of a terrible disaster to the imperial
arms, but there were compensating advantages even in this :
the disaster, as he conceived, had been due to his old enemies—
at any rate it could be ascribed to them with all plausibility.
And he was thus provided with an admirable opportunity to
repay old grudges, of which he took full advantage in the famous
proclamation issued to the army before the commencement of
his new campaign : it is a series of elaborate insults to his
predecessors, as a short quotation may show.

'Soldiers ! with well-equipped fortresses in front and in
rear, a capable general possessing the confidence of his troops
could by the choice of good positions have faced and defeated

the motley levies opposed to you.   Unhappily at the critical
moment timid and downhearted counsels prevailed.   The
fortresses were abandoned or blown up : a hasty and disorderly
retreat gave confidence to the enemy ; and a veteran army,
weak in numbers (it is true) but great in everything that consti-
tutes military character, that army which had fought, bled, and
conquered in every province of Spain, saw with indignation its
laurels blighted, and was forced to abandon its conquests, the
trophies of many sanguinary days of battle.   When at last the
cries of an indignant army stopped the dishonourable flight,
and its chief, touched by a feeling of shame, and yielding to the
general desire, gave battle in front of Vittoria, who can doubt
that a general worthy of his troops could have won the success
merited by their generous enthusiasm, and their splendid sense
of honour ?   Did he make the arrangements and direct the
movements which should have assured to one part of his army
the help and support of the rest ? . . . Soldiers ! I sympathize
with your disappointment, your grievances, your indignation.
I know that the blame for the present situation must be
imputed to others.   It is your task to repair the disaster[1].'

This may have been good ' propaganda ' for the army—it
served to soothe their wounded pride by throwing all blame on
their late commanders.   But there can be no doubt that it was
inspired not so much by this very comprehensible motive as by
long-cherished malice and hatred for the unfortunate Joseph
and Jourdan.   This was quite in keeping with Soult's character.
He was a most distinguished soldier, but a most unamiable
man ; and his memory was as long as his spite was strong.

We have already had much to write on this cold calculating
son of a provincial lawyer—one of the few ' best military
brains,' as his master called him, but also, as King Joseph truly

---

[1] The history of this proclamation is curious. Clarke, or Napoleon
himself, considered it too full of insults of a person who was, after all, the
Emperor's brother. So it had to be disavowed : Soult wrote to Paris that
he had not authorized it, and Clarke had the ingenuity to print in the
French newspapers that it was an invention of the English government,
intended to disgust the Spanish partisans of King Joseph, and to advertise
the ill feeling that prevailed between the French army and the Imperial
family. See Vidal de la Blache, i. p. 138 : as he remarks, the style is all
Soult's, and there is not a trace of foreign diction in it. No Englishman
or Spaniard could have written it.

observed, ' untrustworthy, perverse, dangerous [1].' He served
the Emperor well as long as their interests coincided, but he was
quite ready for any other profitable service. Some thirteen
months later, as the war minister of Louis XVIII, he showed himself a zealous persecutor of Bonapartists [2]. Soult was the most
monstrous of egotists ; at this moment his ambition served his
master well : no general save William III ever won so much
credit from a series of defeats as did Soult in 1813–14 from the
operations that began with the disaster of Sorauren and ended
with the loss of Toulouse. But on the receipt of the news of the
abdication at Fontainebleau he became a zealous Royalist :
eighteen months later he was, as the minister of the Bourbons,
issuing flamboyant proclamations against ' the usurper and
adventurer, Napoleon Bonaparte [3].' Yet in the Hundred Days
he was to be found as the ' usurper's ' Chief of the Staff on the
field of Waterloo ! Proscribed for a short time on account of
this unhappy error in calculation, he was so far back in favour
with the ' powers that were ' as to receive a gift of 200,000 francs
from Louis XVIII in 1820, and the grand cordon of St. Louis from
Charles X in 1825, on the occasion of his coronation at Reims.

But as long as Napoleon I was emperor, Nicholas Soult was
his most valuable lieutenant : their interests coincided, and it
is certain that none of the other marshals would have played
such a creditable losing game on the Pyrenees and the plains of
Southern France against such an adversary as Wellington.

The Army of Spain received the news of his advent with
mixed feelings. There was a considerable faction among his own
old generals of Andalusia, who welcomed back one who had
been an indulgent spectator of their peculations—of which he
himself had set the example. For Soult's acquisitiveness was
portentous—he was ready to snatch at everything from
a shadowy Portuguese crown in Oporto to inferior Murillos in
the convents of Seville. The train of his personal plunder had
excited anger, envy, or derision, according to the temper of the
observer, as it defiled through Madrid, when he quitted Spain
five months back. He had left behind him many adherents,

---

[1] Joseph to Napoleon, 1st February 1813.
[2] See notably the case of General Excelmans.
[3] See especially the proclamation of March 6, 1815.

who followed him for the same motive for which he himself
followed Napoleon. They rejoiced at his return, believing, not
in error, that his patronage would be exercised in favour of old
comrades of the Army of the South, rather than for the benefit
of strangers. Others held that he was to be welcomed because
any leadership would be better than that of King Joseph, and
because his undoubted military talents would be exercised in
the best style when he was working for his own credit, and not
for that of any one else. Like the Emperor, they had a great
belief in his brains. It was difficult to feel much personal
enthusiasm for a chief so self-centred, so cold and hard in his
dealings with subordinates, so ready to shift blame on to other
men's shoulders, so greedy in getting and so mean in spending.
But at any rate he would not be weak like Jourdan, or rash like
Marmont, or simply incapable like Dorsenne or Caffarelli.
A general who served as his senior aide-de-camp for eight
uncomfortable years, and left his staff with glee, sums him up
in the following cruel phrases :

'In war he loved vigorous enterprises, and when once committed
to a scheme stuck to it with obstinacy and force. If I say that
he loved vigorous enterprises I must add that he loved them
provided that they did not involve too much personal danger,
for he was far from possessing the brilliant courage of Ney or
Lannes. It might even be said that he was the very reverse of
rash—that he was a little too careful of himself. This failing
grew upon him after his great fortune had come to him—and
indeed it was not uncommon to meet officers who showed no care
of their lives when they were mere colonels or brigadiers, but
who in later years took cover behind their marshal's bâton.
But this caution visible on the battlefield did not follow him to
the tent, under whose roof he conceived and ordered, often in
the presence of the enemy, movements of great audacity—
whose execution he handed over to officers of known courage
and resolution [1].' Another contemporary makes remarks to
much the same effect, 'Proud of the reputation which he had
usurped, he was full of assurance on the day before a battle :
he recovered that same assurance the day after a defeat. But
in action he seemed unable to issue good orders, to choose good

[1] *Mémoires* of St. Chamans, p. 35.

positions, or to move his troops freely. It seemed as if any
scheme which he had once conceived and written down at his
desk was an immutable decree from heaven, which he had not
the power to vary by subsequent changes [1].'

This is much what Wellington meant when he observed in
familiar conversation that Soult was not equal to Masséna.
' He did not quite understand a field of battle : he knew very
well how to bring his troops on to the field, but not so well how
to use them when he had brought them up [2].'

But on July 12th Soult, with his great opportunity before
him, was in his audacious mood, and it was in all sincerity that
he had written to the Emperor before he assumed his command,
that he would concentrate the army, and retake the offensive
within a very few days, and that he trusted to be able to stop
the movements of Wellington. This was no small promise
considering the state in which the army was handed over to him,
and it is a marvellous proof of his driving power that he actually
succeeded in launching a most dangerous attack on Wellington's
line by the thirteenth day after his arrival at Bayonne.

The detailed orders for the reorganization of the army were
published on July 15th. Soult had started with a general idea
of the lines on which they were to be carried out, and had just
received a more definite scheme from the Emperor, sent off
from Dresden on July 5th in pursuit of him. Napoleon ordered
that not only were the armies of the North, South, Centre, and
Portugal to be abolished—their names were now absurd
anachronisms—but, despite of the great number of troops
available, no army corps were to be created. Evidently he had
come to the conclusion that not only army-commanders, but
even army-corps-commanders might be strong enough to impair
the complete control which he wished to give over to Soult.
He directed that the infantry should be divided into as many
divisions of two brigades and 6,000 men each as the available
total of bayonets could complete. The Marshal was authorized
to work them as he pleased, in groups of two, three, or four
divisions. To command these groups (which were really army-
corps in all but name) he might appoint three officers with the

[1] Maximilien Lamarque, ii. p. 182.
[2] Stanhope's *Conversations with Wellington*, p. 20.

title of lieutenant-general, who would have the divisional
generals under their orders. There were to be no special staffs
for the groups, whose composition the Marshal might alter from
time to time : the lieutenant-generals were only to be allowed
a chief staff-officer and their own personal aides-de-camp, and
their pay was to be no more than 40,000 francs per annum.
Clearly there was to be no recrudescence of the enormous staffs
and liberal perquisites and allowances of the old corps-
commanders.

Artillery might still be short, despite of the large number of
guns sent up to the front from Toulouse and Bordeaux. But
the Emperor directed that each infantry division ought to have
two field batteries, each cavalry division one horse artillery
battery, and that Soult ought to create an army-reserve of two
horse artillery batteries and several batteries of guns of position.
There was to be one general commanding artillery and one
general commanding engineers for the whole army, and (what
was quite as important) one commissary general only, in whose
hands all responsibilities for food and transport were to be
centralized.

In a general way, but not in all details, Soult carried out
these orders. The gross total of the troops under his command
would appear to have been 117,789 of all ranks. But this
included the garrisons of St. Sebastian, Pampeluna, and
Santona, 8,200 men in all : also 5,595 half-trained conscripts
of the Bayonne Reserve, 16,184 sick and detached, and over
4,500 men of the non-combatant services—*ouvriers militaires,*
transport train, ambulance train, &c. Deducting these, he had
available 84,311 fighting men, of whom 72,664 were infantry,
7,147 cavalry, and about 4,000 artillery, sappers and miners,
gendarmerie[1], &c. This total does not include Paris' troops
from Saragossa, who were lying at Jaca, and had not yet joined
the Army of Spain, being still credited to Suchet's Army of
Aragon and Valencia.

Soult created out of these elements nine fighting divisions of
infantry, two of cavalry, and a strong but miscellaneous Reserve

[1] The gendarmerie were those who had come from the ' legions ',
employed in 1811–12–13 as garrisons in Northern Spain. They were
embodied in units, horse and foot, and used as combatants (as at the
combat of Venta del Pozo, for which see p. 71).

Corps, which had the equivalent of five brigades. The plan
which he adopted for the reorganization was to select nine of the
old infantry divisions (of which there had been 14½) and to
keep them as the bases of the new units, drafting into them the
battalions of the other five[1]. Those abolished were the two divisions
(Abbé's and Vandermaesen's) of the Army of the North, Sarrut's
division of the Army of Portugal, Leval's of the Army of the
South, and Darmagnac's of the Army of the Centre. Sarrut
had been killed at Vittoria, Leval had gone to Germany ; but
provision was made for the other three generals whose divisions
were ' scrapped ' : Abbé took over Villatte's old division of the
Army of the South, while Villatte went to command the general
reserve. Vandermaesen was given the division of the Army
of Portugal lately under Barbot, who relapsed into the status of
a brigadier. Darmagnac went with the two French regiments of
his old division to join the surviving unit of the Army of the
Centre, Cassagne's division, and took command of it—Cassagne,
its former chief, disappearing. Lastly, Daricau having been
severely wounded at Vittoria, his division was given to Maransin, whose independent brigade was absorbed. Thus, of the
old divisions, only those of Foy, Conroux, Maucune, Taupin,
Lamartinière, remained under their original leaders : the other
four surviving divisions got new chiefs, whose names are
familiar to us, but who had hitherto been connected with quite
different troops.

Napoleon's ideal of the ' standard ' division of 6,000 men
was not accurately realized, owing to the fact that some corps
had suffered heavily and others hardly at all during the recent
campaign. Putting six regiments into each division, Soult
found that he had created units varying in size from Abbé's
with 8,030 men to Vandermaesen's, with only 4,181. For there
was no uniformity of size among the regiments, which varied

---

[1] As Table XVI in the Appendix shows, Foy's division received two of
Sarrut's regiments : Cassagne's (now Darmagnac's) took all the French
infantry of the old Army of the Centre : Villatte's (now Abbé's) was given
two of Abbé's regiments of the Army of the North : Conroux's division
absorbed Maransin's independent brigade : Barbot's (now Vandermaesen's)
received two regiments of the Army of the North : Daricau's (now
Maransin's) got half Leval's ' scrapped ' division, Taupin the other half
of it : Maucune absorbed one of Vandermaesen's old regiments, Lamartinière one of Sarrut's.

from 1,900 bayonets in three battalions [1] down to 430 in one [2]. Abbé's, Lamartinière's, Conroux's, and Darmagnac's divisions had 7,000 men each, or more ; Foy's, Taupin's, and Maransin's just about 6,000 ; Vandermaesen's and Maucune's not much over 4,000 each. It was still impossible to carry out Napoleon's orders to give each division two batteries of field artillery, only one apiece could be provided ; but, this moderate provision having been made, there remained over for the general artillery reserve two batteries of horse and two of field artillery. The army had in all 140 guns horsed—72 with the infantry divisions, 32 with Villatte's reserve, 12 with the cavalry divisions, 24 as general army reserve. There were also three mountain batteries—two- or three-pounders carried on muleback.

For his chief of the staff Soult chose Gazan, who had long served with him in the same capacity in Andalusia. The late generals-in-chief of the Armies of Portugal, the North and the Centre—Reille, Clausel, and Drouet D'Erlon, naturally took the three lieutenant-generalcies : Soult gave each of them three divisions in charge, but being prohibited from calling these groups ' army corps ', he styled them the ' lieutenancies ' of the Right, Left, and Centre. These terms soon became anomalous—for by the chances of manœuvre the ' Centre '—D'Erlon's group—during the campaign of the Pyrenees fought on the right, the ' left ' (Clausel) in the Centre, and the ' right ' (Reille) on the left wing. The absurd nomenclature of the groups sometimes makes a French dispatch hard to understand : it would have been much simpler to call the three groups army-corps, but this designation was under taboo by the Emperor's special command.

Clausel took the left lieutenancy, because he and his troops, which he had brought back from his long march in Aragon, were actually on the left on June 15th : he had under him the two divisions, those of Vandermaesen and Taupin, which practically represented the bulk of his former column, with Conroux's division which had remained at St. Jean-Pied-du-Port when the rest of the Army of the South went to the Bidassoa. The total of bayonets was 17,218—this was the weakest of the ' lieutenancies ' because the individual regiments recently returned

---

[1] 120th Line of Lamartinière.

[2] 2nd Léger of same, which suffered heavily at Vittoria while under Sarrut.

from Aragon were low in numbers from three months of mountain warfare against Mina.

D'Erlon had the Centre, with the divisions of Abbé and Maransin, both consisting of old Andalusian regiments, and of Darmagnac, who represented the French part of the Army of the Centre. His corps were strong—just under 21,000 bayonets[1].

Reille, late chief of the Army of Portugal, had the remaining three divisions, Foy, Maucune, and Lamartinière, all of them coming from his own old command, and under officers who had long served in that army. Their total strength was 17,235—many of the regiments were low in numbers from the recent fighting in Biscay.

Each of the three ' lieutenancies ' had a light cavalry regiment attached to it—we should have called them corps-cavalry had the name been permitted. They were weak—only 808 sabres between the three—but sufficient for scouting purposes.

Adding the two cavalry divisions of Pierre Soult (the Marshal's very undistinguished but much cherished brother) and Treillard, the Army of Spain had 7,147 sabres, including the remnants of the foreign cavalry—Nassau Chasseurs, Spanish light horse, and Royal Guards, who were something under 1,000 all told.

The very large body of troops under Villatte which Soult had left outside his nine marching divisions, and his three ' lieutenancies ', consisted of a great number of battalions of the recently abolished armies, which were left as a surplus, when the new formations had been brought up to the six-regiment standard. They included of French troops one odd battalion of the Army of Portugal, eleven of the Army of the North, and six of the old Bayonne Reserve. The eighteen battalions were mostly rather weak, and mustered only a little over 9,000 bayonets between them.

In addition Villatte's reserve included all the foreign troops—Neuenstein's *Rheinbund* Germans, who had served so long in the Army of the Centre, St. Pol's Italian brigade, the King's Foot-Guards—a solid body of 2,000 infantry, all Frenchmen, though in Spanish uniform—and the forlorn remnant of the *Afrancesados*—three dwindling regiments under Casapalacios, which had shrunk from 2,000 to 1,100 bayonets during the last month.

---

[1] 20,957 to be exact.

Adding a battalion of foot-gendarmes from the evacuated Biscay garrisons, and another of local National guards, Villatte had over 17,000 infantry—a force as big as Reille's or Clausel's lieutenancies. There was some weak stuff among them [1], but the greater part were experienced troops in nowise inferior to the units of the marching divisions. It is hard to see why Soult did not make up a tenth division out of the best of them : this would still have left Villatte 12,000 men, and would have been very useful in the fighting army. But apparently, as will be seen during the narrative of the campaign of July–August, he intended to use the Reserve in an active fashion, and was foiled by the caution or timidity of Villatte, who discharged the orders given him in a very half-hearted way. This mass of troops was really quite capable of being used as a fighting unit—it had its four batteries of field artillery, the foreign cavalry were allotted to it, and a proportion of sappers and engineers. Even after leaving a detachment—say the *Afrancesados* and one or two of the weakest French battalions—to aid the conscripts to garrison Bayonne, it could have taken the field with 15,000 men of all arms [2].

To assume the offensive with a recently beaten army is dangerous. Many of the regiments which Soult had to use had only a month before recrossed the Pyrenees in a state of complete disorder : they had been entirely out of hand, and had been guilty of outrages among the French peasantry which recalled their worst doings in Spain. The greater number of the senior officers had applied for service in the Army of Germany the moment that they had crossed the frontier : it was refused to nearly all of them. The junior officers would have made similar applications, if they had thought that it would be of any use. Every one of every rank was cursing King Joseph, luck,

---

[1] Not only the *Afrancesados* but some of the Army of the North troops withdrawn from the Biscay garrisons had a poor record, and had disgusted Foy in his recent Tolosa fight. These were high-numbered battalions, recently made up from the Bayonne conscript reserve.

[2] The best proof of the efficiency of the bulk of Villatte's corps is that when Vandermaesen's and Maucune's divisions were cut to pieces in the battles of the Pyrenees, Soult made up a new brigade for each of them out of the Reserve. Joseph's French Guards fought splendidly at San Marcial. The Germans were very steady veteran troops.

the weather, the supply services, the War Ministry at Paris, and his own immediate hierarchical superior : a *sentiment d'ineptie générale* prevailed [1].   A great deal of this demoralization was mere nervous exhaustion, resulting from long marches and semi-starvation extending over many weeks.   After a fortnight of comparative rest and more or less regular rations it commenced to subside.   The whole army consisted of veteran troops proud of their regimental honour and their past victories : they soon persuaded themselves that they had never been given a fair chance in the recent campaign—Soult's clever and malicious proclamation exactly hit off their state of mind.   It was easy to lay all the blame on bad generalship, and to plead that a good half of the troops had not fought at Vittoria : in full force and under a competent leader they would have made mincemeat of the ' motley levies ' of Wellington.   When the whole host was reassembled, after Clausel's arrival, every one could see that the numerical loss in the late disaster had been very moderate : there were more French troops assembled on the Bidassoa than any member of any of the armies had ever seen concentrated before.   Shame and anger replaced dejection in their minds : even the marauders and deserters came back to the Eagles by thousands.   Soult wrote to the Minister of War that the disquieting state of indiscipline which he had discovered on his arrival was subsiding, that marauding had ceased with the distribution of regular rations, and that the morale of the army was satisfactory.

The weakest part of the reorganization was, of course, the transport.   The army had lost all its wheeled vehicles and many of its animals in the disaster of Vittoria : they had not been replaced in any adequate fashion during the four short weeks that followed.   By extraordinary efforts the Commissariat had found food for every one, so long as the main body of the army was encamped between Bayonne and the Bidassoa.   But it would be impossible to start it properly equipped for a long mountain campaign far from its base.   Soult took the desperate risk of starting on July 23 with only four days' rations in hand with the marching columns : all that would be wanted later was to come up by successive convoys sent out from the neigh-

[1] Vidal de la Blache, i. p. 160.

bourhood of Bayonne. And it was little better with munitions
for infantry and artillery alike. The campaign became a time-
problem : unless a decisive success were achieved within the
first four or five days, there was grave danger of the army being
brought to a stop. It would be helpless if it should have used
up all its cartridges in several days of continuous and severe,
but indecisive, fighting : or if bad weather should prevent the
regular appearance of convoys from the rear. This Soult knew,
but thought that his arrangements were calculated to secure
that quick and decisive victory which would justify all taking
of risks.

The plan of campaign which the Marshal chose was one of
the three alternative schemes which the unlucky Jourdan had
formulated during his last days at the front[1]. It will be
remembered that they were (1) to endeavour to raise the siege
of St. Sebastian by massing every available man on the
Bidassoa, and striking at Giron and Graham—who was wrongly
supposed to have only one British division with him. After
driving back Graham as far as Tolosa on the high road, it would
be possible to turn southward and relieve Pampeluna : Clausel's
corps, meanwhile, should demonstrate in Navarre, to distract
Wellington from sending his reserves from the south to the
main point of danger. Both Jourdan on July 5 and Soult on
July 23rd believed, the former correctly, the latter wrongly,
that there were three British divisions engaged in the blockade
of Pampeluna.

(2) To leave a corps of observation on the Bidassoa to contain
Graham, while the rest of the army struck at Pampeluna by the
route of Roncesvalles. This would have the advantage of
raising the siege of that place at once, though the relief of
St. Sebastian would be deferred. But, Jourdan added, it had
three disadvantages—the road was bad and might conceivably
prove impracticable for artillery : the bulk of the British
divisions would probably be found concentrated for a fight to
cover the blockade : and Navarre was a country in which no
army could scrape together food enough to live upon.

---

[1] See above, p. 533. Jourdan to Joseph, July 5. The memorandum
had been made over to Soult. Cf. Clerc, *Campagne du Maréchal Soult,*
p. 46, and Vidal de la Blache, i. p. 182.

(3) To leave a corps of observation on the Bidassoa, and convey the rest of the army into Aragon, by the pass of Jaca, to join Suchet and operate with overwhelming forces on the Ebro against Wellington's flank and rear. This, the operation which Jourdan regarded as the best of the three, had since become impossible, because Paris had abandoned Saragossa, and Suchet had taken his army to Catalonia : on July 17 he was at Tarragona.

Soult's plan was in essence Jourdan's second alternative ; but he complicated it by dividing the army which was to strike at Pampeluna into two columns. Two-thirds of the whole (Reille and Clausel) was to march by the Roncesvalles passes ; D'Erlon with the remainder was to force the pass of Maya and to converge on Pampeluna by the Bastan and the Col de Velate. Jourdan's memorandum contained a special caution against the dissemination of columns, ' je pense que toute opération de plusieurs corps isolés ne réussira pas.' How frequently in military history two columns starting from distant bases have failed to meet on the appointed day is known to every student. It is seldom that a complete success is secured—as at Königgrätz. Much more frequently the enemy against whom the concentration was planned has beaten one corps before the other—delayed by one of the uncountable chances of war—has come upon the scene. And this was to be the case with Soult before Pampeluna.

The advantages of Soult's scheme were very comprehensible. The greatest was that, owing to the existence of a first-class road from Bayonne to St. Jean-Pied-du-Port, he could concentrate the main body of his army upon his extreme left wing long before Wellington could make the corresponding counter-move. In the early days of the operation he could calculate on having an immense superiority of force on the Roncesvalles front. It was more doubtful what would happen on the third or fourth day, if Wellington divined his enemy's plan at the first moment, and ordered a general concentration before Pampeluna, as Jourdan had taken for granted that he would. But Soult considered that he had found means to make such a concentration impossible, by sending D'Erlon and his 20,000 men to pierce the allied left-centre at Maya, and to sweep down the

Bastan. If D'Erlon broke in on the first day, and got possession of the positions that dominate the road-system of the Bastan—Elisondo and the Col de Velate—the northern divisions of Wellington's army would only be able to join the southern divisions in front of Pampeluna by immense détours to the west—by Santesteban and the Pass of Donna Maria, or even by Tolosa and Yrurzun. In all human probability they would arrive too late.

The British commander, as we shall see, did not divine Soult's whole purpose at the first moment, and therefore his general concentration was ordered a day later than it might have been. And the officers who were in charge of his extreme right at Roncesvalles gave way quicker than he had intended. The campaign became a most interesting time problem, which was settled in favour of Wellington in the end, by the fact that his first-arriving northern reserves got to the positions in front of Pampeluna a day before Soult's secondary column under D'Erlon came into touch with the French main body. The subordinate officers on both sides made some extraordinary mistakes, which compromised the plans of their superiors : the worst of them were in the line of slow and irregular transmission of news, which in a mountain country, where all side communications were difficult, and no general view of the situation could be taken by the commander's own eye, sometimes led to ruinous miscalculations at head-quarters. It cannot be said that one side suffered more than the other from this negligence of subordinates.

To proceed to the details. Soult's left wing at St. Jean-Pied-du-Port was ready to start, Conroux and Clausel's old divisions having been cantoned in the neighbourhood of that fortress ever since they arrived in France ; they were only one long march from their objective, the gap of Roncesvalles. At the other end of the line, D'Erlon's three divisions were also within one long march of the Pass of Maya—they already lay with their vanguard at Urdax and their last rear brigade at Espelette. The difficulty lay with the third 'lieutenancy' ; Reille's three divisions of the old Army of Portugal on July 20th were on the lower Bidassoa, holding the front opposite Graham and Giron ; they had to be got to St. Jean-Pied-

du-Port, to join Clausel and co-operate in the main attack [1].
To draw them out of their existing positions without arousing
too much attention at Wellington's head-quarters was comparatively easy. On the night of the 19th–20th four brigades
of Villatte's reserve replaced Reille's troops at the outposts.
On the following day the three fighting divisions concentrated
at St. Jean de Luz and started to march eastward, with orders
to cross the Nive at Cambo, and to get into the great *chaussée*
by Urcaray and Hellette, which leads to St. Jean-Pied-du-Port.
Drawing up a far too optimistic time-chart, Soult had hoped
that they would all be in the neighbourhood of St. Jean-Pied-
du-Port by the morning of the 22nd. As the distance was not
less than 50 miles, this would have been very hard work in any
case, for a long column marching with a large train of artillery,
as Reille was bringing up beside his own pieces three batteries
for Clausel, who had arrived gunless from Aragon. But the
main cause of delay was quite different : though the Bayonne–
St. Jean-Pied-du-Port *chaussée* was excellent, the local cross-road
from St. Jean de Luz by St. Pée to the bridge of Cambo was not,
and torrential rains on the 20th made it into a quagmire [2]. The
troops got on very slowly, and at night the bridge at Cambo
was carried away by a spate, leaving the bulk of Lamartinière's
division on the wrong side of the water. It was repaired ; but
the general result was that the head of Reille's column only
neared its destination late at night on the 22nd, while the rear
division and the guns did not get up till the 24th. The Marshal
had been waiting for them since the morning of the 21st, and
had hoped to start operations on the 23rd. He had been joined
by his two cavalry divisions, brought up from their cantonments
between the Nive and the Adour on that day, so that Reille's
delays put the movement of all the other corps a day late.

On the 24th Soult was able to commence moving up both

---

[1] One asks oneself why Soult did not give Reille the Maya attack,
saving him two-thirds of his journey, and send D'Erlon to join Clausel at
St. Jean-Pied-du-Port, by a march much shorter than Reille was asked
to make.

[2] It is said that persons acquainted with the country told Soult to send
the whole column round by Bayonne, on account of the artillery, but that
he refused. As a matter of fact, Lamartinière's division and some of the
guns *did* go that détour, owing to the broken bridge.

Clausel's and Reille's columns toward the Roncesvalles gap, so
that they should be able to attack it on the 25th at an early
hour. D'Erlon, being already in position in front of Maya, was
only waiting for the signal to march. Villatte had been given
orders which left a good deal to his private judgement, to the
effect that he must simulate an offensive attitude on the
Bidassoa front, but make no real attack till he knew that
D'Erlon had got well forward in the Bastan and that Graham's
flank was threatened. He might then push the latter with
confidence, as the allied troops on the coast would have to give
way, and to raise the siege of St. Sebastian, if their centre in
the Bastan had been broken and driven westward.

It is interesting to find in a dispatch which Soult sent to
Paris on the 23rd his estimate of the position of Wellington's
line of defence. He starts fairly well—Graham with the
1st Division is on the heights beyond the Bidassoa : Oswald
with the 5th Division and a Spanish (it should be a Portuguese)
corps besieges St. Sebastian. The 7th Division under Lord
Dalhousie holds the front Vera–Echalar. Then comes a curious
blunder—the 6th Division under General Hay is on the (French)
left of the 7th Division. Really it was in reserve at Santesteban,
and under Pack ; Clinton, who had only taken over command
after long sick leave on June 22nd, having again fallen ill.
General Hill, with the 2nd Division under W. Stewart, and
Hamilton's Portuguese (Silveira had superseded Hamilton
many months back) is in the Bastan, and holds ' with camps
and batteries ' the passes of Maya and Ispegui. We are assured
that the 3rd and 4th Divisions and a Spanish corps are besieging
Pampeluna. ' There seems to be another division (probably the
8th Division) under a General Bird in position at Altobiscar,
above Roncesvalles. There is an English (Portuguese) brigade
under General Campbell in the Alduides. The Spaniards of the
Army of Galicia guard the Bidassoa from Vera to the sea.'

It will be noted that this reconstruction of Wellington's line
makes the covering force in front of Pampeluna too weak, for
it is believed to consist of ' Bird's ' division (a mistake for Byng's
brigade ?) and the force of Campbell in the Val de Alduides only.
Really the Conde de Abispal's Andalusians had relieved the
3rd and 4th Divisions on July 16–17, and they were free, and

disposable as a reserve to the troops on the Roncesvalles front—Picton being at Olague in the valley of the Lanz, Cole at Viscarret on the Pampeluna–Roncesvalles road : Pack and the 6th Division at Santesteban were only a little farther away. Moreover, Morillo's Spaniards were up in line with Byng. The Light Division makes no appearance in Soult's table, unless he means the 8th Division under ' General Bird ' to represent it.

There is therefore a grave miscalculation when Soult ends by informing Clarke that, after examining the whole Allied line, he has come to the conclusion that the right wing is the weak point, and the one that should be attacked, by a flank movement which he will continue till he has turned its rear. If Wellington's plans had worked out well, there would have happened what Jourdan had foreseen, viz. so vigorous a resistance in the passes by the British outlying troops, that Soult would only have arrived in front of Pampeluna to find the main bulk of Wellington's army offering him battle in front of the besieged city. But, as we shall see, Cole and Picton received Wellington's orders just too late to allow them to carry out the policy which he dictated.

Such were Soult's views of Wellington's situation. It remains to be seen what Wellington made of Soult's intentions. He was from the first conscious that the Marshal's appearance might mean a prompt resumption of the offensive by the enemy[1]. And the movements of the French were reported to him with very fair accuracy and dispatch. As early as the 22nd he was aware that the enemy was weakening his front on the Bidassoa, and that troops were accumulating at St. Jean-Pied-du-Port [2]. On the 24th he knew that the force moved in that direction must be the larger half of the French army. But his judgement on the meaning of this movement was entirely coloured by the fact that he had breached St. Sebastian, and that he believed, like Graham, that it would be stormed successfully on the 24th or 25th. He also knew that Soult was being informed, day by day, of the state of the fortress. On the other hand, he was aware that Pampeluna was quite safe—it had food enough to last for several weeks at least, and he was not pressing it hard,

---

[1] Wellington to Graham, July 22. *Dispatches*, x. p. 559.
[2] Ibid., p. 563, same to same.

as he was pressing St. Sebastian. From this he deduced the conclusion that Soult could not in honour suffer St. Sebastian to be taken almost under his eyes, as it would be unless he intervened. Therefore the moving of troops—even large numbers of troops—towards St. Jean-Pied-du-Port, must be a feint, because the Marshal's obvious duty was to save St. Sebastian—while Pampeluna was in no danger. He read the French manœuvres as an attempt to distract his attention from the Bidassoa. And his idea that a desperate attempt would be made to relieve St. Sebastian seemed to be borne out by the fact that Villatte was making flying bridges at Urogne, and that French boats were running in to the mouth of the Bidassoa from St. Jean de Luz. Still, if reports were correct, the enemy was likely to make a very serious demonstration on the Roncesvalles front. Wellington therefore wrote to Cole on the 23rd that he was not to allow himself to be pushed in too easily towards Pampeluna. ' You should support Major-General Byng in the defence of the passes as effectually as you can, without committing his troops and the 4th Division against a force so superior that the advantage of the ground would not compensate it. You will be good enough to make arrangements further back also, for stopping the enemy's progress toward Pampeluna, in the event of your being compelled to give up the passes which General Byng now occupies. . . . A sure communication should exist with General Sir Thomas Picton, and Sir Thomas should be apprised of any movement of troops, either upon the Roncesvalles road, or upon that of Eugui and the Alduides, in order that he may make such arrangements as circumstances may dictate for giving support, should such an event occur. . . . It is desirable that you should transmit a daily report for the present to Head Quarters [1].'

This was followed up by even more stringent orders on the following day. George Murray wrote to Cole, ' Lord Wellington has desired that I should express still more strongly how essential he considers it that the passes in front of Roncesvalles should be maintained to the utmost. And I am to direct you to be so good as to make every necessary arrangement for repelling effectually any direct attack that the enemy may

---

[1] *Supplementary Dispatches*, viii. p. 113.

make in that quarter. . . . Lord Wellington attaches very little importance to any wider turning movement which the enemy might make upon our right. The difficulties and delays of any wider movement are considerable obstacles, and would retard him sufficiently to give time to make other arrangements to stop his progress [1].'

It would be most inaccurate to say that Wellington was surprised by Soult's offensive at the southern end of his line, as these orders sufficiently demonstrate. At the same time he remained till late on the night of the 25th firmly convinced that the French move in Navarre was a feint or subsidiary operation, and that the real attack would be on the Bidassoa. On the 24th, knowing of the accumulation of hostile troops before Roncesvalles, he wrote to Graham that undoubtedly the enemy is very strong on that side, ' but only because he entertains serious designs to draw away our attention from the side of Irun, and then to attempt to pass the river [2].' And on the same morning he wrote to Giron that 'the enemy's main force has moved towards St. Jean-Pied-du-Port ; but his two pontoon bridges remain at Urogne. It would seem that he intends to distract our attention to the other side, and then to make a try at the river. But as (at 11 a.m.) I no longer hear the guns at St. Sebastian, I am hoping that its business has been settled [3].' It will be remembered that the projected storm on the 24th had been postponed because of the conflagration, so that the cessation of the firing had not the happy meaning that Wellington attributed to it.

On the morning of the 25th, when the unsuccessful attempt on St. Sebastian was actually made, Wellington was up at early dawn, listening once more to the guns, as he strode up and down in the churchyard of Lesaca. Again they stopped, after two hours of furious fire, just as on the preceding day ; and again Wellington hoped that 'the business had been settled'—that the French scheme (as he conceived it) had been foiled, because there was now no garrison at St. Sebastian left for Soult to relieve. But ere noon there arrived a dejected messenger to report that there had been this time no postponed assault, but

[1] Ibid., p. 114.
[2] Wellington to Graham, July 24, *Dispatches*, x. p. 563.
[3] Same morning, to Giron, ibid., p. 564.

a serious attack defeated with very heavy loss. This unhappy
fact upset all Wellington's calculations : if the failure had been
very disastrous, it would result that St. Sebastian must be
reckoned as in no immediate danger ; and Soult's heavy
demonstration in front of Roncesvalles might prove to be no
feint, but a real attempt to relieve Pampeluna. Yet Wellington
still doubted this interpretation of the enemy's move : ' one
can hardly believe that with 30,000 men he proposes to
force himself through the passes of the mountains. The
remainder of his force, one must think, must come into operation on some other point, either to-morrow or the day after [1].'
In fact he still opined that there would be an assault on the
Bidassoa—not understanding that the enemy's surplus, or the
greater part of it—D'Erlon's column of 21,000 men—was
striking at the Maya Pass, and was in possession of it at the
moment when he wrote this dispatch to Graham.

Meanwhile the great thing was to discover exactly what was
the condition of affairs at St. Sebastian, and Wellington rode
over the hills in haste to visit Graham, before any notice of the
attacks of the French at Maya and at Roncesvalles had come
to hand. He spent a long afternoon opposite the fortress, with
the results that have been explained in the preceding chapter.
It was only on his ride back to Lesaca in the dark that he met the
first messenger of evil. His Chief of the Staff, George Murray,
had sent out an officer to tell him that furious firing had been
audible from the side of the Maya passes all through the afternoon. But no explanatory dispatch had been received either
from W. Stewart in command at Maya itself, or from Hill, in
charge of the whole defence of the Bastan. This was astonishing,
as there was a properly established line of communication along
the Bastan to head-quarters ; rumours had come to hand that
the enemy was stopped, but no official report. On reaching
Lesaca an hour later, Wellington found an officer sent by Cole
from Roncesvalles awaiting him, who brought the news that
the French were attacking on that front in overpowering
numbers. But up to midday, when the messenger had started,
no breach had been made in the British line [2].

---

[1] Wellington to Graham, 25th July, *Dispatches*, x. p. 566.
[2] Wellington to Graham, *Dispatches*, x. p. 570.

Late at night news did finally come from the Maya front. Stewart sent a verbal message that he had lost the pass, and though he had regained it for a moment by the aid of a brigade of the 7th Division, Hill had ordered him to fall back. This was confirmed by a letter from Hill, which said that Stewart had been driven out of the pass, but that they were going to try to hold on in a position at Elizondo, ten miles farther down the Bastan. It was owing to absolutely criminal negligence on the part of his subordinates that Wellington learned the details of a fight that had begun at about 11 a.m., only twenty miles away, at no earlier an hour than 10 p.m. But late as it was, he had now at last the information which enabled him to guess at Soult's general design, and to give orders for dealing with it.

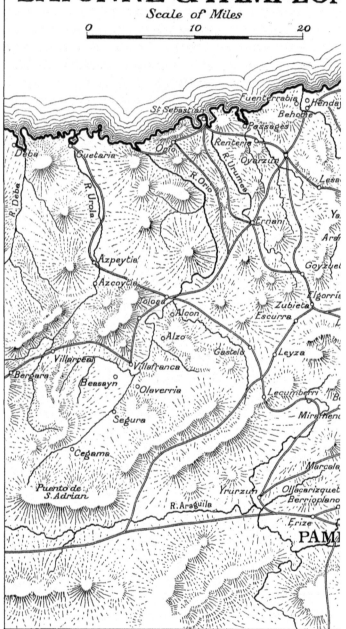

The Country between
BAYONNE & PAMPLON
Scale of Miles

0   10   20

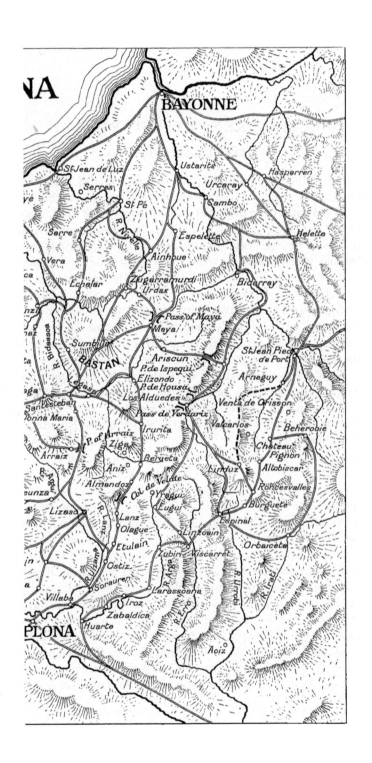

SECTION XXXVIII: CHAPTER III

RONCESVALLES AND MAYA

SOULT, though a day later than he had intended, was ready for his great stroke at the passes by dawn on July 25th. The main blow was to be delivered on the Roncesvalles front, where he had the 34,000 infantry of Reille and Clausel assembled, not to speak of the two cavalry divisions, which would only become useful when he should reach the plain of Pampeluna. So much was D'Erlon's attack on the Maya passes the secondary part of the scheme, that we find Soult informing that general that his advance would probably be facilitated by the arrival in the enemy's camp of the news that Roncesvalles had been forced : this would compel Hill to fall back down the Bastan, and he should be pursued as briskly as possible.

The Roncesvalles business was therefore the more important part of the programme for July 25th. The Marshal had chosen for the routes of Clausel and Reille two roads, which climb up from St. Jean-Pied-du-Port and the valley of the Nive to the bleak plateau above the historic abbey, where the relics of Roland were still shown. Between them lies a broad and deep valley, the Val Carlos, with the mountain stream called the Nive d'Arneguy running down its middle. The eastern road climbs the slopes to the (French) left of the valley : it was practicable for artillery and vehicles, and sappers had been working for the last few days to improve some of its more tiresome curves. This road, after passing the Venta d'Orisson, the last inhabited spot on the north slope, and the ruined fort of Château Pignon, comes to the crest under a hill called Leiçaratheca, immediately in front of the higher position called Altobiscar, where the watershed lies. It then passes for a mile along this watershed known as the ridge of Ibaneta, and descends by curves to the abbey on the Spanish side. The other road, no more than a mountain track in 1813, and quite impracticable for guns or transport, climbs uphill on the western slopes of the Val Carlos, only three or four miles from the better route as the crow flies, but always separated from it by the broad and deep intervening combe. After passing the village of Arneguy, it gets up on to the narrow crest of the mountain, the Airola, which separates the Val Carlos from the Val Haira, the next valley westward. Along this ridge it winds for five or six miles, till the crest joins the main watershed of the Pyrenees at a small plateau called the Linduz, about two miles or so west of the point on the Ibaneta ridge where the other road comes in. A practicable track along the watershed joins them. Since 1813 the whole of the road-geography of this stretch of the Pyrenees has been changed, by the construction of a metalled *chaussée* from Arneguy up the Val Carlos, which did not exist in 1813 : it goes along the slopes, not along the actual crest, like the mere track which Reille's men had to follow on July 25th, and is now a better route than the old high road by Venta d'Orisson and Château Pignon. From the Linduz there is a steep path going straight down into Spain, without joining the Roncesvalles road : it is called the Puerto de Mendichuri, and leads to Espinal. The little plateau has yet another exit ; along the crests to its west comes in a very bad track from the valley of the Alduides, named the path of Atalosti. It is because it lay at such a ganglion of joining ridges, that the Linduz was marked by a ruined earthwork—a relic of the war of 1793–4.

To understand the general lie of the fighting ground, it must be remembered that from the Linduz to Altobiscar is about three miles of saddle-back ridge, lowest in the middle, where the *chaussée* crosses the sky-line at 3,600 feet above sea-level, while the highest point of the Linduz is about 4,200, and that of Altobiscar about 4,900 feet up. The descent into France is much steeper than that into Spain—Burguete and Espinal are only 700 feet below the summit of the pass, Arneguy and the village of Val Carlos on the French side 3,000 feet below it. This is the reason that caused Soult to send his right column along the lofty path on the Airola ridge, from which they could approach the Linduz on a level, instead of bidding them climb up direct from the deep-sunk bottom of the Val Carlos trough.

It should be added that the scenery of the three miles of the Roncesvalles front is not precipitous or Alpine. There are some

outcrops of rock in certain places—e. g. along the front of the
Leiçaratheca hill, but the prevailing aspect is rather like that
of Scottish highland scenery on a large scale.   The slopes are
mostly short slippery grass, not unclimbable for a good walker,
though difficult for the soldier of 1813 carrying the 70 lb. of his
fighting kit and heavy knapsack.   The lower skirts of the hills
are covered in many parts with woods of pine and beech and
stunted undergrowth of oak : in some places these stretch up
right to the summits—the Linduz has thick foliage on its
eastern flank; and the ridge leading to it from the Airola spur
has trees on both sides of the narrow track which winds along
its crest, so that troops ascending it are only intermittently
visible.   Much of the Ibaneta position—the central saddle
between the Linduz and Altobiscar—is covered with bush.
But from the highest summits there are long and clear views over
the woods and the grass-slopes alike—views much more commanding, it may be noted, toward the French than toward the
Spanish side.   So striking is the general effect that, even on the
morning of battle, it fixed itself on the minds of several of
the combatants as a memory not to be forgotten [1] : fighting
has seldom taken place with such a broad and majestic horizon.

Soult knew that his attack would be expected on the high
road—Clausel's troops had been visible to Byng's outposts for
some time, and on the night of the 24th there had been a slight
skirmish of picquets between the Leiçaratheca and Château-
Pignon.   But he was under the impression that he would take
the enemy entirely by surprise in his second attack, that
directed against the Linduz by the obscure and difficult path
along the crest of the Airola mountain, which since the war of
1793–4 had only been used by shepherds and smugglers.   And
on to this narrow path he pushed the full half of his infantry—
the whole of Reille's three divisions.   It is probable that we
must write down the whole of this movement as a mistake : the
track was so bad that it could only be used by daylight—at
night it would have been impossible to discover the way, among
steep slopes and thickets.   There were so many ups and downs,
and the grass slopes on each side were so slippery, that nothing

---

[1] See especially Lemonnier-Delafosse, pp. 211–12, and Wachholz of
Brunswick-Oels, p. 321.

could be done in the dark. The actual result was that the whole 17,000 bayonets of Reille advanced with a front of two men, or even in Indian file, forming a sort of procession many miles long, The head battalion was fighting hard on the Linduz before the tail battalion had begun to stir from Arneguy. Reille had made over his batteries and his regiment of corps-cavalry to Clausel, receiving in return eight mountain guns carried by mules, and a train of pack-beasts laden with infantry ammunition. It is obvious that a movement of this sort could only succeed if the enemy was surprised, since the column had no thrusting-power ; it was all length without breadth, and one brigade ready at the Linduz might hold up the entire three divisions, which would have no space to deploy so as to make their numbers felt. This, as we shall see, is precisely what happened : the Linduz was found in British occupation, and Reille was blocked for the whole day in front of a very inferior force.

On the Château Pignon–Altobiscar road Soult had sent forward the whole of Clausel's force, the three divisions one behind the other, in the order Vandermaesen–Taupin–Conroux. Behind the last infantry division was the cavalry, and then all the guns and transport. Everything on wheels belonging to Reille had been put in at the tail of Clausel's impedimenta. This made a column of interminable length. The conditions were better for an advance on this front than on the western track, since the road was broad and the slopes on each side of it fairly practicable : but there were formidable positions to be carried before the watershed could be reached.

Byng and Morillo had been for three weeks at the Roncesvalles passes, but it was only eight days since they had been put under the command of Cole, who had come up with the 4th Division from his long stay in front of Pampeluna. And it was only on the 22nd that Wellington had sent to Cole the warning that the French main body was moving toward St. Jean-Pied-du-Port, and that he might expect to be attacked. On the 23rd Cole received the stringent orders which have been quoted on an earlier page, but the still stronger message of the 24th seems only to have reached him after the fighting had begun.

While Byng and Morillo were in charge they had evidently

counted on being attacked along the high-road, and possibly also in the depths of the Val Carlos. But no serious attempt had been made to cover the highland path that comes out on the Linduz, much farther west. It was only watched by a picquet—one company of Morillo's men encamped in the ruined redoubt of 1793 on the Linduz. The other points of access were carefully blocked : Byng had a strong first line of defence on the Leiçaratheca hill, whose rocky upper face gave good cover for skirmishers. It was held by the three light companies of his brigade, the attached company of the 5/60th and one battalion[1] and three light companies from Morillo's right-hand brigade. Two miles behind was the real fighting position, occupied by the Buffs and the ' 1st Provisional ' (2/31st and 2/66th), 'with two of Morillo's battalions[2]. Byng's third battalion, the 1/57th, was detached far downhill to the left, on the lower slopes of the Altobiscar, watching the Val Carlos. The third Spanish battalion of Morillo's right-hand brigade, Leon, was detached in a similar fashion to the right, to the foot of the Altobiscar heights, to guard a by-path, which crosses the main chain of the mountains and comes down into the upper valley of the Irati river at the foundry of Orbaiceta.

The remaining battalions of Morillo's left-hand brigade[3] were down in the Val Carlos, on ground south of the village of the same name, in a position blocking the upper and higher end of that deep-sunk depression. They covered the flank of the Altobiscar heights, and were not far from the 1/57th. Their line of retreat, if they should be pushed, was up a very steep path, which comes into the *chaussée* on the Ibaneta ridge[4]. It was this brigade which supplied the picquet on the Linduz, the only precaution taken to cover the extreme left of the Allies' fighting ground. The whole force on the front originally consisted of 2,000 bayonets of Byng's brigade and 3,800 in Morillo's six battalions.

When Cole took over from Byng the general responsibility for the safety of the eastern passes, he brought up his head-

---

[1] Vittoria and light companies of Doyle, La Union, and Legion Estremena.
[2] La Union and the Legion, minus their light companies.
[3] Doyle and 2nd of Jaen.
[4] Sometimes called the Puerto de Val Carlos.

quarters to Viscarret in the valley of the Erro, but placed his first British brigade, that of Ross, at Espinal, in the valley of the Urrobi, on the high road to Roncesvalles, only five miles from the abbey and the ' Puerto ', and three from the pass of Mendichuri leading up to the Linduz. He was thus in a position to reinforce the passes at two or three hours' notice with one brigade, and with his whole 6,000 bayonets in half a day's march. On the night of the 24th, having received both Wellington's first letter of warning and Byng's report that his picquets had been attacked, Cole resolved to bring up his reserves nearer to the front. By the most fortunate of inspirations he directed Ross's brigade to march before dawn—at 2 a.m.—and to occupy the head of the Mendichuri pass and the Linduz.

Ross, obeying orders all the more readily because he had just received Spanish information that the Linduz was going to be attacked next day [1], moved off in the dark, and mounted the Mendichuri, much incommoded on the way by sharp turns where trees had been blown down in a recent storm, and cumbered the path. He had the 20th with him : the 7th was following : the 23rd was left behind at Espinal, to start by daylight and bring on the baggage. Though the distance to the Linduz was only three miles, it took in the darkness more than four hours to reach the summit [2]. There everything was found quiet at dawn—the Spanish picquet in the old redoubt indeed was so sleepy that Ross and his staff rode into them without having been challenged [3]. Dawn had now come ; though nothing suspicious had been observed, the general sent out the Brunswick-Oels company attached to the brigade to reconnoitre along the spur in front, while the 20th piled arms and lay down on the summit, to eat and get some rest after the night

[1] See the very interesting letter of Bainbrigge of the 20th, printed as an Appendix to the regimental history of that corps, p. 390.

[2] Bainbrigge says that it was 7 a.m. before the regiment reached the Linduz, but that it was an hour earlier is demonstrated by the fact that they heard firing at Roncesvalles after arriving. Now Byng's fight on the Leiçaratheca began at 6 a.m. Therefore Ross was on the Linduz earlier.

[3] What became of this Spanish company ? Captain Tovey of the 20th (see history of that corps, p. 408) says that the French ' made the Spanish picquet, who were posted to give us intelligence, prisoners, without their firing a shot '. Another account is that having seen Ross arrive, they quietly went off to rejoin their brigade, without giving any notice.

march. In the far distance to the north-west the tents of Campbell's Portuguese, encamped on the farther side of the Alduides valley were perfectly visible. But shortly after 6 o'clock distant musketry began to be heard from the other flank—the direction of the Leiçaratheca—where the busy day's work was just beginning. It was some time, however, before Ross's brigade came in for their share of it.

Soult's attack, as we have seen, was delivered by two columns each of 17,000 men, and each striking by one narrow road at a vital point of the enemy's defences. There was practically no dispersion of forces on subsidiary enterprises, for the two demonstrations which he made on his flanks on the morning of the 25th were trifling affairs. To distract the attention of Campbell's brigade in the Alduides, he directed all the National Guards of the Val de Baigorry and the other western valleys to assemble on the mountain called Hausa, opposite the Portuguese camp, to light many fires there, as if they marked the bivouacs of a large force, and to show themselves at many points. Little good came of this to the National Guards, for Campbell, an active officer, marched at them without delay, and drove them in helpless rout down the valley. But Soult (unlike the unfortunate local levy) profited perceptibly from the move, for the noise of firing drew down to the Alduides the two British generals responsible for the Bastan—Hill and W. Stewart. And while they were absent, off their own ground, their troops at Maya were attacked, and suffered many things for want of a commander.

A second similar demonstration was made in the valley east of Roncesvalles. Here the local National Guards, backed by a battalion of the 59th under Colonel Loverdo, crossed the main chain of the mountains and attacked Morillo's right flank-guard—the regiment of Leon—at the foundry of Orbaiceta in the Irati valley. The Spaniards defended themselves stoutly, and held their ground all day. But the noise of this skirmishing far to their right rear was decidedly trying to the nerves of Byng and Morillo, who for some time could not be certain that their flank had not been turned by a respectable force. However, nothing came of this skirmish, since it grew evident by the afternoon that the enemy was weak and unable to press forward. It is barely worth putting on record that one battalion detached from the tail of Conroux's division, went up the trough of the Val Carlos, and watched Morillo's left-hand brigade without attempting to close with it.

Having dismissed these feints, concerning which no more need be said, we may proceed to the real fighting. At about 6 a.m. Vandermaesen's division, at the head of Clausel's long column, neared the hill of Leiçaratheca, where the seven British and Spanish light companies were ensconced in the rocky slope commanding the high road. The position had obviously to be stormed by frontal attack if there was reason to hurry, for it could only be turned by very long flanking movements over the steep slopes on each side of the road. General Barbot, commanding the leading brigade, deployed the 1st Line and 25th Léger, and attacked with a swarm of *tirailleurs* the whole front of the hill. The attack failed completely, the defenders being under good cover and perfectly steady. The French, when their first rush had been stopped, threw themselves down among the stones and gorse, and kept up a useless fire upon their almost invisible adversaries. Clausel, after three hours of this profitless bickering, sent in high rage a message to Barbot, that he would have him cashiered, unless he pulled his men together and delivered a serious attack [1]. Meanwhile the French battalions were coming up one after another from the rear, and accumulating behind the single brigade that was engaged. Barbot called back his disordered troops, reformed them in column, put in a fresh battalion, and made a second and a third attack on the hill : all naturally failed—the troops being tired and discouraged. But the matter was finally settled by the divisional general, Vandermaesen, leading off his three rear battalions [2] across the steep hill-side to the east, and turning the Leiçaratheca by a long détour. At the same time Clausel

[1] There is a curious and interesting account of all this in the Memoirs of Lemonnier-Delafosse, aide-de-camp to Clausel, who was twice sent to stir up Barbot, whose conduct he describes in scathing terms (pp. 212–14). Clausel says that the 50th stormed the Leiçaratheca. That it stormed an abandoned position is shown by the figure of its losses. What Clausel does not tell can be gathered from Byng's workmanlike dispatch to Cole, in *Supplementary Dispatches*, viii. pp. 128–9.

[2] Of the 27th and 130th Line.

began to shell the position with six guns brought up from the
rear. When Byng saw his outlying force in danger of being cut
off, he ordered it to retire to his main body on the Altobiscar.
This it did in good time, and when Clausel again advanced
against the Leiçaratheca frontally, with the 50th-Line, while
the flanking column drew in on the right flank, he received only
a few shots from lingering skirmishers, and occupied the position
with the loss of 9 men killed only.

So long had the turning movement taken, that by the time
that the French had got back into order again, and could
advance towards Byng's real fighting ground, it was past
3 o'clock in the afternoon. The Altobiscar position was even
more formidable than that on the Leiçaratheca; Clausel
looked at it, felt it, and did not like it : it was impossible to
turn save by a vast détour : this, he says in his dispatch, he was
preparing to do, by sending his rear division (Conroux) to
circumvent the whole crest of Altobiscar and the still higher
summit to the east of the road, a march of many miles. But
at 5 o'clock a dense mountain fog rose, the enemies became
invisible to each other, and all movement became impossible.
Byng was left unattacked upon his chosen position—though
not destined to stop there. The losses on both sides had been
absurdly small, considering that 17,000 French had faced
6,000 British and Spaniards for eleven hours. But really only
Vandermaesen's division on one side and the Allied light companies on the other had been engaged. Clausel says that he
had but 160 killed and wounded—among the last General
Vandermaesen himself [1]. Byng and Morillo had 120 casualties—
the former remarks that this was an extraordinarily low figure
considering that the French had shelled the Leiçaratheca for
some time—but the cover was good [2]. There were more

---

[1] I confess that I doubt these figures. Martinien's lists show the 27th
Line with seven officer-casualties, the 1st Line with two, the 25th Léger
with three, the 130th with two. Fourteen officer-casualties ought to mean
more like 280 than 160 casualties of all ranks. In the whole Pyrenean
campaign the French army lost 420 officers to 12,300 men—nearly 30 men
to each officer. Clausel asks us to believe that at Roncesvalles the proportion was one officer to twelve men ! Yet, of course, such disproportion
is quite *possible*.

[2] While we have quite a number of good personal narratives of the fight

Spaniards hurt than British : their conduct had been exemplary. Morillo himself had been there, exposing himself with his usual reckless courage.

At the other end of the line the fighting was much more serious. It will be remembered that at 6 o'clock Ross was on the Linduz, with his leading battalion, and a second close behind : the third had only recently started the climb up from Espinal by the Mendichuri. He sent out his light companies to observe the northern slope of the plateau which he had occupied, that of Brunswick-Oels being directed along the wooded spur or crest which forms the western wall of the depression of the Val Carlos. Meanwhile the troops listened to the commencement of the long roll of musketry, which told how Clausel was attacking Byng on the other side of that valley. Three or four hours passed ; General Cole rode by on his way to visit the Roncesvalles front, told Ross to keep a good look-out, and informed him that Anson's and Stubbs's brigade were coming up via Burguete, the former to reinforce the Spaniards at the foundry of Orbaiceta, the latter to the Ibaneta to support Byng. Somewhere about 11 o'clock, according to our best eye-witness, the outlying picquet of the Brunswick company detected dust rolling above the beech copses which masked the crest-path in front of them, and a little later caught intermittent glimpses of troops passing between the trees. It was doubted whether they were French, or some of Morillo's troops retiring from Val Carlos. But about noon, Ross, having been warned to look for trouble, told the Brunswickers to advance and verify the character of the approaching strangers, while he himself called up the left wing of the 20th regiment and followed in support : the rest of the brigade were directed to stand to their arms on the Linduz. The German light company went forward some half a mile on a very up-and-down track, till they got quite close to the oncoming troops, who appeared to be in no particular order, a straggling crowd advancing along

on the Linduz, I have found for the fight on the Leiçaratheca nothing but the official reports of Clausel, Byng, and Morillo, save the memoirs of George L'Estrange of the 31st and of Lemonnier-Delafosse, who is interesting but obviously inaccurate, since he says that the French regiment which carried the hill was the 71st. Not only was it the 50th, as Clausel specially mentions, but 71 was a blank number in the French Army List.

the crest, which is here only thirty yards broad, with trees and bushes on both flanks. When there was no more than eighty yards between the parties the French dressed their front, so as to cover the whole breadth of the ridge, and began to fire. They were the two *compagnies d'élite* of the 6th Léger, the leading battalion of Foy's division, at the head of Reille's column ; close behind them the rest of their battalion was pushing up, as quickly as was possible with men moving on such a narrow track. The sixty Brunswickers, finding themselves in front of such a superior force, fell back, firing, on their supports, pursued by the enemy. General Ross, wanting to gain time for his brigade on the Linduz to deploy, ordered the leading company of the 20th—No. 8, Captain Tovey's—to charge with the bayonet and throw the French back. There followed one of the rarest things in the Peninsular War, a real hand-to-hand fight with the white weapon. The French skirmishers in front gave way into the bushes, clearing the front of the company behind them. Then the two parties, each advancing up one side of a small declivity, met face to face at the top, with only ten yards between them when they came in sight of each other. ' The French instinctively stepped back a pace,' says the Brunswick officer who has left us the best account of this clash, ' several of them made a half turn, as if about to give way ; but their officers, some with appeals, some with threats, and some with curses, kept them to their work. They stood firm, and their bayonets came down to the charge : so did those of Tovey's company. For a few seconds the two sides surveyed each other at a distance of two paces : then one French company officer sprang forward into the middle of the British, and began cutting right and left. He was at once bayoneted, and then the two sides began to fence cautiously with each other, keeping their line and not breaking forward into the enemy's ranks ; it was more like bayonet drill than a charge. I do not think that more than a dozen men fell on either side. After a minute the English captain saw that the French supports were closing in—he shouted ' right about face ', and his men trotted back. When our front was clear of them, our five (four)[1] companies opened fire by platoons, and as the

[1] Four, not five, because the light company of the 20th was absent with

distance was only 100 yards we saw heaps of the French fall at each volley [1].' Tovey's company lost 11 killed and 14 wounded out of about 75 present in this extraordinary adventure, which had given the three rear companies and the Brunswickers time to form up across the crest and in the bushes on each side of it. It is astonishing that a man of the 8th Company got away— clearly the enemy had been too much astonished to pursue as he might have done [2].

The fight on the path that leads to the Linduz now became a very confused and constricted business, with many casualties on both sides, since French and English were firing at each other along a sort of avenue, and could hardly miss. Foy's second battalion, the 1/69th, had now reinforced his first, and finally the left wing of the 20th, badly thinned, gave way and fell back in some disorder to the point where the crest-path debouches on to the Linduz plateau. Here all was ready for defence—the right wing of the 20th, with the regimental colours flying, was waiting ready for the enemy, with the 1/7th in immediate support and the 1/23rd in reserve. When the narrow-fronted French column tried to burst out of the defile, officers in front, drums beating the *pas de charge*, a long-reserved volley smote it, and all the leading files went down. There was a pause before the third of Foy's battalions, the 2/69th, got to the front and tried a similar attack, which failed with even

the other light companies far to the right : so the wing was only four companies strong, or three deducting Tovey's men. Wachholz forgets this.

[1] Wachholz, p. 322.

[2] Tovey fortunately wrote a narrative of this little affair, which may be found in the history of the 20th, p. 408. He says : ' The enemy's light troops opened so galling a fire that Major-General Ross called out for a company to go to the front. Without waiting for orders I pushed out with mine, and in close order and double-quick cleared away the skirmishers from a sort of plateau. They did not wait for us : on reaching its opposite side we came so suddenly on the head of the enemy's infantry column, which had just gained a footing on the summit of the hill, that the men of my company absolutely paused in astonishment, for we were face to face with them. The French officer called to us to throw down our arms : I replied " bayonet away," and rushing on them we turned them back down the descent. Such was the panic and confusion caused by the sudden onset, that our small party (for such it was compared to the French column) had time to regain the regiment, but my military readers may rest assured that it required to be done *double quick*.'

greater loss. For the whole of the rest of the afternoon spasmodic fighting went on at the Linduz. 'The enemy was
visible,' writes one of Ross's brigade, 'several thousands
strong, on the higher part of the spur; every half-hour or so
he sent another company down to relieve his skirmishers. He
always came up in detail and slowly, for there was a tiresome
defile to cross, over a deep cutting in the crest [1], where only one
man abreast could pass. We could always let the head of the
attack debouch, and then attack it and throw it back upon its
supports [2].' No attempt was made to turn the Linduz by its
eastern side, among the steep slopes and thickets at the head
of Val Carlos: all attacks came straight along the spur. Reille
attributes this in his dispatch to the dreadful delays at the rear
of his long column, owing to the narrowness of the path. He
acknowledges that an attempt should have been made to push
on to the Ibaneta, but it was 3.30 before Maucune's first
battalion began to arrive to Foy's assistance, and 5 before the
rear of his division was up. 'By this hour it was too late to
think of turning movements'—even if the fog which stopped
Clausel had not swept down on the Linduz also. As a matter
of fact only Foy's four front regiments—five battalions—were
put into the fight [3]. Similarly on the British side the fight was
sustained only by the 20th, relieved, after its cartridges were all
spent, by the 7th and the 23rd.

Reille does not omit to mention that after the first hour of
fight was over, Cole had begun to show reserves on the Linduz
which would have made any attack by Foy's division, unsupported, quite hopeless. It will be remembered that the commander of the 4th Division had started Anson's brigade for
Orbaiceta, and Stubbs's brigade for the Ibaneta ridge, when first
the attack on Byng was reported, and he had gone to the
Altobiscar himself to watch the progress of affairs on that side.
While he was there Foy's attack on the Linduz developed : Cole

---

[1] This ditch had been cut by the Spaniards in 1793 as an outer protection
to their redoubt on the Linduz.

[2] Wachholz, p. 324.

[3] The 6th Léger, 69th (2 battalions), 76th, and 36th show casualties,
the rear regiments (39th and 65th) none. Nor does Maucune's division.
Similarly on the British side none of Anson's or Stubbs's battalions contribute to the list.

at once rode to the left, to see how Ross was faring, and in consequence sent down-hill to bid Anson abandon his long march to the extreme right, and to turn up the Roncesvalles pass, as Stubbs did also. The British brigade took post on Ross's right ; the Portuguese brigade on the Ibaneta, watching the steep path from the Val Carlos. Up this there presently came the 1/57th and the Spanish battalions which had been near them. Thus Cole showed a continuous line from the Altobiscar to the Linduz, held by 11,000 men placed in a most formidable position not more than three miles long. Nor was this all—General Campbell in the Alduides, after scattering the National Guards who had tried to delude him in the early morning, had heard the firing at Roncesvalles, and (though he had no orders) thought it his duty to march with his five Portuguese battalions toward the sound of battle. Taking the highland track along the upper end of the Alduides, he appeared on Ross's left at 4 o'clock in the afternoon by the so-called path of Atalosti. He was in a position to outflank any attempts that Reille might make to turn Ross's position on the western side.

When the fog fell Soult was in a very unpleasant situation. Having chosen to attack his enemy with narrow-fronted columns of immense depth, over two constricted routes, he had been brought to a complete check. Clausel had driven in Byng's outpost, but was stuck in front of the Altobiscar : Reille had failed to move Ross at all, and was blocked in front of the Linduz. The losses had been negligible, it is true—not much over 500 in all if the Marshal is to be believed. But those of the Allies were still smaller, and the confidence of the men had been raised by the way in which they had easily blocked for some ten hours, and with small loss, an army whose vast strength they could estimate by the interminable file of distant troops crawling up the roads in the rear [1]. If the men, however,

[1] As we have seen already, Clausel puts his loss at the Leiçaratheca at 160, to Byng's and Morillo's 120. At the other end of the line Ross's brigade had lost 216 men—139 of them in the 20th, 31 in the 7th, 42 in the 23rd, 4 in the Brunswick company. [I know not where Napier got his strange statement that this company lost 42 men : their captain, Wachholz, reports 2 killed and 2 wounded.] Foy's six front battalions had lost 10 officers and 361 men. The total Allied loss was about 350, there

were cheerful, their commander was not. Cole estimated the French at 30,000 men and more, and quite correctly : he had himself only 11,000 in line, with 2,000 more of Campbell's Portuguese in touch on his left. Picton's 3rd Division, which lay at Olague on the morn of the 25th, had no doubt started to close up ; but it was a long day's march away, and could not be at Altobiscar or on the Linduz till the 26th. Anything might be happening in the fog which lay deep on the mountains all night. Cole determined ' that he could not hope to maintain the passes against the very great superiority of the force opposed to him—amounting to from 30,000 to 35,000 men [1] ', and that he must retire by night under cover of the mist. Even if his views had been less pessimistic, he would yet have been compelled to retreat by the action of Byng, who had fought heroically all the day, but was obsessed by fears as the fog settled down. He had come to the conclusion that, as the enemy had possession of the path along the eastern hills to Orbaiceta, and had superabundant numbers, he would be using the night to send a large force in that direction, where only the Spanish regiment of Leon was on guard. They could not be stopped, and when down in the valley of the Irati would be able to take Roncesvalles from the rear, and to throw the whole defending force on to the necessity of retiring by the Mendichuri and Atalosti routes, on which retreat would be slow and dangerous. Byng therefore sent a message to Cole that he must needs retire, and was already beginning to draw off his troops, under cover of his light companies, when he received Cole's orders to the same effect. The moral responsibility for the retreat lay equally on both—the technical responsibility on Cole alone, as the superior officer : he might, of course, have ordered Byng back to his old position, which the French had left quite unmolested.

Was Cole's pessimism justified ? Wellington thought not : he wrote to Lord Liverpool ten days later, ' Sir Lowry Cole,

having been a few casualties among Campbell's Portuguese and among the Spaniards at Orbaiceta. The total French loss was not less than 580. Both figures are very moderate. Cole estimated the French casualties at 2,000 men ! Soult wrote that he had almost exterminated the 20th, whose total loss had been 189.

[1] Cole to Wellington, *Supplementary Dispatches*, viii. p. 127.

whose retreat occasioned the retreat of the whole, retired, not because he could not hold his position, but because his right flank was turned. It is a great disadvantage when the officer commanding in chief is absent. For this reason there is nothing that I dislike so much as these extended operations, which I cannot direct myself[1].' And he was no doubt thinking of Cole, no less than of Picton, when he wrote that ' all the beatings we have given the French have not given our generals confidence in themselves and in the exertions of their troops. They are really heroes when I am on the spot to direct them, but when I am obliged to quit them they are children.' Cole was an officer of the first merit in handling troops, as he was to show at Sorauren two days later ; and that he was not destitute of initiative had been sufficiently proved by the advance of the 4th Division at Albuera, where he was practically acting without orders[2]. But there seems no doubt that the scale of the operations in the Pyrenees made him nervous : he was responsible on the 25th July not for a division but for a small army, and he was well aware of the enemy's superiority in numbers. His conduct was the more surprising because he had received before 10 o'clock Wellington's stringent dispatch of the night of the 24th, telling him to ' maintain the passes in front of Roncesvalles to the utmost,' and to disregard any wide turning movements to the east on Soult's part. These orders reached him at the Leiçaratheca, just as he was witnessing Byng's successful repulse of Barbot's brigade. Possibly the excitement of the moment prevented him from thoroughly appreciating their full meaning, and for the rest of the day he was busy enough, riding from front to front on the passes. As he wrote in his first short account of his doings, ' having had no sleep for two nights, and having been on horseback from 4 a.m. till 11 at night, I am somewhat fagged[3].' It is, of course, quite unfair to criticize a responsible officer in the light of subsequent events ; but as a matter of fact Cole was in no danger—the fog endured all that night and far into the morning of the 26th.

[1] Wellington to Liverpool, *Dispatches*, x. p. 596.

[2] See vol. iv. pp. 389–90.

[3] Cole to Murray, Linzoain, July 26th. Wrongly dated July 27th in *Supplementary Dispatches*, viii. p. 124.

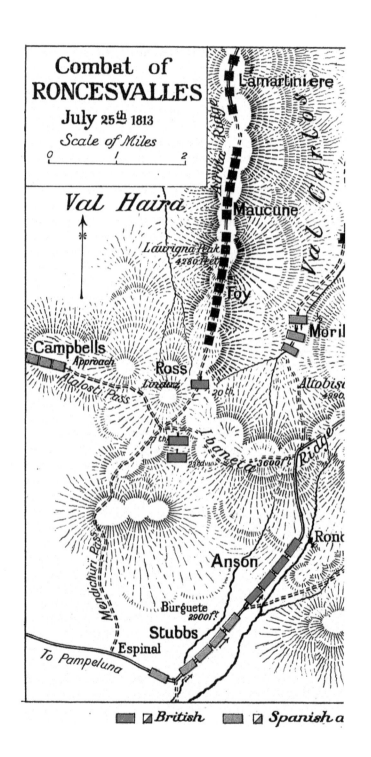

Combat of
RONCESVALLES
July 25th 1813
Scale of Miles
0   1   2

Val Haira

Val Carlos

Arola Ridge

Lamartiniere

Maucune

Laurigna Peak
4280 Feet

Foy

Moril

Campbells
Approach

Ross

Lindux

20th.

Altobis
4990

Atalosti Pass

Ibaneta
3600 ft.

th

23rd

Ridge

Mendichuri Pass

Ront

Anson

Burguete
2900 ft.

Stubbs

Espinal

To Pampeluna

British   Spanish a

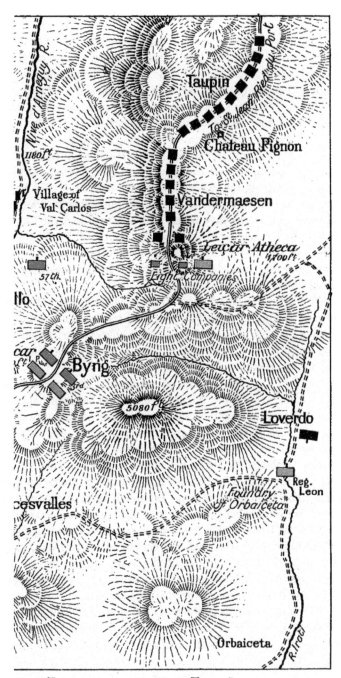

Taupin

Château Pignon

10th 8th leon pied at Port

Vandermaesen

Village of
Val Carlos

1160 ft

57th

Leiçar Atheca
4,400 ft

Eight Companies

No

car
ft

Byng

P
Are

3rd

5080 ft

Loverdo

Reg.
Leon

Foundry
of Orbaiceta

cesvalles

Orbaiceta

R. Iroti

R. Irati

Nive d'Arnegny R.

ind Portuguese ▰ ▨ French

The enemy at Orbaiceta was negligible—one battalion and a few National Guards : Soult sent no more troops on that wretched road. And if he had done so, after the fog cleared on the 26th, they would have taken the best part of a day to get into action. It seems certain that Cole could have held the passes for another day without any great risk ; and if he had done so, Soult's whole plan of campaign would have been wrecked. But, of course, the fog *might* have lifted at midnight : Soult *might* have sent two divisions by a night march to Orbaiceta, and a retreat by bad tracks like the Atalosti would have been slow, and also eccentric, since it did not cover the Pampeluna road, but would have taken Cole to Eugui and the Col de Velate. Nevertheless, looking at the words of Wellington's dispatch of the 24th, it seems that Cole disobeyed orders : he did *not* hold the passes to the utmost, and he did *not* disregard turning movements to the far east.

Both the Linduz and Altobiscar were evacuated in the early hours of the night of July 25th–6th : the French did not discover the move till morning, and by dawn the whole of Cole's force was far on its way down the Pampeluna road entirely unmolested, though very weary.

To understand the general situation on the morning of July 26th, we must now turn back, to note what had been happening in the Bastan during the long hours of Byng's and Ross's fight in the southern passes. The supplementary part of Soult's plan had been to force the Maya defile, and thus to break in the left-centre of Wellington's line of defence, at the same moment that his main body turned its extreme right flank, by forcing its way through the Roncesvalles gap. D'Erlon's three divisions, for whom this task had been set aside, had no long détour to execute, like those of Reille : they were already concentrated in front of their objective ; their leading section was at Urdax, only a few miles from the summit of the Maya ridge ; their most remote reserves at Espelette, in the valley of the Nive, were within one day's march of the British positions.

The orders issued by Soult to D'Erlon on July 23rd ran as follows : ' Comte D'Erlon will make his dispositions on the 24th to attack the enemy at dawn on the 25th, to make himself master of the Puerto of Maya, and to pursue the enemy when he

shall begin his retreat. . . . It is to be presumed that the hostile
forces in the Bastan, in the Alduides, and in the passes of
Ispegui and Maya will draw back the moment that they hear
of [Clausel's and Reille's] movement, or else that they will begin
to manœuvre, so as to leave their present positions ungarrisoned.
Comte D'Erlon will seize the moment to attack them briskly,
and to seize the Maya pass. From thence he will march by
Ariscun on Elizondo, and then on the Col de Velate, or possibly
by Berderis on the pass of Urtiaga, according to the route which
the enemy may take in his retreat. He should remember that
he must try to unite as soon as possible with the main body in
the direction here indicated, and to get into communication
with General Reille. Whatever may happen, he must send
strong detachments to pursue any hostile columns that may
try to get off to their left [westward], to discover their routes,
worry them, and pick up prisoners.'

These are very curious orders, as all their directions depend
on the idea that Roncesvalles will be forced with ease, and that
on hearing of its being lost all the Allied troops in the centre of
Wellington's line will retire in haste. Soult committed himself
to this hypothesis in the words ' it is to be presumed that the
enemy will defend the position of Altobiscar feebly, because he
will see that he is being outflanked by Reille's divisions on the
Linduz, and threatened at the same time, on his right flank by
the detachment and the National Guards who are demonstrating
in the direction of Orbaiceta.'   But what if Roncesvalles were
held for twelve hours against Clausel, if Reille were completely
blocked all day on the Linduz, and if the demonstration on
Orbaiceta proved ineffective ?   In this case the British troops
on the Maya front will *not* hear of disasters in the south, they
will *not* retreat, but stand to fight ; and D'Erlon, far from
having a walk over the pass, as a commencement to a rapid
pursuit of a flying enemy, will have a hard day's work before
him.

This is what was to happen. D'Erlon, instead of running
against an enemy who was about to retreat, and pushing him
forward with ease, met with troops determined to hold their
position, and found himself let in for one of the bloodiest battles
on a small scale that were fought during the whole war. That

he was finally successful, though at a heavy cost, was due
to the mistakes made by the British generals in front of
him.

The disposition of the troops which formed Wellington's
centre was as follows. Hill was in charge of the whole sector,
from the Maya Pass to the head of the Alduides valley. His
force consisted of the 2nd Division (minus Byng's brigade,
detached to Roncesvalles nearly a month back), and of Silveira's
Portuguese division. William Stewart held the left, with the
three available 2nd Division brigades—Cameron's, Pringle's,
and Ashworth's Portuguese. The two British brigades were in
or about the Maya Pass, Ashworth was holding the Ispegui Pass,
seven miles to the east, with one battalion in the defile, and the
others in support on the road from Errazu. Silveira's two
brigades continued the line southward, Da Costa's watching
the Col de Berderis and other minor passes south of the Ispegui,
while A. Campbell's was in the Alduides, on the slopes above
the village of that name. Silveira himself was with Da Costa.
Campbell, as we have already seen, was in close touch with the
Roncesvalles force, and ultimately joined it.

On the other flank the 2nd Division at Maya had as its nearest
neighbour the 7th Division, which was holding the ' Puerto ' of
Echalar. Behind lay the Light Division by Vera, and the 6th
Division, now under Pack, since Clinton's health had again
broken down, in reserve at Santesteban.

Now on the early morning of the 25th the first troops stirring
were Soult's National Guard detachments on the Alduides front,
which (as we have already seen) attracted the notice of Campbell's Portuguese, and suffered for their temerity. Their
activity, most unfortunately, drew the attention of Sir Rowland
Hill in this direction. He rode out from his head-quarters at
Elizondo to visit Campbell, when the demonstration was
reported to him. And he was actually in the Alduides, at the
extreme southern end of his sector, when the French attacked
in force the Maya passes, at its extreme northern end. This was
a pardonable mishap, since he was on his own business. But it
led to his being absent from the real point of danger. Quite
unpardonable, however, was the fact that William Stewart,
commanding the 2nd Division, abandoned his own troops and

went out to join Hill in the same direction [1], toward the front of
Silveira's brigades, attracted by the news of fighting at early
dawn. He would seem to have left no note of his probable
whereabouts at Maya, so that he was sought in vain for many
hours, when his troops were attacked. In his absence the command of his division fell to General Pringle, who had arrived
from England only two days before, to take over the brigade
of which Colonel O'Callaghan of the 39th had been in temporary
charge since the opening of the campaign. Pringle knew
neither the troops nor the ground, and being only a brigadier
had no authority to make new dispositions, when his commanding officer was still technically present, though invisible for the
moment.

The whole responsibility for what happened on the morning
of the 25th, therefore, fell on Stewart. And he must also be
given the discredit of the very inadequate arrangements that
had been made for the defence of the pass. The French at
Urdax were only four miles from the crest, and it was known
that they were in strength close behind—their large camps
about Ainhoue, where Abbé's division was cantoned, were
perfectly visible from the heights [2], and obviously crammed with
men. Considering that he was in close touch with the enemy,
Stewart's precautions were ludicrously incomplete. The Maya
position consists of a broad open grassy saddle, between the
high mountains to east and west—the Alcorrunz peak on
the left and the Aretesque peak on the right. The saddle at
its lowest point is about 2,000 ft. above sea-level—the flanking
heights run up to a thousand feet more. The high road from
Urdax and Zagaramurdi climbs the saddle in its middle, runs
westward along its summit for a mile, and then descends by
a broad curve towards Elizondo on the Spanish side. There is
another lesser track which leads up on to the saddle, from
Espelette ; it gets on to the level of the Col at its extreme
eastern end, under the Aretesque height ; thence, after running
along the crest for a mile, it meets the high road, crosses it, and
continues along the slopes of the Alcorrunz peak, and ulti-

---

[1] See diary of Dr. Henry, who was at Elizondo, and notes how all the
senior officers rode out eastward (p. 161).

[2] Bell, vol. i. p. 102 ; Cadell, p. 161.

mately falls into the by-road from Santesteban to Zagaramurdi. This path, useful for lateral communications east and west, is still known as the *Chemin des Anglais,* from the work which was spent upon it by Wellington's army later in the year, when the necessity for good tracks along the front was better understood than it seems to have been in July. In contemporary records it is generally called the Gorospil path.

The west end of the saddle was not inadequately guarded by Cameron's brigade, which was encamped by battalions on each side of the main *chaussée* close behind the crest, with four Portuguese guns, of Da Cunha's battery, mounted on a commanding knoll whence they could sweep the road. But the east end of the position, under the hill of Aretesque, where the minor road comes in, was almost entirely neglected. There was only a picquet of 80 men placed to cover it, on the spot where the *Chemin des Anglais* gets to the crest of the position. Pringle's brigade, which supplied this picquet, was two and a half miles to the rear, in the low ground about the village of Maya— an hour's march away, for the ascent to the picquet was a climb uphill by a bad path. The only support immediately available for the outpost was the four light companies of the brigade [1], which were encamped on the back-slope of the ridge, about half-way between the hill of Aretesque and the main body of the brigade.

There was much dead ground in front of the Maya position, where it might be approached by ravines and combes whose bottom could not be fathomed by the eye. And in particular the view north-eastward, towards Espelette, was completely blocked by a high round hill half a mile beyond the outer sentries of the Aretesque picquet. With the French only four miles away at Urdax, and seven at Espelette, it is clear that prudence would have dictated constant reconnaissance of all the dead ground. Stewart had made no such arrangements— all that we hear is that the round hill beyond the Aretesque picquet was occasionally visited by Portuguese vedettes. Apparently none had gone out on the morning of the 25th.

D'Erlon would appear to have been well acquainted with

[1] One from each battalion plus the odd company of the 5/60th attached to each 2nd Division brigade.

the general disposition of the British line, as he launched his main attack against the undermanned eastern flank of the position, and did not tackle the strongly held ground on the high road, at its western end, until he was well established on the crest. Darmagnac's division, from Espelette, led the main column, Abbé's division from Ainhoue fell into its rear and followed : both took the *Chemin des Anglais* track, which was blocked from the view of the British picquets by the round hill already mentioned. Maransin's division at Urdax, on the high road, was ordered to mass itself, but to keep under cover, and show no signs of movement till the main body had reached and occupied the eastern end of the saddle. It was then to assail Cameron's brigade, advancing up the high road.

Though the morning was bright and clear, no certain signs of a French attack were seen till 10 o'clock, so carefully did the enemy utilize the ' dead ground ' in front of him. Suspicious movements indeed were observed by the outpost of the 71st on the high road, who noted small bodies of men crossing the sky-line in front of Urdax[1]. And the picquet of the 34th on the Aretesque hill reported to Pringle's brigade-head-quarters that it had seen a small body of cavalry and a larger force of infantry turn the corner of a distant road beyond Ainhoue and disappear again[2]. On both points the enemy had only been visible for a few minutes. Pringle sent up a staff-officer[3] to the Aretesque picquet, who made nothing of the troops that had been detected on that side, but as a measure of precaution ordered up the four light companies of the brigade to join the picquet on the crest. Thus there chanced to be 400 men instead of 80, when D'Erlon discovered himself an hour later. But the five companies were as powerless a guard against the sudden attack of 7,000 men as the one company would have been.

At 10.30 D'Erlon had reached the point, not much over half a mile from the most advanced British sentry, where the head of his column would be forced to come out into the open and

[1] See Hope's *Military Memoirs*, p. 319. Sceptical observers with telescopes said that the objects seen were droves of bullocks.

[2] See Moyle Sherer (who commanded the picquet), p. 257.

[3] Major Thorne, assistant quartermaster-general. Moyle Sherer says that Thorne owned that there was a small column on the move, but that he judged it to be a battalion shifting its quarters, or a relief of outposts.

show itself. His dispositions aimed at a sudden surprise—and effected it. He collected the eight light companies of Darmagnac's division, ordered them to take off and stack their knapsacks, and launched them as a swarm of *tirailleurs* at the position of the British on the Aretesque knoll (or the Gorospil knoll, as Darmagnac calls it in his report). The 16th Léger followed them in column, keeping to the track, while the skirmishers spread out in a semicircle to envelop the knoll. The remainder of the division came on as quickly as it could in support.

The French attacked at a pace that surprised their enemies ; the light companies—they were commanded by Bradbey of the 28th—were desperately engaged within ten minutes of the firing of the first shot. Their flanks being turned, they clubbed together on the higher slopes of the knoll, and around some rocky outcrops on its summit, and held their own for three-quarters of an hour, repulsing several attacks of the voltigeurs and the 16th Léger with great loss, and suffering heavily themselves. Meanwhile the attention of the defenders of the pass being thus distracted, the succeeding battalions of Darmagnac's division hurried up unmolested one after another on to the saddle, and began to deploy. Their general threw the 8th Line across the rear of the knoll, blocking the path which led down to the village of Maya and the camps of Pringle's brigade, and drew out in succession the 28th, 51st, and 54th on the plateau to their right.

Before any succour could arrive [1] the five unlucky companies on the Gorospil knoll were crushed by the concentric attack—six unwounded officers and 140 men were taken prisoners among the rocks at the summit—the other 260 were nearly all killed or wounded. Soon after they had succumbed, tardy reinforcements began to arrive—Pringle had started off his three battalions from the valley to climb the path up to the crest—they arrived at intervals, for their camps were at varying distances from the point of danger, and each acted for itself. The Brigadier himself, finding that he was in general command,

---

[1] Mr. Fortescue (*History of the Army*, ix. p. 258) thinks that the 34th got up in time to join in their last struggle. But Bell of that regiment says ' we laboured on, but all too late—a forlorn hope—our comrades were *all* killed, wounded, or prisoners. The enemy had full possession of the ground.' Bell's *Rough Notes*, i. p. 103.

appears to have ridden up the high road and joined Cameron's brigade at the Maya end of the saddle. From thence he began to send off detachments of that brigade, to co-operate from the flank with the up-hill frontal attack which his own battalions were about to make from the valley.

He found Cameron's brigade under arms, in good order, and unmolested. The Portuguese guns had begun to fire, but not at any enemy, for Maransin was holding back, according to his orders. The shots were signals to give notice to the 7th Division, Ashworth, and other outlying neighbours, that serious fighting had opened in the passes. They do not seem to have commenced till 11 o'clock or even later, for Wellington had ridden off from Lesaca towards St. Sebastian before the cannonade began; and we know that when he started about 11 a.m. no gunfire from the east had been reported. Cameron had already sent off the 50th, the right-hand corps of his brigade, to push along the watershed of the col, and stop the French from any further progress toward the high road. This left only the 71st and 92nd under the Rock of Maya, on the culminating point of the position, awaiting the approach of Maransin, which obviously would not be long delayed.

The second episode of the fight consisted in a series of desperate but ill-connected attempts by four British battalions —the 28th, 34th, 39th, 50th—to push Darmagnac's eight battalions off the foothold on the east end of the col, where they were now firmly established. Abbé's division was not yet on the ground, but was already visible filing up the track which Darmagnac's had already traversed. The three British battalions from the valley arrived in succession, and attacked frontally the mass of French on the crest above them. The 34th came up first and alone. ' It was death to go on against such a host, but it was the *order*, and we went on to destruction, marching up a narrow path with men pumped out and breathless. We had no chance. The colonel, always a good mark, being mounted and foremost, was first knocked over, very badly wounded. Seven more officers were wounded. We persevered, pushed on, made a footing, and kept our ground [1].' But the French held the crest above, and the 34th was brought to a

---

[1] Bell's *Rough Notes*, i. p. 103.

complete standstill. The 39th then climbed up the slope, more to the west, and made a similar unsuccessful push to reach the sky-line. Meanwhile the 50th, coming from the other side along the crest, attacked the French right, and drove in the leading battalion on to the mass, but could get no farther forward, and finally fell back. The last episode of this struggle was a third isolated attack—Pringle had told Cameron to detach the right wing of the 92nd from the Maya position, and to send it on in support of the 50th. Just as the latter recoiled, this strong half-battalion—nearly 400 muskets—came on to the ground on the crest, and at the same moment the 28th, the last of Pringle's battalions to arrive from the valley, climbed the slope and came up diagonally on the right of the 92nd companies. Pringle himself aligned the two corps and led them against the solid mass of French. This advance ended in a most desperate fire-duel at a range of 120 yards, in which the French had the more casualties, but the British line was in the end shot to pieces. Observers from the 28th and 34th speak in the most moving terms of the extraordinary steadiness of the 92nd. ' They stood there like a stone wall, overmatched by twenty to one, until half their blue bonnets lay beside those brave high-land soldiers. When they retired their dead bodies lay as a barrier to the advancing foe. O but they did fight well that day ! I can see the line now of their dead and wounded stretched upon the heather, as the living kept closing up to the centre [1].' It was only when sixty per cent. of these stubborn soldiers had fallen that the senior of the two surviving officers with the wing ordered the remnant to fall back on the 50th, who had reformed in their rear. The 28th, who had been engaged (oddly enough !) with the French 28th, across a dip on the south side of the crest, were cut off from the 92nd, and retreated downhill by the way they had come, towards the village of Maya. So did the 34th, which had been rallied some way down the slope, below the point where they had made their unsuccessful attack, and had been taking long shots uphill against the French flank. So also did the 39th, or the greater part of it [2]. The progress of

---

[1] Bell, i. p. 104.

[2] All this is most difficult to follow, our numerous sources contradicting each other in matters of detail in the most puzzling fashion. For this part

these spent troops downhill was hastened by D'Erlon's detaching two battalions to push them away. They lapsed out of the battle, and retreated towards Maya village, leaving Cameron's brigade alone to maintain the struggle upon the crest—three battalions against three divisions, for Abbé's men were now deploying behind Darmagnac's, and Maransin's long-deferred attack was just beginning to develop.

After the wasted remnant of the right wing of the 92nd had recoiled, the French began to advance along the *Chemin des Anglais*, pushing the beaten troops before them, but were soon brought to a stand for a few minutes once more. For Cameron had detached the right wing of the 71st from the Maya position to follow up the right wing of the 92nd—the system of dribbling in small reinforcements was practised all day—leaving only the two left wings of those regiments to hold the pass against Maransin, who was still an impending danger only. The newly arrived half-battalion, drawn up across the path, delivered a very telling salvo against the front immediately opposed to them—the enemy was now in a mixed mass with no trace of formation, acting like a dense swarm of *tirailleurs*—and brought it to a stop for a moment. But the French, holding back in the centre, spread out on the wings, and began to envelop both flanks of the 71st companies, who had to retire perforce—losing heavily, though not as the 92nd had suffered half an hour before.[1]

of the narrative I have used, beside the dispatch of William Stewart, the books of Moyle Sherer of the 34th, who commanded the Aretesque picquet and was taken prisoner—Sir George Bell of the same regiment, Cadell of the 28th, Hope and Sergeant Robertson of the 92nd, Patterson of the 50th, the two anonymous diarists ' J. S.' and the ' Scottish Soldier ' of the 71st, besides D'Erlon's and Darmagnac's original dispatches, lent me by Mr. Fortescue. I take it that each authority may be followed for the doings of his own corps, but is of inferior weight for those of other units. Patterson says that the 34th was at one time in close touch with the 50th, Cadell that the 28th and 92nd worked together, while Hope says that the 28th was only seen by the 92nd right wing after it had ended its terrible first entry into the fight. Patterson says that he saw O'Callaghan of the 39th fighting along with the 50th in the third episode of the combat, when, according to other sources, that regiment had already retreated south toward the valley with the 34th. Stewart's dispatch only speaks of the 28th and 34th retiring in that direction, not the 39th. A confused fight has left confused memories. I cannot be sure of all the details.

[1] The statement in Napier and succeeding writers that the wounded of

There was now no chance whatever of checking D'Erlon, since the only British troops not yet engaged, the left wings of the 71st and 92nd, were at last feeling the commencement of Maransin's attack, and there were no reinforcements yet visible. Just at this moment, it was perhaps 2 p.m.[1], the long-lost William Stewart at last appeared upon the scene and assumed command. The noise of the guns had reached him in the distant Alduides, and drawn him back to his own business, which he found in a most deplorable condition. A glance round the field showed him that he must give up any hope of holding the Maya pass, and that his only chance was to fight a detaining battle across the high road, in the hope of receiving help from the 7th Division, to whom Pringle had already sent urgent demands for succour.

He accordingly issued orders for the two intact half-battalions on the crest to fall back, and take up a new position below it ; while the weary troops from the old front took shelter and re-formed behind them. Darmagnac's regiments were as much fought out as their opponents, and did not press. Maransin, who had brought up his troops in two columns, one on the road, the other up a ravine to his right, on seeing the way left open to him, did not hurry on, but began to deploy his battalions in succession as they filed up to the saddle of the col. Hence there was a distinct break in the action—half an hour or even more. No disaster was suffered by Cameron's brigade—the only unfortunate incident of the moment of recoil being that the four Portuguese guns were lost. Two had been man-handled with much toil up a rocky slope, from which it was impossible to get them down in a hurry. After firing a round or two of case at the enemy's approaching skirmishers, their gunners

the right wing of the 92nd formed a bank behind which the French advance halted, and stood to receive the fire of the left wing of that same corps, whose bullets hit many of its comrades, comes from the narrative of Norton of the 34th (Napier, V. appendix, p. 442), who was some way off. That the troops which came up were the right wing 71st, and not the left wing 92nd, seems to me proved by the narrative of Hope of the 92nd, who distinctly says that the right wing were relieved by the 71st, and that the left wing were still holding the Maya position and under Stewart, who had just arrived, along with the left wing of the 71st (*Military Memoirs*, p. 210).

[1] He himself in his dispatch only says that it was after 1 p.m.

pushed them over into a ravine and made off [1]. The other two were taken while on the move. Wellington attributed the loss of these four guns, which he much resented (for his army never lost another field gun in action during the whole war), to Stewart, who had, on his arrival, countermanded an order of Pringle's which had directed an earlier retreat for them.

The fourth episode of the combat of Maya, though it included much bloody and obstinate fighting, was not such a desperate business as the long scrambling fight along the *Chemin des Anglais*. D'Erlon halted Darmagnac's troops, who naturally had to re-form, for they were in complete disorder, and had suffered most severely. He now used Maransin's division as his striking force, and when he had got it all deployed attacked Stewart's new position. Abbé's division was brought up to act in support. It was probably well past 3 o'clock when the new fighting began : the delay had enabled Stewart to rearrange a fighting line—the left wings of the 71st and 92nd were drawn up on each side of the *chaussée*, flanked on their left by a company of the latter regiment on a precipitous knoll, where Cameron had placed them before the action began. This company was afterwards reinforced by another from the 82nd, when that regiment came up [2]. About three hundred yards behind, the right wing of the 71st and the 50th, now rallied, made a second line. When Maransin developed his attack, the front line delivered its fire, and fell back in an orderly fashion behind the supports, where it re-formed across the road. The second line repeated this manœuvre. The half-mile of ground given up in these alternate retreats included the camping lines of the 71st and 92nd, where the rows of tents not only broke the enemy's formation, but tempted individuals aside for loot. ' They were plundering on

---

[1] Tulloh (commanding 2nd division batteries) to Dickson, in *Dickson Papers*, p. 1022. Wellington's censure of Stewart may be found in *Dispatches*, x. p. 588, and his reply to the latter's self-defence in xi. p. 107. The details are hard to follow: Wellington says that Pringle ordered the guns to be taken off by the road to Maya—that Stewart directed that they were to go back, and look to ' the mountain road to Elizondo ' as their proper line of retreat. When it became necessary for them to retire at all costs, that road was already in the hands of the French. But I do not know precisely what Wellington meant by the mountain-road to Elizondo. Does it mean the track by which the 28th and 34th had retired ?

[2] See Stewart's Report to Hill, Berueta, July 26.

all hands, cutting down the tents, strewing about the officers' linen, and tearing open their portmanteaux, many of which contained a company's month's pay, while we were obliged to stand at a distance, and view the work of destruction [1].'

The afternoon was drawing on—it was 4.30 or later before Maransin's line re-formed and again advanced : Stewart's front line again retired, but when the enemy followed it he was surprised to be met by a counter-attack. Stewart had just received his first reinforcements—a weak battalion of the 82nd, the nearest troops of the 7th Division, which had long been watching the fight from afar on the Alcorrunz peak, and had just received their divisional general's permission to come in. These new-comers, joining the reserve line, met the leading French battalions with a brisk offensive, which drove them in on their supports. But numbers prevailed, and the fight began once more to roll downhill. At this moment affairs looked black—Stewart had just been wounded in the leg, but still retained the command—he was a splendid fighting man if a careless and tiresome subordinate. Thinking the position hopeless, and a final retreat necessary, he sent messages to the outlying companies of the 82nd and 92nd on the knoll to the left, who were now quite cut off from the rest of the force, to save themselves by striking across the hills. They had been isolated for two hours, had used up all their cartridges, and were defending themselves by the primitive method of pelting the enemy below with whinstones, which lay thick on the hillside [2].

But before the messenger, who had to take a vast détour, could reach this desperate little party, the last episode of the combat of Maya had begun. It was a sufficiently surprising end to the day. At about 6 o'clock there arrived, marching hard along the mountain road which continues the *Chemin des Anglais* westward, two battalions under General Barnes from the 2nd Brigade of the 7th Division [3], which Lord Dalhousie had sent from Echalar on getting the appeal for help. These two units—the 1/6th and Brunswick-Oels—were only 1,500

[1] Robertson, pp. 109–10.

[2] Stewart's dispatch says that it was the 82nd who fought with stones.

[3] This was not the brigade to which the 82nd belonged, but the reserve brigade of the 7th Division, short of one of its units, the 3rd Provisional.

bayonets, and had done nine miles at a hot pace. But they
were fresh troops, and led by a very thunderbolt of war—Barnes
was the brigadier who a few days later made what Wellington
declared to be the most gallant charge that he had seen,
a charge that drew notes of admiration from the most reticent
of pens [1]. They came in diagonally from an unexpected
side road, unseen by the enemy till the moment of contact,
and crashed in upon the leading French battalion with such
an impetus that it was trampled down—losing 15 officers in
a minute. The whole of the rest of the British troops present
cheered, and advanced in the wake of Barnes's men—even the
poor wreck of the right wing of the 92nd, headed by its one
surviving piper. A counter-attack on troops who have already
done much, and are taken by surprise in what seems the
moment of success, is often astoundingly effective—as the war
of 1914–18 has showed. In this case the result was surprising :
Maransin's leading brigade fell back in disorder on his supports,
the latter gave way also, and the whole mass retired uphill, as
far as the camping-ground of Cameron's regiments at the head
of the pass. D'Erlon, wrongly believing that the whole
7th Division had arrived *en masse*, threw a brigade of Abbé's
division across the crest of the col, behind which the beaten
troops took shelter. He expected to end the day with a defensive action, and even recalled a brigade of Darmagnac's troops,
who had been sent down towards the village of Maya, in pursuit
of Pringle's brigade, and who had just got engaged near it with
Ashworth's Portuguese, then retiring by order from the pass
of Ispegui.

But Stewart would have been mad to press on with six
battalions—three of them mere remnants—against eighteen,
and halted on the summit, content to have blocked the pass,
though the enemy had possession of it, and of ground in front
of it on which he stood deployed. The firing continued for a
time, and then died down as the dusk came on. By 8 o'clock
all was over—if D'Erlon had frankly put in Abbé's strong
division of ten battalions, it is clear that he might yet have
turned the fortune of the day. But he did not : hypnotized
by the idea that he had the whole of the 2nd and 7th Divisions

[1] Cf. *Dispatches*, x. pp. 597–8.

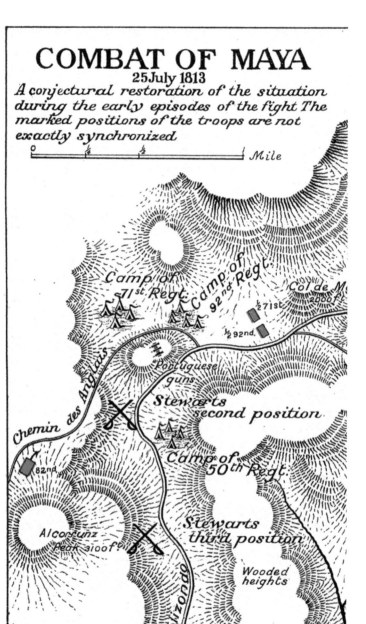

COMBAT OF MAYA
25 July 1813

*A conjectural restoration of the situation
during the early episodes of the fight The
marked positions of the troops are not
exactly synchronized*

0   ¼   ½   1 Mile

Camp of
71ˢᵗ Regt.

Camp of
92ⁿᵈ Regt.

Col de M
2000ᶠᵗ

½ 71ˢᵗ

½ 92ⁿᵈ

Portuguese
guns

Stewarts
second position

Chemin des Anglais

82ⁿᵈ

Camp of
50ᵗʰ Regt.

Alcorrunz
Peak 3100ᶠᵗ

Stewarts
third position

Wooded
heights

To Elizondo

British Troops
French   „ „

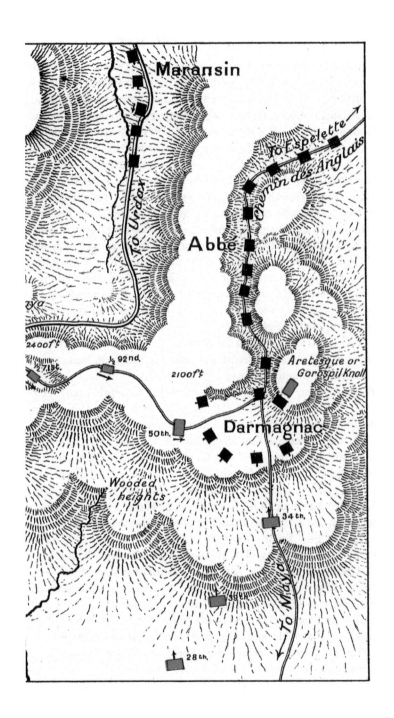

Maransin

To Espelette →

Chemin des Anglais

To Urdox

Abbé

2400 ft

½ 71st.   ½ 92 nd.

2100 ft

Aretesque or
Gorospil Knoll

50th.

Darmagnac

Wooded
heights

34 th.

To Maya →

39th.

28 th.

in front of him, instead of a mere fragment of each. The battle
was well over when General Hill arrived from the Alduides,
bringing with him unlucky news—he had intercepted and read,
at Elizondo, Cole's dispatch to Head-quarters saying that he had
been attacked at Roncesvalles by 35,000 men, and that he was
giving up the pass. Wherefore Hill resolved that he also must
retire, and ordered the weary troops of Stewart and Barnes to
retreat after midnight to Elizondo and cross the upper Bidassoa.
It is scarcely credible that the men who had fought for ten
hours under such conditions on such rough ground, retained
strength to move another furlong—but the order was obeyed,
though many badly wounded men had to be abandoned, and
though the *chaussée* was strewn for miles by dead-beat stragglers,
who dropped out and slept till daylight. They were not disturbed—for D'Erlon made no move till the sun was well up—
he had won the pass and was expecting to have to fight again
at dawn, for the right to emerge from it.

The losses in a fight so honourable to the British battalions,
if so discreditable to British generalship, had been immense in
Cameron's brigade, heavy in Pringle's, appreciable among
Barnes's men, who only struck in at the eleventh hour. The
first-named had lost 800 men out of 1,900 present, of whom
343 belonged to the gallant and unlucky 1/92nd. Pringle's
three battalions had 530 casualties out of 2,000 present, including 140 unwounded prisoners taken on the Gorospil knoll from
its light companies. Barnes and the 7th Division troops had
won a glorious success with a loss of only 140 men. The total
list gives just under 1,500 casualties out of 6,000 men engaged—
of whom 349 were prisoners (200 of them wounded). These are
very different figures from the 3,500 total at which D'Erlon
stated Stewart's loss—but sufficiently distressing. The enemy
had suffered still more, but from infinitely greater numbers—
their commander reported 1,400 casualties in Darmagnac's
division out of 7,000 present, 600 in Maransin's. Abbé was
barely engaged at the eleventh hour : one of his brigadiers
(Rignoux) was hit and only four other officers, with perhaps
100 men. The total reported is therefore about 2,100—no very
formidable proportion out of 20,000 men present. But some
battalions had been badly cut up—the 103rd of Maransin's

division, which bore the first fury of Barnes's attack, had
15 officers killed and wounded out of 20 present ; and the 28th
of Darmagnac's division lost a similar number in sustaining
the attack of the right wing of the 1/92nd and the British 28th.
But this was a two-battalion regiment with 40 officers present.
Nevertheless, D'Erlon's report to Soult sings victory in very
modest terms—he has captured the enemy's position and holds
it at the end of the day—the affair had been one of the most
desperate that he has ever seen—the enemy's loss has been far
greater than his own—but there is no blowing of trumpets.

SECTION XXXVIII: CHAPTER IV

SORAUREN. JULY 26-28

THE first day's fighting in the Pyrenean passes could not be called satisfactory either to Wellington or to Soult. The former had lost both the defiles in which he had intended to make his first stand, and had lost them in a very tiresome fashion—he thought that Maya might have been held at least for twenty-four hours, if there had been a divisional general on the spot to direct the defence: while Roncesvalles had not been forced, but abandoned by Cole, who could certainly have made a longer resistance, if only the orders sent to him had been obeyed. It was, above all things, necessary to gain time for the concentration of the army, and a precious day had been lost—and need not have been lost.

But Soult can have been no better pleased : time, to him also, meant everything; and the orders which he had issued to his lieutenants had presupposed an easy triumph by surprise in the early morning, with a forward march in the afternoon. Instead of this he had won by nightfall a bare foothold on the summit of each pass, after much fighting of an unsatisfactory sort. He, too, had lost a day; and it was only on the morrow that he discovered that both at Maya and at Roncesvalles the enemy had slipped away in the dark, leaving to him the power to debouch from the defiles.

Nevertheless, the Marshal sent on the morning of the 26th a very flamboyant message of victory to his master the Emperor, who then lay at Mayence. Both Maya and Roncesvalles had been forced, D'Erlon had captured five guns and many hundreds of prisoners at the former pass : he himself hoped to be at Pampeluna, and to have raised its siege, by the 27th. These news were sent on from Bayonne by semaphore to Paris and the Rhine, and reached Napoleon on August 1st. At the same time, and by the same rapid method of transmission, arrived General Rey's report of his successful repulse of the assault of

July 25th. It is worth while to turn away from solid history for a moment, in order to see how the Imperial editor of the *Moniteur* utilized this useful material for propaganda. He first wrote to Clarke the Minister of War : ' We can now give the public some account of affairs in Spain. The Vittoria business and the King must not be mentioned. The first note which you must put in the *Moniteur* should run as follows—" His Majesty has named the Duke of Dalmatia as his lieutenant-general commanding his armies in Spain. The Marshal took up the command on July 12, and made immediate dispositions for marching against the besiegers of Pampeluna and St. Sebastian." After that put in General Rey's first letter about the events of the 25th–27th. You had better make some small additions to the number of prisoners and of guns captured, not for French consumption but to influence European opinion. As I am printing General Rey's dispatch in the *Frankfort Journal*, and have made some changes of this sort in it, I send you a corrected copy so that it may appear in the *Moniteur* in identical terms.'

The Emperor's second letter to his Foreign Minister, the Duke of Bassano, sent from Dresden three days later, is even more amusing. ' You had better circulate the news that in conse- quence of Marshal Soult's victory over the English on July 25, the siege of St. Sebastian has been raised, and 30 siege-guns and 200 waggons taken. The blockade of Pampeluna was raised on the 27th : General Hill, who was in command at that siege, could not carry off his wounded, and was obliged to burn part of his baggage. Twelve siege-guns (24-pounders) were captured there. Send this to Prague, Leipzig, and Frankfort [1].'

This ' intelligent anticipation of the future,' for utilization in the armistice-negotiations going on with Austria, could not have been bettered. Unfortunately there arrived next day another semaphore message from Soult of the night of the 26th–27th. The Emperor has to warn Caulaincourt that yesterday's propaganda will not stand criticism. ' I have just got another " telegraphic dispatch " sent on by the

---

[1] ' Lettres de l'Empereur Napoléon non insérées dans la *Correspondance*, publiées par X. Paris and Nancy, 1909,' page 3. It is amusing to find out what Napoleon III omitted of his uncle's letters.

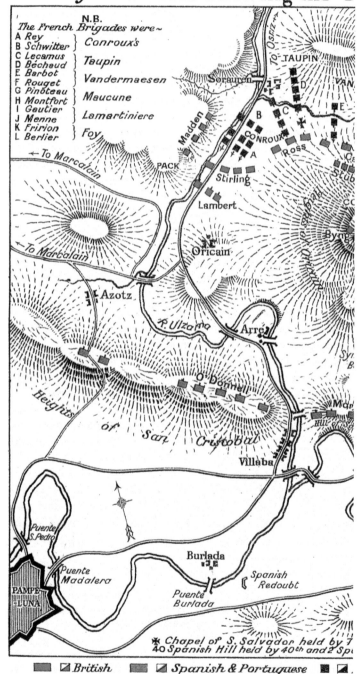

N.B.
The French Brigades were ~

A	Rey	} Conroux's
B	Schwitter	
C	Lecamus	} Taupin
D	Béchaud	
E	Barbot	} Vandermaesen
F	Rouget	
G	Pinôteau	} Maucune
H	Montfort	
I	Geutier	} Lamartiniere
J	Menne	
K	Fririon	} Foy
L	Berlier	

TO TAUPIN

Sorauren

← To Marcalain

PACK

Madden

CONROUX

Ross

Stirling

Lambert

← To Martalain

Oricain

Byn

R. Ulzama

Azotz

Arre

O'Donnell

Heights

of San Cristobal

Villaba

Hill

Puente S. Pedro

Burlada

Puente Madalera

Spanish Redoubt

PAMPE-LUNA

Puente Burlada

✳ Chapel of S. Salvador held by 7
40 Spanish Hill held by 40th and 2 Sp

🟦 ◩ *British*   🟦 ◩ *Spanish & Portuguese*   🟦 ◩

French 0   ½   1   1½ Miles

Empress from Mayence, giving another communication from Soult, written 24 hours after the last, in which he said he would be at Pampeluna on the 27th. The enemy lost many men and seven guns. But nothing decisive seems to have happened. I am impatient for more news, in order to be able to understand in detail Soult's dispositions, and to form from them a general idea of the situation [1].'

Alas for human ingenuity! Soult's next dispatch, of July 29, was not to be of the sort that craved for publicity in the *Moniteur*, even with the most judicious editing.

But to return from Dresden to Biscay, and from the headquarters of the Emperor to those of the 'Sepoy General' whom he had at last begun to recognize as capable of 'des projets très sensés.'

If only Wellington had been at his head-quarters at Lesaca at 11 o'clock on the morning of July 25th, and if William Stewart had been on the spot at Maya, and had sent early news of D'Erlon's attack, many things might have happened differently. Wellington would have had a long afternoon before him to concert operations, and would have possessed information to guide him in drawing up his scheme. Unfortunately he was absent—as we have seen—and only received at 6 o'clock a second-hand report from Lord Dalhousie at Echalar, to the effect that fighting was going on at Maya, with the unfortunate addition that D'Erlon had been repulsed—a most inaccurate summary of what had happened. Later on in the evening, not before 10 p.m., came Cole's first dispatch from Roncesvalles, to say that he and Byng were heavily engaged at 1 o'clock with a large French force, and were holding their own. On these scanty data Wellington felt that no conclusions could be drawn —he wrote to Graham that there must be a great mass of French troops not yet discovered, which would come into action on some other point on the 26th, and that his policy would depend on where that force appeared—he could only account for 30,000 of Soult's men so far. He did not commit himself to any definite guess as to the undiscovered part of the Marshal's plan, but from his other correspondence it is clear that he suspected an attempt to relieve St. Sebastian by an

[1] 'Lettres de l'Empereur Napoléon non insérées dans la *Correspondance*,' p. 18.

attack on the lower Bidassoa—a very possible solution of the problem, but not the correct one [1].

Awaiting further developments, Wellington issued no more orders on the night of the 25th, save one to the Conde de Abispal, directing him to send one of his two infantry divisions from in front of Pampeluna to join Picton and Cole, and to keep the fortress blockaded by the other. The force thus taken away would be replaced by Carlos de España's division, which was marching up from Burgos, and due to arrive on the 26th. In this dispatch Wellington asked the Conde to direct Mina to send up his infantry from Saragossa, and told him that he was intending to order to the front the British heavy cavalry brigades, now cantoned along the Ebro. No other movements were settled that night ; but Wellington was aware that during his absence his Quartermaster-General, George Murray, had directed Lord Dalhousie to have the 7th Division massed at Echalar, prepared to move at an hour's notice, and Charles Alten at Vera to have the Light Division got into a similar readiness. Either would be able to march off at dawn.

Somewhere late in the night [2] Wellington received more news, which made the situation clearer but more unsatisfactory. The true story of the Maya fighting came in from two sources : Hill sent a dispatch dated from Elizondo at some hour after 6 p.m., to say that on getting back from the Alduides he had found Stewart unable to hold the Pass, and had bidden him to retire. Stewart, who was wounded and unable to write, sent a verbal message, which came in about the same time, reporting that Hill had directed him to fall back on Elizondo and Berueta. The officers who brought this information stated that the French were in great force, and that the 2nd Division had been much cut up. No more reports arrived from Cole, so that the result of the Roncesvalles fighting remained unknown.

[1] Wellington's letter to Graham, giving the false report that D'Erlon had been repulsed at Maya, is dated at 10 p.m. The letter to O'Donnell must be a little later, as it repeats this error, but adds that a note has come in from Cole, saying that he was heavily engaged at noon. *Dispatches*, x. pp. 566-7.

[2] The dispatch giving this information (*Dispatches*, x. p. 570) is wrongly dated in the Wellington correspondence. It should be July *26th* at 4 a.m. The hour of the receipt of Hill's and Stewart's reports is not given.

After what must have been a very short and disturbed night's rest, Wellington was in the saddle by 4 a.m. on the 26th, and preparing to ride up the Bastan to visit Hill, and to ascertain the exact measure of the mishap at Maya. Before departing from Lesaca he gave his first definite orders in view of the events of the previous day [1]. Maya being lost, the 7th Division must fall back from Echalar to Sumbilla, on the road to Santesteban : the Light Division must retire from Vera to the west bank of the Bidassoa, and be ready to march either towards Yanzi or towards Santesteban, as might be necessary. Longa's Cantabrians were to block the hill road from the Bidassoa to Oyarzun. Graham was told to hurry on the embarkation of the siege-train from St. Sebastian. Hill was to hold on as long as he could to the position at Irurita, in order to keep touch with the 6th Division, which was directed to feel towards him, and to be ready to join him if necessary. It was to push two of its three brigades to Legasa, on the road from Santesteban along the upper Bidassoa, which would bring them within eight miles of Hill's proposed line of defence at Irurita. The third brigade of the 6th Division was to stand fast at Santesteban, where it would be in touch with Dalhousie, when the latter should have reached Sumbilla.

All these orders, as is obvious, are concerned only with the measures necessary to stop D'Erlon's advance. None of them have any reference to the action of the other French force at Roncesvalles. Till news should come up from Cole and Picton, it was impossible to realize what was going on at that front, or whether the enemy was making his main attack in that direction. There might be still (as Wellington had guessed three days back) a violent demonstration towards Pampeluna, intended to distract a real attempt to relieve St. Sebastian.

And this state of ignorance with regard to the southern theatre of operations was destined to last till late in the afternoon. Either Cole and Picton themselves, or the officers to whom they entrusted their dispatches, were sadly lacking in a sense of the value of the prompt delivery of news. Wellington rode along the Bidassoa for many a mile, till he came on Hill still holding the position of Irurita, and entirely unmolested

[1] All in *Supplementary Dispatches*, viii. pp. 120–1.

by the French. There were now in line the sadly reduced
remnant of the British brigades which had fought at Maya, and
da Costa's and Ashworth's Portuguese, with the three 7th-
Division battalions which had saved Stewart from disaster. The
total made up about 9,000 bayonets. Hill estimated[1] D'Erlon's
force at 14,000 men—a miscalculation, for even after the losses
at Maya there were still 18,000 French in line. The immediate
result of the error, however, was beneficial rather than otherwise, for Wellington considered that Hill was in no particular
danger, and let him stand, while he himself rode southward
towards the lofty Col de Velate, to seek for intelligence from the
Pampeluna front in person, since his lieutenants had vouch-
safed him none. He reached Almandoz, near the crest of the
Pass, in the afternoon, and resolved to establish his head-
quarters there for the night, as it was conveniently central
between the two halves of his army.

Soon after his arrival Wellington, being much vexed at
receiving no news whatever from the south, resolved to send
the 6th Division toward Pampeluna by the Col de Velate as
a matter of precaution—they were to march to Olague in the
valley of the Lanz. The 7th Division was to close in, to take
up the ground where the 6th had been placed, and cover Hill's
left flank[2]. That haste in these movements was not considered a primary necessity, is shown by the fact that Pack and
Dalhousie were told that they need not march till the morning
of the 27th. For the enemy's surprising quiescence at the head
of the Maya pass had reassured Wellington as to any danger on
this side. If D'Erlon, indeed, possessed no more than 14,000
men, Hill with the aid of the 7th Division could easily take
care of him. And the Light Division might still be left near
Lesaca, as a reserve for Graham in case any new mass of French
troops should take the offensive on the Bidassoa.

D'Erlon's conduct on the morning of the 26th was explicable
to himself, though inexplicable to his enemy. He had been
engaged in a most bitter fight, in which he had lost 2,000 men

---

[1] Hill to Murray, *Supplementary Dispatches*, viii. p. 121.
[2] The orders to Pack and Dalhousie may be found in *Supplementary Dispatches*, xix. p. 258-9, dated from Almandoz—obviously before Cole's dispatch had come to hand.

and more. Two British divisions, so he wrote to Soult, were in front of him—the 2nd and the 7th. For he had taken Barnes's brigade for the whole of Dalhousie's unit—the effect of its desperate charge almost justified him in the hypothesis. These troops had been forced to a strategic retreat, but by no means put out of action. They must have been joined, ere now, by the Portuguese column which Darmagnac had sighted on its approach to Ariscun. But there were also troops on his right, of whom he must beware : he knew that Vera and Echalar had been held in strength, and Graham might send reinforcements in that direction, and assemble a heavy force on his flank. Hence he resolved to discover how matters lay by reconnaissances, before committing himself to the march down into the Bastan and then up the Col de Velate which his orders prescribed.

' In my position on the pass of Maya,' he wrote, ' I had on my right all the forces which the enemy had in line as far as St. Sebastian. I had to be prudent, in order not to expose myself to a check in the Bastan, in which the enemy was holding the strongest position. I therefore determined to leave Abbé and Maransin in the pass, with orders to send out reconnaissances towards Santesteban, Echalar, and Mount Atchiola. They would profit by the halt to distribute the half-ration of food which had just come up from Ainhoue. I sent Darmagnac down the road to Ariscun, with orders to push a vanguard to Elizondo, and to explore towards the passes of Ispegui and Berderis, to see if there were any hostile force still on my left.'

An advance of six miles to Elizondo, and that by a mere advanced guard, was all the movement that D'Erlon made this day. It was not till the afternoon that he learnt, by Abbé's reconnaissances, that there were still allied troops on his right —apparently the Light Division opposite Vera, and the 7th at Sumbilla—while Darmagnac reported that the eastern passes were clear, but that Hill was lying across the road beyond Elizondo in great strength. In the evening D'Erlon heard that Soult had forced the pass of Roncesvalles, and was about to advance : this success, he deduced, would make the enemy in front of him give way, in fear that his positions might be taken from behind. So he thought himself justified in ordering a general advance for the morning of the 27th—though Maransin was still to remain for a day at Maya, lest any allied force might move up from the west against the pass. Thus it came that for the whole of July 26th Hill was unmolested, and Soult's plan for a rapid concentration round Pampeluna became almost impossible to carry out. A whole day had been wasted by D'Erlon, though he was not without his extenuating circumstances.

Wellington meanwhile received at Almandoz, probably· at about 8 p.m., the long-expected news from the South. They were, as we know, most unsatisfactory : Cole reported from Linzoain, on the Roncesvalles–Pampeluna road, that he had been driven out of the pass by an army of 35,000 men or more, that he had not yet been joined by the 3rd Division, and was still retreating towards Zubiri, where he understood that Picton would meet him and take over the command. His view of the situation was shown by a remark that if he had not been superseded, and had been compelled to retreat past Pampeluna, he supposed that the road towards Vittoria would have been the right one to take [1]. This most exasperating dispatch only reached Wellington that night by mere chance. The officer bearing it was going to Lesaca, having no knowledge that Army Head-Quarters had left that place : at Lanz he happened to meet the cavalry brigadier Long, whose squadrons were keeping up the line of communication between the two halves of the Army. Hearing from the aide-de-camp of the sort of news that the letter contained, Long opened it and made a copy of it, which he sent to Sir Rowland Hill, before permitting the bearer to go on. Hill received the transcript at Berueta at 6 p.m., and very wisely forwarded it to Wellington at Almandoz. The original was carried on by Cole's messenger to Santesteban, and did not reach Wellington that night.

Thanks to Long's and Hill's intelligent action, the Commander-in-Chief could grasp the whole unpleasant situation at 8 p.m. on the 26th. He sent orders to Picton at once, telling him that the enemy must at all costs be detained : that con-

[1] This letter in *Supplementary Dispatches*, viii. pp. 124–5, is there wrongly dated July 27th (for 26th). Cole, of course, was no longer at Linzoain on the 27th.

sidering the force at his disposal, he ought to be able to check Soult for some time in front of Zubiri : that he would be joined at once by one of O'Donnell's divisions from the Pampeluna blockading force, and shortly by reinforcements coming from the Bastan (the 6th Division). Wellington himself was intending to ride over to the right wing by the next afternoon. Till he should arrive, Picton must send reports every few hours [1]. Unfortunately, Cole and Picton had got things into an even worse state than could have been expected. Just as Wellington was drafting these orders for an obstinate rearguard action, they were at 8.30 p.m. preparing to evacuate the Zubiri position, and setting out on a night march for Pampeluna [2].

To explain this move we must go back to the state of affairs at Roncesvalles on the very foggy morning of July 26th. Cole, Byng, and Morillo had abandoned, as we have already seen [3], their position on Altobiscar and the Linduz under cover of the night, and had all fallen into the Pampeluna road, Ross's brigade descending from the heights by the Mendichuri pass, the other three brigades and Morillo moving by the *chaussée* past the Abbey and Burguete. Anson's brigade formed the rearguard, not having been engaged on the previous day. Morillo's outlying battalion at the Foundry of Orbaiceta safely joined in by a hill path. Campbell's Portuguese retired by the way that they had come, along the Path of Atalosti, but instead of returning to the Alduides followed a mule track to Eugui in the upper valley of the Arga.

Cole's long column, after completing its night march, took a much-needed rest for many hours along the high road near Viscarret. It saw nothing of the French till the early afternoon, when an exploring party of chasseurs ran into the rearguard of Anson's brigade.

What had Soult been doing between early dawn, when his outposts ascertained that there was no enemy in front of them, and three o'clock in the afternoon, when his cavalry rediscovered Cole ? To our surprise we find that he had been attempting to repeat his error of the preceding day—that of sending a whole

[1] To Picton from Almandoz, *Supplementary Dispatches*, xiv. p. 259.
[2] Picton to Murray, 8.30 p.m., *Supplementary Dispatches*, xviii. pp. 121–2.
[3] See above, p. 622.

army corps along a rugged mule track, similar to the one on which Reille's column had been blocked by Ross's brigade. His original order on the 25th had been that Reille, after seizing the Linduz, should turn along the 'crest of the mountains', occupy the Atalosti defile, and push ever westward till he could threaten the Col de Velate, the main line of communication between the two sections of Wellington's army. One would have supposed that the events of the 25th on the Linduz, where one British brigade had checked for a whole day Reille's column of 17,000 men in Indian file, would have taught him the impracticability of such plans. But (as Soult's malevolent critic, quoted already above, observed) when the Marshal had once got his plan drawn up on paper it was like the laws of the Medes and Persians, and must not be altered [1].

While Clausel was directed to use the *chaussée* and pursue Cole along the Pampeluna road past Roncesvalles, Burguete, and Espinal, Reille was once more ordered [2] 'to follow the crest of the mountains to the right, and to try to take in the rear the hostile corps which has been holding the pass of Maya against Count D'Erlon.' The itinerary seems insane : there was a mule track and no more, and Soult proposed to engage upon it a column of 17,000 men, with a front of one file and a depth of at least six miles, allowing for the battalion- and brigade-intervals. The crest was not a flat plateau, but an interminable series of ups and downs, often steep and stony, occasionally wooded. Campbell's brigade had traversed part of it on the 25th, but to move a brigade on a fine day is a different thing from moving an army corps in a fog.

Reille obeyed orders, though the fog was lying as densely upon the mountains as on the preceding night. Apparently Soult had supposed that it would lift at dawn—but it did not till mid-day. Lamartinière's division was left to guard the Linduz and the debouch of the Atalosti path : Foy's, followed by Maucune's, tried to keep to the crest, with the most absurd results. It was supposed to be guided by French-Basque peasants (smugglers, no doubt) who were reputed to know the ground. After going no more than a mile or two in the fog,

---

[1] See above, p. 591.

[2] These are his own words, in his Report of August 2.

the guides, at a confusion of tracks in the middle of a wood, came to a standstill, and talked volubly to Foy in unintelligible Basque. Whether they had lost their way, or were giving advice, the General could not quite discover. In despair he allowed the leading battalion to take the most obvious track. They had got completely off the Atalosti path, and after two miles of down-hill marching found themselves on the *chaussée* not far from Espinal, with the rear of Clausel's corps defiling past them [1]. It would still have been possible to stop the column, for only one brigade had reached the foot of the mountain, and Maucune and Lamartinière were still on the crest. But Reille took upon himself the responsibility of overriding his commander's impracticable directions, and ordered Foy to go on, and the rest to follow, and to fall in to the rear of Clausel's impedimenta. ' Il est fort dangereux dans les hautes montagnes de s'engager sans guides et en brouillard,' as he very truly observed. Justifying himself in a letter of that night to Soult, he wrote that if it were absolutely necessary to get on the crest-path again, it could be done by turning up the Arga valley at Zubiri, and following it to Eugui, from which there were tracks both to the Col de Velate and to Irurita.[2]

Thus ended Soult's impracticable scheme for seizing the Col de Velate by marching three divisions along a precipitous mule track. Even if there had been no fog, it is hard to believe that anything could have come of it, as Campbell's Portuguese would have been found at Eugui well on in the day, and after Reille's column would have been much fatigued. Any show of resistance, even by one brigade, would have checked Foy, and compelled Reille to deploy—an interminable affair, as the fight on the Linduz upon the preceding afternoon had sufficiently demonstrated. But to try this manœuvre in a dense fog was insane, and Reille was quite right to throw it up.

The whole interest, therefore, of the French operation on July 26th turns on the doing of Clausel's column. It advanced very cautiously down the slopes to the Abbey of Roncesvalles, discovering no trace of the enemy save a few abandoned

[1] Foy to Reille, July 26.
[2] Reille to Soult, July 27.

wounded. Having reached the upland valley of Burguete, Clausel sent out cavalry patrols, and found, after much searching in the fog, that Cole had gone off with his whole force towards Espinal. His rearguard was discovered bivouacking along the road beyond that village. When it sighted the French it retired towards Viscarret. Clausel then ordered his infantry to pursue, but they were far to the rear and it was only about 3 p.m. when Taupin's division came into touch with the light companies of Anson's brigade, just as they were falling back on the whole 4th Division, drawn up in a favourable position on heights behind the Erro river, near the village of Linzoain. The day had at last become clear and fine. The 31st Léger, leading the French column, exchanged a lively fusillade with the light companies, while a squadron of chasseurs tried a charge on their flank. But both were driven off, and Clausel halted when he saw Cole waiting for him in order of battle. It was not till he had brought up and deployed two divisions that he ventured to press the Allied front, and nothing serious happened till after 4 o'clock.

Meanwhile Picton had come up from the rear, and joined Cole at Linzoain : the head of his troops had reached Zubiri only three miles behind. The arrival of the truculent general, looking even more eccentric than usual, for he was wearing a tall round civilian hat above a blue undress frock-coat, and was using a furled umbrella by way of riding whip, was taken by the 4th-Division soldiers as a sign of battle[1]. ' Here comes old Tommy : now, boys, make up your minds for a fight ' passed down the ranks[2]. But, oddly enough, this was about the only day in Sir Thomas's military career when he did not take a fair risk. He certainly came up in a bellicose mood, for he ordered Ross's brigade to be ready to move forward when the 3rd Division should have come up to support it. But after riding to the front, and holding a long talk with Cole, he agreed with the latter that it would be dangerous to fight on ground which could be turned on both flanks, with an enemy who was known

[1] The tall hat is vouched for by George L'Estrange of the 31st, and Wachholz from Ross's brigade, the furled umbrella by Bainbrigge of the 20th, all eye-witnesses, whose narratives are among the few detailed accounts of this retreat.

[2] Words overheard by Bainbrigge in his own company.

to have 35,000 men in hand. Only part of the French were up—
Reille's divisions after their stroll in the fog were far to the rear
behind Clausel—so it would be possible to hold on till night,
and slip away in the dark. Picton wrote to Wellington to
report his decision, and does not seem in his dispatch to have
realized in the least that he was contravening the whole spirit
of his commander's instructions of July 23rd with reference to
the 'stopping of the enemy's progress towards Pampeluna in
the event of the passes being given up [1].' He merely stated
that he had received these instructions too late to make it
possible for him to reach Roncesvalles, or to join Cole before the
latter had evacuated his positions [2]. As there was no favourable
ground between the Erro river and the immediate vicinity of
Pampeluna, on which a smaller force could make an effectual
stand against a much larger one, he had determined to retire
at once, and proposed to 'take up a position at as short a distance as practicable from Pampeluna'—by which he meant
the heights of San Cristobal, only two or three miles out from
that fortress. He was thus intending to give up without further
fighting ten miles of most difficult hilly country, where the
enemy could be checked for a time at every successive ridge—
though, no doubt, all the positions could be turned one after
the other by long flank détours. But the net result was that
Picton gave Soult a clear road on the 27th, and allowed him to
arrive in front of Pampeluna on that day, whereas the least
show of resistance between Zubiri and the debouch into the
plains at Huarte, would have forced the French to deploy and
waste time, and they could not have reached the open country
till the 28th. This is sufficiently proved by the extreme difficulty which Soult found in conducting his march, even when he
was not opposed.

---

[1] See Quartermaster-General to Picton, enclosing letter for Cole, sent
off from Lesaca on July 23 (*Supplementary Dispatches*, viii. pp. 112–13),
which must have reached Picton at Olague on the 24th.

[2] This seems a more controvertible plea. Orders went out from Lesaca on
the 23rd, and must have reached Picton not very late in the day on the
24th. Supposing he had marched from Olague on the afternoon of the 24th,
he would have been at Zubiri (only 6 miles off) on that same night, or even
at Viscarret. And from Zubiri to Roncesvalles is not an excessive day's
march for the 25th, especially when firing was to be heard at the front.

So determined was Picton not to fight on the Erro river, or on the Arga, that he did not bring up his own division from Zubiri, but let it stand, only three miles behind the line on which Cole kept up a mild detaining action during the late afternoon hours of the 26th. Soult attacked with great caution, and more by way of flank movements than by frontal pressure. By evening Cole had drawn back one mile, and had 168 casualties, all but four of them in Anson's brigade [1]. Those of the French can hardly have been more numerous : they seem all to have been in Taupin's division [2].

On the afternoon of the 26th Picton had nearly 19,000 men at his disposition [3], Soult had somewhat less, since Reille's column was so far to the rear that it could not get up before dark. There was no wonder, therefore, that the enemy made no resolute attack ; and it can only be said that the Marshal was acting very wisely, for the French force on the ground was not sufficient to move the opposing body, until Reille should have come up ; and Cole and Picton had resolved not to give way before dark. But when the fires of the French, shining for many miles on each side of the road, showed that they had settled down for the night, Cole drew off his division, and retired on Zubiri, where he passed through Picton's troops, who were to take over the rearguard duty, as they were fresh and well rested. Campbell's Portuguese dropped into the line of march from Eugui, by orders issued to them that afternoon, and by 11 p.m. the whole corps was in march for Pampeluna. Its departure had passed wholly unnoticed by the enemy. Meanwhile, Wellington's aide-de-camp, riding through the night from Almandoz, with orders to Picton to maintain the ground which he was abandoning, can only have met the column when it was drawing near its destination.

[1] The remaining four were in the Caçador battalion of Stubbs's Portuguese brigade.

[2] Unfortunately all French losses are given *en bloc* for the six days July 27 to August 1, and the casualties of each day cannot be disentangled. The casualties of Maya and Roncesvalles *can* be ascertained, but not those of the subsequent days.

[3] Viz. about 6,000 of Cole's division, 5,000 of his own, 1,700 of Byng's brigade, 2,500 of Campbell's Portuguese at Eugui, only a few miles away, and something under 4,000 of Morillo's Spaniards.

It was quite early in the morning, though the sun was well up, when the head of the retreating column reached the village of Zabaldica, where the valley of the Arga begins to open out into the plain of Pampeluna, between the last flanking heights which constrict it. In front was the very ill-chosen position which Picton intended to hold, along a line of hills which are quite separate from the main block of the mountains, and stretch isolated in the lowland for some five miles north-west and south-east. These are the hill of Huarte on the right, parted from the mountains by the valley of the Egues river; the hill of San Miguel in the centre, on the other side of the high road and of the Arga river, and on the left the very long ridge of San Cristobal, separated from San Miguel by the Ulzama river, which flows all along its front.

Now these hills are strong posts in themselves, each with a good glacis of slope in its front; the gaps between them are stopped by the large villages of Villaba and Huarte, both susceptible of obstinate defence; and the two flanking hills are covered in front by river-beds—though fordable ones. But they are far too close to Pampeluna, which is but one single mile from San Cristobal: the guns of the fortress actually commanded at a range of only 1,200 yards, the sole road of communication along the rear of the position. Cassan's garrison of 3,000 men was not large enough to furnish men for any large sortie—though he made a vigorous sally against O'Donnell's blockading division on the 27th, and destroyed some of its trenches [1]. But no army should fight with a hostile fortress less than two miles in its rear, and commanding its line of retreat: it is surprising that such an old soldier as Picton chose this ground—presumably he was seduced by the fine position for both infantry and guns which it shows looking towards the enemy's road of arrival.

Apparently Cole had a better eye for ground than Picton, for as they were riding together between Zabaldica and Huarte, he pointed out to his senior the advantage that would be gained by throwing forward the left wing of the army to a position much more remote from Pampeluna, the hill of Oricain or Sorauren, which faces the San Cristobal ridge from the other

[1] See Belmas, iv. p. 803.

side of the Ulzama river [1]. This height is the last roll of the
mountains, but almost separated from their main *massif*: it is
only joined to the next summit by a high *col* at its right centre.
For the rest of its length it is separated from its neighbour-
height by a well-marked ravine. Its flanks are guarded by the
beds of the Arga to the right and the Ulzama to the left. It is
well under two miles long, about 1,000 feet high, and except at
the Col has a very formidable front of steep slopes, covered with
gorse and scattered bushes. The whole formed a strong and
self-contained position, whose weak point was that it was
rather too much in advance of the Huarte–San Miguel heights,
which trend away southward, so that when the army was
drawn out its right was much ' refused,' and its left very much
thrown forward. It was also inconvenient that the access to
the crest from the rear was bad, a steep climb by sheep-tracks
from Oricain or Arre, up which all food or munitions would have
to be brought. From the north there was a slightly better path
to the summit from Sorauren, leading up to the small pilgrimage
chapel of San Salvador on the left end of the crest. But this
would be of more use to the assailants than to the defenders of
the heights. Between the Col and the river Arga, and close
above the village of Zabaldica, there was a spur or under-
feature of the main position, which formed a sort of outwork
or flank protection to it. At the moment when the retreating
army was passing on towards Huarte, this spur was being held
by two Spanish battalions, part of the division which O'Donnell,
by Wellington's orders, had detached to reinforce Picton. It

---

[1] Napier says (v. p. 225), and all subsequent historians have followed him,
that Picton originally intended to place Cole on a line between Oricain and
Arleta, i. e. on the low back-slope of the ridge. This seems to me almost
incredible, as this ground is all running downhill, completely commanded
by the much loftier crests about the Col. Surely no one, according to
the tactical ideas of 1813, would take up a defensive position half-way
down a slope whose summit is abandoned to the enemy. I can find no
authority save Napier (who was not in the battle) for this curious statement. And I am justified, I think, in holding that the San Miguel hill
was the place where Picton intended to place Cole, by the narrative and
sketch-map of Wachholz of Ross's brigade, who places the first position
of the 4th Division on a well-marked hill immediately to the right of
Villaba, and close to the 3rd Division's ground at Huarte. This *must*
mean San Miguel.

was perhaps the sight of this small force in a very good position which suggested to Cole that the right policy was to prolong his line in continuation of it, across the Col and as far as the chapel above Sorauren.

Having allowed Cole to take up his new advanced position, Picton drew out the 3rd Division on the hill to the right of Huarte, with its flank eastwards covered by four brigades of cavalry, which had come up by Wellington's orders from their cantonments on the Ebro[1]. Morillo's Spaniards continued the line westward along the Cerro de San Miguel, as far as Villaba : from thence the San Cristobal ridge was occupied by the greater part of the division which O'Donnell had drawn from the blockading lines—all, in fact, save the two battalions in advance on the hill by Zabaldica. Later in the day two battalions more were added from the besieging force, for Carlos de España's division from Castile had arrived, and relieved part of the troops which had hitherto been observing Pampeluna. Byng's brigade was told off to support the 4th Division, and took post on the rear of the summit of the Oricain hill, half a mile behind Cole. The actual fighting line on the left was composed of Anson's brigade on the Col, next to the Spaniards on the lower spur, of Campbell's Portuguese upon the central stretch of the heights (except one battalion which was sent to support the Spaniards below)[2], and of Ross's brigade holding the left. Stubbs's Portuguese were in rear of Campbell's, except the 7th Caçadores, which was detached to the front and held the ground about the chapel of San Salvador. The divisional battery (Sympher's of the K.G.L.) was placed far down the right side of the hill, below and behind Byng's brigade, in a position from which it could sweep the high road from Zabaldica to Arleta. Cole's tactical dispositions were in the complete Wellingtonian style, with the light companies and caçadores thrown out some way down the slope, far in advance of the main force, whose battalions were drawn back well behind the sky-line, so as to be invisible till the last moment to enemies storming the hill. Soult followed up the retreating Allies at such a slow pace that

[1] R. Hill's, Ponsonby's, the Hussar brigade, and D'Urban's Portuguese, Fane's brigade, which was observing on the side of Aragon, did not arrive this day.   [2] One of the 4th Line.

the whole of Picton's troops were settling into their ground before the enemy came in sight [1].

The slow advance of the French was due to the accumulation of such a large force in a narrow valley provided with only one road. The Marshal made an attempt to relieve the congestion, by ordering that the *chaussée* should be left to Clausel and to the cavalry and impedimenta in his rear, while Reille's divisions should move on the east bank of the Arga by local paths between the villages. The excellent intention of securing room for both columns to move freely had no good result. Clausel arrived in front of Zabaldica by 9 a.m.[2] But Reille was nowhere in sight. His report fully explains his absence : he had obeyed orders by turning up into the hills a mile and a half beyond the village of Erro. 'This direction rendered the march of the three divisions extremely slow and difficult. They found no road, and had to tramp through brushwood, climb steep slopes, or to follow tracks obliterated by recent rain. At last Count Reille took the decision to abandon the high ground. The 1st Division (Foy) dropped down to the village of Alzuza on the extreme left. The 7th Division (Maucune) re-descended into the valley of the Arga, a little above Iroz, where it bivouacked. The 9th Division (Lamartinière) also came down into the valley opposite Larrasoana, and kept along the high road to Iroz,' where it fell in with the rear of Clausel's column late in the day. The only result of Soult's precaution had been to put Reille out of the game on the 27th, just as on the 26th.

For the whole of the morning hours, therefore, Soult had only Clausel's corps at his disposition, a fact which accounts for the unenterprising character of his action. But that the 27th was a very slack day on the French side was not Clausel's fault. On arriving at Zabaldica, and discovering that the heights of Oricain were held in strength, he did not wait for the Marshal's orders, but began to form a line of battle parallel to Cole's front, along the mountain opposite. Halting Conroux's division on the high road in face of the hill held by the Spaniards, he pushed Taupin's and Vandermaesen's divisions up the slopes,

---

[1] Reille's report of August 1st.

[2] Clausel in his report says that he arrived in time to see the 4th Division cross the hill of Oricain.

with cavalry detachments feeling the way in front of them, till they had lined the whole ridge, and their right was overlooking Sorauren and the valley of the Ulzama. He then sent down to ask the Marshal's leave to attack, saying that he could see from the summit behind his line large baggage trains moving away along the Vittoria road in the plain of Pampeluna, and bodies of troops in motion northward [1]—the enemy was about to raise the siege, and was only offering a rearguard action in order to cover the retreat of his impedimenta. If pressed he would give way at once [2].

Soult did not believe this, and very rightly; but being pressed by repeated messages he mounted up to the heights behind Clausel's front at 11 a.m.: if he had chanced to notice it, he was just in time to see a solitary horseman ride up the north-western slope of the hill of Oricain, and to hear the whole of the Allied troops aligned opposite him burst out into a storm of tempestuous cheering. Wellington had come upon the ground. Soult heard the noise, but (as his dispatches show) did not guess its precise cause. He thought that reinforcements had just come up for Cole.

The story of Wellington's eventful ride from Almandoz to Sorauren is a very interesting one. Much irritated at receiving no further news from Picton, he had mounted at sunrise and ridden over the Col de Velate, taking with him only George Murray, his Quartermaster-General, his Military Secretary Fitzroy Somerset, and three or four other officers: the bulk of the head-quarters staff was to follow at leisure. On arriving at Lanz, the first village on the south side of the pass, they heard rumours of Picton's continued retreat, though they do not seem to have met the aide-de-camp whom he had sent off on the preceding night to report it. This news was so unexpected and vexatious that Wellington halted for a moment, to send back orders to Hill to the effect that it was conceivable that affairs might go badly on the Pampeluna front. If so, the whole right or

[1] Perhaps Carlos de España's division, arriving from the south.

[2] All this from the very interesting narrative of Clausel's aide-de-camp Lemonnier Delafosse (p. 220), who bore the first message to Soult, and was (like his chief) much irritated by the Marshal's caution and refusal to commit himself. Clausel had got a completely erroneous notion of the enemy's intentions—like Ney at Bussaco.

southern wing of the army might have to swing back to the line Yrurzon–Tolosa, and Hill would have to direct his own two divisions, and also Dalhousie, and Pack, with all the artillery and baggage, to fall back westward on Lizaso and Lecumberri, instead of coming over the Col de Velate towards Pampeluna. The Light Division, too, might have to leave the neighbourhood of the Bastan, and to retire to Zubieta on the Oyarzun–Lecumberri road, in order to keep up the touch between the main army and Graham's force in front of St. Sebastian. The latter general, however, was not to move, unless matters went very badly indeed, as the blockade of St. Sebastian must be kept up till the last possible minute. But previous orders were to stand, unless and until the Commander-in-Chief should send new ones: in particular Pack and the 6th Division were expected at Olague, and the batteries of Silveira's division and the Light Division might come on to Lanz, as there was an artillery road from Olague by which they might be turned off eastward if it became necessary [1].

On getting five miles farther down the road, Wellington halted for another moment at Olague, to leave word that the 6th Division [2], when it arrived, was to hold that place till further notice, and especially to look out for a possible movement of the French across the hills from Eugui, which must be blocked at all costs. Pack must turn all wheeled transport, batteries, convoys, &c., arriving from the Col de Velate off the high road to Pampeluna, and send them westward by the side road Olague–Lizaso, at which last-named village everything must wait for further orders. The closest and most frequent communication must be kept up with Hill's corps, which would be wanting to use this same road. Finally, Pack, after resting his division and giving it its noonday meal, must be ready to march again at a moment's notice in the afternoon [3].

[1] Quartermaster-General to Sir R. Hill, *Supplementary Dispatches*, viii. pp. 259–60.

[2] Wellington to Pack, *Supplementary Dispatches*, viii. p. 122, wrongly dated 1 o'clock—it should be 10 o'clock. Wellington was at Sorauren by 11.

[3] Final destination not given—clearly it might be down the high-road to Pampeluna; but if Picton had retreated still further and raised the siege, it might be to Lizaso, to join Hill and the rest.

Three miles farther down the road, at Ostiz, Wellington found waiting for him General Long, with some of the squadrons of his Light Dragoons, who were dispersed all along the lines of communication, keeping touch with all divisions. Long gave the alarming information that Picton had abandoned the Linzoain and Zubiri positions during the previous night, and was now in the immediate neighbourhood of Pampeluna, where he was intending to fight on the San Cristobal heights. The French were known to be in pursuit, and a collision might occur at any moment—indeed might have occurred already, but no firing had yet been heard.

Ostiz is only four miles from Sorauren and six from Villaba ; there was probably time to reach the fighting ground before an action might commence. Wellington directed his Quartermaster-General to stop behind, and make preparations for turning all troops off the Lanz valley road on to the Lizaso road, if he should receive further orders in the next hour—everything depended on what was going on six miles away. He then went off at racing speed down the *chaussée*, gradually dropping behind him all his staff except Fitzroy Somerset—their horses could not keep up with his thoroughbred. Turning the corner half a mile from Sorauren, he suddenly came on the whole panorama of battle. Cole's line was visible on the right-hand heights stretching away from the Chapel of San Salvador to the Col above Zabaldica. On the opposite mountain Taupin's and Vandermaesen's divisions were moving along the crest towards Sorauren and the Ulzama valley : cavalry vedettes were pushing ahead of them all over the slopes, looking for paths or British outposts. They were only a mile away at most. There was just time, and no more, to join Cole and take over the direction of affairs. Wellington put on full speed till he reached Sorauren bridge, and then (with his usual cool-blooded calculation of risks and moments) dismounted, and wrote a short order to Murray in pencil, using the cap-stone of the bridge end as his table. While he was writing the thirteen hurried lines, he was much distracted by well-intentioned peasants, who flocked around him with shouts that the French were coming down into the other end of the village. But the dispatch reads clearly enough. Murray is informed that the high road is blocked by the presence of the French at Sorauren ; all troops, therefore, must turn off on to the side-road Olague–Lizaso, both Pack and the artillery, and also Hill's corps. The latter must march at once from the Bastan, and get across the Col de Velate by nightfall if it could, leaving a rearguard to hold the pass against any possible pursuit by D'Erlon. The 7th Division near Santesteban should also come across by the Puerto de Arraiz to Lizaso. Orders for the further movements of all troops would be sent to Lizaso as soon as possible [1].

Fitzroy Somerset dashed out of the village at its northern end with the completed dispatch, just as the French chasseurs came exploring into its other end. He was not seen, or at least not pursued, and Murray received the orders, which made Lizaso the concentration point of all the central divisions of the army in half an hour, and set to work to amplify them and to forward them to their destinations. As Wellington very truly observed, several hours were gained by sending back Somerset by the straight road, and in particular the 6th Division was able to reach Lizaso by dark, and to get a good rest for the march of the next day to the battle-field [2].

[1] Wellington described his ride to Larpent, his Judge-Advocate General, a week later, in the following terse language (Larpent, p. 242) : ' At one time it was rather alarming, certainly, and a close run thing. When I came to the bridge of Sorauren I saw French on the hills on one side, and it was clear that we could make a stand on the other hill, in our position of the 28th, but I found that we could not keep Sorauren, as it was exposed to their fire and not to ours. I was obliged to write my orders accordingly at Sorauren, to be sent back instantly. For if they had not been dispatched back directly, by the way I had come, I must have sent them four leagues round, a quarter of an hour later. I stopped therefore to write accordingly, people saying to me all the time, " The French are coming ! " " The French are coming ! " I looked pretty sharp after them every now and then, till I had completed my orders, and then set off. I saw them just near the one end of the village as I went out of it at the other end. And then we took up our ground.' Wellington then added, in a confidential moment, that there need have been no fuss or trouble, if only Cole had kept sending the proper information on the 26th and 27th. If only his intention of going right back to Pampeluna had been known earlier, the 6th and 7th Divisions could have been up on the 27th, and Hill's corps too, which had been kept at Irurita and Berueta for 36 hours, because the situation in the south was concealed by Cole's reticence. ' We should have stopped the French much sooner.'

[2] French critics expressed surprise that Wellington did not tell Pack to fall on Clausel's flank and rear. But the 6th Division, attacking from

Meanwhile, Wellington, now all alone, rode up the steep track which rises from Sorauren to the pilgrimage-chapel on the height above, and was presently among the skirmishing line of O'Toole's Caçadores, who were holding that corner of the front. His familiar but unobtrusive silhouette—the short frock-coat, small plumeless cocked hat fitting down tight over the great Roman nose, and wiry thoroughbred—was at once recognized—the Portuguese set up the cry of ' Douro,' with which they were wont to greet him—recalling the first victory in which English and Portuguese co-operated, and also his first title of nobility : the noise swelled into the hoarse cheers of the British soldier as it passed up the line towards the Col. The 4th Division, which had been grumbling bitterly since it had been on the retreat, suddenly felt the atmosphere change. ' I never can forget the joy which beamed in every countenance when his Lordship's presence became known. It diffused a feeling of confidence throughout all ranks. No more dispiriting murmurs on the awkwardness of our situation : now we began to talk of driving the French over the frontier as a matter of course [1].' Wellington halted in front of Ross's brigade, and for a long time studied the French movements through a telescope. He easily made out Soult himself, who was conferring with Clausel and other staff-officers in a conspicuous group. Napier says that he observed that the Marshal would have heard the cheering, and would try to make out what it was about, before taking any serious step : ' that will give time for the 6th Division to arrive, and I shall beat him.' There is no corroboration for this story, though it may be true : Napier was in England on July 28th, and speaks only from hearsay. But an eye-witness present on the spot says that General Ross, as his chief continued to focus the French staff, ventured the remark that ' this time Soult certainly meditates an attack,' to which Wellington, with the glass still to his eye, replied, ' It is just probable that *I* shall attack *him* [2]. And this thought

Olague, would have been out of touch with the rest of the army, and Wellington did not believe in attacks by isolated corps uncombined with the main army, and unable to communicate with it. See Dumas' *Campagne du Maréchal Soult*, p. 163.

[1] Bainbrigge's narrative in Smyth's *History of the XXth*, p. 396.

[2] Ibid. Bainbrigge was standing close to both.

seems to be corroborated by a remark which Wellington made six days after to Judge Larpent, to the effect that he should and could have done more on the 27th [1]. The French army was but half arrived—only Clausel's three divisions were up, and Reille was at 11 a.m. still miles away. The enemy was tempting Providence by marching across the Allied front, just as Marmont had done at Salamanca a year before.

Whether Soult was stopped from an early attack, by guessing that the cheers on Cole's front implied the arrival of Wellington, seems more than doubtful. There is, of course, no trace of such an idea in the French dispatches—naturally it would not have been mentioned. But the one personal narrative which we have from a member of the group of Soult's staff-officers whom Wellington was eyeing, is to the effect that Clausel was at the moment trying to persuade the Marshal to attack at once, though only half his force was up, that Soult utterly refused to do so, spread out his maps, and finally took his lunch and a nap after it. ' Clausel meanwhile leaning against an oak was literally beating his forehead with rage, muttering " Who could go to sleep at such a moment " [2].'

What is certain is that Soult's dispatch to Paris says that he had discovered that Wellington had arrived *in the afternoon*, which would seem to show that he did not know by personal observation that he had come up at 11 a.m. He says, also, that at the moment of his own arrival the Allies had 30,000 men in line, including all the blockading troops from Pampeluna, which rendered it necessary to make a thorough examination of their position, and to get up all the divisions [3]. To discover the exact ground on which the enemy intended to fight, it proved necessary to make demonstrations or partial attacks.

Two of these were executed : the spur held by the two Spanish battalions, above Zabaldica, was so close in to the French position, that it was thought worth while to make an attempt to occupy it. A regiment of Conroux's division was sent up from the village to storm it, but was handsomely repulsed, when near the top of the slope, by a charge in line of

[1] Larpent, p. 243.
[2] Lemonnier-Delafosse, p. 219.
[3] Soult to Clarke, July 28.

these corps (Principe and Pravia of O'Donnell's Andalusian Reserve). Clausel's report says that his men 'took the hill but could not keep it,' but many British eye-witnesses on the slope above say that the summit was never reached. Clausel estimates the loss of his regiment at 100 men, Soult gives the more liberal estimate of 200. The repulse showed plainly enough that the whole hill of Oricain was to form part of the Allies' position, and that they intended to fight for every inch of it.

Late in the afternoon Soult directed Foy, who had now reached Alzuza on the extreme French left, to demonstrate against the heights of Huarte, so as to discover the end of the British line, and the strength in which it was held. Foy sent forward two regiments in column down the slope toward the Egues river, while showing the rest of his troops on the hill behind. When the French got within cannon shot, Picton brought up the whole 3rd Division to the crest, and R. Hill's and Ponsonby's heavy cavalry showed themselves in front of the village of Gorraiz, covering his flank. The divisional battery fired a few rounds at the columns, which at once swerved and retired in haste. Foy could report that the Huarte heights were held in strength, and by all arms.

This was the last incident of the day—shortly afterwards a heavy thunderstorm swept down from the Pyrenees, darkened the twilight, and drenched both armies. The same thing had happened on the eve of Salamanca—and was to happen again on the eve of Waterloo.

Far more important than the trifling skirmishes of the afternoon were the arrangements for the morrow—orders and dispatches, which the rival commanders were evolving during the evening hours. Soult felt himself still blocked in the valley of the Arga and wanted to deploy—was it possible to get his long column of guns and cavalry out of the defile—and if so, how ? Was there a possibility of extending to the left beyond Foy's present position, or to the right beyond Sorauren, the limit of Clausel's occupation ? Or must the Oricain heights be captured at all costs before the army could get into a proper order of battle ? Could any immediate help be expected from D'Erlon, whose tiresome letter of the 26th had come to hand, showing that he was no farther forward than Elizondo on that night ? He was not doing his best to occupy the enemy in his front, and there was a danger that Hill might arrive at Sorauren long before the corps that had been set the task of occupying his attention.

There would appear to have been something like a council of war at the French head-quarters in the evening, in which Clausel, Reille, Gazan, the Chief of the Staff, and probably other officers took part. Clausel wished to extend the line northward up the valley of the Ulzama, and to turn the flank of the whole Oricain position. The objection to this was that the transport and guns could not follow over the mule-tracks which must be used ; they were blocked in the Arga valley as long as the Allies held the heights commanding the main road. Moreover, reports had come in that British troops were descending on to Sorauren by the Lanz valley road, who would take in flank any attempt of Clausel to turn the Oricain position. (This seems to refer to the arrival of the 6th Division at Olague, but Long's cavalry was also visible up the *chaussée*.) And an extension of the French right to the heights westward would make the whole line of battle very long and weak : how could Reille's three divisions take over the whole ground from Sorauren to Alzuza ? After much discussion Soult decided in favour of a concentric attack on the whole Oricain position by five of his six divisions, while only Foy should remain out on the left, observing and containing the British force on the Huarte hills. Clausel's three divisions should attack Cole's line from Sorauren to the Col, two of Reille's divisions should co-operate, by assailing the Col and the Spaniards' Hill south of it. Some guns should be got to the front if possible, and Foy should be lent some cavalry, who must climb over the hills to cover his flank. Details would have to be settled on the morrow, also the transference of troops, who could not move in the dark over steep and unknown ground. Yet there was an uneasy feeling that too much time had been lost already—Soult notes a rumour that Wellington had announced the approach of four more British divisions. Even the arrival of D'Erlon could not compensate for this, and it did not look as if D'Erlon was likely to appear early on the 28th.

356·6   X X

Wellington moved the troops who were on the ground very little that evening—only relieving the Portuguese battalion which was in reserve on the hill above Zabaldica by a British regiment of Anson's brigade—the 40th Foot—and sending two of O'Donnell's battalions to Ollocarizqueta, to watch the mountain road west of Sorauren, by which it was conceivable that Clausel might try to turn the hill of Oricain. He had got news that French troops had been seen beyond Sorauren, and did not want to have them prying too close behind this flank, or observing the paths by which he intended to bring up his reserves on that side.

For his main attention that afternoon was devoted to drawing up the orders for the divisions coming from the Bastan, which he had promised to send to Murray, in the note that Fitzroy Somerset bore from the bridge of Sorauren. At 4 o'clock he sent off the all-important dispatch [1]. It will be remembered that his last orders provided for the successive arrival at Lizaso of the 6th and 7th Divisions, of the whole corps of Hill, and of the artillery, and divisional baggage trains of all the troops.

Pack was to start from Lizaso at dawn, and to move as rapidly as possible along the country road by Marcalain to Ollocarizqueta, which goes along the back of the hills that form the right bank of the valley of the Ulzama. At the last-named village (which he would find held by two Spanish battalions) he would be only five miles from Cole's flank, and in a position to strengthen or cover it. A supplementary note [2] warned Pack that if any French were found anywhere on the way he must not let himself be turned off; even if it came to leaving the road and taking to mountain tracks, the 6th Division *must* arrive at its destination. The artillery and the reserve of infantry ammunition were to follow Pack, unless serious opposition were offered to him, in which case they must return to Lizaso, and from thence turn on to Yrurzun.

Dalhousie and Hill had already had orders to march on Lizaso, the one by the Puerto de Arraiz, the other by the Velate. Both had a long march, but Wellington hoped that they might reach Lizaso during the night of the 27th–28th. If the men

[1] *Supplementary Dispatches*, viii. p. 123.
[2] Ibid., p. 124.

were not over-fatigued, all three divisions should follow Pack to Ollocarizqueta, after being given a suitable time of rest. All impedimenta likely to hinder rapid marching, and the wounded from the Maya fight, were to be directed from Lizaso to Yrurzun. Murray had already, acting on the orders of the Sorauren Bridge dispatch of 11 a.m., sent the route for Lizaso to Hill and Dalhousie, adding some precautions of his own, to the effect that they should leave small rearguards at the passes, to detain D'Erlon if he should come up. Moreover, he had spread out the 1st Hussars of the K.G.L. along the roads, to keep up touch between all the divisions on the move, and also between Lizaso and the Light Division, now at Zubieta. The only addition made by Wellington's new orders was the all-important one that everything of the fighting sort that came to Lizaso was to march for the main army, but all baggage for Yrurzun.

Of the arrangements thus made, that for Pack worked perfectly—he was at Ollocarizqueta with the 6th Division before 10 a.m. on the morning of the 28th. But Hill and Dalhousie were detained in the passes by the storm of the evening of the 27th, and only reached Lizaso so late on the 28th that they were of no use in the fighting of that day. As Wellington observed to Larpent [1], they could both have got into the battle of Sorauren if they had been given a longer march on the 26th, but ignorance of Cole's and Picton's retreat had prevented him from starting them early enough. However, the 6th Division alone sufficed to settle the matter.

The morning of the 28th was fine and bright—the storm of the preceding night seemed to have cleared the clouds from the hills, and the eye could range freely over a very wide landscape. Not only was the battle front of each army visible to the other, but from the high crest on or behind each position, a good deal could be made out of what was going on in the rear. This was more the case with the French line than with the British: Wellington's usual plan of keeping his main force behind the sky-line had great efficacy on such lofty ground as that of the heights of Oricain.

Soult spent the long hours of the July morning in moving his troops to the positions which had been selected on the previous

---

[1] See above, p. 661.

X X 2

night. Conroux's division, abandoning Zabaldica, marched over
the hills in the rear of Clausel's other divisions, and occupied
Sorauren village—relieving there some of Taupin's battalions,
which shifted a little to their left. To replace Conroux at
Zabaldica Lamartinière came up from Iroz, and deployed one
brigade (Gauthier's) in front of the Spaniards' Hill, while the other
(Menne's) remained in reserve beside the Arga, with two regiments across the high road and the third on the slopes east of
the river. Maucune's division, starting up the slopes from the
rear of Iroz, took post on the heights immediately opposite the
Col, with its right touching the left of Vandermaesen. Two
regiments were in front line exactly in face of the Col, a third
somewhat farther to the left, keeping touch with Lamartinière's
brigade near Zabaldica. The other brigade (Montfort's) was
placed in reserve farther up the mountain [1]. Pierre Soult's
light cavalry regiments disentangled themselves from the long
cavalry and artillery column in the rear, and picked their way
up the heights southward till they reached Foy's position, from
which they extended themselves to the left, till they reached as
far as the village of Elcano. Four howitzers were chosen out
of the batteries in the rear, and brought forward to the front of
Zabaldica, a position in which it was hoped that their high-
trajectory fire might reach effectively the Allies on the Col and
the Spanish Hill. These were the only French cannon used that
day, except some mule-guns employed by Clausel on the side of
Sorauren.

The greater part of these movements were perfectly visible
to Wellington, though some of them were intermittently screened
from sight when the marching columns dipped into dead ground,
or were passing through thickets. They took up so many hours
that he wrote to Graham at 10.30 that it looked as if Soult was
not inclined to attack. Meanwhile, the only British force on
the move was the 6th Division, which had been marching since
daylight, and arrived about 10 a.m. at Ollocarizqueta. On
getting news of its presence, Wellington ordered it to move by
a country road which comes across a crack in the hills west of
the Ulzama not far from the village of Oricain, and after
reaching that river to keep its Portuguese brigade on the

---

[1] Reports of Maucune and Lamartinière dated August 3rd and 4th.

western bank, its two British brigades on the eastern, and so
to advance till it should arrive facing Sorauren, prolonging
Cole's left in the lower ground, and covering him from any
attempt to turn his flank. About noon Pack's leading troops
began to appear—these were Madden's Portuguese on the left
of the division, working along the hillside west of the Ulzama.

Now the ' zero ' hour for the general attack on the whole
Allied front had been fixed by Soult for 1 o'clock, but long before
that hour Clausel was informed by an exploring officer, whom
he had sent to the hills on the other side of the Ulzama, beyond
his right, that a heavy British column was visible coming from
the direction of Marcalain, obviously to join the British left [1].
Now the French general had been thinking of turning Cole's
flank on this side, and had actually got troops some little way
up the Ulzama valley beyond Sorauren. But hearing of Pack's
approach and of his strength, he determined that he must now
turn his attention to fending off this move against his own
flank, and that the effort would absorb no small portion of his
troops. Conroux's division had been originally intended for
the attack of the north-west corner of the Oricain heights, to
the right (French) of the chapel, while Taupin was to make the
chapel itself his objective ; Vandermaesen was to strike at the
centre of Cole's position, and Maucune to attack the Col. But
Clausel determined that, in order to make the general frontal
attack feasible, he must at once stop the forward march of
Pack, and keep him at a distance, while the other divisions
made their great stroke. Accordingly he called in his right wing
detachments, and having concentrated Conroux's strong division (7,000 bayonets) he ordered it, at 12.30, to deploy across
the valley of the Ulzama below Sorauren and advance in two
lines of brigades against the approaching British column. This
movement—probably a necessary one—brought on the first
clash of battle, half an hour before the appointed time for the
general movement. Clausel at the same moment sent word to
the other divisions to attack at once ; but they were not quite
ready, the fixed hour not having yet been reached.

But Conroux pushed up the valley farther than was prudent,
for when he was some half a mile beyond Sorauren, he found

[1] Clausel's report of August 2.

himself encompassed on three sides—Madden's Portuguese pushing forward along the hill on the other side of the river, turned in on his right flank, some of Ross's skirmishers on the slopes west of the chapel of San Salvador came down and began to fire upon his left flank, while the main body of the 6th Division—Stirling's brigade deployed in front line, Lambert's supporting in column—met him face to face in the low ground. The concentric fire was too heavy to be stood, and Conroux had to give back, fighting fiercely, till he had the support of the village of Sorauren at his back : there the battle stood still, for Pack had orders to cover Cole's flank, not to attack the enemy's[1].

Meanwhile, the general frontal attack was being delivered by the other French divisions, starting from the right, as each got forward on receiving Clausel's orders to anticipate the fixed hour and advance at once. Hence the assault was made in échelon of brigades from the right, Taupin's two brigades being a little ahead of Vandermaesen's, and Vandermaesen's perceptibly earlier on the hill than the brigade of Maucune which attacked at the Col. The separate assault by Lamartinière on the Spaniards' Hill is definitely stated by that general to have been

[1] There is a most curious and difficult point in this history of the first phase of the action. Clausel says, and he is of course a primary authority, that though Conroux was already deeply engaged with the 6th Division, ' was being fired on from all sides, was suffering severe losses, and had already had one of his brigadiers disabled ' [Schwitter], he told him that he must join in the attack ' swerving to the left so as to mount the hill in the direction originally assigned to him ', which was done and Conroux immediately repulsed. I cannot see how this was physically possible. How could Conroux, if already disadvantageously engaged with the 6th Division, and ' fired at from all sides ', break off this fight and attack any point of the hill of Oricain ? If he had gone away in that direction, *who was there to hold Sorauren against Pack's people, who were pressing in on it, and (as Clausel says) only a musket-shot away from it ?* As far as I can make out, Conroux must have been sufficiently employed in fending off Pack and maintaining Sorauren, so as to cover the flank of the other divisions, for the next hour or two. No other authority but Clausel gives any hint that Conroux got away from Pack and joined in the general assault. And I am constrained to think that Clausel (strange as it may seem) is making a misstatement—and that when Conroux is said to have been ordered to attack the hill by swerving to the left, he can only have been keeping off Pack. I note that Vidal de la Blache and Mr. Fortescue try to accept Clausel's story, but that General Beatson (*With Wellington in the Pyrenees*, pp. 170–2) ignores it.

made at 12 o'clock—earlier, apparently, than the others—but he is contradicted by Reille, in command on this front, who says that it started *vers une heure*. This is much more likely to be correct.

The assault on the hill of Oricain bears a remarkable likeness to the battle of Bussaco, both being attacks by a series of brigade columns on a steep hill, with every disadvantage except numbers to the assailant. Cole's position was singularly like that of Picton in the battle of 1810, the main differences being that the hillside was not quite so steep or quite so high, and was strewn with clumps of brushwood in its lower slopes, while the Bussaco ground only shows heather and a little gorse. At the Portuguese fight the defenders of the hill had some help from artillery—at the Navarrese fight none. On the other hand, Cole had a shorter line to defend, and more men to hold it. Reynier attacked with 13,000 infantry—Clausel with 20,000—including in each case unengaged reserve brigades. Picton held the slopes of San Antonio de Cantaro with 6,800 men—Cole had about 11,000 at Oricain—the proportional difference therefore between the attacking and the defending force was much the same [1]. By an odd chance no less than four French regiments climbed both these deadly hills (17th Léger, 31st Léger, 47th and 70th Line); but the only officer who has left us his narrative of both fights does not chance to have compared them, though he was a competent observer and a fluent writer [2]. None of Cole's regiments, on the other hand, had been engaged at Bussaco, though eight of them were present on that field in unattacked sectors of Wellington's line.

The direction of the attack of the six French brigades which mounted the hill of Oricain was such that in their first advance Taupin's right brigade (Lecamus) attacked Ross; his left brigade (Béchaud) came in where Ross's and Campbell's lines met : both Vandermaesen's were opposed to Campbell's centre and right ; Maucune's front brigade tackled Anson at the Col,

---

[1] I include, in reckoning Picton's force at Bussaco, his own division and the three battalions of Leith's first brigade which brought him help. In Cole's Oricain figures are reckoned the 4th Division, Byng's brigade, Campbell's Portuguese, and two Spanish regiments.

[2] Lemonnier-Delafosse of the 31st Léger.

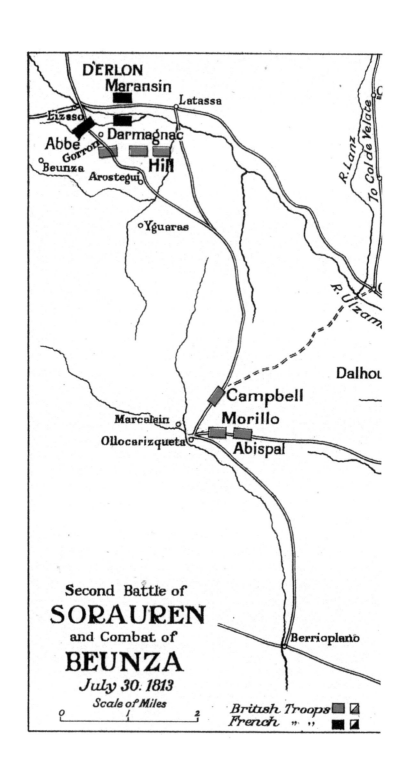

D'ERLON
Maransin
Latassa
Elzaso
Abbe
Darmagnac
Gorron
Beunza
Hill
Arostegui
Yguaras

To Col de Velate
R. Lanz

R. Ulzam

Dalhou

Campbell
Morillo
Marcalain
Ollocarizqueta
Abispal

Berrioplano

Second Battle of
SORAUREN
and Combat of
BEUNZA
July 30. 1813
Scale of Miles
0   1   2

British Troops
French   „ „

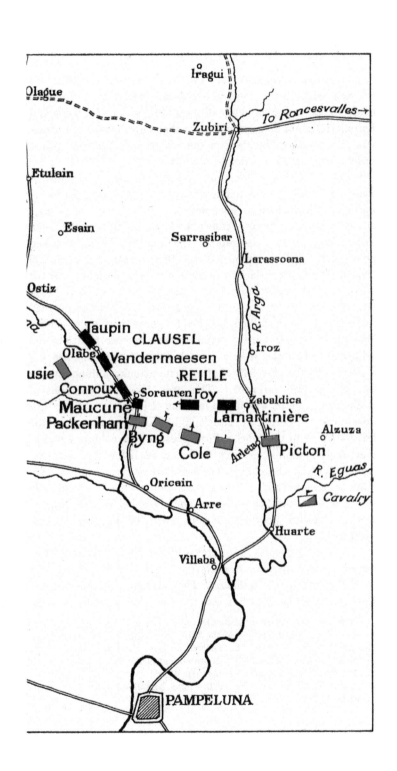

Iragui

Olague

To Roncesvalles →

Zubiri

Etulain

Esain

Sarrasibar

Larassoana

R. Arga

Ostiz

Taupin

CLAUSEL

Iroz

Olabe

Vandermaesen

usie

REILLE

Conroux

Sorauren Foy

Zabaldica

Maucune

Lamartinière

Packenham

Alzuza

Byng

Cole

Arletao

Picton

R. Eguas

Oricain

Cavalry

Arre

Huarte

Villaba

PAMPELUNA

and Gauthier of Lamartinière's division assailed the 40th and the Spaniards on the slopes above Zabaldica. The six brigades made 15,000 bayonets in all—the rear brigades of Maucune and Lamartinière not being counted, for they never closed. Conroux was paired off against Pack in the low ground, fighting against numbers not much inferior to his own.

Lecamus's brigade, starting from a short distance south of Sorauren, made for the north-west corner of the heights,—its four battalion columns screened by their eight *compagnies d'élite* in a dense swarm [1], much thicker than the usual French skirmishing line. This column, the first up the hill, pushed before it the light companies of the British 20th and 23rd, and the 7th Portuguese Caçadores, and won its way nearly to the crest, when it was charged by Ross with the whole Fusilier Brigade and thrown violently down hill. It was not pursued far, and ultimately rallied, but was for some time out of action. The Fusiliers had hardly resumed their former position and reformed, when the second French column came up the hill a little way to the left of the last attack, aiming at the Chapel of San Salvador. This was the five battalions of Béchaud's brigade, which had in front of it the line of the 10th Caçadores, supported by Ross's right-hand battalion and the left battalion of Campbell's Portuguese. This column actually reached the summit, driving the Caçadores before it, and established itself by the chapel, but was finally thrown down by a flank attack of Ross's left-hand battalions, while it was heavily engaged with the 7th Fusiliers and Campbell's 10th Line in front. It rallied only a short way down the hill, as there was no pursuit.

This fight was still in progress when Vandermaesen's two brigades came up the hill, each in a single column preceded by a heavy screen of *tirailleurs*. They came into collision with Campbell's centre and left, drove in his Caçadores [2] and light

[1] This exceptional use of grenadiers in the skirmishing line, I get from an observation of Bainbrigge of the 20th, who expresses his surprise that the troops with whom he was engaged, though acting as *tirailleurs*, were not light infantry, but men in tall bearskin caps like the Guard, ' some of the finest-looking soldiers I ever met ' (p. 400).

[2] The 10th Caçadores, Campbell's light battalion, was a very weak unit of only 250 bayonets.

companies, and forced their way right to the summit, after a very sharp exchange of fire. Cole was obliged to send up Stubbs's Portuguese to strengthen the line, which held for some time, but finally gave way on its left, where the 10th Line broke, thus exposing the flank of Ross's 7th Fusiliers, its next neighbours along the crest. At the same time Béchaud's brigade, now rallied, came up the hill for a second attack on Ross, whose line, or at least the right-hand part of it, lost ground and fell back in some disorder. At the same moment the French column beyond Vandermaesen—Maucune's front brigade—was attacking the Col. 'At that instant,' wrote Clausel to Soult, ' I had, despite all the difficulties of the enterprise, some hope of success [1].'

The combat seems to have stood still for a perceptible time—the French troops had established themselves on a long strip of the crest, and were slowly pushing back Campbell's left and Ross's right, which had suffered severely and were in bad order. But the enemy was also in great confusion—the columns and the skirmishing line had dissolved into irregular crowds. The men were absolutely exhausted by the steep climb which they had just made; and the blasting volleys which they had received before reaching the crest had laid low a very large proportion of the officers, who had led with reckless courage. There was no impetus left in their advance, which was slow and irregular.

The decision of the fight seems to have started on the very highest point of the hill, where Maucune's front brigade was attacking Anson. Here the French never won the crest, and were thrown back with extreme violence and terrible loss. The laconic report of the division merely says that ' the advance was a complete failure : the troops were repulsed at every point, and returned to their original position with the loss of 600 to 700 men and a colonel [2].' The whole strength of the three attacking battalions had been only 2,200 men, and all the casualties coming in ten minutes, the column was too hard hit to rally. Nor did Maucune choose to send in his rear brigade, which was the only intact reserve on the French heights. After watching this complete failure of the central assault from behind

---

[1] Clausel's report of August 2.
[2] D'Haw of the 34th Léger.

Anson's line, and noting the demoralization of the enemy, Wellington took the very bold step of ordering two of Anson's three battalions [1], the 3/27th and 1/48th, to descend from their own ground, and fall on the flank of Vandermaesen's division, which was advancing slowly and in disorder, pushing back Campbell's and Stubbs's Portuguese. He left only the 2nd Provisional (2nd and 2/53rd) to hold the high point from which Maucune had just been repulsed. At the same time Byng's brigade, hitherto kept in reserve a quarter of a mile back, on the centre of the hill, was ordered to advance and support Ross.

The diagonal down-hill charge of the 3/27th and 1/48th was swift and irresistible, when falling on the flank of a disordered mass. A French observer on the opposite mountain noted and admired it. ' The enemy's reinforcements, which he launched against our divisions, charged at a running pace, but with such order and unity that looking on from a distance one might have thought it was cavalry galloping. Hardly had they repulsed the troops on their right, when they ran in on the centre, and after the centre on to the left. . . . Our men came back four times to the assault, but what could three divisions do against an army perfectly settled down into its position, which had only to receive the shock of troops already half discomfited by exhaustion and by the obstacles of an inaccessible hillside [2].' Wellington merely says, ' I ordered the 27th and 48th to charge first that body of the enemy which had first established itself on the heights (Vandermaesen) and next those on the left (Béchaud) : both attacks succeeded, and the enemy was driven down with immense loss.'

Byng's brigade was in time to give assistance in the last part of the attack, but was only slightly engaged ; its three battalions had no more than 70 casualties among them [3], while the 27th and 48th counted no less than 389—a sufficient proof of the sort of resistance which they respectively met.

With the general repulse of the French brigades which had

---

[1] The fourth battalion of the brigade, the 1/40th was detached below on the Spaniards' Hill.

[2] Lemonnier-Delafosse, pp. 227–8.

[3] The Buffs lost only 2 men, the 1st Provisional (2/31st and 2/66th) only 5—so can hardly have been engaged,—but the 1/57th had 63 casualties.

established themselves on the crest, the crisis of the battle was
over. But sporadic fighting continued for an hour more, owing
to the gallant obstinacy of the French officers, who at several
points of the line rallied their battalions and brought them up
the hill again for partial and obviously futile attacks.   As
Wellington had forbidden all pursuit, the enemy had full power
to reassemble half-way down the hill and to try his luck again.
But since the men were tired out, and quite understood that if
a general assault by six brigades had failed, isolated pushes by
individual regiments were hopeless, there was no conviction in
these later attacks.   About four o'clock Soult sent orders that
they must cease, and that all troops must return to their original
positions.

. It remains to speak of three side-shows of the battle, one of
which was of great interest and some importance.   It will be
remembered that when the great advance took place about
1 a.m., Gauthier's brigade at Zabaldica was told to storm the
spur opposite, now held by the British 40th and the Spanish
battalions Pravia and Principe.   There was some artillery
preparation here, the howitzers beside the village having been
directed to open a high-trajectory fire on the hill.   It had,
however, no effect, and the infantry were put in ere long.
As to what happened British and French accounts show a
satisfactory agreement.   Gauthier first sent up the 120th, a
strong three-battalion unit, keeping the 122nd (two battalions)
in reserve.   The attack was frontal, and in one column—
possibly the presence of Sympher's battery to the right rear,
sweeping all the slopes above the Arga river, prohibited any
flank extension to turn the position.

Reille, who directed this attack in person from Zabaldica,
says that the regiment went up the hill with a very strong screen
of skirmishers (no doubt all the six *compagnies d'élite*) but in
great disorder, the pace having been pressed too much up a very
steep ascent, so that the whole arrived at the crest in a mass.
The enemy, who had been waiting behind the sky-line, suddenly
appeared at the critical moment, and opened such a heavy and
effective fire that the 120th crumpled up and rolled down hill.
The Allies, contented with the result of their salvo, did not
pursue, but stepped back behind the crest.   Gauthier rallied

the defeated regiment half-way down the slope, and brought
up the 122nd to assist : he then repeated the assault over the
same ground, and with better success, for the 120th reached
the crest, and broke up a Portuguese regiment (it was really
two *Spanish* battalions), and came to a deadly musketry contest
with the English regiment posted on the highest ground.   There
was a fusillade almost muzzle to muzzle, but the French regiment finally gave way ' whether from the disadvantage of the
position or from over-fatigue after twice climbing such steep
slopes '.   The 122nd, coming up just too late, then delivered a
similar attack, and suffered a similar repulse.   Both regiments
were then rallied half-way down the slope, and kept up from
thence a scattering fire, until Soult's orders came to withdraw
all the line, in consequence of the defeat of Clausel's divisions.
This exactly tallies with the narratives of the British officers of
the 40th, who also speak of three attacks, the first easily foiled—
a mere rush of skirmishers—the second very serious, and
rendered almost fatal by the incomprehensible panic of the
Spaniards, who, after behaving very well both on the previous
day and during the first attack, suddenly broke and fled—' all
attempts to rally them being ineffectual '—over the whole face
of the hill behind.   The rout was only stopped by a desperate
charge against the front of the leading French battalion, which
was successful contrary to every expectation and probability.
For the 40th, who had suffered considerable loss in the combat
of Linzoain two days before, had only 10 officers and 400 men
in line, and were attacking a column of nearly 2,000 men.   This
column had been cast down hill, and the men of the 40th had
barely been reformed—they showed a great wish to pursue and
came back reluctantly—when the third French attack, that of
the 122nd, was delivered with resolution and steadiness but
without success.   Even then the fight was not over, for after
an interval the enemy came up the hill again, in disorder but
with drums beating and eagles carried to the front, the officers
making incredible efforts to push the men forward.   They did
not, however, get to the crest, but, after rolling up to within
twenty-five yards of it, stood still under the heavy musketry
fire, and then fell back, completely ' fought out [1].'

[1] The above narrative is reconstructed from Reille's two reports (the

Reille's report declares that Gauthier's brigade only lost ' 50 killed and several hundred wounded '—say 350 in all—in this combat. The British 40th had 129 casualties—the Spanish battalions on their flanks 192. If a brigade of five battalions and 3,300 bayonets allowed itself to be stopped by a single battalion in the last phases of the combat, after suffering a loss of only one man in nine, there must have been something wrong with it, beside bad guidance. One would suspect that Reille is understating casualties in the most reckless fashion.

While this fight was going on by the banks of the Arga, there was another in progress on the other flank of the hill of Oricain, on the banks of the Ulzama. The 6th Division had been intermittently engaged with Conroux's troops during the whole time of the French assaults on the heights. When it was seen that Clausel's men were ' fought out ' and falling back, Pack made an effort to utilize the moment of the French débâcle by capturing Sorauren. He brought up his divisional guns (Brandreth's battery) to a position close to the village, and sent forward the light companies of the two British brigades to press in upon its south side, while Madden's Portuguese, on the other bank of the river, tried to get into it from the rear on the north side. The attack failed, indeed was never pushed home, Sorauren being too strongly held. The guns had to be drawn back, many horses and some gunners having been shot down. Pack himself was severely wounded in the head, and Madden's brigade lost 300 men. Wellington sent down from the hill to order the attack to cease, for even if Sorauren had been taken, the rest of his front-line troops were in no condition to improve the advantage[1].

While this was going on upon the extreme left, an almost bloodless demonstration was in progress on the extreme right, where Foy, as on the previous day, had been ordered to keep Picton employed. He showed his infantry in front of Alzuza, and pushed forward the considerable body of light cavalry

divisional report of Lamartinière, however, is useless) and from narratives of Stretton of the 40th in Maxwell's *Peninsular Sketches*, and Mills in the history of the regiment by Smythies.

[1] There is little about this affair in the British narratives. Diarists were rare in the 6th Division. The only point of interest I found in them is the mention of mule-guns used by the French.

which had been lent him to his left flank by Elcano, till their skirmishers had got into collision with those of the British Hussar Brigade, along the river Egues. There was much *tiraillade* but few casualties on either side ; the 10th Hussars were driven across the river, but were replaced by the 18th, who kept the French in check for the rest of the day. Pierre Soult showed no intention of closing, and Stapleton Cotton had been warned by Wellington that his four brigades were intended for flank-protection not for taking the offensive. The afternoon, therefore, passed away in noisy but almost harmless bickering between lines of vedettes. Foy in his report expressed himself contented with having kept a larger force than his own occupied all day.

Thus ended this second Bussaco, a repetition in its main lines of the first, and a justification of the central theory of Wellington's tactical system. Once more the line, in a well-chosen position, and with proper precautions taken, had proved itself able to defeat the column. The French made a most gallant attempt to storm a position held by much inferior numbers, but extremely strong. They were beaten partly—as all the critics insisted— by the fact that men who have just scaled a hill of 1,000 feet are inevitably exhausted at the moment when they reach its crest, but much more by the superiority of fire of the line over the column when matters came to the musketry duel. The French generals had learnt one thing at least from previous experience —they tried to sheathe and screen the column by exceptionally heavy skirmishing lines, but even so they could not achieve their purpose. The only risk in Wellington's game was that the enemy's numbers might be too overwhelming—if, for example, the 6th Division had not been up in time on July 28th, and Clausel had been able to put in Conroux's division (7,000 extra bayonets) along with the rest, operating against Ross's extreme flank, it is not certain that the heights of Oricain could have been held. But Wellington only offered battle, as he did, because he was relying on the arrival of the 6th Division. If he had known on the night of the 27th that it could not possibly come up in time, he would probably have accepted the unsatisfactory alternative policy of which he speaks in several dispatches, that of raising the siege of Pampeluna and falling back on Yrurzun. ' I hope we should in any case have beaten the French at last, but it must have been further back certainly, and probably on the Tolosa road [1].'

Soult is said to have felt from the 26th onward—his original project of a surprise followed by a very rapid advance having failed—' une véritable conviction de non-réussite [2].' We could well understand this if he really believed—as he wrote to Clarke on the evening after the battle—that Wellington had 50,000 men already in line. But this was an *ex post facto* statement, intended to explain his defeat to the Minister ; and we may be justified in thinking that if he had really estimated the hostile army at any such a figure, he would never have attacked. His long delay in bringing on the action may be explained by the fact that Reille's divisions were not on the field before evening on the 27th, and that on the 28th it took many hours to re-arrange the troops on a terrain destitute of any roads, rather than by a fear of a defeat by superior numbers. It might have been supposed on the 27th that he was waiting for the possible arrival of D'Erlon, but on the morning of the 28th he had heard overnight from his lieutenant, and knew that he could not reach the battle-front on that day. In his self-exculpatory dispatch to Clarke, Soult complains that D'Erlon told him that he was blocked by British divisions at Irurita, ' but I have no doubt that these are the same troops which fell upon General Clausel's flank this afternoon [3].' In this he was wrong—D'Erlon was speaking of Hill's and Dalhousie's divisions, while it was Pack (whom D'Erlon had never seen) that rendered a French success at Sorauren impossible.

The loss of the Allied Army was 2,652—of whom 1,358 were British, 1,102 Portuguese, and 192 Spaniards. The heaviest casualties fell on the 3/27th in Anson's brigade, who first repulsed Maucune, and then swept away Vandermaesen, and the 1/7th in Ross's brigade, the regiment whose flank was exposed by the breaking of the 10th Portuguese—which corps

---

[1] Larpent, p. 221. Cf. Napier, v. p. 226 : ' That will give time for the 6th Division to arrive, and I shall beat him '—words true in thought but perhaps never spoken by Wellington.

[2] Lapéne, p. 80.

[3] Soult to Clarke, report of the battle.

also, as was natural, was very hard hit. But all the front-line battalions, both British and Portuguese, had considerable losses. Soult (as at Albuera) made a most mendacious under-statement of his casualties, putting them at 1,800 only. As Clausel alone had reported about 2,000, Maucune about 700, and Lamartiniére at least 350, it is certain that the Marshal's total loss was over 3,000—how much over it is impossible to say, since the only accessible regimental casualty-lists include all men killed, wounded, or missing between July 25th and August 2nd. But the chances are that 4,000 would have been nearer the mark than 3,000 [1].

[1] See statistics in Appendix XXII.

SOULT'S RETREAT, JULY 30–31. THE SECOND BATTLE
OF SORAUREN

WHILE the battle of July 28th was being fought, the outlying
divisions of both Soult's and Wellington's armies were at last
beginning to draw in towards the main bodies.

Hill, as we have already seen, had received the orders written
by Wellington on Sorauren bridge at 11 a.m. by the afternoon
of the same day, and had started off at once with his whole
force—the three 2nd Division brigades, Silveira's one brigade,
and Barnes's three battalions of the 7th Division. His directions
were to endeavour to cross the Puerto de Velate that night, so
as to sleep at Lanz, the first village on the south side of the pass.
He was to leave a detachment at the head of the defile, to check
D'Erlon's probable movement of pursuit. The supplementary
order, issued at 4 p.m. from the heights of Oricain, directed Hill
to march from the place where his corps should encamp on the
night of the 27th (Lanz as was hoped) to Lizaso, abandoning the
high road for the side road Olague–Lizaso, since the former was
known to be cut by the French at Sorauren. If the men were
not over-fatigued when they reached Lizaso, Hill must try to
bring them on farther, to Ollocarizqueta on the flank of the
Sorauren position, where the 6th Division would have preceded
them.

Similarly Dalhousie with the 7th Division (minus the three
battalions with Hill) was to march that same evening from
Santesteban over the Puerto de Arraiz on to Lizaso, to sleep
there and to march on Ollocarizqueta, like Hill, on the morning
of the 28th, if the state of the troops allowed it. All the baggage,
sick, stores, and other impedimenta from the Bastan were also
directed on Lizaso, but they were to go through it westward
and turn off to Yrurzun, not to follow the fighting force to Ollocarizqueta.

None of these directions worked out as was desired, the main
hindering cause being the fearful thunderstorm already recorded,
which raged during the twilight hours of the evening of the

Y y

27th. Hill had started from Irurita, as directed, keeping as a rearguard Ashworth's Portuguese, who were intended to hold the Puerto de Velate when the rest of the column should have crossed it. He was nearing the watershed, in the roughest part of the road, where it has many precipitous slopes on the left hand, when the storm came down, completely blotting out the evening light with a deluge of rain, and almost sweeping men off their feet. One of Barnes's officers describes the scene as follows : ' So entangled were we among carts, horses, vicious kicking mules, baggage, and broken-down artillery, which lined the road, that we could not extricate ourselves. Some lighted sticks and candles only added to the confusion, for we were not able to see one yard beyond the lights, owing to the thick haze, which seemed to render darkness still more dark. In this bewildered state many who could not stand were obliged from fatigue to sit down in the mire : to attempt going on was impossible, except by climbing over the different vehicles that blocked the road. In this miserable plight, I seated myself against a tree, when weariness caused me, even amidst this bustle, mud, and riot, to fall fast asleep [1].' All sorts of disasters happened : one of Tulloh's 9-pounders went over the precipice with the shaft animals drawn down with it, when the side of the roadway crumbled in [2]. Ross's battery lost another gun in a similar way, owing to the sudden breaking of a wheel, and many carts and mules blundered over the edge. The only thing that could be done was to stick to the track, sit down, and wait for daylight, which was fortunately early in July.

When it came, the drenched and miserable column picked itself up from the mire, and straggled down the defile of the Velate, passing Lanz and turning off at Olague towards Lizaso, as ordered. Troops and baggage were coming in all day to this small and overcrowded mountain village, in very sorry plight. It was of course quite impossible for them to move a mile farther on the 28th, and Hill had to write to Wellington that he could only hope to move his four brigades on the early morning of the 29th.[3]

---

[1] Narrative of Captain G. Wood of the 1/82nd, pp. 192–3.
[2] See *Dickson Papers*, Tulloh's letter, p. 1022.
[3] Hill to Quartermaster-General, *Supplementary Dispatches*, viii. p. 142.

Lord Dalhousie had fared, as it seems, a little better in crossing the Puerto de Arraiz ; he had a less distance to cover, but the dispatch from Sorauren bridge only reached him at 7 p.m. when the rain was beginning. With laudable perseverance he kept marching all night, and reached Lizaso at 12 noon on the 28th, with all his men, except a battalion of Caçadores left behind to watch the pass. The condition of the division was so far better than that of Hill's column, that Dalhousie wrote to Wellington that he could march again in the late afternoon, after six hours' rest, and would be at or near Ollocarizqueta by dawn on the 29th [1], though two successive night marches would have made the men very weary. This the division accomplished, much to its credit, and reached the appointed destination complete, for Hill had returned to it the three battalions which had saved the day at Maya on the 25th.

Lizaso on the afternoon of July 28th was a dismal sight, crammed with the drenched and worn-out men of seven brigades, who had just finished a terrible night march, with large parties of the Maya wounded, much baggage and transport with terrified muleteers in charge, and a horde of the peasants of the Bastan, who had loaded their more precious possessions on ox-wagons, and started off to escape the French. It took hours to sort out the impedimenta and start them on the Yrurzun road. There was a general feeling of disaster in the air, mainly owing to physical exhaustion, which even the report of the victory of Sorauren arriving in the evening could not exorcise. Rumours were afloat that Wellington was about to retire again, despite of the successes of the afternoon. However, the day being fine, the men were able to cook and to dry themselves, and the 7th Division duly set out for another night march.

It was fortunate that the retiring columns were not troubled by any pursuit either on the 27th or the 28th. The storm which had so maltreated Hill's column seems to have kept the French from discovering its departure. Darmagnac had moved forward on the 27th from Elizondo to ground facing Hill's position at Irurita, but had not attempted to attack it, D'Erlon having decided that it was ' *très forte par elle-même, et inatta-*

---

[1] Dalhousie to Quartermaster-General, ibid.

quable, étant gardée par autant de troupes.' So badly was touch
kept owing to the rainy evening, that Hill got away unobserved,
and it was only on the following morning that Darmagnac
reported that he had disappeared. This news at last inspired
D'Erlon with a desire to push forward, and on the morning of
the 28th Abbé took over the vanguard, passed Almandoz, and
crossed the Velate, with Darmagnac following in his rear, while
Maransin—kept back so long at Maya—came down in the wake
of the other divisions to Elizondo. The head of Abbé's division
passed the Puerto de Velate, pushing before it Ashworth's
Portuguese, who had been left as a detaining force. Abbé
reported that the pass was full of wrecked baggage, and that
he had seen guns shattered at the foot of precipices. D'Erlon
says that 400 British stragglers were gleaned by the way—no
doubt Maya wounded and footsore men. On the night of the
28th Abbé and Darmagnac bivouacked at and about Lanz,
Maransin somewhere by Irurita. He left behind one battalion
at Elizondo [1], to pick up and escort the convoy of food expected
from Urdax and Ainhoue.

The light cavalry [2] who accompanied Abbé duly reported
that Hill had not followed the great road farther than Olague,
but had turned off along the valley of the upper Ulzama to
Lizaso ; his fires were noted at evening all along the edge of
the woods near that village. One patrol of chasseurs, pushing
down the main road to Ostiz, sighted a similar exploring party
of Ismert's dragoons coming from Sorauren, but could not get
in touch with them, as the dragoons took them for enemies and
decamped. However, the two bodies of French cavalry met
again and recognized each other at dawn on the 29th, so that
free communication between the two parts of Soult's army was
now established.

D'Erlon has been blamed by every critic for his slow advance
between the 26th and the 29th. He was quite aware that it was
slow, and frankly stated in his reports that he did not attack
Hill because he could not have turned him out of the position of
Irurita, not having a sufficient superiority of numbers to cancel
Hill's advantage of position. This is quite an arguable thesis—
D'Erlon had, deducting Maya losses, some 18,000 men : Hill,

----

[1] 28th Léger.   [2] 22nd Chasseurs.

counting in Dalhousie who had been placed on his flank by
Wellington for the purpose of helping him if he were pressed,
had (also deducting Maya losses) four British and three Portuguese brigades, with a strength of about 14,000. If Cameron's
and Pringle's regiments had been terribly cut up at Maya,
Darmagnac's and Maransin's had suffered a perceptibly larger
loss, though one distributed over more units. D'Erlon was
under the impression that Hill had three divisions with him,
having received false information to that effect. If this had
been true, an assault on the position of Irurita would have been
very reckless policy. It was *not* true—only two divisions and
one extra Portuguese brigade being in line. Yet still the event
of the combat of Beunza, only three days later, when D'Erlon's
three divisions attacked Hill's own four brigades—no other
allied troops being present—and were held in check for the
better part of a day, suggests that D'Erlon may have had good
justification for not taking the offensive on the 26th or 27th,
while the 7th Division was at Hill's disposition. The most odd
part of his tactics seems to have been the way in which he kept
Maransin back at Maya and Elizondo so long : this was apparently the result of fear that Graham might have something to
say in the contest—an unjustifiable fear as we know now, but
D'Erlon cannot have been so certain as we are ! The one
criticism on the French general's conduct which does seem to
admit of no adequate reply, is that in his original orders from
Soult, which laid down the scheme of the whole campaign, he
was certainly directed to get into touch with the main army as
soon as possible, though he was also directed to seize the pass of
Maya and to pursue Hill by Elizondo and the Puerto de Velate.
If he drew the conclusion on the 26th that he could not hope to
dislodge Hill from the Irurita position, it was probably his duty
to march eastward by the Col de Berderis or the Col d'Ispegui
and join the main body by the Alduides. It is more than doubtful whether, considering the character of the country and the
tracks, he could have arrived in time for the battle of Sorauren
on the 28th. And if Hill had seen him disappear eastward, he
could have marched to join Wellington by a shorter and much
better road, and could certainly have been in touch with his
chief before D'Erlon was in touch with Soult. Nevertheless, it

cannot be said that the French general obeyed the order which
told him that ' *il ne perdra pas de vue qu'il doit chercher à se
réunir le plutôt possible au reste de l'armée* [1].' And orders ought
to be obeyed—however difficult they may appear.

At dawn on the 29th, therefore, Soult's troops were in their
position of the preceding day, and D'Erlon's leading division
was at Lanz, requiring only a short march to join the main body.
But Wellington was in a better position, since he had already
been joined by the 6th Division, and would be joined in a few
hours by the 7th Division, which, marching all night, had reached
Ollocarizqueta. Hill, with his four original brigades, was at
Lizaso, as near to Wellington as D'Erlon was to Soult. The
only other troops which could have been drawn in, if Wellington
had so originally intended, were the brigades of the Light Division, for which (as we shall see) he made another disposition.
But omitting this unit, and supposing that the other troops on
both sides simply marched in to join their main bodies on the
29th, it was clear that by night Wellington would have a
numerical equality with his adversary, and this would make
any further attempts to relieve Pampeluna impossible on the
part of Soult.

This was the Marshal's conviction, and he even overrated the
odds set against him, if (as he said in his dispatch to Clarke) he
estimated his adversary's force on the evening of the 28th at
50,000 men, and thought that several other divisions would
join him ere long. In face of such conditions, what was to be
the next move ? Obviously a cautious general would have
decided that his bolt had been shot, and that he had failed. He
had a safe retreat before him to Roncesvalles, by a road which
would take all his cavalry and guns ; and D'Erlon had an
equally secure retreat either by Elizondo and Maya on a good
road, or by the Alduides, if absolute security were preferred to
convenience in marching. The country was such that strong
rearguards could have held off any pursuit. And this may have
been the Marshal's first intention, for in his letter to Clarke,
written on the evening after the battle, before he had any knowledge of D'Erlon's approach, he said that he was sending back his
artillery and dragoons on Roncesvalles, since it was impossible

[1] Soult's general orders of July 23rd.

to use them in Navarre, and that he was dispatching them to the Bidassoa ' where he could make better use of them in new operations, which he was about to undertake '. He was intending to remain a short time in his present position with the infantry, to see what the enemy would do. No news had been received of D'Erlon since the 27th, when he was still at Elizondo, declaring that he could not move because he was blocked by a large hostile force—' the same force, as I believe, which fell on Clausel's flank to-day.' Further comment the Marshal evidently judged superfluous [1]. The column of guns and baggage actually marched off on the night of the 28th–29th.

But early on the morning of the 29th D'Erlon's cavalry was met, and the news arrived that he was at Lanz, and marching on Ostiz, where he would arrive at mid-day, and would be only five miles from Sorauren. This seems to have changed the Marshal's outlook on the situation, and by the afternoon he had sketched out a wholly different plan of campaign, and one of the utmost hazard. As the critic quoted a few pages back observed, he recovered his confidence when once he was twenty-four hours away from a defeat, and his strategical conceptions were sometimes risky in the extreme [2].

The new plan involved a complete change of direction. Hitherto Soult had been aiming at Pampeluna, and D'Erlon was, so to speak, his rearguard. Now he avowed another objective— the cutting of the road between Pampeluna and Tolosa, with the purpose of throwing himself between Wellington and Graham and forcing the latter to raise the siege of St. Sebastian [3]. He had now, as he explained, attracted to the extreme south nearly the whole of the Anglo-Portuguese divisions : there was practically a gap between Wellington, with the troops about to join him, and the comparatively small force left on the Bidassoa. He would turn the British left, by using D'Erlon's corps as his vanguard and cutting in north of Lizaso, making for Hernani or Tolosa, whichever might prove the more easy goal. He hoped

---

[1] Soult to Clarke, from Zabaldica, evening of the 28th.

[2] See St. Chamans, quoted above, p. 590.

[3] Expressed most clearly, perhaps, in the Orders issued by the Chief of the Staff, Gazan, to the Corps-Commanders on July 29 : ' L'intention du Général en Chef est de se porter avec toute l'armée sur la communication de Pampelune à St. Estevan.'

that Villatte and the reserves on the Bidassoa might already be at Hernani, for D'Erlon had passed on to him an untrustworthy report that an offensive had begun in that direction, as his original orders had directed. The manœuvre would be so unexpected that he ought to gain a full day on Wellington— D'Erlon was within striking distance of Hill, and should be able to thrust him out of the way, before the accumulation of British troops about Sorauren, Villaba, and Huerta could come up. There was obviously one difficult point in the plan : D'Erlon could get at Hill easily enough. But was it certain that the rest of the troops, now in such very close touch with Wellington's main body—separated from it on one front of two miles by no more than a narrow ravine—would be able to disentangle themselves without risk, and to follow D'Erlon up the valley of the Ulzama ? When armies are so near that either can bring on a general action by advancing half a mile, it is not easy for one of them to withdraw, without exposing at least its rear-guard or covering troops to the danger of annihilation.

Soult took this risk, whether underrating Wellington's initia-tive, or overrating the manœuvring power of his own officers and men. It was a gross tactical error, and he was to pay dearly for it on the 30th. In fact, having obliged his enemy with a second Bussaco on the 28th, he presented him with the opportunity of a second Salamanca two days after. For in its essence the wide-spread battle of the 30th, which extended over ten miles from D'Erlon's attack on Hill near Lizaso to Wellington's counter-attack on Reille near Sorauren, was, like Salamanca, the sudden descent of an army in position upon an enemy who has unwisely committed himself to a march right across its front.

Soult made the most elaborate plans for his manœuvre— D'Erlon was to move from Ostiz and Lanz against Hill : he was lent the whole of Treillard's dragoons, to give him plenty of cavalry for reconnaissance purposes ; Clausel was to march Taupin's and Vandermaesen's troops behind Conroux, who was to hold Sorauren village till they had passed him. Conroux would then be relieved by Maucune's division from the high ground opposite the Col, and when it had taken over Sorauren from him, would follow the rest of Clausel's troops up the high road. Maucune's vacant position would be handed over to

Foy and Lamartinière. The former was to evacuate Alzuza
and the left bank of the Arga, where he was not needed, as the
column of guns and baggage, with its escort of cavalry, had got
far enough away on the road to Zubiri and Roncesvalles to be
out of danger. He was then to go up on to the heights where
Maucune had been posted during the recent battle, as was also
Lamartinière. The latter was to leave one battalion, along with
the corps-cavalry (13th Chasseurs) of Reille's wing, on the high
road north of Zabaldica, as an extra precaution to guard against
any attempt by the enemy to raid the retreating column of
impedimenta [1].

Finally, some orders impossible to execute were dictated—
viz. that all these movements were to be carried out in the
night, and that both Clausel and Reille were to be careful that
the British should get no idea that any change in the position
of the army was taking place ; one general is told that ' *il
opérera son mouvement de manière à ce que l'ennemi ne puisse
aucunement l'apercevoir*,' the other that ' *il disposera ses troupes
à manière que l'ennemi ne puisse soupçonner qu'il y a de change-
ment ni de diminution*.' Reille was to hold the line Sorauren–
Zabaldica for the whole day of the 30th, and then to follow
Clausel with absolute secrecy and silence. Now, unfortunately,
one cannot move 35,000 men on pathless hillsides and among
woods and ravines in the dark, without many units losing their
way, and much noise being made. And when one is in touch
with a watchful enemy at a distance of half a mile only, one cannot prevent him from seeing and hearing that changes are going
on. The orders were impracticable.

Such were Soult's plans for the 30th. Wellington's counter-
plans do not, on the 29th, show any signs of an assumption of
the offensive as yet, though it was certainly in his mind. They
are entirely precautionary, all of them being intended to guard
against the next possible move of the opponent. The troops
which had suffered severely in the battle were drawn back into
second line, Byng's and Stubbs's brigades taking over the
ground held by Ross and Campbell. The 6th Division—now
under Pakenham, Pack having been severely wounded on the
previous day—occupied the heights north-west of Sorauren,

---

[1] Ordre du 29 Juillet ; see also Gazan to Reille of same date.

continuing the line held on the 28th to the left. Both Cole and
Pakenham were told to get their guns up, if possible. And when
Lord Dalhousie came up from Lizaso after his night march,
his division also was placed to prolong the allied left—two
brigades to the left-rear of the 6th Division, hidden behind a
high ridge, the third several miles westward over a hill which
commanded the by-road Ostiz–Marcalain—a possible route for
a French turning movement [1].

Originally Wellington had supposed that Hill would reach
Lizaso earlier than Dalhousie, and had intended that the 2nd
Division should come down towards Marcalain and Pampeluna,
while the 7th remained at Lizaso to protect the junction of roads.
But the storm, which smote Hill worse than it smote Dalhousie,
had settled matters otherwise. It was the latter, not the former,
who turned up to join hands with the main army. Accepting
the change, Wellington directed Hill to select a good fighting
position by Lizaso, in which he should place the two English
brigades of the 2nd Division and Ashworth, while Da Costa's
Portuguese were to move to Marcalain [2], close to the rear
brigade which the 7th Division had left in the neighbourhood.
Thus something like a covering line was provided for any move
which D'Erlon might make against the British left. Wellington
was feeling very jealous that day of attempts to turn this flank,
and took one more precaution which (as matters were to turn
out) he was much to regret on the 31st. Orders were sent to
Charles Alten to move the Light Division from Zubieta towards
the high road that goes from Tolosa to Yrurzun via Lecumberri.
In ignorance of the division's exact position, the dispatch
directed Alten to come down so far as might seem best—Yrurzun
being named as the farthest point which should be taken into
consideration [3]. This caused Alten to move, by a very toilsome
night march, from Zubieta, where he would have been very
useful later on, to Lecumberri, where (as it chanced) he was not
needed. But this was a hazard of war—it was impossible to

[1] Quartermaster-General to Dalhousie and Hill, *Supplementary Dispatches*, viii. p. 151.

[2] Ibid., Q.M.G. to Hill, p. 152. In this Da Costa's brigade is called the Conde de Amarante's *division*, but Campbell had not yet joined Da Costa.

[3] Q.M.G. to Alten, *Supplementary Dispatches*, viii. pp. 150–1.

guess on the 29th the unlikely place where Soult's army was about to be on the 31st. Another move of troops to the Yrurzun road was that Fane's cavalry brigade, newly arrived from the side of Aragon, was directed to Berrioplano, behind Pampeluna on the Vittoria road, with orders to get into touch with Lizaso, Yrurzun, and Lecumberri.

Obviously all these arrangements were defensive, and contemplated three possible moves on the part of the enemy— (1) a renewal of the battle of the 28th at and north of Sorauren, with which the 6th and 7th Divisions could deal; (2) an attempt to turn the allied flank on the short circuit Ostiz-Marcalain; (3) a similar attempt by a larger circuit via Lizaso, which would enable the enemy to get on to the roads Lizaso-Yrurzun, and Lizaso–Lecumberri, and so cut the communication between Wellington and Graham. The third was the correct reading of Soult's intentions. To foil it Hill was in position at Lizaso, with the power to call in first Da Costa, then the 7th Division, and much later the Light Division, whose whereabouts was uncertain, and whose arrival must obviously come very late. But if the enemy should attack Hill with anything more than the body of troops which had been seen at Ostiz and Lanz (D'Erlon's corps), Wellington intended to fall upon their main corps, so soon as it began to show signs of detaching reinforcements to join the turning or enveloping column.

Soult's manœuvre had duly begun on the night of the 28th–29th by the retreat of the artillery, the wounded, the train and heavy baggage towards Roncesvalles, under the escort of the dragoon regiments of Pierre Soult's division, whose chasseur regiments, however, remained with Reille as ' corps cavalry '. On the news of this move going round, a general impression prevailed that the whole army was about to retire by the road on which it had come up. This seemed all the more likely because the last of the rations brought from St. Jean-Pied-du-Port had been distributed on the battle-morning, and the troops had been told on the 29th to make raids for food on all the mountain villages on their flanks and rear. They had found little save wine—which was more a snare than a help. The perspicacious Foy noted in his diary his impression that Soult's new move was not made with any real hope of relieving St. Sebastian or cutting the Allies' communication, it was in essence a retreat ; but, to save his face, the Marshal was trying to give it the appearance of a strategic manœuvre [1]. This was a very legitimate deduction—it certainly seemed unlikely that an army short of food, and almost equally short of munitions, could be asked to conduct a long campaign in a region where it was notorious that it could not hope to live by requisitions, and would find communication with its base almost impossible. It was true that convoys were coming up behind D'Erlon—one was due at Elizondo—but roads were bad and appointments hard to keep. There were orders sent to Bayonne on the 28th for the start of another—but how many days would it take before the army got the benefit ?—a week at least. Men and officers marched off on the new adventure grumbling and with stomachs ill-filled.

The result of Soult's orders was to produce two separate actions on the 30th—one between D'Erlon and Hill behind Lizaso, in which the French gained a tactical advantage of no great importance, the other on the heights along the Ulzama between Wellington's main body and Clausel and Reille, in which the French rear divisions were so routed and dispersed that Soult had to throw up all his ambitious plans, and rush home for safety as fast as was possible.

The more important action, generally called the Second Battle of Sorauren, may be dealt with first.

At midnight Clausel's two divisions on the heights, separated from Cole's position by the great ravine, moved off, leaving their fires burning. By dawn they had safely arrived on the high road between Sorauren and Ostiz, and were ready to move on towards D'Erlon when the third division—Conroux's—should have been relieved at Sorauren village by Maucune. But this had not yet been accomplished, even by five in the morning : for Maucune's troops having woods and pathless slopes to cross, in great part lost their way, and were straggling in small bands over the hills during the night. They had only two miles to go in many cases, yet when the light came some of them were still far from their destination and in quite unexpected places. Conroux had disentangled one brigade from Sorauren, while the other was still

[1] Foy (Girod de l'Ain), p. 219.

holding the outposts, and Maucune was just beginning to file some of his men behind the barricades and defences, when the whole of the village received a salvo of shells, which brought death and confusion everywhere. During the night Pakenham and Cole, obeying Wellington's orders, had succeeded in getting some guns up to the crest of the heights—the 6th Division had hauled six guns up the hill on its left : they were now mounted in front of Madden's Portuguese, only 500 yards from their mark [1]. Of the 4th Division battery [2] two guns and a howitzer had been dragged with immense toil to the neighbourhood of the chapel of San Salvador, overlooking Sorauren, the other three guns to a point farther east, opposite the front from which Vandermaesen had attacked on the 28th.

This was apparently the commencement of the action, but it soon started on several other points. Foy had evacuated Alzuza at midnight, but having rough country-paths in a steep hillside as his only guides in the darkness, had not succeeded in massing his division at Iroz till 5 a.m. He then mounted the heights in his immediate front, pushing before him (as he says) fractions of Maucune's division which had lost their way. His long column had got as far as the Col and the ground west of it, when —full daylight now prevailing—be began to be shelled by guns from the opposite heights—obviously the other half of Sympher's battery [3].

Meanwhile Lamartinière's division (minus the one battalion of the 122nd left to watch the Roncesvalles road) had moved very little in the night, having only drawn itself up from Zabaldica to the heights immediately to the left of the Col, where it lay in two lines of brigades, the front one facing the Spaniards' Hill, the rear one a few hundred yards back. Foy, coming from Iroz, had marched past Lamartinière's rear, covered by him till he got west of the Col. This division was not shelled, as Conroux, Maucune, and Foy had all been, but noted with disquiet that British troops were streaming up from Huarte

---

[1] These guns did not belong to Brandreth's battery, the divisional artillery of the 6th Division, but oddly enough to Cairnes's battery, which belonged to the 7th. See Duncan's *History of the Royal Artillery*, ii. p. 190.

[2] Sympher's, of the K.G.L.

[3] Foy in Girod de l'Ain, p. 220.

on the Roncesvalles road, with the obvious intention of turning its left, and getting possession of the main route to France.

Wellington, as it chanced, was in the most perfect condition to take advantage of the mistake which Soult had made in planning to withdraw his troops by a march right across the front of the allied army in position. The night-movements of the French had been heard, and under the idea that they might portend a new attack, all the divisions had been put under arms an hour before dawn. The guns, too, were in position, only waiting for their mark to become visible—it had been intended to shell the French out of Sorauren in any case that morning. Wellington had risen early as usual, and was on the look-out place on the Oricain heights which he used as his post on the 28th and 29th. When the panorama on the opposite mountain became visible to him, he had only to send orders for a general frontal attack, for which the troops were perfectly placed.

Accordingly, the 6th Division attacked Sorauren village at once, while the troops on the Oricain heights descended, a little later, in two lines—the front one formed of Byng's brigade, Stubbs's Portuguese, and the 40th and Provisional Battalion of Anson's—while Ross's brigade and Anson's two other battalions (the troops which had taken the worst knocks on the 28th) formed the reserve line. Preceded by their skirmishers, Byng's battalions made for Sorauren, Cole's marched straight for Foy's troops on the opposite hills [1]. Farther to the right Picton had discovered already that there was no longer any French force opposite him, and had got his division assembled for an advance along the Roncesvalles road. He would seem to have been inclined to go a little farther than Wellington thought prudent, as there was a dispatch sent to him at 8 a.m. bidding him to advance no farther, until it was certain that all was clear on the left, though he might push forward light troops on the heights east of the Arga river. He did not therefore get into touch with

---

[1] That the firing began at dawn immediately is stated by Larpent, p. 210. That the troops were under arms before daylight is noted by the anonymous *Soldier of the 42nd*, p. 199. The attack by the 6th Division on Sorauren was appreciably before the descent of Cole and Byng from the heights of Oricain.

Lamartiniére on the mountain above Zabaldica for some time after Foy and Maucune had been attacked.

Meanwhile it was not only to the old fighting-ground of the 28th that the attack was confined. Wellington ordered Lord Dalhousie to emerge from the shelter of the hills beyond the left of the 6th Division, and to assail the troops below him in the Ulzama valley—that is Taupin's and Vandermaesen's divisions, halted by Clausel some way short of Ostiz, when the sound of firing began near Sorauren.

The French units which were in the greatest danger were the three divisions of Conroux, Maucune, and Foy, all suddenly caught under the artillery fire of an enemy whom they had not believed to possess any guns in line. Troops marching in column are very helpless when saluted in this fashion. Foy writes ' we had not been intending to fight, and suddenly we found ourselves massed under the fire of the enemy's cannon. We were forced to go up the mountain side to get out of range ; we should have to retreat, and we already saw that we should be turned on both flanks by the two valleys on our left and right. . . . General Reille only sent part of my division up on to the high crests after its masses had been well played upon by an enemy whose artillery fire is most accurate [1].' Now Foy could, after all, get out of range by going up hill—but Maucune and Conroux were in and about a village which it was their duty to hold, since they had to cover the retreat of Foy and Lamartinière across their rear. If Sorauren were lost, Reille's two left divisions would be driven away from the main army—perhaps even cut off. Yet it was a hard business to hold a village under a close-range artillery fire from commanding ground, which enfiladed it on both sides, when the enemy's infantry intervened. Pakenham sent Madden's Portuguese round the village on the north—where they drove in one regiment [2] which Conroux had thrown out as a flank guard on the west bank of the Ulzama, and then proceeded to push round the rear of the place. At the same time the left wing of the troops which had descended from the chapel of San Salvador (Byng's brigade) began to envelop Sorauren on the eastern flank. And frontally it was attacked by the light companies of Lambert's brigade of the 6th Division.

---

[1] Girod de l'Ain, p. 221.   [2] 43rd Line (2 battalions).

Conroux's first brigade (Rey's) had succeeded in getting away to the north of the village before it was completely surrounded, and, after bickerings with Madden's Portuguese and other 6th Division troops, finally straggled across the hills to Ostiz. His other brigade, however, and all Maucune's division were very nearly exterminated. They made an obstinate defence of Sorauren for nearly two hours, till the place was entirely encompassed : Maucune says that he cleared a way for the more compromised units by a charge which retook part of the village, and then led the whole mass up the hill. The bulk of them scraped through, but were intercepted by 4th Division troops in the hollow hillside above. One whole battalion was forced to surrender, and great part of two others; there were 1,700 unwounded prisoners taken, of whom 1,100 belonged to Maucune and 600 to Conroux's rear brigade [1].

Maucune's division was practically destroyed : having reported 600 casualties on the 28th, he reported 1,800 more on the 30th, and as his total strength was only 4,186, it is clear that only 1,700 men got away. The general and the survivors rallied in to Foy on the heights above, along with the wrecks of Conroux's second brigade, which lost 1,000 men : the first brigade, though less hard hit, seems to have had 500 or 600 casualties, and many stragglers. Altogether both divisions were no longer a real fighting force during the rest of the campaign.

Meanwhile, there had been a distinct and separate combat going on farther up the Ulzama valley. When the fighting in and about Sorauren began, Clausel had halted Vandermaesen's and Taupin's division at a defile near the village of Olabe, knowing that if he continued on his way towards Ostiz and Olague Reille's wing would be completely cut off from him. Having seen suspicious movements in the hills on his left, he sent up two battalions from Vandermaesen's division to hold the heights immediately beyond the river and cover his flank.

---

[1] Maucune's 34th Léger reports 13 officers and 531 men prisoners out of a strength of 773. Why does Captain Vidal de la Blache, usually accurate, give this as Maucune's total loss in prisoners ? (cf. p. 251). His other battalions contribute another 550. Conroux's 55th and 58th Line give respectively 282 and 348 prisoners—the other regiments smaller but appreciable lists of captured.

The precaution was wise but insufficient : somewhere about 8.30 a.m. the British 7th Division, having received its orders to join in the general attack, came up from its concealed position in the rear, and fell upon the covering troops, who were driven off their steep position by Inglis's brigade, and thrown down on to the main body of Clausel's troops in the valley. There was close and bloody fighting in the bottom, ' a small level covered with small bushes of underwood,' but after a time the French gave way. Vandermaesen's men soon got locked in a stationary fight with Inglis's battalions, but the two other 7th Division brigades (Le Cor and Barnes) which had not descended to the river and the road, were plying Taupin's column with a steady fire from the slope of the opposite bank, which made standing still impossible [1]. Having to choose between attacking or retreating, Clausel opted for the easier alternative, and drew off. In his report to Soult he gives as his reason the fact that Sorauren had now been lost, that Reille's troops were streaming over the hills in disorder, and that it was no use waiting any longer to cover their retreat, which was not going to be by the road, but broadcast across the mountains. Accordingly he disengaged himself as best he could, and retreated up the *chaussée* followed by the 7th Division, which naturally took some time to get into order. Inglis's brigade followed by the road, presently supported by Byng's troops, who came up from the side of Sorauren at noon : the other two brigades kept to the slopes on the west of the river, turning each position which Clausel took up [2]. By one o'clock he was back to Etulain, by dusk at Olague, where he was joined by Conroux and the 3,000 men who represented the wreck of his division. Vandermaesen had been much mauled—and had left behind 300

---

[1] Interesting accounts of this fight may be found in the narratives of Wood of the 82nd, Green of the 68th, and Wheeler of the 51st—all in Inglis's brigade. They are, however, most confused, none of them having much notion of how or where they came into the general scheme of the fight. All speak of the steepness of the ground.

[2] I cannot make out for certain when Le Cor's Portuguese joined Dalhousie on the 30th, coming from the Marcalain road, where they had been placed on the previous evening. Probably not early, as they had 64 casualties only (mostly in 2nd Caçadores), while the other brigades had 200 apiece. The fact that the losses are nearly all in the light battalion shows that a skirmishing pursuit was the task of Le Cor's men.

prisoners, while many stragglers from his division, and more from both of the brigades of Conroux, were loose in the hills. It is doubtful whether Clausel had more than 8,000 men out of his original 17,000 in hand that evening. The survivors were not fit for further fighting [1].

Meanwhile, Reille was undergoing equally unpleasant experiences. He had stopped behind to conduct the retreat of Foy's and Lamartinière's divisions, when the unexpected cannonade, followed by the advance of the British infantry, showed that he was not to get away without hard fighting. When Pakenham attacked Sorauren, and Cole a little later crossed the ravine to assail Foy's position, Reille tried for some time to maintain himself on the heights, but soon saw that it was impossible. He sent Maucune permission to evacuate Sorauren—of which the latter could not avail himself, for he was pressed on all sides and no longer a free agent. And having thus endeavoured to divest himself of responsibility for the fate of his right division, he gave orders for the retreat of the two others not by any regular route, but straight across country, up hill and down dale. The reason for haste was not only that Cole was now pressing hard upon Foy's new position, but that Picton was visible marching hard for Zabaldica, with the obvious intention of turning Lamartinière's flank. There was an ominous want of any frontal attack on this division—it was clear that Picton intended to encircle it, while Foy on the other flank was being driven in by Cole, and there was a chance of the whole wing being surrounded. Accordingly, at about 10 o'clock by Lamartinière's reckoning, he began to give way in échelon of brigades, much hindered after a time by Picton's light troops, who had now swerved up into the hills after him,

[1] Clausel's report is (perhaps naturally) very reticent, and would give a reader who had no other sources to utilize a very inadequate account of the day's work—no one could possibly gather from it that Conroux lost 600 prisoners and Vandermaesen 300, or that the whole corps was in great disorder. For a picture of Conroux's division scattered over the hills, and its general storming at the fugitives, see Lemonnier-Delafosse, p. 232.

The hours at which events took place on Clausel's wing are hard to settle. I follow him in making the artillery begin to play on Sorauren *long* before 7, the infantry attack soon after that hour, and the loss of Sorauren about 9.

and pestered each battalion when it turned to retreat [1]. Foy
reports that his rear brigade and part of his colleague's division
were at one moment nearly cut off, and that he ran some danger
of being taken prisoner. It evidently became a helter-skelter
business to get away, and the French can have made no serious
resistance, as Picton's three brigades that day had only just
110 casualties between them [2]. The retreat was made more
disorderly by the arrival of a drove of some 4,000 fugitives of
Conroux's and Maucune's divisions, accompanied by the latter
general himself, who had escaped over the hills from Sorauren,
and ran in for shelter on Foy's rear.

At about one o'clock Reille's divisions, having outdistanced
their pursuers by their rapidity, halted in considerable disarray
in a valley by the village of Esain [3], where Reille tried to restore
order, and to settle a practicable itinerary, with the object of
rejoining Clausel. For reasons which he does not specify, he
marched himself by a road down the valley, which would lead
him to Olague, but told Foy to take a parallel track farther up
the slope which should take him to Lanz, higher in the same
valley. The partition was obviously made in a very haphazard
fashion, for while the bulk of Lamartinière's division, and the
poor remnant of Maucune's which preserved any order, accompanied the corps-commander, Foy found that he was being
followed by two stray battalions of Gauthier's brigade of Lamartinière, and by a great mass of stragglers, largely Conroux's men,
but partly also Maucune's and Lamartinière's.

Reille got to Olague at dusk and joined Clausel, but brought
with him a mere wreck of his corps, probably not 6,000 men.
For Foy never appeared—and never was to appear again during
the campaign. He explained, not in the most satisfactory way,
that part of his track lay through woods, where the sense of
direction is lost, that he was worried by the reappearance of
British light troops, who had to be driven off repeatedly, and
that the stragglers smothered his marching columns and led

---

[1] So Lamartinière, who admits that there was ' un peu de désordre '
but confesses much less than Foy, for whose account see Girod de l'Ain,
p. 221.

[2] Picton's division lost 89 in Brisbane's brigade, 20 among Power's
Portuguese, none in Colville's brigade.

[3] So Foy. Reille thinks that it was Sarrasibar, 3 miles farther east.

them astray. Anyhow, he found himself at dusk at Iragui in the upper valley of the Arga, instead of at Lanz in the upper valley of the Ulzama—having marched ten miles instead of the five that would have taken him from Esain to Lanz. Picton's light troops were still in touch with him, and he resolved that it was hopeless to try to struggle over mountains in the dark. Dropping into the pass that leads from Zubiri to the Alduides (the Puerto de Urtiaga), he marched for some hours more, bivouacked, and next morning descended into French territory[1]. He sent off the stragglers to St. Jean-Pied-de-Port—they sacked all the mountain villages on their way[2]—and took his own division at leisure down the Val de Baigorry to Cambo—having lost only 550 men out of his 6,000 in the whole campaign. Some critics whispered that, seeing disaster behind him, *il a su trop bien tirer son épingle du jeu*, and had saved his division, regardless of what might happen to colleagues—just as on the eve of Vittoria he had refused to join Jourdan, and had managed a safe retreat for himself. That it was not absolutely impossible to get away to the Bastan was shown by the fact that the two stray battalions of Lamartinière's division which had followed Foy in error, branched off from him at Iragui and got to Almandoz, Elizondo, and the pass of Maya. Another lost party—the battalion and cavalry regiment which Lamartinière had left to cover the Roncesvalles road[3]—turned off at Zubiri and followed Foy's route by the Alduides and Baigorry. Reille's ' main body ' was a poor remnant by the night of the 30th, after all these deductions had come to pass.

It must not be supposed that the operations of Pakenham, Dalhousie, Cole, and Picton during the morning of the 30th were left to the personal initiative of these officers. Wellington's orders for the first move had been made on the spur of the moment, as the position of the French became visible at dawn. But after the capture of Sorauren, probably between 9 and 10 a.m., he issued a definite programme for the remainder of the day's operations.

---

[1] Girod de l'Ain, p. 223.

[2] See Vidal de la Blache, p. 280, for complaints by the French *maires* of atrocities committed.

[3] See above, p. 681.

Picton was to pursue the enemy who had gone off north-eastward (Lamartinière) toward the Roncesvalles road. He was given two squadrons of hussars, and told to take his divisional battery with him.

Cole was to act on the *massif* between the Arga and the Ulzama, keeping touch with Picton on one flank and Pakenham on the other : if the enemy in his front (Foy and the wrecks of Maucune) made a strong stand, he was not to lose men by violent frontal attacks, but to wait for the effect of Picton's turning movement, ' which will alarm the enemy for his flank.'

Up the main road Ostiz–Olague there were to march Byng's brigade, the 6th Division, and O'Donnell's troops from the San Cristobal position (some six battalions). The 6th Division was to take its divisional battery with it.

Dalhousie should operate on the east bank of the Ulzama, keeping touch with Byng and Pakenham—he would be in a position to turn all positions which the French (Taupin and Vandermaesen) might take up, if they tried to hold back the main column on the high road. Like Cole, he was not to attempt anything costly or hazardous.

Finally, and here later news caused a complete alteration of the programme, Hill was to ' point a movement ' from Lizaso on Olague and Lanz, if the situation of the enemy made it possible. Attacked himself by the superior numbers of D'Erlon's corps, Hill was (of course) unable to do anything of the kind. Wellington seems to have suspected that he might be too weak for his task, and in the general rearrangement of the army sent him not only Campbell's Portuguese brigade (which properly belonged to the division of Silveira, who was in person with Hill but only with one brigade, Da Costa's), but also the Spanish battalions which O'Donnell had detached to Ollocarizqueta on the 27th [1], and finally Morillo's division. These 7,000 men were started from their positions before noon, but did not arrive in time to help Hill [2]. A separate supplementary order went off to Charles Alten to tell him that the

---

[1] See above, p. 664.

[2] All this in Q.M.G. to Hill, &c., in *Supplementary Dispatches*, viii. pp. 154–5, where it is stupidly printed *after* the evening orders given at 9 p.m.

Light Division would not be wanted at Lecumberri, and should return to Zubieta.

The whole of this series of orders is purely offensive in character, and, as is easily seen, presupposes first that a large section of the French army is retiring on the Roncesvalles road, but secondly that the main body is about to go back by Lanz, the Col de Velate, Elizondo, and Maya. Hence the heaviness of the column directed on the *chaussée*: if Wellington had dreamed that Soult was intending to send nothing back by the Roncesvalles road, and had started a vigorous attack on Hill that morning, the orders given would have been different.

Meanwhile, during the hours which saw the destruction of Clausel's and Reille's divisions, Soult himself was urging on D'Erlon's corps to overwhelm Hill, and hoping for the early arrival of Clausel's to lend assistance. Reille he had left behind as a containing force, and did not expect to see for another twenty-four hours. Soult informs us that he left Zabaldica and the left wing so early that he had no reason to expect the trouble which was about to break out behind him. He noticed Maucune's division beginning to file into Sorauren, and passed Clausel in march on Ostiz, before the British guns opened, i. e. before 6 o'clock in the morning. But they must have been sounding up the valley before he reached D'Erlon on the heights by Etulain : he resolved to pay no attention to the ominous noise, being entirely absorbed in the operation which he had in hand.

D'Erlon was already in movement, by the valley of the Ulzama, and had just been joined by the cavalry, which had come up from the Arga valley by cross roads in the rear [1]. It was, of course, no use to him in the sort of engagement on which he was launched. The Marshal instructed him to push on and hurry matters, as there were reports from deserters that three hostile divisions were on their way to reinforce the British force at Lizaso. Accordingly D'Erlon, having discovered his enemy's position with some little difficulty, for it lay all along the edge of woods, delivered his attack as soon as his troops were up.

---

[1] Soult says by way of Zubiri, Eugui, and Lanz, which seems a vast circuit—this march must surely have been made on the preceding evening : in the dark it would hardly have been possible.

Hill, on news of the French advance reaching him, had evacuated Lizaso, which lies in a hole, and had drawn up his four
brigades along a wooded ridge half a mile to the south, with the
village of Gorron in front of his left wing, and that of Arostegui
behind his right wing. The Portuguese brigade of Ashworth
formed his centre : on the right was one regiment of Da Costa's
brigade which had been called up from the Marcalain road, on
the left the other and the remains of Cameron's brigade, which
had suffered so heavily at Maya : Fitzgerald of the 5/60th was
in command, the brigadier having been wounded on the 25th.
Pringle's brigade (under O'Callaghan that day, for Pringle was
acting as division-commander vice William Stewart wounded
at Maya) was in reserve—apparently distributed by battalions
along the rear of the line. The edge of the woods was lined
with a heavy skirmishing line of light companies, and the
Caçador battalion of Ashworth's brigade. Altogether there
were under 9,000 men in line.

D'Erlon determined to demonstrate against Hill's front with
Darmagnac's division, who were to hold the Portuguese closely
engaged, but not to attack seriously. Meanwhile Abbé was to
assail the Allied left, and also to turn it by climbing the high
hills beyond its extreme flank, in the direction of the village of
Beunza. He had ample force to do this, having the strongest
division in Soult's army—8,000 bayonets—and the only one
which had not yet been seriously engaged during the campaign.
Maransin followed Abbé in support. The arrangements being
scientific, and the force put in action more than double Hill's,
success seemed certain.

It was secured ; but not so easily as D'Erlon had hoped.
Darmagnac, so Soult says, engaged himself much more deeply
than had been intended. Finding only Portuguese in his front,
he made a fierce attempt to break through, and was handsomely
repulsed. Meanwhile Abbé, groping among the wooded slopes
to find the flank of Fitzgerald's brigade, missed it at first, and
attacking the 50th and 92nd frontally, saw his leading battalions
thrown back. But he put in more, farther out to the right, and
though the British brigade threw back its flank *en potence*, and
tried to hold on, it was completely turned, and would have been
cut off, but for a fierce charge by the 34th, who came up from

the reserve and held the enemy in check long enough for the rest to retire—with the loss of only 36 prisoners (two of them officers). The retreat of the left wing compelled the Portuguese in the centre to give back also—they had to make their way across a valley and stream closely pursued, but behaved most steadily, and lost less than might have been expected—though some 130 were cut off and captured. The right wing pivoted, in its withdrawal, on an isolated hill held by Da Costa's 2nd Line, which was gallantly maintained to the end of the day. The centre and left lost more than a mile of ground, but were in good enough order to take up a new position, selected by Hill on a height in front of the village of Yguaras, where they repulsed with loss a final attack made by one of Darmagnac's regiments which pursued too fiercely [1]. D'Erlon was reforming his troops, much scattered in the woods, when at 4 p.m. there arrived from Marcalain the head of Campbell's Portuguese brigade, followed by Morillo's and O'Donnell's Spaniards. Their approach was observed, and no further attacks were made by the French. D'Erlon winds up his account of the day by observing, quite correctly, that he had driven Hill out of his position, inflicted much loss on him, and got possession of the road to Yrurzun. So he had—the Allies had lost 156 British and about 900 Portuguese, of whom 170 were prisoners. The French casualties must have been about 800 in all, if we may make a rough calculation from the fact that they lost 39 officers—10 in Abbé's division, 29 in Darmagnac's [2].

But it is not to win results such as these that 18,000 men attack 8,000, and fight them for seven hours [3]. And what was the use of such a tactical success, when meanwhile Soult's main

[1] 75th Line. Darmagnac says in his report that its colonel attacked the second position without orders. Martinien's lists show that it lost 16 officers—presumably therefore over 300 men.

[2] See casualty tables in Appendix. Maransin had no losses, having never been engaged. Hill made an astounding blunder in estimating his total loss at 400 in his report to Wellington. Nine British and 36 Portuguese officers were hit—exactly the same number as the French officer-casualties.

[3] Hill had Fitzgerald's and O'Callaghan's British brigades—2,600 deducting Maya losses, Da Costa's brigade 2,300, Ashworth's 2,800, and some squadrons of Long's light dragoons—about 8,000 in all. D'Erlon had, also deducting 2,000 Maya losses, over 18,000 infantry in his three divisions—not to speak of the cavalry division just arrived.

body had been beaten and scattered to the winds, so that Reille and Clausel were bringing up 14,000 demoralized soldiers, instead of 30,000 confident ones, to join the victorious D'Erlon ?

This unpleasant fact stared Soult in the face, when he rode back to Olague to receive the reports of his two lieutenants. It was useless to think of further attempts on the Tolosa road, or molestation of Graham. D'Erlon's three divisions were now his only intact force, capable of engaging in an action with confidence : the rest were not only reduced to a wreck in number, but were ' spent troops ' from the point of view of morale. The only thing to be done was to retreat as fast as possible, using the one solid body of combatants to cover the retreat of the rest. All that Soult afterwards wrote to Paris about his movements of July 31 being the logical continuation of his design of July 30—' de me rapprocher de la frontière pour y prendre des subsistances, avec l'espoir de joindre la réserve du Général Villatte [1],' was of course mere insincerity. He changed his whole plan, and fled in haste, merely because he was forced to do so.

One strange resolve, however, he made on the evening of July 30. The safest and shortest way home was by the Puerto de Velate, Elizondo, and Maya ; and Clausel's and Reille's troops at Olague and Lanz were well placed for taking this route. This was not the case with D'Erlon's men at Lizaso and the newly won villages in front of it. Instead of bidding the routed corps hurry straight on, and bringing D'Erlon down to cover them, the Marshal directed Reille and Clausel to leave the great road, to cut across by Olague to Lizaso, and to get behind D'Erlon, who would hold on till they were past his rear. All would then take the route of the Puerto de Arraiz and go by Santesteban. This was a much more dangerous line of retreat ; so much so that the choice excites surprise. Soult told Clarke that his reason for taking the risk was that D'Erlon had got so far west that there was no time to move him back to the Velate road—which seems an unconvincing argument. For Clausel and Reille had to transfer themselves to the Puerto de Arraiz road, which would take just as much time ; and D'Erlon could not retreat till they had cleared his rear. The

[1] Soult to Clarke, August 2.

real explanation would seem to be that Soult thought that the British column on the Velate road, being victorious, would start sooner and pursue more vigorously than Hill's troops, who had just been defeated. If Reille and Clausel were pressed without delay, their divisions would go to pieces : D'Erlon, on the other hand, could be relied upon to stand his ground as long as was needful. If this was Soult's idea, his prescience was justified.

SECTION XXXVIII: CHAPTER VI

SOULT'S RETREAT, JULY 31-AUG. 3

WHEN Soult's orders of the evening of July 29th had been issued, there was no longer any pretence kept up that the Army was executing a voluntary strategical movement, *planmässig* as the German of 1918 would have expressed the idea, and not absconding under pressure of the enemy.

At 1 o'clock midnight Clausel's and Reille's harassed troops at Olague and Lanz went off as fast as their tired legs would carry them, and leaving countless stragglers behind. D'Erlon could not retire till the morning, when he sent off Darmagnac and Maransin to follow the rest of the army, retaining Abbé's division as his rearguard, which held the heights north of Lizaso for some time after their comrades had gone.

Wellington's orders issued at nightfall [1] were such as suited Soult fairly well, for the British general had not foreseen that which was unlikely, and he had been deceived to some extent by the reports which had come in. The deductions which he drew from what he had ascertained were that a large body of the enemy had retreated eastward, and would fall into the Roncesvalles road, but that the main force would follow the Velate–Elizondo *chaussée*. That Soult would lead all that survived to him of his army over the Puerto de Arraiz passes, to Santesteban, had not struck him as a likely contingency. Hence his detailed orders overnight were inappropriate to the facts which appeared next morning. He directed Picton to pursue whatever was before him on the Roncesvalles road— thinking that Foy and Lamartinière would escape in that direction ; but lest they should have gone off by Eugui and the Col de Urtiaga he directed Pakenham to take the 6th Division from Olague, when it should have reached that place, across the hills to Eugui, from whence he could join Picton

---

[1] *Supplementary Dispatches*, viii. pp. 152–3.

if necessary. Campbell's Portuguese were to turn off in the same direction and make for Eugui and the Alduides. Unfortunately, Picton was thus set to pursue nothing, while Pakenham was twelve hours behind Foy, and never likely to catch him.

The main pursuit was to be urged on the *chaussée* leading by Olague and Lanz to Elizondo, whither it was supposed that Soult would have taken the bulk of his army. From Ostiz and the neighbourhood Byng and Cole were to march in this direction, conducted by Wellington himself, while from the other side Hill was to lead thither his own four brigades, and the Spanish reinforcements which had reached him at the end of the combat of Beunza.

Only Dalhousie and the 7th Division were directed to take the route of the Puerto de Arraiz, and this not with the object of pursuing the main French army, but rather as a flanking movement to favour the operation allotted to Hill. And Dalhousie, unfortunately, was not well placed for the march allotted to him, since he was near Ostiz, and had to get to his destination by a cross march via Lizaso.

A separate note for Charles Alten, written at the same time as the rest of the orders, but not sent out till the following morning, directed the Light Division to march back to Zubieta, where it would be able to communicate with the column that went by the Puerto de Arraiz, i.e. that of Dalhousie [1], and be well placed for flank operations against the retreating enemy.

The net result of all this was to send over half the available troops—Picton, Pakenham, Campbell, Byng, and Cole—on roads where no enemy would be found. And Hill's force would have suffered the same fate, if it had not been in such close touch with D'Erlon that it could not help following, when its enemy's route became evident. Unfortunately—as Soult had perhaps calculated—Hill had troops whose ranks had been terribly thinned, and who were tired out by an unsuccessful action fought on the preceding afternoon.

The day's work was unsatisfactory. Picton, of course, found out at Zubiri that everything that had been on the Roncesvalles

---

[1] *Supplementary Dispatches*, viii. p. 154, written at Ostiz, 30th July, many hours after the preceding note to Alten, also written on the 30th but from Villaba. It is endorsed by G. Murray, Lizaso, 11 a.m., 31st July.

road—the small detachment already spoken of [1], and a mass of stragglers—had turned up toward Eugui and the Alduides on the preceding night. And Cole discovered that Foy had passed the Puerto de Urtiaga a whole march ahead of him. Wellington, with the column on the great *chaussée*, pressed rapidly across the Velate and reached Irurita, with the exasperating result that he discovered that only 500 to 1,000 French had passed that way [2]. On the other hand, he had news from the west that an immense mass of the enemy had gone by the Puerto de Arraiz, with Hill and Dalhousie after them. There were doubts whether the pursuing force was not dangerously small—at any rate, it would have to be cautious. And it was tiresome that the position of the Light Division was still unknown—it might (or might not) have a chance of falling on the flank of Soult's long column, either at Santesteban or at Sumbilla. Wellington's own troops had marched far and fast from Ostiz to Irurita, but there was in the evening enough energy left in Byng's brigade for a short push farther. News came in that a great convoy of food from St. Jean de Luz had just reached Elizondo, where it had halted under the protection of the regiment which D'Erlon had left there on the 27th. By a forced march in the evening Byng's flank companies surprised and captured the whole—a good supply of bread, biscuit, and brandy—the escort making off without resistance. The brigadier had the heads of the brandy casks stove in, before the weary troops could get at them, ' it was a sight to see the disappointed soldiers lying down on their faces and lapping up the liquor with their hands [3].'

All this, of course, was unimportant. The real interest of the doings of July 31st lay on the road from Lizaso to the Puerto de Arraiz. Hill, as was natural, was late in discovering that the whole of the French army had passed across his front, since Abbé's division still lay at eight in the morning in battle-order blocking his way. But having got the news of the decisive success won by his chief on the preceding day, Hill had to attack the hitherto victorious enemy in front of him, knowing that the

---

[1] One battalion and one cavalry regiment, see above, p. 681.
[2] Wellington to Q.M.G., Irurita, 3 p.m.
[3] Narrative of L'Estrange of the 31st, p. 121.

general situation was such that they could not possibly stand. His advance was not made till 10 a.m.—a sufficient proof of the difficulty of resuming the offensive with tired and beaten troops. When once, however, it began, the 2nd Division showed that if its numbers were wasted, its fighting power was still strong. And the delay in its attack allowed of the arrival of the 7th Division, who were able to co-operate in a way that would have been impossible if the fighting had started at daybreak.

On the other hand, the hours between dawn and 10 a.m., during which his retreat was unmolested, were invaluable to Soult, whose army was jammed in the passes in a most danger- ous fashion. He had taken the lead himself, with the two cavalry divisions and the baggage, ordering Reille, whose troops were the most demoralized of all, to follow, with Clausel in his rear—D'Erlon stopping behind as rearguard to hold back the enemy. Now cavalry moves slowly in an uphill climb on a narrow road ; while worn-out mules and pack-horses go much slower still, and are always breaking down and obstructing the route. The result was a complete block in the defiles : when Reille heard firing commencing in the rear, he grew so anxious that he ordered his infantry to push on anyhow, and thrust their way through the baggage by force [1]. This naturally made matters still worse. Clausel found a better plan : the Puerto de Arraiz gives its name to what is really not a single path, but three parallel ones of various merit, all crossing the same dip in the main crest of the Pyrenees within a short distance of each other. They come together again on the north side of the watershed near the village of Donna Maria, whence some writers call the whole group ' the Donna Maria passes.' Clausel leaving the best and most obvious track to the others, crossed by the most eastern of the three, the Puerto de Arraiz proper, while the cavalry, Reille, and D'Erlon took the western route which is locally known as the Puerto de Eradi, and comes down more directly on to Santesteban.

When Hill's attack began to develop from Lizaso, D'Erlon ordered Abbé's division to give ground, before it was too closely pressed, but halted it for a stand again, on heights by the Venta

[1] In his report, as he explains, ' je m'occupai de déblayer la route, qui était encombrée d'équipages et de cavalerie.'

de Urroz, six miles farther north, at the foot of the passes. Darmagnac and Maransin were visible higher up the crest, where they were waiting till the road should be clear in front of them.   It was now nearly two o'clock, and Dalhousie's division was nearing the front, and was visible closing towards Hill's right.   Undoubtedly the proper game was to await its arrival, and use it to turn Abbé's flank.   But Hill directed his leading troops to prevent the enemy from withdrawing, and the vanguard was this day in charge of the reckless William Stewart, who despite his Maya wound had come back to his troops, and appeared with his damaged leg strapped to his saddle in a roll of cushions.   He ordered Fitzgerald's brigade to attack at once frontally : this was really wicked ; the three battalions had lost nearly half their numbers at Maya, and 150 men more at Beunza on the preceding afternoon.   They were a mere wreck—under 1,000 bayonets : the position opposite them was a steep wooded hill, held by the most intact division of the whole French army, over 7,000 strong.   The attack was delivered with great courage, but was hopeless from the first, and repelled with loss [1].   Stewart then repeated it, throwing in Pringle's brigade as it came up from the rear, to support Fitzgerald's, and turning on two guns, which had been brought up with much difficulty, to shell the woods beside the road.   A second attack was thus delivered with equal want of success.   But Dalhousie's troops having now come up on the right [2], a third push was successful, and Abbé went back, and retired behind Darmagnac, who now took over the rearguard. The hours gained in this combat had sufficed to clear the road, and on the further advance of the British, D'Erlon's corps gave back rapidly but in good order, and was in full retreat down the northern watershed when a dense fog came on, and caused Hill to halt his troops.   Stewart's first wholly unnecessary frontal attack had resulted in the loss of the acting-brigadier, Fitzgerald, wounded and a prisoner [3], and of nearly 200 casualties

[1] D'Erlon in his report of August 3 says that ' the majority of the enemy's soldiers were drunk,' an involuntary tribute to their wild pluck.

[2] The 7th Division had a steep scramble and a tough fight ; see the diary of Green of the 68th, p. 162.

[3] A fact mentioned only by D'Erlon and by Rigaud's history of the 5/60th, Fitzgerald's corps.

among his three weak battalions—91 in the 92nd Highlanders
alone, who having put 750 men in line at Maya on the 25th
came out of action on the 31st with only 250 surviving. The
7th Division had 117 casualties distributed between six English
and Portuguese units—and the total loss in the combat was
387, including a score of prisoners. That Stewart himself was
again wounded and sent to the rear, after only twelve hours at
the front, was a testimonial to his courage, but a very fortunate
event for the 2nd Division. The French cannot have lost much
over 200 men [1].

Having thus cleared the passes, Hill thought it was his duty
to carry out Wellington's original orders of the preceding night [2],
by closing in towards the main body on the Maya *chaussée* ; he
did so by taking a hill track called the Puerto de Sangre, which
runs from Arraiz to Almandoz. Of course this was a grave
mistake, as troops were wanted rather on the Santesteban than
on the Elizondo road. Hill must not be too much blamed, as Wellington might have sent him new orders to keep to the direction
of the enemy's retreat, and did not. The danger involved in this
move was that only the 7th Division was left to pursue Soult's
main body, and the force in the upper Bastan was unnecessarily
increased. The responsibility rests with Wellington, who, even
after reaching Irurita in the afternoon and finding practically
no traces of enemy in the Bastan, could not believe that the
French had gone off *en masse* by the passes to Santesteban. He
would make no sweeping changes in his plan till he got full
information. ' I shall make the troops dine, and see what is to
be done in the evening ' was his message to Murray [3]. The
evening brought Hill's news, and by dawn Wellington was much
more clear about the situation—' as far as I can judge the
enemy have six divisions between Doña Maria and St. Estevan.
There are three divisions certainly about Eugui and Ronces-

---

[1] So I deduce from there being precisely 10 officer-casualties in Abbé's
regiments, according to Martinien's lists.

[2] Hill and the Quartermaster-General, George Murray, had settled at
11 a.m. that Wellington's original order was only ' momentarily suspended '
and not cancelled, by the necessity for driving in ' the column of the enemy
now retiring by the Donna Maria road.' *Supplementary Dispatches*, viii.
p. 163.

[3] *Supplementary Dispatches*, viii. p. 159.

valles [1].' The distribution of the French was even still mis-judged—there were troops representing eight divisions, not six, in the Central Bastan valley. And only one division, Foy's, had passed eastward ; though so many lost detachments and bands of stragglers had followed it, that an impression of much larger numbers had been produced.

Despite of Wellington's misconceptions, Soult's position at Santesteban that evening was most uncomfortable. His cavalry scouts had brought him news that there was a heavy British column on his right flank, at Elizondo in the Upper Bastan (Cole and Byng). His rearguard had been fiercely attacked by another column (Dalhousie and Hill). There were large possibilities of the arrival of other foes from the north and west, if Graham had not been kept employed by Villatte. And it was growing most obvious that the story which D'Erlon had reported, to the effect that the Reserve Division had crossed the Bidassoa, and was advancing, could not be true. For cavalry patrols pushing down the river towards Vera could not find any signs of friendly troops, and had been fired on by Spanish outposts—Longa's men. When Soult next wrote to Paris he spoke out with much bitterness on the criminal torpidity of Villatte, who might at least, without risking anything, have occupied Vera and the gorge of the Bidassoa, and have tried to get into touch with the army in the field. It must be remem-bered that down to the 30th all Soult's communications with his bases at Bayonne and St. Jean-Pied-du-Port had been either by Maya or by Roncesvalles. He had thrown up the latter line when he marched north ; the former was now closed to him by the reported arrival of a large hostile force at Elizondo. The only way home was by the road down the Bidassoa by Sumbilla to Echalar ; and now it turned out that there was no certainty that this road might not have been blocked by detachments from Graham's army. The situation was anything but hopeful, and a complete disaster was by no means outside the bounds of possibility. One thing was certain—the army must get out of the Santesteban cul-de-sac as soon as possible, and by the only road that was not known to be intercepted. But prompt flight

---

[1] Wellington to O'Donnell, Irurita 6 a.m., on the 1st August. *Supple-mentary Dispatches*, viii. p. 163.

was rendered difficult by the presence at head-quarters of two divisions of quite useless cavalry, a convoy of many thousands of wounded, and the baggage of eight divisions.

At evening on the 31st the Marshal had been so much disturbed by the news of the presence of the British at Elizondo, from whence they could descend on Santesteban by following the road along the Bidassoa, that he had thrown out the whole of Reille's surviving infantry (perhaps 6,000 men) to cover the road by the river against any attack. But the enemy did not move that night—Wellington was resting his men and waiting for news. Dalhousie had halted on the heights by the Puerto de Arraiz when the fog came down at 5 p.m., and did not follow D'Erlon down to the valley.

Hence Soult had the power to arrange for a flitting before dawn, on the only possible route—a gorge twelve miles long where the road follows the rocky bed of the Bidassoa in all its curves, with the water on its left and steep wooded hills on its right. The line of march was headed by one infantry battalion of Reille's corps to clear the way [1], then came Treillard's dragoons [2], six regiments, taking up an intolerable length of road, then the remains of Lamartinière's division [3], then the wounded followed by the baggage train, then the handful of men that represented the wrecked division of Maucune, then (apparently) Pierre Soult's cavalry [4]. D'Erlon's corps was to follow—in the order Abbé, Maransin, Darmagnac, followed by another mass of baggage. Clausel's wing was directed to bring up the rear, with the task of holding back any pursuit either from the direction of Elizondo or that of the Donna Maria passes. It was certain that there was danger from both sides— so the start was made early—at 2.30, long ere dawn. Reille was

[1] 1/120th Line of Lamartinière.

[2] Who were picked up by Reille some miles north of Santesteban, having been sent forward on the Sumbilla road overnight, in charge of the convoy of wounded. See Reille's Report.

[3] Reduced to five battalions, since it had detached one regiment to the head of the column, and was short of two battalions which had escaped by Almandoz, and one which had escaped by Zubiri and Eugui following Foy. See above, pp. 699–700.

[4] The chasseur regiments only—the dragoons having escorted the artillery to Roncesvalles. Place in the column not quite certain—but see the narrative of Lemonnier-Delafosse for P. Soult's presence.

directed to lead the column along the river as far as the bifur-cation of the routes to Vera and to Echalar, where he was to take the latter, and turn off from the Bidassoa : for the last stage into France was to be made over the Puerto de Echalar and not over the more westerly Puerto de Vera. Apparently D'Erlon was ordered to branch off at Sumbilla with his infantry alone, and to take a separate mountain-track to Echalar, which few maps mark. This is, at any rate, Soult's statement ; but as D'Erlon makes no mention of such directions, and did not actually go that way (though Clausel did), the order matters little to the historian.

The unpleasant possibilities of the situation of the French on the night of July 31st–August 1st seem to have been more clearly discerned by Soult than by Wellington—as was natural, since the Marshal knew much better the exact state of his own army. There was a positive danger that it might be enveloped from all sides on the following day. But Wellington does not seem to have contemplated so great an operation, though he had a clear notion that the enemy might be much incommoded and harassed if all went well. He had hopes that something might be done by means of the Light Division—whose position was still, most unluckily, a matter of doubt. He had written on the preceding afternoon to Charles Alten to say that if he had got back to Zubieta, he ought to be told that a large body of the enemy was marching by the Donna Maria passes : ' it is very desirable that you should endeavour to head them at St. Estevan. If you should find that you cannot head them there, you might at Sumbilla, or you might cut in upon their column of march : they are in the greatest disorder. The head of our troops is here at Irurita, and others are following the enemy by Doña Maria. Communicate this to Sir Thomas Graham, via Goizueta [1].' It is quite clear that there is no idea of encirclement in this order, but only one of molestation. And it is equally obvious that Wellington had no idea of using any of Graham's forces to block the gorge of the Bidassoa. His message to that general on the 31st is, ' we are going to act immediately against a column which is retiring by the Doña Maria road. We have plenty of troops in the proper direction,

[1] To Alten, 12 noon, from near Almandoz. *Dispatches*, x. p. 574.

and if we can overtake the column, I hope its rear will suffer considerably [1].' Graham is asked for no help ; and, what is more curious, Wellington in his last preceding letter had told him that he attached no importance to keeping possession of Vera, at the actual gorge of the Bidassoa. ' I have a letter from General Giron, expressing apprehensions of the consequences to his position of losing Vera. The fact is, that Vera is no object to anybody. The heights are important for the communication with Lesaca by the valley of the Bidassoa, and the heights on the other side open the *débouché* into France. But the loss of both would not affect the position of Irun, if the passages through the rocky heights on the right of Irun are well guarded, for which Longa is allotted : and that is what it is most important to take care of.' This, it is true, was written on the 30th, before Wellington had ascertained that any French force was to retire by Santesteban. But it coincides completely with Graham's contemporary letter to his commander, expressing exactly the same opinion. ' General Giron seems anxious, on hearing of Soult's being repulsed, to undertake an offensive operation against the Puerto de Vera, which I could not encourage, being persuaded that his troops would not succeed, against so strong a post, and that his failure would be very prejudicial.'

In fact it is clear that Graham and Wellington both discouraged the idea of sending a considerable force to the gorge of the Bidassoa, which a day later would have proved of incalculable importance. A single division placed on the crossroads to Vera and Echalar by the bridge of Yanzi would have cut Soult's only line of retreat. His infantry, no doubt, or great part of it, could have escaped over the mountains, but the whole of his cavalry and train, and no doubt many infantry also, must have been captured. To make matters easy for the enemy, Soult had placed at the head of his interminable column useless dragoons, and the smallest and most demoralized of his corps of infantry. Neither Reille's wasted divisions nor Treillard's cavalry could have cut their way through 5,000

---

[1] *Dispatches*, x. p. 573.

[2] Graham to Wellington, July 30, 5 a.m. *Supplementary Dispatches*, viii. p. 156.

steady troops at the mouth of the defile. And D'Erlon could not have got up—the road in front of him for miles being blocked with baggage and helpless horsemen, and his rear harassed by vigorous pursuit.

Unfortunately, however, when Longa complained that he was too weak on the heights opposite Vera, and reported that the French were turning back, and that his post at the bridge of Yanzi would be attacked, no more was done to strengthen him than the moving of one brigade of Barcena's division to the heights by Lesaca, from which a single battalion was sent down to the Yanzi position. Yet this solitary unit had no small effect on the events of August 1, caused a panic among the enemy, and delayed Soult's march for hours. What would have happened if Graham and Giron had sent down a solid force (e.g. one British and one or two Spanish brigades) it is impossible to say with accuracy, but the results must have been tremendous.

There can be no doubt that the legend according to which Wellington schemed for the complete encirclement of Soult's army on the 1st of August, though early and well supported, is inaccurate. The form which it takes in Napier [1], Larpent, and Stanhope's *Conversations with the Duke of Wellington*, is that on the evening of the 31st arrangements were being made for a concentric attack on Soult, but that they were foiled, under Wellington's own eyes, by a party of marauding British soldiers, who strayed near the French camp, and were taken prisoners. Their appearance from the Elizondo side betrayed, it is alleged, to Soult that he was outflanked, and caused him to march in the night instead of at dawn—by which time he would have been surrounded. Unfortunately for the legend, we have Soult's own contemporary dispatch of August 2 to prove that the news of the presence of the British at Elizondo was brought him by a cavalry patrol, which reached the village just as it and the convoy in it were captured by Byng's brigade. They got away, but could not tell him whether the convoy-escort

---

[1] Napier (v. p. 243) and Stanhope (pp. 71-2) both say that they had the anecdote from the Duke himself—but wrote many years after 1813. But Larpent's absolutely contemporary diary also has the tale (p. 218) written down on August 3, only two days after the supposed event.

had, or had not, escaped. Moreover, much earlier in the day,
Reille had warned the Marshal that the British were coming up
in force on the Velate–Elizondo road—so the whole story falls
through.

Wellington's limited ambitions of August 1 are made clear
by his dispatch written at 6 in the morning, which says that
he is sending the 4th Division on to Santesteban ' with the
intention of aiding Dalhousie's advance, and to endeavour to
cut some of them off.' It is true that he adds, ' I sent in tripli-
cate to the Light Division at Zubieta yesterday, to desire that
General Alten should move toward St. Estevan, and at all
events get hold of Sumbilla if he could. But I have heard
nothing of him [1].' He was therefore not relying on certain help
from the Light Division, or from Graham or from Longa,
though advices of the situation were sent to all three. Of the
troops under his own hand he only sent the 4th Division to join
the hunt. Cole was directed to push the French on the north
bank of the Bidassoa, while Dalhousie was pressing them on
the south bank. Byng was told to remain stationary, till Hill's
column should come up from Almandoz, ' when I shall know
better how things are situated on all sides, and how far Sir
Rowland has advanced.'

The 4th Division, starting early despite of its long march on
the preceding day, was attacking the French rear by seven
o'clock in the morning—7th Division diaries would seem to
show that Dalhousie was much later in closing. We have,
oddly enough, no good account of the fight that ensued from
any British source [2] ; but Clausel's narrative enables us to
understand pretty well what happened. At dawn Vandermaesen's division had been left as rearguard on the hill facing
Santesteban on the north side of the Bidassoa, with Taupin's
in support, while Conroux's was trying to make its way towards
Sumbilla, but found the path blocked by D'Erlon's baggage in
front. Wherefore Clausel directed his brigadiers to give up any
idea of keeping to the road, and to march along the slopes above
it, so long as was possible. When the British appeared, they

---

[1] Wellington to O'Donnell. *Supplementary Dispatches*, viii. p. 163.
[2] Some good diarists had been wounded at Sorauren, and fail us after
the 28th July.

attacked with long lines of skirmishers, keeping to the hillside and attempting to turn Vandermaesen's flank on the high ground. The French, therefore, also extended themselves uphill, but reached the crest only after the enemy had just crowned it. ' On this ground, where no regular deployment could take place, the side which had got to the top first had every advantage.' Vandermaesen's battalions evidently broke up, as we are told that they got into trouble, ' continuing a retrograde movement high up the mountain among horrid precipices,' and were only rallied on two of Taupin's regiments above the gorge of the defile between Santesteban and Sumbilla, where Clausel had to halt perforce, because there was a complete block in front of him—Darmagnac's division of D'Erlon's corps was halted there from absolute inability to proceed, owing to trouble in front. The French narrative then describes an hour of incoherent fighting on the slopes above Sumbilla, in which Darmagnac's troops on the road below were also engaged. It ended with the retreat of all Clausel's three divisions across the hills, each taking its own way by foot-tracks up a different spur of the Atchiola range, and arriving in succession in the upland valley of Echalar by separate routes. The British did not follow, but stuck to Darmagnac and the baggage-train down in the road, whom they continued to press and persecute. All this reads like a serious fight and a deliberate retreat—but the critical historian must remark that to all appearances Clausel is glozing over a complete *débandade* and a disorderly flight across the mountains—for that there was no real resistance is shown by the casualty list of the pursuing British. The 4th Division brigades, English and Portuguese, lost that day precisely three men killed and three officers and 42 men wounded among their twelve battalions—i. e. there can have been no attempt at a stand at any time in the morning—and from the first moment, when Vandermaesen's flank was turned, the enemy must have continued to make off over inaccessible ground as hard as he could go. If he had tried to hold the pursuers back, the 4th Division would have shown more than 48 killed and wounded. The 7th Division had no casualties at all, so evidently did not get to the front in time to do more than pick up stragglers and baggage. The same impression of mere flight is produced by the French lists of officers killed and hurt—six in Vander-maesen's division, one in Conroux's, none in Taupin's—this should, on the usual proportion between the ranks, repre-sent perhaps 150 or 160 as the total loss of Clausel's corps [1]. Obviously then, we are facing the record of a flight not of a fight ; and the conduct of these same divisions on the following morning, when attacked by Barnes's brigade—of which, more in its proper place—sufficiently explains the happenings of August 1st.

So much for the chronicle of the rearguard. That of the vanguard is much more interesting. Reille, as has been before mentioned, was in charge of the advance, which consisted of one battalion of the 120th Regiment, followed by Treillard's dragoon division, the baggage of the corps, and the main convoy of wounded ; the rest of the infantry was separated by a couple of miles of impedimenta from the leading battalion. There was no trouble, though progress was very slow, until, late in the morning, the head of the column arrived near the bridge of Yanzi, where a by-path, leading down from that village and from Lesaca, crosses the Bidassoa. The bridge of Yanzi was, as has been mentioned above—the extreme right point of the long observation line which Longa's Spaniards had been holding since July 25th. The village above it, on the west bank, a mile uphill, was occupied by a battalion of Barcena's division of the Galician Army, lent to Longa on the preceding day—the 2nd Regiment of Asturias [2]. But there were two companies of Longa's own on outlying picket at the bridge, which had been

---

[1] One of the French officers killed on August 1, Hutant of the 59th, is registered as ' tué en défendant l'aigle.' Now with such absurdly small casualty lists as those shown above, the eagle can only have been in danger if the regiment was ' on the run.'

[2] I had immense difficulty in identifying this battalion, which belonged to Barcena's division, as Wellington mentions in his letter to Lord Liver-pool of August 4 (*Dispatches*, x. p. 598). But Wellington calls it there a cazadore battalion, which it was not, but an old line battalion. The trouble was first to find the composition of Barcena's division in July 1813, and then to hunt in Spanish regimental histories (those of the Conde de Clonard) for a claim by any of those corps to have been at the bridge of Yanzi on August 1. Alone among all the regiments Asturias makes this claim—but the corps-historian says not one word about its meritorious service—evidently unknown to him.

barricaded but not broken.   The road from Santesteban bifur-
cates a short distance upstream from the bridge, the left-hand
branch following the bank of the Bidassoa to Vera, the right-
hand one diverging inland and uphill to Echalar.   The route
of the French was not across the bridge, since they were not
going to Lesaca or Yanzi, nor past it, since they were not going
to Vera ;   they had to turn off eastward at the cross-roads,
almost opposite the bridge but a little south of it, and to follow
the minor road which leads up to Echalar along the south bank
of the Sari stream, on which that village stands.   When Reille's
battalion at the head of the marching column came to the cross
roads, it was fired upon by the Spanish post at the bridge.   This
created some confusion :   the critic can only ask with wonder
why Reille, who had six cavalry regiments under his orders,
had not sent out vedettes along the roads far ahead, and become
aware long before of the obstruction in his front :   evidently,
however, he had not.   After the first shots were fired, there was
a general stoppage all down the column.   The battalion at its
head could see that the Spaniards were very few, and prepared
to dislodge them.   Meanwhile the dragoons had halted and
many of them, at places where the river was level with the road,
walked their horses into the stream, to let them drink.   Suddenly there came a violent explosion of musketry from the
front—the bridge was being attacked and forced.   But to those
far down the road, who could not see the bridge, it sounded as
if the enemy was assailing and driving in the solitary battalion
on which the safety of the whole army depended for the
moment.   A great part of the dragoons shouted ' right about
turn,' and galloped backward up the pass without having
received any order [1], till they plunged into General Reille and
his staff, moving at the head of Lamartinière's division, and
nearly rode them down.   The column of infantry blocking the
road stopped the further progress of the foremost fugitives, who
got jammed in a mass by the impetus of squadrons pressing

---

[1] Reille says in his report that the order ' halt,' issued at the head of
the column, was repeated down the column of dragoons and turned in the
noise and confusion into ' demi tour '.   Whereupon the rear regiments
thought the column was cut off, and galloped back in panic.   ' Halte ' is
not very like ' demi tour '—but there was no doubt about the panic.

behind them. Reille could not make out the cause of the panic,
but filed the 2nd Léger out of the road and sent them past the
dragoons by a footpath on the slope, by which they got to the
bridge. It was found that the Spaniards had been driven from
it, and forced to retire up the west bank of the river, the way
to Echalar being clear. Thereupon the battalion of the 120th,
followed by the 2nd Léger, turned up the road, and after them
the leading regiments of dragoons. The officers in charge at
the front forgot that their enemies might return, and left no one
to guard the bridge. Hence, when Reille came up in person a
little later, he was vexed to find that the Spaniards had re-
appeared on the rocky farther bank of the river half a mile
above the bridge, and were firing across the ravine at the
passing cavalry, causing much confusion and some loss. Unable
to cross the river, which had precipitous banks at this point, he
ordered that the next infantry which arrived—the 2nd battalion
of the 120th—should deploy on the slopes above the road, and
keep down the enemy's fire by continuous volleys. He also
directed another battalion to cross the bridge, and work up-
stream till they should come on the flank of the Spaniards, and
then to drive them away. This was done, and the rest of the
dragoons, Lamartinière's infantry, and the head of the column
of baggage filed past the cross-roads and went on towards
Echalar—with Reille himself in their company. He had left
a battalion at the Yanzi bridge, with orders to hold the pass,
but had little expectation of seeing it molested again, taking
the enemy for a mere party of guerrilleros.

But worse was now to come. The Spanish companies which
had been driven off were now reinforced by the main body of
the regiment of Asturias, which, coming down from Yanzi
village, made a vigorous attack on the bridge, swept back the
French battalion which was holding it [1], and began firing into
the baggage train which was passing the cross roads at that
moment. The bulk of it turned back in confusion, and rushed
up the defile, soon causing a complete block among the convoy
of wounded and the division of Maucune, which was the next
combatant unit in the line of march. The Spaniards held the

---

[1] We learn from Lamartinière's report that it was one of the 118th
regiment.

bridge for more than two hours, during which complete anarchy prevailed on the road as far as Sumbilla, where D'Erlon's rear-guard, the division of Darmagnac, was now engaged in skirmishing with the British 4th Division. The real difficulty was that owing to the bad arrangement of the order of march, it took an inordinate time to bring fresh troops from the rear up to the head of the column ; while Reille, now safely arrived at Echalar and busy in arranging his troops in position there, does not seem to have thought for a moment of what might be going on behind him [1]. Maucune's division (a mere wreck) came up at last, thrusting the baggage and wounded aside : its general confesses that ' it fought feebly with the Spaniards at the bridge—its loss was not more than 30 men. The division was so weak, its men so short of cartridges, that it was necessary to wait for one of Count D'Erlon's divisions to come up, before the road could be cleared [2].' He does not add—but his corps-commander [3] gives us the fact—that ' the 7th Division ended by quitting the road and throwing itself into the mountains in order to avoid the enemy's fire,' i. e. it went over the hills in disorder, and arrived at Echalar as a mob rather than a formed body. Abbé's troops, at the head of D'Erlon's column, at last got up, after a desperate scramble through the mass of baggage, wounded, and (apparently) cavalry also, for some of Pierre Soult's regiments seem to have been marching after Maucune. ' Jammed between the river, whose right bank is very steep, and the mountain, whose slopes are wooded and impracticable, the soldiers shoved the train aside, upsetting much into the river, and turning the disorder of the movement to profit by pillaging all that they could lay their hands upon [4].' At last Abbé got four or five battalions disentangled [5] and formed them to attack the bridge, which was carried by the 64th Regiment after a struggle which did the Asturians much credit—the French

---

[1] He declares in his report that he never heard of the trouble until nightfall.   [2] Report of Maucune, dated August 3.

[3] Report of Reille.

[4] Report of the Right Wing—dated that night, August 1.

[5] D'Erlon complains that he found no French troops whatever facing the bridge—i. e. the 118th and Maucune had disappeared long before his front battalion got up. The battalions engaged were the 5th Léger and 63rd and 64th Line—whose officer-casualties for that day were 1 killed and 8 wounded.

units engaged showed a loss of 9 officers, probably therefore of some 200 men [1]. Leaving a couple of battalions to guard the bridge and the knoll beyond it, Abbé hurried the rest of his division towards Echalar, the baggage following as it could, mixed with the troops that were coming up from the rear. Thus the greater part of D'Erlon's corps got through ; but there was still one more episode to come in this day of alarms and excursions. Darmagnac's division, at the rear of all, had reached the cross-roads, and had relieved Abbé's battalions at the bridge by a covering force of its own, when a new and furious fire of musketry suddenly broke out from the slopes above, and a swarm of green-coated skirmishers rushed down the heights, carried the knoll and the bridge below it, and opened fire on the passing troops—Darmagnac's rear brigade—and the mass of baggage which was mixed with it. This marked the arrival—when it was too late—of the much tried British Light Division, whose unfortunate adventures of the last three days it is necessary to explain.

It will be remembered that Wellington had sent orders to Charles Alten, on the 29th July, that he should move from Zubieta to such a point on the Tolosa–Yrurzun road as might seem best—possibly Lecumberri. This dispatch travelled fast, and Alten marched that same night to Saldias—a short stage but fatiguing, as marches in the dark are prone to be. Next day —the 30th—the Light Division made an extremely long and exhausting march by vile mountain roads to Lecumberri, hearing all day incessant cannonading and musketry fire to their left—this was the noise of the second battle of Sorauren and the combat of Beunza. Unfortunately Alten was in touch neither with Hill nor with Head-Quarters, and though he reached Lecumberri at dark on the 30th, got no news of what had happened till late on the afternoon of the 31st, when one of Wellington's aides-de-camp rode in, ' more dead than alive from excessive fatigue [2],' bearing the order issued late on the

[1] The best account of all this is in Graham's report, *Supplementary Dispatches*, xiv. p. 261.

[2] All these marches are mainly detailed from the excellent narrative of Quartermaster Surtees of the 3/95th, pp. 223–6, supplemented by that of Captain Cooke of the 1/43rd.

30th for the return of the division to Zubieta. He brought the news of Soult's defeat—but Wellington and every one else had supposed that the French would go back by the Puerto de Velate, and Alten's orders were merely to get into communication with the 7th Division, sent on the side-operation by the Puerto de Arraiz, which was at the time of the issue of the order thought comparatively subsidiary[1]. The Light Division marched that evening to Leyza—eight or nine miles on a mountain road —not a bad achievement for the dark hours, but critics (wise after the event) whispered that Alten might have got to Saldias, eight miles farther, if he had chosen to push the men. It, at any rate, made a mighty difference to the fate of the campaign that Wellington's next orders, those issued from Almandoz at noon on the 31st, found the Light Division not near Zubieta but at Leyza, when they were handed in during the small hours before dawn on the 1st.

This dispatch, as will be remembered, told Alten that Soult had retired by the Puerto de Arraiz and Santesteban, and was obviously going home through the gorge of the Bidassoa, by Vera and Echalar. He was directed to 'head off' the enemy at Santesteban, if that were possible, if not at Sumbilla seven miles farther north—or at least to 'cut in upon their column of march' somewhere [2]. All this would have been quite possible, if Wellington had not on the 29th sent the Light Division on the unlucky southward march from Zubieta to Lecumberri. This misdirection was at the root of all subsequent misadventure. We may add that it would still have been possible, if the dispatch sent off in the early morning of the 31st to bid the division come back to Zubieta, had contained any indication that the enemy was retiring by Santesteban, or that haste was necessary. But it had only directed Alten to 'put his division in movement for Zubieta,' but to keep up his touch with Lecumberri, and told him that Dalhousie would be marching by the passes of Donna Maria [3]. The Almandoz note, which contained the really important general information and detailed

---

[1] See above, p. 700.　　　　　　[2] See above, p. 707.
[3] See above, p. 710. It was written at Ostiz on the night of the 30th, but only sent off by G. Murray from Lizasso on the morning of the 31st.

orders, wandered about for many hours in the sabretache of
an aide-de-camp who could not know where Alten was, and
found him after many hours of groping in the night at Leyza,
and not at Zubieta. From the latter place, only six miles from
Santesteban, the operation directed by Wellington would have
been possible to execute in good time—from Leyza (on the
other side of a difficult pass, and many miles farther away) it
was not. This simple fact settled the fate of the Light Division
on August 1.

Alten put his men under arms at dawn on that morning, and
marched, as ordered, for Santesteban via Zubieta ; having
passed the latter place and got to Elgorriaga, four miles farther
on, he received the news that the enemy had left Santesteban
early, and could not be headed off there. Wellington's alternative scheme dictated an attempt to break into Soult's line of
march at Sumbilla, so the Light Division was put in motion by
the very bad country road over the mountain of Santa Cruz
from Elgorriaga to Aranaz and Yanzi. The men had already
gone a full day's journey, and were much fatigued. They had
(it will be remembered) executed a night march from Lecumberri to Leyza only twelve hours back. The Santa Cruz path
was heart-breaking—officers had to dismount and walk up
to spare their horses : the men went bent double under their
knapsacks : the day was one of blazing August sunshine : the
track was over big stones embedded in deep shale—one sufferer
compared his progress to striding from one stepping-stone to
another [1].

On reaching the crest of the Santa Cruz mountain, opposite
Sumbilla, at four in the afternoon, the Light Division at last came
in sight of the enemy—a dense and disorderly column hurrying
along the road from Sumbilla northward, pressed by the 4th
Division, the bickering fire of whose skirmishers could be seen
round the tail of the rearguard. They were separated from the
observer's point of view by the cañon of the Bidassoa, here very
deep and precipitous—the Santa Cruz mountain is over
3,000 feet high. It would have taken much time to scramble
down the steep path to Sumbilla, and the enemy was already
past that village. Alten, therefore, resolved to push for the

[1] See Cooke, i. p. 315.

bridge of Yanzi, seven miles farther on, with the hope of cutting off at least the rearguard of the French.

But this seven miles was too much for men already in the last stages of fatigue from over-marching and want of food. ' When the cry was set up " the enemy," the worn soldiers raised their bent heads covered with dust and sweat : we had nearly reached the summit of the tremendous mountain, but nature was quite exhausted. Many men had lagged behind, having accomplished thirty miles over rocky roads interspersed with loose stones. Many fell heavily on the naked rock, frothing at the mouth, black in the face, and struggling in their last agonies. Others, unable to drag one leg after the other, leaned on the muzzles of their firelocks, muttering in disconsolate accents that " they had never fallen out before " [1].'

This was a heart-breaking sight for the divisional commander, who could see both the opportunity still offered him, and the impossibility of taking full advantage of it. After a short halt the troops, or such of them as could still keep up, were started off again to shuffle down the shaly track on the north side of the mountain. At the foot of it, by a brook near the village of Aranaz, the 2nd Brigade was told to halt and fall out—it was a trifle more exhausted than the 1st Brigade, because it had endured more of the dust, and more of the delay from casual stoppages and accidents, which always happens in the rear of a long column. Alten carried the survivors—the 1st and 3rd battalions Rifle Brigade, 1/43rd, and 1st Caçadores—as far as Yanzi, and then turned them down the road to the Bidassoa, which is screened by woods. The French were taken wholly by surprise : the Rifle battalions carried the knoll above the bridge, and the bridge itself, without much difficulty. The 43rd and Caçadores spread themselves out on the slope to their right and opened fire on the hurrying mass below them.

' At twilight,' wrote a captain of the 43rd whose narrative was quoted by Napier, but is well worth quoting again, ' we overlooked the enemy within a stone's throw, and from the summit of a precipice : the river separated us : but the French were wedged in a narrow road, with rocks enclosing them on one side and the river on the other. Such confusion took place

[1] Cooke, i. pp. 315–16.

among them as is impossible to describe. The wounded were
thrown down in the rush and trampled upon : the cavalry drew
their swords and endeavoured to charge up the pass to Echalar[1],
the only opening on their right flank. But the infantry beat
them back, and several of them, horse and man, were precipi-
tated into the river. Others fired up vertically at us, while
the wounded called out for quarter, and pointed to the
numerous soldiers borne on the shoulders of their comrades
on stretchers composed of the branches of trees, to which were
looped great-coats clotted with gore, or blood-stained sheets
taken from houses to carry their wounded—on whom we did
not fire [2].'

The officer commanding in the French rear finally got out a
battalion behind a stone wall, whose fire somewhat covered the
defiling mass. All the bolder spirits ran the gauntlet through
the zone of fire and escaped up the road to Echalar [3]. The
weak, the wounded, and the worn-out surrendered to the
leading troops of the 4th Division, who now closed in on them.
About 1,000 prisoners were made, largely soldiers of the train
and other non-combatants, but including stragglers from nearly
every division in Soult's army. There was no pursuit—the
Light Division troops could not have stirred a step : the
4th Division were almost as weary after a long day's hunt.
The casualties of both had been absurdly small—3 officers and
45 men in Cole's regiments, 1 officer and 15 men in Alten's. The
Spanish battalion engaged in the afternoon must, of course, have
lost on a very different scale during its highly creditable operations ; but its casualties have, unluckily, not been recorded.
The French may have had 500 killed and wounded, and 1,000
prisoners—but this was the least part of their loss—the really
important thing was that thousands of men were scattered in
the hills, and did not rally to their eagles for many days. That
night Soult's army was not only a demoralized, but a much
depleted force.

Wellington was, not unnaturally, dissatisfied with the day's
work. ' Many events,' he wrote to Graham, ' turned out for us

[1] Some, therefore, of P. Soult's chasseurs must have been with the
rearguard.
[2] Cooke, i. p. 317.   [3] Surtees, p. 226.

unfortunately on the 1st instant, each of which ought to have been in our favour : we should have done the enemy a great deal more mischief than we did during his passage down this valley [1].' For one of these things, Alten's late arrival, he was himself mainly responsible [2] : for the others—Longa's and Barcena's strange failure to detach more troops to help the regiment of Asturias at Yanzi [3], and Dalhousie's late arrival with the 7th Division—which never got into action or lost a man—he was not.

It must be confessed, however, that Wellington's intentions on August 1st are a little difficult to follow. One would have supposed that he would have devoted his main attention to a direct attempt to smash up Soult's main body—but he never allotted more than the 4th, 7th, and Light Divisions to that task—while he had obviously another idea in his head, dealing with a larger scheme for the destruction of the enemy. At 9.30, when he had occupied Santesteban, he sent orders to Byng, then at Elizondo, to bid him to march at once on the Pass of Maya, and to throw an advanced party into Urdax, on the French side of the defile. At the same time Hill, at Irurita, is desired to follow Byng, occupy Elizondo, and—if his troops can bear the strain—advance even to the Pass of Maya. Should this prove possible, Byng, when relieved by Hill, should descend into France as far as Ainhoue on the Nivelle. The 2nd Division, and the Portuguese division attached to it, would follow him next morning. Hopes are expressed in the dispatch that Pakenham and the 6th Division—last heard of at Eugui on the 31st—would be in a position to combine their operations with those of Hill [4].

This descent into the valley of the Nivelle from the Maya pass must surely have been imagined with the idea of encircling the

[1] *Dispatches*, x. p. 591.

[2] Probably also we must add the responsibility for Hill and the 2nd Division being at Elizondo this day, owing to the false march which they had made—on Wellington's orders—from the Puerto de Arraiz to the Velate road.

[3] Wellington in *Dispatches*, xi. p. 7, blames Barcena for this—one would have supposed that Graham and Giron were still more responsible, as they were in higher command.

[4] Orders for Q.M.G. from Santesteban, 9.30 a.m. *Supplementary Dispatches*, viii. p. 164.

whole French army at Echalar, for Ainhoue was well in Soult's rear, and troops placed there could cut him off from the direct road to Bayonne. On the same evening Wellington was dictating a dispatch to Graham telling him that he hoped to be at Maya next morning, and beyond the frontier : Graham was therefore to prepare to cross the Bidassoa and attack Villatte with his and Giron's full force, including cavalry and guns, leaving St. Sebastian blockaded by the necessary minimum detachment [1]. Meanwhile Alten, Dalhousie, and Cole were to mass in front of the enemy's position at Echalar. The only possible meaning that can be drawn from these orders, when read together, is that Wellington had now developed the complete encircling scheme for Soult's destruction, which he had *not* thought out on July 31.

But the scheme was never put into execution. On August 2 Byng was halted at Maya, Graham received no order to pass the Bidassoa, and all that was done was to execute an attack on Echalar—attended with complete success, it is true, but only resulting in pushing Soult back towards the Nivelle, where there was no intercepting force waiting to waylay him. Somewhere between 8 p.m. on the 1st and dawn on the 2nd Wellington, for reasons which he did not avow to his staff or his most trusted lieutenants, gave up the greater game, which had in it immense possibilities : for Soult had no longer an army that could fight—as events at Echalar were to prove a few hours later. Minor causes for this great piece of self-restraint can be cited. One was that Hill and Pakenham turned out not to be within easy supporting distance of Byng, so that the dash into Soult's rear could not be executed with a sufficient force. If this operation were not carried out, Graham's became useless. Certainly a reflection on the extremely depleted condition of the 2nd Division, which had suffered such heavy losses at Maya, Beunza, and the Venta de Urroz, helped to deter Wellington from using this exhausted force for his main stroke. Writing to Graham two days later, he mentioned its condition as a cause of delay, along with a general dearth of musket ammunition and shoes. But the main reason, as we shall see

[1] Wellington to Graham, 8 p.m., from Santesteban. *Dispatches*, x. p. 574.

later, lay rather in the higher spheres of European politics, and the explanation was reserved for the Minister of War in London alone. Next morning no general attack was delivered : Wellington did not go to Maya, but merely joined the 4th and Light Divisions on the Bidassoa. The great scheme was stillborn, and never took shape.

Soult had gathered the wrecks of his army on the range of mountains behind Echalar, where the Spanish-French boundary line runs. The cavalry had been at once packed off to the rear. The infantry took up a position. Clausel's three divisions were in the centre—Vandermaesen holding the village with a company, and with his main body—certainly not 2,000 men that day—across the road on the slope above. Conroux's division was on Vandermaesen's right : Taupin's, in reserve to both the others, on the crest where the frontier runs. Reille's corps—still more depleted than Clausel's, continued the line westward—Lamartinière's division next to Conroux's, as far as the Peak of Ivantelly : Maucune's—the most dilapidated unit in a dilapidated army—holding the ground beyond the Ivantelly, with a flank-guard out on its right watching the road from Vera to Sarre. D'Erlon's divisions—still by far the most intact units of the whole command, were on Clausel's left, prolonging the line eastward and holding a commanding position on the mountain side as far as the Peaks of Salaberry and Atchuria. It is doubtful whether the Marshal had 25,000 men in line that day in his eight divisions—not because the remainder were all casualties or prisoners, but because the long retreat, with its incessant scrambling over mountain sides, had led to the defection of many voluntary and still more involuntary stragglers. The former were scattered over the country for miles on every side, seeking for food and for ' a day off '—the latter had dropped behind from sheer exhaustion : there had been no regular distribution of rations since July 29th, and the first convoy of relief had been captured by Byng at Elizondo on the 31st.

Wellington had only 12,000 men available in front of a very formidable position—hills 1,500 or 1,800 feet high, with the peaks which formed the flank protection rising to 2,100 or 2,300. Under ordinary circumstances an attack would have been insane. Moreover, his troops were almost as wayworn as those of Soult : the Light and 4th Divisions had received no rations since the 30th, and the latter had lost a good third of its strength in the very heavy fighting in which it had taken the chief part between the 25th and the 30th. But their spirits were high, they had the strongest confidence in their power to win, and they were convinced that the enemy was ' on the run ' —in which idea they were perfectly right.

The plan of attack was that the 4th and 7th Divisions should assail the enemy's centre, on each side of the village of Echalar, while the Light Division turned his western flank. This involved long preliminary marching for Alten's men, despite of their awful fatigues of the preceding day. They had to trudge from the bridge of Yanzi and Aranaz to Vera, where they turned uphill on to the heights of Santa Barbara, a series of successive slopes by which they ascended towards the Peak of Ivantelly and Reille's flank. Just as they began to deploy they got the first regular meal that they had seen for two days : ' The soldiers were so weak that they could hardly stand ; however, our excellent commissary had managed to overtake us, and hastily served out half a pound of biscuit to each individual, which the men devoured in the act of priming and loading just as they moved off to the attack [1].' The morning was dull and misty—a great contrast to the blazing sunshine of the preceding day, and it was hard to get any complete view of the position— clouds were drifting along the hills and obscuring parts of the landscape for many minutes at a time. This chance put Wellington himself in serious danger for a moment—pushing forward farther than he knew, with a half-company of the 43rd to cover him, he got among the French outposts, and was only saved by the vigilance of his escort from being cut off— he galloped back under a shower of balls—any one of which might have caused a serious complication in the British com- mand—it is impossible to guess what Beresford would have made of the end of the campaign of 1813.

While the Light Division was developing the flank attack, the front attack was already being delivered—somewhat sooner than Wellington expected or intended. The plan had been for

[1] Cooke, i. 819.

the 4th Division to operate against the French right—the 7th against their centre and left centre. Cole, however, was delayed in getting forward by the immense block of French débris along the narrow defile from Sumbilla to the bridge of Yanzi. ' For two miles there were scattered along the road papers, old rugs, blankets, pack-saddles, old bridles and girths, private letters, hundreds of empty and broken boxes, quantities of entrenching tools, French clothes, dead mules, dead soldiers, dead peasants, farriers' tools, boots and linen, the boxes of M. le Général Baron de St. Pol [1] and other officers, the field hospital of the 2nd Division (Darmagnac's), and all sorts of things worth picking up—which caused stoppage and confusion [2].'

Now the 7th Division did not follow the spoil-strewn river road, but cut across from Sumbilla towards Echalar, over the same hill-tracks which Clausel's divisions had taken on the preceding afternoon, when they escaped from the pursuit of Cole's skirmishers. Hence it chanced that they arrived in front of Echalar on a route where the enemy was keeping no good watch, long before the 4th Division came up from the bridge of Yanzi and the Vera cross-roads. The mists on the hills had kept them screened—as Clausel complains in his report. Lord Dalhousie now carried out a most dangerous manœuvre—a frontal attack on an enemy in position by a series of brigades arriving at long intervals—without any co-operation having been sought or obtained from the troops known to be on his left. ' Bravery and success,' as a Light-Division neighbour observed, ' certainly far exceeded judgement or utility [3].' What led the commander of the 7th Division to this astounding escapade was the obvious unpreparedness of the enemy. ' We caught them,' he wrote, ' cooking above, and plundering below in the village. I thought it best to be at them instantly, and I really believe Barnes's brigade was among them before their packs were well on [4].'

The leading troops, and the only ones which really got into action, were the three battalions (1/6th, 3rd Provisional [5], and

---

[1] A brigadier in Maransin's division.
[2] Larpent's diary, p. 214.   [3] Harry Smith, i. p. 115.
[4] Dalhousie to Cairnes in *Dickson Papers*, ed. Leslie, p. 1020.
[5] 2/24th and 2/58th.

Brunswick-Oels) of Barnes's brigade—led by that same fighting general who had stopped the rout at Maya with two of these same battalions. Barnes got his line formed, and attacked uphill against the front of Conroux's division, long before Inglis's brigade was ready to follow, or Lecor's Portuguese had even got down from the hill path into the narrow valley of the Sari stream. With such speed and vigour was the assault delivered, under a frontal fire from Conroux's men, and a flank fire from Vandermaesen's on the right, that Inglis's brigade, which was aiming at the village of Echalar, never had the chance of getting near its enemy. The advancing line suffered severely as it climbed—nearly 300 casualties—but when it came against the front of Conroux, and delivered its first volley, the enemy simply melted away [1]. As Clausel writes in apology, ' the resistance ought to have been greater, and in the ordinary state of the army, that is to say when a better spirit prevailed, it would never have been possible for the enemy to establish himself in this fashion on a section of the main chain of the Pyrenees. This day the morale of the troops was bad [2].' It must be remembered that Conroux's was the division which had suffered so heavily in the village of Sorauren both on the 28th and the 30th of July. Several of its battalions were skeletons—all much thinned. Still there must have been 3,000 men yet present out of the original 7,000—and they turned and fled before the uphill attack of 1,800 or less. Nor was this the end of the disaster. Clausel tried to hurry Vandermaesen's division to the succour of Conroux's. But the manœuvre failed : the French General says that Conroux's flying troops ran in upon Vandermaesen's, that confusion followed, and that he was obliged to let the whole mass roll back to seek shelter with Taupin's division in the reserve line [2].

At this moment the leading brigade of the 4th Division, that of Ross, at last appeared on Dalhousie's left, and began to

---

[1] Wellington thought this the most desperate and gallant charge he had ever seen. *Dispatches*, x. p. 591.

[2] Report of Clausel, August 2. ' Les troupes relevées n'ayant pu, malgré les efforts des généraux Conroux et Rey, s'arrêter sur la position indiquée, et s'étant jetées sur celles qui repoussaient l'attaque de la direction d'Échalar, il s'ensuivit un peu de confusion, et on fut obligé de les laisser aller jusqu'à l'hauteur de la division Taupin.'

skirmish with Lamartinière's line [1] : demonstrations began—
probably by Lecor's Portuguese—against the front of Maransin[2],
D'Erlon's right-hand division.   But these were of no importance
in comparison with the effect of the turning of Reille's end of
the line by the Light Division.   This was almost as startling in
effect as Barnes's dealings. with the French centre.   Having
reached the front on the heights of Santa Barbara, below the
Peak of Ivantelly, Alten brushed aside Maucune's feeble
skirmishing line, and let loose five companies of the Rifle Brigade
supported by four of the 43rd against the dominating peak of
the Ivantelly, the most prominent feature of the French position.
Clouds swept down along the hills at this moment, and the
supporting companies lost sight of the front line. ' An invisible
firing commenced, and it was impossible to ascertain which
party was getting the better of the fight : the combatants were
literally contending in the clouds [3].'   But when the 43rd came
up, they found that the rifle companies had dislodged the
2nd Léger, Lamartinière's flank regiment, from the precipitous
crest, and were in full possession of it. As they lost only 1 officer
and 26 men in taking a most formidable peak, it is clear that
the enemy's resistance must have been very ineffective [4].

All was now confusion on the French right wing—Reille
speaks of himself as wandering about in a fog with three
battalions of Lamartinière's, and meeting no one save the
brigadier Montfort, who was bringing up a mere 200 men to try to
reinforce the troops on the Ivantelly.   The soldiers were profiting
by the mist to go off to the rear, and could not be kept together.
' On se tirailla faiblement, et nos troupes se retirèrent sur la

[1] Ross's brigade had a few casualties in each battalion—37 in all.

[2] ' Devant la division Maransin je n'ai vu que des tirailleurs,' says Clausel.
From the sequence of brigades in the 7th Division, I think these must
have been Lecor's people.

[3] Cooke, i. p. 320. Both he and Surtees mention that the evicted French
battalion was the 2nd Léger—a fact not to be found in the reports of
Lamartinière or of Reille.

[4] The total French loss was probably not very great—as happens when
troops give at once, and are not pursued.   Conroux's division only records
5 officer-casualties, Vandermaesen's 8—which should mean a total
casualty list of 300 or so.   But it is astonishing to find Reille reporting
that Maucune lost only about 20 men ; if so, the flank-guard cannot have
stood at all.

route de Sarre.' With his centre smashed in, and his right dispersed, Soult could do nothing but retire. The remains of Clausel's and Reille's divisions fell back on the road to Sarre. D'Erlon, who had never been attacked, could not use this route, but made his way along the crest of the mountains to Zagaramurdi, Urdax, and Ainhoue. What would have been his fate if he had found there not the picquet which (by Wellington's order) Byng had thrown forward to Urdax, but the whole of Byng's and Hill's troops blocking his retreat—as would have been the case if the great scheme drawn up on the night of August 1 had been carried out ? But the Pass of Maya had not been utilized that day, and D'Erlon had only to drive away 50 men.

There was no pursuit : if there had been it would seem that the whole French army would have broken up, for it had shown itself this day no longer able to fight. ' The spirit not only of the men but of the officers,' wrote Reille next morning, ' has been very bad during these last days. The absolute want of food must be the excuse for this state of things.' The condition of the army was deplorable—Maucune's division showed less than 1,000 men holding together. The 1st Line of Vander-maesen's had precisely 27 men with the eagle—yet had lost only 4 officers and 193 men in action—where were the remaining 400 ? Other units could show a few hundred men but absolutely or practically no officers—the 55th Line of Conroux had lost every one of 13 officers, the 51st Line of Darmagnac 12 out of 17, the 34th Léger of Maucune 30 out of 35; these were exceptionally hard cases, but in all the divisions save those of Foy and Abbé (the least engaged during the short campaign), the proportion was appalling. For the infantry of the whole army it was 420 casualties among 1,318 officers present. Soult wrote to Clarke on the last day of the campaign : ' I deceived myself in the strangest way when I told your Excellency that the troops had their morale intact, and would do their duty. I mistook the sentiment of shame for their recent disaster (Vittoria) for that of steadfastness. When tested, they started with one furious rush, but showed no power of resistance. . . . Since I first entered the service I have seen nothing like this. It reminded me of the behaviour of the levy *en masse* of 1792. The spirit of

these troops must be terribly broken to have permitted them
to behave in this fashion.   One general told me that he had
overheard men remarking, when we were near Pampeluna, that
they had better not fight too hard, because it would be preferable to get back to the frontier rather than to be led off into
the middle of Spain [1].'   These were cruel and spiteful words—
the army had fought with excellent courage, till after July 30th
it had convinced itself that the Marshal had got wrong with all
his calculations, that the game was up—that they were being
taken on a wild goose chase without rations in the most desolate
and rocky region of Europe.   But by August 2 Soult was not
far out in his statement—on that day the greater part of his
army was a spent force.   If Wellington had resolved to pursue
with vigour, he could have pushed it as far as he pleased.
Perhaps the great encircling scheme with which his mind dallied
for a few hours on the night of August 1 might have resulted in
its surrender or complete dispersion.

This was not to be.   On August 3 Wellington halted, and
commenced to rearrange his troops on much the same principles,
and in much the same positions, that he had selected before.   He
wrote to Graham next day that he was perfectly well aware of
the objection to taking up a defensive position in the Pyrenees,
but that an advance was too risky [2].   It was not so much the
prospect of the wastage of his troops, even in successful operation, that deterred him, though this was the point on which he
insisted in his letter to Graham, but the general political situation of Europe.   The eternal Armistice of Plässwitz was still
holding up operations in Germany : it was still possible that
the Allied Sovereigns might make a selfish peace with Napoleon,
and permit the Emperor to expand Soult's army *ad infinitum*
with sudden reinforcements.   What would then become of the
Anglo-Portuguese host, even if it had won its way not only to
Bayonne but to Bordeaux ?   All this he had considered, and
wrote to the Secretary for War in Whitehall that ' as for the
immediate invasion of France, from what I have seen of the
state of negotiations in the North of Europe, I have determined
to consider it only in reference to the convenience of my own

[1] Soult to Clarke, August 2, and August 6.
[2] *Dispatches*, x. p. 591.

operations. . . . If peace should be made by the Powers of the
North, I must necessarily withdraw into Spain.' No advance,
however tempting the opportunity, should be made until he was
certain that war had recommenced in Saxony [1]. Meanwhile,
' Soult will not feel any inclination to renew his expeditions—
on this side at least.'

So the army settled down to hold once more the line of the
Pyrenees, and to resume the siege of St. Sebastian. On
August 3 the Head-quarters were once more at Lesaca, as they
had been on July 25—how many things had happened in the
interval ! Hill and the 2nd Division, now rejoined by the long-
missing brigade of Byng, as also Silveira's Portuguese, were in
the Maya passes once more. The 3rd Division was holding the
Roncesvalles defiles, the 4th and 7th were at Echalar, the 6th
in the Alduides (replacing Campbell's Portuguese in that remote
valley); the Light Division lay on the heights opposite Vera.
Morillo's Division was in the Bastan behind Hill, the part of
the Army of Reserve of Andalusia which O'Donnell had carried
to the front, when he left the rest before Pampeluna, was at the
moment near the bridge of Yanzi. The remainder of that army
and Carlos de España were continuing the blockade of Pampeluna.

The total losses of the Allies during the nine days' ' Campaign
of the Pyrenees ' had amounted to slightly over 6,400 officers
and men for the English and Portuguese [2]. The Spanish loss
could not add over 600 more—at Sorauren it was 192 ; Morillo's
casualties at Altobiscar, and those of the regiment of Asturias
at Yanzi bridge are the only unknown quantities, and can
hardly have reached 400. The distribution among divisions and
corps was odd—the 3rd and Light Division had practically
negligible casualties : the former under 120, the latter under 50.
The main stress fell on the 2nd and 4th Divisions, the former
with 2,000 British and 350 Portuguese casualties, the latter
with 1,400 and 300 respectively. But it must be remembered

---

[1] Ibid., x. p. 611. August 7.

[2] 6,440 to be exact. Of which 4,708 were British and 1,732 Portuguese.
The latter figure is worked out from the detailed Portuguese returns in
Appendix No. XXI, and is perceptibly lower than Wellington's original
estimate of 2,300 : stragglers no doubt had been rejoining.

that the 2nd Division had (including Byng) four brigades, the 4th Division only three. Every unit in both was severely tried ; the most terrible return was that of the 1/92nd with its 26 officers and 445 men killed, wounded, and missing. But this was a strong battalion of 750 bayonets, and I am not sure that the 284 casualties of the 20th and the 296 casualties of the 3/27th, both in the 4th Division, do not represent almost as great a proportional loss, as these were both much smaller corps.

The 6th Division was engaged on two days only, at the two battles of Sorauren, and had the appreciable number of 450 British and 370 Portuguese casualties. The 7th Division fought on three days—at second Sorauren, at the Combat of the Venta de Urroz, and at Echalar, and three of its battalions also saved the day at Maya—with a loss in all of 750 British but only 60 Portuguese. Lastly, we must name the two Portuguese brigades of Silveira's division, of which Campbell's fought at Sorauren, Da Costa's at Beunza, with a loss to the former of 350 and to the latter of 280 men. The general fact emerges that the 2nd and 4th Divisions lost between them 4,350 men out of the total 7,000—no other division had so many as 1,000 casualties.

The official list of French losses is not quite complete, as it includes only the infantry and cavalry units—but such casualties as may have been suffered by the general staff, the artillery (very little engaged) sappers, and train can have added comparatively little to the total, though a good many men of the train were taken at Yanzi on August 1. The figures given work out to 12,563—1,308 killed, 8,545 wounded, and 2,710 prisoners. The last-named total should probably be brought up to 3,000 in order to include individuals of the non-combatant corps captured in the retreat. The divisions suffered in very unequal measure : Foy and Abbé got off very lightly, because the one was practically not engaged at first Sorauren, nor the latter at Maya—they lost respectively only 550 and 750 men. Vandermaesen's and Maucune's Divisions—each a small unit of only 4,000 men, had the crushing losses of 1,480 and 1,850 respectively, and were dissolved when the campaign was over, and re-formed to a large extent with battalions drawn from the

Bayonne reserve. Darmagnac and Conroux each lost well over 2,000 men out of 7,000—their divisions having been terribly cut up, the one at Maya the other at Sorauren. Maransin and Taupin each return over 1,000 men lost out of 6,000 ; Lamartinière just under 1,000 out of 7,000. The cavalry, barely engaged and quite useless, had only 67 casualties to report.

But to get at Soult's fighting strength on the last day of the retreat, it is not sufficient merely to deduct the 12,563 casualties from the 59,000 which took the field in Navarre. The eight divisions collected on the 2nd August were short not only of their own casualties, but of Foy's division, which had gone off on an eccentric line of retreat, as had several smaller detachments [1]. But the great deficit was that of at least 8,000 or 10,000 stragglers, who rejoined at their leisure during the next ten days. The cavalry and artillery had all gone to the rear, and it is doubtful if the last stand at Echalar was made with so many as 25,000 weary infantry. If the Marshal had been faced with an opponent who had no political *arrière pensée* to hold him back, he would have been doomed to absolute destruction. Only a wreck of his army would have escaped, and Wellington might have driven the remnants as far as he pleased —even to the gates of Bordeaux.

But the British General had made his ' great refusal ' on the night of August 1st–2nd, and had resolved that the tempting scheme for invading France, which had flitted before his eyes for a few evening hours, must be postponed. He would risk nothing till he should get certain information that the war had begun again in Germany. And as the news of the rupture of the Armistice did not reach him till September 3rd, he was condemned to another month of waiting. He turned back to his old policy of June—St. Sebastian and Pampeluna must be reduced. When they should have fallen, it would be time enough to see whether the general European situation had made the invasion of France a feasible enterprise.

---

[1] e. g. the troops on the Roncesvalles road, the two battalions of Lamartinière which followed Foy, and Maransin's 28th Léger from Elizondo—at least 2,500 in all.

APPENDICES

I

BRITISH LOSSES AT THE SIEGE OF BURGOS
SEPTEMBER 20—OCTOBER 21, 1812

Sept. 20th, storm of the Hornwork of St. Michael. Total casualties 421 (of whom the 42nd lost 2 officers and 33 men killed, 5 officers and 164 men wounded = 204 ; the 79th lost 5 men killed, 2 officers and 32 men wounded = 39 ; the Portuguese lost 3 officers and 17 men killed, 5 officers and 88 men wounded = 113 ; the other 67 casualties were divided among the remaining battalions of the 1st Division).

Sept. 21st, casualties 42 ; Sept. 22nd, 39 ; Sept. 23, 158 (of which 76 in the Guards Brigade and 44 in the K.G.L. brigade of the 1st Division, and 29 among the Portuguese).

Sept. 24th, casualties 39 ; Sept. 25th, 38 ; Sept. 26th, 32 ; Sept. 27th, 53 ; Sept. 28th, 26 ; Sept. 29th, 9 ; Sept. 30th, 29 ; Oct. 1st, 11 ; Oct. 2nd, 20 ; Oct. 3rd, 9 ; Oct. 4th, 16 ; Oct. 5th, 224 (of these 224, which really belong to the storm of the outer enceinte on the evening of Oct. 4th, the 2/24th had 68 casualties, no other battalion more than 15).

Oct. 6th, casualties (French sortie of night of 5th) 142 ; Oct. 7th, 33 ; Oct. 8th (2nd French sortie in which 133 in the K.G.L. Brigade were killed or wounded), 184 ; Oct. 9th, 18 ; Oct. 10th, 61 ; Oct. 11th, 24 ; Oct. 12th, 17 ; Oct. 13th, 9 ; Oct. 14th, 3 ; Oct. 15th, 18 ; Oct. 16th, 12 ; Oct. 17th, 18 ; Oct. 18th, 48 ; Oct. 19th (the last assault), 170 (of whom 85 in the Guards Brigade and 84 in the K.G.L. Brigade of the 1st Division).

Oct. 20th, 47 ; Oct. 21st, 9.

General Total : 24 officers and 485 men killed
68 ,, ,, 1,445 ,, wounded
42 ,, missing = 2,064

II

THE FRENCH ARMIES IN SPAIN : OCTOBER 15, 1812
[From the return in the *Archives Nationales*, Paris.]

I. ARMY OF THE SOUTH. MARSHAL SOULT

	Officers.	Men.
1st Division, Conroux : 9th Léger, 24th, 96th Line (each 3 batts.) : 3 battalions Marine Troops . . .	203	5,615
2nd Division, Barrois [1] : 8th Line, 16th Léger, 51st, 54th Line (each 3 batts.)	201	4,801

[1] Cassagne succeeded Barrois shortly after.

	Officers.	Men.
3rd Division, Villatte : 27th Léger, 63rd, 94th, 95th Line (each 3 batts.)	209	5,888
4th Division, Leval : 32nd, 43rd Line (4 batts. each), 55th, 58th Line (3 batts. each)	259	7,794
5th Division, D'Erlon [1] : 12th Léger (4 batts.), 45th Line (3 batts.), 28th Léger, 88th Line (2 batts. each)	202	5,016
6th Division, Daricau : 21st Léger, 100th Line (3 batts. each), 64th, 103rd Line (2 batts. each)	187	4,308
Cavalry Division, Perreymond : 2nd Hussars, 5th, 10th, 21st, 27th Chasseurs, 7th Lancers (in all, 20 squad.)	144	2,349
Cavalry Division, Digeon : 2nd, 4th, 14th, 17th, 26th, 27th Dragoons (in all, 20 squadrons)	148	2,956
Cavalry Division, Pierre Soult : 5th, 12th, 16th, 21st Dragoons (14 squadrons)	121	1,712
Artillery, and Artillery Train and Park	122	3,511
Engineers and Sappers	17	851
Gendarmerie and Équipages Militaires	9	592
État-Major	313	—
Total present	1,816	45,393
Gross total of Army including 64 officers and 1,904 men detached, and 60 officers and 6,293 men in hospital :	1,940	53,590

II. ARMY OF THE CENTRE

	Officers.	Men.
The King's French Guards : no figures given, but about		2,500
Darmagnac's Division : 28th and 75th Line (3 batts. each), 2nd Nassau and Baden (2 batts. each), Frankfort (1 batt.)	199	5,039
Palombini's Division : 4th and 6th Italian Line (2 batts. each), 2nd Italian Léger (3 batts.), Dragoons of Napoleon and two batteries	142	3,050
Casapalacios' Spanish Division (3 batts., 3 squadrons)	167	1,263
Treillard's Cavalry Division : 13th, 18th, 19th, 22nd Dragoons, Westphalian *chevaux légers*, Nassau *chasseurs*	114	1,679
Artillery, Engineers, and Train	12	596
Various detachments	12	403
Total present	646	14,530
Gross total of Army, including État-Major 55 officers, 32 officers and 655 men detached, and 14 officers and 1,900 men sick, is	747	17,075

[1] After D'Erlon was removed to command the Army of the Centre, this division was at different times under Remond and Semélé.

III. ARMY OF PORTUGAL. GENERAL SOUHAM

	Officers.	Men.
1st Division, Foy : 6th Léger (1 batt.), 39th, 69th, 76th Line (2 batts. each)	151	3,492
2nd Division, Clausel : 25th Léger, 27th, 50th, 59th Line (2 batts. each)	130	4,506
3rd Division, Taupin [late Ferey], 31st Léger, 26th, 70th Line (2 batts. each), 47th Line (3 batts.) . .	184	6,064
4th Division, Sarrut : 2nd and 4th Léger, 36th Line (2 batts. each)	130	4,000
5th Division, Maucune : 15th, 66th, 82nd, 86th Line (2 batts. each)	165	5,097
6th Division, Pinoteau [late Brenier] : 17th Léger, 65th Line (2 batts. each), 22nd Line (1 batt.) . .	87	2,730
7th Division, Bonté [late Thomières] : 1st and 62nd Line (2 batts. each), 101st Line (1 batt.) . . .	109	2,425
8th Division, Chauvel [late Bonnet] : 118th, 119th, 120th Line (2 batts. each), 122nd Line (3 batts.) .	180	4,437
(Each infantry division includes its artillery and train.)		
Cavalry Division, Curto : 3rd Hussars, 13th, 14th, 22nd, 26th, 28th Chasseurs	115	2,048
Cavalry Division, Boyer : 6th, 11th, 15th, 25th Dragoons	70	1,303
Horse Artillery and train attached to cavalry . .	5	292
Artillery Reserve and Park	37	1,822
Engineers	7	274
Gendarmerie and Équipages Militaires . . .	33	1,102
Attached to the Army of Portugal—		
Cavalry Brigade, Merlin, of the Army of the North, 1st Hussars, 31st Chasseurs	53	693
Infantry Brigade, Aussenac, detached from the Bayonne Reserve : 3rd and 105th Line (2 batts. each), 64th, 100th, 103rd (1 batt. each) . .	110	3,308
Total present	1,566	43,860
Gross total of Army with 150 officers and 4,574 men detached, and 53 officers and 11,113 men in hospital :	1,769	59,547
		61,316

IV. ARMY OF ARAGON AND VALENCIA. MARSHAL SUCHET

1st Division, Musnier : 1st Léger (3 batts.), 114th Line (2 batts.), 121st Line (3 batts.), Neapolitans (2 batts.)	180	5,403
2nd Division, Harispe : 7th, 44th, 116th Line (2 batts. each)	104	4,011
3rd Division, Habert : 14th, 16th Line (2 batts. each), 117th Line (3 batts.)	158	4,817

	Officers.	Men.
Cavalry Division, Boussard : 14th Cuirassiers, 24th Dragoons, 4th Hussars, 1st Neapolitan Chasseurs .	01	1,831
Artillery and train	21	858
Engineers	11	411
Gendarmerie and Équipages Militaires . . .	6	529

Troops attached to the Army of Aragon

	Officers.	Men.
Reille's Division : 10th Line (4 batts.), 81st (3 batts.), 9th *bis* of Hussars, artillery	147	4,393
Severoli's Division : 1st Italian Line and 1st Italian Léger (2 batts. each), 5th Léger (French) (1 batt.), and Italian artillery	151	3,758
Brigade from Catalonia : 3rd Léger, 11th, 20th Line (2 batts. each), 1st Italian Chasseurs . . .	130	3,719
Total present	1,038	30,980
Gross total of Army, including 131 officers and 3,884 men detached, and 24 officers and 4,287 men in hospital :	1,193	39,151

V. ARMY OF THE NORTH. GENERAL CAFFARELLI

	Officers.	Men.
Division Abbé : 5th Léger (3 batts.), 10th Léger, 3rd, 52nd, 105th Line (2 batts. each), 20th Dragoons, and artillery	219	6,878
Division Vandermaesen : 34th Léger (1 batt.), 34th, 40th Line (3 batts. each), 113th, 130th Line (2 batts. each), 4th Suisse (1 batt.), 6 *bataillons de marche* = 18 battalions in all	388	12,197
Brigade Dumoustier : 4 batts. Young Guard, and 2 of National Guards	100	3,976
Cavalry Brigade Laferrière : Lancers of Berg (2 squadrons), 15th Chasseurs (3 squadrons), Gendarmerie (6 squadrons)	37	1,625
Government of Navarre (garrison of Pampeluna) detachments	45	1,644
Government of Biscay, all *régiments de marche* and detachments	264	9,431
Government of Castile (garrison of Santoña) detachments	43	1,342
Total present	1,151	36,465
Gross total of Army, including 41 officers and 5,176 men in hospital, is	1,192	41,641

VI. ARMY OF CATALONIA. GENERAL DECAEN

	Officers.	Men.
Division Quesnel (at Puyerda), 102nd Line (2 batts.), 116th Line (1 batt.), and detachments . . .	123	3,502
Division Lamarque : 60th and 79th Line (3 batts. each), Regiment of Wurzburg, and detachments . .	137	3,491
Brigade Petit : 67th Line (3 batts.), 32nd Léger (1 batt.)	66	1,553
Division Maurice Mathieu (Barcelona) : 115th Line (4 batts.), 18th Léger (2 batts.), 1st of Nassau (2 batts.), and detachments	185	6,180
Garrisons of Figueras, &c. : 60th, 86th Line, and 32nd Léger (1 batt. each), and detachments . . .	160	3,646
Garrison of Tarragona (Bertoletti) : 20th Line (1 batt.), 7th Italian Line (1 batt.)	63	1,451
Garrison of Lerida (Henriod) : 42nd Line (3 batts.), and detachments	70	1,639
Brigade Espert (flying column) : 5th Line (3 batts.), 23rd Léger (2 batts.)	89	2,988
Artillery, Sappers, Gendarmes, Équipages Militaires, &c.	55	4,194
Total present, under arms	948	28,514
Gross total of Army, including 107 État-Major, 26 officers and 369 men detached, and 44 officers and 6,045 men in hospital, is	1,125	34,928

VII. BAYONNE RESERVE

All consisting of detachments or régiments de marche .	172	7,072
Adding 134 detached and 600 in hospital, gross total is :		7,978

Total Army of Spain, therefore, on October 15 amounts to :

    7,516 officers, 206,814 men present with the colours
        326   ,,   11,520 ,,   detached
        236   ,,   35,414 ,,   in hospital.
GENERAL GROSS TOTAL = 8,185 officers and 253,748 men.

III

STRENGTH OF WELLINGTON'S ARMY DURING AND AFTER THE BURGOS RETREAT

The subjoined statistics show the marching strength of the Anglo-Portuguese divisions of Wellington's army at the commencement of the Burgos Retreat (Oct. 23) and some days after its termination (Nov. 29). There had been, immediately after the army reached Ciudad Rodrigo, certain transferences of units from one division to another, which are duly noted. The figures give only rank and file ; to get the fighting strength one-eighth should be added to cover officers, sergeants, and drummers.

	Present under arms. Oct. 23.	*Present under arms.* Nov. 29.
1st Cavalry Division .	2,827	2,909 (2nd Hussars K.G.L. has joined.)
2nd Cavalry Division	1,947	1,625 (2nd Hussars K.G.L. has left.)
1st Division	3,970	4,002 (1st & 3rd battalions First Guards have joined, but Stirling's brigade has been transferred to the 6th Division.)
2nd Division .	7,915	6,591
3rd Division .	4,229	3,860 (2/87th from Cadiz has joined.)
4th Division .	4,487	3,861 (1/82nd has joined.)
5th Division .	3,638	3,732 (2/47th from Cadiz has joined.)
6th Division .	3,380	5,228 (The division has been joined by Stirling's brigade and also by the 1/91st.)
7th Division .	4,298	3,358
Light Division	3,428	3,775 (2 companies 3/95th and the 20th Portuguese have joined.)
Hamilton's Portuguese Division	4,719	4,076
Pack's Portuguese Brigade .	1,681	1,105
Bradford's Portuguese Brigade .	1,645	881
	48,124	45,003
Artillery, Train, Staff Corps, &c.	2,500	2,300

The fall in numbers would have been much greater but for the joining of Skerret's force from Cadiz (3/1st Guards, 2/47th, 2/87th, 20th Portuguese, and two companies 3/95th) and of the 1/1st Guards and 1/91st from England, and the 1/82nd from Gibraltar—in all, nearly 6,000 men.

It may be worth while to give here the statistics of the Spanish troops which were acting with Wellington's and Hill's armies during this period. They were by their October morning states:

' 6th Army ' or Galicians (Santocildes):

1st Division (Barcena) .	6,810 (5 of the 15 battalions of this division were not at the front.)
2nd Division (Cabrera) . .	4,749
3rd Division (Losada) . .	4,213
Cavalry Brigade (Figuelmonde)	1,356 (5 of the 9 squadrons of this brigade were not at the front.)

5th Army (Estremadurans and Castilian) :

Morillo's Division . . .	2,371	(Acting with Hill's Corps.)
Carlos de España's Division .	3,809	(ditto.)
Penne Villemur's cavalry .	992	(ditto.)
Julian Sanchez's cavalry .	1,159	(Acting with Main Army.
Total Spanish troops .	25,459	

IV

LOSSES IN THE BURGOS RETREAT

The casualties in action between October 23rd and November 19th are easily ascertainable, and quite moderate. But the loss in 'missing', by the capture of stragglers, marauders, and footsore men, was much higher than is generally known. I believe that the annexed table, from the morning state of November 29th, is now published for the first time. It gives only the *rank and file* missing, but these are almost the whole list: officers and sergeants did not straggle or drop behind like the privates. I believe that the total of officers missing was 25, of sergeants 56 British and 29 Portuguese : we have also to add 43 British and 32 Portuguese drummers, &c., to the general list, which runs as follows :

	British.	Portuguese.	Total.
1st Cavalry Division .	192	—	192
2nd „ „ .	101	8	109
1st Division Infantry . .	283	—	283
2nd „ „ . .	302	260	562
3rd „ „ . .	184	230	414
4th „ „ . .	308	19	327
5th „ „ . .	453	359	812
6th „ „ . .	96	74	170
7th „ „ . .	357	243	600
Light „ „ . .	92	163	253
Portuguese. Hamilton's Division	—	221	221
„ Pack's Brigade .	—	293	293
„ Bradford's Brigade	—	514	514
Total	2,368	2,374	4,752

The abnormally high totals of the 5th Division and 7th Division are to be accounted for in different ways. The former had 150 prisoners taken in action on the day of the combat of Villa Muriel (October 25) ; the latter contained the two battalions that always gave a high percentage of deserters, the foreign regiments of Brunswick-Oels and *Chasseurs Britanniques*. It will be noted that the 2nd Division has also a high total, but as it had nearly double the numbers of any other division (7,500 men to an average 4,000 for the others) it did not lose out of proportion to its strength. It will be noted that the Portuguese lost more heavily in relation to their total numbers than the British—their ' missing ' were about the same as those of the British, but they only had about 20,000 rank and file in the field as against about 30,000 British. This excessive loss in missing was due entirely to the fact that the cold and rain of the last ten days of the retreat told much more heavily upon them. They were not so well clothed or fed as the British, and fell behind from exhaustion. Bradford's brigade, though never seriously in action, lost 500 men out of 1,600 by the roadside, much the heaviest percentage in the whole army.

The losses in killed and wounded as opposed to 'missing' seem to make up the following moderate figures, to which the heavy fighting about Venta del Pozo and Villa Muriel during the first days of the retreat made much the heaviest contribution.

Killed : 9 officers, 180 men. Wounded : 54 officers, 699 men—i. e. the total of 951. This does not, of course, include the *prisoners* taken at Venta del Pozo or Villa Muriel, who are counted among the 'missing' reckoned in the prefixed table. The losses in killed and wounded at Alba de Tormes and San Muñoz are less than might have been expected ; those in the other skirmishes at Valladolid, Tordesillas, &c., quite negligible.

V

THE CAMPAIGN OF CASTALLA : APRIL 1813

Sir John Murray reports his army to have consisted of the following elements :

Infantry : British, German, Anglo-Italian, Calabrese 8,274 officers and men

Sicilian ' Estero ' Regiment . . .	1,136	,, ,,
Whittingham's Spanish Division (6 batts.) .	3,901	,, ,,
Roche's Spanish Division (5 batts.) . .	4,019	,, ,,
Cavalry : British, Spanish, and Sicilian . .	886	,, ,,
Artillery, &c.	500	,, ,,
	18,716	,, ,,

The units appear to have been brigaded as follows :

Advance Guard, General Adam : 2/27th, 1st Italian Levy, Calabrese Free Corps, Rifle Companies of 3rd and 8th K.G.L.

J. Mackenzie's Division : 1/27th, 4th and 6th Line K.G.L., Sicilian Estero Regiment (2 batts.).

Clinton's Division: 1/10th, 1/58th, 1/81st, De Roll-Dillon, 2nd Italian Levy.

Cavalry : 20th Light Dragoon (2 squadrons), Foreign Hussars (1 troop), 1st Sicilian Cavalry, four Spanish squadrons [1].

Whittingham's Spaniards : Cordova, Mallorca, Guadalajara, 2nd of Burgos, 5th Grenadiers, 2nd of Murcia.

Roche's Spaniards : Volunteers of Aragon, Alicante, Chinchilla, Volunteers of Valencia, Canarias.

Artillery : British companies of Holcombe, Thompson, Williamson and Lacy ; Portuguese company of Cox, one Sicilian company (three of these companies were holding the forts of Alicante).

[1] Attached to Whittingham. Regiments of Olivenza and Almanza.

VI

SUCHET'S ARMY AT CASTALLA: APRIL 13, 1813

[RETURN OF APRIL 1.]

	Officers.	Men.	Total.
1st Division, General Robert [for Musnier, absent] :			
1st Léger (2 batts.)	38	1,443	1,481
114th Ligne (2 batts.)	36	1,498	1,534
121st Ligne (2 batts.)	34	1,252	1,286
3rd Léger (2 batts.) [1]	16	767	783
	124	4,960	5,084
2nd Division, General Harispe :			
7th Ligne (2 batts.)	31	1,298	1,329
44th Ligne (2 batts.)	26	1,160	1,186
116th Ligne (2 batts.)	35	1,502	1,537
	92	3,960	4,052
3rd Division, General Habert :			
14th Ligne (2 batts.)	42	1,189	1,231
1/16th Ligne [2]	21	614	635
1/117th Ligne [2]	27	829	856
	90	2,632	2,722
Cavalry, General Boussard :			
Two squadrons 4th Hussars	21	408	429
13th Cuirassiers	25	523	548
24th Dragoons (2 squadrons)	20	427	447
	66	1,358	1,424
Artillery : four batteries	10	282	232
TOTAL	376	13,192	13,568

[1] 3rd Léger, properly belonging to Lamarque's brigade from Catalonia, was short of four companies left in garrisons.

[2] The second battalions of these corps were left behind, along with the 11th and 20th Ligne, two squadrons of 4th Hussars, one of 24th Dragoons, the 3/5th Léger, and some 250 Italian Light Horse, to hold down the kingdom of Valencia.

VII

BIAR AND CASTALLA LOSSES : APRIL 12–13, 1813

	Killed. Offi-cers.	Men.	Wounded. Offi-cers.	Men.	Missing. Offi-cers.	Men.	Total.
Staff	1	—	2	—	—	—	3
Adam's Brigade :							
2/27th Foot	—	18	2	90	—	2	112
1st Italian Levy		23	3	49	—	28	103
Calabrese Free Corps	—	8	2	49	—	—	59
Rifle Companies 3rd & 8th K.G.L.	1	7	2	23	—	2	35
Mackenzie's Division :							
1/27th Foot	—	2	—	18	—	—	20
4th Line K.G.L.	—	3	—	9	—	—	12
6th Line K.G.L.	—	1	—	5	—	—	6
Sicilian ' Estero ' Regiment	—	1	—	8	—	—	9
Clinton's Division :							
1/58th Foot	—	1	—	5	—	—	6
De Roll-Dillon	—	4	1	20	—	9	34
Whittingham's Spanish Division :							
Cordova, Mallorca, Guadalajara, 2nd Burgos, 5th Grenadiers, 2nd of Murcia	2	73	4	183	—	—	262
20th Light Dragoons	—	—	—	1	—	—	1
Sicilian Cavalry	—	—	—	—	—	1	1
R.A. and drivers	—	—	—	5	—	—	5
Portuguese Artillery	—	—	—	3	—	—	3
TOTAL	4	141	16	468	—	42	671

VIII

WELLINGTON'S ARMY IN THE VITTORIA CAMPAIGN
MARCHING STRENGTH, MAY 25, 1813 [1]
CAVALRY

	Officers.	Men.	Total.
R. Hill's Brigade : 1st & 2nd Life Guards, Horse Guards	42	828	870
Ponsonby's Brigade : 5th Dragoon Guards, 3rd & 4th Dragoons	61	1,177	1,238
G. Anson's Brigade : 12th & 16th Light Dragoons	39	780	819
Long's Brigade : 13th Light Dragoons	20	374	394
V. Alten's Brigade : 14th Light Dragoons, 1st Hussars K.G.L.	49	956	1,005
Bock's Brigade : 1st & 2nd Dragoons K.G.L.	38	594	632
Fane's Brigade : 3rd Dragoon Guards, 1st Dragoons	42	800	842

[1] In Portuguese Units officers and men are given together.

	Officers.	Men.	Total.
Grant's Brigade : 10th, 15th, 18th Hussars .	63	1,561	1,624
D'Urban's Portuguese Brigade : 1st, 11th, 12th Cavalry	—	685	685
6th Portuguese Cavalry (Campbell) . . .	—	208	208
Cavalry Total .	354	7,963	8,317

INFANTRY

1st Division, General Howard [1] :

	Officers.	Men.	Total.
Stopford's Brigade : 1st Coldstream, 1st Scots Guards, one company 5/60th . . .	56	1,672	4,854
Halkett's Brigade : 1st, 2nd, 5th Line K.G.L., 1st & 2nd Light K.G.L.	133	2,993	

2nd Division, Sir Rowland Hill :

	Officers.	Men.	Total.
Cadogan's Brigade : 1/50th, 1/71st, 1/92nd, one company 5/60th	120	2,657	10,834
Byng's Brigade : 1/3rd, 1/57th, 1st Prov. Batt.[2], one company 5/60th . . .	131	2,334	
O'Callaghan's Brigade : 1/28th, 2/34th, 1/39th, one company 5/60th	122	2,408	
Ashworth's Portuguese : 6th & 18th Line, 6th Caçadores	—	3,062	

3rd Division, General Sir Thomas Picton :

	Officers.	Men.	Total.
Brisbane's Brigade : 1/45th, 74th, 1/88th, three companies 5/60th	125	2,598	7,437
Colville's Brigade : 1/5th, 2/83rd, 2/87th, 94th .	120	2,156	
Power's Portuguese Brigade : 9th & 21st Line, 11th Caçadores	—	2,460	

4th Division, General Sir G. Lowry Cole :

	Officers.	Men.	Total.
W. Anson's Brigade : 3/27th, 1/40th, 1/48th, 2nd Prov. Batt.[3], one company 5/60th .	139	2,796	7,816
Skerret's Brigade : 1/7th, 20th, 1/23rd, one company Brunswick	123	1,926	
Stubbs's Portuguese Brigade : 11th & 23rd Line, 7th Caçadores	—	2,842	

5th Division, General Oswald [for General Leith] :

	Officers.	Men.	Total.
Hay's Brigade : 3/1st, 1/9th, 1/38th, one company Brunswick	109	2,183	6,725
Robinson's Brigade : 1/4th, 2/47th, 2/59th, one company Brunswick . . .	100	1,961	
Spry's Portuguese Brigade : 3rd & 15th Line, 8th Caçadores	—	2,372	

[1] The other Guards' Brigade, 1st and 3rd batts. of 1st Guards, was left at Oporto and did not rejoin till August.

[2] 2/31st and 2/66th.

[3] 2nd and 2/53rd.

	Officers.	Men.	Total.
6th Division, General Pakenham [for General Clinton] :			
Stirling's Brigade : 1/42nd, 1/79th, 1/91st, one			
company 5/60th	127	2,327	
Hinde's Brigade : 1/11th, 1/32nd, 1/36th, 1/61st	130	2,288	7,347
Madden's Portuguese Brigade : 8th & 12th Line,			
9th Caçadores	—	2,475	
7th Division, General Lord Dalhousie :			
Barnes's Brigade : 1/6th, 3rd Prov. Batt.[1], nine			
companies Brunswick-Oels . . .	116	2,206	
Grant's Brigade : 51st, 68th, 1/82nd, Chasseurs			
Britanniques	141	2,397	7,287
Lecor's Portuguese Brigade : 7th & 19th Line,			
2nd Caçadores	—	2,437	
Light Division, General Charles Alten :			
Kempt's Brigade : 1/43rd, 1st & 3rd/95th	98	1,979	
Vandeleur's Brigade : 1/52nd, 2/95th .	63	1,399	5,484
Portuguese 17th Line, 1st & 3rd Caçadores	—	1,945	
Silveira's Portuguese Division :			
Da Costa's Brigade : 2nd & 14th Line . .	—	2,492	
A. Campbell's Brigade : 4th & 10th Line, 10th			5,287
Caçadores	—	2,795	
Pack's Portuguese Brigade : 1st & 16th Line, 4th			
Caçadores	—	2,297	2,297
Bradford's Portuguese Brigade : 13th & 24th Line,			
5th Caçadores	—	2,392	2,392
R.H.A. and Drivers	23	780	
Field Artillery, Train, Ammunition column, &c. .	100	2,722	
K.G.L. Artillery	17	335	
Portuguese Artillery	—	330	
Engineers and Sappers	41	302	
Staff Corps	21	126	
Wagon Train	37	165	

	British.	Portuguese.	Total.
Total Cavalry . . .	7,424	893	8,317
„ 1st Division . .	4,854	—	4,854
„ 2nd Division . .	7,772	3,062	10,834
„ 3rd Division . .	4,977	2,460	7,437
„ 4th Division . .	4,974	2,842	7,816
„ 5th Division . .	4,353	2,372	6,725
„ 6th Division . .	4,872	2,475	7,347
„ 7th Division . .	4,850	2,437	7,287
„ Light Division . . .	3,539	1,945	5,484
„ Silveira's Division . .	—	5,287	5,287
„ Pack's and Bradford's Brigades .	—	4,689	4,689
„ Artillery and Train . .	3,977	330	4,307
„ Engineers, Staff Corps, &c. . .	892	—	892
	52,484	28,792	81,276

[1] 2/24th and 2/58th.

This is, I believe, the first complete return of Wellington's army in the Vittoria campaign ever published. My predecessors in Peninsular history sought in vain for the 'morning states' which should have accompanied Wellington's dispatches to Lord Bathurst, and which are mentioned in those dispatches. In previous years, down to December 1812, they are generally found annexed to the covering letter, in the bound volumes at the Record Office. I should have fared no better than other seekers, but for the admirable knowledge of the contents of the Office possessed by Mr. Leonard Atkinson. He remembered that there existed some separate packages of 'morning states', which had been divorced from the rest of Wellington's sendings, and not bound up with them. When sought, they turned out to be the missing figures of 1813, tied up unbound between two covers of cardboard. Mr. Atkinson's happy discovery enables me to give the prefixed statistics, which permit us to know Wellington's exact strength just as the campaign of Vittoria was starting.

IX

SPANISH TROOPS UNDER WELLINGTON'S COMMAND JUNE—JULY 1813

STATES OF JUNE 1
I. FOURTH ARMY (GENERAL GIRON)

	Officers.	Men.	Total.
Morillo's Division	172	4,379	4,551
Losada's Galician Division (6 batts.) .	295	5,560	5,855
P. Barcena's Galician Division (7 batts.) . .	235	4,908	5,143
Porlier's Asturian Division (3 batts.) .	124	2,284	2,408
Longa's Division (5 batts.) . . .	130	3,000	3,130
Penne Villemur's Cavalry (7 regts.) . .	194	2,434	2,628
Julian Sanchez's Cavalry (2 regts.) . .	90	1,200	1,290
Artillery	20	400	240
Total of June 1 .	1,263	24,165	25,425

II. LEFT IN CASTILE, REJOINED ON JULY 28

	Officers.	Men.	Total.
Carlos de España's division of 4th Army (5 batts.)	175	3,167	3,342

III. JOINED ON JULY 16

THE 'ARMY OF RESERVE OF ANDALUSIA' (CONDE DE ABISPAL)

	Officers.	Men.	Total.
Echevarri's Division (7 batts.)	237	6,380	6,617
Creagh's Division (7 batts.) . . .	273	6,181	6,454
C. G. Barcena's Cavalry Brigade (2 regts.) .	39	789	828
Artillery	10	274	284
Total of later arrivals . . .	734	16,791	17,525

The General Total of the Spanish troops which actually joined Wellington between May 26 and July 28 was therefore 46,292. This does not include Mina's irregulars operating in Aragon and Eastern Navarre.

X

THE FRENCH ARMY AT VITTORIA

ARMY OF THE SOUTH. RETURN OF MAY 29, 1813.

[From Paris Archives, lent me by Mr. Fortescue.]

	Officers.	Men.	Total.
1st Division, Leval :			
Brigade Mocquery : 9th Léger, 24th Line	63	2,516	2,579
Brigade Morgan : 88th Line, 96th Line .	43	2,056	2,099
Divisional battery and train . .	3	163	166
Divisional Total	109	4,735	4,844
2nd Division, Cassagne : lent to Army of the Centre.			
3rd Division, Villatte :			
Brigade Rignoux : 27th Léger, 63rd Line	39	2,539	2,578
Brigade Lefol : 94th Line, 95th Line .	50	3,063	3,113
Divisional battery and train . .	4	179	182
Divisional Total	93	5,781	5,874
4th Division, Conroux :			
Brigade Rey : 32nd and 43rd Line .	78	3,591	3,669
Brigade Schwitter : 55th and 58th Line	47	2,670	2,717
Divisional battery and train . .	4	189	193
Divisional Total . .	129	6,460	6,589
5th Division, brigade Maransin only :			
12th Léger, 45th Line . . .	58	2,869	2,927
6th Division, Daricau :			
Brigade St. Pol : 21st Léger, 100th Line	53	2,658	2,711
Brigade Remond : 28th Léger, 103rd Line	45	2,939	2,984
Divisional battery and train . .	3	237	240
Total . . .	101	5,834	5,935
TOTAL 4½ INFANTRY DIVISIONS	490	25,679	26,169
Cavalry :			
Pierre Soult's Division :			
2nd Hussars, 5th, 10th, 21st Chasseurs	74	1,428	1,502
One battery H.A. and train . .	4	165	169
Tilly's Division :			
2nd, 4th, 14th, 17th, 26th, 27th Dragoons .	88	1,841	1,929
Digeon's Division :			
5th, 12th, 16th, 21st Dragoons .	80	1,612	1,692
One battery H.A. and train .	3	174	177
Total cavalry .	249	6,220	6,469

	Officers,	Men.	Total.
Artillery Reserve : two batteries and train .	5	365	370
Artillery Park : two companies Field Artillery, one company pontoniers, artificers, train .	17	696	713
Engineers : two companies sappers, two miners, and train	11	619	630
Gendarmerie	4	101	105
Wagon train	2	63	65
Total auxiliary troops . . .	39	1,844	1,883
État-Major of the Army and the divisions	115	—	115
GENERAL TOTAL OF ARMY OF THE SOUTH .	893	33,743	34,636

ARMY OF THE CENTRE AT VITTORIA

RETURN OF MAY 29 FOR CASSAGNE'S DIVISION ; OF MAY 1 ONLY FOR THE REST, EXCEPT FOR THE ROYAL GUARDS AND SPANIARDS, AS SEE NOTE.

	Officers	Men	Total
1st Division, Darmagnac :			
Brigade Chassé : 28th & 75th Line . .	35	1,759	1,794
Brigade Neuenstein : 2nd Nassau, 4th Baden, Frankfort	101	2,577	2,678
Divisional Total	136	4,336	4,472
2nd Division, Cassagne :			
Brigade Braun : 16th Léger, 8th Line . Brigade Blondeau : 51st Line, 54th Line	95	5,114	5,209
Total Infantry .	231	9,450	9,681
Cavalry :			
Treillard's Division : 13th, 18th, 19th, 22nd Dragoons	44	994	1,038
Avy's Light Cavalry : 27th Chasseurs, Nassau Chasseurs	22	452	474
Total Cavalry . .	66	1,446	1,512
Artillery (3 batteries) and train	13	488	501
Engineers (1 company sappers)	2	129	131
Wagon train, &c. . . .	3	195	198
Total Auxiliary Arms	28	812	830
The King's Spanish Army [1] :			
Royal Guards, General Guy :			
Grenadiers, tirailleurs, voltigeurs of the Guard	80	2,300	2,380
Hussars and Lancers of the Guard . .	25	400	425

[1] These figures are estimated from what was still surviving of each unit when Soult reorganized the army in July 16. The Royal Guards infantry had then 2,019 men, the line cavalry 64 officers and 500 men, the line

	Officers.	Men.	Total.
Line :			
Regiments of Castile, Toledo, *Royal Étranger*	70	2,000	2,070
Cavalry : 1st & 2nd Chasseurs, Hussars of			
Guadalajara	70	600	670
Artillery : one battery . . .	3	90	93
Total King's Army	248	5,390	5,633
TOTAL ARMY OF THE CENTRE .	603	17,098	17,691

ARMY OF PORTUGAL

NO RETURN AVAILABLE LATER THAN MAY 1.

	Officers.	Men.	Total.
4th Division, Sarrut :			
Brigade Fririon : 2nd Léger, 36th Line .			
Brigade Menne : 4th Léger, 65th Line .	146	4,656	4,802
Divisional field battery and train .			
6th Division, Lamartinière :			
Brigade Gauthier : 118th Line, 119th Line	71	2,496	2,567
Brigade Menne : 120th Line, 122nd Line	102	3,866	3,968
Divisional field battery and train	3	173	176
Total Infantry Divisions	322	11,191	11,513
Cavalry :			
Division Mermet :			
Brigade Curto : 13th & 22nd Chasseurs .	39	863	902
Brigade ? : 3rd Hussars, 14th & 26th			
Chasseurs	42	857	899
Division Boyer :			
6th, 11th, 15th, 25th Dragoons .	67	1,404	1,471
Total Cavalry .	148	3,324	3,472
Reserve Artillery :			
One H.A., four field batteries . . .	11	379	390
One company Pontoniers, train, artificers, &c.	10	763	773
Engineers : two companies sappers . . .	5	190	195
Gendarmerie	5	169	174
Wagon train, mule train, &c. . .	35	898	933
Total auxiliary arms . .	66	2,389	2,455
GENERAL TOTAL OF ARMY OF PORTUGAL . .	536	16,904	17,440

Allowing for wastage May 1 to June 21, there may probably have been 14,000 of all arms at Vittoria—say 9,500 infantry, 2,800 cavalry, 1,700 auxiliary arms.

---

infantry 1,168, though it had lost over 300 men at Vittoria and a much greater number from desertion. I take it that to allow 300 extra men at the battle for the Guard infantry, 100 more for the Line cavalry, and 800 more for the Line infantry cannot be far out.

Adding the totals of the three armies as above, we should get 2,032 officers and 68,231 men. But deductions of course must be made :

(1) For decrease from May 1 to June 21 in the Armies of Portugal and the Centre, and from May 29 to June 21 in the Army of the South by normal wastage, and in the two former by drafts sent back to France in May.

(2) For casualties in action since the campaign opened.
The latter would not be large, only Digeon's Dragoons and Villatte's and Sarrut's infantry divisions having been seriously engaged during the retreat. The Burgos explosion cost Villatte over 100 men. We need not allow more than 1,500 as an ample estimate for casualties in action.

The normal wastage, and the deduction for drafts sent to France in May are more difficult to calculate, but I think we shall not be far out in taking 3,000 as an outside allowance for the latter—which affects only the Armies of Portugal and the Centre, since we have a May 29th Return for Gazan's Army, which of course sent nothing away after that date. And in healthy months, such as May and early June, the deficit from extra sick would not be large—indeed as many men may have rejoined as convalescents as went into hospital, since (except Villatte at Salamanca) the troops had never been pressed or overmarched. It would be generous to allow 5,000 for ' wastage '.

If so, the French had 63,000 men at Vittoria, but deducting non-combatants (train, artificers, &c.) there would be 9,000 horse, over 46,000 men in the infantry divisions, and about 1,300 gunners with the field and horse batteries not included in the infantry divisions, also 1,000 sappers. This makes over 57,000 fighting men actually available. There must also be a small addition for stray units of the Army of the North known to have been present—not less than 500 nor more than 1,000. All attempts to bring down the French force present to 45,000 men (*Victoires et Conquêtes*, vol. xxii) or 39,000 infantry and 8,000 horse (Jourdan) or ' barely 50,000 men ' (Picard) are inadmissible.

XI

BRITISH AND PORTUGUESE LOSSES AT VITTORIA

I. BRITISH LOSSES

	Killed.		Wounded.		Missing.		
	Offi-cers.	Men.	Offi-cers.	Men.	Offi-cers.	Men.	Total.
1st Division, General Howard :							
Stopford's Brigade { 1st Coldstream Guards, 1/3rd Guards .			No casualties.				
Halkett's Brigade { 1st,2nd,5th LineK.G.L. —	1	—	1	—	—	2
1st Light K.G.L. . —	1	1	7	—	—	9
2nd Light K.G.L. . —	4	—	39	—	—	43
Divisional Total . . —	6	1	47	—	—	54

		Killed.		Wounded.		Missing.		
		Officers.	Men.	Officers.	Men.	Officers.	Men.	Total.

2nd Division, General Sir W. Stewart :

		Officers	Men	Officers	Men	Officers	Men	Total
Cadogan's Brigade	1/50th Foot .	—	27	7	70	—	—	104
	1/71st Foot . .	3	41	12	260	See below [1]		316
	1/92nd Foot .	—	4	—	16	—	—	20
Byng's Brigade	1/3rd Foot . .	—	8	7	96	—	—	110
	1/57th Foot. .	—	5	2	21	—	—	28
	1st Provisional [2] Batt.—		3	2	35	—	—	40
O'Callaghan's Brigade	1/28th Foot. .	—	12	17	171	—	—	199
	2/34th Foot. .	—	10	3	63	—	—	76
	1/39th Foot.	—	26	8	181	—	—	215
Divisional Total .		3	136	58	913	—	—	1,110

3rd Division, General Sir Thomas Picton :

		Officers	Men	Officers	Men	Officers	Men	Total
Brisbane's Brigade	1/45th Foot . .	—	4	4	66	—	—	74
	74th Foot . .	—	13	4	66	—	—	83
	1/88th Foot . .	—	23	5	187	—	—	215
	5/60th Foot (3 comp.)	—	2	2	47	—	—	51
Colville's Brigade	1/5th Foot . .	2	22	6	133	—	—	163
	2/83rd Foot .	2	18	4	50	—	—	74
	2/87th Foot . .	1	54	12	177	—	—	244
	94th Foot .	—	5	6	56	—	—	67
Divisional Total . .		5	141	43	782	—	—	972

4th Division, General Sir Lowry Cole :

		Officers	Men	Officers	Men	Officers	Men	Total
W. Anson's Brigade	3/27th Foot . .	—	7	3	32	—	—	42
	1/40th Foot .	—	5	3	34	—	—	42
	1/48th Foot .	—	1	—	18	—	—	19
	2nd Provisional [3]	—	4	—	6	—	—	10
Skerrett's Brigade	1/7th Foot .	—	2	—	2	—	—	4
	20th Foot .	—	3	—	1	—	—	4
	1/23rd Foot .	—	1	—	3	—	—	4
Divisional Total .		—	23	6	96	—	—	125

5th Division, General Oswald :

		Officers	Men	Officers	Men	Officers	Men	Total
Hay's Brigade	3/1st Foot . .	—	8	7	96	—	—	111
	1/9th Foot . .	1	9	—	15	—	—	25
	1/38th Foot .	—	—	1	7	—	—	8
Robinson's Brigade	1/4th Foot .	1	12	6	72	—	—	91
	2/47th Foot .	2	18	4	88	—	—	112
	2/59th Foot .	—	11	8	130	—	—	149
Divisional Total .		4	58	26	408	—	—	496

[1] About 40 prisoners of the 1/71st are lost among the general total of 223 ' missing and stragglers ' : these were the only actual prisoners lost in the battle. See p. 416 of this volume.

[2] i. e. 2/31st and 2/66th.

[3] i. e. 2nd and 2/53rd.

	Killed. Offi-cers.	Killed. Men.	Wounded. Offi-cers.	Wounded. Men.	Missing. Offi-cers.	Missing. Men.	Total.
7th Division, General Lord Dalhousie :							
Barnes's Brigade			No casualties.				
Grant's Brigade — 51st Foot	1	10	—	21	—	—	32
68th Foot	2	23	9	91	—	—	125
1/82nd Foot	1	5	3	22	—	—	31
Chasseurs Britanniques	—	29	2	109	—	—	140
Light Company Brunswick-Oels[1]	1	—	—	5	—	—	6
Divisional Total	5	67	14	248	—	—	334
Light Division, General Charles Alten :							
Kempt's Brigade — 1/43rd Foot	—	2	2	27	—	—	31
1/95th Rifles	—	4	4	37	—	—	45
3/95th Rifles	1	7	—	16	—	—	24
Vandeleur's Brigade — 1/52nd Foot	1	3	1	18	—	—	23
2/95th Rifles	—	—	1	8	—	—	9
Divisional Total	2	16	8	106	—	—	132
CAVALRY.							
R. Hill's Brigade (Household Cavalry)			No casualties.				
Ponsonby's Brigade	—	—	—	2	—	—	2
G. Anson's Brigade — 12th Light Dragoons	1	3	—	8	—	—	12
16th Light Dragoons	—	7	1	13	—	—	21
Long's Brigade	—	—	—	1	—	—	1
V. Alten's Brigade			No casualties.				
Bock's Brigade	—	1	—	—	—	—	1
Fane's Brigade — 3rd Dragoon Guards	—	3	1	4	—	—	8
1st Royal Dragoons	—	—	—	1	—	—	1
Grant's Brigade — 10th Hussars	—	6	—	10	—	—	16
15th Hussars	—	10	2	47	—	—	59
18th Hussars	1	10	2	21	—	—	34
Total Cavalry	2	40	6	107	—	—	155
Royal Horse Artillery	—	4	1	35	—	—	40
Field Artillery	—	5	—	18	—	—	23
K.G.L. Artillery	—	2	—	5	—	—	7
Royal Engineers	—	—	1	—	—	—	1
General Staff	—	—	8	—	—	—	8
GENERAL TOTAL	21	498	192	2,764	—	—	3,475

N.B.—In addition we have, undistributed under corps, 223 rank and file missing, of whom all except about 40 of the 1/71st were stragglers, not prisoners.

[1] Brunswick-Oels Head-Quarters were in the 7th Division, but companies were distributed all around the Army. These casualties partly belong to outlying companies, not to Head-Quarters.

II. PORTUGUESE LOSSES

		Killed.		Wounded.		Missing.		Total.
		Officers.	Men.	Officers.	Men.	Officers.	Men.	
Ashworth's Brigade (2nd Division)	6th Line	—	1	—	10	—	1	12
	18th Line	—	—	—	1	—	—	1
	6th Caçadores	1	1	—	7	—	—	9
Power's Brigade (3rd Division)	9th Line	3	43	9	157	—	—	212
	21st Line	3	55	8	115	—	6	187
	11th Caçadores	—	3	2	7	—	—	12
Stubbs's Brigade (4th Division)	11th Line	1	36	6	109	—	1	153
	23rd Line	—	20	3	35	—	—	58
	7th Caçadores	—	9	4	21	—	—	35
Spry's Brigade (5th Division)	3rd Line	—	2	3	8	—	—	13
	15th Line	—	6	3	19	—	—	28
	8th Caçadores	—	13	2	25	—	—	40
Lecor's Brigade (7th Division)	7th Line	—	—	—	—	—	6	6
Light Division	1st Caçadores	—	2	—	2	—	—	4
	3rd Caçadores	—	—	—	1	—	—	1
	17th Line	—	7	1	20	—	—	28
Silveira's Division	Da Costa's Brigade	No casualties.						
	A. Campbell's Brigade	—	2	—	1	—	7	10
Pack's Brigade	1st Line	—	3	—	—	—	—	3
	16th Line	1	10	2	24	—	—	37
	4th Caçadores	—	16	1	18	—	—	35
Bradford's Brigade	13th Line	—	—	—	1	—	16	17
	24th Line	—	—	—	3	—	3	3
	5th Caçadores	—	4	—	5	—	2	11
Cavalry : in 6th Regiment		—	—	—	2	—	—	2
Artillery		No casualties.						
Total Portuguese Losses		9	233	44	592	—	43	921

III. SPANISH LOSSES

	Killed.		Wounded.		Missing.		Total.
	Officers.	Men.	Officers.	Men.	Officers.	Men.	
All in Morillo's and Longa's Divisions	4	85	10	453	—	—	562

TOTAL ALLIED LOSSES

	Killed.		Wounded.		Missing.		Total.
	Officers.	Men.	Officers.	Men.	Officers.	Men.	
BRITISH	20	489	192	2,749	—	223	3,675
PORTUGUESE	9	233	44	592	—	43	921
SPANISH	4	85	10	453	—	—	562
Total	33	807	246	3,794	—	266	5,158

XII

FRENCH LOSSES AT VITTORIA : JUNE 21

[From the Official Returns, lent me by Mr. Fortescue.]

ARMY OF THE SOUTH

	Killed.		Wounded.		Prisoners.		'Disparus.'		Total.
	Offi-cers.	Men.	Offi-cers.	Men.	Offi-cers.	Men.	Offi-cers.	Men.	
Leval's Division .	4	98	17	395	4	133	—	108	759
Villatte's Division .	—	43	2	212	—	22	—	—	291
Conroux's Division .	5	74	27	712	4	265	—	—	1,087
Maransin's Brigade .	3	80	21	510	4	63	—	—	681
Daricau's Division .	3	89	20	389	1	49	—	280	833
Pierre Soult's Cavalry	—	—	3	—	—	—	—	3	6
Digeon's Dragoons .	—	18	11	69	1	3	—	—	102
Tilly's Dragoons .	—	2	—	19	1	3	—	—	25
Artillery . . .	2	20	—	366	—	100	—	—	488
Engineers, &c. . .	1	2	—	2	—	23	—	—	28
Total . .	18	426	101	2,074	15	661	—	391	4,300

ARMY OF THE CENTRE

	Killed.		Wounded.		'Prisoners or missing.'		Total.
	Offi-cers.	Men.	Offi-cers.	Men.	Offi-cers.	Men.	
Darmagnac's Division .	9	96	33	414	3	791	1,346
Cassagne's Division . .	—	9	6	70	—	178	263
Treillard's Dragoons .	—	6	1	17	—	56	80
Avy's Chasseurs .	—	2	1	3	—	51	57
Artillery : no Returns	?	?	?	?	?	?	?
Engineers	—	—	—	—	—	4	4
Casapalacios' Spaniards .	5	20	12	21	—	300	358
Total . . .	14	133	53	525	3	1,380	2,108

ARMY OF PORTUGAL

Sarrut's Division . .	2	51	26	505	4	224	812
Lamartinière's Division .	7	70	30	362	1	116	586
Mermet's Light Cavalry .	—	18	8	42	—	29	97
Boyer's Dragoons . .	1	16	8	80	—	—	105
Artillery, Engineers, &c. .	?	?	?	?	?	?	?
Total . . .	10	155	72	989	5	369	1,600
GENERAL TOTAL OF THE THREE ARMIES	42	714	226	4,188	23	2,801	8,008

No return (as usual) from King Joseph's Royal Guards, who had, however, as Martinien's lists show, 11 officers killed and wounded, probably therefore 150 to 200 casualties in rank and file. Also no returns from Artillery of Armies of the Centre and Portugal, from whom Martinien shows 9 officer-casualties, or from the fractions of the Army of the North present (3rd Line, &c.); the last show 3 officer-casualties in Martinien. It is obvious that the official total is several hundreds too small.

XIII

SIR JOHN MURRAY'S ARMY ON THE TARRAGONA EXPEDITION: JUNE 1813

Advanced Guard Brigade. Colonel Adam :
  2/27th, Calabrese Free Corps, 1st Anglo-Italian Levy, one company Rifles of De Roll.

1st Division. General William Clinton. Brigadiers Houstedt and Haviland-Smith :
  1/58th, 2/67th, 4th Line Battalion K.G.L., Sicilian ' Estero ' regiment (2 batts.).

2nd Division. General John Mackenzie. Brigadiers Warren and Prevost :
  1/10th, 1/27th, 1/81st, De Roll-Dillon, 2nd Italian Levy.

Whittingham's Spanish Infantry :
  Guadalajara, Cordova, 2nd of Murcia, Mallorca, 5th Grenadiers.

Cavalry :
  Two squadrons 20th Light Dragoons, two squadrons Brunswick Hussars, one troop Foreign Hussars.

Artillery :
  Two British and one Portuguese Field Batteries ; one company British and one Portuguese attached to Battering Train.

STATISTICS OF ABOVE. JUNE 4, 1813

[No regimental totals available.]

Infantry :	Officers.	Men.
British, German Legion, De Roll-Dillon, 1st and 2nd batts. Anglo-Italian Levy, Calabrese Free Corps	345	8,040
Sicilian Estero Regiment	67	1,041
Whittingham's Spanish Infantry . . .	228	4,624
Cavalry	37	764 [726 horses]
Artillery	53	767
Engineers and Staff Corps	9	77
Total .	739	15,313

XIV

SUCHET'S ARMY AT THE TIME OF SIR JOHN MURRAY'S TARRAGONA EXPEDITION

I. THE ARMY OF VALENCIA. MORNING STATE OF JUNE 16, 1813

	Officers.	Men.	Total.
1st Division, General Musnier [at Perello near Tortosa]: 1st Léger (2 batts.), 114th Line (3 batts.), 121st Line (2 batts.) . . .	100	4,063	4,163
2nd Division, General Harispe [at Xativa]: 7th, 44th, 116th Line (2 batts. each) . . .	97	3,967	4,064
3rd Division, General Habert [at Alcira]: 14th, 16th, 117th Line (2 batts. each) . . .	118	4,002	4,120
3/5th Léger	18	601	619
Brigade detached from Catalonia, General Lamarque: 3rd Léger, 11th Line (2 batts. each), 20th Line (2 batts.)[1], 1st Italian Chasseurs (1 squadron)	89	3,240	3,329
Cavalry, General Boussard: 4th Hussars (4 squadrons), 12th Cuirassiers (4 squadrons), 24th Dragoons (3 squadrons), Neapolitan Chasseurs (2 squadrons)	84	1,895	1,979
Cavalry from the Army of the Centre: 1 squadron Westphalian Chasseurs.	11	163	174
Artillery and Artillery Train	20	1,201	1,221
Sappers	8	366	374
Gendarmerie, Équipages Militaires, &c. . .	9	681	690
Italian Division Severoli [at Buñol]: 1st Ligne and 1st Léger (2 batts. each), and divisional artillery	57	2,008	2,065
Total	611	22,187	22,798

II. GARRISONS OF ARAGON (GENERAL PARIS)

10th Ligne (2 batts.), 81st Ligne (3 batts.), 8th Neapolitans	87	3,302	3,389
12th Hussars (3 squadrons) . .	26	370	396
Artillery	6	245	251
Gendarmerie (6 companies) .	28	1,105	1,133
Chasseurs des Montagnes . .	26	658	684
Spanish troops .	7	151	158
Total	180	5,831	6,011

[1] Pannetier's flying column, which tried to relieve Tarragona, consisted of 3/5th Léger, and two battalions each of 20th Line and 3rd Léger, with the Westphalian chasseurs: a little under 3,000 men.

III. THE ARMY OF CATALONIA. MORNING STATE OF JUNE 16

	Officers.	Men.	Total.
Division of Cerdagne, General Quesnel : 102nd Line (2 batts.), 143rd Line (4 batts.), and details	113	2,961	3,074
Division of Upper Catalonia, General Lamarque : 32nd Léger and 60th Line (1 batt. each), 3rd Provisional Regiment, and details . .	60	2,459	2,519
Arrondissement of Gerona, General Nogués : 60th Line (2 batts.), 115th Line (1 batt.), and details	100	2,964	3,064
Beurmann's Brigade : 115th Line (2 batts.), 23rd Léger (2 batts.), and details	62	2,400	2,462
Petit's Brigade : 23rd Ligne (1 batt.), 67th Line (2 batts.), Wurzburg (1 batt.), and details .	87	1,972	2,059
Arrondissement of Barcelona, General Maurice Mathieu : 5th Line (2 batts.), 79th Line (2 batts.), 18th Léger (2 batts.), 1st of Nassau (2 batts.), 29th Chasseurs (1 squadron), and details . .	162	6,857	7,019
Garrison of Lerida, General Henriot : 42nd Line (2 batts.), and details	39	1,404	1,443
Garrison of Tarragona : 20th Line (1 batt.), 7th Italian Line (1 batt.), and details . . .	60	1,456	1,516
Gendarmerie (6 companies) . . .	33	1,015	1,048
Artillery and Train . . .	17	1,152	1,169
Sappers and Miners . . :	5	186	191
Total	738	24,826	25,566

N.B.—The Cavalry (29th Chasseurs, and an odd squadron of 1st Hussars) was distributed in troops and half-troops all round the brigades, the only solid bodies being one squadron with Beurmann's brigade, and one at Barcelona. The total number of sabres was 670 only.

XV

SPANISH ARMIES ON THE EAST COAST: JUNE 1, 1813

FIRST ARMY (General COPONS).

1st Division (Eroles) : 5 batts. and 2 squadrons	202	4,357	4,559
2nd Division (?) : 7 batts. and 2 squadrons	309	5,124	5,433
Garrisons : 5 batts. and details . . .	272	5,497	5,769
Total	783	14,978	15,761

	Officers.	Men.	Total.
SECOND ARMY (General ELIO).			
1st Division (Mijares) : 6 batts. . . .	230	4,125	4,355
2nd Division (Villacampa) : 4 batts., 2 squadrons	209	4,355	4,564
3rd Division (Sarsfield) : 5 batts., 2 squadrons .	206	5,178	5,384
4th Division (Roche), 5 batts. . . .	199	4,237	4,436
5th Division (theEmpecinado): 4 batts.,2 squadrons	135	4,113	4,248
6th Division (Duran) : 4 batts., 3 squadrons .	199	5,264	5,463
Cavalry Brigade : 2 regiments . . .	61	953	1,014
Artillery	41	741	782
Engineers and Sappers	31	228	259
Total .	1,311	29,294	30,605
THIRD ARMY (Duque DEL PARQUE).			
1st Division (Prince of Anglona) : 8 batts. .	210	4,982	5,142
2nd Division (Marquis de las Cuevas) : 7 batts. .	187	3,438	3,625
3rd Division (Cruz Murgeon) : 7 batts. . .	118	2,656	2,774
Cavalry Brigade (Sisternes) . . .	42	664	706
Artillery, &c.	21	323	344
Total .	578	12,013	12,591

XVI

THE ARMY OF SPAIN AS REORGANIZED BY SOULT : JULY 1813

N.B.—Numerals appended to a regiment's name give the number of battalions in it, when they exceed *one.* ,

Officers and men present.

1st Division. FOY.

Brigade Fririon : 6th Léger. Late Foy's Division Army of
        69th Line (2).   Ditto.   [Portugal.
        76th Line.   Ditto.
Brigade Berlier : 36th Line (2).   Late Sarrut's Div. A. of P.
        39th Line. Late Foy's Div. A. of P.
        65th Line (2).   Late Sarrut's Div. of P.

5,922

2nd Division. DARMAGNAC.

Brigade Chassé : 16th Léger. Late Darmagnac's Div. Army of
        8th Line.   Ditto.   [the Centre.
        28th Line (2).   Late Cassagne's Div. A. of C.
Brigade Gruardet : 51st Line. Ditto.
        54th Line.   Ditto.
        75th Line (2).   Ditto.

6,961

Officers and men present.

3rd Division. ABBÉ.
Brigade Rignoux : 27th Léger. Late Villatte's Div. Army of
    63rd Line. Ditto.   [the South.
    64th Line[1] (2). Late garrison of Vittoria A.ofN.
Brigade Rémond : 5th Léger (2). Late Abbé's Div. A. of N.   8,030
    94th Line (2). Late Villatte's Div. A. of S.
    95th Line. Ditto.

4th Division. CONROUX.
Brigade Rey : 12th Léger (2). Late Maransin's Brigade A. of S.
    32nd Line (2). Late Conroux's Div. A. of S.
    43rd Line (2). Ditto.   7,056
Brigade Schwitter : 45th Line. Late Maransin's Brigade A. of S.
    55th Line. Late Conroux's Div. A. of S.
    58th Line. Ditto.

5th Division. VANDERMAESEN.
Brigade Barbot : 25th Léger. Late Barbot's Div. A. of P.
    1st Line. Late garrison of Burgos, A. of N.[2]
    27th Line. Late Barbot's Div. A. of P.
Brigade Rouget : 50th Line. Ditto.   4,181
    59th Line. Ditto.
    130th Line (2). Late Vandermaesen's Div. A.
              [of N.

6th Division. MARANSIN.
Brigade St. Pol : 21st Léger. Late Daricau's Div. A. of S.
    24th Line. Late Leval's Div. A. of S.
    96th Line. Ditto.   5,966
Brigade Mocquery : 28th Léger. Late Daricau's Div. A. of S.
    101st Line (2). Ditto.
    103rd Line. Ditto.

7th Division. MAUCUNE.
Brigade Pinoteau : 17th Léger. Late Maucune's Div. A. of P.
    15th Line (2). Ditto.
    66th Line. Ditto.
Brigade Montfort : 34th Léger. Late Vandermaesen's Div. 4,186
             [A. of N.
    82nd Line. Late Maucune's Div. A. of P.
    86th Line. Ditto.

8th Division. TAUPIN.
Brigade Béchaud : 9th Léger (2). Late Leval's Div. A. of S.
    26th Line. Late Taupin's Div. A. of P.
    47th Line (2). Ditto.   5,981
Brigade Lecamus : 31st Léger. Ditto.
    70th Line (2). Ditto.
    88th Line. Late Leval's Div. A. of S.

[1] But originally an A. of S. regiment, transferred to A. of N. in January.
[2] Originally an A. of P. regiment, but transferred to A. of N. in January 1813.

Officers and men present.

9th Division. LAMARTINIÈRE.

Brigade Menne : 2nd Léger. Late Sarrut's Div. A. of P. ⎫
   118th Line (2).   Late Lamartinière's Div. A. ⎪
   119th Line (2).   Ditto.   [of P. ⎬ 7,127
Brigade Gauthier : 120th Line (3). Ditto.   ⎪
   122nd Line (2). Ditto.   ⎭

Reserve (General VILLATTE).

Brigadiers : Thouvenot and Boivin.

(1) 1/4th Léger. Late Sarrut's Division A. of P.   .   . ⎫
   1 & 2/10th Léger. Late Abbé's Division A. of N. .   . ⎪
   3/31st Léger. Late garrison of Vittoria A. of N. .   . ⎪
   1/3rd Line. Late Abbé's Division A. of N.   .   .   . ⎪
   2/34th Line. Late Vandermaesen's Division A. of N.   . ⎪
   1 & 3/40th Line. Late Vandermaesen's Division A. of N. ⎪
   1/101st Line. Late garrison of Vittoria A. of N.   .   . ⎬ 9,102
   1 & 2/105th Line. Late Abbé's Division A. of N. . ⎪
   4/114th Line (detachment). Old Bayonne Reserve   . ⎪
   4 & 5/115th Line. Old Bayonne Reserve   .   .   . ⎪
   4/116th Line. Old Bayonne Reserve   .   .   .   . ⎪
   4/117th Line. Old Bayonne Reserve   .   .   .   . ⎪
   3/118th Line. Old Bayonne Reserve   .   .   .   . ⎪
   3/119th Line. Late Biscay garrisons   .   .   .   . ⎭
      Total : 17 battalions.

(2) Foreign troops :

Neuenstein's German Brigade, 4th Baden, 2nd Nassau (2),
   Frankfort 2,066
St. Paul's Italian Brigade 2nd Léger, 4th and 6th Line . 1,349
Casapalacios' Spanish Brigade—Castile, Toledo, Royal
   Étranger   1,168
King Joseph's Guard (General Guy). 3 regiments   . 2,019
(3) Gendarmes *à pied* of the 4th and 5th Legions .   .   . 900
National Guards 650
                                            ———
      Total of Reserve 17,254

This total, as is obvious, much exceeds the 12,654 given as the total of the Reserve by the tables which Soult sent to Paris on July 16 as representing his available troops. These tables omit the following French battalions which were all undoubtedly on the Pyrenean frontier in July 1813 as they formed parts of the armies of the North and Portugal or of the old Bayonne Reserve in the returns of May, and are all found again present in the returns of September—1/3rd Line, 2/34th Line, 1 & 2/40th Line, 1 & 2/105th Line, 4/116th Line, 4/117th, 2/10th Ligne : i. e. 8½ battalions, which easily account for the 4,600 men short in Soult's total. After the battles of the Pyrenees, in which Maucune's and Vandermaesen's divisions were so cut up that they had to be re-formed with new units, the following battalions, whose existence is concealed by Soult in his July table, were drafted in to them—1 & 3/40th Line into Vandermaesen's division, 1/3rd, 1 & 2/105th, 2/10th Léger, into Maucune's. Obviously then, they were available, though omitted. The 4/116th and 4/117th (a fragment of four companies) came into the fighting divisions later, but must have been somewhere behind the Bidassoa all the time (having belonged to the old Bayonne Reserve).

	Officers and men present.
Cavalry :	
Acting as Corps-cavalry with the field army : 13th, 15th, 22nd Chasseurs	808
P. Soult's Division : 5th and 12th Dragoons, 2nd Hussars, 5th, 10th, 21st Chasseurs, Nassau Chasseurs, Spanish Cavalry	3,981
Treillard's Division : 4th, 14th, 16th, 17th, 21st, 26th Dragoons	2,358
Total cavalry	7,147

This makes the total available for service in the field :

Infantry	72,664
Cavalry	7,147
Total	79,811

while Soult only gave himself credit for 69,543, including the Reserve, for his field army.

In addition, there were half-trained conscripts at Bayonne 5,595. Garrisons of San Sebastian 3,185, Santona 1,465, Pampeluna 3,550 = 8,200. Also sick 14,074, and detached 2,110.

Finally, ' Troupes non comprises dans les organizations,' or ' troupes hors ligne,' i. e. artillery, engineers, sappers, gendarmerie à cheval, train, équipages militaires, &c. = 9,000. Gross total about 122,367.

XVII

BRITISH LOSSES AT MAYA : JULY 25, 1813

	Killed.		Wounded.		Missing.		Total.
	Offi-cers.	Men.	Offi-cers.	Men.	Offi-cers.	Men.	
2nd Division Staff . .	—	—	2	—	—	—	2
Cameron's Brigade :							
1/50th Foot . . .	3	21	10	158	2	55	249
1/71st Foot . . .	2	16	4	120	1	53	196
1/92nd Foot . . .	—	34	19	268	—	22	343
Pringle's Brigade :							
1/28th Foot	1	8	6	112	1	31	159
2/34th Foot	1	21	4	54	6	82	168
1/39th Foot	2	10	7	111	2	54	186
Two companies 5/60th, attached to above brigades . .	2	5	—	11	1	25	44

	Killed.		Wounded.		Missing.		Total.
	Offi-cers.	Men.	Offi-cers.	Men.	Offi-cers.	Men.	

7th Division troops :

	Killed Officers	Killed Men	Wounded Officers	Wounded Men	Missing Officers	Missing Men	Total
1/6th	—	2	2	17	—	—	21
1/82nd	—	8	4	67	—	—	79
Brunswick-Oels . . .	—	8	3	15	—	15	41
Total of the three brigades	11	133	61	933	13	337	1,488

BRITISH LOSSES AT RONCESVALLES

N.B.—Only those of Ross's and Campbell's brigades are available in detail, those of Byng's brigade are nowhere found, but are known to have been slight—under 100 in all. It is most curious that not one officer-casualty appears to have occurred either in the 1/3rd or in the 1st Provisional Battalion, Byng's only units engaged at Roncesvalles.

Ross's Brigade :

	Killed Officers	Killed Men	Wounded Officers	Wounded Men	Missing Officers	Missing Men	Total
1/7th Foot	1	6	—	24	—	—	31
20th Foot	1	14	8	105	—	11	139
1/23rd Foot	—	6	4	32	—	—	42
1 company Brunswick-Oels .	—	2	—	2	—	—	4

Portuguese Brigade (A. Campbell) :

	Killed Officers	Killed Men	Wounded Officers	Wounded Men	Missing Officers	Missing Men	Total
11th Line ⎫ .							
23rd Line ⎬ . .	—	3	—	20	—	6	29
7th Caçadores ⎭							

XVIII

BRITISH LOSSES AT SORAUREN : JULY 28

2nd Division :

		Killed Officers	Killed Men	Wounded Officers	Wounded Men	Missing Officers	Missing Men	Total
Byng's Brigade	1/3rd Foot . .	—	—	—	2	—	—	2
	1/57th Foot . .	—	2	2	59	—	—	63
	1st Provisional Batt. (2/31st & 2/66th) .	—	—	1	4	—	—	5
	Brigade Total . . .	—	2	3	65	—	—	70

3rd Division : no losses.

4th Division (Cole) :

		Killed Officers	Killed Men	Wounded Officers	Wounded Men	Missing Officers	Missing Men	Total
Anson's Brigade	3/27th Foot . .	2	41	9	195	—	7	254
	1/40th Foot . .	1	19	4	105	—	—	129
	1/48th Foot . .	2	10	8	104	—	11	135
	2nd Provisional Batt. (2nd & 2/53rd)	—	1	1	18	—	—	20
Ross's Brigade	1/7th Foot . .	1	46	10	159	1	—	217
	1/20th Foot . .	1	23	5	79	—	—	108
	1/23rd Foot . .	2	16	4	59	—	—	81
	1 company Brunswick-Oels	—	1	—	3	—	1	5
	Divisional Total	9	157	41	722	1	19	949

	Killed. Offi-cers.	Men.	Wounded. Offi-cers.	Men.	Missing. Offi-cers.	Men.	Total.
6th Division (Pack):							
Stirling's Brigade — 1/42nd Foot	—	3	—	19	—	—	22
1/79th Foot	—	4	1	30	—	—	35
1/91st Foot	—	12	6	92	—	2	112
1 company 5/60th	—	1	—	4	—	—	5
Lambert's Brigade — 1/11th Foot	—	5	4	42	—	—	51
1/32nd Foot	—	—	1	23	—	—	24
1/36th Foot	—	—	2	16	—	—	18
1/61st Foot	—	2	2	58	—	—	62
Divisional Total	—	27	16	284	—	2	329
Artillery	—	—	—	6	—	—	6
General Staff	2	—	2	—	—	—	4
Total British	11	186	62	1,077	1	21	1,358
Total Portuguese	3	160	45	850	—	44	1,102
GENERAL TOTAL	14	346	107	2,034	1	65	2460

XIX

BRITISH LOSSES AT SECOND SORAUREN: JULY 30

	Killed. Offi-cers.	Men.	Wounded. Offi-cers.	Men.	Missing. Offi-cers.	Men.	Total.
2nd Division:							
Byng's Brigade — 1/3rd Foot	1	3	1	25	—	—	30
1/57th Foot	—	2	2	33	—	—	37
1st Provisional Batt. (2/31st & 2/66th)	1	5	6	52	—	—	64
Brigade Total	2	10	9	110	—	—	131
3rd Division (Picton):							
Brisbane's Brigade — 1/45th Foot	—	—	1	7	—	—	8
5/60th (4 companies)	—	2	1	28	—	—	31
74th Foot	1	6	4	38	—	—	49
1/88th Foot	—	—	—	1	—	—	1
Brigade Total	1	8	6	74	—	—	89

Colville's Brigade : no casualties.

	Killed. Offi-cers.	Men.	Wounded. Offi-cers.	Men.	Missing. Offi-cers.	Men.	Total.
4th Division (Cole):							
Anson's Brigade — 3/27th Foot	—	—	—	—	—	—	—
1/40th Foot	—	—	1	6	—	—	7
1/48th Foot	—	—	—	—	—	—	—
2nd Provisional Batt. (2nd & 2/53rd)	—	—	—	6	—	—	6
Brigade Total	—	—	1	12	—	—	13

		Killed.		Wounded.		Missing.		
		Offi-cers.	Men.	Offi-cers.	Men.	Offi-cers.	Men.	Total.
Ross's Brigade : no casualties.								
6th Division (Pakenham) :								
Stirling's Brigade	1/42nd Foot	—	1	—	7	—	—	8
	1/79th Foot	—	1	—	17	—	—	18
	1/91st Foot	—	1	1	7	—	—	9
Lambert's Brigade	1/11th Foot	—	2	—	20	—	1	23
	1/32nd Foot	—	3	2	28	—	—	33
	1/36th Foot	—	6	1	19	—	—	26
	1/61st Foot	—	1	2	10	—	—	13
Divisional Total		—	15	6	108	—	1	130
7th Division (Dalhousie) :								
Barnes's Brigade	1/6th Foot	—	—	1	5	—	1	7
	3rd Provisional Batt. (2/24th & 2/58th)	—	1	—	2	—	—	3
	Brunswick-Oels (9 companies)	—	2	—	1	—	14	17
Inglis's Brigade	51st Foot	—	2	—	22	—	—	24
	68th Foot	1	3	3	16	—	—	28
	1/82nd Foot	—	9	7	76	—	—	92
	Chasseurs Britanniques	1	12	9	19	—	4	45
Divisional Total		2	29	20	141	—	19	211
Artillery		—	1	—	8	—	—	9
GENERAL BRITISH TOTAL		5	62	42	448	—	20	583

Portuguese total unascertainable ; the casualties of 2nd Sorauren and Beunza, fought on the same day, being lumped together in the return at 1,120. But at 2nd Sorauren they were fairly light : from the fact that Stubbs's Portuguese brigade had 6 officer-casualties this day, Lecor's 4, and Madden's 3, it might be guessed that the ' other ranks ' casualties may have been about 300 in all.

COMBAT OF BEUNZA. JULY 30

	Killed.		Wounded.		Missing.		
Fitzgerald's (late Cameron's) Brigade :							
1/50th	—	3	2	14	2	9	30
1/71st	—	8	1	28	—	13	50
1/92nd	—	9	1	26	—	1	37
Pringle's Brigade :							
1/28th	—	—	—	—	—	—	—
2/34th	1	5	1	15	—	9	31
1/39th	—	—	—	3	—	—	3
General Staff	—	—	1	—	—	—	1
Cavalry (14th Light Dragoons and 1st Hussars K.G.L.)	—	—	1	2	—	2	5
Total	1	25	7	88	2	34	157

Portuguese losses heavy. Ashworth's brigade had 12 officer-casualties, Da Costa's 18; this at the usual rate should mean about 600 casualties of all ranks.

XX

BRITISH CASUALTIES IN MINOR ENGAGEMENTS: JULY 31—AUGUST 2, 1813

COMBAT OF VENTA DE URROZ (or DONNA MARIA). JULY 31

		Killed.		Wounded.		Missing.		Total.
		Officers.	Men.	Officers.	Men.	Officers.	Men.	
2nd Division, Staff .		—	—	1 [1]	—	1 [2]	—	2
Fitzgerald's Brigade	1/50th Foot .	—	6	—	26	—	14	46
	1/71st Foot .	—	2	1	34	—	—	37
	1/92nd Foot .	—	12	6	69	—	4	91
Pringle's Brigade	1/28th Foot	—	1	—	1	—	—	2
	2/34th Foot .	—	1	—	13	—	2	16
	1/39th Foot .	—	—	—	4	—	—	4
7th Division :								
Inglis's Brigade	51st Foot	—	5	—	40	—	6	51
	68th Foot	—	5	—	25	—	—	30
	1/82nd Foot .	—	—	—	3	—	—	3
	Chasseurs Britanniques	—	9	1	15	—	8	33
Total	.	—	41	9	230	1	34	315

COMBAT OF ECHALAR. AUGUST 2

		Killed.		Wounded.		Missing.		Total.
		Officers.	Men.	Officers.	Men.	Officers.	Men.	
General Staff .	.	—	—	1	—	—	—	1
4th Division :								
Ross's Brigade	1/7th Foot .	—	—	—	4	—	—	4
	20th Foot .	1	—	3	26	—	—	30
	1/23rd Foot	—	—	—	3	—	—	3
7th Division :								
Barnes's Brigade	1/6th Foot .	1	12	3	119	—	3	138
	3rd Provisional Batt.	—	15	9	115	—	2	141
	Brunswick-Oels .	—	1	4	7	—	2	14
Light Division :								
1/43rd . .	.	—	—	—	1	—	—	1
1/95th . .	.	—	1	1	10	—	—	12
3/95th . .	.	—	1	—	13	—	—	14
Total . . .	.	2	30	21	298	—	7	358

[1] General William Stewart, commanding the Division.

[2] Colonel Fitzgerald, 5/60th, commanding a Brigade.

XXI

PORTUGUESE LOSSES IN THE BATTLES OF THE PYRENEES

	Killed. Offi-cers.	Men.	Wounded. Offi-cers.	Men.	Missing. Offi-cers.	Men.	Total.	
Da Costa's Brigade :								
2nd Line .	3	85	9	81	—	21	200	} All at Beunza, July 30.
14th Line .	1	23	5	36	—	19	84	
A. Campbell's Brigade :								
4th Line .	2	24	7	78	—	3	114	} Almost all at two battles of Sorauren.
10th Line .	2	75	7	116	—	13	213	
10th Caçadores .	—	3	3	12	—	10	28	
Ashworth's Brigade (2nd Division) :								
6th Line .	—	29	5	63	—	8	105	} All at Beunza, July 30.
18th Line .	1	51	4	82	—	12	150	
6th Caçadores .	1	13	1	37	—	10	62	
Lecor's Brigade (7th Division) :								
7th Line .	—	—	—	—	—	4	4	} Almost all at 2nd Sorauren, July 30.
19th Line .	—	—	2	—	—	—	2	
2nd Caçadores .	1	12	1	44	—	—	58	
Madden's Brigade (6th Division) :								
8th Line .	—	—	—	3	—	—	3	} At the two battles of Sorauren.
12th Line .	2	53	2	208	—	4	269	
9th Caçadores .	—	15	3	86	—	—	104	
Power's Brigade (3rd Division) :								
9th Line .	—	—	—	—	—	2	2	} All at 2nd Sorauren.
21st Line .	—	5	—	9	—	—	14	
11th Caçadores .	—	1	—	5	—	—	6	
Stubbs's Brigade (4th Division) :								
11th Line .	1	34	1	105	—	1	142	} At the two battles of Sorauren.
23rd Line .	1	17	6	26	—	—	50	
7th Caçadores .	2	47	5	67	—	—	121	
Total .	16	489	60	1,060	—	107	1,732	

No Artillery losses save those at the combat of Maya, which were about 15. No Cavalry losses at all, though D'Urban's brigade was in the field at Sorauren.

N.B.—It will be noted that these losses are appreciably lower than those stated in Wellington's general return. The figures given above are from Beresford's corrected returns at Lisbon.

XXII

FRENCH LOSSES IN THE CAMPAIGN OF THE PYRENEES

[From Soult's Official Return, lent me by Mr. Fortescue.]

	Killed. Offi-cers.	Men.	Wounded. Offi-cers.	Men.	Prisoners. Offi-cers.	Men.	Total.
I. REILLE'S WING :							
1st Division (Foy) . .	6	78	9	393	—	69	555
7th Division (Maucune) .	14	189	27	500	25	1,102	1,857
9th Division (Lamartinière)	10	79	16	657	3	216	981
Total Reille's Wing	30	346	52	1,550	28	1,387	3,393
II. D'ERLON'S ' CENTRE ' :							
2nd Division (Darmagnac)	13	191	65	1,925	1	30	2,225
3rd Division (Abbé) . .	9	130	21	560	1	29	750
6th Division (Maransin) .	11	105	34	783	—	126	1,059
Total D'Erlon's ' Centre '	33	426	120	3,268	2	185	4,034
III. CLAUSEL'S WING :							
4th Division (Conroux) .	16	145	35	1,432	12	747	2,387
5th Division (Vandermaesen)	16	153	30	978	2	301	1,480
8th Division (Taupin) .	6	125	38	1,007	—	26	1,202
Total Clausel's Wing	38	423	103	3,417	14	1,074	5,069
IV. Cavalry . . .	—	12	2	33	1	19	67
GENERAL TOTAL OF ARMY	101	1,207	277	8,268	45	2,665	12,563

No figures for Artillery, Engineers, Train, or other auxiliary services, or for General Staff. Martinien's lists supply 4 casualties of generals (Conroux, Schwitter, Rignoux, Meunier), and 12 of staff officers. There must have been appreciable casualties in the other services, especially men captured from the Train at the Yanzi disaster.

Soult's figures are always unreliable (as witness Albuera). The details above contain some ' moral impossibilities '—e. g. the Return gives 63rd Line of Abbé's Division 193 casualties, *not including one officer*. But Martinien's lists supply one officer-casualty at Maya, two at Beunza, two at Yanzi. Similarly 58th Line of Conroux has in the Official Return 473 casualties, including only 5 officers—1 wounded and 4 prisoners. A reference to Martinien shows 2 officers killed (one the colonel !) and 5 wounded—adding the 4 prisoners we get 11 officer-casualties to 473 men : quite a possible percentage, which Soult's is not.

Captain Vidal de la Blache (i. p. 280) gives a casualty list differing slightly from the above. It runs : Foy 556, Maucune 2,457, Lamartinière 981, Darmagnac 2,225, Abbé 253 [quite impossible], Maransin 1,059, Conroux 2,387, Vandermaesen 1,480, Taupin 1,202, Cavalry 72 ; total 12,671.

INDEX

Abbé, general, governor of Navarre, fails to relieve Taffalla, 262; joined by Barbot, 263; by Taupin, 264; at Maya, 629; at Beunza, 703; at Venta de Urroz, 710; at Yanzi, 723.

Aboville, Auguste Gabriel, general, his explosion at Burgos, 358.

Adam, Frederick, colonel, at combat of Biar, 287–90; at Castalla, 291–7; protests against abandonment of the siege of Tarragona, 511.

Alava, Miguel, general, wounded at Villa Muriel, 80.

Alba de Tormes, combat of, 122–3; defended by major José Miranda, 125.

Albeyda, combat of, 282.

Alcoy, combat of, 282.

Alicante, Maitland at, 4, 162; Mackenzie commands Anglo-Spanish army at, 58, 163; Bentinck's proposal to withdraw troops from, 220; Murray at, 275; Bentinck brings back expeditionary force to, 521.

Alten, Charles, major-general commanding Light Division, left in command at Madrid, 4; in the Bastan, 540; moves the Light Division to Lecumberri, 690; ordered to harass Soult's retreat, 715–24; at Yanzi, 727; at Ivantelly, 735.

Alten, Victor, major-general, on retreat from Madrid, 98, 119, 130, 135, 144; pursues Villatte, 317, at Vittoria, 395, 419; in the Vittoria pursuit, 458.

Altobiscar, combat of, see Roncesvalles.

Alvarez, Pedro, colonel, his defence of Castro-Urdiales, 272–3.

Anson, George, major-general, his brigade on the Douro, 9–10, 15; on retreat from Burgos, 68; at Venta del Pozo, 71–6.

Anson, William, major-general, at Vittoria, 419; at Sorauren, 656, 673; at second Sorauren, 694.

Aranjuez, evacuated by Hill, 97.

Ariñez, village of, in battle of Vittoria, taken by Picton, 418–21.

Artificers, Royal Military, converted into Royal Sappers and Miners, 26; at siege of Burgos, 50.

Ashworth, Charles, brigadier-general, at Vittoria, 419; in the Bastan, 530; at Maya, 626; at combat of Beunza, 703.

Astorga, long siege of, 6–12; surrenders to Castaños, 11; Foy at, 11.

Aussenac, general, joins Souham, 54; operations of his brigade, 116 note; in Biscay, 267.

Avy, Antoine, general, at Vittoria, 393, 411, 428.

Babila Fuente, combat of, 319.

Balaguer, fort, besieged by Murray, 491; fall of, 499.

Ballasteros, Francisco, general, Wellington's orders to, 58, 59; his attempted coup d'état, 60, 61, 66, 178, 198; exiled by the Cortes, 62; Wellington's comments on, 300.

Barbot, general, his troops defeated at combat of Lerin, 263; checked at Roncesvalles, 615.

Barnes, Edward, major-general, his gallant counter-attack at Maya, 637; at second Sorauren, 697; charge of his brigade at Echalar, 733.

Bathurst, Henry, Earl, Secretary for War, correspondence of Wellington with, 12, 25, 28, 64, 112, 117, 164 note, 197, 211, 214, 217, 219, 220, 225–6; establishes Beresford's claims to seniority over Graham and Cotton, 230; Wellington sends plan of campaign for 1813 to, 301–4; Wellington's remarks after Vittoria, 453, 468; suggests Wellington's transfer to Germany, 558.

Bayas, skirmish on the, 379.

Behobie, bridge of, broken by Foy, 487.

Bejar, Foy's failure at, 240–1.

Bentinck, Lord Frederick, at siege of Tarragona, 507, 511.

Bentinck, Lord William, sends troops to Alicante, 164; proposes to withdraw them, 222–3; sends a raiding force to Tuscany, 223 ; recalls troops from Alicante to Sicily, 284 ; arrives to take command at Balaguer, 520 ; his dispatches to Wellington and Bathurst, 521.

Beresford, Sir William, marshal, his management of army in Portugal, 210 ; Wellington's choice of, as successor to himself, 228 ; Duke of York's decision against his claims, 229 ; Lord Bathurst establishes his right to seniority, 230 ; receives Wellington's plan of campaign for 1813, 303.

Bertoletti, general, commands at Tarragona, 492 ; defends the town against Murray, 496–514.

Beunza, combat of, 703, 704 ; casualties at, 739.

Biar, combat of, 288–90.

Bilbao, taken and lost by the Spaniards, 254 ; again attacked, 254 ; relieved by Palombini, 261 ; again attacked by Spaniards, 267.

Bloye, captain (R.N.), at Castro-Urdiales, 271–2, 273.

Bock, Eberhard, general, on retreat from Burgos, 69 ; at combat of Venta del Pozo, 71–4 ; brings his brigade to join Graham, 323 ; crosses the Esla, 330 ; at Vittoria, 396, 437.

Bourbon, the Cardinal, appointed head of Spanish Regency, 205–7.

Boyer, general, at combat of Venta del Pozo, 72–4 ; ordered to return to France, 246 ; his raid across the Esla, 327 ; at Vittoria, 404, 436 ; summoned to join Napoleon, 531.

Bradford, Henry, brigadier-general, sufferings of his brigade on retreat to Rodrigo, 154 ; at Vittoria, 396, 424, 437 ; at combat of Villareal, 474, 475 ; at combat of Tolosa, 478 ; at St. Sebastian, 567, 571.

Brisbane, Thomas, major-general, his brigade at Vittoria, 413, 418, 421.

Burgos, description of, 21–4 ; siege of, 17–51 ; relieved by Souham, 68 ; Wellington's comments on, 299 ; operations round, in June, 1813, 346–63 ; abandoned by King Joseph, 357.

Burgoyne, John, major (R.E.), senior engineer at Burgos, 18 n., 28 n., 30 n., 41 n. ; his observations, 44–5, 47, 49–51 ; his notes on siege of St. Sebastian, 573, 578.

Byng, John, major-general, at Vittoria, 400, 419 ; at Roncesvalles, 557, 611 ; retires, 622–3 ; at Sorauren, 656, 673 ; at second Sorauren, 694.

Cadiz, Wellington at, 201–6.

Cadogan, Hon. Henry, colonel, at Vittoria, 400 ; death of, 401.

Caffarelli, Louis Marie, general, commands Army of the North, 2 ; strengthens Burgos, 23 ; joins Souham at Briviesca, 48–54 ; in pursuit of Wellington, 85 ; returns to Burgos, 111 ; opposed by the Guerrilleros, 166 ; his failure to restore order in Biscay, 191–3, 252–8 ; superseded by Clausel, 193 ; returns to France, 217, 262.

Cameron, John, colonel, succeeds to Cadogan's brigade at Vittoria, 417, 419, 429 ; in pursuit of the French, 439 ; in the Bastan, 530 ; at Maya, 542, 626, 633, 634.

Campbell, Archibald, major-general, at Roncesvalles, joins Ross, 621 ; at Sorauren, 656 ; at Beunza, 704.

Campbell, Colin, captain, his account of storm of St. Sebastian, 580, 581, 582.

Campbell, James, general, at Alicante, 162 ; supersedes Clinton, 165, 275 ; superseded by Murray, 275.

Carvajal, Spanish minister of war, Wellington's letter to, 198–200.

Casapalacios, general, commanding Franco-Spaniards at Vittoria, 394–426 ; under Soult, 595.

Cassagne, general, at Vittoria, 393, 402, 414, 429 ; his division in the Bastan, 534.

Cassan, general, governor of Pampeluna, 528.

Castalla, battle of, 291–6.

Castaños, Francisco Xavier, general, commands Army of Galicia, joins Wellington before Burgos, 15–16 ; on retreat, 64, 156 ; winter quarters of, 184 ; Wellington's approval of, 199 ; appointed captain-general in Galicia, Castile, and Estremadura, 305 ; deposed by Regency, 523.

Castro-Urdiales, fortified by the Spaniards, 260 ; Clausel at, 265 ; siege and storm of, 271–3.

Chinchilla, siege of, 63 ; taken by French, 66.

Ciudad Rodrigo, Wellington's retreat on, 153 ; winter quarters at, 180.

Clarke, Henri, duc de Feltre, French minister of war, appoints Masséna to command Army of Portugal, 33 ; orders withdrawal from Madrid, 243 ; recalls troops to France, 248, 249 ; his orders to Clausel, 259 ; forwards King Joseph's complaints to Russia, 88 ; lectures the king on his strategy, 243, 248, 249 ; his views on the Northern insurrection, 252 ; urges the king to send troops to Biscay and Navarre, 259–60 ; his misconceptions of Wellington's strength and designs, 245, 251 ; his instructions to King Joseph after his retreat into France, 546.

Clausel, Bertrand, general, commands Army of Portugal, 2 ; reorganizes his army, 6–8 ; advances to Valladolid, 8–9 ; retreats northward, 14, 15, 17 ; superseded by Souham, 33 ; in operations round Salamanca, 124–42 ; supersedes Caffarelli with Army of the North, 193, 258, 262 ; his failure to subdue the North, 259, 270 ; his pursuit of Mina, 268, 269, 334 ; ordered to join King Joseph, 386 ; fails to reach Vittoria before the battle, 454 ; evades Wellington's pursuit, 460–9 ; reaches Saragossa, 465 ; arrives in France, 469, 527 ; appointed to command of the left wing under Soult, 594 ; at Roncesvalles, 615 ; at Sorauren, 657, 663, 665–77 ; in second battle of Sorauren, 692–7 ; retreat, 707 ; at Sumbilla, 718 ; at Echalar, 734.

Clinton, Henry, general commanding 6th Division, 2 ; joined by Wellington, 13 ; at Burgos, 42 ; Wellington's dissatisfaction with, 52 ; resumes command of 6th Division, after Vittoria, 462 ; pursues Clausel, 463, 464.

Clinton, William, major-general, takes command at Alicante, 164 ; superseded by Campbell, 165, 275 ; at battle of Castalla, 291–7 ; at Tarragona, 492, 565 ; thwarted by Murray, 509–10.

Collier, Sir George, captain (R.N.), blockades St. Sebastian, 567 ; lands naval guns, 569.

Cole, Sir Lowry, major-general, retreats from Madrid, 102 ; at Roncesvalles, 585, 604, 611, 617, 620 ;

Wellington censures his retreat, 622, 623 ; at combut of Linzoain, 651 ; at Sorauren, 656 ; at second Sorauren, 694.

Colville, Hon. Charles, major-general, at Vittoria, 411, 417, 429, 435.

Conroux, general, at Vittoria, 401 ; alarmist reports of, 538, 540 ; at Sorauren, 663, 668 ; in second battle of Sorauren, 692–6 ; at Sumbilla, 719 ; at Echalar, 734.

Constantin, Foy defeats Silveira at, 11.

Copons, Francisco, captain-general of Catalonia, commands 1st Army in Catalonia, 308 ; co-operates with Murray, 49, 504 ; Murray's pledge to join him in defending the Gaya, 507 ; abandoned by Murray, 513 ; threatens Mathieu's force, 518.

Cortes, intrigues in the Spanish, 202–3.

Cotton, Sir Stapleton, lieut.-general, at combat of Venta del Pozo, 70–4 ; in command at combat of Villadrigo, 76 ; Wellington's estimate of, 229 ; his ambitions as to the command in the Peninsula, 229–30.

Croker, John Wilson, records Wellington's plan for driving the French out of the Peninsula, 359–60, 454 note.

Curto, Jean-Baptiste, general, pursues Wellington from Burgos, 69, 71 ; at combat of Venta del Pozo, 71–4 ; at Vittoria, 426, 436.

Da Costa, general, his operations in the Bastan, 537 ; at Maya, 626 ; at Beunza, 704.

Dalhousie, George, Earl of, lieut.-general, insubordinate action of, 152 ; commands 7th Division at Vittoria, 409, 422 ; his responsibility for errors, 449 ; blockades Pampeluna, 539 ; marches to Lizaso, 683 ; at second Sorauren, 695 ; at Venta de Urroz, 711 ; at Echalar, 733.

Daricau, general, in pursuit of Wellington, 149 ; marches toward Valencia, 280 ; withdraws from Zamora, 327 ; pursued by Wellington, 331 ; at Vittoria, 393, 401.

Darmagnac, general, at Vittoria, 393, 413, 417, 428 ; at combat of Araquil, 461 ; at Maya, 629 ; at

Irurita, 683, 684 ; at Beunza, 703 ; at Venta de Urroz, 711 ; at Sumbilla, 719.

Decaen, Charles, general, commands French Army of Catalonia, 308 ; prepares to withstand Murray, 502–4 ; his ineffective operations, 517.

Denia, abortive expedition to, 163, 164.

D'Erlon, Jean Baptiste Drouet, comte, in pursuit of Hill from Madrid, 99 ; supersedes Souham in command of Army of Portugal, 129 ; his operations on the Tormes, 132 ; brings Army of the Centre to Valladolid, 339 ; at Vittoria, 401, 418 ; abandoned by Gazan, 431 ; retires, 433 ; disorderly retreat of, 439 ; retreats by the Col de Velate, 521 ; in the Bastan, 530 ; ordered to join Reille on the Nivelle, 584 ; appointed to command Centre of Army under Soult, 594 ; ordered to force the pass of Maya, 624 ; captures the position, 624–39 ; at Irurita, 683, 684 ; his delays, 685 ; attacks Hill, 702 ; at combat of Beunza, 703 ; retreats to France, 736.

Desprez, colonel, sent by King Joseph to Russia, 88 ; his report of the Moscow retreat, 241, 242.

Dickson, Alexander, colonel (R.A.), at Vittoria, 419, 428 ; at St. Sebastian, 565.

Digeon, Alexandre, general, pursuing Wellington's army, 144 ; on the Esla, 327, 328 ; abandons Zamora, 330 ; pursued by Wellington, 331 ; at Vittoria, 393, 404, 426 ; covers Reille's retreat, 436.

Donkin, Rufane, major-general, Q.M.G. to Murray, 292–5 ; his misleading dispatch, 508 ; plans re-embarkation from Tarragona, 509 ; remonstrates with Murray, 511.

Douglas, Sir Howard, colonel, 11, 14 ; sends guns for the siege of Burgos, 39, 41 note.

Dubreton, general, governor of Burgos, successful defence of, 23–51 ; relieved by Souham, 68.

Duran, José, brigadier-general, 255, 280–1.

D'Urban, Benjamin, major-general, views on the siege of Burgos, 51 ; on retreat from Madrid, 98, 119, 130, 132, 156, 159 ; brings his Portuguese brigade to join Graham, 324–5 ; crosses the Esla, 330 ; at Vittoria, 394, 419.

Ebro, crossed by Wellington, 362, 363 ; operations on, 364.

Echalar, combat of, 732 ; casualties at, 739.

Elio, Francisco, general, commanding in Valencia, 66 ; combines with Hill, 95, 98–110 ; retires to Alicante, 162–4 ; his army in Murcia, 277 ; on the Xucar, 283, 285 ; his mismanagement at Villena, 287, 288 ; co-operates with Murray, 298, 488, 502.

Empecinado, the (Juan Martin), brigadier-general, 100, 109 ; occupies Madrid, 110 ; in East Castile, 255, 256, 281.

Erskine, Sir William, general, at combat of Ocaña, 93 ; his suicide, 315.

Esla, passage of the, 329.

España, Carlos de, general, 98, 100, 112, 184, 305, 315, 656.

Fane, Henry, major-general, pursues Villatte, 317 ; at Vittoria, 394.

Ferdinand, King of Sicily, his abortive coup d'état, 284–5.

Fletcher, Sir Richard, colonel R.E., directs siege of St. Sebastian, 565, 578.

Forjaz, Miguel, secretary of state in Portugal, Wellington's correspondence with, 208.

Foy, Maximilien, general, his raid on Zamora, 10–11 ; joins Clausel, 12 ; in pursuit of Wellington after Burgos, 78, 83, 84 ; at Salamanca, 141–2 ; his views on the campaign, 168 ; on Wellington, 174, 180 ; at Avila, 187 ; abortive effort to surprise Bejar, 240 ; operations in Biscay, 271–4, 337, 365 ; receives orders to join King Joseph, 378 ; decides against joining the army at Vittoria, 470 ; harassed by Longa, 472 ; at combat of Tolosa, 477–82 ; regarrisons St. Sebastian, 484 ; falls back on the Bidassoa, 485 ; burns Behobie bridge, 487 ; on the Linduz, 619, 649 ; at Sorauren, 664 ; at second Sorauren, 693 ; retreats into France, 699–700.

Fraile, the (Agostin Nebot), guerrillero chief, 280.

Freire, Manuel, general, opposes Soult's advance on Madrid, 93 ;

ordered to join Ballasteros, 100 ; with Elio and the Empecinado, 109 ; in Andalusia, 162, 165, 307 ; succeeds Castaños in command of the 4th Army, 524.

Freneda, Wellington at, 194–213.

Fuenterrabia, castle of, seized and burned by Mina's bands, 263.

Gaudin, colonel, defeated by Mina at combat of Lerin, 263.

Gauthier, general, at combat of Villa Muriel, 79 ; at Sorauren, 675.

Gazan, countess, sent by Wellington to France after Vittoria, 445.

Gazan, Honoré, general, succeeds Soult, 247 ; orders Leval to evacuate Madrid, 339 ; with Army of the South at Arminion, 379 ; at Vittoria, 390 ; defence of his action, 402, 417 ; his retreat from Gomecha, 430–1 ; retires by the Pass of Roncesvalles, 523 ; ordered to take command in the Bastan, 534 ; retreats before Hill, 536 ; abandons Maya, 543 ; chief of the staff to Soult, 594 ; in the Pyrenean campaign, 665.

Giron, Pedro Agostin, general, nephew of Castaños, commands 4th Army, 306 ; his operations in Biscay, 368, 381 ; marches to Vittoria, 381, 396 ; sent in pursuit of French, 454 ; returns to guard Vittoria, 471 ; joins Longa, 473 ; at combat of Tolosa, 479 ; superseded in command of 4th Army by the Regency, 524 ; at Irun, 557.

Gomm, William, captain, his criticism on siege of St. Sebastian, 583, 584.

Gordon, James Willoughby, colonel, Q.M.G., errors of, 135–8, 146, 180 ; his treacherous conduct while on Wellington's staff, 224–6; dismissed, 226.

Graham, Sir Thomas, general, resigns his claims of seniority over Beresford, 230 ; moves across the Douro, 303 ; operations of his column, 322–33 ; in operations round Burgos, 354–62 ; at combat of Osma, 374 ; at Vittoria, 395 ; his attack on Reille, 405 ; on the Upper Zadorra, 424–35 ; discussion of his tactics at Vittoria, 447–8 ; in pursuit of French in Biscay, 456 ; attacks Maucune, 474 ; attacks and

drives Foy from Tolosa, 477–82 ; besieges St. Sebastian, 564–86.

Grant, Colquhoun, colonel, at combat of Morales, 331 ; at Vittoria, 395, 413, 419, 435 ; nearly captures King Joseph, 441.

Grant, William, brigadier in 7th Division, at Vittoria, 422–3.

Guernica, combats of, 266.

Guerrilleros, the, activity of, 189, 190 ; Napoleon's failure to estimate importance of, 257 ; their operations in the spring of 1813, 258–78.

Guingret, captain, his exploit at Tordesillas, 83, 84.

Halkett, Colin, brigadier commanding K.G.L., on retreat from Burgos, 69, 83 ; at Vittoria, 425.

Hallowell, Benjamin, admiral, bombards Tarragona, 496, 498 ; protests against Murray's reembarkation, 509, 512 ; effects the embarkation, 514 ; dissuades Murray from another attack on Tarragona, 516 ; hails Bentinck's arrival, 520 ; his dispatch to Wellington, 521.

Harispe, Jean Isidore, general, defeats Spaniards at combat of Yecla, 286–7 ; at battle of Castalla, 292 ; left by Suchet in command in Valencia, 500.

Harrison, John B., colonel, defends Bejar against Foy, 240–1.

Hay, Leith, captain, his notes on Vittoria campaign, 336, 364 ; exchanged on eve of Vittoria, 397, 416.

Hill, Robert, major-general, commanding cavalry brigade at Vittoria, 395, 419 ; in pursuit of Gazan, 439 ; guards town of Vittoria, 441, 455.

Hill, Sir Rowland, lieutenant-general, warns Wellington of King Joseph's advance on Madrid, 66, 67, 93 ; his retreat from Madrid, 96–110, 118 ; in operations round Salamanca, 113–42 ; on retreat to Rodrigo, 137–53 ; his orders for 1813, 303 ; operations of his column, 314–18 ; halts at Salamanca, 319 ; takes command of southern wing of Wellington's army, 320 ; forces Reille to withdraw before him, 356–7 ; at Vittoria, 395 ; blockades Pampeluna, 527 ; in the Bastan, 530 ; drives out Gazan, 536 ; absent from the combat of Maya, 585,

626 ; abandons the pass of Maya, 638 ; marches to Lizaso, 681–2 ; attacked by D'Erlon at Beunza, 702–5 ; in pursuit of Soult, 708–9; re-occupies pass of Maya, 738.
Huebra, combat of the, 149.

Inglis, William, major-general, his brigade at second Sorauren, 697.

Jones, John, colonel (R.E.), notes on siege of Burgos, 25, 28 *n.*, 35 *n.*, 41 *n.*, 49, 50 *n.*, 171 *n.* ; and on St. Sebastian, 566.
Joseph Napoleon Bonaparte, King of Spain, advances on Madrid, 66 ; joined by Soult and Suchet, 87 ; his quarrel with Soult, 88, 89 ; in pursuit of Hill, 99, 108 ; before Salamanca, 124 ; his accusations against Soult, 140 ; returns to Salamanca, 141 ; marches on Madrid, 155 ; Napoleon's criticism of, 169 ; his return to Madrid, 184–6 ; receives news of Napoleon's retreat from Russia, 239–40 ; abandons Madrid, 247 ; at Valladolid, 335 ; summons Clausel to join him, 356 ; abandons Burgos, 357 ; at Miranda, 366 ; retires on Vittoria, 377 ; reconnoitres the position with Jourdan, 397 ; orders retreat, 433 ; escapes from British cavalry, 441 ; at Salvatierra, 451 ; at Pampeluna, 462 ; fixes his headquarters at St. Jean de Luz, 532 ; orders concentration at St. Jean-Pied-du-Port, 541 ; superseded by Soult, 550 ; his fall, 567 ; retires to Mortefontaine, 552 ; appreciation of, 552–6.
Jourdan, Jean Baptiste, marshal, with King Joseph, 87 ; in pursuit of Hill from Madrid, 106, 108 ; in operations round Salamanca, 124–39 ; returns to Salamanca, 141 ; returns to Madrid, 186 ; orders concentration of forces to oppose Wellington, 337–9 ; at Burgos, 354–8 ; misconception of Wellington's movements, 372–3, 387–8, 398 ; his dispositions at Vittoria, 401–7 ; comment on Gazan's disobedience, 431 ; orders retreat on Pampeluna, 433 ; his remarks on the battle, 452 ; estrangement from King Joseph, 532 ; disgraced by Napoleon, 556 ; later history of, 556.

Kempt, James, major-general, at combat of San Millan, 375 ; his passage of the Zadorra, 407–8 ; at Vittoria, 418.

La Hermandad, stormed by Vandeleur, 423.
Lamartinière, general, joins King Joseph, 355, 365 ; at Vittoria, 404, 435 ; abandons Vera, 544 ; on the Linduz, 649 ; at Sorauren, 668 ; at second Sorauren, 693 ; at Yanzi, 722 ; at Echalar, 735.
Lameth, general, at Santoña, 266, 271.
Larpent, Francis, appointed Judge-Advocate General, with the army, 238 ; reports Wellington's plans for encircling Soult, 717.
Lerin, combat of, 263.
Leval, Jean François, general, evacuates Madrid, 340 ; at Vittoria, 393, 401, 413, 429 ; in the Bastan, 535, 539.
Linduz, defence of the, by Ross's brigade, 618.
Linzoain, combat of, 653.
Liverpool, Robert, Earl of, prime minister, his relations with Wellington, 214–16 ; Wellington's correspondence with, 300 ; he suggests transferring Wellington to Germany, 558–61.
Long, Robert, major-general, in operations round Salamanca,135 ; informs Wellington of Soult's movements, 647.
Longa, Francisco, colonel, his activity in the North, 253, 254 ; surprises Palombini at Poza, 261 ; escapes from Sarrut, 274 ; on the Ebro, 370 ; brings his division up before Vittoria, 381, 387, 396 ; in the attack on Reille, 405, 424 ; seizes Durana, 427 ; sent to Biscay in pursuit of Maucune, 454, 471 ; harasses Foy's retreat, 472, 475 ; at combat of Tolosa, 478–80 ; captures garrison of Passages, 486 ; at Yanzi, 720–4.

Mackenzie, John, general, commanding at Alicante, 58, 163 ; superseded by Clinton, 164, 275 ; at battle of Castalla, 291–7 ; at Tarragona, 492 ; protests against Murray's abandonment of siege, 511 ; his advance on Valdellos, 515.
Mackenzie, Mr., British secret agent, offers Russian troops for the Peninsula, 220, 221.

Madrid, evacuated by Hill, 106 ; occupied by King Joseph, 108 ; evacuated by him, 109, 110 ; occupied again for the winter, 186 ; King Joseph leaves it, 218, 247 ; the French abandon it for the last time, 340.

Maitland, Hon. T., major-general, commanding at Alicante, 4, 163, 275.

Maransin, Jean Pierre, general, at Vittoria, 392 ; at Maya, 542, 629 ; at Beunza, 703 ; at Venta de Urroz, 711 ; at Echalar, 735.

Marmont, Auguste, marshal, Duke of Ragusa, Napoleon's criticism of, 169 ; estimate of, 172–3 ; his remarks on the War of Spain, 257.

Masséna, André, marshal, Prince of Essling, abortive appointment of, to command in Spain, 33.

Mathieu, Maurice, general, governor of Barcelona, demonstrates against Murray, 503–5 ; relieves Tarragona, 517.

Maucune, general, attacks Wellington before Burgos, 64, 65 ; enters Burgos, 68 ; in pursuit of Wellington, 70–9 ; repulsed at combat of Villa Muriel, 79–82 ; in operations round Salamanca, 130; at combat of San Millan, 375 ; escorts a convoy from Vittoria, 386 ; resists Graham's advance, 475 ; attacks the heights of Sorauren, 671 ; his division routed at second Sorauren, 692 ; at Yanzi, 723 ; and at Echalar, 735.

Maya, first combat of, 542, 585 ; second combat of, 617–39.

Medico, El, guerrillero leader, at Toledo, 97.

Melville, Robert, Lord, fails to supply help for blockade of St. Sebastian, 567–8.

Mendizabel, Gabriel, general commanding Seventh Spanish Army, 253 ; opposes Clausel, 262 ; at Castro-Urdiales, 265 ; acts in conjunction with Graham near Tolosa, 478, 481 ; at siege of St. Sebastian, 523, 566.

Mermet, Julien, general, at Vittoria, 404, 427.

Mijares, Francisco, general, defeated at combat of Yecla, 286.

Mina, F. Espoz y, his operations round Pampeluna, 55 ; holds Navarre, 191, 255 ; Napoleon's remarks on, 259 ; opposes Abbé, 262 ; defeats Barbot at combat

of Lerin, 263 ; defeated and dispersed by Clausel, 269 ; threatens Clausel's retreat, 461, 463.

Miranda, José, major, defends Alba de Tormes, 125–32.

Morales, combat of, 331.

Morillo, Pablo, general, 98, 112, 119, 134, 184, 305–11, 315 ; at Vittoria, 394, 400, 419, 429 ; in pursuit of the French, 439 ; blockades Pampeluna, 527 ; at Roncesvalles, 611, 614 ; sent to assist Hill, 704.

Murray, Sir George, general, restored to Wellington as Q.M.G., 226 ; his advice as to pursuit of Clausel, 455 ; dispatches orders before Sorauren, 667.

Murray, Sir John, general, supersedes Campbell at Alicante, 275 ; his campaign against Suchet, 281–98 ; wins battle of Castalla, 293–6 ; his failure to carry out Wellington's plans, 311 ; his orders from Wellington, 488 ; embarks, 490 ; his half-hearted attack on Tarragona, 493–4 ; his miserable hesitations, 505–9 ; re-embarks troops, 511 ; abandons Copons, 513 ; his futile advance on Valdellos, 515 ; superseded by Bentinck, 520 ; his explanations to Wellington, 511 ; court-martial on, in 1814, 521, 561.

Napier, William, colonel, historian, his comments on Clausel's retreat, 18 and note, 40 n. ; on siege of Burgos, 49, 77 ; on Wellington's retreat to Rodrigo, 133, 145 n., 149 n. ; on Wellington's campaign of 1812, 170 ; his criticism of Jourdan at Vittoria, 389 ; reports Wellington's account of his scheme for encircling Soult, 717.

Napoleon, Emperor, nominates Reille to command army of Portugal, 33 ; receives news of Joseph's quarrel with Soult, 89 ; his dissatisfaction with conduct of the War in Spain, 168–9, 218 ; his disastrous retreat from Russia, 185, 215, 239, 241 ; supersedes Caffarelli by Clausel, 193 ; his delusions regarding the war in Spain, 250, 251 ; his victories at Bautzen and Lützen, 355, 360 ; anger at Foy's re-crossing the Bidassoa, 487 ; receives the news of Vittoria,'547 ; his appreciation of Wellington's schemes on the

Pyrenean frontier, 557 ; his perversions of Soult's dispatches, 640, 641.

O'Callaghan, Hon. R. W., colonel, at Vittoria, 401, 419 ; at Maya, 542 ; at Beunza, 703.
Ocaña, combat of, 93.
O'Donnell, Enrique, Conde de Abispal, succeeds Ballasteros in command of Army of Andalusia, 63, 307 ; takes the forts of Pancorbo, 528 ; blockades Pampeluna, 528 ; marches to join Hill, 704.
O'Donoju, Juan, general, Spanish minister of war, 205 ; Wellington's censures on, 347.
Ompteda, Christian, colonel K.G.L., at Tolosa, 480.
Osma, combat of, 373–4.
Oswald, John, major-general, his insubordination on the Burgos retreat, 150–2 ; at Vittoria, 424–6, 437 ; at St. Sebastian, 567, 571, 578, 583.

Pack, Denis, major-general, marches on Burgos, 3, 17 ; at siege of Burgos, 26, 47, 48 ; retreats from Burgos, 67 ; in operations round Salamanca, 134 ; at Vittoria, 396, 424, 437 ; at combat of Villareal, 475 ; at combat of Tolosa, 478 ; at Sorauren, 666, 677.
Paget, Sir Edward, general, sent to Spain as second-in-command, 53 ; attacks Maucune, 65, 66 ; taken prisoner on Salamanca retreat, 147.
Pakenham, Sir Edward, majorgeneral, offers Wellington siegeguns for Burgos, 40 ; takes command of the 6th Division, left at Medina de Pomar, 370 ; opposed to Clausel at Vittoria, 459 ; superseded by Clinton, 462 ; replaces Pack, 689.
Palencia, stormed by Foy, 78–81.
Palombini, general, operations of his Italian division in Castile, 260, 261 ; and in Biscay, 265–7 ; at Santoña, 265 ; at Guernica, 266 ; at siege of Castro-Urdiales, 271, 274.
Pampeluna, King Joseph at, 462 ; siege of, 528–9.
Pancorbo, forts of, reduced by O'Donnell, 528.
Pannetier, general, attempts to relieve Tarragona, 501, 514–15.

Paris, general, defends Saragossa, 468 ; evacuates it, 599.
Parque, The Duque del, successor of Ballasteros, commanding Army of Andalusia, 63, 307, 311 ; co-operation with Murray, 489, 502 ; attacks on the Xucar, 515.
Passages, harbour, arrival of Wellington's siege train at, 569.
Pastor, El, guerrillero chief, 254, 266, 267, 365.
Pellew, Sir Edward, admiral, makes naval demonstration off the coast of the Ampurdam, 503 ; brings Bentinck to take command at Balaguer, 520.
Penne Villemur, Conde, cavalry general, 98, 119, 132.
Picton, Sir Thomas, lieut.-general, at Vittoria, 409 ; crosses the Zadorra with the 3rd Division, 411 ; at Ariñez, 418 ; joins Cole at Linzoain, 651 ; at second battle of Sorauren, 698 ; pursues Foy, 698–9.
Plässwitz, Armistice of, 360 ; its effect on Wellington's policy, 525, 737.
Ponsonby, Hon. William, majorgeneral, brings his brigade to join Graham, 323 ; at Vittoria, 395, 419.
Popham, Sir Home, commodore, sends ammunition to Wellington at Burgos, 39 ; offers guns, 40 ; his operations on coast of Biscay, 54, 55, 57, 58 n., 176, 177, 253–4.
Porlier, Juan Diaz, general, heads Asturian insurgents, 254 ; at combat of Tolosa, 478.
Poza de la Sal, combat of, 261.
Prevost, William, colonel, sent to take the Col de Balaguar, 491, 500 ; rejoins Murray, 514, 515.
Pringle, William Henry, majorgeneral, at Villa Muriel, 80–1 ; at Maya, 626 ; at combat of Beunza, 703.
Provisional Battalions, controversy concerning, 232–3.
Puente Larga, combat of, 102–5.

Ramsay, Norman, captain R.A., unjust treatment of, 456–8.
Regency of Portugal, dealings of, with Wellington, 207–8, 209.
Regency of Spain, dealings of, with Wellington, 201–4 ; displaced, 205 ; its successors, 205.
Regent, the, George, Prince of Wales, creates Wellington fieldmarshal, 442.

Regent of Portugal, Prince John, 206–7.

Reille, Honoré Charles, general, commanding Army of Portugal, his failure to cope with the guerrilleros, 190 ; sends Boyer across the Esla, 327 ; his position before Burgos, 354 ; retreats before Hill, 356, 357, 367 ; at combat of Osma, 373, 374 ; at Vittoria, 393, 404, 435, his orderly retreat, 436–9, 451 ; sent to guard the frontier of France, 459 ; abandons the bridge of Behobie, 487 ; appointed to command the right wing of the army under Soult, 594 ; checked on the Linduz, 617–21, 649 ; at Sorauren, 665, 675 ; at second Sorauren, 695 ; retreat, 698 ; at combat of Yanzi, 720–4 ; at Ivantelly, 735.

Rey, Emanuel, general, at Vittoria, 401 ; governor of St. Sebastian, 483, 567 ; his gallant defence, 570, 574, 586.

Robinson, Frederick, major-general, at Vittoria, 406.

Roche, Philip K., general, commands Spanish division at Alicante, 275 ; at battle of Castalla, 291.

Roncal, combat of, 269.

Roncesvalles, combat of, 608–20.

Ross, Robert, major-general, at Roncesvalles, 613 ; at Sorauren, 656, 662 ; at second Sorauren, 694 ; at Echalar, 734.

Rouget, general, defends Bilbao, 267 ; at combat of Tolosa, 481.

Salamanca, operations round, 111–42 ; recovered by the Allied Army, 317.

Sanchez, Julius, in retreat from Burgos, 67, 68, 69 ; at Ciudad Rodrigo, 153 ; operations in Castile, 305, 315 ; in pursuit of French, 364.

San Miguel, hornwork of, at Burgos, stormed, 27 ; blown up by Wellington, 48 ; again destroyed by the French, 355.

San Millan, combat of, 375.

San Muñoz, combat of, 149.

Santocildes, José Maria, general, commanding Galician army on the Douro, 6 ; evacuates Valladolid, 9 ; joins in pursuit of Clausel, 16.

Santoña, relieved by Palombini, 265.

Sar.ut, general, 270 ; joins King

Joseph before Vittoria, 365 ; killed at Vittoria, 404, 425.

Scovell, George, major, Wellington's cypher-secretary, appointed to command Staff Corps Cavalry, 2, 37.

Silviera, Francisco, Conde de Amarante, driven from Zamora by Foy, 11 ; takes command of the Portuguese Independent Division, 314 ; at Vittoria, 395, 419 ; in the Bastan, 527, 536 ; at the combat of Beunza, 626.

Skerrett, John B., major-general, joins Hill with his column, 95 ; evacuates Aranjuez, 97 ; at combat of Puente Larga, 102–5 ; at Vittoria, 419.

Smith, Charles, major, engineer at St. Sebastian, 565, 569, 578.

Somers-Cocks, Captain the Hon. John, storms San Miguel, 27, 28 ; killed at Burgos, 38.

Somerset, Lord Fitzroy, carries Wellington's message from Sorauren, 660.

Sorauren, first battle of, 654–80 ; second battle of, 692–706 ; casualties at, 738, 739.

Souham, Joseph, general, supersedes Clausel in command of Army of Portugal, 33 ; receives reinforcements, 54, 55 ; advances to relieve Burgos, 64–8 ; enters Burgos, 68 ; his pursuit of Wellington, 68–85 ; joins Soult, 121 ; superseded by Drouet, 129.

Soult, Nicolas, Jean de Dieu, marshal, duke of Dalmatia, evacuates Andalusia, 2, 56 ; advances on Madrid, 66 ; his quarrel with King Joseph, 87–9 ; in pursuit of Hill, 99–121 ; unites with Army of Portugal and Army of the Centre, 121 ; ineffective attack on Alba de Tormes, 122, 123 ; operations round Salamanca,124–39 ; King Joseph's accusations against, 140 ; his pursuit of Wellington, 140–51 ; turns back on the Huebra, 151 ; Napoleon's estimate of, 169 ; at Toledo, 187 ; recalled to France, 217, 243 ; supersedes Joseph, 550, 587 ; his proclamation to the troops, 588 ; character and career of, 589–91 ; reorganizes the army, 591–8 ; seizes Maya and Roncesvalles, 620 ; his report to Napoleon, 640 ; repulsed at Sorauren, 663–80 ; retreat, 681–705 ; his discouragement, 736–7.

Soult, Pierre, general, in pursuit of Hill, 105-8 ; crosses the Tormes, 131 ; King Joseph's strictures on, 140 ; at Vittoria, 393, 428 ; at Sorauren, 668.

Spry, William, brigadier-general, at St. Sebastian, 573, 586.

St. Sebastian, Rey governor of, 483 ; Foy's attempt to reinforce it, 484 ; blockade of, 485 ; siege of, 562-86 ; natural features of, 562 ; abortive storm of, 575-82 ; its siege abandoned, 586, 606.

Staff Corps Cavalry, formation of the, 237.

Stapleton Cotton, see Cotton.

Stewart, Sir William, lieut.-general, his disobedience during the retreat from Salamanca, 150-2 ; Wellington's complaints against, 226, 227; absent at the time of the attack on Maya, 626, 627 ; returns to take command, 634 ; at combat of Venta de Urroz, 711.

Stuart, Sir Charles, British minister member of Regency of Portugal, 209 ; Wellington's correspondence with, 211, 221.

Stubbs, George, colonel, commanding Portuguese brigade, at Vittoria, 414, 419 ; at Sorauren, 656 ; at second Sorauren, 694.

Suchet, Louis Gabriel, duke of Albufera, marshal, advances on Madrid, 66 ; his quarrels with King Joseph and Soult, 88, 89 ; gathering of Spanish and British armies against, 162-6 ; precarious position of, 279-81 ; his campaign against Murray, 281-98, 488-500 ; defeated at battle of Castalla, 292-309 ; marches to relieve Tarragona, 501 ; finds his advance blocked by Fort Balaguer, 515 ; withdraws across the Ebro, 516.

Sumbilla, combat of, 718, 719.

Tarragona, defences of, 493 ; siege of, 496 ; relieved by Mathieu, 517.

Thackeray, Frederick, major, senior engineer at siege of Tarragona, 497 ; protests against Murray's abandonment of the siege, 511.

Thouvenot, general, governor of Vittoria, 378, 470.

Tiebas, combat of, 262.

Tolosa, combat of, 477-81.

Tomkinson, William captain 16th Light Dragoons, his diary of events on the Douro, 6 n., 14 n.,

15 n., 16 n., 18 n., 28 n., 38 n. ; on Reille's retreat, 438.

Tordesillas, exploit of Captain Guingret at, 83.

Toro, French garrison of, relieved by Foy, 10 ; junction of Wellington and Hill at, 331-3.

Torquemada, riotous scenes at, 77.

Torrens, Henry, colonel, military secretary to Duke of York, Wellington's correspondence with, 224.

Tovey, George, captain, bayonet charge of his company on the Linduz, 618.

Treillard, Jean Paul, general, at Vittoria, 428 ; at Sorauren, 688.

Vacani, Camillo, historian, with Palombini, 264-8 ; his account of Tarragona, 496.

Valdemoro, riotous scenes at, 102, 105.

Valladolid, occupied by Clausel, 9 ; his eviction by Wellington, 14 ; abandoned by Wellington, 84 ; King Joseph makes it his capital, 247 ; evacuated by the French, 344.

Vandeleur, J. Ormsby, major-general, at combat of San Millan, 375 ; at Vittoria, 412 ; storms La Hermandad, 423.

Vandermaesen, general, at Roncesvalles, 615 ; at Sorauren, 668 ; at second Sorauren, 695 ; at combat of Sumbilla, 718 ; at Echalar, 734.

Venta del Pozo, combat of, 71-4.

Venta de Urroz, combat of, 711 ; casualties at, 739.

Vera, abandoned by Lamartinière, 544.

Villacampa, Pedro, general, acts under Elio, 280, 281, 298.

Villadrigo, combat of, 75.

Villafranca, combat of, 475.

Villa Muriel, combat of, 79-82.

Villareal, combat of, 473.

Villatte, general, driven from Salamanca, 316-19 ; at Vittoria, 393, 402 ; attacks Morillo and the 71st, 415 ; retirement of, 416, 429 ; Soult's complaints of, 718 ; commands Bayonne reserve, 595 ; his torpor, 602, 713.

Villena, castle of, capitulates to Suchet, 287, 288.

Vittoria, battle of, 384-450 ; retreat of the French from, 433-50.

Wachholz, Ludwig, captain, notes of, 432 ; on combat of the Linduz, 618-19.

Waldron, John, captain, exploit of, at Castalla, 295.

Wellesley, Hon. Henry, ambassador to Spain, his correspondence with Wellington, 196–7, 525 ; his dealings with the Regency of Spain, 205.

Wellesley, Richard, marquis, resigns from Perceval Cabinet, 214.

Wellington, Arthur Wellesley, Marquis of, marches to Burgos, 3 ; crosses the Douro, 12–18 ; his pursuit of Clausel, 16–20 ; siege of Burgos, 21–51 ; his instructions to Hill, 57 ; retreats from Burgos, 66–86 ; orders Hill to retire from Madrid, 99 ; his reasons for retreat, 111 ; operations round Salamanca, 111–37 ; retreats on Ciudad Rodrigo, 137–53 ; his strictures on officers commanding divisions and brigades, 156–61 ; criticism of his campaigns of 1812, 170–6 ; at Freneda, 194 ; made Generalissimo of Spanish armies, 196–204 ; at Cadiz, 201 ; on Portuguese finance, 211–13 ; his relations with Whitehall, 214–24 ; with the Duke of York, 223–4 ; intrigues of Gordon against, 224–6 ; his plan for campaign of 1813, 299–305 ; plan for Tarragona expedition, 308 ; leaves Hill in command of Southern Army, 320 ; joins Graham, 329 ; occupies Toro, 331–3 ; his plan for transferring British base to the Bay of Biscay, 348–9 ; for driving the French out of the Peninsula, 359 ; his operations on the Ebro, 364–82 ; plan of attack at Vittoria, 394 ; his derogatory remarks on his army, 452, 453 ; marches for Navarre, 455 ; severity towards Norman Ramsay, 456–8 ; pursues Clausel in vain, 467 ; his orders for

Murray's expedition to Tarragona, 488 ; dissatisfaction with Murray, 521 ; influence of Armistice of Plässwitz on his plans, 525–6 ; in the Bastan, 537–43 ; in correspondence with Bathurst and Liverpool, rejects their suggestion of transfer to Germany, 558, 561 ; controversy with Melville, 567–8 ; goes to St. Sebastian, 585 ; his dispositions for the defence of the Pyrenees, 603–6 ; concentrates against Soult, 647, 659 ; his ride to Sorauren, 658–62 ; prepares to attack Soult, 694 ; at second Sorauren, 694–701 ; pursuit of Soult, 707–40 ; renounces advance into France, 737–40.

Whittingham, Sir Samford, general, his Spanish division, 163, 276 ; at combat of Albeyda, 282 ; at battle of Castalla, 293, 294 ; in the Tarragona expedition, 492.

Wimpffen, Louis, general, Spanish chief of the staff to Wellington, 201.

Xixona, plot to betray, 279.

Yanzi, combat of, 720–4.

Yecla, combat of, 286–7.

York, Frederick, Duke of, his relations with Wellington, 223 ; opposes Beresford's claims to seniority, 228, 229 ; disapproves of Provisional Battalions, 232–4.

Yrurzun, combat of, 461.

Zadorra, the river, its importance in battle of Vittoria, 384 ; crossed by Kempt, 407 ; by Picton, 411 ; Reille's defence along, 435.

Zamora, French garrison of, relieved by Foy, 11 ; occupied by Daricau, 327 ; occupied by Graham, 330.

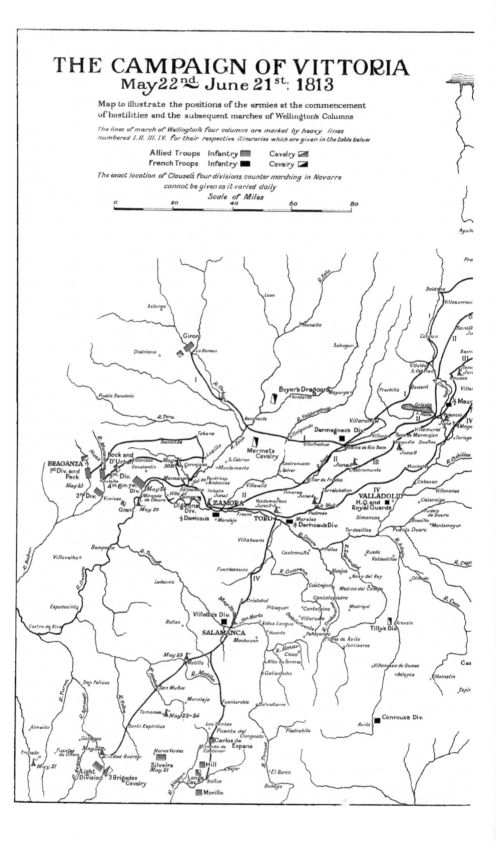

THE CAMPAIGN OF VITTORIA
May 22nd ~ June 21st: 1813

Map to illustrate the positions of the armies at the commencement
of hostilities and the subsequent marches of Wellington's Columns

*The lines of march of Wellington's four columns are marked by heavy lines
numbered I. II. III. IV. for their respective itineraries which are given in the table below*

Allied Troops Infantry ▬ Cavalry ▱
French Troops Infantry ▬ Cavalry ▱

*The exact location of Clausel's four divisions, counter marching in Navarre
cannot be given as it varied daily*

Scale of Miles
0   20   40   60   80

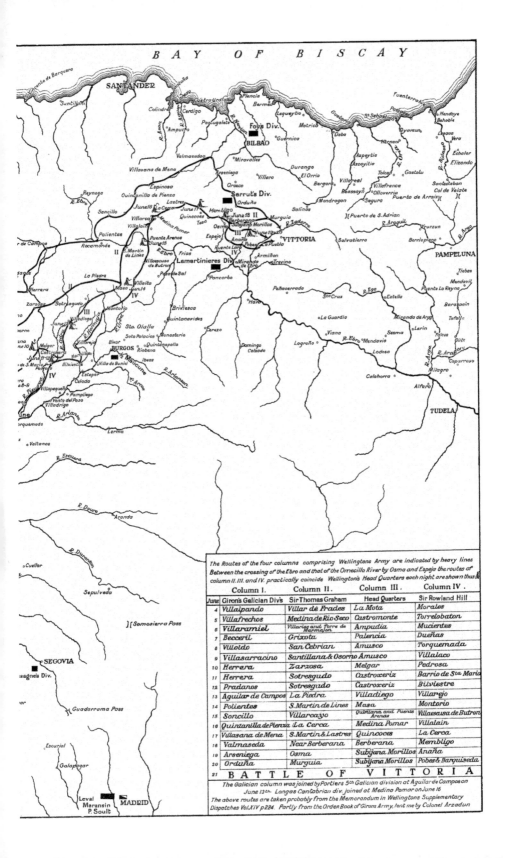

The Routes of the four columns comprising Wellingtons Army are indicated by heavy lines. Between the crossing of the Ebro and that of the Omecillo River by Osma and Espeja the routes of column II. III. and IV. practically coincide. Wellington's Head Quarters each night are shown thus ▲

June	Column I. Giron's Galician Div's	Column II. Sir Thomas Graham	Column III. Head Quarters	Column IV. Sir Rowland Hill
4	Villalpando	Villar de Frades	La Mota	Morales
5	Villafrechos	Medina de Rio Seco	Castromonte	Torrelobaton
6	Villaramiel	Villariegand Torre de Marmojon	Ampudia	Mucientes
7	Becceril	Grixota	Palencia	Dueñas
8	Villoldo	San Cebrian	Amusco	Torquemada
9	Villasarracino	Santillana & Osorno	Amusco	Villalaco
10	Herrera	Zarzosa	Melgar	Pedrosa
11	Herrera	Sotresgudo	Castroxeriz	Barrio de Sta. Maria
12	Pradanos	Sotresgudo	Castroxeriz	Bilviestre
13	Aguilar de Campos	La Piedra	Villadiego	Villarejo
14	Polientes	S.Martin de Lines	Masa	Montorio
15	Soncillo	Villarcayo	Quintana and Puente Arenas	Villaesusa de Butron
16	Quintanilla de Pienza	La Cerca	Medina Pomar	Villalain
17	Villasana de Mena	S.Martin & Lastras	Quincoces	La Cerca
18	Valmaseda	Near Berberana	Berberana	Membligo
19	Arseniega	Osma	Subijana Morillos	Anaña
20	Orduña	Murguia	Subijana Morillos	Pobes & Barquiseda
21	BATTLE OF VITTORIA			

The Galician column was joined by Portiers 5th Galician division at Aguilar de Campos on June 13th. Longas Cantabrian div. joined at Medina Pomar on June 16
The above routes are taken probably from the Memorandum in Wellingtons Supplementary Dispatches Vol.XIV p.224. Partly from the Order Book of Girons Army, lent me by Colonel Arzadun.

Lightning Source UK Ltd.
Milton Keynes UK
UKHW020625240222
399174UK00001B/3